THE STUDY OF PERSONALITY

An Interdisciplinary Appraisal

THE STUDY OF PERSONALITY

An Interdisciplinary Appraisal

EDITED BY

EDWARD NORBECK

DOUGLASS PRICE-WILLIAMS

WILLIAM M. McCORD

RICE UNIVERSITY

HOLT, RINEHART AND WINSTON, INC.

New York   Chicago   San Francisco   Atlanta   Dallas   Montreal
Toronto   London

Copyright © 1968 by Holt, Rinehart and Winston, Inc.
All rights reserved
Library of Congress Catalog Card Number: 68–18432
2686657
Printed in the United States of America
1 2 3 4 5 6 7 8 9

BF
698
.S77

CANISIUS COLLEGE LIBRARY
BUFFALO, N. Y.

FOREWORD

We wish to express indebtedness to many people for their aid in the preparation of this book and in planning and conducting the symposium on which it is based. First, we give heartiest thanks to all of our speakers and authors, whose willing cooperation made our task easy. We are also thankful to the many people who participated as members of the symposium audience, often traveling long distances to do so.

We offer thanks for encouragement and aid of varying kinds to President and Mrs. Kenneth S. Pitzer of Rice University, Trenton W. Wann, Chandler Davidson, Frederick C. Gamst, Frank Hole, Edwin Harwood, Wayne Wheeler, Edwin Willems, Hifa Rezak, Deni Seinfeld, Jackie Miller, Marian Haesly, Jean Adams, William Ainley, Alma Beman, Gary Bohlken, Russell Clark, Don des Jarlais, Katherine Ellison, William Gordon, Michael Karchmer, Charles Kasdorf, Clive Kileff, Suzanne Kitchen, Colleen McGee, Brian Mustain, Gail O'Connell, Robert Olasov, William S. Red, Carolyn Schum, Janice Tate, Howard Thompson and members of his staff, Josephine Williams, Frank Zumwalt, and to our wives.

A special word of acknowledgment is due to professional colleagues at colleges and universities throughout the United States who gave counsel in planning the symposium and to colleagues who were invited to participate in the symposium but were unable to do so at the onset or who, after initial acceptance, later were obliged to withdraw because of ill health or other unexpected obstacles. These scholars are Gordon W. Allport, Orville G. Brim, William Caudill, Cora DuBois, Erich Fromm, Erving Goffman, Dell H. Hymes, Alex Inkeles, John I. Lacey, Alexander H. Leighton, Gardner Lindzey, Don Martindale, Robert K. Merton, Rhoda Metraux, Wilbert E. Moore, Talcott Parsons, David Riesman, Arnold Rose, and Sherwood L. Washburn.

We are indebted to Rice University and the National Science Foundation for financial support of the symposium.

                                                                                                 E. N.
                                                                                               D. P.-W.

Houston, Texas   W. McC.
February 1968

CONTENTS

Foreword   v

1. Introduction   1
   EDWARD NORBECK, DOUGLASS PRICE-WILLIAMS,
   and WILLIAM M. MCCORD,
   Rice University

PART ONE   *Theoretical Standpoints*

2. Psychological Views of Personality and Contributions to Its Study   15
   GARDNER MURPHY,
   The Menninger Foundation

3. Anthropological Contributions to the Theory of Personality   41
   ANTHONY F. C. WALLACE,
   *University of Pennsylvania
   and Eastern Pennsylvania Psychiatric Institute*

4. Sociological Views and Contributions   54
   ANSELM STRAUSS,
   University of California Medical School

5. Personality from a Psychoanalytic Viewpoint   65
   WESTON LA BARRE,
   Duke University

6. The Philosophy of Science and the Study of Personality   88
   DOUGLASS PRICE-WILLIAMS,
   Rice University

7. National Character Revisited: a Proposal for Renegotiating the Concept   103
   DANIEL BELL,
   Columbia University

8. The Method of the Study of Persons   121
   BERT KAPLAN,
   University of California, Santa Cruz

PART TWO *The Formation of Personality*

9. Personality and the Biological Nature of Man   137
   JOHN O. ELLEFSON,
   Stanford University School of Medicine

10. Toward a Neuropsychological Theory of Person   150
    KARL H. PRIBRAM,
    Stanford University School of Medicine

11. Genetics and Personality   161
    WILLIAM R. THOMPSON,
    Queen's University, Kingston, Ontario

12. Influences of Childhood and Adolescence   175
    MARY ELLEN GOODMAN,
    Rice University

13. The Self and Adult Socialization   194
    HOWARD S. BECKER,
    Northwestern University

14. Personality Change in Middle and Old Age   209
    WILLIAM E. HENRY,
    The University of Chicago

15. The Consequences of Early Bilingualism in Cognitive Development and Personality Formation   218
    A. RICHARD DIEBOLD, JR.,
    Stanford University

16. The Study of Personality in Primitive Societies   246
    JOHN J. HONIGMANN,
    University of North Carolina

PART THREE *Personality under Stress and Change*

17. Cultural Factors in Mental Illness — 279
    E. D. WITTKOWER,
    McGill University
    G. DUBREUIL,
    Université de Montréal

18. The Family and Personality in Crisis — 296
    A. B. HOLLINGSHEAD,
    Yale University

19. The Personality of Social Deviants — 311
    WILLIAM M. MCCORD,
    Rice University

20. Psychocultural Adaptation — 326
    GEORGE D. SPINDLER,
    Stanford University

21. Achievement and Innovation in Culture and Personality — 348
    GEORGE A. DE VOS,
    University of California, Berkeley

Closing Address

22. Problems and Progress in the Study of Personality — 373
    MARGARET MEAD,
    American Museum of Natural History

Biographical Sketches of Authors — 383

Index — 389

THE STUDY OF PERSONALITY

An Interdisciplinary Appraisal

1

Introduction

Edward Norbeck
Douglass Price-Williams
William M. McCord

The collection of papers in this volume are written versions of addresses given at Rice University on November 5th and 6th, 1966, in a symposium bearing the same name as this volume. Many symposia on the subject of personality have been conducted during the past two decades, but they have most commonly concerned specialized subtopics and they have not included all of the scholarly fields in which the study of personality has been important. The objectives of our symposium were to review and appraise knowledge and theories concerning personality in all of these fields of study in a manner comprehensible to educated persons who are not specialists in the subjects concerned.

Such a summing up was thought to be desirable for several reasons. No summary and appraisal of this scope has previously been attempted, although much research on the subject of personality has been conducted during the past three or four decades. Increasing scholarly specialization added to the rapid accumulation of knowledge makes it difficult for even the specialist to keep abreast of developments in scholarly disciplines other than his own that bear on his subject of interest. The interested layman cannot without the greatest difficulty gain an overall view because the many pertinent publications are often written in technical language and are scattered widely in the professional journals. A periodic taking of stock also allows the professional scholars to make judgments of their progress, of strengths and weaknesses in their work; and interdisciplinary stocktaking offers obvious opportunities for cross-fertilization.

An influencing factor in planning the symposium was the nature of the audience, which we conceived as composed of university students and faculty members, educated laymen, and professional scholars in the social sciences. To reach the objectives of the symposium, distinguished scholars were invited to summarize their knowledge in short addresses representing an impartial distillation of theories and knowledge concerning their subjects. Time and funds available for such an enterprise expectably placed limits on the number of fields and subjects that might be covered. A total of twenty-one subjects was finally decided upon, representing the fields of psychology, psychiatry, anthropology, and sociology. Introductory addresses summarizing the viewpoints and contributions of each of these fields were followed by addresses on important subtopics, and the symposium ended with an address giving a general appraisal of the history and present status of the study of personality in the social sciences.

The success of the symposium far exceeded expectations, making clear that the subject of personality holds much interest for the educated public as well as for the scholar. During the four sessions of the symposium conducted over two days on the Rice University campus, audiences averaged approximately 1500 persons, about half of whom came from communities other than Houston. Professional social scientists attending as members of the audience were drawn from all parts of the nation.

In addition to giving addresses before an audience, speakers in the symposium were requested to prepare for publication in this volume longer written versions of their oral presentations that provided appropriate scholarly references and bibliographies useful as guides to additional reading. Our goal for this volume was a collection of papers written in a style suitable for the educated person, layman or specialist, who has no special knowledge of the subjects under discussion. In most instances, the papers published here are then expanded versions of the authors' addresses. The closing address by Margaret Mead, which depended in part upon the contents of the preceding addresses, is a transcription of her oral delivery.

We were pleased and encouraged to find that the scholars invited to participate as speakers and authors found our ideas about the nature of the symposium agreeable, and we are most grateful for their fine cooperation. A few words on the selection of the participants in the symposium seem appropriate. For the most part, distinguished, mature scholars were invited to take part. It was thought desirable, however, to avoid a roster composed entirely of distinguished senior statesmen, and younger scholars of distinction and promise were also included. As a matter of historical interest, Margaret Mead (see her closing address) has requested that we record the names of all scholars who had been invited to participate. As she accurately states, only a few declined our invitation. During the period of a year or so between the time when our invitations were extended and the date of the symposium, a few substitutions of participants were made because ill health or other unexpected events made participation impossible for those originally invited. Names of scholars who were invited to participate but were unable to do so and of others who gave counsel or served other roles in connection with the symposium appear in the Foreword. We shall note here only that the paper written by E. D. Wittkower and G. Dubreuil was delivered by Wittkower, and that Irven DeVore participated as a speaker but not as an author. The paper on DeVore's subject in this volume was

3 *Introduction*

written by John O. Ellefson. Of the twenty-two authors, nine are identified primarily as psychologists or psychiatrists, eight as anthropologists, and six as sociologists.

With the idea that they will be helpful to readers, we give below brief explanatory notes on the arrangements of the papers in this volume and remarks on their contents. Papers are grouped under three major headings, "Theoretical Standpoints," "The Formation of Personality," and "Personality Under Stress and Change," to which a summarizing address of conclusion is added. These major headings embrace principally writings that concern, first, views of personality and contributions toward its study of the major fields of the social sciences; second, factors that influence the formation of personality; and, third, the personalities of social and psychiatric deviates, and personality as related to sociocultural change. Our divisions are not mutually exclusive, and certain papers clearly overlap our classifications. For example, although all papers directly or indirectly concern matters of theory, we have placed under this heading only writings directed toward the subject that represent concepts of an entire discipline or subdiscipline. The paper by Karl H. Pribram might be labeled as an account of the views and contributions of neuropsychology and neurophysiology. We have classified it as a paper concerning biological factors related to personality, and have placed it with other writings that deal primarily with the formation of personality. Other papers might similarly be reclassified. The group of writings on personality under stress and change concern chiefly sociocultural factors influential in shaping personality, but the papers form a closely related subgroup and for this reason are set apart.

Many links appear in papers that concern different subjects and are widely separated in the book. Certain concepts, themes, and issues appear over and over again, and these are informative about the current state of the study of personality. One of the most commonly recurrent issues, expressed in the opening and concluding papers and in many others, restates an objective of this symposium. This is a plea for greater cooperation between fields and subfields of specialization. An examination of the entire collection of writings in this book shows, however, very considerable cooperation and cross-fertilization among disciplines. Concepts such as self-identity, derived from psychology, appear as central ideas in sociological writings, for example, and no paper fails to show strongly the influence of concepts derived from disciplines other than those with which their authors are identified. Certain concepts, independently formulated in different fields of study, are closely similar or analogous, and explicit attention is called to such "convergences" by some of our writers. Gardner Murphy observes that none of the five principal methods of psychology was devised by a professional psychologist, and similar circumstances apply to other fields.

An outstanding characteristic of all the groups of papers, especially evident in writings presenting theoretical viewpoints of the various scholarly fields, is a differing point of reference in conceptions of personality. Most commonly, psychologists and psychiatrists among our authors use the individual as their point of reference, whereas anthropologists and sociologists, whose study most frequently concerns groups, tend toward a modal concept of personality. Perhaps one of the most useful potential contributions of this book is the attention it calls to this difference of viewpoint, of which many scholars seem unaware. As a result, they are prone to see fault and error in the research and theories of colleagues who proceed with different assumptions toward different goals. Other recurrent themes and issues will be discussed in the remarks that follow concerning individual parts of the book.

Part One, "Theoretical Standpoints" shows the manifold nature of inter and intradisciplinary approaches to the study of personality. The writers include three psychologists, two sociologists, and two anthropologists, one of whom concerns himself with Freudian psychology. Three principal and closely related themes run through these seven papers:

(1) The relationship of concepts of personality to methods of investigation
(2) The distinctions (a) between the individual and the modal personality, and (b) between the "inner" person or self and the personality within a social or cultural context
(3) The importance of sociocultural variables in influencing personality.

The opening paper by Gardner Murphy has as its prevailing theme the mutual predetermination of concept by method and of method by concept in psychological studies of personality. Murphy shows how certain traditional methods of psychology have influenced concepts of personality, so that the concepts "are the children of the methods." Murphy's writing, in accordance with the prevailing interests and methods of psychology, concerns principally the personality of the individual. Anselm Strauss, representing sociology, writes of personality in a modal sense and of what goes on outside of persons and among persons. Following the line of thought presented by Murphy, we may see in the paper by Strauss a sociological illustration of the relationship between concept and method. Indeed, it might be said that the reason why sociology avoids an "inside" concept of personality, whether individual or modal, is because the methods suited for its study lie outside the scope of the traditional methods of sociology. Weston LaBarre also brings out the interplay of concept and method in his exposition of classical Freudian psychoanalysis. He points out the difficulty of replication in psychoanalytic study and, in its place, makes a plea for participant witnessing either as analyst or analysand, thus illustrating the subjectivity of concepts and techniques of psychoanalysis. Psychoanalysis may, in fact, be described as an outstanding example of the relationship between methods and concepts, since the concepts were formulated on the basis of information derived from specialized techniques of clinical interaction such as free association and transference.

In his delineation of national character, Daniel Bell also points to the relationship between method and concept. He observes that the four concepts of national creed, national image, national style, and national consciousness are not attributes of the personalities of individuals, but are ideas derived from methods other than techniques for directly measuring personality, "compounds of history, traditions, legitimations, values, customs, and manners which have been codified more or less consciously in texts, observations, or folklore." Only the modal personality of a nation, an abstraction of the attributes of individuals, is derived by techniques designed to assay personality.

The interdependence of concept and method relates closely to the second common theme we have noted in this group of papers, the distinction between individual and modal concepts of personality and the related distinction between the inner person or "self" and the person in a sociocultural context. We have already noted that the issue of modal versus individual personality appears implicitly or explicitly in many papers throughout the book. Douglass Price-Williams deals primarily with this subject, urging that the distinction always be kept in mind, that is, whether the point of reference is the individual or a modal abstraction. Price-Williams also points out an added weakness of some students of personality who, without apparent awareness of doing so, shift their point of reference from the individual to the modal and vice versa. Bell and Anthony F. C. Wallace consistently present modal views of personality, and Wallace emphasizes that his subject is human nature in general rather than any narrower concept of personality. Wallace sees studies of individual societies or cultures not as subordinate to any supraordinate theory of personality formulated on the basis of circumstances in Western society but as coordinate to a supraordinate concept that should represent human nature in general. Wallace also reminds us of the primate nature of man and of his innate physiological characteristics, subjects that are the exclusive interest of papers that follow in Part Two. Strauss brings out the sociological view of personality within a social context, observing that such interest in the individual as sociology may show generally inclines to the study of social variables affecting the behavior of individuals rather than the study of individuals themselves.

The question of the distinction between the "inner" personality and the individual in a context also concerns the third of the themes running through these papers, the importance of sociocultural context. Murphy outlines the issue in discussing the problem of personality integration, observing that if it can be shown that individuality is not the individuality of the organism but of the context, ". . . have we not lifted the discussion to a realm in which personality can be directly observed, and at the same time, intuitively and conceptually grasped?" Price-Williams, in similar vein, questions whether it is possible even to view personality apart from context; that is, whether the concept of trait can be separated from sociocultural milieux. Following existentialist thought, Bert Kaplan also deals with this subject, holding that the proper concept of personality should be based upon the individual facing a situation and not an investigation of the "constituted self" behind the observable appearances. Only LaBarre's chapter on basic concepts of psychoanalysis seems at all to depart from the view that the appropriate view of personality is in a sociocultural context, and even in the psychoanalytic approach social contexts are involved, of parent-child, husband-wife, analyst-patient, and the like.

A lesser but recurrent theme of the papers in this section is the problem of definition of concepts. Since the point of reference in concepts of personality varies, it is expectable that definitions of personality vary accordingly. Our contributors so observe, noting the great number of definitions of personality and related concepts and their impreciseness, and explicitly or implicitly urging interdisciplinary cooperation as a corrective measure.

Another common attribute of these papers discussing theories and contributions of the disciplines concerned with personality is worthy of note. No author praises his own field, and most authors urge that various kinds of action be taken for improvement. Strauss gives an appraisal of the contributions of sociology as being slight, a view which we think merits special comment. Although we align ourselves with Strauss in the view that sociology, like other fields, could do more, we believe that its contributions to date have been substantial, and we suggest that the various papers by sociologists in this volume support our opinion.

Many of the foregoing remarks have concerned methods of research in the study of personality, but our volume includes no writing expressly intended to describe and appraise the various methods and techniques developed for study. Omission was deliberate on the grounds that adequate treatment of this subject could not be achieved without greatly enlarging the symposium and book, and we therefore limited our concern with methodology to its theoretical aspects.

Part Two, "The Formation of Personality" is arranged principally along what may be called developmental lines, beginning with three writings on biological factors related to the formation of personality that are followed by three papers concerning sociocultural influences to which individuals and groups are exposed from childhood through old age. This group of papers concludes with two writings on language and personality and on the study of personality in primitive societies.

In our planning of the contents of the symposium, we sought to include discussion of biological influences relating to personality of both individuals and mankind in general. John O. Ellefson, writing as a primatologist,

7 Introduction

deals with hereditary biological factors connected with personality among the nonhuman primates, discussing observed differences in personality among individuals, groups, and species, and offering suggestions to account for them. On the basis of these observations of behavior, and of interpretations of reasons for intra and interspecific differences, he draws inferences about the nature of early man and factors involved in the formation of human personality. It is noteworthy that his interpretations of factors influencing the personalities of nonhuman primates coincides in considerable part with prevailing ideas about the formation of human personality. If the word "culture" is substituted for the term "ecology" in Ellefson's exposition, the similarity is very close. Unlike other contributors, Ellefson is dealing with more than one species of living forms. His idea that the differing modal personalities of the several species of nonhuman primates have adaptive value in an evolutionary sense is nevertheless similar to ideas about congruence between human personality and culture that appear implicitly in most of the other papers in this volume.

Karl H. Pribram discusses individual differences in behavior and differences at different times among individuals, and advocates the study of affective, "nonbehavioral" reactions—that is, the internal mental reactions of people—that are important in attributes of personality such as strength of character, creativity, introversion, and extroversion. He urges interdisciplinary cooperation, calling special attention to ideas and research in neuropsychology and neurophysiology which parallel, complement, and reinforce observations of the social sciences regarding personality and offer the promise of amplifying and clarifying ideas about cultural factors influential in forming personality. Individual, hereditary differences among human beings as these relate to personality are treated by W. R. Thompson in a paper that directly or indirectly relates to all other writings in this book. Thompson presents an historical review emphasizing modern trends in the study of genetic inheritance of various behavioral traits customarily called traits of personality. In an attempt to distinguish between genetic and nongenetic influences on personality, he makes use of studies of nonhuman mammals as well as of man and gives special attention to studies of human twins.

In the papers that follow by Mary Ellen Goodman, Howard S. Becker, and William E. Henry, the subject shifts from biological influences on personality to sociocultural influences to which human beings are exposed as they pass from infancy and childhood through adolescence, adulthood, and old age. Writing on influences on personality during childhood and adolescence, Goodman reviews and summarizes research and thought on this subject in psychology, psychiatry, and sociology as well as in her own field of anthropology. She gives pointed attention to a subject which we have not previously mentioned that recurs in many other papers, the importance of features of form (the who, when, and how of child rearing) as distinguished from features of content (what a child learns—goals, ideas, values).

Howard S. Becker reviews and summarizes studies of adult socialization in the framework of a theory of symbolic interaction which includes a discussion of the concept of self and of changes in the self during the adult years of life. Becker discusses from a sociological viewpoint the kinds of changes of the self taking place under the impact of different social circumstances and the socializing institutions operating to produce the changes. William E. Henry, also presenting a sociological viewpoint and writing long lines similar to those of Becker's paper, concerns himself with hanges in personality that cover and bridge middle and old age. Becker points out contrasts between these two periods of the normal human life span, discusses associated changes in social life, and presents a tentative formulation of types of life styles among adults. His presentation makes use of the concepts such as identity, agency, communion, investment, and disengagement, ideas that recur in various other papers in similar and differing context and sometimes under different names or in somewhat variant forms.

In a specialized paper on early bilingualism as related to personality, A. Richard Diebold, Jr., touches upon an important question not otherwise dealt with in this volume, the relationship between personality and the modes of characteristic thought and action that may inhere among speakers of particular languages. Diebold's use of data on bilingual individuals provides another example of convergence of techniques, resembling the technique discussed by Thompson of studying twins in attempts to distinguish between what is genetically transmitted and what is acquired. As is generally characteristic of the entire body of studies of the relationship between language and personality, Diebold's paper presents no firm conclusions but offers evidence suggesting that speakers of different languages live in different worlds of reality.

John J. Honigmann's paper on the study of personality in primitive societies is extremely informative and is also in good measure a history of the scientific study of personality that begins with the Cambridge Anthropological Expedition to Torres Straits in 1901. Honigmann's paper cuts across a wide range of cultural factors relating to personality and presents a valuable cross-cultural summary of the study of personality in primitive society that points out weaknesses as well as noting progress. The tabulation which Honigmann provides of primitive societies on which one or more comprehensive studies relating to personality are available should be a valuable aid to students of the subject.

Most of the articles in this volume concern personality among socially and psychiatrically normal persons, and thus they reflect the major concern of research and theory on the subject of personality. Part Three, "Personality Under Stress and Change" includes three papers that concern personality among psychiatric and social deviants and two papers concerning personality and cultural change. "The universe is change;" Marcus Aurelius, the stoic Emperor of Rome once wrote, "our life is what our thoughts make of it." We live in an era of stress and change; a time which—despite predictions of modern prophets of gloom—probably does not differ strikingly from the epoch when Aurelius witnessed the decline of the Roman Empire. There is, however, one important difference. Today, as the following essays indicate, social scientists systematically examine the stresses of life and attempt to determine what "our thoughts make of it." Modern social science has gone beyond Marcus Aurelius—not in the sense of surpassing his wise meditations—but rather by making careful, comparative investigations of conditions of human life which can be replicated by human beings other than the original observers.

In the first paper in Part Three, for example, E. D. Wittkower and G. Dubreuil, a psychiatrist and an anthropologist respectively, review nearly one hundred studies concerning the effect of culture upon mental disorder. They draw on research done by many social scientists thousands of miles apart, and thus they are able to examine the cultural context of mental disorder as it exists throughout much of the world. Their discussion of causative circumstances, the types of stress arising in particular cultures, and of common elements found in mental disorder thus covers small primitive societies as well as great, industrialized nations. Wittkower and Dubreuil argue correctly that no society has produced a Rousseauian utopia where all men live in a state of primitive pleasure devoid of problems, and point to the problems of mental disorder that characterize particular cultures. As do other contributors in Part Three, they point out that the line between the "normal" and the "abnormal" is thin, and that much can be learned about the normal from the study of the abnormal.

A. B. Hollingshead presents a classical example of empirical research concerned with human reaction to the universal problem of illness. He examines the ways in which families withstand the pressures produced by the serious illness of a family member, and demonstrates that families which were emotionally stable before the onset of the sickness can best handle the multiple problems incurred by the illness.

William M. McCord reviews research conducted by himself and other scholars on three types of people—violent criminals, alcoholics, and psychotics—who have succumbed to unbearable stresses in their lives, and presents a summary and discussion of social factors involved in these forms of deviation from normality. Drawing upon the Cambridge-Somerville Study, McCord was able to analyze subjects long before they committed crimes, became alcoholics, or entered mental hospitals as psychotics. Like other contributors, he emphasizes that society itself defines what it regards as acceptable and nonacceptable behavior. McCord emphasizes the need for cooperation between the social sciences and physical sciences, such as biochemistry and genetics, in attempts to understand the nature of forms of psychosis, such as schizophrenia. As does Margaret Mead in the concluding chapter of this volume, he urges that the findings of the social sciences he put to practical use in informing the public and in aiding to arrive at decisions in matters of public policy.

In a paper that links research and theory on the subjects of cognition, motivation, and acculturation, George D. Spindler writes concerning a major problem confronting most human populations of the world today, the problem and processes of psychological adaptation to changing conditions of society and culture. He provides a fine example of anthropological research that concerns the basic personality structure of members of two Indian tribes, the Menomini and the Blood, whose ways of life have undergone great acculturative change. The Menomini control aggression, have little desire for achievement, remain fatalistic in the face of stress, and exhibit quiet endurance when confronted with problems. The Blood differ markedly in all of their reactions to similar problems. Making use of the concepts of identity and cognitive control, Spindler traces the relation between the personalities characterizing the two tribes and the sociocultural conditions under which they live, which he sees as interdependent. He also discusses reactive movements, such as new religions, as ways of searching for identity and reestablishing cognitive control over one's environment under conditions of change.

Spindler's discussion relates in the subject of motivation and in many other ways to the paper that follows by George A. DeVos, who concerns himself with personality as related to innovative change. Comparing interpretations of circumstances in Japan formulated by himself and coworkers with those offered by other scholars treating the United States and other societies of the world, DeVos presents a provocative discussion of the problem of understanding motivation toward achievement. He shows that the drive toward achievement is similar among citizens of Japan and of the United States but points out notable differences in its goals and in the associated sociocultural circumstances that foster and support this value. DeVos' discussion of failure to achieve and associated problems of juvenile delinquency, crime, and other forms of social deviation among depressed minority groups closely relates to subjects dealt with by McCord.

All of the papers in Part Three may be regarded as illustrations of interdisciplinary research that examine the relationships between culture, social structure, and personality, and their authors freely cross the traditional lines of the disciplines. Like most of the other contributors to this volume, the authors of these papers generally advocate interdisciplinary cooperation—and their contributions provide evidence that such cooperation is indeed taking place.

In her concluding address, Margaret Mead gives an historical summary of developments over the four decades since personality became established as a subject of scientific inquiry and calls attention to new or enlarging horizons that include neurophysiological research on the brain, modern techniques for efficient retrieval of information, and the application of knowledge to problems of modern life. She calls attention to relevant subjects that are well represented and poorly represented in the collection of papers published in this volume, adding insights and observations of her own. Mead concludes her address with pleas in which the editors of this volume join. She urges that the social sciences combine knowledge and methods to form a united science of behavior, and that they "put things together" to meet the challenge of practical problems imposed by the rapid change the world is now undergoing.

It is our hope that this volume will stimulate further interdisciplinary cooperation and that, as guidelines for continued development of research on personality, the future will see additional symposia of the kind we have attempted here. We regard as a privilege our role as planners of the symposium and editors of this volume.

PART ONE
Theoretical Standpoints

2

Psychological Views of Personality and Contributions to Its Study

Gardner Murphy

It is convenient to define personality as that which makes a person distinctively himself; it is equivalent, then, to individuality. We shall use the term in this sense.

However, this definition—adequate for the psychology of today—is inadequate from the point of view of the biological sciences and medicine, and is inadequate also from the point of view of the social and cultural sciences. It is my hope that for the present, various disciplines may be used simultaneously, each with its own approach; but that we shall learn something in our work together which will carry us toward a more appropriate multidisciplinary definition. Please regard all my factual and theoretical efforts as guided by the hope that ultimately the narrowness and specificity of the psychological approach can be merged in and find "membership character" within a larger whole.

I

A place is needed for what Gordon Allport (1937) has called the *idiographic,* and likewise a place for the *nomothetic*. The idiographic is the approach of the biographer and the historian who tell us, in the language of Plutarch or Boswell, just what a man was really like in his heart of hearts. The nomothetic will find its interest in the laws, principles, or dynamics of personality growth and function, in the things that make men what they are, and in the lawfulness of the passage through Shakespeare's seven ages of man, or the eight modern ages of Erik Erikson; looking in the genes, or the endocrine organs, or the operant conditionings, or the perceptual learning processes, or the psychoanalytic dynamics, for the way in which the complex of laws and principles makes possible the response of a particular individual to a particular situation. Allport's two approaches can indeed be reconciled. But "the work draws blood." If the interest is essentially idiographic, it weeps to see its Goethe or its Joan of Arc lost in abstract laws and principles; and if the interest is essentially nomothetic, there is a feeling that the resources of science have been sold short for the sake of a vivid picture. The nomothetic law-seeking scientist will agree that the heart of man calls for pictures. "But if we are to have pictures," he says, "let Michelangelo paint them. Let Beethoven or Wagner or Tchaikovsky tell us how the divine message came to him. But," he adds, *"scientists* have a different task—indeed the universal task—of observing, generalizing, formulating principles." It is because the nomothetic scientist recognizes the limitations of abstract science that he insists so vigorously that it shall do all that it can do, while recognizing the precious role sustained by the idiographic.

Even if I had the supreme gift of a great biographer, my message would not be quite the one demanded on an occasion like this, in which laws of personality formation and functioning are, I believe, sought conjointly by the various sciences of man. I believe that when the story is all told the nomothetic effort will give not a small, but a large place in personality study to the researches into history, literature, and the arts, and also a deeper intuitive grasp of what it is that Euripides, Dante, Shakespeare, and Walt Whitman had to say about their own experience as they lived through it, or as they put it in eternal form through the mouths of their characters.

II

The scientific effort to study personality has proved to be extraordinarily difficult. It is a labor fraught with conflict, frustration, the discovery of one's limitations and mistakes, the endless necessity for backtracking and doing over, and the certainty that one will not only fail one's contemporaries, but fail oneself in the process. Of course, anyone who talks about personality is going to fail. But Boswell, while he failed, made for himself a glorious place as a father of biography. William James (H. James 1920), as we learn from his letters, could discover the richness of human interchanges in a manner which he knew he could never write into a systematic psychology. During the last few centuries, many men of wisdom, like Immanuel Kant and William James, have met the effort towards a scientific psychology with utter incredulity. "A nasty little science," said James. Such men are sure that the world of abstractions, laws, and principles applies only to inert matter, or at best to those aspects of "matter in the living state" which are closest to physics and chemistry; and of all the searching words of scepticism or hostility they have directed to the efforts to make a science of psychology, they have been most profoundly and earnestly hostile to the attempt at a science of personality. Those of us who believe that such a science can be coaxed into existence and given a dignity and even a meaning worthy of a philosopher are out of step with contemporary science in many ways.

The trouble lies partly in the fact that personality is far more complex than most of the phenomena of the life sciences; another lies in the fact that there are profound cultural biases in each period which cause personality to be looked upon in a way plainly reeking with all the difficulties of the sociology of knowledge and cultural relativity; and third, plainly and patently, that the conscious and unconscious dynamics of the individual investigator of personality wreak havoc with his most devoted and most disciplined scientific efforts. All of the pitfalls which the various kinds of relativity have pointed out, the fact that—as Einstein says—there is no "privileged position," the fact—as Freud made clear—that one cannot outgrow one's own deeply ingrained personal outlook when one looks upon either persons in general, or the theory of the person in particular—all this makes the challenge peculiarly severe. There are culturally ingrained and personally colored considerations which determine what can and what cannot be done with the concept of personality, and if we know that our theory is sound, we know that its very soundness inexorably rules out the possibility of our achieving the objectivity which we seek.

No less obvious, however, is the fact that the challenge must be accepted. We live in an era in which we are learning a great deal about the facts that belong to the physical sciences, while we still know tragically little about the facts that have to do with human psychology, and least of all about the facts that have to do with the individuality from which growth, creativity, and leadership must spring. Mallory said that he climbed Everest because it was there. The psychologist must study personality first of all "because it is there."

As I browse through the great libraries of the world, the Widener Library at Harvard, the Library of Congress, the Library of the British Museum, I am again and again impressed by the fact that science is made chiefly not by advance in content, but by advance in method. Newton could not have solved introductory problems of celestial mechanics until he had invented the method of the calculus. Helmholtz could not discover the nature of tone qualities without inventing metal resonators, and showing how they were to be used. Max Planck could not give us quantum theory except by investigating the dynamics of black-body radiation. Pavlov could not give us the behavior world of classical conditioning without the conditioned response method. Freud could not give us the theory of the unconscious without working through the psychoanalytic method.

Indeed the predetermination of concepts by methods is one of the general, almost universal, realities of modern science. You will find in the Widener Library, for example, a vast graveyard of psychological ideas, stimulating and challenging in their era, but without a method which could give them life; while even rather meager and humble experimentalists have proved capable of building a structure of experimental psychology—a house in which personalities like Wertheimer or Hull or Tolman can look out of the windows upon an exciting and vast domain.

The glory and the bane of modern life is the scientific method. The nurse, the social worker, no less than the physician and the engineer, the critic of literature, indeed, even the critic of music and the fine arts, lives or dies by his method, and his method becomes more and more like the method of science. Dip for a moment, for example, into the fascinating world of cultural anthropology and prehistory, and the challenging and maddening world of the analysis of historical artifacts, records, and documents, and see what is happening to them all by methods of dating through carbon 14. You will find that science has descended upon the earlier, cruder methods as the lava of Vesuvius descended upon Pompeii.

With the death of the old comes a new life. The world is suddenly caught, disciplined, and forced into order by the very nature of the message of science. There is a great deal of "playing dead" and a great deal of "playing deaf," particularly among some students of personality who are more at home in the generous tradition of an impressionistic type of literary and artistic criticism. They were content because it was their life to say that a painting must or must not have been painted by Rembrandt because of its atmosphere, or because of the personality which was breathed into it. Unfortunately, they set up arguments like this against the simple realities of analysis of paint and of canvas, and if the kind of paint used is simply incompatible with the given interpretation, the scientific method must—however grudgingly—be accepted. It will be my thesis that intuition will gain rather than lose, will become richer rather than poorer by this acknowledgement of the role of science. My primary point is that the method of science sweeps like a homogeneous glacier-like process down over the whole of the world, and that it does certain things to the people who study personality in their social settings which can never be undone by any alternative, never reversed by another method, however suggestive and however valuable.

I have said that method predetermines the subject matter of the special disciplines. But what would really be better would be to say that there is a mutual predetermination of concept by method, and of method by concept. The concepts which belong to Western European culture serve, in large degree, to shape the mind of the person who invents a method. The method leads back into the structure of the science he is creating. It is, in general, a time-space system of ideas—strictly a time-space-mass-energy system of ideas, still essentially Newtonian—that underlies the structure of physical science, and the modern physical science working through the theory of the nucleus, the theory of energy, quantum theory, the theory of new and challenging aspects of time and of space, has been forced upon the modern thinker. The new concepts, frightfully abstract as they are, have worked their way back to guide and limit the invention of new methods which will confirm or modify them.

Now personality is ultimately the beneficiary or the victim, depending upon your point of view, of this preoccupation with method. It was first the experimental method—the nineteenth century gift of biological sciences—that made psychology look for analogies between the nature of the individual man and the cell, and ultimately the nucleus of the atom. Ultimately the personality theory of today is a distillation of modern physics applied to the organism and the cell, and then the electrical particle working back and forth from the large to the small and from the small to the large, until we convince ourselves that personality is a special time-space structure basically analogous to the time-space structure with which the physicists and the chemists are at home. Our operationism (Bridgman 1946), our factor analysis (Guilford 1936), our definitions of the nature of psychological processes—whether behavioristic (Skinner 1936), Gestalt-like (Koffka 1935), or psychoanalytic (S. Freud 1949)—make personality simply the most complex expression of what we have come to regard as self-evident and real at the level of the smallest knowable things. There is a two-way relation between conceptual assumptions and methodological assumptions, and the method which leads to these concepts—the method of observation, dissection, verification, replication, and ultimately combination and integration—is a method which we assume must be right for personality because personality is like other real things studied in nature.

III

But let us look more closely at the five great methods of modern psychology: the cross-cultural, the developmental, the clinical, the experimental, and the quantitative. I will note some of their interdependences and the possibilities for their integration.

I will begin with the cross-cultural method partly because I delight in a collaborative effort with those from other disciplines. Partly it is because we must recognize the dependence of our twentieth-century Western science upon the particular form and quality of cultural evolution from which we happen to benefit, and by which, incidentally, we are likewise somewhat blinded. We are dialectically led onward toward greater methodological sophistication. The cross-cultural method shows clearly that the specific conceptions of personality presupposed in the West are conceptions traceable in large measure to the preliterate concepts of the Mediterranean societies, and later by Greek, Hebrew, and Christian ideas, which were somewhat integrated under the Roman and the Holy Roman Empires. Some of the most elemental and obvious ideas about personality, as the West has seen the issue, are the idea of free will in the sense of indeterminism, the idea of aloofness from the very core of the cosmos, the bold conception that "I am the master of my fate, I am the captain of my soul," the idea of individualism contrasted to group responsibility, and in general the idea of the sharp separation likewise between the soul and the body, and between psychological law and physiological law. Modern Western psychology has made some of these ideas whipping boys to be eliminated to make place for other ideas which are still their blood-relatives. Place all these Western ideas in juxtaposition with the ideas from the *Upanishads* or the *Gita,* or either Indian or Chinese Buddhism, and you will see what I mean by the cultural predetermination of the frame of reference within which we work. The East has had trouble in understanding these "individualistic" ideas.

The methods of the cultural sciences are also methods influenced, as I tried to show above, by the whole methodological development of the physical sciences. The cross-cultural method, like most other methods, is analytic before it is synthetic. It assumes that the basic dynamics of things seen in the large must be the same as the basic dynamics of things as seen in the small. There is a basic isomorphism of all the aspects of reality. A doctrine such as William James' "pluralistic universe" (1909), a piecemeal or loose-jointed affair in which the different parts are autonomous from the rest, is related to Western individualism, and perhaps even, to the loneliness of the pioneer facing the wilderness. But, however that may be, the cross-cultural method, though it comes first in our presentation, comes as the heir of a long methodological series dating from at least as far back as Galileo, and indeed going back to the Greek atomists and the generous relativism of Herodotus. For Herodotus knew that the men of different city states and of different cultural areas must grow and develop as different kinds of entities upon the face of the earth. He knew this in a way utterly different from the way in which the Indian philosophers knew of the changeless and eternal *atman* within each manifest individuality. It was because Herodotus saw things in a cross-cultural way—if I am allowed a little exaggeration—that we who belong to his own tradition see things in a cross-cultural way.

The comparative method comes second. It was invented, I suppose, by Aristotle's taxonomy of plants and animals. It was given its modern form by the use of accessory sense organs like the microscope, and by functional concepts like "adaptation to the environment," which were in the air in the time of Malthus and Erasmus Darwin. As usual, the concepts and methods interacted, and it was in the acute observational powers, the incredible capacity for discerning what lay hidden, that Charles Darwin's functionalism, his conception of the survival of the fittest, with adaptation to the environment, came to life. Just as Herodotus' cross-cultural method shows that persons must be different in differing environments, so the biological method, turning inward, showed through the microscopes of the year 1900 the reality of the process of mutation which, before long, viewed through the Columbia University microscopes of T. H. Morgan, gave the "theory of the gene." Evolutionism was, of course, the great idea of the last hundred years, ready to suffer many changes as genetics, embryology, and the investigation of the growth process offer keys to individual temperament, individual intellectual endowment, individual capacity for impulse control and delay. Morphology can define structure. Passing rapidly beyond the crude but useful morphologies which found temperament to be a reflection of bodily organization, the methods of the biological sciences have become available to the student of individual personality.

We come third to the developmental method. It is hard for us to realize, as we look at the biology of Aristotle, that the biology of modern times is a very distinctive new departure in being a developmental science, a time science, a science of the derivation of one thing from another, in an orderly intelligible sequence. Life can hardly be conceived in cross-section terms. The development of the race and of the individual directs our attention to the passage of the present into the past, and of the future into the present, in a manner suggesting concepts such as fulfillment, purpose, and aim. Even if these processes be regarded as completely blind, they point, in a sense, to something ahead along the path. The species works, so to speak, towards a particular kind of an adaptation to environment, as an individual in growth works towards the filling of a particular adult form.

Here Kurt Lewin (1935) put his hand upon a very fundamental difference between the physical sciences, with their ahistorical or cross-sectional approach, and those psychological and sociocultural sciences which are concerned with developmental dynamics. The reason I emphasize this point is that there is nothing more characteristic of modern psychology than its developmentalism, its passionate devotion to a sequential or time-related dynamic. Even the most narrow experimentalist, technically preoccupied with the sheer factual situation, the sheer "is-ness" of what he confronts, is *mainly* interested in the learning process or the *growth* process, or perceptual *development,* or the climax and dissipation of tension, or any one of another hundred aspects of time sequential observations. The great master of our own time in matters psychological, Sigmund Freud, wrote a developmental psychology from the time of his observations on little children in the nineties to his preoccupation with the little infant Moses in the bulrushes (1939), as he completed the eighth decade of his own life; and developmental sequences in terms of psychosexual stages, or phases in the personal evolution of id, ego, and superego are absolutely essential to the conceptual structure. The sequence of interpersonal interchanges in the patient-therapist relationship constitute a methodological approach to the transference and therapeutic processes as a whole.

If I asked you who is the greatest of living psychologists, you might meditate, and say, "Jean Piaget." I would reply: "If so, is it not because of what he calls epistemological genetics? Is it not because of the developmental character of his whole work?" Is not the primary philosophical question regarding personality development as such, the question whether growth is a matter of articulation of parts which stick together to form higher synthesized structures, or, on the other hand, a matter of confluence or progressive mutual adjustment of parts, that which we might call emergence? Indeed, is not the primary question for personality philosophy the question of reductionism versus emergence, and is the solution not to be found mainly in the methodological sophistication with which the growth process is to be viewed?

But we come, fourth, to the clinical method and its handmaid, the testing movement. The clinical method of personality study was well developed in western Europe in the latter half of the nineteenth century, consisting largely of vivid sketches of individual sufferers whom the medical men characterized with a few brief strokes and subjected to some crude method of neurological or performance testing in the service of differential diagnosis. They began to say that disease is not external to the personality, but often an expression or an exaggeration of what is already there. Manifestations became clearly defined, and the development of new diagnostic categories and of new test instruments had, of course, to go hand in hand. It was here that the greatness of Alfred Binet became evident because, in fact, Binet had been a tester of intellectual powers, and a sophisticated student of ego organization, long before he was charged by the French Minister of Public Instruction in 1904 to differentiate the clinical group of the mental defectives from those capable of doing the normal work of the schools. It was a clinical purpose that Binet's work served, and it was a methodological sophistication, with fifteen years of prior work with testing, that made possible the 1905 scale. Here, incidentally, the evolutionary approach had already made an important beginning, for it was the work of early evolutionists like Galton and Cattell that had been responsible for the development of the psychological test prior to the time of Binet.

Again, it was the clinical preoccupation with people of different types that led the Swiss psychiatrist, Hermann Rorschach (1941), to his ingenious experiments with the perception of inkblots. The cross-cultural viewpoint was expressed in the amazing wisdom which he manifested in studying the differences between the Swiss of different cantons. But the great consummation of the clinical method was Sigmund Freud's development of the psychoanalytic method by which the free association of disturbed patients led to the discovery and disentanglement of unconscious conflicts, and pointed to the capacity for reintegration. The method has, of course, leavened psychology deeply and broadly, and has been intimately fused with ingenious experimental procedures. The work of Harry Murray (1938), notably in the studies entitled "Explorations in Personality," perhaps most vividly shown in the Thematic Apperception Test, brings out the way in which the perceptual life reveals the dynamic organization of the person. Murray saw, as had Rorschach, that the psychological dynamics of the individual, the way in which he makes sense of what is presented to him, can offer a major source of light upon the adjustmental dynamic, the unconscious conflicts, and the potential sources of integration within the person. In fact, these three giants—Binet, Rorschach, and Murray—have shown clearly once, and I hope for all, that no manipulation of data about overt behavior can ever be a really meaningful clue to the person unless the dynamic of his own perceptual interpretation of life is included.

Next comes experimentation. It may seem odd in any modern psychological discussion to defend the experimental method. The experimentalists usually consider themselves the aristocracy, the élite among psychological investigators, and it may be odd to say a word in their defense, as if they needed it. On the other hand, experimentation has tended to be belittled by many social scientists, by humanists, and by those interested in the philosophy of human life, as if somehow the attempt to control various aspects were pernicious to the liberation of the human spirit. Objections from the right and from the left are characteristic of an era which does not know how to look at itself, which suspects on the one hand that too much exactness is being demanded, and on the other hand that it is only exactness that counts. From the experimentalists' viewpoint, you must limit the number of variables. From the clinicians' viewpoint, most experimentalists leave out *contexts* and *complexities*.

What the experimentalist, however, can learn to do if well taught is to disentangle problems soluble by action from problems that are soluble only by conceptualization and mathematization. He has insisted on acting in an appropriate way with regard to his situation, has laid out his independent and dependent variables, has selected his miniscule details of the life situation, has attempted an orderly formulation of possible interrelations between such details. All of this could be illustrated by Pavlov's (1928–1941) development of "classical conditioning" techniques, essentially techniques for holding constant, in the life of an experimental animal, a great deal that must not be left to chance; and by using measured amounts of stimulation and measured responses to such stimulation in connection with a conceptualization regarding the stimulation of the central nervous system. The operant conditioning developed in the last three decades by Skinner (1936) has made systematic attempts to note behavioral changes under the impact of known stimulating conditions. When judged by the productivity and the systematic influence of the theories of learning associated with this method, the fact that it is going stronger each day makes it absolutely ridiculous to belittle it.

I will grant to many humanistic and phenomenological friends that human life may be oversimplified when viewed through these particular lenses. But it is the very nature of science to oversimplify, to create abstractions which can only be made viable when related to many other abstractions of many sorts to create a scientific picture as a whole, and then brought back to the doorstep with the idiographic method, as already noted. Every time we teach an adult, or a child, or ourselves anything at all, there are elements of classical and of operant conditioning involved, and it would be utter folly to deny ourselves the fullest possible understanding of the principles of learning that are beginning to be clear thereby.

We can legitimately object if classical and operant conditioning are offered as the only kinds of learning process. As Edward Tolman (1949) vigorously said and well documented: "There is more than one kind of learning." For example, another kind of learning pointed out simultaneously over a half-century ago by an American experimentalist named Whitman (1919) and an Austrian psychiatrist named Freud (1949), shows that there is a tendency for any stimulus object which gives satisfaction to a drive to attain a high priority in control of the organism's life, so that other stimuli which originally have had the same effect upon the life of the organism lose this capacity, and are made permanently secondary to the one which first repeatedly satisfied the drive. This principle was named by Freud the principle of *investment;* the life energies are invested in whatever comes along so that it has a priority, a love value, an attention value which later competing objects cannot obtain. "First love," if you like; "old friends are the dearest." Life may be guided by what happened to come first. Freud's term *investment* is usually replaced—unfortunately —by a Greek term *cathexis,* which means approximately "taking hold of." The animal psychologists have been finding during these same decades that the object which gratifies a bird or mammal, when aroused and ready for it, may similarly get the advantage of primacy, never to be displaced by other objects of the same general quality. The animal or bird thus follows the human investigator rather than members of its own kind. The investigator has the first chance. The principle was formulated in terms of a German word which means almost literally "impregnation," not quite correctly translated into English by any single word, but rendered ordinarily by the term *imprinting*.

Now Freud's term "investment" and the Tinbergen-Lorenz term "imprinting" refer to functionally overlapping groups of observations. We do not dare say that investment and imprinting are identical, but they certainly point to the same types of biological realities. It has been generally realized that learning phenomena of the broad type indicated here are not easily fitted within the framework of either classical or operant conditioning. Personally, I think that they are of enormous importance, and following Pierre Janet (1925), I have called them phenomena of "canalization." I think the important thing at this time is not names, but the accumulation of more experimental work. I notice, incidentally, a successful replication of an early study of acquired tastes which seems to show quite clearly that among a group of equally well-accepted foods, those which are "practiced"—repeatedly given to hungry subjects—develop an advantage over other foods which originally were comparable in satisfying quality (Hartley and Perelman 1963). It looks as if the phenomenon were analogous to the imprinting-investment phenomenon.

I do not think we know yet whether perceptual learning, in the sense of progressive modification of a way of perceiving anything, expresses the same laws which appear at a motor or functional level. It certainly looks as if R. S. Woodworth (1947) was right in pointing out that the reinforcement process occurs at the perceptual level before it can have any effect at the motor terminal. But I will content myself then with the statement that there seem to be several kinds of learning processes revealed by the experimental method.

Here is a very curious paradox: When you use a systematic method, you commit yourself to the concepts that are intrinsic to it, and you must see them through. You commit yourself, for example, when you use the experimental method, to the idea of independent and dependent variables, and to the manipulation of the independent variable through a range of values, ordinarily quantitative values, in order that you may observe the outcome in the dependent variables. This, of course, involves a certain conception of how the universe is made if you are going to experiment upon it, and this means that if the experiment is successful, there is a certain sort of validation that the universe was, at least for these particular purposes, made as you assumed it was made. A large part of our modern knowledge of nutrition and of medicine, our ability to cure gout, and prevent smallpox derives from successful application of this kind of experimental thinking.

But here is the paradox: If you once open the door to let nature in, and you use an experimental method which allows her to come in, she will come in and she will take up the house. Or, as the Germans say, "Give the devil a finger and he will take the whole hand." The experimental method has been bringing into psychology, particularly into personality study, a number of things which we do not like at all. The classical illustration is the use of experimental manipulations and words by the followers of Mesmer, who had a very definite theory about animal magnetism and who did succeed in quieting many nervous sufferers. Later, Charcot produced anesthesias and paralyses and then removed them by devices which were full-fledged experimental methods. In other words, experimental methods bring into the house the most disreputable phenomena such as the whole bag and baggage of hypnosis, which the experimentalist would never have welcomed if he had understood what he was doing. I think experimental hypnosis has shown, in the last twenty years (Brenman and Gill 1947; Hilgard 1965), a motley throng of phenomena which we cannot interpret even with maximal use of the conventional concepts as to how organisms are built. I would add that the whole field of parapsychology confronts us with the same difficulties, for, as Donald Hebb (1958) has pointed out, if the rules of experimental practice were followed and if we were dealing with any ordinary experimental problem that finds a place within the tightly structured systems in which most of us are at home, we should have to admit telepathy, clairvoyance, precognition, and the rest of the disturbing and disreputable band of practices.

Every one of the five methods I have thus described makes use of *quantification*. It goes beyond the sheer statement that a phenomenon is present or absent, and tells how much of it is present and whether two classes of observations vary directly or inversely. It tells whether an experimental group and a control group differ in consequence of the fact that the control group is not subjected to the same factors as the experimental group. In other words, we are moving, as Herman Ebbinghaus' experiments on memory clearly showed almost a hundred years ago, into a realm where the universal mathematical language of science must be applied to psychological data unflinchingly, exactly as if physiology or morphology were involved. It is not surprising in these terms that the most important single methodological device for personality study in the closing nineteenth century was the system of mathematical techniques developed by G. T. Fechner (1860) and his collaborators, known as psychophysics, dealing with the quantitative relations between physical stimuli and psychological results. Also, there is nothing surprising about the fact that the most important single mathematical tool to get into personality study in the early years of the present century is the product-moment correlation method of Karl Pearson, showing the degree of concomitance of two sets of measures. When it began to be clear that the mathematics suitable for very large populations is not the same as that suitable for small samples, the influence of a plant geneticist, Ronald A. Fisher (1935), began to be heavy, and within a few years this mathematician-geneticist planted a bomb under the whole conception of one independent variable and its immediate straight-line consequences as seen in the dependent variables, and introduced the tremendously exciting, dramatic, and valuable method known under the term "analysis of variance," with subordinate methods and applications. Fisher undertook to show that the solutions to quantitative problems were often quite easily discoverable by working with a system of interrelated measures, with due regard to probability theory, and the likelihood of various types of errors. Along with Darwin, Pavlov, and Freud, you could very well say that R. A. Fisher is a source of fundamental revolution in psychological research method, and in particular in the investigation of personality structure. There is almost no personality research being published today which does not at least make some use of the system of ideas represented by R. A. Fisher.

Incidentally, it is interesting that none of the five revolutionary new methods of today was devised by a professional psychologist. Most of the methods which have proved most novel and successful for personality study have come to us from biology, medicine, physiology, psychoanalysis, and mathematics.

IV

So much for methods. We turn now to concepts. I indicated previously that I would suggest a way in which methods and concepts could be shown to be directly interdependent, or translatable one to the other. I must show that the concepts to be described are the children of the methods used.

The first of the concepts to underscore is that individuality has its being in a social context. There is indeed St. John of the Cross, or as William James (1902) said, "individual men in their solitude." History, as Carlyle (1928) said, can be conceived as the record of the "lives of great men." Today, however, we clamor for context. On the face of this earth evolved not so much a lot of separate lives, but life; and not a lot of separate birds, mammals, primates, but species. The life of the species came before the life of those specific accidents of time and place which brought individuals into existence. Individuals owe their everything, their being, to a context. They may occasionally leave a footprint on the sands of time, but whether they do or do not, to understand them involves understanding their time, place, and function. These are the concepts that precede, as well as accompany, the cross-cultural approach and the cross-cultural approach makes more specific the matter of social contexts of individuality.

Viewed in the same broad evolutionary scheme, one can see why behaviorism has had its enormous vogue. If behaviorism were in court, and we asked it to swear to tell "the truth, the whole truth, and nothing but the truth," we should certainly have to settle for a compromise, telling us by its most vigorous methods, nothing but the truth; but we should be very foolish to ask it to tell us the whole truth. In the very nature of the case, behaviorism had to be seclusive and selective; had to start with the picture of life on the face of the earth, as just described; had to ask why creatures survived and why creatures evolved into new forms; had to emphasize behavior, and the behavior had to be seen in the context of the behavior of other living things. It was not ready for a study of the inner world of behaving organisms. It was, moreover, committed to the conception of science at the beginning of this century, with its passionate belief in the reality of things observed, and the unvarying and relentless reality-orientation of the method which science exemplified. The concept of objectivity—and incidentally, the general lack of any recognition of cultural relativity—made it possible to believe that the behavioral observation was a self-contained reality, both for the person investigated and for the social context in which he appeared. The conditioned-reflex method became involved in the general understanding of behaviorism, so that the behaviorist had to believe in the central importance of conditioning models. Psychological reality had to be conceptualized in behavior terms. The behaviorist felt himself oriented in the direction of a behavioral philosophy which had no place for any biological realities but only for behavioral realities.

A counterpoint to this emphasis was to be found, capable simultaneously of negating the behavioral emphasis and negating the piecemeal analysis to which the conditioned reflex gave its flavor. The double protest in the form of Max Wertheimer's Gestalt psychology set up a personality theory based upon perceptual dynamics, rather similar in some ways to that toward which Hermann Rorschach was working his way, a conception that was the reverse of the method of analysis, and the mere juxtaposition of parts. Wertheimer and his associates believed that the parts of personality, or of anything else, are not really parts at all, but are aspects that can be understood only in the light of the whole (Koffka 1935). They have "membership character"; that is, they take on a quality depending upon the exact time and place of their appearance in a psychological act. Just as the color that you see in a sunset depends upon the evening sky as a whole, so the whole gentleness or fury or amusement which you see in a face are reflections of the total form and movement of the person whose face it is. So, as in the experiments of Wolff (1943) and Arnheim (1928), the face, the hands, the moving figure are seen dynamically and interpreted correctly in the light of a structured whole in which there really are no parts in the traditional Euclidean sense. These ideas remain fundamental in the personality research of present years, in which thousands of different diagnostic instruments, like those devised by Binet, Rorschach, and Murray, give results that the sage clinician of Gestaltish persuasion sees as reflecting aspects which have membership character in the person as a whole. These concepts utilized in personality theory are engaged in endless barter and interchange with general psychology. Concepts about the nature of perceptual and cognitive processes, for example, even when applied in the laboratory without any special concern for personality as such, must for the Gestaltist be consistent with Gestalt theory, for it calls the tune for a general theory of perception-cognition, and not just for a theory of personality as such. Just as personality theory, as developed by a behaviorist, has a place in the very large behavioral scheme that the behaviorist regards as the duty of science to develop, so the specific personality attributes which are visible to the naked eye of the Gestaltist must be those in which general Gestalt principles are applicable.

It follows, I believe, that the newer methods of personality research must take a direction given mostly by the conceptual preferences of the systematizers. The systematizers are aware of the gradual disappearance of introspection, but also of the recent rise of phenomenology. Introspection was the direct confrontation of one's own experience, whether percept, memory, image, concept, affect, or whatnot, and that is what phenomenology is concerned with. But introspection had the besetting sin of over-concern with detailed or atomized particles, so that to be modern, against the background of Gestalt psychology, we must gently remove the atomistic bias, and restate our faith in and love for nonatomized introspection, look at our whole experience and glory in it. Thus we become phenomenologists ready to take the whole of experience and make the most of it for science, for therapy, and for education. Where the behaviorist is unwilling to allow us concern with immediate experience, we seek a tenuous compromise by talking about "hypothetical constructs and intervening variables." These are conceived to lie between the stimulus impact and the resulting behavioral response. This allows those who believe in phenomenology, of course, to say that this is exactly what they are interested in, namely what goes on between the stimulus and the response, while it allows the behaviorist, often cordial to this protective language, to make clear that it is behavior he is concerned with.

Social psychology, as a behavioral science, is caught by this paradox: for to be a behavioral scientist one must talk as behaviorists talk, but one desperately needs to study social experience too. The ingenious experimental work of Muzafer Sherif (1936), showing that each of us perceives as the group about him perceives, though thoroughly assimilable within a behavioral analysis, is nevertheless in its essence a reinstatement of human perception, memory, affect, and other personal realities within the context of the social group, small or large. It presents, in other words, a face both to phenomenological analysis and to behavioral analysis. The same is true of the very different conceptual system of J. L. Moreno (1934), with its concern for the rich inner world of "tele" or subjective interpersonal responses, and for the choice process, and the interaction process which characterize the theater of life both on the experimental stage and as we live it. Kurt Lewin (1935), too, is big enough to have developed a system that faces both ways, that accepts both methods and concepts of behavioral analysis, and of the world of craving and fantasy which play so large a part in the social dynamics portrayed in his interpersonal models.

Another system of ideas which have been highly valuable as bridging over from phenomenology to behavioral analysis has to do with the renewed excitement about the sensory life in and for its own sake. I refer to the studies of sensory deprivation and enrichment, studies emanating from Hebb (1958) at McGill University, and now leavening psychology everywhere, in which we ask ourselves what the role of the individual pattern of stimulation may be for the task orientation and the behavioral adequacy of the person. At the same time we ask ourselves, on a broad educational front, what the sensory and cultural enrichment of infant and childhood experience may mean to a generation determined to release a larger share of the latent potentials of those who go through our neighborhood and school experience. These are concepts which latch on to the older introspection, to the newer phenomenology, and to Hebb's concern with the meaning of various kinds of sensory stimulation for the arousal and stimulation of personal resources.

In the same vein, one of the most modern and inescapable of the trends which pervade our life as psychologists—the trend to information and communication theory—is making use today of all the resources of a perceptual psychology and its individual character, and of a psychology of behavior responses. Clinical problems are being restated right and left in terms of communication-information theory. It is beginning to be realized that what a person perceives, feels, and decides to do can be made more clear and treated with greater exactness insofar as the basic communication process is itself better understood. The person is both giver and receiver in the communication process (Thayer 1966), and what he understands and does about it can be stated in terms of the signal and the noise, the resulting message and the action which he causes in his fellow next along the line. This seems to illustrate the fact that every modern movement in psychology has to have its impact on personality; personality, because it deals with everything, has to receive and find a way to use everything that is going on.

v

Much of what I have to say suggests that everything in psychology is directly related to the study of personality. There are, however, three massive ideas which cannot be so easily treated. These are three aspects of the investigation of personality which are uniquely related to the preoccupation with personality itself and *not* really parts of general psychology. These three, as I understand them, are the problem of self, the problem of uniqueness of the stimulating situation, and the problem of the uniqueness of the integrated response.

By the problem of the self I mean the problem of the nature of that confrontation which each individual makes with his own individuality. It is the problem which the West European languages recast in the form of the personal pronoun—the "I" and the "me," "*le moi*," "*das ich*." Generally, the inclination of most psychologists today is to believe that this is a perceptual problem; that is, the problem of the mode in which the organized individual, the organism, let us say, becomes aware of and comes to terms with itself. This is not necessarily the dynamic problem of self-enhancement or self-defense; those issues come later. First, rather, it is a perceptual problem, the discovery by the little child of hands and feet, mouth and words, of the relation of his own totality to the totality of those about him. This perceptual problem belongs to personality study, and nowhere else—

indeed, to that aspect of personality that is truly multidisciplinary in which, from William James (1890) or James Mark Baldwin (1895), we move through the writings of E. Claparéde (1925) and G. H. Mead (1934), of Dewey and Bentley (1949) and Wolfgang Köhler (1960), and the struggle with the old Kantian and today's post-Kantian problems of the empirical and observable "me," as contrasted with the perhaps transcendental "I."

Note here the extraordinary contrast in shadings as we change from these structural problems to the dynamic problems of acting in a certain way because one sees oneself in a certain way: the activities of self-enhancement, the beautification and protection of the self-image, the more complex mechanisms of defense. Here we rapidly turn to dynamics rather than perceptual structure. In this dynamics we find ourselves using an almost military psychology in which defense is often the primary task. Freud, writing in German, had in mind a dynamic problem which he designated by the expression *"das ich"*—close enough for all practical purposes to our English word, the "I." The translator, however, in a typical preoccupation with philosophical difficulties, uses not the modern West European languages, but the Latin, and calls "das ich," the "ego." I will not blame him for this, but you will note the delicate way in which the matter of plain perceptual speech, describing what you see before you, has been deftly relegated to the kitchen, and a respectable guest with a Latin name, who is hard to look straight at and harder still to see through, has been seated at the dinner table. This "ego," this fellow with the dynamics, this fellow with the obscure gestures and something under his coat and in his clenched hands which we dare not try to penetrate is of course a name for a system of operations, not simply a perceptual object. It is as if I tried to describe the game of baseball to you, and I had exactly one word, let us say "blob," to describe both the bat and the ball. It is the purpose of the game to use the blob to hit the blob. So we get into the sufferings and difficulties of the student of psychology who wants to know whether he may not just replace the word "self" by the word "ego" whenever he comes across it. Why yes of course he can. There is no harm *provided* that he knows what he means by "ego." If we have a term to describe the self as observed, with all its rich significance for personality, if we have the term "self" as any biographer or autobiographer must be concerned with it, if we have the term "self" to mean all that you know as you know yourself, then why do we need a word like "ego," which relates to dozens of other problems such as bucking when you feel that you have been offended, or having a strong will and getting the appellation of ego strength, and so on? The problem of the nature of the self is definitely not soluble today, but at least it can be defined as a problem of what the individual can know regarding his own constitution, habits, attitudes; and we can quite conveniently, if we like, use the term "ego" to describe the processes by which this picture of the self is magnified, inflated, protected by socially active dynamic functions. Ego mediates between drives and environment; it *uses* the environment. We can treat ego functions as Sigmund Freud (1949) and Anna Freud (1946) have treated them.

I said that the self is one of the three problems that belongs distinctly to personality study and does not belong in a miscellaneous way to every problem in psychology; it is a part of the specific language of personality study as such. The second of these problems, with its own vocabulary related to personality as such, is the investigation of the situational pressures upon the individual, called by Murray (1938) the "press," called by social scientists the "ecology," or more vaguely the "environment." I think of W. I. Thomas (1928) on "defining the situation at a given time"; I think of the Chicago ecological studies; I think of Hartshorn and May's (1928) "situationism" in the study of honest and dishonest behaviors in children, depending upon the situation acting upon them; I think of the "demand properties" of a situation for animals and men as developed by von Uexküll (1957) and others among the comparative psychologists; the fact that a chair can have a demand quality of "jumping in" for a dog; and a stripped-down and souped-up car may have a step-on-the-gas demand quality for its young owner; I think of the dawning awareness of personality students that what is observed is not a function only of the *person,* shielded within his own shell, his skin, but of the total situation "at a given time" interacting with him. Kurt Lewin (1935) put it well by saying, in his equation, that behavior is a function of the person and the environment; and the "transactionism" of Dewey and Bentley (1949) shows that there is no autonomous life of a person, not even a conceptual life of a person, except in endless reciprocity, give and take, mutual exchange, dyadic communication with his surroundings. It is no longer the living individual who is the bearer of personality, but rather the interflowing, mutually interacting processes which make up the observable personal field. This concept, developed thirty or forty years ago by experimental embryologists, grasped and vividly developed by Kurt Lewin (1935), philosophically adumbrated by Dewey and Bentley (1949), and experimentally enriched by feedback theory in its various forms, has made personality a functional reality, a system of observable responses—you might call them interresponses—in which the perceptual-cognitive-affective life is part of the total behavior life enmeshed within the behavior life of others. Each individual is endowed with a personal inner world as well as with the objectively observed interacting world in which it is embedded. This development, largely the work of those whom I have just mentioned, is the most promising of the multidisciplinary conceptions of personality offered in recent years. It is not my invention, but I am personally deeply committed to it (Murphy 1966).

I wish, however, to draw your attention to some difficulties. If one accepts this conception of personality, one must sacrifice the prevailing viewpoint in the biological and social sciences, the preferred conceptual and mathematical methods which characterize the modern period, and the assurance that we are talking, in the name of science, about the same individuals who are definite personalities and who will not meet the requirements of personality as defined above. What kind of perverse masochism makes me offend you at this moment, offer you bread for a stone, and ask you to give up the enlightened vistas which I seemed, a few minutes ago, to offer as the best that modern science has given us?

Well, I am afraid there is only one reason for doing all these perverse and inappropriate things; namely, that the conception of personality as a self-contained entity, an encapsulated whole, capable of being pinpointed and described by science, goes badly with the world of reality which it is our desire to describe, explain, and even occasionally predict or control. You never saw one of these self-contained organisms that the psychology books talk about, any more than you saw a cloud with a completely sharp edge, or a fire with flames sharply separated from the area around them. The air which you breathe in and out gets sorted out and part of it as oxygen combines with parts of your body; there is never, in the inspiration or the expiration, a sharp distinction between you and your environment. The body temperature similarly shows a gradient, and when you step outdoors on a cold winter night, the environment invades you just as your body invades it. As Henri Bergson pointed out, the furthest visible star gets into your eyes and brain. The situation around you makes a continuing impress upon you; changing, modulating, remaking you. We have never fully paid our respects to the natural world around us, partly because, the individualistic tradition has made us proud of everything that we can sharply separate from the rest. The dyadic, the ecological, the transactional aspects of human life have been regarded as too cheap, too poor to aspire to that magnificent individualism which stands forth in Caesar, in Mohammed, in Luther, in Michelangelo, in Tchaikovsky. But if it should happen to be true that personality is molded by, enclosed with, all that is there around the organism, and that it is knowable only in its commerce with the environment about it, then we shall make a pretty serious mistake in ignoring this fact for the sake of the rugged self-sufficiency of the self-contained self.

This idea about wholeness, this idea about the total integration, even this idea about the phenomenologically unified self, defies, draws away from empirical reality. Magnificent as are the Emersonian joys in self-sufficiency, they will work only for a kind of personality which is encysted, encapsulated from its life as a person in a social world.

Have I not implied that the picture on the wall is as much a part of you as the vital cells at the roots of your fingernails; have I not said that the chords of Beethoven's *Appassionata* sonata are as much *you* as is the true inwardness of *you*. I have said all this because I believe that there is an isomorphic relation, an interchange relation, a process of mutual acceptance and support between environment and man.

Is the identifiable personality not, in reality, simply the living organism? Are its limits not the same? Is not its core and substance and organization the same? Is the personality that is offered us by this transactional theory, this field theory, something a bit foggy, a bit messy, that spills over into the environment, something that lacks the sharp heroic quality of complete self-sufficiency, and a boundary line which all can see? Indeed the question may be asked: What are we to do with the true uniqueness of the individual personality? Perhaps the answer lies in studying the uniqueness of each encounter, each *sequence* of individual encounters. These encounters have the virtue of being observable, while the person lifted out of his series of encounters is simply not observable. A snapshot is not as good as a motion picture, and a motion picture without context is not as good as one *with* context; for what we want is the fullness of the personal process.

The critical test lies in the third great problem that I asked you to consider—the problem of the nature of personality integration. If it can be shown that individuality is not the individuality of the organism, but of the transactions, the field relationships which it sustains with interpersonal and transactional members of its world, have we not lifted the discussion to a realm in which personality can be directly observed, and at the same time, intuitively and conceptually grasped? Can Rembrandt be defined without Saskia and Titus, without the world of Renaissance medicine, the world of empire building, and the world of competitive bidding for paintings that wrecked the fortune which he had amassed? Do not the endless Rembrandt self-portraits show that this most profoundly self-observant of men knew that he was a part of all that he had met? The critical test would lie in the life of a man or woman conceived first in terms of the continuity of the organism, and second in terms of the continuity of the intimate relationships which made the life. I would challenge all comparisons, in looking at human biographies, that they are the records of transactions, that they have no meaning when the transactions are surgically removed in the essence of the search for the kind of self-sufficient wholeness which Emil Ludwig, for example, has tried to apply to a science of biography. Individuality, whether as a cross section or as a developmental sequence, is a fulfillment of what that kind of a person could become in that kind of environment, and what that environment could become for a particular person. There is no Socrates without Athens, and no Athens without Socrates; no Vienna without Beethoven, and no Beethoven without Vienna; no Thoreau without Concord, and no Concord without Thoreau. There are indeed, within the genes and within the earliest mother-child responses, possibilities and potentialities which have a self-contained meaning like the thread spun and snipped off by the Fates. These potentialities are releaseable only by specific intimate interactions, and these interactions are unique on the face of the globe. This is just as much the case with the group as with the individual. The Essenes of the Dead Sea scrolls, the guilds of Chartres Cathedral—here personality is really fulfilled, and a group of personalities define one another. This is the real meaning of role playing, the psychodrama, the group dynamics of today, the group atmosphere, the leadership; the companionship, so to speak, with the other members of the group, and the unique individual potentials are merged in a unity. It is only this unity of one's various inner potentials, interacting with the rich rainbow of situational possibilities which can really be called personality. The principle of "membership character" applies just as much to the person as to the swatch of color or the tone in the melodic sequence, and no less, the colors and tones of the social environment. Context and entity are interdependent in their definition.

VI

What shall we say about the assets, the achievements, of the personality study of today? An *evaluation* of the achievements in today's personality research will, of course, also have "membership character" in our total conception of what today's psychology is all about. To define these achievements today I would say first—in negative terms—that they are inadequate relative to their potentials, chiefly because of the poor isolation of the pieces, the clinical poorly articulated with the experimental and the developmental poorly articulated with the cross-cultural. Personality has been fractionated by the narrowness of method. Few indeed of the experimental studies see the clinical realities, and few indeed of the clinical studies see the experimental possibilities. It was not at all accidental that a clinician of Harry Murray's stature saw, in the concluding chapter of *Explorations in Personality,* the vista of a program of experimental personality research. It is still unfulfilled. The separations and dislocations are largely the result of the estrangement of the clinical and the experimental, no less than the estrangement of the biological and the cross-cultural.

Secondly, there are the growing pains and the acute frustrations engendered by concepts bigger than the imagination of the methodologist. Our students are not taught, as a rule, to be creative in the search for methods. They are taught the methods that already exist. This has been true throughout the lifetime of experimental psychology and of the mathematical methods that have attended it. The reason why it was Pearson and Fisher rather than psychologists who introduced the great mathematical innovations was that the psychologists had been trained in genuflection before the standardized and ritualized methods of an age. One would think that perhaps the wisdom of the clinician would have saved us, but almost everywhere the clinician learns his trade in terms of standard practices. He learns "how to give the WISC"; "how to give the Rorschach." It is a generally recognized scandal that clinical findings are only replicable to a very limited degree, transferred from one setting to another, say from a psychoanalytic to a Rogerian setting, or even from one psychoanalytic center to another; for what has been built in is not the sensitivity to personality, but the sensitivity to trouble signs, psychopathological indicators, and all the garbage of what Maslow would call a rubricizing method. One of the things that clinicians have thought they have learned is that the trouble lies within the person, and most of the wisdom of situational and field analysis has fallen on deaf ears. All of this is evident even at the conscious level, but the tangled skein of partisan ideas between different schools of thought traps the individual clinician into loyalty, and what is even worse, into the perception of only a certain kind of realities which slip through the mesh of the particular net in which he is unconsciously selecting what is to be caught. Clinical training can, and often does, become a form of ossification, exactly as can any of the other methods, including the experimental and the cross-cultural. Procrustes is our hero, in deference to whom we must be methodologically lopped off by every millimeter which does not fit the standard measure of the dimension involved. Having set up the pure and correct method, and getting caught by it, we complain of the complexity of our subject matter, and make it the prime source of our difficulties. Boscovich remarked that "what appears to be complexity in nature is deficiency in our mathematics." You can solve a problem with arithmetic, with several yards of paper on which to work out your answer, but you can also solve it on a thumbnail by means of calculus. You can often solve a personality problem if you can bear to see its whole context and solve it simply. Or you can create a bibliography of a hundred pieces, using a method which admits only one kind of data and forces you to go foraging over the earth to get the data; this information is not even organized so that you can realize that it is related to data already gathered by others using the same method as yours. From anthropology, or from embryology, or from child development, appear facts, for example, about the growth of cognition which are here and there being juxtaposed, but still all too timidly sought by a single method, as if it were a real achievement to do a thing the hard way. "Look, Mom, no hands!"

To carry out the thought one step further, the cutting edge of fresh research and conceptualization today is mostly the recognition of the same basic problem in different guises; as William James said, genius is the capacity to recognize remote similarities. And genius is rare. Why does it come about that the brilliant integration of methods and concepts comes mostly from those who came from outside of psychology—Freud, Pavlov, Fisher? I think it is because we train psychologists in psychology, and the psychology in which we train them is already sifted, molded, polarized so that only information which fits a cliché of today can get through. If it is in the notebooks of Leonardo da Vinci, it is not psychology. If it is published in the newest issue of the *Journal of Experimental Psychology,* you can be very sure that it is psychology. Indeed now that we have a *Journal of Experimental Research in Personality,* we can be sure what is really psychology.

VII

I will allow myself a moment at the end for normative issues; going on beyond questions of fact, I will ask what *should* or *ought* to happen—foolish prophet that I am—knowing that all of you, and myself too, will expect the effort to backfire. I will nevertheless say that the attempt to use the language of "should, ought, and must" regarding personality is a way of damaging, or even destroying, both the idiographic and the nomothetic methods which I have tried to apply. Problems of health and disease are real problems from the point of view of a normative practitioner like a physician; but for a psychologist who is interested in personality as a product of a very complex evolving nature, it would be bold—and I think premature—to say that any personality as such is *better* than any other personality, or to say that his father *ought* to have given him better discipline, or that his mother *ought* to have let him wander where he wanted to wander. We can certainly say that differences result from different methods, and there is an enormously important place in human life for the normative approach. But I am suggesting that to mix the normative approach with the factual approach produces, in personality study, the same kind of confusion which appears from similar efforts in biology and in sociology.

I vividly remember the generous professor at Yale who told us about parasitism and the damage worked upon the body of the host, and then explained that in view of the dire need of the parasite there were cases of "justifiable parasitism." We have similar questions constantly buzzing around our ears with regard to what is good and bad about education, and about law, and about our ethical system as a whole. Good for whom? Good how? Good in what context? What are the functional realities? These are the questions I suggest for the scientific approach, and even these efforts are likely to suffer from Victorian egocentrism unless terms like "should, ought, must, good, right" are defined in terms of occasions and consequences. Man's enormous capacity for moral judgments can lead him either into a sadistic, inquisitorial attack upon his fellows in the certainty that he is right, or into a generous concern with the welfare of his species; and we can help—if we keep our eyes clear—to produce generosity, sympathy, and mutual respect if those are the things that we want. We will do this better if we kept our factual and our normative language clear so that each can talk to the other, at least until something far more wise can be said about ethics than is being said in this generation. Can we not appropriately hope that greater knowledge about personality will add somewhat to the effectiveness with which our normative efforts are carried out? The cognitive struggle is great enough even without being constantly clogged by the effort to solve a factual and a normative question by the same method.

VIII

So what are the prospects for sound research on personality in our era? They depend mainly upon greater breadth of training of our young scientists, and a wider concern with the contexts within which significant events occur. The removal of arbitrary boundaries between conceptual areas will mean more and more of what Kirtley Mather has called "outrageous hypotheses." The history of science shows that most great steps have been taken not by systematically checking every factual box to be sure that each contains what it is supposed to contain, but rather by conceiving new kinds of boxes. It is this, I hope, which such a conference may serve to encourage; this which I hope all the multidisciplinary approaches will tend to nurture. This cannot be done within the authoritarianism of a curriculum committee, or a departmental leeadership, or a university system which is primarily concerned with the conservation of treasured truth from the past, or with the indoctrination of students into the accredited folklore of observation and interpretation. We have been running fast, but, like Alice in Wonderland led by the Red Queen, perhaps not running fast enough to do more than stay where we are. In the meantime the destructive capacities of scientific weaponry increase the closely kept, but altogether harrowing, possibilities of bacteriological and chemical warfare as political power overshadows by at least a thousand to one the power of science in the courts of national and international aspirations for peace. Lack of knowledge about human beings is not a trivial, but a major, threat to life. Lack of knowledge about personality is perhaps the central core of the issue that is most relevant for us today: the issue of understanding what human beings can become under a new set of social arrangements. The personality of the contemporary human being offers a generic problem in self-liberation. And here looms a special case: the personality of the leader; the leader capable of understanding and giving fulfillment to potentialities. This is a major opportunity for intellectual "risk-taking"; the major challenge to the investigator, the student, and the layman. For we shall be saved, if at all, by learning to recognize and to nurture a kind of leadership which is responsive everywhere to the human growth potential.

BIBLIOGRAPHY

ALLPORT, G. W., *Personality: A Psychological Interpretation*. New York: Holt, Rinehart and Winston, Inc., 1937.

ARNHEIM, R., "Experimentell-psychologische Untersuchungen zum Ausbruchsproblem," *Psychologie Forschung,* Vol. 11, 1928, pp. 2–132.
BALDWIN, J. M., *Mental Development in the Child and the Race.* New York: The Macmillan Company, 1895.
BRENMAN, M., and M. M. GILL, *Hypnotherapy; A Survey of the Literature, with Appended Case Reports and an Experimental Study.* New York: International Universities Press, Inc., 1947.
BRIDGMAN, P. W., *The Logic of Modern Physics.* New York: The Macmillan Company, 1946.
CARLYLE, T., *On Heroes, Hero Worship, and the Heroic in History.* New York: Oxford University Press, 1928.
CLAPARÈDE, E., "Does the Will Express the Entire Personality?" in C. M. Campbell, et al. (eds.), *Problems of Personality: Studies in Honor of Morton Prince,* pp. 39–43. New York: Harper & Row, Publishers, 1925.
DEWEY, J., and A. F. BENTLEY, *Knowing and the Known.* Boston: The Beacon Press, 1949.
FECHNER, G. T., *Elemente der Psychophysik.* Leipzig, 1860.
FISHER, R. A., *The Design of Experiments.* Edinburgh and London: Oliver and Boyd, Ltd., 1935.
FREUD, A., *The Ego and the Mechanisms of Defense.* New York: International Universities Press, Inc., 1946.
FREUD, S., *An Outline of Psychoanalysis.* New York: W. W. Norton & Company, Inc., 1949.
FREUD, S., *Moses and Monotheism.* London: Hogarth Press, Ltd., 1939.
GUILFORD, J. P., *Psychometric Methods.* New York: McGraw-Hill, Inc., 1936.
HARTLEY, E. L., and M. A. PERELMAN, "Deprivation and the Canalization of Responses to Food," *Psychological Reports,* Vol. 13, 1963, pp. 647–656.
HARTSHORN, H., and M. A. MAY, *Studies in Deceit.* New York: The Macmillan Company, 1928.
HEBB, D. O., *A Textbook of Psychology.* Philadelphia: W. B. Saunders Company, 1958.
HILGARD, E. R., *Hypnotic Susceptibility.* New York: Harcourt, Brace & World, Inc., 1965.
JAMES, H. (ed.), *The Letters of William James.* New York: Longmans, Green & Co., Inc., 1920.
JAMES, W., *A Pluralistic Universe.* New York: Longmans, Green & Co., Inc., 1909.
———, *The Principles of Psychology* (2 vols.) New York: Holt, Rinehart and Winston, Inc., 1890.
———, *The Varieties of Religious Experience.* New York: Longmans, Green & Co., Inc., 1902.
JANET, P., *Psychological Healing.* Paris: Alcan, 1925.
KOFFKA, K., *Principles of Gestalt Psychology.* New York: Harcourt, Brace & World, Inc., 1935.
KÖHLER, W., *Dynamics in Psychology.* New York: Grove Press, Inc., 1960.
LEWIN, K., *A Dynamic Theory of Personality.* New York: McGraw-Hill, Inc., 1935.
MEAD, G. H., *Mind, Self and Society.* Chicago: University of Chicago Press, 1934.
MORENO, J. L., *Who Shall Survive?* Nervous and Mental Disorder Monograph, 1934.
MURPHY, G., *Personality: A Biosocial Approach to Origins and Structure.* New York: Basic Books, Inc., 1966.

MURRAY, H. A., et al., *Explorations in Personality*. New York: Oxford University Press, 1938.
PAVLOV, I. P., *Lectures on Conditioned Reflexes* (2 vols.). New York: International Publishers Co., Inc., 1928–1941.
RORSCHACH, H., *Psychodiagnostics*. New York: Grune & Stratton, Inc., 1941.
SHERIF, M., *The Psychology of Social Norms*. New York: Harper & Row, Publishers, 1936.
SKINNER, B. F., *The Behavior of Organisms: An Experimental Analysis*. New York: Appleton-Century-Crofts, 1936.
THAYER, L. (ed.)., *Communication: Concepts and Perspectives*. ("Proceedings of the Second International Symposium on Communication Theory and Research.") Washington, D.C.: Spartan Books, 1966.
THOMAS, W. I., "The Behavior Pattern and the Situation," *Publications of the American Sociological Society*, Vol. 22, 1928, pp. 1–13.
TOLMAN, E. C., "There is More Than One Kind of Learning," *Psychological Review*, Vol. 56, 1949, pp. 144–155.
VON UEXKÜLL, J., "A Stroll Through the Worlds of Animals and Men," in C. H. Schiller (ed.), *Instinctive Behavior: The Development of a Modern Concept*, pp. 5–80. New York: International Universities Press, Inc., 1957.
WHITMAN, C., "The Behavior of Pigeons," *Carnegie Institute of Washington Publications*, Vol. 257, 1919, p. 3.
WOLFF, W., *The Expression of Personality*. New York: Harper & Row, Publishers, 1943.
WOODWORTH, R. S., "Reinforcement of Perception," *American Journal of Psychology*, Vol. 60, 1947, pp. 119–124.

3

Anthropological Contributions to the Theory of Personality

Anthony F. C. Wallace

Anthropologists have been avid consumers of theories of personality of other disciplines and of their methods for the study of personality. Our investigations of character and socialization have by and large depended upon the application of psychological concepts and techniques to the study of individuals in communities other than Vienna. This sort of work always confirms its guiding axiom that individual personality develops differently in different cultural settings. But little has been done to construct and test any particularly anthropological theory of personality.

In a sense, of course, one can say that the anthropologist who assays to present a formulation of a national character and the socialization processes responsible for it is developing and testing a theory of personality particular to a given society. He is developing a theory of Iroquois, or Samoan, or Japanese, or Russian personality coordinate with, let us say, Freud's theory of Viennese personality. But as a matter of fact, these local theories are not really coordinate; they are derivative because they use the original concepts of Freud, or whomever, rather than new ones unique to the society under study.

But the theories of personality upon which anthropology has recently depended are themselves based on, and rationalized by, beliefs about human nature which are drawn in part from earlier anthropological knowledge. Freud and other psychoanalytic thinkers, for example, have appealed repeatedly to the testimony of nineteenth-century primatology and cultural anthropology for confirmation of their beliefs in such things as the collective unconscious, the native irrationality and destructiveness of man, and other supposedly essential attributes of human beings. The difficulty with psychoanalysis is not that because the theory was evolved in Vienna it must necessarily be considered valid only for Viennese. The mechanisms of defense may indeed operate in very much the same way in Vienna and in Iroquoia. But what they operate on, and why they have to operate at all, may be different in both Vienna and Iroquoia from what nineteenth-

42   Theoretical Standpoints

century assumptions about human nature would suggest. The original contributions of anthropology have been, and potentially are, less to personality psychology *per se* than to this somewhat broader and more inclusive field of interest—the nature of human nature. In this paper, therefore, I shall not direct attention to the applications which anthropologists have made of psychoanalytic concepts, of psychological tests and measurements, and of other schemes and techniques given us by our colleagues. I shall be talking about human nature.

What sort of statements should a description of human nature contain? They should be statements which, first, are not culturally restricted; that is, they must be true of people in *any* culture. Second, they should not be bounded by species; that is, although they must be true for human beings in all societies, they need not be true *only* for human beings. Third, they should be relevant to statements about group as well as individual behavior; they should be relevant to theory about culture, social organization, demography, and so forth. And fourth, they need not be readily classifiable into statements about personality, cognition, physiology, and other conventional fields of behavioral science.

Let us go on now to consider some statements, and questions, about human nature which seem to be suggested by anthropology (and by the findings of other fields as well) today. Hazardous as this exercise may be, it is important from time to time to ask the most general question "What kind of people are people?" rather than the more specific, "What kind of people are the Iroquois?"

NEGATIVE CONTRIBUTIONS: THE ANECDOTAL VETO

The traditional contribution of anthropology to the study of human nature is the anecdotal veto. The anecdotal veto is the announcement by an anthropologist or other far traveler that some proposition advanced by Western folk wisdom, or by a luckless professor of psychology or sociology, is not true among the so-and-so. The anecdotal veto sometimes is very irritating to professionals in other fields (and even to other anthropologists) because it seems unfair that a plain and unassuming theory should be slain by an exotic fact. One of the classic examples of the anecdotal veto was Margaret Mead's demonstration that the European kind of adolescent turmoil could not be considered a universal stage in human development because it did not occur during coming of age in Samoa (Mead 1939). A more controversial challenge to conventional wisdom was presented by Bronislaw Malinowski when he indicated that the oedipus complex could not be considered universal because among the Trobriand Islanders the mother's brother, rather than the father, was the significant male disciplinarian in the boy child's life and the focus of his hostility (Malinowski

1927). Similar confrontations of general assumptions are mounted by evidence that some primitive peoples do not seem to have a latency period (Roheim 1932:1–224); that some fail to recognize the true connection between sexual intercourse and pregnancy; that there have been social groups which do not observe an incest taboo between siblings; that the nuclear family may not be ubiquitous (Spiro 1954: 839–846).

In general, the threat of anthropology's anecdotal veto has led to an awareness among most educated people that statements about human nature cannot be statements that are invalid in even one culture, however underdeveloped, and that human nature—which means *our* nature—is remarkably plastic and allows for far more various arrangements than had been suspected a century ago. The merits of particular vetoes have been debated but the very debate has rested on the assumption that an exception, in this arena, does invalidate the rule. And respect for the veto has prompted many psychiatrists and social psychologists to undertake pious pilgrimages to other cultures, there to discover for themselves that American college student subjects for psychology experiments do not represent the whole human race, that the sight of the primal scene does not always arouse castration anxiety in children, or that being raised in a kibbutz nursery does not invariably lead to an emotionally stunted adult personality.

But the services of anthropology as a pruning hook, while valuable, are not the main contribution of the field to the study of human nature. Let me suggest what seem to me to be some of these main contributions under five broad headings: the primate nature of man; the physiological parameters of personality; the theory of identity; processes of personality change; and the cognitive structure (and parameters) of culture.

THE PRIMATE NATURE OF MAN

We may revise Huxley's minimal description of man as an "erect, featherless biped" to something a little more mammalian: Man is an erect primate with not much hair but lots of brains. Man's standing posture, achieved by an appropriate evolution of the pelvis, has freed his hands for the use and manufacture of tools; and tools have led to technological culture and the further selection for brain size necessary to maintain and support language and other symbolic forms of communication (Washburn 1960). But the social implications of being a primate, and a mammal, are also interesting and particularly germane to the subject of human nature.

Man, as men constantly remind each other, is a social animal. So are most other animals, not only primates, but the rest of the mammals, birds, reptiles, fish, and even insects. Animals differ from one another largely not as to whether or not they are social but what sort of social life they lead. Most animals have two sexes and reproduce by sexual congress; as a result they maintain a sort of minimal sociality with respect to sex and reproduction. Some animals, including all primates, also sleep, travel, play, and forage for food in groups; thus community and sex-and-reproduction groups, where they occur, invariably overlap. What seems to distinguish human sociality is a consequence of the slowness with which the central nervous system of the infant develops after birth. The human infant characteristically remains radically dependent for several years upon one or more mature females, who in turn depend for their and the infant's support upon a combined community and sex-and-reproduction group which includes males. Human survival, in consequence, requires the prolonged maintenance of highly stable groups of adults. The mechanisms which make possible this permanence of groups are, apparently, intense emotional ties between mothers and their own offspring, between adults of both sexes and immature or dependent individuals in general, and between and among mature adults.

Just what are these "emotional ties" which are naturally characteristic of man? This is perhaps the most important single question to be asked about human nature; it is also the most difficult to answer. But certain minimal statements can be made. Human infants need to be handled, caressed, touched by warm skin, or they will fail to develop, sicken, or even die (Spitz 1947), and the desire for such comfort remains throughout life. Human beings, who are not restricted in their sexuality by an oestrus cycle, are from childhood to old age continuously involved, in one manner or another, in sexual relationships. Adult human beings continuously play with and work for each other and for the young, sharing food, and protecting their group from danger.

Although most animals, including the primates, display aggressive dominance behavior, and although this behavior is readily institutionalized, there is little evidence to suggest that *destructive* aggression occurs often within nonhuman primate communities except under such peculiar circumstances as confinement or severe overpopulation and (as we shall suggest in the next section) as a result of difficulties in the formation and maintenance of a satisfying identity. Nor is there much to suggest that destructive aggression between nonhuman primate communities, even over territorial rights, is a natural and inevitable process (Devore 1965). To the contrary, it seems to me, the occurence of destructive aggression within and between nonhuman primate groups is a temporary reactive product of fear except under the circumstance of widespread damage to identity processes in which chronic internalized fear (of a kind experienced in man as a threat of self-esteem) becomes endemic. In view of the apparently nondestructive inclinations of most other primates, one must ask whether man's notorious propensity for hostility may not also be a consequence of his extreme vulnerability to fear induced by disorders of identity processes.

THE PHYSIOLOGICAL PARAMETERS OF PERSONALITY

There is another aspect of human nature, of a biological sort, which is worth mentioning. This is the variability of the physiological parameters of the functioning of the human central nervous system (CNS), particularly the brain. The most obvious example is the course of physical maturation from birth to death. There are also cyclical changes such as those associated with menstruation, pregnancy, parturition, and lactation. There are more or less regular diurnal cycles of fatigue, sleep, thirst, hunger, and elimination which, if interfered with, are quickly followed by intense physiological stress. And the physiological adaptation to stress itself may lead to regressive changes in affect and cognition. There are the multitudinous effects of nutritional deficiencies of one kind or another which affect the functioning of central nervous system—protein deficiencies in kwashiorkor, vitamin deficiencies in pellagra and beri-beri, mineral deficiencies leading to various other neurologically relevant conditions such as calcium deficiencies resulting in hypocalcemic tetany (Wallace 1961:255–295). Degenerative diseases like diabetes and arteriosclerosis can have gross effects on the CNS and so do infectious diseases like yaws, syphilis, malaria, and trypanosomiasis. Tumors, injuries, and surgical intervention may affect the endocrine system directly or indirectly. Fevers may be accompanied by delirium, low temperature by sleepiness. The CNS is directly affected, sometimes permanently, by a number of poisons such as lead and carbon monoxide for example. Drugs like caffeine, alcohol, mescaline, opiates, barbiturates, marijuana, LSD-25, tranquilizers, energizers, and the hallucinogenic compounds contained in various mushrooms and plants have been and are widely used in many cultures for the purpose of altering CNS function for medical and religious purposes. Variations in oxygenation affect CNS function: in the hyperventilation syndrome, gross changes in muscular and brain function occur; and the major difficulties in maintaining CNS stability at high altitudes and under high pressures are well known.

In other words, although the human central nervous system is well buffered against physical and chemical assault, it varies extensively in its mode of operation during any person's life span in relation to a host of chemical factors. These chemical factors in turn may vary directly in response to physical insult to the organism or as a result of a chain of psychological events which evoke physiological responses that affect the chemical milieu. The human brain is not a machine which is either on or off and, when it is on, operates always at the same level of efficiency and always in the same way. Its level and mode of function are noticeably different in all healthy human beings during sleep, during intoxication, and during "normal" waking states. Occasionally mode and level of function vary to such a degree that the organism must be considered temporarily or even chronically ill. There are reasons to suspect that such severe and chronic mental disorders as schizophrenia and depression involve anomalies of body chemistry; and one cannot dismiss any such anomalies that may be found as merely the result of a "deviant" genetic predisposition. Genetic properties may in some persons lower the threshold of vulnerability but all human beings have thresholds sufficiently low, in many dimensions, to experience under provocation disorders symptomatically identical to those in genetically more prone individuals.

Now it is an interesting question whether, in his artificial and man-made cultural environment, man is more subject now to unwanted interferences with his body chemistry than he was millennia ago. Man's ancestors, in the course of evolution in the wild, evolved physical means of adaptation to considerable changes in temperature, sunlight, oxygen pressure, and the hunting and collecting way of life. But culture, and particularly industrial culture, would seem to involve a variety of "side effects" that may affect man neurologically in ways with which he is not physically prepared to cope as well as he would like. Man with culture must deal with the physical poisons he creates (such as lead, carbon monoxide, and drugs); with rapidly enveloping epidemics of infectious disease; with the degenerative diseases of older years to which larger and larger numbers become vulnerable; with the nutritional difficulties of large populations of agriculturalists. In an urban industrial society like the United States, the actual cost and potential dangers of CNS disorders are fearsome. The most extraordinary measures must be constantly taken by hospitals, physicians, courts, police, jails, and so on to "protect society" from persons, temporarily or chronically suffering from gross disorders of the central nervous system, who are driving cars, who possess various lethal weapons, and who raise children. One must suspect, in fact, that it is on the almost invisible processes of neurologically relevant physiology that natural selection is currently at work most actively, now that all but gross anatomical variation has, with the invention of culture, become nearly irrelevant to survival and reproduction.

IDENTITY

A main contribution of anthropology to the study of personality as such has been to help in the development of identity theory. By identity I mean simply an image of self; and I think it is generally assumed by students of human personality that all human beings maintain such images of self, that these self-images are the focus of strong emotion, and that people are accordingly motivated to enhance self-esteem or at least to avoid loss of self-esteem. As Hallowell has pointed out, the development of a sense of self must have occurred early in human evolution (Hallowell 1959). And no doubt the observation that people have self-images is one of the first psy-

47 Anthropological Contributions to the Theory of Personality

chological generalizations made by man. The history of the concept of identity in the theory of personality has thus, in a sense, been a history of the rediscovery of the obvious. But what is obvious is not always easy to understand.

Early psychoanalytic theory introduced the notion of identity almost casually. It was assumed without question that the awareness of unwanted images of self might arouse intense fear and anxiety and that the organism would develop various mechanisms of defense to prevent such images of self from becoming conscious. The psychoanalysts who developed ego psychology were especially interested in identity; Erikson, who in particular has contributed to this area, studied anthropology with Kroeber, did fieldwork among the Yurok Indians of California and published on the relation between body image and world view in that tribe, and later of course published comparisons of Sioux and American cultures (Erikson 1959). Kardiner, in his development of the theory of "projective systems," and in his work on American Negro personality structure, relied heavily on the use of identity processes; Kardiner had earlier worked closely with anthropologists, including Cora DuBois and Ralph Linton, in the famous Columbia seminars (Kardiner and Ovesy 1951). Erich Fromm has also relied on anthropological considerations (Fromm 1951). One may mention also the sociologist Erving Goffman, who has studied identity processes in psychiatric institutions, and who published his early position paper in the *American Anthropologist* under the title "Deference and Demeanor" (Goffman 1956).

A concern with identity and its processes grows naturally out of the tradition in cultural anthropology of recording a complex of identity-relevant information under such categories as "values," "themes," "world view," "ethos," and "national character." These materials include statements of what kind of person it is considered desirable to be, what kind is not so desirable, what kind of person the people of the given society think they really are, and what deprivations, defenses, and compensations are required by the presence of this identity structure. Notable are both the variability of models of identity, from one culture to another, and also the fact that people in all cultures are able to articulate such values. But what is perhaps most impressive to the anthropologist is the importance of these identity models in any theory which attempts to account for socialization, for intercultural relations, and for rapid culture change. Some of us have attempted more or less systematically to delineate the implications of treating identity as a cognitive and motivational system in various situations of social interaction (Wallace and Fogelson 1965; Wallace 1965; Goodenough 1963).

The principal theoretical issues raised by such efforts would seem to be two. First, what is the motivational calculus in identity dynamics, given the assumption that in all human beings there is a positive motive to bring the real identity closer in the individual's perception to his model of the ideal identity, and a negative motive to separate the real identity as much as possible from his model of the feared identity? Does this calculus, for instance, follow dissonance theory? And second, what relation do identity dynamics have to other motivational processes? Answers to these questions are partially given by well-worn, but valid, clichés about primary and secondary narcissism, mechanisms of defense, libidinal maturation, parental imagos, ego and superego processes, castration anxiety, the varieties of identification, and so on. Probably identity dynamics also are implicit in the ontogeny of primate dominance behavior in general and thus are extremely ancient phylogenetically. Man's notorious difficulty with identity problems thus may have something to do with having both a large brain and a propensity for developing dominance relationships. But while these formulations may help to account for the origin of identity models in the individual and for the energy with which identity enhancement is pursued, they do not adequately explain, it seems to me, the interaction between the identity motivations, once launched, and motives associated with other appetites. Too much of human psychopathology and interpersonal and intergroup conflict is carried on in terms of identity processes to permit their treatment entirely as epiphenomena of other instincts, needs, drives, or what have you.

Why is it, for example, so difficult for two warring nations locked in an identity struggle, as are the United States and North Vietnam, to disengage? Evidently neither side can possibly, within a lifetime, expect to win anything of economic value sufficient to offset the losses already suffered, let alone those to be expected; nor can either side really lose much of political or military value by an armistice. Both parties are motivated by the desperate fear of losing some priceless aspect of their identity; this fear precludes both sides from making any of the moves which would end the struggle. To call such stable systems of mutual destruction the game of "chicken" played with millions of lives is not to use a metaphor but to draw attention to a homology. Effective resolutions of this kind of deadly embrace, into which human beings seem all too prone too fall, are more likely to come when we have a better understanding of how identity processes work as ongoing systems of motivation.

SOCIALIZATION

Anthropologists have always been interested in enculturation and socialization: the processes by which the infant learns his culture and develops a personality appropriate to that culture. Some of this work, particularly that conducted by John Whiting and his associates, has had the aim of testing the validity of psychoanalytic and other theories of human development by statistical analysis of cross-cultural regularities in customary behavior

(Whiting and Child 1953). Another tradition, exemplified best by Margaret Mead and her colleagues (Mead 1939), by Melford Spiro (1958), and Francis L. K. Hsu (1963), has sought to avoid the difficulties of dealing with scoring cultures on dimensions of custom taken out of context, and has concentrated on the thorough analysis in individual cultures of the rich matrix of patterned experience through which the child's human nature grows into cultural character. Still another tradition, most clearly expressed by Kardiner (1939), emphasizes the role of socialization processes in determining the "projective system" (religion, mythology, and even such distortions of the "maintenance" system as may be represented in perpetual war, chronic poverty, and overpopulation). Although these various studies do support the general assumption that early experience powerfully affects adult behavior, and that people in any society are able to make the next generation pretty much like themselves, they leave this reader with the uncomfortable feeling that we still do not know very well how it is all accomplished. The effect of any particular experience, such as separation from the mother or swaddling or severe bowel training, is so heavily dependent on so many other events over so long a span of time that neither statistical associations nor the identification of recurrent themes or patterns in socialization experience yields much conviction that the mechanisms of change are understood. Punishment, reward, and repetition are no doubt involved. But efforts to apply learning theory by the recording of reinforcement methods in either general socialization (Whiting 1941) or language learning (Chomsky 1959:26–58) have not been convincing at all because it is too difficult to identify the reinforcing acts, to identify them as rewarding or punishing, to assign them weight and to demonstrate what behavior, overt or covert, these reinforcements reinforce. Furthermore, children are diabolically creative and can invent new meanings for old forms. Learning by conditioning of some sort of course occurs but just how it occurs, over a period of fifteen or twenty years, may not be as simply described as is bar pressing in rats—and that is not really simple either.

Perhaps the most fruitful zone of inquiry for anthropologists has been the study of ritual, particularly of those dramatic rites of passage which in many societies occur about the time of puberty. On such ritual occasions the initiate is expected during a brief time to achieve a reorganization of motive and knowledge so that he can abandon an earlier role, and identity, and adopt a new one; and the initiators (including both ritual practitioners and audience) are expected to begin to respond to the new role with behavior that rewards its performance. Ritual has long, and properly, been interpreted as a symbolic expression of internal conflict and its resolution; but it is interesting to consider it as a mechanism of personality change. It would be worth investigating the general hypothesis, first, that rites of passage, along with related experiences in "brain-washing," religious conversion, mystical experience, hypnosis, and perhaps some forms of psychotherapy, are indeed effective in producing temporary and sometimes long-lasting personality change in a brief period of time, and second, that the success of the ritual procedure rests on prior symbolic learning of the new pattern and the effective dissociation of the individual from meaningful cues associated with earlier learnings by the use of such devices as isolation, sensory deprivation, drugs, and physical and emotional stress. During the period of dissociation the initiate is instructed to attach motivational value to the new pattern and to execute it (Wallace 1966).

Certainly most cultures do work on the assumption, naively arrived at to be sure, that major personality change can be accomplished in this way. Such changes, when they are conceded to occur at all, are often regarded merely as pathological in secular professional groups in Western cultures, because of their association with paranoid forms of religious and political enthusiasm. The process of ritual precipitation of rapid personality change could, however, be used in more constructive ways if it were more thoroughly understood.

COGNITION

But the main business of cultural anthropology is, after all, ethnography: the description of culture. Accordingly, the unique contribution of anthropology to the study of the psychological aspects of human nature is the specification of what a person must know in order to be able to perform the actions which are described in the ethnography of his group. The ethnographer reports that Eskimo hunters build snow houses, describes such houses, and the manner of their construction. He also answers, or tries to answer, the questions, What are the cognitive operations that an Eskimo must be able to perform in order to build such a house? What does the Eskimo have to know about the properties of various kinds of snow? How is the snow cut? How large can the blocks be? What is their shape? How are they handled? In what sequence must the operations be performed? The ethnographer, in other words, sets a problem for the psychologist: here is a description of what these people do and what they can tell me of what they know about doing it; your theory of learning, and model of cognitive process, need to be adequate to these specifications.

Much conceptual effort, but not much experimental work, has been done by anthropologists in an effort to clarify the problem of describing the cognitive structure of culture. The work of linguists in describing language has inspired a number of ethnographers to undertake what is sometimes called "formal analysis" of culture content. One kind of formal analysis is represented by the technique of "componential analysis" (Hammel 1965). This technique aims to elucidate the semantic structure of terminologies—for instance, of kinship terminology, which is found in every language. Appropriately carried out, such an analysis not merely enables the anthropologist to predict correctly to which object the native user will apply which term, but to identify the particular cognitive calculus—the underlying taxonomy—that the native user actually employs in deciding which term to use and what the characteristics are of objects to which a term has been applied. Such a "psychologically real" taxonomy is constructed according to definable logical principles—has a certain semantic geometry as it were—and also a measurable size. Thus the analysis of culture content, by the application of mathematical models in the manner of Kemenyi and others (1963), and by techniques like those of linguistics and componential analysis, will ultimately permit making more general statements about both cultural variation and cross-cultural consistency in the cognitive operations involved in culturally institutionalized behavior.

The implication of these exercises for the study of human nature, and of personality in particular, is not difficult to discern in general. Personality structures are composed of internal representations of objects, and situations, and processes, which are affectively valued, and decisions about behavior are made according to the nature of the structure. There is no reason to suppose at the outset that the abstract geometry of such structures, and the calculi for their use, differs fundamentally according to whether the "objects" involved are kinship terms, real people, or the various dimensions of identity. (But the discovery that radically different principles divide cognition-in-personality from other kinds of cognitive process would certainly be very interesting). Thus the analysis of the size and structure of the calculi embodied in culture should provide important leads to the study of behavior viewed from other perspectives, such as that of personality theory. One would ask, for instance, whether Miller's "Magical Number 7" (1956), and my "2^6 Rule" (Wallace 1961:458–464), proposed as statements of the upper limits of convenient size for paradigmatic contrast or discrimination groups, apply also to taxonomic and discrimination tasks involved in personality processes. Do human beings strive with equal fervor to increase organization by maximizing both the orderliness and complexity of experience in both human relations and technology? Such questions need not be parceled out among culture, personality, cognition, perception, learning as if they were mutually insulated areas of knowledge; they are questions about human nature.

CONCLUSION

In conclusion, I should like to suggest explicitly what I have already implied in discussion: that an effort to define the nature of human nature is needed for the advancement of utopian thinking. As Margaret Mead once pointed out in a wise article, we do need to create more vivid utopias (1957). And utopias need to be founded on a knowledge, not just of separate disciplines, nor of particular cultures, but of human nature. Not all utopian cultures are viable; utopias based on inadequate conceptions of human nature especially are not viable. A utopia which assumed that human babies could be raised in incubators for the first three years would, so far as we know, be doomed. Human nature is plastic but not infinitely so; and where the limits of plasticity have been defined, ethics are no longer relative but absolute. So the utopian thinker had better be right on his assumptions about human nature.

BIBLIOGRAPHY

CHOMSKY, NAOM, Review of *Verbal Behavior* by B. F. Skinner, *Language*, Vol. 35, 1959, pp. 26–58.
DeVORE, IRVEN (ed.), *Primate Behavior: Field Studies of Monkeys and Apes.* New York: Holt, Rinehart and Winston, Inc., 1965.
ERIKSON, E. H., "Identity and the Life Cycle," *Psychological Issues*, Vol. 1, 1959.
FROMM, ERICH, *The Forgotten Language.* New York: Holt, Rinehart and Winston, Inc., 1951.
GOFFMAN, ERVING, "Deference and Demeanor on Mental Hospital Wards," *American Anthropologist*, Vol. 58, No. 3, 1956.
GOODENOUGH, WARD H., *Cooperation in Change.* New York: Russell Sage Foundation, 1963.
HALLOWELL, A. I., "Behavioral Evolution and the Emergence of Self," in *Evolution and Anthropology: A Centennial Appraisal.* Washington, D.C.: The Anthropological Society of Washington, 1959.
HAMMEL, E. A. (ed.), "Formal Semantic Analysis." *American Anthropologist* Special Publication, Vol. 67, No. 5, PL 2, 1965.
HSU, FRANCIS L. K., *Caste, Clan, and Club.* Princeton, N.J.: D. Van Nostrand Company, Inc., 1963.
KARDINER, ABRAM, *The Individual and His Society.* New York: Columbia University Press, 1939.
KARDINER, ABRAM, and LIONEL OVESY, *The Mark of Oppression.* New York: W. W. Norton & Company, Inc., 1951.
KEMENYI, J. G., J. L. SNELL, and G. L. THOMPSON, *Finite Mathematics*, appendices by R. Bush and Weyl. Englewood Cliffs, N.J.: Prentice-Hall, Inc., 1963.
MALINOWSKI, BRONISLAW, *Sex and Repression in Savage Society.* New York: Humanities Press, Inc., 1927.
MEAD, MARGARET, *From the South Seas: Studies of Adolescence and Sex in Primitive Societies.* New York: William Morrow & Company, Inc., 1939.
————, "Toward More Vivid Utopias," *Science*, Vol. 126, pp. 957–961, 1957.
MILLER, GEORGE, "The Magical Number Seven, Plus or Minus Two." *Psychological Bulletin*, Vol. 63, No. 2, 1956.
ROHEIM, GEZA, The Psychoanalysis of Primitive Cultural Types. *International Journal of Psychoanalysis*, Vol. 13, 1932, pp. 1–224.
SPIRO, MELFORD, "Is the Family Universal?" *American Anthropologist*, Vol. 56, 1954, pp. 839–846.
————, *Children of the Kibbutz.* Cambridge, Mass.: Harvard University Press, 1958.
SPITZ, RENE, "Anaclitic Depression," in *The Psychoanalytic Study of the Child*, Vol. 2, pp. 313–342. New York: International Universities Press, Inc., 1947.

WALLACE, ANTHONY F. C., "Identity Processes in Personality and in Culture." University of Colorado Symposium on Cognition (1965), in press.
———, *Religion: An Anthropological View*. New York: Random House, Inc., 1966.
———, "Mental Illness, Biology, and Culture," in Francis L. K. Hsu (ed.), *Psychological Anthropology*, pp. 255–295. Homewood, Ill.: The Dorsey Press, 1961.
———, "On Being Just Complicated Enough." *Proceedings of the National Academy of Sciences*, Vol. 47, 1961, pp. 458–464.
———, and Ray Fogelson, "The Identity Struggle," in Ivan B. Nagy and James L. Framo (eds.), *Intensive Family Therapy*. New York: Harper & Row, Publishers, 1965.
WASHBURN, S. L., and F. C. HOWELL, "Human Evolution and Culture," in Sol Tax (ed.), *The Evolution of Man*. Chicago: University of Chicago Press, 1960.
WHITING, JOHN, and IRVING CHILD, *Child Training and Personality*. New Haven, Conn.: Yale University Press, 1953.

4

Sociological Views and Contributions

Anselm Strauss

A month ago I found myself in a situation rather similar to the one in which I am today. The occasion was a symposium on "normality"—a subject of absorbing interest to the assembled psychiatrists and psychologists. As the sole sociologist among the speakers, I admitted then that sociologists have little interest in normality and do not much study it. Insofar as they study something akin to it, they call it "deviancy," and raise rather different types of queries about it than psychiatrists and psychologists do about normality.

Today with less conviction—but only a little less—I have to admit that my colleagues evince rather little interest in what ordinarily goes by the name of personality. That is not a technical term to sociologists. Unlike the psychologists, we have no area of specialization called "personality." Very few of our publications feature the term in their titles, so that if we should ever computerize our writings for quick bibliographic reference the search for articles on personality would yield little. Even in our monographs you would be much frustrated if you were to look for technical references to personality or personality variables. Our introductory textbooks usually include a major section on personality, but typically it is preceded and followed by more fully developed sociological topics. And in the personality section most of the literature drawn on is likely to be written by psychologists or psychiatrists.

It is also safe to assert that no major sociologist ever has gained his reputation through research on personality. While one influential theorist, Talcott Parsons, has done considerable theorizing about personality—leaning on one type of psychoanalytic theory—this aspect of his writing has generated few validating studies even among sociologists who customarily follow his lead. You might be startled also to know that in the widely read book *Sociology Today* (a compilation of papers delivered at the 1957 sociological meetings) virtually no items are indexed under personality (Merton 1959). One paper, "Personality and Social Structure" by Alex Inkeles, is mainly a plea to introduce personality variables into sociological research in coordination with the sociological variables. Inkeles' footnotes direct us mainly to the writings of anthropologists, psychologists, and psychiatrists.

But what of sociologists who work in the speciality known as social psychology? There, more than in other sociological areas, there is considerable focus on phenomena that psychologists, psychiatrists, and anthropologists would regard as relevant to their own interests in personality. Yet these sociologists too are sufficiently oriented to the prevailing sociological issues that their personality-relevant work has a distinctly sociological cast. Typically they write about topics like adult socialization, the self, self conceptions, status and roles, role playing and role taking, careers, group identifications, identity.

Why is there a failure—sometimes even a refusal—by sociologists to focus on personality, to bother with or to invent methods of studying personality, and to concern themselves much with personality and personality variables? Short of a special study, no clear answer can be given to that question; but of course I shall hazard one. Certainly the answer does not lie in sociologists' ignorance of sister fields or of the research methods pioneered in them. The history of social psychology gives a strong hint about why, even when sociologists are aware of nonsociological literature, they do not necessarily use it in their own work.

Social psychology has been a major branch of American sociology since shortly before the turn of the century. In the early nineties, W. I. Thomas signaled the importance of understanding the psychological aspects of group relations. He was one of many sociologists who believed that society could not be studied without attention to what individuals might contribute to the functioning of groups and institutions—and, inversely, what the latter contribute to their members. So from the beginning American sociology produced a literature about those matters, and key figures like Thomas, Cooley, Park, and George H. Mead all contributed to the sociologists' social psychology. There was a parallel evolution in psychology, especially after 1920, but generally there was little traffic across the boundaries of sociology and psychology.

In the past thirty years or so interdisciplinary mergers have been prophesied and occasionally institutionally promoted—as at Michigan and Harvard—but, as I read the results, for the most part the two social psychologies have continued to face toward their major fields. Social psychologists who have been trained mainly as sociologists have continued to face toward the magnetic north of sociology. The writings of anthropologists on matters of personality perhaps have drawn their interest even less than writings by psychologists specializing in personality or social psychology. Psychiatry also has left sociologists relatively unaffected, except insofar as men like Goffman have attacked prevailing psychiatric practice and by implication psychiatric theory, or have studied practice and institutions by standard sociological methods. Those studies are made almost always with an eye on what contributions might also be afforded to sociological theory. It looks then as if sociologists have been so gifted with issues from their discipline that they are still focused on those issues. Even Inkeles, whom I mentioned before, is no exception. Sociologists who specialize in other areas are perhaps even less inclined to be interested in personality variables or personality study.

Coming now more closely to grips with the topic of this symposium, I suggest also that few sociologists are primarily interested in what goes on *"inside"* the person. Insofar as they are interested in persons, they are more inclined to study the social variables that affect individuals' behavior than to study individuals themselves. In fact, sociology grew up in Europe and America explicitly opposed to the psychologizing of society, and sociologists opted either for study of society without a focus on individuals or study of social influences on individuals. Put in over-simple terms: it is possible to focus on what goes on *inside* of persons, or *outside* of persons, or *among* persons. Sociologists are professionally oriented—biased if you will—toward the second and third of those approaches. Here is a good example: in a review of "Personality and Situational Factors in Prejudice," Simpson and Yinger conclude, "There is now widespread, if not universal, agreement that collective behavior in intergroup relations cannot be explained by what is 'in' individuals. Men are role-playing creatures; they act in structured situations; to an important degree they behave in terms of their obligations and group-defined interests" (Merton 1959:580). Personality thus dispensed with, they go on to consider situational and structural variables.

The sociological bias was recently brought home strikingly to me. At a working conference devoted to hammering out a long interview guide, to be used in a study of TB patients and TB clinics, there was an atmosphere of relative harmony. Occasionally the psychologists and the sociologists teased each other because their respective professional skirts were showing, but finally there was a disruptive clash between a psychologist and a sociologist. The latter, who probably was more hospitable to psychological variables than most sociologists, was joined by an anthropologist. Both objected strongly to getting certain personality data. After all, it was the structural variables that would most efficiently bring the change of behavior that we all wished might be the outcome of the research.

Sociologists, I think we must conclude, really have little interest in, and virtually nothing to contribute to, what is commonly referred to as the structure of personality. They might some day; they do not now. As I hope to make clear to those of you who are not well acquainted with sociological writing, such interest as we have in relations among persons or in the social variables that influence persons is almost always in the service of our analyses of group and organizational functioning.

Let us now look at a few kinds of analyses made by sociologists when their analyses are concerned with psychological rather than purely organizational phenomena. I shall first discuss studies of work and occupational careers. E. C. Hughes, whose teaching and writings have been instrumental in stimulating an interest in work and careers, emphasized that they take place within specified social and occupational contexts. A student of his, Rue Bucher, who is interested in medical specialties, has published an illuminating paper about pathologists (Bucher 1962). She discovered that there were—this was about six years ago—two groups of American pathologists, one oriented toward research and the other toward clinical practice in hospitals. Each group has been somewhat differently trained, works in a different organizational setting, has contact with different clients or colleagues, relies on somewhat different techniques when doing research, holds different attitudes toward work and toward pathology, and even has a different conception of what pathology "is" and of themselves as pathologists. The research pathologists are located mainly in the medical schools, where pathologists traditionally have worked for many decades. As teachers and researchers, they trace their lineage back to the great nineteenth-century pathologists. And they are oriented chiefly toward their research colleagues in neighboring medical specialties and sciences. The clinical pathologists are a much newer group. They work mainly in community hospitals, where they are rapidly becoming the representatives of a powerful and aspiring clinical specialty. They model themselves after internists and surgeons, with whom they have close relationships. In detailing the careers of men in these two professional "segments," Bucher highlights how the career steps are related to the organizational contexts. While she is interested in the differential types of individuals produced, and perhaps recruited, by each segment, typically she is much more interested in the patterns of work, values, and social relationships that are characteristic of each segment, as well as in the relation of each segment to the other.

In such studies of careers, emphasis falls now on one structural feature and now on another. For instance, the researcher's focus can be on relationships with clients, as for instance on those which the solo lawyer has with the people whom he services. The focus can also be on how an organization deals with failure at various phases of typical careers, as in Martin's study of one corporation's resources for moving people geographically and vertically when confronted with their incompetency or failing abilities (Martin 1956). Emphasis may be on how organizations recruit, shape, employ, and dismiss their young men, as in Smigel's study of the Wall Street lawyer (Smigel 1964). The sociologist can also choose to emphasize the educational or socialization aspects of the initial years of a career, as in the Becker-Geer-Hughes study of medical students (Becker 1961). A central concept of this study was "student culture," which helped students to "get by" with a maximum of collective support and a minimum of personal stress.

Such studies may dwell on what work and participation in an organization may do to the person—and vice versa—but that is not usually a major feature of the research. Rather, the sociologist wants to know about those things mainly because he wishes to know about the functioning of the occupation or the organization. Yet we would probably all agree, those studies *are* relevant to questions of identity, of self-images, of personal styles and individual action. The sociologist's eye, however, is almost always on the "big picture" rather than on the microscopic study of persons.

Insofar as his intent is to study persons, he tends to be interested in social interaction rather than with what is ordinarily called "interpersonal interaction." For the sociologist, persons rarely are just persons; they represent organizations or groups and "occupy," as the saying goes, various social positions and "play" the associated roles. Thus social interaction is viewed as occurring among representatives of social positions, of groups and organizations. For instance: in various situations the same man may act as a corporation official, as an upper-middle class fellow, as a husband, and as a lay member of the Catholic Church. And he acts toward others who are related to his various social positions and statuses in determinable ways.

I shall give one or two examples of systematic studies of social interaction before turning to some theoretical issues raised by such studies. Melville Dalton has written about types of patterned interaction that are characteristic of top labor officials and corporation officials (Rose 1962). He analyzed the interaction between those elites at the local levels, as well as between each elite and its national counterpart; also between each local elite and its rank-and-file associates. These patterned interactions are the product of recurrent situations in which each elite finds itself with respect to the above-mentioned groups. Sociologists would tend to call Dalton's analysis a "structural analysis" because he has carefully uncovered those structural elements of unions and corporations which typically affect the behavior of people holding various social positions in those organizations. Insofar as interaction among these men affects their perspectives, perceptions, and sense of identity—and they *are* affected—then Dalton also is interested in what this audience today might call matters of personality.

I turn to another analysis of interaction, one which seems less obviously structural but is quite as structural. In a study of what he calls "deviance disavowal," Fred Davis carefully analyzed how people with visible stigmas (the blind, the crippled, and so on) typically manage the course of conversation and action with nonstigmatized persons when they meet each other for the first time (Davis 1961). Typically, the encounter has a great potential for causing embarrassment. The nonstigmatized person has trouble keeping his eyes off the stigma and may not know how to handle conversation with the stigmatized person. The latter may also be embarrassed and humiliated if he cannot keep his disability out of the center of attention. He wishes to keep the conversation normal and to keep relationships as they would be if he were not afflicted.

Davis has described various strategies employed by the stigmatized person, but his main interest was in the phases through which interaction proceeds when the strategies and tactics are successful. The first stage is "fictional acceptance" whereby each person pays studied inattention to the stigma. The second stage is "breaking through" or "facilitating" the "normalized role taking." The third stage is "institutionalization of the normalized relationship." In general, the stigmatized person attempts first to keep the interaction in the fictional mode; then gradually he engineers matters to a final phase where it is "openly fitting and safe to admit to certain incidental capacities, limits and needs." A sociologist would not think of such interaction as "interpersonal" but as interaction characteristic of people who are members of opposing categories, respectively the stigmatized and the nonstigmatized—such as sociologists study interaction between Negroes and whites, or politicians and constituents.

Furthermore, we might think of this research as dealing with a particular structural context which has at least four additional features besides the ones mentioned explicitly by Professor Davis. First, this is an initial encounter and not a later or successive encounter. Second, the stigmatized person is experienced and the normal person is inexperienced at these encounters. Third, visible stigmata are involved rather than invisible ones which might possibly become known to the normal person if the interaction were inexpertly managed. Fourth, the stigmatized person wishes to keep the interaction normalized—but sometimes he might wish to profit from his stigma. Each of those additional structural features would lead to interaction with different characteristics than those described by Davis. Change any of those structural conditions and not only does the interaction become different but so does the potential for its temporary or lasting impact on the interacting persons.

An even more typical sociological approach to interaction and incidentally to what is called "role conflict" and "group membership" is exemplified by a study reported a few years ago by Lewis Killian (1952). People caught in tornadoes and explosions were afterward interviewed. The interviews showed "conflict between loyalties to the family and to the community" which operated to direct people's actions during the disasters. There were also "dilemmas arising from conflicting roles derived from memberships in other groups." For instance, there was a conflict between loyalty as an employee of an organization and to "fellow employees as friends and human beings." As is typical of such sociological studies, Killian was interested in the role conflicts and how they were resolved. Each type of conflict was securely linked, in his analysis, with the social positions of the actors in this collective drama. Therefore, the reader gets a pretty clear picture of how people with differential group memberships acted in specifically patterned ways. In a general sense, we could say about Killian's analysis that it too is concerned with the question of personality insofar as it bears on the tug of loyalties and group identifications.

These kinds of studies indicate why sociologists have been concerned with more abstract questions such as: What is the nature of role playing and of role taking? Probably all American sociologists are familiar with George H. Mead's pioneering discussion of role taking as imagining what one's act will look like to the other person when viewed from the other's perspective. Mead's associated idea of role playing was that a person organized his activity in accordance with his anticipations of how other persons might respond to his acts, as well as in accordance with a continuing assessment of their actual responses.

Fairly recently Ralph Turner has followed up in two directions on Mead's earlier analysis (Rose 1962; Turner 1956). First, he has emphasized the idea of role playing as a process, in contrast with the more static notion that persons occupy social positions and then act in accordance with the roles called for by those positions. He also has made role playing a more complex process than in Mead's analysis by distinguishing between taking the other's attitude toward oneself and taking his attitude toward anyone else, including presumably himself. Turner also distinguishes among the standpoints from which I may view the other's attitude: from my own standpoint, from a third party's, and from that of the other person himself. (Turner, incidentally, terms this last standpoint "identifying.")

Better known is Erving Goffman's analysis of a feature of role playing which he terms "impression management" (Goffman 1959). When a person takes the role of another and then organizes his own overt behavior to elicit from the other the desired role-taking response, this is impression management. This management may be completely sincere or coldly manipulative; it may be done consciously or virtually without awareness. Impressions are created by a large variety of communicative devices and interactional tactics and by the use of external props such as clothing and arrangements of furnishings—books, furniture, pictures. Goffman makes his analysis complex by noting that audiences are frequently aware of their management. They may go along with the performance or may negate it by sabotage, heckling, and other forms of disrespect. They may see through the formal facade but carefully act to convince the impression manager that they do not; or both audience and he may act with a kind of mutual pretense.

Gregory Stone has pushed analysis of role playing still further (Rose 1962). Theorizing from data on the use of clothing, he notes that people select what clothes they will wear and how they will wear them so as to get others to make the proper identifications of themselves. In a general statement of this phenomenon, he remarks that "identifications of one another are facilitated by appearance and are often accomplished silently or unverbally." In managing one's appearance with clothes, one attempts to get validation for his conception of himself, and at the same time helps the other to act appropriately in the given social situation. If the other responds in a way that is discrepant with one's conception of self, then there is likely to be some movement toward the "redefinition of the challenged self." To show how complex Stone's analysis is, I shall only mention that he distinguishes among the following four functions of selecting and wearing specific clothing: (1) The person announces his identity; (2) he shows his value; (3) he expresses his mood; (4) he proposes some attitude. Such analyses as the ones I have discussed are valuable extensions of our conceptions of role taking and role playing. It is safe to predict that this general line of theorizing will continue to affect sociological research.

I shall end now on a personal note. This will allow you perhaps to discount partly my interpretation of sociologists' handling of personality, while allowing me to reaffirm the interpretation. The difference between a sociological approach and a psychological one can be seen quite dramatically in a research area in which I have been working for several years. Because I am at a medical center, I have noted that the medical nursing care given to patients who lie dying in hospitals is beset with difficult problems for the hospitals and wards, along with the careers of staff members and the courses of illness; all have an impact on the interaction observable among patients, families, and staff. My colleagues (Barney Glaser and Jeanne Quint) and I are interested in the consequences of the interaction for the hospital itself, as well as for the various dramatis personae. In contrast, psychologists and psychiatrists who study death characteristically have studied how people feel about death—what their attitudes toward death are. They do not study dying as a process that takes place over time, or by noting the interactions between the dying person and others who live and work around him.

One of the major publications to come out of our research is a study of how the social organization of nursing schools, in conjunction with that of hospitals, results in specifiable sets of consequences for the work and identities of nursing students (Quint 1967). Another publication traces the interplay between structural conditions and interaction during the course (or "trajectory") of dying (Glaser 1968). Finally—and here I shall say something more detailed—we have made an intricate analysis of the phenomena which, above all, most people seem most interested in when they talk about dying (Glaser 1965). I refer to something which we call "awareness contexts." Sometimes patients know they are dying; sometimes they suspect it; sometimes they never know. The same is true of their relatives. Hence we coined the term "awareness context," which is the total combination of what each interactant in a situation knows about the identity of the other and his own identity in the eyes of the other. This total awareness is the context within which successive interactions are guided over periods of time, whether long or short. We distinguished four principal types of awareness context which are immensely relevant to the situations we were studying. An *open* awareness context obtains when each interactant is aware of the other's true identity (in this case the patient is dying) and his own identity in the eyes of the other. A *closed* awareness context obtains when one interactant does not know either the other's identity or the other's view of his identity. A *suspicion* context is when one interactant suspects the true identity of the other or the other's view of his own identity, or both. A *pretense* context is when both are fully aware but pretend not to be. In linking these awareness contexts with interaction, we proceeded in accordance with the following directives given to ourselves.

(1) give a description of the given type of awareness context;
(2) give the structural conditions under which it exists;
(3) give the consequent interaction;
(4) give changes of interaction that occasion transformations of awareness context, along with the structural conditions for the transformation;
(5) give the tactics of various interactants as they attempt to manage changes of context; and
(6) give some consequences of the initial context for the various interactants and for the ward and hospital.

Here is how this set of directives worked for the closed awareness context:

1. Hospitalized patients frequently do not recognize their impending death while the staff does. Thus interaction between them occurs within a closed awareness context about the patient's true (dying) identity.

2. At least four major structural conditions determine this closed context. First, most patients are not especially experienced at recognizing the signs of impending death. Second, the hospital is magnificently organized, both by accident and design, for hiding the medical truth from the patient. Third, physicians are supported in their withholding of information by professional rationales, such as: "Why deny them all hope by telling them?" Fourth, ordinarily the patient has no allies who can help him discover the staff's secret; even his family or other patients tend to withhold such information if privy to it.

3. To prevent the patient's comprehension of the truth, the staff utilizes a number of "situation as normal" tactics. They seek to act in his presence as if he were only ill. They talk to him as if he were going to live. They converse about his future, thus enhancing his belief that he will regain his health. By such indirect signaling they offer him a false biography.

To supplement these tactics they use additional ones to guard against disclosure. They carefully guard against the patient's overhearing any conversation about his real condition. The also engage in careful management of expressions, controlling their facial and bodily gestures so as not to give the show away. Almost inevitably they attempt, not always consciously, to reduce the number of potentially disclosing cues by reducing time spent with the patient or by restricting their conversations with him.

4. In such collusive games the teamwork can be phenomenal but the dangers of disclosure to the patient are very great. Unless he dies quickly or becomes permanently comatose, he tends to begin to suspect or even clearly understand how others identify him. Patients do overhear occasional conversations about themselves. Personnel unwittingly may flash cues, or make conversational errors, which arouse his suspicions. Day and night staff may give him contradictory information or divergent clues. In short, various of the original structural conditions that sustain closed awareness now begin to disappear, or are counteracted by new structural conditions that make for suspicion or open awareness.

5. Some interactants may wish to move him along into other types of awareness context. If so, they can employ certain interactional tactics which are, for the most part, merely the opposites of the nondisclosure tactics. Intentionally, a staff member may give the game away, wholly or partly, by improper management of face, by carefully oblique phrasing of words, by merely failing to reassure the patient sufficiently about a hopeful prognosis, and so on.

6. The closed awareness that surrounds the patient has many significant consequences for him and the staff. Because the patient is unaware of the others' view of his identity, he cannot act as if he were aware of dying. Thus, he cannot talk to close kin about his fate. He cannot assuage their grief. Nor can he act toward himself as if he were dying, by facing his expected death, however he may face it, or doing the things he might do if he knew he were dying—like drawing up wills or "making up" with people with whom he has quarreled.

The kinsmen and hospital personnel are saved from certain stressful scenes that accompany open awareness about death, but they are also blocked from participating in various satisfying rituals of passage to death. Wives cannot openly take farewells of husbands; personnel cannot share the sometimes ennobling acceptance of death which a patient evinces if he is aware of impending death.

My chief reason for giving these details is to underscore the sociological style that makes this kind of research and theorizing at least somewhat different from that found in other fields. I do not doubt that psychologists or psychiatrists could supplement our work with valuable research of their own, perhaps using personality variables, but the research would be supplementary and directed toward different theoretical issues. Another reason why I discussed this research was to indicate that such studies of interaction and social structure are undoubtedly relevant to matters which other behavioral scientists call "personality." But I do not think I should do the job, at least not here, of tying up the threads of the various frames of reference. I feel, in fact, the need to go on record, saying that we need *more* approaches to such matters rather than eclectic or combined approaches.

BIBLIOGRAPHY

BECKER, HOWARD S., BLANCHE GEER, EVERETT HUGHES, and ANSELM STRAUSS, *Boys in White*. Chicago: University of Chicago Press, 1961.
BUCHER, RUE. "Pathology: A Study of Social Movements within a Profession," *Social Problems*, Vol. 10, No. 1, 1962, pp. 40–51.
DALTON, MELVILLE, "Cooperative Evasions to Support Labor-Management Contracts," in A. Rose (ed.), *Human Behavior and Social Processes*, pp. 267–84. Boston: Houghton Mifflin Company, 1962.
DAVIS, FRED, "Deviance Disavowal: The Management of Strained Interaction by the Visibly Handicapped," *Social Problems*, Vol. 9, No. 2, 1961, pp. 120–132.
GLASER, BARNEY, and ANSELM STRAUSS, *Dying in Hospitals*. Chicago: Aldine Publishing Company, 1968.
———, *Awareness of Dying*. Chicago: Aldine Publishing Company, 1965.
GOFFMAN, ERVING, *The Presentation of Self in Everyday Life*. New York: Doubleday & Company, Inc., Anchor, 1959.
INKELES, ALEX, "Personality and Social Structure," in R. Merton, L. Broom, and L. Cottrell (eds.), *Sociology Today*, pp. 249–276. New York: Basic Books, Inc., 1959.
KILLIAN, LEWIS, "Significance of Multiple-Group Membership in Disaster," *American Journal of Sociology*, Vol. 57, 1952, pp. 309–14.
MARTIN, NORMAN, and ANSELM STRAUSS, "Patterns of Mobility within Industrial Organizations," *Journal of Business*, Vol. 29, 1956, pp. 101–110.
MERTON, R., L. BROOM, and L. COTTRELL, (eds.), *Sociology Today*. New York: Basic Books, Inc., 1959.
QUINT, JEANNE, *The Nurse and the Dying Patient*. New York: The Macmillan Company, 1967.
SIMPSON, GEORGE, and MILTON YINGER, "The Sociology of Race and Ethnic Relations," in R. Merton, L. Broom, and L. Cottrell (eds.), *Sociology Today*, pp. 376–399. New York: Basic Books, Inc., 1959.
SMIGEL, ERWIN, *The Wall Street Lawyer*. New York: The Free Press, 1964.
STONE, GREGORY, "Appearance and the Self," in A. Rose (ed.), *Human Behavior and Social Processes*, pp. 86–118. Boston: Houghton Mifflin Company, 1962.
TURNER, RALPH, "Role Taking, Role Standpoint, and Reference Group Behavior," *American Journal of Sociology*, Vol. 61, 1956, pp. 316–328.
———, "Role Taking: Process Versus Conformity," in A. Rose (ed.), *Human Behavior and Social Processes*, pp. 20–40. Boston: Houghton Mifflin Company, 1962.

5

Personality from a Psychoanalytic Viewpoint

Weston La Barre

It may seem strange, in this symposium, to deal specifically with the psychology of Freud, since his influence on our times is so far-reaching and so profound. In the words of the poet Auden about Freud, "If often he was wrong and at times absurd, to us he is no more a person now but a whole climate of opinion." [1] This very fact of widespread familiarity with psychoanalytic theory, often at second or third hand or even more remotely, does not guarantee, however, the accuracy of these widespread notions, for we are deeply motivated to distort some of Freud's findings. Therefore it may be well to summarize this difficult psychology from the original sources.[2] I wish to make clear at the outset that I think Freud did make some errors —for example, in *Totem and Taboo*, in his projection of the Oedipal conflict into the purely mythological past history of mankind, in his "primal horde" theory, and again in the so-called "hydraulic theory of the libido" which supposes that libidinal energy, different in amount for each individual, can be freely transferred from one organ system to another.[3] But his contribution remains the core of modern psychiatry, while parts of it are widely shared in all modern psychologies.

There are four characteristics of Freudian psychology which originally set it off from other psychologies:

(1) Psychoanalysis is the first psychology to take seriously the whole human body as a place to live in.[4] The specific experiences of this body and the vicissitudes of learning about this body adaptively as various parts of it become biologically important—especially in relation to the culturally structured attitudes and requirements of a given society—shape profoundly the individual personality.[5] Personality is partly learned: its individual structure is shaped by individual experience to an amazing degree. Nevertheless, psychoanalysis is profoundly biological about basic "species-specific" givens, and sensitively oriented to the concrete social and cultural sources of learning.

(2) Psychoanalysis is the first psychology to preoccupy itself with the

purpose (as opposed to the processes) of thinking. The pre-Freudian notion was that thinking was simply an obvious and rational way of discovering the nature of reality. Psychoanalysis has dealt a hard blow to this unexamined and comfortably confident faith, much as Copernican theory dealt a fatal blow to earth-centered astronomy, and Darwinian evolution to man-centered biology. To Freud, thinking is a far more complex matter of making peace among three competing forces. The first datum of psychology is the conscious mind. "I think, therefore, I am," said Descartes, and all of us are convinced of the reality of our own minds. But the conscious mind has been rejected by some psychologies as too "subjective" a thing to study, hence behaviorism, for one, discarded the subject matter of psychology at the very beginning. Freud called this subjective, conscious, adaptive, *executive* part of the mind the "ego." But the ego, as we shall see, must serve three masters, and is not solely the obedient subject of reality alone.

First of all, there are the imperious organic demands of this kind of animal body, demands which may be deferred and disciplined but never finally frustrated if the organism is to stay healthy, alive, and reproduce itself. For example, the gratification of conscious thirst can within limits be postponed, but without water ultimately, the animal dies.[6] The sum total of these organic demands on the psyche is called the "id." When id needs are repressed, we have *neurosis* and conflicts of various kinds, with the "return of the repressed" in the form of distorted symptoms which both punish and gratify.

Secondly, the ego must adapt the organism to external reality from which the organism derives its biochemical energy, for no organism can survive unless adapted to its environment. If the ego loses its adaptive relation to reality, we have *psychosis*. And thirdly, the ego must adapt to the moral demands of a specific traditional society, not all of which demands are necessarily life enhancing or even rational. The influence of moral reality is precipitated within the mind as an arduously learned conscience or "superego." If the individual does not incorporate these moral demands emotionally and forcefully, but is only intellectually aware of his tribal customs in the way a visiting anthropologist might coldly and bloodlessly know about the customs of an alien society that do not apply to him, then we have the *psychopath*, who may be well oriented to physical reality and thoroughly indulgent of his id impulses but who is morally sick. These relations may be diagrammed simply as indicated in figure on p. 67.

The ego therefore must serve three masters at the same time: the organic id, the environmental reality, and the social superego—and the shirking of each ego task gives us, respectively, neurosis, psychosis, and psychopathy. In this view, then, the ego is not master in its own house, the mind.[7] The *purpose* of thinking is to achieve homeostasis, to preserve some kind of equilibrium or *modus vivendi* among these three kinds of demands made upon it. As everybody knows, the task is not easy or automatic.

The ego has a number of defenses which all of us use at one time or another—rationalization, denial, projection, intellectualization, and the like—but chronic overuse brings problems. Rationalization is finding good reasons for unreasonable positions we wish to hold, despite our perhaps unconsciously "knowing better," which only increases the flow of rationalizations. The extreme of this self-serving indulgence in fantasy is schizophrenia. Denial is simply "turning one's back" psychologically on unpleasant facts—a characteristic ego defense in hysteria. Projection is pretending the forbidden impulse is not inside but outside one's own mind—like the hysteric old maid who looks constantly and with delicious fearfulness for the burglar under the bed she unconsciously wishes were in bed with her.

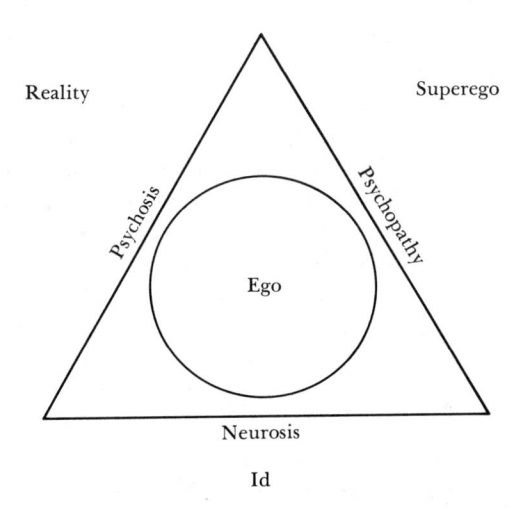

```
                    /\
                   /  \
         Reality  /    \  Superego
                 /      \
                / ∙∙∙∙∙∙ \
               / ∙      ∙ \
        Psychosis ∙  Ego ∙ Psychopathy
             / ∙      ∙ \
            / ∙∙∙∙∙∙∙∙ \
           /_____\
              Neurosis
                Id
```

The lustful burglar has the wicked wish, not she! For, see, how busily she preoccupies herself with seeing that this wish is not accomplished? She seemingly can have her cake and eat it too: she can spend all her time in delectable fantasy, and yet not be guilty. But her symptom both punishes and gratifies. Her *phobia* is what she unconsciously desires but consciously denies and projects—and she never gets her man.[8] Fantasy is fun and not dangerous; and yet it does not really gratify in the end.

The ego has other mechanisms of defense, for example "conversion." The conversion hysteric can convert conscious psychic pain into as-if physical illnesses, thus achieving the characteristic "belle indifference" of the conversion hysteric, but keeping the surgeon needlessly busy cutting out one naughty organ after another. The conversion hysteric can (and often does), with smiling face and evident pleasure, give a long "organ recital" of dreadful illnesses, any one of which, if organically real, might put her at death's door, instead of allowing her to walk around and pridefully talk about it. Her "belle indifference" or surprising emotional unconcern comes from the conversion (projection) of psychic stress into a pseudo-organic illness, which *functionally substitutes* for conscious anxiety. That is, the pain of operations gives punishment, but she may get sympathy too—and she has gotten rid of the symbolically wicked organ. But only symbolically. She will soon need another operation because this masochistic process has meant no dynamic cure of the *psychological* problem. Ultimately she may shop around for a surgeon (surgeons have unconscious motivations too) and have a needless hysterectomy, after which, commonly, she may have a psychotic breakdown.

Our insight into the meaning of the psychic game of the "burglar under the bed" or the hypochondria of the conversion hysteric is one reason why we get so impatient with the neurotic. We correctly perceive that the neurotic partly enjoys the symptom, hence we regard even real suffering as somehow "phony" and dismiss the neurotic as an "old crock" whose problem "exists only in the imagination." No, not in the imagination; only in the memory. Neurotics are literally sick of the past. The psychiatric problem is how to discover that past, examine and understand it. It is true the neurotic seems like the famous Hellenistic sculpture of Laocoön, in which a brawny man and his two sons struggle extravagantly with a snake, but if they would just *let go* they could probably step out of the coils and walk away. However, in this incomplete judgment we forget two facts: first, the neurotic clings to his symptoms because of what they *do for him,* protecting him from frightening insight, often plus the "secondary gain" of removing him from frightening situations and eliciting pity or indulgence—at the same time that they morally punish him with guilt and psychically needed anguish and anxiety. The patient seems to say to the analyst, "Take anything, but just let me keep my symptoms!" Secondly, because of *resistance,* the insight of an analyst or friend is by no means equivalent to insight on the part of the patient himself. The very correctness of the insight arouses his defense mechanisms. Anyone who has uselessly tried to tell a neurotic plain and obvious facts about himself knows well what "resistance" is and may agree that it takes skilled professional help to cope with it. Resistance is often extremely easy to see in other persons, and just as often impossible to see in oneself. Thus "self-analysis" is impossible beyond a very modest point, because a kind of psychic blindness arises when one gets close to really anxiety-arousing points. Similarly, resistance to "certain parts of psychoanalysis" is likely to be part-identification with the neurotic at these points because the insights apply to us too.

We have seen that in phobic hysteria there is projection of a disclaimed portion of the psyche to the outside, and in conversion hysteria projection of psychic into physical pain. Projection of erotic and aggressive impulses is also present in males, especially in paranoia. Instead of recognizing his own hostility, the paranoiac projects it into other people and then claims they are persecuting him ("persecutory mania"). Instead of recognizing his own (forbidden) unconscious wishes, he claims someone else is making "unwanted" sexual advances to him. Since the hysteric's unconscious wish is merely heterosexual, she can often get along with the relatively shallow and transparently naive defense of simple denial. But since the paranoiac's unconscious wish is homosexual, he needs the far more elaborated defenses of a completely rationalized "paranoid system" for he can afford no chink in his psychic defenses or body-image—other people would otherwise wickedly "poison" him or "stab him in the back." (Such fears are not without symbolic meaning.) Pathological jealousy means he unconsciously feels the attractiveness of another man but projects this onto his own wife and falsely blames her for being attracted to him. Or, instead of recognizing his own inadequacy, he fantasies compensatory omnipotence ("megalomania"), as overprotested as he needs it to be. Or, instead of recognizing his inability to love, he believes that every woman *loves him* ("erotomania"). Likewise, paranoid suspiciousness imputes to other people one's own denied aggressive and hostile impulses, which later can be consciously felt because now "justified." The paranoiac Hitler displayed all these mechanisms in classic textbook forms.[9]

The variety of defense mechanisms is almost endless. In displacement of anger toward his boss, the man bullies his wife, she nags the child, and the child kicks the cat. Intellectualization and isolation are characteristic of compulsion neuroses and obsessions, which are sometimes almost as intricate as paranoid systems, though their dynamics are otherwise somewhat different. Too tyrannical a conscience or superego may crush the ego into a *depression*, in which the Ego feels weak, rejected, unlovable and unloved, helpless, and "no good." Or a rebellious ego-id team, trying to run away from an overly severe superego, can end up in the pseudo-blithesome "vacation from conscience" of frantic *mania*.

(3) The third distinguishing characteristic of psychoanalysis is that it is the first psychology to pay significant attention to the *symbolic content* of thought. The neurotic symbol is something that is not, but conveniently stands for, the upsetting reality. We can immediately see the great usefulness of the symbol, for example in dreams, where the wish may disguise itself behind the mask of the symbol, and thus achieve gratification at the same time it gets past the dream censor and hoodwinks the superego. Of course the conflict may arouse too much anxiety, and we wake up, often with the mild malaise of guilt mixed with a smug naughty sense of surreptitious gratification. Similarly in more severe conflicts, the nightmare, terror-laden, may call upon the conscious ego for help and we wake up frightened. But most of the time dreaming seems to be another homeostatic device of the mind, this one specifically to preserve sleep. Beyond dream use, massive symbol using is one of the prime adaptive characteristics of *Homo sapiens*, and no human psychology that ignores the nature of symbolizing can hope to be a complete or even adequate psychology.

The nature of symbolizing now seems to be so widely recognized that many people indulge in amateur symbol hunting as a kind of parlor game. The dangers in this are multiple and complex. For one, there exists no absolute "universal dictionary" of previously-agreed-upon dream symbols or of any other kind of symbol supposedly inherent in human minds. Hence *ad hoc* "interpretation" risks being simply wrong intellectually. It is the nature of symbol equations to be invented by man, not discovered in nature—for all that they may be unconsciously shared by people in the same society and learned like the rest of culture. Hence cross-cultural "interpretations" may simply miss the point methodologically and rise from the wrong culture base. Again, common sense can always say "Come now, X is not *really* equal to Y!"—and be right, even though we correctly perceived what the person meant it to mean unconsciously, but have now aroused someone's resistances, perhaps the subject's. Again, who is doing the symbolizing? Insofar as an unconscious meaning is not truly resident in the symbol producer's mind, we are clearly projecting a meaning of our own, the only possible source now being one's own mind. We are then not so much discovering the contents of another psyche as naively and unwittingly exhibiting one's own. Finally, *what are we doing* in this allegedly "psychoanalytic" gambit of symbol chasing: are we being voyeuristic, punitive, aggressive, seductive, hostile, oneupsman, exhibitionistic, or what? Such "wild analysis" of the amateur can be each of these unseemly activities, when lacking the constant self-scrutiny of the "counter-transference" in himself as a trained analyst does it. Since the professional analyst must often spend actual weeks in discovering an unconscious meaning *through his patient's voluminous free associations* in order to be able to demonstrate it unequivocably and massively to him later, nothing is quite so painful to the sophisticate as to witness amateur symbol mongering. Besides, *motives* for doing this in the parlor are not the same as those in the doctor's office—in addition to the shameless inadequacy of the methodology. In the same manner, and for much the same reasons, nothing so much sets the professional anthropologist's teeth on edge as to hear a glib interpretation of the "symbolism" of a piece of primitive art, when the speaker knows nothing whatever about the man or the tribe that made it but is merely improvising *ad hoc* folklore; whereas the anthropologist may have spent patient months tracing *in native minds* the ramifications of a new and alien symbolic system. No one with genuine knowledge of the individual and cultural nature of symbolism would permit himself the fatuous absurdity of public amateur "interpretations." Nor, justly, is he likely to convince.

(4) A fourth characteristic of psychoanalysis involves a profound irony. We are all familiar with some of the Victorian generation's defense against Darwinian evolution. This defense is one of the shabbiest of all argumentative dodges: it consists in an unacknowledged understanding of what a

man said, with clever purpose distorting it, and then using it to demolish a straw man of one's own devising. For example, the cliché about Darwin was, "You don't think your grandfather was an ape, ha ha!, do you?" As a matter of fact, Darwin was looking for a "missing link" at each branching between man's ancestry and that of modern apes. It is a cheap triumph to demolish one's own nonsense.

But the same gambit is still commonly used against psychoanalysis. Even now, people sometimes say, "Freud thinks everything is sex, ha ha!, and you and I both know this isn't so." However, Freud long argued, and evidently without much success, that there are *other kinds of sensual pleasure* besides the sexual (genital), for example the oral pleasure of the baby's lustful suckling at his mother's breast, which we still retain in modified form in the pleasure of eating, drinking, smoking, gum chewing, talking, and the like. There is also evident pleasure in urination and defecation, but half the time we say this is not true, so Freud is wrong, and half the time we acknowledge it but call Freud a nasty man for dreaming it up.

This is what I mean by saying that we are sometimes deeply motivated defensively to distort the findings of Freud. He tells us many things we do not want to know, and against these we liberally use all the familiar defense mechanisms, including readily-joined-in ridicule insofar as we share the same aversion to self-knowledge. In this we are again like the proverbial old maid. When the analyst finally points out that she seems, on much evidence, to have real (and even legitimate) sexual wishes, she calls him a "dirty old man" (denial), probably lusting after her himself (projection)—an especially terrible matter because the analyst unconsciously represents her (forbidden) father. Similarly, the paranoid patient, or person, gets into a long "logical" argument in which he is able to rationalize everything, however preposterous. And the psychopath, in turn, falsely alleges that "Freud says you should act on all your impulses or you'll be neurotic—" this at the precise moment when the analyst is trying to point out that what the psychopath really needs is a few well-contrived inhibitions and ego-disciplined sublimations. One's peculiarly distorted view of Freud's findings may therefore be diagnostic of one's basic personality.

This brings us to the chief difficulty of Freud's psychology. Are we to suppose that people become anguishingly insane over nice, innocuous, genteel matters that we can complacently converse about in the parlor? No! People go mad over really upsetting matters like forbidden incestuous impulses, deeply unconscious homosexual wishes, murderous rage, and other such unseemly feelings. We all have forbidden wishes, hopefully to a lesser degree and in more manageable forms, hence our anxieties are inevitably aroused by Freud's explanations, and hence our various defense mechanisms bristle in violently argumentative form. At this point we can only quote Shakespeare, "Methinks the lady doth protest too much"—or in more homely fashion discern that "Where there's smoke, there's fire."

Freud first pointed out what now seems obvious to many: that there are a number of body zones besides the genital one, all capable of giving sensual pleasure, zones in fact primordially more activated and physiologically significant in time than the genital. Diffuse skin erotism is present very early, although in humans it is perhaps not so significant as it is in lower animals. There is also positive, and sometimes intense, pleasure in seeing and hearing, smelling and touching and tasting. But none of these is primary in the libidinal sense. It is because of traumatic relinquishment, painful vicissitudes in experiencing, overindulgence, or repression of these libidinal pleasures that so many people protest so fiercely their nonexistence; and because it is often so hardly won, or precarious, they protest the exclusive primacy of genital pleasure. And yet pregenital gratifications are always part of genital forepleasure (kissing, seeing, touching, and so on), such that the forepleasure is a kind of recapitulation of the libidinal history of the individual and an autobiography of the relative importance of these for the individual.

The primary libidinal zones are those of the various portal skins of the body, where pleasure is associated with successful accomplishment of an adaptive physiological duty or need. Primary in the suckling is the oral zone, where libidinal pleasure accompanies the satisfaction of its primary need to take in and to grow; the eye and ear are later adjuncts of "oral incorporation" as a process. Reciprocally, the normal woman obtains deep physical gratification in nursing a baby. The mutual gratification-frustration gamut of these experiences shapes the individual, quite irrationally and preverbally, as either an "oral optimist" or an "oral pessimist" in his emotional expectations of the world. Later appearing, about the time the individual begins to walk and talk and to achieve a more active body mastery, social demands invading individual body autonomy come into conflict over the anal zone; the residual emotional tone of this experience has much to do with individual awareness of self-not-self discrimination and attitudes of dominance-submission in larger social contexts later. Urethral disciplines become associated with pride, shame, and ambition. The phallic phase, about which more will be said later, is perhaps still an "imprinting" period for sexual identification and introjection of psychic maleness or femaleness; this is the time of enthusiastic discovery and valuation of one's own sex, and appropriate sex typing through emulation, learning, and identification (only when a fixated self-sex admiration becomes genitalized does it become perverse). Associated with the phallic is the oedipal phase, when the child discovers a significant figure (father) beyond the gratifying-demanding mother of the oral-anal phases; it is the emotional paradigm for all future superego relations with society; for example, individual attitudes toward religion are a revealing Rorschach of the peculiar resolution of the oedipal conflict, which underlies all rational or rationalized superstructures built intellectually upon it (war, politics, and the like). The psychological phase of genital primacy is quite the last of all. Of course none of these phases should be thought of as stations on a railway line, for they coexist and intermingle and in some form persist; but they do follow much the same sequence in most individuals.

There is a familiar phrase—"As the twig is bent, so is the tree inclined" —to which we often pay lip service, but which psychoanalysis insists on taking seriously and literally. There must be the concrete "twig," the physical body and nervous system of the baby; it is "bent" by environmental forces and grows thereafter in the distorted form; and the way the personality is "inclined" can be seen in overt symptoms. Psychoanalysis points to specific parts of the human body significant in pleasure-rewarded learning of adaptive and necessary physiological acts; it notes characteristic features in the human environment of primary importance, the mother and father; it describes the relation of body demands (id) to the conscious mind (ego), and of the ego to society (superego) and the physical world (reality). Taking these simple postulates, psychoanalysis relentlessly pursues their corollaries, upsetting and surprising as these may be. Psychoanalysis is positivistic, empirical, phenomenological, and concrete.

Individual personality, then, according to psychoanalytic psychology, is a structure incorporating all the experiences of the ego in meeting these components of psychological reality. Each later psychological phase builds on the victories and defeats of earlier ones. Each earlier phase shapes the later, for example, oral gratification-frustration certainly influences the process of undergoing social discipline in the anal period; in turn, anal rebelliousness may carry over into and color oedipal conflict; and the resolution of phallic-oedipal problems deeply conditions the genital constitution of the individual.

Further, every neurosis, psychosis, and psychopathy is a major fixation at or regression to some growth stage, and represents continuing unresolved conflicts (now repressed) at one or a combination of the pregenital phases. Schizophrenia is the lack of libidinal reality of the outside world, resulting from primary frustration of oral dependency needs and the acquired fixed habit of fantasying magic-symbolic libidinal gratification instead. The schizophrenic has not been loved into, rewarded into accepting the gratifying reality and the frustrating separateness of the now present, now absent mother; he must be for himself the whole world narcissistically and libidinally. Schizophrenia is hard to cure because it represents traumata at a very archaic level of ego development, with at best only precarious development in later phases; disturbance at the pre-verbal oral object level means that in schizophrenia it is very difficult to make human contact with the therapist. Alcoholics, often literal "bottle-babies," still seek the magic ego-enhancing liquid potency, now ambiguously masculine-feminine; they commonly marry dominating women who want a phallus without a man behind it, and whom the alcoholic punishes with his provocative infantilism.

Though partly an oral disturbance, alcoholism is far easier to cure than schizophrenia because there is often relatively strong growth in later phases that enables the therapist to work with and build on them.

Compulsive obsessives, fixated mainly at the anal level, are somewhat less difficult to work with than schizophrenics because of a further matured ego; but they still do much magic-symbolic thinking, have relatively feeble ego boundaries, and maintain massive resistance to the influence of another person: compulsive obsessives still struggle for complete anal-omnipotent management of the whole world as if the only reality were the body and body contents. Manic-depression is the fluctuating self-image learned from ambivalent parents in early oral-anal and other conditioning, with consequently very unstable superego-ego tonuses; depression is more susceptible to therapy than mania because of greater accessibility to outside influence, though in depression the ego is weak, whereas in mania the ego is in full flight from any constrictions. Paranoia is the (chiefly male) struggle for the father's archaic-level omnipotence and love. Hysteria (chiefly female) is oral-dependent, colored phallic conflict over possession of the father; hence the frequency of oral-pregnancy fantasies (stomach-baby) in hysteria, *anorexia nervosa* or eating disturbances, and so on—but hysteria is relatively easier to treat by therapy because of ready suggestibility and accessibility to a father authority. (Freud early used hypnosis in hysteria, but decided that only "symptomatic" or "transference" cure could result if there is no participation of the conscious ego of the patient; nevertheless, because of the relative transparency of hysteric defenses, he was able to learn much initially from hysterics). Perversions are phallic-period fixations in oral, anal, or other pregenital zone terms; they represent "genitalization" of basically oral and anal libido. And, finally, psychopathy is a superego pathology representing only part identification and conflict with a hated (and possibly hating) father; understandably the therapist encounters built-in difficulties in working with psychopaths.

These "pure type" classic syndromes can of course also be mixed symptomatically, for there is nothing to prevent idiosyncratic mixtures of libidinal traumata in individual patients; because of this conception, analysts are less interested in pigeonholing syndromes than in understanding dynamics. By contrast with the types described above, the "genital character"—obviously another pure-type construct, since no individual has enjoyed problemless growth—can have all kinds of libidinal cakes and eat them all too. Through cumulative "amphimictic" growth in all stages he can enjoy food, drink, and people without distorting irrational components, disabling guilt, and psychic energy tied up in major unfinished battles raging in the unconscious. The mature person can enjoy lustily all body functions without antisocial hostility, be appropriately aggressive or accommodative in proper proportion and contexts, and achieve full maleness or femaleness without fear of body damage as the consequence of enjoying it. The mature person has learned to love from loving parents, whom he now sees realistically as persons and not as fearsome images in child-written dramas. Freud's definition of the mature person is one who is able to work and to love, because work we are fitted for achieves sublimation of all pregenital needs, and genital needs can be expressed directly in love.

Although following each unwelcome insight into its ultimate ramifications in many varieties of individual makes psychoanalysis both difficult intellectually and disturbing emotionally, Freud maintains that complexity is inherent in the human data and may not be oversimplified out of existence. Freud further observed that nearly all psychic events are "overdetermined." That is, they have many complex and simultaneously operating causes. This complexity is demonstrated in the fact of "condensation" that may occur in a single dream symbol (another reason for not indulging in facile *ad hoc* interpretations). That is, a single symbol may quite uncannily "condense" into itself a fantastic amount of meanings when its implications are followed out in free association. The semantic complexity is an analogue of the complexity of the brain and the complexity of life experience itself.

Overdetermination and condensation mean that single-cause statements are oversimplified and probably wrong. Hence those who insist on thinking in terms of single-cause formulas have an easy straw man to set up and destroy. In each individual there is a *complex* of causes, though the component causes may differ and operate in different people in different contexts. Hence the findings of psychoanalysis are difficult to *generalize* when each case is in some way unique. By contrast, one atom of an isotope of oxygen may behave *identically* with another; therefore they are in one-to-one comparability with one another and can be meaningfully discussed numerically since numbers properly can summarize and generalize only comparables. Persons who can deal only with complex data when falsely denuded to numbers will always be frustrated with the semantic irreducibility of words and meanings to numbers: the denotations and connotations are endlessly rich, like a psychiatric "complex." Psychological data are more like words than numbers. Verbal-minded people are more apt in handling psychoanalytic data, therefore, than are number-minded people. Number-minded temperaments are likely to have a vast impatience with psychoanalysis on "purely scientific" grounds. Unfortunately, the content of the oedipus complex, for example, may be almost tiresomely similar in one patient after another, and yet each person remain unique in his complex.

Such summary formulas as the analyst is able to make about the universal human oedipus complex—beyond its anxiety-arousing nature—must therefore lack the overwhelming convincingness of the countless corroborating details present in a single specific case. Probably no person has ever been emotionally convinced of the reality of the oedipus complex until he has encountered it analytically in himself—though the cold intellectual fact remains that *every known human group has the nuclear incest-taboo.* The anthropological fact is somehow easier to accept than the psychiatric consequences of the same fact. Every human being faces the oedipal predicament, and yet every single oedipus complex is somehow unique. It is not that analysts are number-shy mystics but that their data do not admit of simplified reductionism. The analyst even thinks that reductionism falsifies his data, since it is the dynamic configuration that is significant. The numbering of uniquenesses ignores their significant quiddity.

If the normal reader's resistance has not yet been aroused by our rapid review of the dynamics of the various neuroses, psychoses, and psychopathies (since he shares none of these dynamics in disabling or unfaceable degree), or by our uncompromising insistence on the reality of the oedipus complex (which is, in fact, in every human being), perhaps we can make the fact of resistance psychologically real by discussing now material certain to arouse anxiety by reason of the universality of another complex. This is an area of common experience that has been or still is acutely painful to every one of us. It is the *castration complex,* though this differs in males and females.

At some time early in life, every little boy and every little girl becomes aware of the physical differences of the other sex. For the boy this means that there are persons who do not have what he has, external genitals, a situation he can only believe results from their having lost this "normal" and taken-for-granted, indeed pleasure-giving, part of his body. The lack raises the frightening possibility that he could and might lose his too, either in punishment for guilty wishes or in punishment for forbidden pleasure. Since there are several pleasure zones in the body, castration anxiety is part of a larger "separation anxiety" from the source of gratification. At birth he suffered the "birth trauma" of losing complete gratification and protection in a physiological Eden, where every metabolic wish was continuously granted. Now he had to learn new methods of blood oxidation, heat control, nourishment and elimination (perhaps colic is so common a problem because of some difficulty in learning all at once the intricate process of digestion). As a weanling he lost the mother's breast. In toilet training he had to learn not especially welcome discipline concerning his own body contents—and now he may lose his pleasure-giving genitals also (thus castration means for the child the specific loss of the penis, not the testes).

For the little girl, sexual difference means that she has lost what boys have, either unfairly or as a punishment. Thus she feels deprived, inferior and envious, and may even fantasy that somehow the organ will one day magically grow back. The appearance of bleeding at menstruation commonly reactivates the female castration complex at puberty, and she may feel deeply frightened at this new "proof" of her "mutilation." The uncontrollability of the flow may also reactivate cleanliness-training problems again and arouse shame. Residually, even when a grown woman she may still feel some deep fear of body damage in sexual intercourse or childbirth. (Men, too, can fear genital damage at intercourse, in the fantasy of the "vagina dentata" and the general dangerousness of woman). Because her presumed "deprivation" has always been the case, most women are able to recapture memory of earlier "penis envy," though in many women the complex becomes repressed early and comes out in various irrational symbolic demands for "equality" with men. "Female courage" has nothing to lose; besides, she can always exploit her advantages as a woman.

In males, however, because damage to or loss of external genitals is still a dreaded and real possibility, the male castration complex is characteristically very deeply repressed. The poignancy of male strength and courage lies in the fact that he still remains tenderly vulnerable. The castration complex in males may be further complicated by a usually still more deeply repressed envy of women and their lot, envy of their greater retention of the permitted passivity and dependence which he also enjoyed as a child, but which he has had to replace with more dangerous, aggressively competitive activity; envy of the female breast, rudimentary in him, but its pleasure potential dimly discernible in analogy to penis pleasure; and even envy of the female's ability to have a baby, which both sexes early fantasy in the oral-anal terms of body experience of these other zones. The terribleness of his envy consists in its sometimes being a monstrous wish, desperately defended against, to get rid of the whole problem entirely; and there are actually some few cases where men have had themselves surgically made "women."

The normal adult, however, comes to "possess" a mate. This is no idle metaphor, but a psychological reality. A man can take endless pride in what his "possession" is, a woman who has everything he lacks and cannot do—women can take mere groceries and miraculously turn them into delicious food. Remaining drab himself, he can still obtain much gratification in enhancing her femininity with clothes, furs, jewels and home, and display his successful masculine prowess at the same time. His emotionally married identification with her can even be sexual, for a loving husband commonly has great anxiety at the birth of a child (the *couvade* or "male childbirth" drama is fairly common among primitive peoples also). Consciously, he may have some guilt at what his aggressive male sexuality has "done to" her; unconsciously, his own womb-envy and castration anxiety may be aroused, even to the point of a literal new "separation anxiety" in potentially losing his pleasure-giving object at childbirth.

Conversely, a woman symbolically obtains a penis in her man. Remaining modestly feminine herself, she may still obtain great vicarious pleasure in the male aggressiveness of her man, boast of his successes, and suffer with his defeats (a woman can tenderly identify especially with defeat, for she has intimately known pain and loss in her own body). Curiously, for many normal women, having a child unconsciously symbolizes obtaining a penis; certainly in her sons she gains further foils for her vicarious enjoyment of masculinity and her fomenting of it in males she loves. Perhaps men marvel at the truly astonishing ability of feminine women to identify with loved males only because man's own conscious masculinity must deny his unconscious feminine component, so that he must loudly boast he "just cannot understand women." (But he has, when she had a baby, his. And psychological fatherhood consists a great deal in learning from women.)

Sexual difference is not dangerous after all, either to men or to women, when "possession" of a mate of the other sex represents a further amphimictic triumph. In the "genital character" that achieves a firm and unfearing self-possession of his or her sexual identity, castration anxiety is transcended. The individual loves being a man or a woman. And what is wrong with loving another different body as much as one's own? The castration complex will of course vary in individuals, depending on whether the boy has been overtly threatened with penis loss, either "playfully" in teasing or more seriously as the consequence of masturbation; whether he has been overthreatened by having a seductive hysteric mother or insecure brutal father; or whether the girl has been properly prepared for menstruation—and depending on a host of other factors, including each parent's conscious and unconscious evaluation of his own and the other sex, parental preference for another sex in the child, and so on.

The castration complex here becomes implicated again with another involving the parents, the ubiquitous oedipus complex (often called "Electra complex" in females). The child of either sex normally has *loved oral-dependently* the mother as a source of physiological gratification. When sexuality supervenes, if a boy, the child must now give up this first love object, to retain his physical maleness in competition with the more powerful father, who properly possesses the mother as a genital but not alimentary property as the child had. To achieve psychological genitality, as described above, the boy must find substitute female objects for his love or else give up the heterosexual aim entirely and remain fixated at the same-sex-loving phallic level, as a male homosexual who stays childishly attached to mother and pretends he passively loves men orally as a pseudo-child or anally as a pseudo-woman. To become masculine like his father, the boy must give up the father's sexual love object and find another like her; he must also change his body modality of relating to females from the passive-oral to the active-genital. (Here again is manifest the fact of different zone modalities of loving, since all love is a tender concern for the source of any kind of libidinal gratification.)

The girl child, on the other hand, must change the sex of her love object from mother to father. Since she has already suffered "castration," a girl commonly has closer to consciousness her sexual fantasy about an early love of her father, a new and more powerfully protective figure for her feminine dependency, and as a male one who is able to give her a baby. But in resolving the "Electra" competition with mother—less frightening than the boy's oedipal conflict with the father—she must next find another male than father to love. Female sexuality is consequently more complex and derived. It is also more secret and hidden, for whereas a male can never deny or be in doubt about sexual arousal, a girl may sometimes actually not know.

Boys are perhaps more fiercely embattled in growing up. They must go farther from childhood and change the most in relation to women from passive dependence to aggressive dominance; and they must constantly prove that they have made the masculine journey from child to man. But male love for women, given the fact of motherhood, is psychologically simple and transparent. The girl's coming to love men is a more intricate process and, in terms of early need gratification, more obscure than male love of women, or a female's love of her own femininity, both via mother. Why men love women is no problem: they loved their mothers. Why women love men is highly problematical. One supposition is that the girl simply transfers her childhood dependency from mother to father (Why? Because he is a stronger and more dominating protective figure of both mother and daughter, or because as a male he is more loving and indulgent of his daughter?) Another supposition is that women love men because men have what they lack, or that only a man can give them a baby. But in this, as in other explanations, psychoanalysis can perhaps properly be accused of being a male-centered psychology, for women are not just unmales but *sui generis* in their own right. Still another explanation is that the encompassing narcissistic self-love of motherhood that includes her baby also includes mothering loved men, for women have more ways of loving than men do. Perhaps men are debarred from this understanding simply because they do not have female bodies. Feminine sexuality is certainly hard to understand!

The psychological fact of experiencing different bodies, in any case, explains a number of differences in sexual temperament. Men must learn courage in order to face and to transcend castration anxiety and to achieve their masculinity and psychophysical "integrity." Nevertheless, it is the male, often the most masculine one, who is most threatened by any surgical operation or other symbolic body mutilation. In being male he is still most vulnerable. Women, already knowing pain in menstruation, defloration, and childbirth, are more stoic in facing this kind of pain—indeed may be more accustomed to making the masochistic symbolic "bargain" with guilt in surgical operations—because pain has often been followed with pleasure and triumphs of feminine fulfilment. Thus women are sometimes polysurgical hysterics, men almost never.

Again, male masturbation is commonly more guilt laden than female masturbation, and more rigorously suppressed. The male superego is also commonly more stern and uncompromising; the female can more easily say that the rules do not apply to her because of anatomical "injustice" and therefore she has "something coming to her." Besides, males take in masculine superego demands primarily from males (chiefly father) and hence fulfil their masculinity in this process of introjection; but the process applies less to women (fathers indulge daughters more than sons, and the Electra complex and counter-complex are more direct than is oedipal *rivalry* over the mother), and women take in part of the superego from females (that is, femininity from the mother). Male sexuality *overwhelms* obstacles, because the normal man resolves his castration complex by accepting that, once the male-imposed incest rule is respected, then active male sexuality will go unpunished by castration. The female castration complex is resolved by accepting femininity and *acquiring* a penis-bearing man. Therefore female sexuality *accepts* a gift, because the normal woman wants a baby and knows only accepting a male can give her one and thus fulfil her basic femininity. Men fear being unable to *perform* (being unable to love); women fear *being unloved* (being unlovable). Women are concrete personalists; they first love *this* man and *this* child because these symbolize narcissistic possessions or gains, although they may later generalize their love socially, but still concretely and personally. After giving up the mother—a more intense love, because more physiological, than the girl's love for her father—men are abstractionists and generalists, and perhaps poorer monogamists than women. Men can manifest fierce respect for abstract and artificial oedipal hierarchies such as those in the military, which women find merely ridiculous or incomprehensible and seek constantly to undermine on personal grounds. Male narcissism is derived and intensely symbolic; female narcissism is more primary and physical. Men are more commonly the symbolic creators of money, symbolic dominance-prowess, science, art, and social structures (law, the state), because only women can naively and obviously really create (grow a baby). Hence men must constantly *prove* their masculinity and fear its loss or impugning, whereas women (once having transcended the castration complex) can more passively and complacently *be* feminine. Sexual differences in social role, therefore, are not so much intellectual as motivational and emotional: individuals may differ in their position on a masculine-feminine gamut and yet still manifest definitely masculine versus feminine characteristics and trends. Besides, every individual introjects from both parents: the doctor may borrow a more-than-typical male compassion for other people from his mother while yet insisting intensely on male dominance and fatherly control of his patients; a woman can be a formidable politician while yet employing feminine wiles too.

An acknowledged and perhaps inescapable scientific difficulty with psychoanalysis is the "nonreplicability" of its data (quite apart from the uniquenesses of each case). One must be present, either as analyst or analyzand, in order to *witness the data*. And, because of our normal resistances and our thinking (falsely) that we "know ourselves," it is really impossible intellectually to translate the analyst's public scientific generalizations into their full visceral-emotional reality—as when, with shock and surprise, we discover they apply to us in every inescapable detail. Both proselytizing analyzand and reluctant unanalyzed persons must admit, in all fairness, that psychological revelation and the psychiatrist's pointing out its significance both occur in a private, privileged, protected situation with no one else present; hence it is difficult to convey the transactions publicly or fully enough—again, even apart from the quite understandable defenses normal people have against insight into such fearsome and terrible things. However, for some degree of understanding, all we need do is to attend any clinical "Grand Rounds" on a psychiatric case, or listen carefully with an open mind to any psychotic in the State Hospital—in each instance deciding in safe psychological privacy whether our ability to see is not first an insight into ourselves—at least to be convinced that really desperate and dangerous matters are involved. It is in fact a demonstration of our own equilibrium and strength if we can listen without being overwhelmed by anxiety. For this reason, every psychiatrist must be carefully and exhaustively trained to know himself, since we can only afford to see clinically what we have first acknowledged in ourselves.

Psychoanalysis has several assumptions it now shares with other psychologies. First is *psychic determinism*. Everything that happens in the mind is part of a lawfully determined universe. Every psychic event has causes and effects, as inevitable as brain chemistry, no matter how multiple and obscure and complex these events are, and no matter how difficult to discover and to discern and to discuss completely. Any attempt at heated, special pleading that at least *this* event is "purely accidental" or "meaningless" points, in that very protest, the relentless finger of evidence. Consequently, full classic psychoanalysis has a very clear understanding of how and why some "neo-Freudians" like Rank and Jung and Adler have each erected their own unanalyzed portions into a system, even though they have all made contributions that can be accepted into the analytic tradition.[10]

Another discovery psychoanalysis now shares widely with other psychologies is that all that goes on in the conscious mind does not exhaust the whole activity of the mind. There is an *unconscious* part of the psychic economy that can be demonstrated in such phenomena as hypnosis, dreams, memory, multiple personality, and the like. The only uniqueness nowadays is that psychoanalysis uses the technique of "free association" in which the patient is allowed freely to fantasy and to say absolutely anything he wants to. Everyone these days knows about the many brilliant and successful *alternative* research techniques of the clinical psychologists in uncovering the same unconscious content of the mind—the Rorschach

Test, the Thematic Apperception Test, and many other projective techniques. To understand these techniques is inevitably to respect them. They are justifiably regarded as powerful diagnostic tools. Therapeutically, however, old-fashioned id analysis insists that the *conscious insight of the patient* into his psychic mechanisms is necessary if the executive ego is to take charge, now with a fuller awareness and understanding of the problem.[11]

This understanding comes only from a long and patient process in which the subject brings out one example after another of a behavior which, after a while, the analyst invites the patient to compare, and then to decide for himself whether these mechanisms are really there and characteristically do operate—but only against the most intense resistance of the subject to reopening old wounds. Defense mechanisms intervene between joint sharing of these details and the belated acknowledgement of their reality. The analyst does not have to argue or indoctrinate, because the data are now open-facedly there and will certainly come up again another time. The insight of the analyst is not automatically equivalent to the patient's.

Strangely, "free association" has to be learned, the relentless intellectual and emotional honesty of saying without censorship anything that comes into the mind, however ugly, ridiculous, shameful, aggressive, obscene, or seemingly trivial. Every patient must learn this through long preliminary testing out and gradually coming to trust his psychiatrist—that absolutely anything the patient says is heard without punishment or judgment, rejection or moral indignation from the analyst. Then emerges the extraordinary phenomenon of "transference." Transference is often misunderstood to mean "falling in love" with the analyst, but this is erroneous and misses the real point of the phenomenon. What happens is that as the analyst is more and more experienced by the patient as a neutral listener who does not demand the usual adaptive and sail-trimming social protocol, gradually in more and more pure form the patient begins to treat him *as if he were* the person who was critically important to the particular problem in the past.

Examining the transference is a *research technique,* for here are laid bare the now uncensored feelings of the patient toward his parents and siblings as a child. The analyst does not fatuously think that all his patients are in love with him. On the contrary, he knows that what the patient projects onto the blank screen *has nothing to do* with the analyst's real private personality—a useful knowledge when the analyst has to absorb unjust and abusive comments as well as expressions of twisted kinds of love. In order to remain less a real person, the analyst commonly sits out of sight behind the patient lying relaxed on the couch; also, the trained analyst constantly examines his own feelings of "counter-transference" for what his free-floating attention and understanding of his own unconscious can teach him about the patient—with all of which he scrupulously refrains from burdening the patient. Thus, at the patient's protestations of love, he is likely, to the surprise and edification of the patient, to point out ambivalent components of the patient's "love."

Curious and unexpected phenomena emerge in the transference: commonly the patient treats the male analyst as if he were, say, a tenderly overprotective mother, or a female analyst as if she were a sternly authoritative father. The content of every transference statement is, in this, similar to the Rorschach Test: any "meaning" is not in the meaningless cards or the faceless nonperson of the analyst but only in the mind of the projecting subject. Again, a transference from parent to therapist may not necessarily be a loving one, since sometimes children hate their parents. A transference can be violently "negative" (hate filled) in feeling and still yield useful data, if that was the problem with the parent, though a positive transference is easier to deal with therapeutically and the patient is less likely precipitately to leave off the analysis. Meanwhile, the analyst knows that the patient's hatred does not really apply to him either, though he has painfully to teach through his neutrality that he is not in fact the hateful parent. Slowly the patient realizes that his transference statements are only his real feelings laid bare. The analyst has mirrored back the patient's own psychological visage.

It is true, of course, that transference-like phenomena do occur outside analysis, since we meet each unknown new person with our habitual feelings and experiences from the past. It is sometimes startling to realize how we unconsciously collect people to play roles in our private dramas, say, an angry, arbitrary father in a little-known but really quite benevolent and decent boss. "Falling in love at first sight" can be elicited by a single cue of similarity to the parent loved in the past (the girl has red hair like mother's) and "punch the button" for projective fantasy. But such "love" cannot, by definition, proceed from a full knowledge of the actual personality of the unknown "loved" one, and he who marries in haste can repent in leisure. "First love" is rather like a Rorschach, in which we learn mostly about ourselves, painfully, when the part-transference collapses through accumulating knowledge of the object. Authentic love can occur only in knowing both subject and object, and both accepting both mutually. Thus, to speak loosely of transference to mean affection in ordinary social situations is of course merely silly.

There is one further difficulty. Freud believed that every neurosis—and every person is technically neurotic to some degree—is a frustration of and impediment to normal growth. The neurosis is a protective scab over the crippling wound. At one time in the individual's past, the anxiety of new and then insoluble problems overwhelmed the weak but growing adaptive ego of the child. That is, he became "fixated" (massively or mildly) at that stage in his development, and still struggles now with the same buried and unresolved problem that other persons normally will have solved. Thus the "normal" person quite truly does not actively suffer from an "oedipus complex" in the sense that it cripples him from loving other women than the mother; but he nevertheless did once face the oedipal *predicament* which is the lot of every man. The normal man quite commonly encounters, if he is fortunate, maternal tenderness and sometimes arbitrarily loving acceptance in the woman he loves; but she is not his mother, and he is not her son. Similarly, a normal woman quite commonly encounters, if she is fortunate, paternal strength and loving protectiveness in her husband; but he is not her father, and she is not his child. It is only that mature love has its roots deep in childhood.

By contrast, the neurotic's ego is *functionally mutilated* in its ability to solve the problem, whatever it is, because the whole overwhelming conflict was finally repressed into the unconscious. And there it still boils explosively, like a soup pot with the lid tightly on, now coming out as a symptom, now as intense anxiety, and again as neurotic "acting out."[12] The whole job of therapy is to discover the old forgotten griefs and terrifying experiences and frightening impulses and woefully lost battles, then to face and understand them with the more mature resources of the now older person; first to rely on the unafraid analyst, and then to let the strengthened ego of the patient take over again the continuing task of running his own life. There is no magic in it, only intellectually honest and emotionally sincere struggle, pain, and hard work. No one can be expected to understand Freud unless he is willing and able to make, in some fashion, the perilous and frightening journey into the past. But if he can and does, he will see all these things for himself.

NOTES

(1) W. H. Auden, *The Collected Poems of W. H. Auden,* New York: Random House, Inc., 1945, p. 166. This poet has a precise and sure knowledge of what Freud was about.
(2) The main sources are Freud's *Interpretation of Dreams* (*Complete Psychological Works of Sigmund Freud,* edited by James Strachey, "Standard Edition," London: Hogarth Press, Ltd., 1953, Vols. 4 and 5; *Collected Papers of Sigmund Freud,* New York: Basic Books, Inc., Vol. 3, 1959; and Avon Books [paperback]) ; *Three Contributions to the Theory of Sex* (New York and Washington: Nervous and Mental Disease Publishing Company, 1930; also in *The Basic Writings of Sigmund Freud,* New York: Modern Library, 1938, pp. 181–549, but the Strachey translations are to be preferred, in the Basic Books paperback and *Standard Edition*) ; and also Freud's *The Ego and the Id* (London: Hogarth Press, Ltd., 1927), *Beyond the Pleasure Principle* (London: Hogarth Press, Ltd., 1922), *Civilization and Its Discontents* (London: Hogarth Press, Ltd., 1930) — the last three long essays also to be found in the *Standard Edition.* After Freud, the classical psychoanalytic works are *Selected Papers of Karl Abraham* (London: Hogarth Press, Ltd., 1927) ; Sandor Ferenczi, *Further Contributions to the Theory and Technique of Psycho-Analysis* (London: Hogarth Press, Ltd., 1926) ; Ernest Jones, *Essays in Applied Psycho-Analysis* (London: Hogarth Press, Ltd.,

1923), and *Papers on Psycho-Analysis* (Baltimore: Williams and Wilkins Co., 1912, also Beacon [paperback]). The best introduction to Freud is by Karin Stephen, *Psychoanalysis and Medicine, A Study of the Wish to Fall Ill* (London: Cambridge University Press, 1939); the best single-volume compendium, but for the advanced student, is Otto Fenichel, *The Psychoanalytic Theory of Neurosis* (New York: W. W. Norton & Company, 1945). A remarkable biography is by Ernest Jones, *The Life and Work of Sigmund Freud* (New York: Basic Books, Inc., 3 vols., 1953–1957; also available in paperback in abbreviated form).

(3) The "primal horde" theory of the "cyclopean family" I reject on anthropological grounds: recent primatological studies have cast doubt upon it; and the animal-hunting *Australopithecines* must already have had nuclear families within the necessarily cooperating group of male hunters of large or swift game. (Weston La Barre, *The Human Animal*, Chicago: Phoenix Books [paperback], 1960, p. 346. Kroeber, at his death the acknowledged premier anthropologist in the world, in a famous review of *Totem and Taboo* quite fairly calls it a "Just So" story, and Freud's view of totemism is universally rejected now by anthropologists as an etiological myth. Nevertheless, if we can discriminate between Freud's insight and his faulty anthropology, *Totem and Taboo* still has much to teach us. The so-called "hydraulic theory of the libido" seems to me improbable on anatomical, neurophysiological, and biological grounds alike. In this I believe I am joined by most psychologists.

(4) Psychoanalysis has not statistically dismembered man into artificial and subjectively selected fragments, where critical remaining differences of the "comparables" are masked or ignored, as well as significant traits of the whole configuration lost, but has kept its eye steadily on live, whole, functioning human beings in real situations. Psychoanalysis has not retreated into a disguised neurophysiology that ignores "subjective" *psychological* events. And psychoanalysis has not converted itself into an overtly infrahuman animal psychology. Since rats do not have the nuclear family, incest taboos, the oedipus complex, culture, conscience, psychoses (though experimental psychologists, taking their cue from psychoanalysis, have been able to make rats and other animals neurotic), language, or articulate symbolism, it can be well argued that none of these critical human features can be encountered or discussed meaningfully in rats. Further —human defense mechanisms being what they are—the "controlled experiment" will likely control out of the experimental situation any of the dangerous and unpleasant discoveries that might edify us about humans; at best, such experiments can only "test," often in methodologically inappropriate ways, hypotheses provided by psychoanalysis, already sufficiently established clinically. Like anthropology in its nonmanipulative study of functioning groups, psychoanalysis is a naturalistic, "bird-watching" science that does not manipulate its subjects into contrived situations, but only observes. Nevertheless, purely observational studies can still be scientific: astronomy is, and without pushing one star out of orbit.

(5) Since psychoanalysis is body-oriented, and since the human body is functionally a cross-cultural phenomenon, it is not surprising that culture-and-personality studies of group *ethos* also began within a psychoanalytic framework. The preoccupation of psychoanalysis with the purposes and symbolic content of thought further fits it, uniquely among psychologies, for the study of myth and religion. It is a pity that "social anthropology" has degenerated into a kind of "kinship algebra" obsessed with structure, since many of these human relationships might possibly have functional significance psychoanalytically.

(6) Not all organic needs, of course, ever become conscious. If, for example, from hard exercise, the CO_2 level of the blood rises, a special chemoreceptor at the

entrance to the heart increases the rate of heartbeat to increase oxygen replacement in the red blood cells pumped to the lungs. There are many such automatically homeostatic "feedback" devices in the body, described in W. B. Cannon's valuable book on *The Wisdom of the Body* (New York: W. W. Norton & Company, 1932). Indeed, the forebrain may only be another such, and phylogenetically latest, homeostatic device, needed only for new or physiologically uncontrolled problems.

(7) Reality figuratively says "This is the way things are." The id says, stubbornly and obdurately and blindly, "I want." The superego says, "You should (or should not)." But only the ego says "I shall (or shall not)." Reality and superego and id all tend to be heard as "You must" though it is only our (possibly mistaken) *view* of reality that seems to require this; the demands of conscience may sometimes be circumvented, especially if defined irrationally, but the price of conscious circumvention may be guilt or shame; and the id may be satisfied with many *alternative* sources of calories and other necessities, and not necessarily a specific food consciously desired. Only the ego is saddled with existentialist *epistemological* problems.

(8) It is a dangerous mistake to think simply that "she needs a man" because if she really did have one then she might be precipitated into psychosis—because that is what her symptom is for, to protect her from recognizing she has expanded the prohibition of an incestuously loved man (father, or sometimes brother) to include all men. The attempt by the would-be omnipotent "therapist" simply to wrest away symptoms may leave the neurotic denuded of necessary protective defenses and drive him into deeper difficulty. Well-meaning "advice" from a friend, though insightful (and especially *if* insightful), can often do great damage if this psychiatric principle is not taken into account.

(9) The "blood purge" of his former crony Ernst Roehm was a classic instance in Hitler of "homosexual panic" often found in seemingly meaningless murders or random paranoid massacres of many persons. The contrived "Reichstag fire" was a paranoid maneuver to project guilt and "justify" attack, as was the alleged "persecution" of Sudeten Germans, followed by the invasion of Czechoslovakia and a later mass murder of Jews that was the most psychotic enormity in all recorded history. The cult of "der schöne Adolf" in which all Nordic women were supposed to be in love with Hitler was a classic case of erotomaniac fantasy. Hitler's sexual life can also be called in question: he was evidently a nonpracticing, unconsciously homosexual paranoid fanatic, with only a feeble or dubious heterosexuality. These and other paranoid symptoms are abundantly documented in Konrad Heiden, *Der Fuehrer* (Boston: Houghton Mifflin Company, 1944) and elsewhere.

(10) For example, Jung's early psychoanalytic understanding of schizophrenia is a magnificent and permanent contribution. By the same token, we can criticise Freud himself for being too "Jungian" in projecting the oedipal situation once and for all back into the mythological past—whence it reaches us as a kind of Lamarckian "acquired characteristic" of the "folk unconscious"! Similar critiques can be made of Rank and Adler, and at the same time some of these apply to Freud. Any "orthodoxy" arrived at by many highly critical and keen minds lies in the unavoidable facts of human nature.

(11) In the adjective "old-fashioned" I refer to classical id-analysis, which is so lengthy and expensive that, given the shortage of qualified analysts, this is nowadays best confined to research persons and those who wish to become psychiatrists. Modern "ego-analysis," though harder to conduct in the sense that it requires superlative skill of the analyst in picking out major items to deal with, often does not require "total" insight in the patient for a cure. But it is

more economical of time and money, though not of pain. Furthermore, much therapy is not technically "analysis" but merely "psychoanalytically oriented therapy." Indeed, many primitive techniques of curing, if dynamically sound and despite irrational native rationale, can result in cure without the conscious insight of either patient or therapist. For evidence of this, see Ari Kiev (editor), *Magic, Faith, and Healing* (New York: The Free Press, 1964), and Marvin K. Opler (editor), *Culture and Mental Health* (New York: The Macmillan Company, 1959).

(12) Again there is a gross misconception current about "acting out." Properly speaking, this means that the patient is not able to verbalize his problem but "acts out" his conflict in real life outside the analysis, and then tells the analyst about it later. Though not an ideal method of communication, and sometimes dangerous, acting out does provide the analyst, and the patient, with significant data which they can use by analyzing it. To use "acting out" loosely to mean merely *manifesting one's neurosis* unfortunately has become a current cliché for people who do not know what it means.

6

The Philosophy of Science and the Study of Personality

Douglass Price-Williams

The philosophy of science is associated traditionally with the examination of theories, concepts, methods, and aims in the physical, biological, and social sciences. It is concerned with such matters as epistemological assumptions, verifiability and testability, the logic of measurement, and specific analysis of key notions such as causation. In the present context of this symposium, the pretentious title of this contribution disguises a modest trial to clarify some of the problems that occur in what has come to be labeled as the field of culture and personality or personality in culture. As it is an integral intention of this paper to delve into the meaning of the two central terms, a tolerance is requested for their introduction without definition. In any case, it is probably a fruitless task to lay down definitions *ab initio*. In 1952 Kroeber and Kluckhohn listed 150 definitions of culture and in 1937 Gordon Allport enumerated 50 for personality (Kroeber and Kluckhohn 1952; Allport 1949). If you consider their relationship to one another, then there are 7500 ways of defining culture and personality. The *via definitiva* is not the path I wish to take; it turns too easily into the *via dolorosa*.

ISSUES

There are two separate groups of theses which recur throughout the writings of the theorists in the field of personality and culture:

(1) That the individual influences, creates, molds, fashions his culture. This will be called the individualist issue.
(2) That the individual is influenced, created, molded, fashioned *by* his culture. This will be called the culturological issue.

Some writers have dwelt singly and persistently on one of the two sets of theses. Most others have tended to shift from one to the other, and have regarded their study as one of interactionism. Although interactionism reflects true *descriptive* statements it leaves open the question of what is to be *explained* thereby.[1] I shall maintain that there are these two *explanatory* theses, which I will simply call the individualist thesis and the culturological thesis.

The view that the individual shapes culture has adopted over the years a spectrum of positions. In general, the principle involved is that of methodological individualism. The principle states that "the ultimate constituents of the social world are individual people who act more or less appropriately in the light of their dispositions and understanding of their situation. Every complex social situation, institution, or event is the result of a particular configuration of individuals, their dispositions, situations, beliefs, and physical resources and environment" (Watkins 1957; see also Hayek 1948 and Popper 1952). There is a species of this principle called *psychologism* which says "that all large-scale social characteristics are not merely the intended or unintended result of, but a *reflection* of, individual characteristics" (Watkins 1957). What I am calling the individualist view held both the genus and the species positions. Let me give some examples. Take Ruth Benedict's early statement (1928): "The cultural situation in the Southwest is in many ways hard to explain. With no natural barriers to isolate it from surrounding peoples, it presents probably the most abrupt cultural break that we know in America. All our efforts to trace out the influences from other areas are impressive for the fragmentariness of the detail; we find bits of the weft or woof of their culture, we do not find any very significant clues to its pattern. From the point of view of the present paper this clue is to be found in a fundamental psychological set which has undoubtedly been established for centuries in the culture of this region, and which has bent to its own uses any details it imitated from surrounding peoples and has created an intricate cultural pattern to express its own preferences. It is not only that the understanding of this psychological set is necessary for a descriptive statement of this culture; without it the cultural dynamics of this region are unintelligible."

In commenting on the early papers of Ruth Benedict, Singer (1961:23) makes the point that she had a cultural and not a psychological problem as her starting point: "She wanted to know how and why the culture of the Southwest Pueblos differed so strikingly from its neighboring cultures." This position of the early Benedict is a clear case of psychologism, differing in no way in principle from Plato's view that the character of the *polis* was a reflection of the character of the kind of soul predominant in it. (Holding an individualist view does not, as I said earlier, negate holding a culturological view. And we find in another early paper of Benedict [1934] a typical statement of cultural determinism to the effect that "The vast majority of the individuals in any group are shaped to the fashion of that culture. In other words, most individuals are plastic to the molding force of the society into which they are born.")

Returning to discussion of the individualist view, we may find examples of reductionist theses that are more explicit. In making the distinction between primary and secondary institutions—of which the primary institutions (the early experiences of the individual) are thought to be the more influential in molding the range of beliefs of a society—Kardiner could write (1939:484) that "if the character of the human mind is integrative, then it follows that the earliest constellations are basic, and if they proved expedient they will form the groundwork of all subsequent integrations, because they become a part of the individual's appreciation of reality." As a matter of fact, Kardiner's formulation approaches entanglement with a branch of studies, namely, that of socialization, to which I shall address myself later. Spiro, (1961:468) writing from a vantage point of the passage of over twenty years since Kardiner's views were presented, is more dogmatic about the reductionist thesis: "By focusing on personality dynamics and on social behavior (rather than on cultural traits or social culture) these (personality and culture) studies have impressed upon some anthropologists, at least, the realization that cultures and/or social systems do not lead an independent existence of their own; that their operation and maintenance are dependent to a marked degree on their internalization (either as cognitive or as affective variables) within the personalities of the members of society. . . ."[2] In bringing out these quotations, I do not wish to imply that their authors entertain simple-minded notions of causation. My intent is to show that among some personality and culture theorists a position of methodological individualism is held, which stands against collectivist ideas, theses of superorganicism, societalism, and the like.

The individualist thesis is not a simple one; as I have said, it has a spectrum of positions. If one traces the history of the personality and culture movement, he gains the impression that original aims of understanding the relationship between culture and personality became minimized in the search for clarification of the basic concept of personality. As a consequence, emphasis was placed more and more on the method and tools rather than on what might be revealed by using them. The descriptive problem of what is meant by typical, modal, or basic personality became a target in itself. The names of DuBois, Wallace, Gladwin, and Sarason are milestones on the path of probing questions regarding sampling, validity, proper testing of individuals, and so on. In addition, formulating concepts such as "fit," coherence, correlation and matching between the individual and his culture became ends in themselves. One is tempted to speculate on reasons for this change. There is of course the obvious reason, which most commentators have observed, that the proper study of individuals requires appropriate methods of interrogation. This explains the emphasis on sampling and validity. But it does not explain the other shift to theories of congruence. The individualist stand became an essay in isomorphism; the problem was to discover the similarity in form of culture and of the individual.

The early history of the personality and culture movement can be understood by reference to the historical tradition in American anthropology and the dominant role which Boas played in it. *Pari passu* with the reconstruction of histories of peoples, Boas was also interested in formulating psychological principles of cultural growth (Eggan 1954). In the years to follow, historical diffusionist studies became influenced by—or at least the two were concurrent with—the comparative method and its structural-functional orientation. The growth in the United States of social anthropology coming from British scholars like Radcliffe-Brown had its effect on American anthropology as a whole. Within the culture and personality movement the effect was twofold. First, where it had been the custom to show connections between elements of culture, such as economy, law, and kinship, the tendency now was to match in a similar manner traits of culture with features of personality. To assay a paraphrase, it might be said that the aim was to interpret personality as being identical with an institutional feature, so that it could be fitted into the interdependent framework of society like any other social structure. Second, as a consequence, the concept of personality moved away from concern with individual differences and biological aspects of personality. What the new position needed was not a concept of the individual personality but one of a generic personality. Another effect was the use of such terms as "socially required personality patterns," "cultural character," and "tribal character." Nobody had suggested the drastic move of doing away with the concept of personality altogether; instead, there was a tendency to bifurcate the term, leaving the unexplained residue to biologically minded psychologists. All this is readily understandable, save one feature: there was almost exclusive reliance on psychological tools associated with the study of the individual. I refer of course to projective techniques, a major subject to which I shall return in the last section of this paper.

Nevertheless, concern with past events did not completely disappear with the shift towards problems of isomorphism. Or perhaps it might be better said that it disappeared in one guise only to reappear in another. I referred earlier to the fact that one of Kardiner's formulations approached a third issue—socialization. Kardiner's "secondary institutions" are thought of as projective systems—beliefs and representations (mythology, art, folklore, and religious beliefs). If the influence of the individual on culture is thought of as the way in which an individual *acquires* certain kinds of social behavior, then certainly understanding basic personality structure is a study of socialization. As such, this represents a quite distinct study, that of how the individual learns and adjusts to his milieu. Socialization is a quite legitimate and respectable study, but it does not, in itself, represent an *is-*

sue that stands or falls with debate or research. Nobody has to argue that socialization is a serious study. It may lead to theses which fall under the heading of either the individualist or culturological theses; the study of socialization should not be identified with either standpoint. Particularly, it should not be confused with the individualist view. To acquire cultural habits and adjust to a cultural ethos may be *necessary* prerequisites for influencing, fashioning, or molding that culture; they certainly are not *sufficient* conditions for doing so. Moreover—a point which Spiro has so ably made—distinctions have to be drawn between cultural heritage, cultural heredity, and culture itself. Under this analysis, the development of personality and the acquisition of culture are one and the same learning process (Spiro 1951:42). If, then, one identifies the study of socialization with the individualist camp, truly Spiro can write of the natural history of a false dichotomy. The focus on socialization, it might be further noted, breaks away from considerations of personality per se. Anxiety, guilt, and motives as a whole tend to be treated as mechanisms in their own right. Take Whiting and Child (1953:34–35): "the practice of severe weaning leads the typical child in some societies to develop a motive of anxiety in response to oral activities. This motive persists into adulthood". . . ."the connection is traced through a hypothetical motive . . . and the continuation of this motive from childhood into adulthood. Such a motive and its continuation may be appropriately labelled as examples of personality processes." In this passage Whiting and Child have not completely weaned themselves from the concept of personality, but it is clear that their use of the words "appropriately labelled" is only an act of terminological grace. Nothing would have been spoiled in their formulation if the last sentence had been dropped.

The individualist stand, then, has displayed a number of subtheses within its range, which have altered over the years. What began as a search for historical explanation turned into quasi-psychological questions about personality, which in turn sparked off a quest for similarity of form.

The culturological thesis has also begat its subtheses, and they are more clearly demarcated. They concern, I believe, only three matters:

1. Modifications of generalizations about human nature.
2. The effect of culture on personality traits.
3. The effect of culture on psychological functions.

Of these, the first two have been associated mainly with psychologically minded anthropologists, the third with experimental psychologists interested in cultural factors. The history of the first two is sufficiently known and appreciated. The great contributions of Malinowski and Margaret Mead are sufficient to remember in relation to the first. The numerous empirical studies using projective techniques are in themselves historical ac-

93   The Philosophy of Science and the Study of Personality

counts. The third subthesis, however, may need a brief historical mention as it is generally considered to be outside the customary area of personality and culture. This is quite correct: it is outside. But I am considering the influence of cultural factors on the *individual,* and the introduction of psychological functions (as distinct from personality traits) is basic to the conclusions to which I will be drawn about the relationship between the individual and his culture. The famous Torres Straits expedition at the turn of the century (Haddon 1901) marked the first systematic attempt to gain knowledge about so-called primitive peoples' psychological functions relating to vision, perception, and classificatory behavior. It is a historical curiosity that this first trial did not lead to further exploration by psychologists. This may have been due to the deflection of social psychology towards the model of classic experimental psychology in its parochial concern with an available tive set of subjects. At any rate, apart from a few sporadic studies, we have to wait until this decade for further systematic inquiries of the effect of culture on psychological functions (Segall *et al.* 1963, 1966; Bruner *et al.* 1966). The search has been for cultural factors which influence perception and thinking and retention. Explanation is offered in terms of such concepts in the study of perception as salience and familiarity, and, in the study of thinking, of contrast, and of manipulation. In other words, the explanatory terminology is tied in to the various theoretical schemes relating to the study of these processes. Culture comes in as the presence or absence of factors that arouse or dampen the explanatory mechanisms, but there is no special concern for culture as a phenomenon in itself.

Apart from this brief mention of the third subthesis, I propose to deal less with historical accounts than with an analysis of the important conceptual problems which the culturological issue introduces. This revolves around the possibility or impossibility of subtracting the individual from his milieu, the distinction between orientation and function in psychology, and the crucial concept of trait. In essence, I shall argue that so long as the concept of trait is followed, an external referent has always to be attached, and this makes for confusion in any distinction between individuality and culture. I shall further argue that the concept of personality within culture and personality has been narrowly conceived, and shall show what implications follow if an explanation is allowed that is based upon this narrow conception.

ORIENTATION AND FUNCTION

Three scholars of quite different backgrounds have voiced a similar concern as to whether one can consider psychological traits apart from the social matrix. The first was the well-known plea of Rivers (1926): "How can you explain the workings of the human mind without a knowledge of the social setting which must have played so great a part in determining the sentiments and opinions of mankind?" (pp. 10–11) The second is Nadel who in his *Foundations of Social Anthropology* resurrected an old polemic between Westermarck and Rivers over the blood feud, which had given rise to Rivers' plea. Nadel referred to the distinction between a social analysis and a psychological analysis as being expressed in quite different language, or, I would prefer to say, metalanguages. The social analysis uses what Nadel called object language, while the psychological analysis uses function language. Nadel then goes on to state (1951:595):

> .... inasmuch as the psychological analysis pays attention to the content of mental events rather than to the processes involved it will only duplicate the findings of the social enquiry. This becomes important when the object-reference of mental processes is not, or not directly, to concrete things or events (such as modes of behavior), but to thoughts or beliefs about things and events.

The third person to be paraded is Karl Popper who in a fairly lengthy passage reiterates much of what the first two have said.

> If all regularities in social life, the laws of our social environment, of all institutions, etc., are ultimately to be explained by, and reduced to, the 'actions and passions of human beings', then such an approach forces upon us not only the idea of historic-causal development, but also the idea of the *first steps* of such a development. For the stress on the psychological origin of social rules or institutions can only mean that they can be traced back to a state when their introduction was dependent solely upon psychological factors, or more precisely, when it was independent of any established social institutions. Psychologism is thus forced, whether it likes it or not, to operate with the idea of a *beginning of society,* and with the idea of a human nature and a human psychology as they existed prior to society. . . . It is a desperate position because this theory of a pre-social human nature which explains the foundation of society—a psychologistic version of the 'social contract'—is not only an historical myth, but also, as it were, a methodological myth (Popper 1952:92–3).

Popper thus comes close to the Marxian epigram which he quotes at the head of that chapter from which I have quoted: "It is not the consciousness of man that determines his existence—rather, it is his social existence that determines his consciousness." And indeed Popper concludes: "Men—i.e. human minds, the needs, the hopes, fears, and expectations, the motives and aspirations of human individuals—are if anything, the product of life in society rather than its creators" (p. 93).

These three quotations are tantamount to statements of cultural determinism; as such they are unnecessarily drastic. Instead of a mold theory one could substitute the lesser thesis of a cultural cloak.[3] Nevertheless the argument is still forceful. If these three people are correct in any degree it still should represent a sharp shock to *psychologists* concerned with personality. For probably the majority of books and articles written on personality by psychologists either ignore the social milieu altogether or give it sparing treatment in an end chapter. Exclusion of the social milieu, while questionable from an ontological viewpoint, nevertheless avoids the methodological difficulty which personality and culture theorists have to face. The difficulty concerns the distinction between orientation and function, and we find the distinction crucial when the concept of *trait* is to be distinguished from the concept of *attitude*. Whereas the distinction between trait and type has been well treated in the literature and can be well understood in terms of a hierarchial relationship, it is harder to find discussion relating trait to attitude. Allport is one of the few who have gone into the relationship full tilt:

> Both attitude and trait are indispensable concepts. Between them they cover virtually every type of disposition with which the psychology of personality concerns itself. Ordinarily *attitude* should be employed when the disposition is bound to an object of value, that is to say, when it is well aroused by a well-defined class of stimuli, and when the individual feels towards these stimuli a definite attraction or repulsion" (Allport 1937:295).

Hall and Lindzey, in discussing Allport's definitions of these two terms, comment:

> The generality of the trait is almost always greater than that of the attitude; in fact, as the number of objects increases to which the attitude refers, it comes to resemble a trait more and more. The attitude may vary in generality from highly specific to the relatively general, while the trait must always be general. Second, the attitude usually implies evaluation (acceptance or rejection) of the object towards which it is directed while the trait does not" (Hall and Lindzey 1957:264).

In the discussion of traits by psychologists interest has dwelt mainly on the aspect of consistency. All sorts of classifications have been made: common and unique traits; dynamic and ability traits; surface and source; environmental mold and constitutional; cardinal, central, and secondary traits. Allport and Odbert (1936) once laboriously made a list of 17,953 words which served as trait terms in the English language, and classified them according to whether they were neutral terms designating personal traits, terms primarily descriptive of temporary moods or activities, weighted terms conveying social or characterial judgments, or judgments of personal conduct, or designating influence upon others, or a miscellaneous batch designating physique, capacities, and developmental conditions. Also added in the classification were metaphorical and doubtful terms. Allport thought that only the first group could be thought of as traits in the strict sense of the word, and admitted that the attempt to distinguish "neutral terms" from social judgmental terms was often difficult: "In spite of our efforts to locate only neutral terms some of the terms appearing . . . do seem to imply censorial judgment. In America to say that John is self-assured, inventive, or decisive, is to praise him; in some societies he would stand condemned" (1937:308). Two observations need to be made about traits. The first may seem banal but it has some point when I pick up the concluding threads later; namely, that they come from everyday language and are thus interpersonal in nature. The second observation is that traits have a built-in orientation about them, as it were. The reason for mentioning Allport and Odbert's study was to show the attempt of crystallizing a metalanguage from the ordinary language of everyday living by subtracting socially evaluative and judgmental terms, thus leaving a residue of "true" traits. Allport admits that even this was not always possible, but the confession is laid on the basis of distinction between descriptive and judgmental terms. Allowing that Allport's attempt was partially successful, it is difficult to go down the list of true traits without being able to add the words "toward" or "about" in order to clarify the meaning. Again, as we have noted, the main difference between traits and attitudes lies in their range of generality. Both are *vectoring concepts*. The difference lies in the magnitude associated with the direction, traits having a larger range of application if range is regarded as similar to magnitude.

I now return to the starting point of this section: is it possible to conceive of the human mind apart from the milieu in which it is embedded? The conclusion to which one is drawn is that this is operationally impossible so long as the basic concept of trait is adhered to. As long as this is done, however circuitous and drawn out the route is, one returns to Nadel's quandary of social and psychological analysis. This conclusion has implications to which I will return later. In the meantime, a reference to Jung's scheme of personality may represent a clue as to the way in which this quandary may be avoided. Jung (1933) reintroduced the well-known terms of introversion and extraversion into psychological theory. Often books on personality have called these terms personality traits, but actually Jung thought of them as attitudes or orientations. He then related them to four *psychological functions:* thinking, sensing, feeling, and intuition, thereby making an eightfold scheme of types. Soon after this typology was formulated, the anthropologist Seligman (1924) tried to apply the orientation part of the scheme—introversion and extraversion—to whole tribes. Significantly from the point of view raised here, he made no mention of the psychological functions.[4] The theoretical advantage of Jung's scheme, whether or not one agrees with his actual choice of functions and attitudes, is that there is a clear distinction between psychological functions or processes and the orientation toward or from the milieu in which these processes find their expression. With traits the distinction is, at the very least, not so clear. I should, however, like to make clear that these remarks about traits are in the context of personality as it coincides with culture. The history of the study of traits has had too honorable mention in the history of psychology (see Allport 1966 for the most recent summary) to dismiss it entirely in so cavalier a fashion as may have been done here. All the same, I believe these arguments are cogent and become particularly focal when traits are placed fully in the wider framework of social context and not restricted to the personality construct minus the milieu.

THE WIDER FRAMEWORK

Perhaps the really striking thing that a psychologist notes in observing the culture and personality school is the restriction of both the meaning extended to personality and the methods employed to its literary and clinical aspects. As late as 1961 Spiro (1961:490) was advocating that studies in culture and personality make use of role theory. Since the idea of role playing can be dated back at least to George Herbert Mead's lectures at the University of Chicago in the early 1900s, why did this suggestion not come earlier in the history of culture and personality studies? It is all speculative, but a number of answers may be found. First, there is the question of the discipline concerned. The concept of role was allied to sociology and social psychology, not ethnology. This involves the unit of study. Role becomes an operational concept only when *society* and/or a social system is contrasted with culture. A second reason may be that anthropology allied itself to the early meanings given to personality which were synonymous with characterological notions current from the fifteenth through the eighteenth centuries. The idea of national character was already well implanted in the scholarly world in the nineteenth century, if not earlier. A third reason is more subtle, and relates to the impact of psychoanalytical ideas on anthropology and the concomitant use of projective techniques. The impact led to a quest for explanation in terms of internalization. Like any other construct in social science that we seem to flagellate to pieces, role has undoubtedly run its course over a plethora of meanings. It is still true, however, that whereas the modern version bites into the whole person pretty deeply, early interpretations were of role *playing,* with overtones of putting on and off like a Roman mask. The concept of role had a public and not a private access. It clearly would not serve to deal with the internal and consistent springs of action conceived by theoreticians seeking explanation for social facts within the individual. Personality, as generally conceived, was a more promising candidate. Particularly so when it was reinforced with the depth significance of psychoanalytic thought. Much of the psychoanalytic *impedimenta* has been lost in transit. It is interesting to note, on the other hand, that the *superego* has lost none of its original force, and provides for scholars such as Talcott Parsons (1961) ideas of the internal mechanism for the external processes of social control.

Almost exclusive reliance on two types of personality assessments—projective techniques and the use of documentation—went together with the picture of personality just presented, perhaps only because the administrative procedures are relatively simple. Yet one is struck with the variety of other methods of assessing personality that are available. There are questionnaires and inventories of all kinds; rating scales attached to observational procedures; check lists; psychometric measures applied to attitudes and values linked to the study of personality; situational tests; experimental methods relating to psychological functions; and physiological indicators. The dependency on the clinical and literary image of personality has undoubtedly been such because of the methods used. What would happen to this image if other methods were introduced? To take an extreme example: a type of visual illusion, the spiral aftereffect, has been found to vary significantly in two different groups of people, classified as different personality types by different procedures (Claridge 1960). What would happen to the matching problem of personality and culture if this measure were used in the study of the Kaska, Tuscarora, or Great Plains Indians? Another example is the phenomenon in psychology called reminiscence (a sudden resurging of retention after a long period of forgetting). This too has been associated with personality types. There have also been studies of different cognitive styles (Witkin 1962; Gardner 1953) associated with personality typologies. Some of these (Witkin 1966; Mercado, Diaz-Guerrero, and Gardner 1963) have been applied cross-culturally. The result seems to be a far more complex picture of personality than might be desired by certain writers in culture and personality. To explain this remark, it is necessary to mark the part that personality typologies have in certain branches of psychology, and it is worthwhile contrasting this with the part they serve in the social sciences. Whereas personality is used as an atom of explanation in individualistic minded social science—that is, at the lowest level of explanation—in psychology it serves as a superordinate construct of a hierarchy of operations. In such areas as the study of cognitive styles, the superordinate construct amounts to no more than a nominalistic convenience to specify a group of procedures. Personality is saved from a semblance of unreality only by the fact that the typology is supported by a quite different set of methods, at the observational level. For example, the construct 'repressers' are supported both by experimental methods pertaining to thinking and retention and to the usual clinical observations. But obviously a number of possible personality constructs can be built up in this way. If the range of methods of personality assessment is extended in the personality and culture field, there is the likelihood of a number of personality constructs, all probably valid and operational within the same culture. This means that the unit with which personality needs to be tied must cut across the defining boundaries which are usually introduced. Already the "social side" of culture and personality studies is bursting at the seams. We have cultural and national character; social character or personality; tribal character; institutional personality; political, religious and occupational personality types; slave personality, and so on. A veritable cartography of personality is thus generated. There is no reason why the fractionation might not continue unto the smallest unit possible.

Another movement, now developing, turns away from this position and has two lines of thought. One line concentrates on social organizations, more in the sociological sense than in the early anthropological sense of the term. Social mechanisms are taken as the target of inquiry. Special attention is given to mechanisms of social control, factors of social change (for example, acculturation), attitudes towards authority, forms of equilibrium and disequilibrium within a society, and similar matters. The other line focuses on the *inter*personal level, and has deep philosophical implications. More than one serious student of the subject has wondered whether there is in fact something that can be called personality at all, if what we call personality is not, in effect, the product of interpersonal relations.[5] This idea dates back, I suppose, to the philosophy of G. H. Mead; in a more modern form it can be found in the writings of Harry Stack Sullivan (1953; see also Mullahy 1949; 1952) and Daniel Miller (Miller 1961), and has had restirrings within the framework of social psychology (see Asch 1959). As a matter of fact the older social psychology had approached this idea, but it was formulated in a way that was objectionable. Asch states: "Why was the group mind thesis put forward by able men? It started with a serious problem—with the clarification of group characteristics and group membership. It had its roots in a formulation by no means strange today, namely, that one cannot understand an individual by studying him solely as an individual; one must see him in his group relations" (p. 369). Reacting against the logical affront of the group mind (misunderstood though it might have been), the social psychology of the twenties and thirties took social factors merely as any other stimulus, a trigger to set off responses in the individual. The dominant stimulus-response psychology of the day encouraged this view. A thoroughgoing theory of interpersonal relations for psychology emerged only very recently, one of the best examples being Heider's *tour de force* (1958).

Radcliffe-Brown (1957) once temptingly spoke on an "intermediate science," dealing with the relation of culture to the individual, but which, in his view, would have to await further development of the laws of psychology and the laws of sociology. An intermediate science might well lie in the close-knit architecture of interpersonal relations. The resulting structure cannot wholly depend on sociological support, such as can be found in the Cooley approach, nor can it depend wholly on the kind of psychological interpretation of interpersonal relations that can be found in Newcomb's social psychology (1950). It is rather to be found by treating interpersonal relations as a *psychological dyad,* a unit *sui generis* (Sears 1951). I suggest that a future for the further study of personality and culture lies in this promising region.

NOTES

(1) In this connection, the following quotation from Kroeber (1952) originally given in an address in 1948 has some interest. "What 'culture and personality' as a field of study seems to be, in its purest form, is what has just been described as the interaction of persons and their enveloping culture. Really to pursue this study, it is obviously first necessary to understand pretty well what the culture is and what the persons are like. It would be vain to hope that worthwhile results will eventuate from operating with an indeterminately variable X matched against an indeterminately variable Y. Kluckhohn, prominently identified with the 'culture and personality' movement, has recently proposed shifting its focus from the mutual interaction of these two factors, as just described, to a focus within personality, as this is affected by hereditary constitution, by social environment, by society, and by culture. This would make personality the real subject of investigation, and culture only one of several factors impinging on it. This is less, and rather more one-sided, than a true culture-and-personality field as it has just been envisaged." (p. 133).

(2) For people who have rejected the notion of culture as having an independent existence, and who have turned to psychological interpretations, the words of Karl Popper contain cold comfort: "Psychologism is, I believe, correct only in so far as it insists upon what may be called 'methodological individualism' as opposed to 'methodological collectivism'; it rightly insists that the 'behavior' and the 'actions' of collectives, such as states or social groups, must be reduced to the behavior and to the actions of human individuals. But the belief that the choice of such an individualistic method implies the choice of a psychological method is mistaken, even though it may appear very convincing at first sight (Popper 1952:91).

(3) This refers to a similar debate on the deterministic effect of language on thought. The strong position of Whorf holds that language determines or molds thought; the lesser position is that language follows the form of thought, on the analogy of a cloak around the body.

(4) This did not escape Seligman. In a footnote to his printed address (p. 16) he pointed out that Jung's earlier communications on psychological types, only the extraverted and introverted types were contrasted, feeling being identified with the former, and thinking with the latter. The eightfold scheme came later. The significant point is that Seligman was moved to say that it was the earlier formulation of Jung that he accepted in his paper.

(5) The extent to which the influence of interpersonal effects can go is shown by considering the result of the classic study by Brown and Lenneberg (1954) on the influence of language on cognition. They found that recognition of colors depended on the codability of the color name. Using factor analysis, for an analysis of codability, it was found that the factor with the highest saturation was interobserver agreement.

BIBLIOGRAPHY

ALLPORT, GORDON, *Personality: A Psychological Interpretation*. London: Constable & Company, Ltd., 1949. First printed 1937 in U.S.A.

———, "Traits Revisited," *American Psychologist*, Vol. 21, No. 1, 1966, pp. 1–10

ALLPORT, GORDON, and H. S. ODBERT, "Trait-names: A Psycho-lexical Study," *Psychological Monographs,* Vol. 47, No. 211, 1936.
ASCH, SOLOMON E., "A Perspective on Social Psychology," in Sigmund Koch (ed.), *Psychology: A Study of a Science,* Vol. 3: Formulations of the Person and the Social Context, pp. 363–383. New York: McGraw-Hill, Inc.
BENEDICT, RUTH F., "Psychological Types in the Cultures of the Southwest," in *Proceedings of the 23rd Congress of Americanists,* 1928, pp. 572–581. Chicago: University of Chicago Press, 1930. Reprinted in Margaret Mead (ed.), *An Anthropologist at Work. Writings of Ruth Benedict,* pp. 248–261, Boston: Houghton Mifflin Company, 1959.
———, "Anthropology and the Abnormal," *Journal of General Psychology,* Vol. X, No. 2, 1934, pp. 59–82. Reprinted in Margaret Mead (ed.), *An Anthropologist at Work. Writings of Ruth Benedict,* pp. 262–283. Boston: Houghton Mifflin Company, 1959.
BROWN, R., and E. H. LENNEBERG, "A Study in Language and Cognition," *Journal of Abnormal and Social Psychology,* Vol. 49, 1954, pp. 454–462.
BRUNER, JEROME S., et al., *Studies in Cognitive Growth.* New York: John Wiley & Sons, Inc., 1966.
CLARIDGE, G., "The Excitation-Inhibition Balance in Neurotics," in H. J. Eysenck (ed.), *Experiments in Personality.* London: Routledge & Kegan Paul, Ltd., 1960.
EGGAN, FRED, "Social Anthropology and the Method of Controlled Comparison," *American Anthropologist,* Vol. 56, 1954, pp. 743–763.
GARDNER, RILEY W., "Cognitive Styles in Categorizing Behavior," *Journal of Personality,* Vol. 22, 1953, pp. 214–233.
HADDON, A. C. (ed.), *Reports of the Cambridge Anthropological Expedition to Torres Straits.* London: Cambridge University Press, 1901.
HALL, CALVIN S., and GARDNER LINDZEY, *Theories of Personality.* New York: John Wiley & Sons, Inc., 1957.
HAYEK, F. A., *Individualism and Economic Order.* Chicago: University of Chicago Press, 1948.
HEIDER, FRITZ, *The Psychology of Interpersonal Relations.* New York: John Wiley & Sons, Inc., 1958.
JUNG, CARL G., *Psychological Types.* New York: Harcourt, Brace & World, Inc., 1933. Published in England 1923.
KARDINER, ABRAM, *The Individual and His Society.* New York: Columbia University Press, 1939.
KROEBER, A. L., "The Concept of Culture in Science," in A. L. Kroeber (ed.), *The Nature of Culture,* pp. 118–135. Chicago: The University of Chicago Press, 1952.
———, and C. KLUCKHOHN, "Culture: A Critical Review of Concepts and Definitions," *Papers of the Peabody Museum of American Archeology and Ethnology,* Vol. 47, No. 1, 1952, p. 181.
MERCADO, S. J., R. D. DIAZ-GUERRERO, and R. W. GARDNER, "Cognitive Control in Children of Mexico and the United States," *Journal of Social Psychology,* Vol. 59, 1963, pp. 199–208.
MILLER, DANIEL, "Personality and Social Interaction," in Bert Kaplan (ed.), *Studying Personality Cross-Culturally,* pp. 271–298. New York: Harper & Row, Publishers, 1961.
MULLAHY, P. (ed.), *A Study of Interpersonal Relations.* New York: Hermitage House, Inc., 1949.
———, *The Contributions of Harry Stack Sullivan.* New York: Hermitage House, Inc., 1952.

NADEL, S. F., *The Foundations of Social Anthropology.* New York: The Free Press, 1951.
NEWCOMB, T. M., *Social Psychology,* pp. 34–35. New York: Holt, Rinehart and Winston, Inc., 1950.
PARSONS, TALCOTT, "Social Structure and the Development of Personality," in Bert Kaplan (ed.), *Studying Personality Cross Culturally,* pp. 165–199. New York: Harper & Row, Publishers, 1961.
POPPER, KARL R., *The Open Society and Its Enemies.* Vol. 11, The High Tide of Prophecy: Hegel, Marx and the Aftermath. London: Routledge & Kegan Paul, Ltd., 1952.
RADCLIFFE-BROWN, A. R., *A Natural Science of Society.* New York: The Free Press, 1957.
RIVERS, W. H. R., *Psychology and Ethnology.* New York: Harcourt, Brace & World, Inc., 1926.
SEARS, R. R., "A Theoretical Framework for Personality and Social Behavior," *American Psychologist,* Vol. 9, 1951, pp. 476–483.
SEGALL, M. H., D. T. CAMPBELL, and M. J. HERSKOVITS, "Cultural Differences in the Perception of Geometric Illusions," *Science,* Vol. 139, 1963, pp. 769–771.
———, *The Influence of Culture on Visual Perception.* Indianapolis: The Bobbs-Merrill Company, Inc., 1966.
SELIGMAN, C. G., "Anthropology and Psychology: A Study of Some Points of Contact," *Journal of the Royal Anthropological Institute,* Vol. 54, 1924, pp. 13–46.
SINGER, MILTON, "A Survey of Culture and Personality Theory and Research," in Bert Kaplan (ed.), *Studying Personality Cross-Culturally,* pp. 9–90. New York: Harper & Row, Publishers, 1961.
SPIRO, MELFORD E., "Culture and Personality. The Natural History of a False Dichotomy," *Psychiatry,* Vol. 14, 1951, pp. 19–56.
———, "An Overview and a Suggested Reorientation," in Francis L. K. Hsu (ed.), *Psychological Anthropology. Approaches to Culture and Personality,* pp. 459–492. Illinois: The Dorsey Press, Inc., 1961.
SULLIVAN, HARRY STACK, *The Interpersonal Theory of Psychiatry.* New York: W. W. Norton, and Company, Inc., 1953.
WATKINS, J. W. N., "Historical Explanation in the Social Sciences," *The British Journal for the Philosophy of Science,* Vol. VIII, No. 30, 1957, pp. 104–117.
WHITING, J. W. M., and I. L. CHILD, *Child Training and Personality.* Yale: Yale University Press, 1953.
WITKIN, H. A., et al., *Psychological Differentiation.* New York: John Wiley & Sons, Inc., 1962.
———, "Cultural Influences in the Development of Cognitive Style," Paper presented at a Symposium on "Intercultural Studies of Mental Development," International Congress of Psychology, Moscow, 1966.

7

*National Character Revisited: a Proposal for Renegotiating the Concept**

Daniel Bell

I

The idea of national character—at least, of distinctive group differences—is as old as the first traveler who ever encountered another society, and lived to tell about it on returning to his own. Herodotus, who explored Egypt as far as the headwaters of the Nile, was among the first to write about national character. He pointed out that the people of a nation behaved in similar ways and had similar institutions and artifacts. Plato, one might say, had a distinct theory of "modal personality" deriving from the character of the polis. For him, the division of classes in a city corresponded to the different parts of the soul, and just as each man had a rational, spirited and appetitive dimension of the soul, so a particular city, because of the predominance of one type of individual, had a distinct character. In *The Republic,* Socrates remarked:

> It would be ridiculous to imagine that among peoples who bear the reputation for being spirited, like the inhabitants of Thrace, Scythia and the north generally, the spirited character does not come from the individual citizens, or that it is otherwise with the love of learning which would be chiefly ascribed to this country, or with the love of riches, which people would especially attribute to the Phoenicians and the inhabitants of Egypt. . . . we may take this as a fact and one not hard to comprehend.[1]

But the first skepticism about the clean-cut nature of the concept is also to be found in Greece. Theophrastus, Aristotle's successor as the director of

---

* I am indebted to Alex Inkeles for the clarification of some ideas, and for an advance copy of the revision of his essay (with Daniel Levinson) on National Character for the *Handbook of Social Psychology.*
[1] *The Republic,* Book IV, #435, trans. by A. D. Lindsay. Everyman's Library Edition, p. 152.

the Lyceum, and perhaps the first social scientist, wondered why it was that although all Greece had the same climate and all Greeks had the same kind of education, nevertheless all Greeks did not have the same structure (*taxis*) of character-traits (*tropos*). To satisfy that curiosity, as Professor Richard McKeon tells us,[2] Theophrastus started to study human nature (*physis*) and to distinguish and compare kinds of dispositions. Theophrastus planned to investigate good and bad dispositions, but his work *The Characters,* as it has come to us, analyzes thirty bad characters, and we have no evidence that he had extended his investigation to good characters.

Yet despite all the difficulties of definition, a sense of national character persists because in human society there is an awareness of group differences. Other than in the hitherto small milieux where cosmopolitanism is accepted as a way of life, the strangeness of another is often an affront to oneself, unless it can be treated as exotic and therefore outside the pale, or unless the outsider is regarded as an object, as a curiosity, and treated as being intrinsically inferior. Much of the history of the world is a history of hostility between groups, and there has therefore been a constant need to mobilize in-group sentiments against an enemy. Since much of human personality involved a repression of socially defined undesirable impulses, an important mechanism of self-maintenance is the projection of ill-concealed, undesirable traits, or feared impulses onto the outsider. The most telling example of such projection was the attributing of syphilis, when it was first brought to Europe from the American continent, as variously the French, Italian, or Spanish disease, depending on what "other" country a man was from.

The idea of group character, of course, antedates the idea of a nation, for the nation is in fact a very recent entity. Historically, the basic idea of group character was *race,* a presumed descent from some common lineage through the blood, and often marked by some distinctive physiognomic features or coloring. Much of human history has been a history of conquests, and the differences between groups—in vigor, courage and hardiness—were attributed by the victors to the superiority of the racial stock, whether it was the Aryans against the Dravidians, the Latins over the Spanish, the Celts over the Saxons, and so on.

The modern conception of national character has its roots largely in the nineteenth century, when the efforts of nationalities to gain independence, and of imperialist powers to justify their right of rule over others, were fused with racial theory. Against the Enlightenment, with its emphasis upon universal reason, modern romanticism, beginning with Herder,

---

[2] I take this illustration from a paper by Richard McKeon, on "Character and the Arts and Disciplines," prepared for the Seventeenth Conference on Science, Philosophy and Religion, 1966, to be included in the forthcoming volume of the proceedings.

sought to justify group differences and cultural diversity on the grounds of language and history and race. Lionel Trilling has cogently summed this up:

> ... in [Matthew] Arnold's day the racial theory, stimulated by a rising nationalism and a spreading imperialism, supported by an incomplete and mal-assumed science, was almost undisputed. The conception of race served to sustain oppressed nationalities in their struggle for freedom (Italy, Poland), to unify diversified states in their attempt at integration and power (Germany), and to justify powerful imperialistic nations in their right to rule others. The theory, sprung from the desk of the philosopher and the philologist, had an unfailing attraction for the literary and quasi-religious mind; the conception of a mystic and constant "blood" was a handy substitute for the *soul.*
> ... there were many to foster and elaborate the notion of a racial constant—Gobineau, who gave it its greatest impetus, who explained the enormous superiority of the blond northerners over the other Whites and of the Whites over the Blacks and Yellows; Moses Hess, who contrasted the eternal differences of Rome and Jerusalem; Heine, who followed Hess and Ludwig Börne in making firm the distinctions between Hellenism and Hebraism; Disraeli, who set Saxon industry against Norman manners and Jewish culture against Baltic piracy; Stendhal, Meredeith, Mme. de Staël, Carlyle, J. A. Fronde, Kingsley, J. R. Green, Taine, Renan (from whom Arnold got much of his interest in the Celts), Saint-Beuve—all built the racial hypothesis into their work. *Indeed, the list could be made to include nearly every writer of the time who generalized about human affairs.* And if some used it for liberalizing purposes, as Arnold himself did, still by their very assent to an unfounded assumption they cannot wholly be dissociated from the quaint, curious and dangerous lucubrations of Houston Stewart Chamberlain, Richard Wagner, Woltmann, Treitschke, Rosenberg and the whole of official German thought in the present day. It is not, after all, a very great step from Arnold's telling us that the Celt is by "blood" gay, sensual, anarchic, to Treitschke's telling us that the Germans excel Latins in artistic appreciation because when a Latin reposes in the woods he crassly lies on his stomach whereas "blood" dictates to the German that he lie, aesthetically, on his back.[3]

For the past forty years, the entire weight of modern social science has been devoted to demolishing the idea of race as a meaningful concept in history or social relations, and to denying the idea of any intrinsic group superiority. Though Lord Bryce could say, in his *Race Sentiment as a Factor in History,* that in the thought and imagination of every civilized people there is "an unquestionable racial strain" and that "race sentiment is one of the elements that go to make up national sentiment and national pride and help to make people cohesive," a nation, according to the British historian Ernest Barker, "is not the physical fact of one blood, but the mental fact of one tradition." In the effort to separate the two terms of

---

[3] Lionel Trilling, *Matthew Arnold* (New York: W. W. Norton & Company, Inc. 1939), pp. 234–235. (Second emphasis added.)

race and nation, it has been argued that race is a biological term, the continuity of a physical type, which is largely unrelated to nationality, language, or custom, while a nation is designated by historical and social characteristics that are altered over time by custom or even by deliberate induced change. Thus, there is no German or American race, but there is a German or American nation, no Aryan race but Aryan languages, no Roman race but a Roman civilization.[4]

But the idea of history and tradition was itself too variable, and modern social anthropology soon substituted the idea of *culture* for *race,* arguing that a group could best be defined not by physical characteristics but by normative patterns which are prescriptive of behavior, and that the varying integration of such normative patterns provides the boundaries of the group or its culture. For the idea of group superiority, the anthropologists argued for a relativism that gave to each culture its own justification for the working out of patterns functional to the needs of the people who comprise the culture.

The advantages of this approach are quickly evident. Descriptions in terms of culture allow for an identification of specific patterns of behavior which are prescriptive for the members of the society; by relating these patterns to personality, one provides a mechanism for the interplay of the individual and the society as well as for identifying the means of continuity and change. The theory seemed to promise the integration of biology, psychology, and anthropology in a meaningful way. It stipulated, in sum, that societies have patterned, regularized ways of meeting sociobiological needs which are more or less integrated through some normative structure (religion, values, or beliefs) and that these ways are transmitted, in defined patterns, through the children, who, by internalizing the norms, learn the modes of society. In this fusion of anthropology and psychology, most often Freudian psychology, social analysts became sensitive to the way in which different cultures shape basic psychosexual and other primal drives—aggression, self-conceptions, identifications with parents and with authority, modes of handling death, and the like—and the way in which individual and group variations in personality reshape cultural norms for the next generation. Out of these inquiries there developed in the late 1930s and early 1940s the field called culture and personality.

---

[4] For a succinct discussion of this problem, see Louis L. Snyder, *The Meaning of Nationalism* (New Brunswick, N.J.: Rutgers University Press, 1954), Chap. II. Lord Bryce's book, it may be noted, was published in 1915, and Sir Ernest Barker's, *National Character and the Factors in Its Formation,* in 1927. But one could still find distinguished anthropologists, usually physical anthropologists, arguing, as Sir Arthur Keith did in 1931, that when a land is peopled with a mixture of old races, a new effort at race building is initiated sooner or later. "A nation always represents an attempt to become a race; nation and race are but different degrees of the same evolutionary movement." (Sir Arthur Keith, *Ethnos, or The Problem of Race,* cited in Snyder, p. 17.)

The major book of this early period was Ruth Benedict's *Patterns of Culture* (1934), which sought to present holistic descriptions of cultures in psychological terms, though the appellations themselves, such as Apollonian or Dionysian, were metaphors borrowed from Nietzsche, to emphasize polar configurations. Her emphasis was not on the individual but, as characterized by Geoffrey Gorer, "on the psychological coherence of the varied *institutions* which make up a society." And, as Inkeles and Levinson have commented, Dr. Benedict "did not make a clear conceptual distinction between the sociocultural system and the personality as a system, but rather appears to have assumed that the psychological coherence of the individual personality was isomorphic with the psychological coherence of the culture." [5]

The linking of the individual with the cultural pattern was made largely by the psychoanalyst Abram Kardiner (in his *The Individual and Society*, 1939), who, working with the anthropologist Ralph Linton, formulated the idea of the "basic personality structure" as a means of explaining the relationship of the individual to the society. For Kardiner, *basic* did not mean the deepest aspect of a person, but the modal or common type which is most congenial to the prevailing institutions and ethos. As Inkeles and Levinson put it: ". . . the basic personality structure consists of those dispositions, conceptions, modes of relating to each other, and the like, that make the individual maximally receptive to cultural ways and ideologies, and that enable him to achieve adequate gratification and security within the existing order." [6]

The shift from "culture" (or even from "society") to the "nation" as the unit that shapes character received its impetus during World War II, when a number of anthropologists and psychiatrists tried to describe the psychological makeup of the Germans, the Japanese, and the Russians, in holistic terms, as a guide to policy. In extreme formulations Richard Brickner and Bertram Schaffner described the Germans as an authoritarian nation whose character resulted from the dominant position of the father in the German family, while Brickner went so far (in *Is Germany Incurable?*) as to call the Germans a pathological nation. Henry V. Dicks, the British psychiatrist, drew a picture of "an ambivalent compulsive character structure with the emphasis on submissive/dominant conformity" which draws sanc-

---

[5] The history of the development of the culture-and-personality field is developed at great length in the comprehensive monograph "National Character: The Study of Modal Personality and Sociocultural Systems," by Alex Inkeles and D. J. Levinson, in the *Handbook of Social Psychology*, Vol. 2, edited by Gardner Lindzey (Reading, Mass.: Addison-Wesley Publishing Company, Inc.), 1954, and there is little need for me to review the developments here. I have taken certain central features of this history as the basis for my own proposals developed later in this essay. I quote here from the ms. of the paper to appear in the revised edition of the Lindzey volume, p. 4.

[6] Lindzey, Vol. 2, p. 17.

tion for aggressive outbursts "from superego leader figures (Bismarck, Kaiser, Hitler). . . ." More cautiously, Erich Fromm stated that "the Nazi ideology and practice satisfies one part of the population and gives direction . . . to those . . . who were resigned and had given up faith in life and their own decisions." In her wartime study of Japan, a study of "culture from a distance," Ruth Benedict drew a picture of a society highly controlled, rigidly organized, esthetic in its preoccupations, yet capable of wild outbursts of savagery, a picture summed up in the title of her book *The Chrysanthemum and the Sword.* If Japanese culture was regarded largely as "anal," the Russian culture—specifically the culture of Great Russia—was regarded by Gorer and Rickman, and Margaret Mead, as "oral"—a culture in which individuals were subject to wild manic-depressive swings, from sullen, stubborn, and passive feelings to large outbursts of rage and storming emotions. In a more differentiated picture, Henry Dicks and Nathan Leites, in separate studies, sought to show how a new elite—purposeful, organized, controlled—was seeking to reshape the traditional Russian character, which had been given vivid literary form in such types as Platon Karatayev, Myshkin, Alyosha Karamazov, and Oblomov.

The difficulty with so many of these studies was implicit in the enterprise itself; that is, the amophous definitions of nation and character. Not only was there a tendency, at least in the early studies, to assume a single personality mode for the population of any given society. There was the more important ambiguity stemming from the lack of any real agreement on what constituted *personality* itself. Equally, there was no discussion of the *nation* as a concept: *What,* if anything, makes the nation a distinctive boundary, marking it off, the way a culture presumably does, as a particular configuration of norms, or manners, or personalities sufficiently different from that of other nations? This elision of "culture," with the substitution of "nation" as the unit of action, was rarely examined critically. It is to these two problems—the use of such units as "character" (or "personality") and "nation"—that we now turn.

II

Character, in the original sense of the term, meant an impress or stamp, an idea borrowed from the minting of coins, by which types are differentiated and classified. The central points, therefore, are the distinctive elements of recurrent behavior which define personality and the principles which differentiate them or create relevant typologies.

Modern efforts to define character at the most abstract and general level provide few statements of boundaries; they become, as the French say, *une palissard*—so many words. Thus, according to Erich Fromm, "character in the dynamic sense of analytical psychology is the specific form in which human energy is shaped by the dynamic adaptation of human needs to the particular mode of existence of a given society. Character, in its turn, determines the thinking, feeling and acting of individuals." Social character, further, "comprises only a selection of traits, the essential nucleus of the character structure of most members of a group that has developed as the result of basic experiences and mode of living common to a group." For Fromm, the social character, by internalizing external necessities, harnesses human energy for the tasks required by a given economic and social system.[7]

The difficulty with this definition is the imprecision of the key terms—*energy, dynamic, basic*—and the reification of the economic and social system as "requiring" specific modes of conformity. Not only does the effort suffer from these defects, but it in no way accounts for variations of character, perhaps because it does not allow for variations in the social and cultural systems which the individual confronts.

When one descends from this level of generality to more specific efforts to define *personality*, one is led to a number of different forests, each of which provides different configurative patterns. The most influential theory has been the psychoanalytic, because, more than any other theory, it has posed the problem of how an individual learns to handle his impulses, and how, either through the oedipal or some other situation, he learns to confront authority. The specific virtue of psychoanalytical theory is that it has sought to define specific types of personality. In the classic psychosexual formulations, individuals were either oral, anal, or genital. In Fromm's variation, they were sadomasochistic or autonomous. Jungian theory had its complex pairings, in which individuals were fundamentally introverted or extroverted; within these there were dominant or secondary constellations of intuition, intelligence, sensation, and emotion as character traits. Psychoanalytic ego theory, organized around the basic defense mechanisms that individuals characteristically employ to handle conflicts and to achieve integration, posited either a passive-aggressive dimension, an autonomous-authoritarian dimension, or, in the subtle stage theory of Erikson, fixations that revolve around the antinomies of trust-mistrust, autonomy-shame, and integration-role diffusion.

A second, and somewhat different, approach has attempted to organize personality theory around "self-conceptions." David Riesman has become famous for his historical description of the shift from the "inner-directed" to the "other-directed" character type, though the complete panoply includes at one end of the continuum the "tradition-directed," and at the other, as a possibility rather than a historic actuality, the "autonomous" type. Riesman's early effort to relate these, variously, to stages of population cycle or to urbanization has been abandoned, and the terms, still power-

---

[7] Cited in Inkeles and Levinson 1954, p. 278.

fully suggestive, remain as analytic types. In the same direction, Gordon Allport's concept of "self-realization," while not purely typological, does derive from development theory and allows one to see, presumably, at what stage of development an individual has been able to rise towards the goal of being a self-determining person.

A third kind of personality theory, which has been popular in recent years, centers around the conception of "needs" and the means of realizing them. An early effort along these lines was the idea of the "four wishes" developed by W. I. Thomas, in which it was posited that each individual has a basic need for security, recognition, the search for new adventures, sex, and the like. More recently, A. H. Maslow has suggested that various human needs can be organized along hierarchical lines in which certain satisfactions must come before others.

Clifford Geertz has levelled against some of the recent personality theories the criticism that they once again neglect the enormous range of cultural variability.[8] However, a more difficult problem is that few of the personality theories are organized around some standard analytical scheme—categories of authority, self, primary dilemmas, cognitive functions, expressive behavior—which allow for cross-cultural or cross-societal comparisons. As Inkeles and Levinson have summed up the problem:

> Ideally the personality theory used in this field should have certain basic characteristics. Its assumptions and concepts should comprise an explicitly formulated, coherent whole. It should largely determine the empirical description and analysis of modal personalities; that is, it should generate a relatively standardized analytic scheme—a descriptive-interpretative language—in terms of which modal personalities can be delineated. The variables in the analytic scheme should be *psychologically significant,* in the sense that they represent intrapersonal characteristics that play an important part in determining the individual's thought and behavior; and *socially relevant,* in the sense that they influence the individual's readiness to maintain or change the existing sociocultural system. The theoretical framework should be comprehensive and universally applicable, so as to ensure maximal richness in the analysis of a single society and maximal cross-societal comparability of findings.
>
> It is evident at the outset that "individual psychology" does not yet provide personality theories that meet the above criteria to a satisfactory degree. This lack has been one of several major hindrances to the systematic description of modal personality structures, and must be kept in mind in any critical appraisal of the work to date.[9]

If the concept of personality has been nebulous, the term *nation* as a visible unit to circumscribe character has been almost completely unexam-

---

[8] Clifford Geertz, "The Impact of Culture on the Study of Man," John R. Platt, editor, *The Nature of Man* (Chicago: University of Chicago Press, 1965).
[9] Inkeles and Levinson, 1967 ms., pp. 28–29.

ined. A nation is a political and territorial unit capable of kindling or evoking emotional loyalty as a symbol, but its shifting contours over periods of time, and its very newness as a social unit, raise the very question whether there has been sufficient continuity of generational time to provide for those enduring and stable personality characteristics which presumably mark or carry the imprint of "national character." E. H. Carr, who headed a study group of the Royal Institute of International Affairs that was trying to formulate a definition of nationalism, wrote in 1945:

> The nation is not a definable and clearly recognized entity. . . . Nevertheless the nation is . . . far more than a voluntary association; and it embodies in itself . . . such natural and universal elements as attachments to one's native land and speech and a sense of wider kinship than that of family. The modern nation is a history group.[10]

The word *patriotism* first cropped up in the eighteenth century, and *nationalism* appeared only in the nineteenth. In French, *nationalisme* is to be found first in 1812. The oldest example of *nationalism* in English dates from 1836, and then, as Johann Huizinga points out, "remarkably with a theological significance, namely for the doctrine that certain nations have been chosen by God."[11] H. L. Featherstone, in *A Century of Nationalism,* reviewed the different movements and the attempts to establish the bases of nationalism and concluded that "nationalism is not capable of scientific definition."

A nation in a social-psychological sense is a quest for solidarity, the fusion of politics and culture, in which loyalties once given to tribe or place, race or religion are given to some more inclusive unity. But whether this unity ever achieves a sufficient homogeneity to provide for consistent normative or prescriptive patterns is an empirical matter. The tensions of earlier, parochial loyalties in the one direction and the syncretism of culture or the commonalties created by industrialization in another, make problematic the idea that "the nation" is itself a sufficiently encapsulating and durable crucible of distinctive personality-defining cultural patterns.

In the "new nations" of Africa and Asia, it is clear that primordial and local territorial attachments make it difficult, if not impossible, to talk of a "Nigerian" character or even of a "Burmese" character, if one includes as part of Burma not only the Burmans but the Kachins, the Shans, and dozens of other smaller peoples who are part of the state. In the same way the idea of a Yugoslav national character falls by the wayside when one is

---

[10] E. H. Carr, *Nationalism and After* (New York: The Macmillan Company, 1945), p. 40, cited in Karl W. Deutsch, *Nationalism and Social Communication* (M.I.T. Press and John Wiley, 1953), p. 13.
[11] "Patriotism and Nationalism in European History," in Johann Huizinga, *Men and Ideas* (New York: Meridian Books, 1959), p. 99.

confronted with the significant differences among the Serbs, Croats, Slovenes, Montenegrins, Bosnians, Herzogovinians, and even the smaller enclaves of mountain and valley people included in the political nation. But even in "old," long-established historic nations such as England, which presumably have some kind of definable character, one finds, in cutting below the stereotype of the quiet, reserved, law-abiding "national" character, distinctive regional differences which are more real and recognizable to the English themselves. In a description of the impact of the Beatles on English life, James Morris comments:

> Their Mersey accent, which not long ago would have seemed to most Englishmen perfectly barbaric, now falls with an attractive bite upon the ear. . . . In a country so long hag-ridden by class, they are classless—that is to say, they don't care, or make clear what their social background is. . . . they have managed to make the whole subject of personal origins, so long an obsession of the English, irrelevant to themselves. In the past, a regional character in England has almost always stood for broad comedy—Yorkshire knockabout, tedious Scotch japes about kilts and stinginess or that perennial of the music halls, the cheeky Cockney. The Beatles have neither exploited nor disguised their Lancashire origins. . . . If, for the English, regional and class character has loomed so large in their images of one another, at what point does one find fruitful the idea of an "English" national character? [12]

The question of class variation may at times be as important as local or regional variations of a "national" character. If character is organized pri-

---

[12] Perhaps the *locus classicus* of this type of demurrer is the observation of Stephen Potter—an example of the anecdotal veto of a concept—that you can puncture any generalization about a foreign country by saying, "Yes, but what about the South?" And to a remarkable degree the demurrer seems to hold. In the United States there is the classic division between the North and the South. The differences are equally striking in France and in Italy: the Midi is quite different from the lands of the Seine and the Somme, and Calabria is another world from Milan. Spain has Andalusia and Catalonia, Ireland has Erin and Ulster, England has Lancashire and London, Germany has Prussia and Bavaria, Russia has Moscow and Kiev.

But what is true of Europe and the United States is true of Asia as well. China has Canton and Peking (and some observers have pointed out that the Kuomintang came from the south and the Communists from the north, and the latter have exploited the hatred of the south, though Mao is a southerner); India has Madras and Delhi, Korea its south and north, and Vietnam *its* south and north, differences long established and not merely the result of recent political divisions.

The south is not just geography, but also, seemingly, a frame of mind. Southern Germany (Bavaria) is north of Milan and Turin, but is "south." Southern France is north of bustling Catalonia and of most Italian cities, but it is also "south," more akin to southern Italy in tempo than to northern France.

The only two countries where none of this apparently applies are Poland and Israel: Poland may be the only country with a true national character because Poland is eternally a question, while Israeli character is summed up, typically, in a joke—for example, where there are two Jews there are three political parties. In fact, most definitions of national character, because of the aggressiveness of the subject, begin with a joke.

marily around the repression or regulation of human drives, one of the distinctive aspects of the lower classes from the Roman plebs to the *Lumpenproletariat* of the present has often been the relatively unrestrained "acting out" of impulses, the failure to internalize the norms that distinguish middle-class behavior from that of other classes. Much of this is equally true of bohemians, lazzaroni, hoboes, and others who consciously exempt themselves from the prevailing norms of the society and often create a "counter-society" of their own. In what way are such elements an aspect of the "national" character?

The question of trans-national boundaries is one that arises out of the impact of industrialization and of increasing cultural contact. Long ago Veblen and Dewey pointed out the imprint of distinct occupational marks: miners, seamen, timber workers, and scientists all have distinct occupational traits which, despite national boundaries, may make them more alike than different. But lacking such cross-cultural studies, we have no evidence to decide either way. Martin Meyerson has suggested that the character of cities and landscapes reflects national temperamental differences.[13] The large, open piazzas of Italy, he says, reflect the gregariousness of the Italian people; the quiet residential squares of England, and the growth of English cities without focus, derive from the piecemeal empiricism and private desires of Englishmen. The great boulevards of France, linear in character, are consonant with an affinity for display, while the countryside has an almost Cartesian character, captured in the cubelike landscapes of Cezanne; the separation of private and public spheres is reflected in Japanese urban arrangements: within the home the garden is serene, the house is spotless; without, the city is shapeless, disorderly, higgledy-piggledy, the landscape a tangle of overhead wires and laundry lines. And in America: there is the skyscraper, bigger and better, taller and higher, even when there is no direct economic motive or, as in Chicago, where the sandy subsoil made skyscraper construction difficult.

Persuasive though this may be, at least as literary metaphor, such styles reflect a time when social change was crescive, responding to the collective interaction of thousands of individuals. Yet today, when choice is more conscious and esthetic design is derived from the mingling of many styles, how do distinctive national styles reflect specific national temperaments? Just as in art, there is in architecture an "international style," and its mandarins, Gropius, Le Corbusier, Niemeyer, Saarinen—a German, a Frenchman, a Brazilian, and an American—have become the shapes of urban design. In the syncretism of the modern world, do the French intellectual and the French petty-bourgeois have more in common than a French and an English intellectual do?

---

[13] Martin Meyerson, "National Character and Urban Development," in *Public Policy*, Yearbook of the Harvard Graduate School of Public Administration, Vol. XII, 1963.

And if one is to introduce variations in locale and class, what is one to say about changes over time, especially if the idea of character implies some stable and enduring features through generations? Here is Weston La Barre's description of "the character structure of the average Chinese," written twenty years ago:

> . . . they lack any strong visceral disciplines such as are so insistent and strong in the "Protestant Ethic". . . . The internalization of the super ego is weak, the sense of sin nearly absent . . . The ego is sturdy and reality oriented in the direction of the physical world, but in the patriarchical family it is relatively thin skinned in its response to the human world. The average Chinese is cheerful, dignified, discreet, poised, unanxious, proud, secure, realistic and kindly.[14]

Apart from the awkward notion of an "average Chinese," how is one to square such an observation with the Red Guards of today, rampaging, shouting, deifying Mao?

The accounts one has of English character in the seventeenth and eighteenth centuries—lusty, brawling, boisterous in the style of Tom Jones—do not fit easily into the picture of young Christian gentlemen fashioned by Thomas Arnold or the English working class shaped by the Methodist and Wesleyan influences. If one is to accept Geoffrey Gorer's explorations of English character, much of this metamorphosis was accomplished quite sharply in the Victorian period because a new example was set by changes in the life of the Court, and through the creation of a metropolitan police system, wherein sober young men were deliberately chosen as models of deportment for the English working classes.

What these sundry examples suggest is that as quickly as one can define a "national character" (based, as has often been the case, on impressionistic description, or skewed samples), one can just as quickly find qualification (and disqualification), variation and counter-tendencies. How, then, is it possible to thread one's way through such a contradictory maze?

III

In 1949 Kluckhohn and Murray asserted that "the statistical prediction can safely be made that a hundred Americans, for example, will display certain defined characteristics more frequently than will a hundred Englishmen comparably distributed as to age, sex, social class and vocation." The difficulty with this statement is the ambiguous ground term "certain defined characteristics." If this means certain behavioral traits, it may possibly be true at any specific time. But since behavioral traits change after a

---

[14] Weston La Barre, "Some Observations on Character Structure in the Orient: The Chinese." *Psychiatry*, 1946, 9, pp. 375–395.

time, and the study of *character*, not *characteristics*, implies relatively enduring personality components, the proposition is less satisfactory. As Inkeles and Levinson, in trying to save the concept of national character, argue, the general definition does not involve "phenotypic, behavior-descriptive terms. Rather they are higher level abstractions that refer to stable, generalized dispositions or modes of functioning and may take a great variety of concrete behavioral forms. . . . Since one of the main analytic functions of the concept of national character is to enable us to determine the role of psychological forces in societal patterning and change, it must be defined conceptually as a *determinant* of behavior rather than concretely as a *form* of behavior. And it must have some stability or resistance to change; for characteristics that change easily under everyday situational pressures can hardly be of major importance as determinants of either stability or organized social change." [15]

The effort to deal with the problem of variation or contradictions led Ralph Linton (in *The Cultural Background of Personality*, 1945) to refer to character as a distributive concept that is common or standardized to some degree among individuals in a given society. Thus, on a statistical basis Linton was led to the idea of national character as *modal* personality structures. In this way he accepted the fact of wide individual differences but simply stated that a modal personality structure is one that appears with more considerable frequency than others, and thus there may be several modes in any distribution of variants.

The idea of modal personality structure is the foundation of the effort by Inkeles and Levinson to reformulate the idea of national character. They write:

> Our general definition of national character does *not* posit a heavily unimodal distribution of personality characteristics. National character can be said to exist to the extent that modal personality traits and syndromes are found. How many modes there are is an important empirical and theoretical matter, but one that is not relevant to the definition of national character.
>
> Particularly in the case of the complex industrial nation, a *multimodal* conception of national character would seem to be theoretically the most meaningful as well as empirically the most realistic. It appears unlikely that any specific personality characteristic, or any character type, will be found in as much as 60–70 percent of any modern national population. However, it is still a reasonable hypothesis that a nation may be characterized in terms of a limited number of modes, say five or six, some of which apply to perhaps 10–15 percent, others to perhaps 30 percent of the total population. Such a conception of national character can accommodate the subcultural variations of socioeconomic class, geosocial region, ethnic group and the like, which appears to exist in all modern nations.[16]

---

[15] Inkeles and Levinson, 1967, pp. 20–21.
[16] Inkeles and Levinson, p. 24.

But if one is to differentiate modal personalities, one needs a standardized analytic scheme to distinguish systematic responses from one group to another. And, as Inkeles and Levinson write, "We do not yet have an adequate basis in personality theory, and certainly not in empirical knowledge for producing a set of variables sure to have universal applicability and significance. And, in any case, a scheme which is limited to a relatively few, universally relevant variables would necessarily omit much that is important in any one society." [17]

Inkeles and Levinson do go on to suggest a set of dimensions illustrative of the kind of standard analytic issues that a comprehensive scheme would have to include. They assert that such issues should meet the criteria of being distributed universally and that the patterning of responses should indicate the readiness of an individual to accept or change a given sociocultural mode. Thus, they suggest such issues as "relation to authority," "conception of self," "primary dilemmas or conflicts—and ways of dealing with them," "modes of cognitive functioning," "styles of expressive behavior," and the like. In all, however, a workable scheme might contain about 30 to 40 categories in which one would group responses to identify the modal personality types.

In their review, and particularly in their 1967 revision, Inkeles and Levinson have given us the *conditions* for establishing a concept of "character" and for allowing "modal personality types" as frequency distributions of given character configurations within a population. But what is striking about their essay (particularly the 1954 version) is the avoidance of any discussion of the *nation* as the realistic unit of the society that is in some interactive relation with the personality. At any crucial moment of their discussion, their term is the *sociocultural system,* and the question is fairly begged whether the nation is or is not the effective unit of a sociocultural system. In effect their essay, though entitled "national character," is actually a sophisticated discussion of the traditional "culture and personality" field, rather than of the more elusive problem of "national character." [18]

---

[17] Inkeles and Levinson, p. 73. They remark further: "National character research is thus faced with a dilemma central to current personality research generally. A standardized analytical scheme can, at its best, add to the technical rigor and theoretical value of our investigation. Premature standardization, on the other hand, may seriously impair the flexibility and inclusiveness of analysis, and at its worst leads to rigorous measurement without concern for the theoretical meaning or functional significance of the variables measured."

[18] In a letter to the author, Inkeles wrote: ". . . within certain limits a nation state may have a population displaying almost no significant 'common' modes, modes restricted to special subgroups but not shared among the subgroups as a set, or having a few or even many common psychological traits on a wide scale. This latter case is more to be expected to the degree the population is culturally (ethnically) homogeneous and has been for a long time. But even when a national population has not been 'culturally' homogeneous originally, to the extent that communication, mass media, or

National Character Revisited

To clarify the meaning of "character" or "personality" helps to make more meaningful the differentiations *within* a population of various modal types, but it is not necessarily helpful to define *national character* as the predominance, simply, of a modal *personality* type. In common parlance, for example, writers talk of a style of action which is not derived from a frequency distribution of personality but refers to something more characteristic of the ways in which nations confront problems. In a recent essay on "Strategic Thinking," Professor John Chapman of the University of Pittsburgh talks of military doctrine as having national character, so that the French style is dubbed Cartesian, the American pragmatic, and the British empirical. Robert Bowie of Harvard, in a book on foreign policy which stresses the need for persistence, points out that this goes against the American grain: "Our impatience, our pragmatism, our zeal for novelty," he claims, "all argue against it." Or when Santayana writes, metaphorically, that Americans are "inexperienced in poisons," he means that in a confrontation with styles of intrigue or diplomacy, certain modes of action are repugnant, an attitude summed up in the refusal of Henry Stimson, even when he was Secretary of War, to countenance a permanent espionage agency. In one sense such expressions deal with what might be called the *character of a nation,* not *national character*. It is a mode of thinking which is often possible because of our anthropocentric use of the word *nation* itself. As Paul Valéry remarked:

> A nation is characterized by its sovereign rights and property. It owns, buys, sells, fights, tries to live and thrive at others' expense; it is jealous, proud, rich or poor; it criticizes others; it has friends, enemies and sympathies; it is either artistic or inartistic and so on. In a word, nations are persons to whom we at-

---

common institutions diffuse certain influences and encourage the emergence of certain qualities in the population, to that extent you may foster a modal national character. England and France, and the Scandinavian countries probably best represent the first model. Indeed, in them you tend to have both ethnic original culture and common institutional experience working in the same direction. The United States is probably the best case of the amalgam model although it is approximated in Argentina and Brazil. Canada is a two-culture case. Yugoslavia and Nigeria are cases where there is no 'national character' in the personality sense, only a series of regional or cultural characters linked by political hegemony in a 'nation.' But the Yugoslavs probably hope to achieve more of the common culture than the Soviets have introduced.

"You must also keep in mind our strict use of the term 'mode.' A pattern may be modal, therefore serve to define the distinctive national character, even if only a modest percent of the population possesses it. For example, on a test of sadism only twenty percent of the Germans might score high. If this were still 2 or 3 times as many as the proportion in any other national character, we would consider sadism part of the German national character. Of course, many problems arise: what if all 20 percent of the sadistic Germans come from one region, from one religious or ethnic subgroup, or from one class? How meaningful is it then to call this national character?" (November 15, 1966).

tribute sentiments, rights and duties, virtues and vices, wills and responsibilities, according to an immemorial habit of simplification.[19]

But such "simplification" often tends to confuse more than to clarify. In seeking to determine what various authors mean when they talk of national character, it may be helpful to distinguish different dimensions of the problem which contain diverse referents and diverse levels of action. I would distinguish, therefore, five different elements that are often lumped together and confused as national character when writers use the term. These are:

(1) the National Creed
(2) the National Imagoes
(3) the National Style
(4) the National Consciousness
(5) the Modal Personalities

Of these, the first four are not personality attributes of individuals but compounds of history, traditions, legitimations, values, customs, and manners which have been codified more or less consciously in texts, observations or folklore, and which have become reference points for discussion by the native and the foreigner. The fifth is "national character" as Inkeles and Levinson have defined the subject. Within this space I can discuss each of these only briefly.

The national creed—I take American life for its ready examples—is the implicit or explicitly approved set of values which tends to legitimate behavior in a society and, when made conscious, to define its purposes. In the United States the distinctive values would be individualism, achievement, and equality of opportunity. Material wealth is regarded as good and as a sign of achievement. Because of the emphasis on achievement, there is also an attitude of "nothing sacred," so that old institutions or old buildings are not regarded as having any intrinsic value and can be demolished. In this respect a positive attitude toward change gets built into the society, and "progress" becomes a positive value. In a different sense, the program of the Communist Party becomes the national creed of the Soviet Union and achievement is defined not by individual criteria but in the enhancement of the community. Within this framework, ideology is a conscious selection of aspects of the value system in order to mobilize people toward the achievement of goals.

National imagoes are the diverse folk, historical, and literary characters who embody modes of response to life situations. Often they provide styles

---

[19] Paul Valéry, *Reflections on the World Today* (New York: Pantheon Books, 1948), p. 82.

of response to existential situations—to ways of confronting death, or meeting danger; sometimes they provide "approved" models, the "positive heroes," in a society because they represent the dominant values; often they provide "deviant" models for groups that cannot identify with the major values of the society.

In Russian literature one finds sharply delineated types who become imagoes for various persons: Ivan Karamazov, Stavrogin, Rakhmetov (the steel-willed revolutionary hero of Cherneyshevsky's *What Is To Be Done*, who became a conscious model for Lenin), and others. In the United States one finds such diverse figures as Daniel Boone, Huck Finn, Horatio Alger, Charles A. Lindbergh, and the various imagoes of a popular culture such as Frank Sinatra or Elvis Presley.

It is a mistake, however, to try to find the dominant or characteristic imagoes in the serious literature of a country. We are told that the nineteenth century "American," for example, was optimistic, cheerful, confident of his mastery over nature; yet the major writers of the period—Poe, Hawthorne, Melville, and James—were deeply pessimistic, metaphysical, dark and brooding, and had an "adversary" relation to the society. It is more often in popular literature, in the Western, the detective story, or in science fiction, where issues are presented in simple black-and-white, that better clues to the approved modes are to be found.

The national style is often the political style of the leadership of a country. It is a distinctive way of meeting the problems of order and adaptation, of conflict and consensus, of individual ends and communal welfare that confront any society. It is a distillation of the national values and the various imagoes that have functioned in the past, and must square itself with the traditions and history of a country. The "moralism," for example, of the American political style derives from the particular Protestant conception that treats action as the product largely of individuals (rather than "social forces"), and judges individuals as "good guys" and "bad guys." The Bolshevik political style—or, as Nathan Leites has called it, "the operational code"—is an amalgam of specific character maxims (to be controlled, purposeful, and so on) blended with a combat posture derived from a *Weltanschauung* or Ideology about its position vis-à-vis its opponents.[20]

When a nineteenth century writer such as Walter Bagehot wrote: "All

---

[20] The literature on these questions is discursive. For a discussion of the American creed and values, see Gunnar Myrdal, *An American Dilemma*, and the essay by Talcott Parsons and Winston White in *Culture and Social Character*, edited by S. M. Lipset and Leo Lowenthal. On imagoes, see David Riesman, *The Lonely Crowd*, and Martha Wolfenstein and Nathan Leites, *Movies: A Psychological Study*. On national style, see *The National Style*, edited by Elting E. Morison, particularly the essay by W. W. Rostow, *The Operational Code of the Politburo* by Nathan Leites, and my essay in *The Radical Right*.

nations have a character, and that character when once taken is, I do not say unchangeable—religion modifies it, catastrophe annihilates it—but the least changeable thing in this ever-varying and changeful world," he is in effect writing about national style. When Graham Greene talks of the "Quiet American," and other writers, such as those previously cited, talk of the character of military doctrine or of foreign affairs, they, too, are describing elements of the national style.

National consciousness—I follow here the usage of Karl Deutsch—is the self-conscious attachment of individuals to specific group symbols in an effort to differentiate themselves directly from other groups. It is what Franklin H. Giddings, of an older generation of sociologists, called the "consciousness of kind," and what is called today "national identity." This can either be crescive, as in the slow-growth and intercommunication of persons who seek a wider and more inclusive loyalty; it may be contrived, as in the efforts of leaders of various new states to forge a national identity.[21]

National character, in the popular sense of the term, has usually meant that compound of mannerisms and customs which travelers have observed, beginning in the time of Herodotus. Such observers, and one recalls Tocqueville as the most acute, are often shrewd and arresting, but after a time (compare the distance between Frances Trollope and Simone de Beauvoir) they quickly degenerate into stereotypes that become self-reinforcing. If one is to distinguish between personality configuration and the values, styles, and imagoes of a country as influences which in one way or another shape individual responses, then the idea of modal personality types can serve as the ground for the dimension of *character* in the idea of national character. But if one also seeks to maintain the idea of the *nation* as a meaningful unit of a sociocultural pattern, then one cannot eschew the examination of the national creed, imagoes, style, and consciousness as components of the cultural pattern. It is in this effort, perhaps, by searching out the interplay between personality and the components I have sought to specify, that we might yet be able to find some viable meaning in the ambiguous phrase "national character."

---

[21] Karl Deutsch, *National and Social Communication*, pp. 144–151. Deutsch, seeking to "operationalize" his concept, describes consciousness "as the interplay and feedback of secondary symbols in an information-processing system."

8

The Method of the Study of Persons

Bert Kaplan

All modern methods of psychodynamic personality study are characterized by the same basic vector: namely, the movement from an observed action or behavior of a person to the reality which underlies it. The psychodiagnostic activity of the psychologist seeks to travel in a reverse direction from the processes which resulted in the observed action or behavior. It thus may be said that the modern "method" of personality study, regardless of what technical means are utilized to elicit or observe actions, or what rules or principles are followed in inferring the underlying "facts," is a simple unitary one, and that the apparent diversity of personality study methods is relatively unimportant compared to the general, almost universal agreement about the nature and character of the task of personality study. The intention of this paper is to examine and assess this basic task, putting aside for the moment the question of the best technical means for accomplishing it. In approaching the subject in this way I am perhaps taking the term "method" in a somewhat broader way than was intended by the organizers of this symposium. I do so with the sense that a "method" has a greater importance than to be merely the technical means of accomplishing a particular aim, and that it comprehends and contains its ends or aims within itself. To consider the question of method is to consider the activity as a whole. A method, in the expanded sense in which I am using the word, is a way of proceeding, an idea or an attitude which regulates the spirit of one's relationship to what is studied, and a language or conceptual apparatus for talking about it. The question of method elevated in this way is nothing less than the question of the nature of the project which one is engaged in.

I shall consider the question of the "method" of personality study in relation to certain philosophical problems that have been raised, primarily in German and French philosophy, regarding the "method" of the human sciences in general. The distinction between the *Naturwissenschaften* or natural sciences, and the *Geisteswissenschaften* or human studies was an important theme in the writing of such philosophers as Novalis, Schleiermacher, and Dilthey, which focused specially on the methods of history and sociology. It owes a special debt to the demonstration of Descartes that the reality of consciousness is of a totally different order than that of material substances. If the criteria of matter are spatiality and causal determinism, the criterion of the mental phenomena is knowing or thinking. Descartes' dualistic theory posited two kinds of reality, a *res extensa* and a *res cognita*. Of the latter Descartes wrote in the *Meditations* (Descartes 1955: 152), ". . . I am . . . a real thing and really exist, but what kind of thing? I have answered: a thing that thinks." Descartes, in his classic search for something of which he could be certain, found this certainty only in his own thinking and concluded, "I am certain that I am a thinking thing."

Novalis, believing that the human sciences should be based on a thorough study of human nature, called for a *reale Psychologie* or *anthropologie* which could study man, not in the same spirit and by the same methods as things were studied but in the way appropriate to the phenomenon of humanness. Schleiermacher proposed a special hermeneutic or theory of interpretation for the human disciplines which took up the question of the conditions that made a correct understanding of human products and acts possible. Like Dilthey, who followed him, he reacted against the Kantian thesis of the noumenal reality which could never be reached so far as it pertained to human beings. Kant held that the transcendental self is that which knows and thus it could never be the object of knowledge. Both Schleiermacher and Dilthey returned repeatedly to the idea that we *can* reach the reality of human experience in a way that we cannot do for physical things. While our knowledge of the latter, according to Kant, is confined to what our minds constitute, human experience can be understood because it is the one object which we can know by acquaintance as well as by description. We know the mind, because it is what we are. This notion is carried further by Vico, who holds that knowledge of the human is the only real knowledge that is possible since it is only this reality that a human mind can understand, anything else being totally alien to it. We can therefore know only what we ourselves make, or what we ourselves are.

Descartes' method of systematic doubt led him to the idea of his own existence as a thinking and doubting substance, the reality of his doubting coming to be the first reality he could be certain of. His aim, however, was not to doubt but to attain certainty. He said,

> "Because I wished to give myself entirely to the search after truth, I thought that it was necessary for me to adopt an apparently opposite course and to reject as absolutely false everything concerning which I could imagine the least ground of doubt" (Descartes 1931:100).

The modern scientific method has much in common with Descartes' method of systematic doubt, raising the question of the possibility of the psychologist's turning to his own activity as the certain ground and starting place of his inquiry.

The more usual starting place has been the belief in the being of that which is studied. Science, including psychology, takes for granted the reality of the objects and events that are studied. This "believing in," or faith that what is studied is part of a natural order existing independently of the observer, has been called the natural attitude by Edmund Husserl and his followers, and naive realism by other philosophers. This attitude exempts from the method of systematic doubt what Aristotle thought to be the fundamental aspect of anything under investigation, its being. On this fundamental question the attitude of the scientist turns from doubt to presupposition. The "world" of the natural attitude contains a thinker who is an existing being, a variety of psychic events which are also presupposed as existing within a natural order, and a set of objects or real things that belong within the same order. One could indefinitely extend the list of those events whose existence within this order is presupposed. It includes all of the processes that psychologists are concerned with, starting from the person himself, his ego or self, his motives, his perceptions, his behavior and the objects to which he is directed. Psychological events then are located within the natural order and are believed to be real in the same way that everything else in this order is real. Of particular importance to this symposium, the ego or the self, the I which is the initiator of actions, is real in this way also.

Rigor in psychology ordinarily means a disbelief in whatever cannot be observed by more than one investigator. Another kind of rigor, however, is a concern that the beginnings of any inquiry have some sure ground. Philosophy has been called the science of beginnings, the study of how to begin, or of how to make a new beginning. A new beginning is a beginning without presuppositions.

The Cartesian method of reaching such a sure ground was the method of doubt. Edmund Husserl has proposed a related but somewhat different method which has come to be known as the phenomenological reduction. Husserl states that it was not necessary to deny or to be skeptical about the truth of a presupposition in order to put it out of action. It is sufficient merely to suspend or abstain from belief in it. What is to be gained from the general application of this method? Husserl (1962) proposes that this method be applied in radical fashion to the world of everyday experience and to the whole of the natural world.

> Thus all sciences which relate to this natural world, though they stand never so firm to me, though they fill me with wondering admiration, though I am far from any thought of objecting to them in the least degree, *I disconnect them all, I make absolutely no use of their standards, I do not appropriate a single one of the propositions that enter into their systems, even though their evidential value is perfect, I take none of them, no one of them serves me for*

a foundation—so long, that is, as it is understood, in the way those sciences themselves understand it, as a truth *concerning the realities of this world* (p. 100).

By thus holding in suspension or bracketing the general thesis of the natural standpoint, it is possible to withhold judgment about the facticity of the whole fact world, to disbelieve in the being of the world and of everything in it. The purpose of this drastic step is to discover the world without presuppositions. By bringing the thesis of the natural attitude to light, and holding it in abeyance, a new world appears: namely, the world as it is available to our consciousness. The experienced or phenomenal world is thus for the first time made available to us as the ground of the natural world, rather than as the imperfect representation of it. This requires a changed attitude toward the world, but equally and more profoundly, it asks us to change our attitude toward experience. This change is summarized succinctly by Sartre in the first paragraphs of *Being and Nothingness:*

> Modern thought has realized considerable progress by reducing the existent to the series of appearances which manifest it. Its aim was to overcome a certain number of dualisms which have embarrassed philosophy and to replace them by the monism of the phenomenon. . . . "In the first place we certainly thus get rid of that dualism which in the existent opposed interior to exterior. There is no longer an exterior for the existent if one means by that a superficial covering which hides from sight the true nature of the object. And this true nature in turn, if it is to be the secret reality of the thing, which one can have a presentiment of or which one can suppose but can never reach because it is the "interior" of the object under consideration—this nature no longer exists. The appearances which manifest the existent are neither interior nor exterior; they are all equal, they all refer to other appearances, and none of them is privileged. . . .
> The obvious conclusion is that the dualism of being and appearance is no longer entitled to any legal status within philosophy. The appearance refers to the total series of appearances and not to a hidden reality which would drain to itself all the *being* of the existent. And the appearance for its part is not an inconsistent manifestation of this being. . . . But if we once get away from what Nietzsche called "the illusion of worlds-behind-the-scene," and if we no longer believe in the being-behind-the-appearance, then the appearance becomes full positivity; its essence is an "appearing" which is no longer opposed to being but on the contrary is the measure of it. For the being of an existent is exactly what it appears (pp. iv).

It is not appropriate on this occasion to explore the significance of this change for the whole range of psychological questions to which it is relevant. The problem of personality study and its method, however, has a particular salience among these questions.

The suspension of belief in the real things in the world may include disbelief in a structure that is the object and foundation of the science of personality study, namely, the personality itself. It is in fact a widely held view in modern phenomenology that the suspension of belief in the thesis of the natural standpoint necessarily involves holding in abeyance the belief in the reality of the self. Although Husserl's own writings are filled with ambiguity on this question, it is clear that he does subject the empirical ego to the reduction, thereby rendering problematic its "reality" and making possible the appearance of the phenomenal ego, or of the ego which is present in experience. The consequences for the method of personality study of this rendering the empirical ego problematic is the chief question of this paper. Other areas of psychology deal with the constitution of the perceived world and with various specific psychological phenomena. Personality theory and study however are concerned with the reality of the person himself, and with his reality as a person. Thus the effects of rendering the "person" problematic should be felt first by those concerned with personality study, since the latter experience the "loss" of the object they are attempting to describe and explain. The phenomenon of the person as it actually is immanent in experience will presumably replace this lost object, but the student of personality may be forgiven the anxiety he must experience at the moment at which the reality of personality is lost and the phenomenon of personality has not yet appeared.

I had this experience myself about ten years ago when I completed the experimental study which led me into the train of thought presented here and to the discovery of the phenomenological tradition in philosophy. Initially this research sought to determine whether the productivity of subjects taking the Rorschach test could be increased. One of the conditions investigated was the repetition of the test with the request for additional responses. This request in general failed to increase the number of Rorschach responses given but it led to the discovery of a related condition which led to useful results. It was found that if the test were repeated with the instruction that only new responses different from those already given would be acceptable, subjects would give a whole new series equal in number and variety to those given on the original attempt. It was found further that a second protocol could be elicited looking somewhat like the first but with different responses. Also that a third and fourth and sometimes as many as nine or ten protocols could similarly be obtained. This somewhat unexpected finding became the basis of the 1956 study reported by Stanley Berger and myself (Kaplan and Berger 1956). The situation of having not one Rorschach picture to interpret but four to six different ones from the same subject was a somewhat startling one, especially since the protocols were considerably different from each other. The initial statistical study of the stability of seventeen Rorschach variables through the four performances indicated both a certain amount of consistency and a change, but a comparison of psychogram patterns revealed that when pairs of tests of the same subjects were compared, the pattern of movement, form and color responses remained the same in only 18 percent of the pairs.

Since the mixed findings left a certain amount of ambiguity regarding the relative preponderance of the stability of the performance as opposed to its changeability, a second study was conducted by Berger (1957). Berger sought to resolve the question by determining whether two Rorschach protocols of the same person were similar enough so that they could be matched by experienced psychologists. A series of judges were given a Rorschach protocol and asked to choose which of three other protocols were given by the same person. Ten of the judges were undergraduate psychology students, twenty were second-year psychology graduate students, and twenty were highly trained clinical psychologists from the staff of the Menninger Clinic and Topeka Veterans' Administration Hospital. Fifty judges each attempted five sortings. Only five of the fifty judges were successful at a significantly better than chance level. For all judgments pooled, the successes were at the .02 level of significance, with 42 percent successes as compared with a chance expectation of $33\frac{1}{3}$ percent. However, only the naive judges had successes that were significantly greater than the chance expectation. Neither the partly trained nor the expert group had a level significantly greater than chance. A further finding was that judges were on the whole more confident of their judgments when they were incorrect than when they were correct. The results were interpreted as indicating that the task was difficult and could be accomplished with only a negligible amount of success if any at all. It was concluded that the two protocols of the same person were in fact quite different from each other.

What is the psychologist to think when there are two or more protocols each purporting to reflect the same personality? One possibility is to decide that one of the protocols is the genuine one and the others spurious. This has actually been the reaction of many psychologists, who feel that only the initial protocol is the real one, the others being obtained under changed conditions. A second interpretation is that personality patterns are so complex that each protocol can provide no more than a part of the total personality picture. Other studies indicate, however, that individuals are able to go on producing new Rorschach responses almost indefinitely, so that while subjects do stop after one, two, or three hundred responses (to a single card), they are always *able* to produce another one. The capacity to reorganize the blot materials into a new percept appears to be inexhaustible and depends only on the person's willingness to apply energy to this purpose. It seems always *possible* to give another response to the question "What kind of person are you?" that is implicit in the Rorschach situation.

The consequence of these and a series of other similar studies was to lead me toward a "doubt" about the reality of personality as the source and underlying meaning of observed behavior and thus to a position vaguely similar to that reached by the bracketing of the general thesis of the natural standpoint and the real existence of an empirical ego. Somewhat incongruously at a time when almost all personality theorists are vigorously defending the reality of inner states against the skepticism of behavior theorists like B. F. Skinner, for whom only what is directly observable by the psychologist about other people is admissible as real, phenomenology appears to be joining in this skepticism.

This situation is worth commenting on and attempting to clarify. Both behavior theory and phenomenology hold in abeyance "belief in" the reality of a personality system which is the source of acts or behavior. Behavior theory will not admit such a reality because it cannot be seen. What is real for it are environmental events and the behavior of organisms, and both may be said to belong to the same natural order. Skinner (1964) says, for example:

> If psychology is a science of mental life—of the mind, of conscious experience—then it must develop and defend a special methodology, which it has not yet done successfully. If it is, on the other hand, a science of the behavior of organisms, human or otherwise, then it is part of biology, a natural science for which tested and highly successful methods are available (p. 79).

It seems that what is at issue in Skinner's behaviorism is chiefly the attempt to adhere rigorously to the natural standpoint and a sensitivity to the complications and difficulties of treating the mental life in these terms.

The phenomenological approach is sensitive to exactly the same conceptual difficulties, but rather than excluding the difficult phenomenon of mind, it faces them resolutely and attempts to "develop and defend a special methodology" which will be the method of a new science of lived experience, a science which does not begin by presupposing the metaphysics of the natural standpoint but begins rather with the certain ground of being as phenomenon. Since Kant demonstrated to almost everyone's satisfaction that all constructions of the world, including scientific ones, are constituted within experience and have as their ground not the noumenal order but the categories of mind and experience itself, the Skinnerian view that the natural order is all-encompassing and whatever does not conform with its rules does not exist, is no longer convincing.

Dynamic psychology has attempted to defend the reality of the psychological by insisting on the reality of the "inner man" or ego. This ego is not the ego of Freud but rather ego as the source of all actions, and as the knower. In other words, it is the subject of all human predicates. Modern dynamic psychology has taken as a matter of first importance the defense of the reality of the ego against the skepticism of the behaviorist, who doubts that it exists because he can't see it. This view is taken chiefly because through it, mental phenomena can be grounded and located in the world of the natural standpoint.

The basic categories in terms of which we think of anything real—substance, quality, property, and relationship—were given to us by Aristotle. These categories comprehend both animate and inanimate matter.

According to Aristotle, anything that is, or has being, has that being as substance. The occupying of space thus becomes the basic, indeed the only mode of existence. The actual is synonymous with the geographical. The Aristotelian metaphysics has been described as an exposition of the subject-predicate structure in the Greek language. Any statement begins by specifying in the subject the substance or real thing that is being talked about. The remainder of the statement predicates a quality of the subject or its relation to other subjects. The subject has a true nature or being of its own irrespective of what in particular is predicated about it. However, this essence is also the ground of its individual appearances and is "realized" or made manifest in them. The essence is also described as potentiality for all of the predicates that can be made for it tending toward the manifestation of these predicates. This mode of thinking is carried over to thinking about living beings. The various activities of man are predicates which express his nature and potentialities. The tendency for this nature to unfold in actions is the equivalent of the tendency of substance to manifest itself in its qualities.

Modern psychology has inherited the subject-predicate structure for its sentences also, and it seems almost impossible to say or think anything except in this form. Nevertheless, certain phenomenologists, most particularly Jean-Paul Sartre, have made a bold effort to dispense with the ego as the source of motives and acts and to conceive of a consciousness which exists without this ground. The intent of this effort is simply to be consistent in suspending judgment about *all* questions of fact, including presuppositions of the factuality of the ego, so that the phenomenal reality can stand forth fully.

What would a psychology of personality and of personality study be like without the concept of an empirical ego? What would be the method of such a psychology? The first step toward the realization of such a method is to discard the method of the psychology of the natural standpoint, namely, the movement from the phenomena of consciousness and action to the inner reality which they manifest. When this inner reality has been placed in brackets, consciousness and its structure stand forth in full positivity. It becomes necessary—and possible—to deal with the phenomenon itself. We have in psychology been so accustomed to dealing with any phenomenon by inquiring into its antecedents, its consequences and its relations with other phenomena, and in general acting as though it could be defined by these external relationships, that the possibility of an inquiry into the phenomenon itself comes as something of a surprise, and finds us without a ready method. We can "explain" an aggressive act by postulating the motive of aggression and that motive by antecedent experiences, but it is difficult to step into this chain of explanation and investigate the act itself, or the motive itself. In the next pages I propose to suggest the outlines of the method for the inquiry into the phenomenon itself in the belief that this method is not merely an alternative to present practice, but that it is a step in the direction of deepening psychological analysis.

The general method I am proposing may be characterized at the outset as an "ontological" method. That is, it aims directly at what the phenomenon "is" or at the question of its being. Perhaps the best analogy is to the method of chemistry, which seems able to pull apart whatever substance it is concerned with, analyze its structure, its components, and the manner of its constitution. The latter particularly is crucial since the significant moment for any phenomenon is the moment when it comes into being or "appears." A suggestion made by Joseph Lyons in his recent book, *Psychology and the Measure of Man*, (Lyons 1963:253) is that instead of utilizing the test responses "to learn something about the real, or true, version of the person who faces him across the desk [as though] the person who faces the psychologist, insofar as he is a test subject, is somehow not really real [but] . . . at best a valuable or useful representative of his own true self. . . . the test response may be described and examined in its own right." Instead of asking what the response represents one can ask what it is.

The easiest and quickest way to appreciate the nature of a test response is to imagine oneself giving it. One of the first things that will be felt is the ambiguity which Vernon recognized in the 1930s when he said that there is "a fundamental difficulty which cannot be evaded, namely—the subject who knows his personality is under investigation cannot react normally" (Vernon 1934:174). The test response occurs under the "stare" of an observer. It does not flow spontaneously and directly from some inner wellspring but rather is what Goffman calls a "performance." It may also be a "front" or "that part of the individual's performance which regularly functions . . . to define the situation for those who observe the performance" (Goffman 1959:22). The response serves, it appears, less to express "personality" than to constitute a personality that does not exist. It is a commonplace in psychology that motives are known by the end-states that actions move toward. It has remained for Sartre (1956:437) to interpret the motive as the movement toward a future that does not yet exist. The motive does not cause the act, he says, but is the act. One might equally well say that the act is a motive, in the sense that both are movement toward the end.

In phenomenology, the concept of intentionality has dealt with this question. Husserl borrowed the concept of intentionality from Franz Brentano (1874), who attempted to be explicit about the difference between physical and mental phenomena. The former, he said, manifest extension and a spatial location. Mental phenomena are clearly located in time, but more important, they are *Vorstellung*, or the presenting of something which they themselves are not. The term intentionality was introduced to indicate the essential character of a mental phenomenon as a constituting phenomenon. Brentano seems to have had in mind the constituting by the mental act of its objects, as when we perceive a tree and thus constitute the perceived tree, but Husserl extended the concept to the noetic act of constituting the subject or self.

In the personality study situation, the subject by his test response constitutes for the psychologist a self which can be taken as the source of all acts. Psychologists, with only occasional exceptions, have been content to discover this constituted self. The intentionality of the response, however, is not this self, but the constituting or positing of it. It would appear, therefore, that the proper psychological attainment is the appreciation of the intentionality of the act. Wilhelm Dilthey proposed that the method of the *Naturwissenschaften* or natural sciences is explanation or the construction of theories to account for what is observed. The method proposed for the *Geisteswissenschaften,* or human studies, is understanding. Because what is studied is a human phenomenon, and we know what a human phenomenon is because we ourselves are human, it is possible to know an act, or the product of an act, from the inside. We can live our way into it. The hermeneutic, or method of interpretation of Schleiermacher, was to move from the printed text or action of an author as it is available to the observer, to the "inner form" or meaning that is involved in the "germination" or constitution of the text. We can understand because by living ourselves into the author's act we can reconstruct the path by which it was created.

I believe this is the proper method of personality study. The intentionality of the act or test response can only be understood if we put aside the aim of discovering what caused it. The act's own reality is a movement from a deprivation or absence of being to a full, determined, completed, finished fact. As Joseph Lyons suggests (1963), the procedure of the inquiry in the Rorschach test is the prototype of the kind of clinical investigation in which this reconstruction is performed. The vital center of the inquiry is the phenomenon of reflection, the return to a human reality in the mode of knowingly placing oneself into it again. This reconstruction or recreation makes great demands on the humanness of the investigator. The impossibility of a mechanical mode which treats the subject as an object and which is itself object-like or computer-like is amply clear, since such a mistaken presupposition moves the investigation in the wrong direction. But movement in the correct direction is not sufficient. It is not enough for the psychologist simply to open his eyes and expect that he will see his subject's reality. The visual senses operate in this way, but the intentionality of the act cannot be *seen*. It can only be reached by a movement into the mode of action. According to Hegel and Marx, a human existence is produced by work, and entering into the existence and actions of another person is especially hard work. Real reflectiveness does not flow easily and spontaneously out of natural inclination. The psychologist's task is possible but difficult, as any true task should be. Confronting it, we have a right to feel encouraged at the prospect of real attainments, but also chastened at the amount of labor, effort, and commitment that it will require. Becoming a real psychologist is not an easy achievement because above all it requires the psychologist himself to become thoroughly humanized. On the other hand, labor at the task of understanding the human being is precisely the kind of humanizing work which is the condition for this transformation.

What significance does this "method," if I may call it that, have for the issues in the culture and personality field that many of us here are concerned with? The immediate impression is that it offers the prospect of incredibly great difficulties for application cross-culturally. To the work of living oneself into the actions of another person is added the work of living oneself into another culture. The latter is the anthropologist's equivalent of the task I have been outlining. There is no reason why someone who has performed this work should not then undertake the psychological task. On the other hand, I can see no possibility whatsoever of success for the psychologist who does not either in preparation, or simultaneously, understand feelingly his subject's cultural milieu. Vico's words seem relevant:

> In the thick darkness . . . there shines the eternal and never failing light of a truth beyond all question: that the world of civil society has certainly been made by men, and that its principles are therefore to be found within the modifications of our own human mind. Whoever reflects on this cannot but marvel that the philosophers should have bent all their energies to the study of the world of nature, which, since God made it, He alone knows, and that they should have neglected the study of the world of nations, or civil world, which, since men had made it, men could come to know (1961: p. 52).

It is a Hegelian notion that man recreates nature by his work and that the transformed man-made order is the cultural order. The vast construction we call culture in which man realizes infinitely more of the possibilities of his freedom than he could in his own individuality, is also the product of his intentionality. The same constitutive process that is involved in action and the products of action is present in the creation of culture. Cultural phenomena are not dead, inert forms, they are the embodiment of human activities and values. History therefore is human history, or the history of the modifications of the human mind. Society is a form taken by human life when men acknowledge each other's reality. The method of the human sciences, and in the present context this means the culture and personality field, is the description and understanding of the form of humanness which is incorporated into human institutions.

The study of motivational processes has had an important role in cross-cultural studies of personality, since the problem that has appeared the most critical to theorists has been the character of the motivation of social performance and the role of motivational processes in social systems. In the last few years there has been a marked trend toward emphasizing the part that cognitive processes play in social cohesion, but the contribution to culture-personality studies that psychologists are expected to make still focuses on the description of motivational processes.

I believe this theoretical formulation takes both culture and personality as existing in the world of the natural attitude. In such a realm the only questions that can be asked are questions of causal relations. For a turn-of-the-century German philosopher of the human sciences like Dilthey, however, a cultural phenomenon was the embodiment of a particular form of historical consciousness or knowledge of world and self. Thus Husserl (1965) stated the phenomenological version of the culture and personality problem as follows:

> We pose the question: what constitutes the characteristic structure of the European mind? . . . We are obviously dealing here under the term "Europe" with the unity of life, activity and creativity of the human spirit, with all their aims, interests, concerns and efforts, with the forms their aims have taken, with institutions and organizations. . . . all inwardly bound together . . . in the unity of a characteristic mental structure. In this way there is attributed to persons, to associations of persons, and to their cultural achievements an all-uniting character."

In closing I return briefly to the question of method. I have interpreted the term expansively. The great methods for the attainment of certainty have been reason, doubt, faith, experiment, empiricism, and one or two others. The method we have been discussing can, properly be called reconstruction. It is a returning to an event that has occurred and repeating it with the addition of reflection and understanding. The new structure is the old one brought into the light of comprehension and meaningfulness. It is a method which produces a deepened human existence.

BIBLIOGRAPHY

BERGER, STANLEY, *Similarities of Rorschach Records Obtained Through Re-Testing Procedures as Indicated by the Ability of Judges to Match Protocols.* Ph.D. Thesis, University of Kansas, 1957.

DESCARTES, RENE, *Discourse on Method,* translated by Elizabeth Haldane and G. R. T. Ross. New York: Dover Publications, Inc., 1931.

———, *Meditations,* trans. by Elizabeth Haldane and G. R. T. Rose, from *The Philosophical Works of Descartes.* New York: Dover Publications, Inc., 1955.

EPSTEIN, SEYMOUR, ELIZABETH LUNDBORG, and BERT KAPLAN, "Allocation of Energy and Rorschach Responsivity," *Journal of Clinical Psychology,* Vol. 19, No. 3, 1956, pp. 304–309.

GOFFMAN, ERVING, *The Presentation of Self in Everyday Life.* New York: Doubleday and Company, Inc., Anchor, 1959.

HUSSERL, EDMUND, *Philosophy and the Crisis of European Man* in Jean T. Wilde and William Kimmel (trans. and eds.), *The Search for Being,* pp. 378–

413. New York: The Noonday Press, a subsidiary of Farrar, Straus and Giroux, Inc., 1965.
HUSSERL, EDMUND, *Ideas,* trans. by W. R. Boyce Gibson. New York: Collier Books, 1962.
KAPLAN, BERT, and STANLEY BERGER, "Increments and Consistency of Performance in Four Repeated Rorschach Administrations," *Journal of Projective Techniques,* Vol. 20, No. 3, 1956, pp. 304–309.
LYONS, JOSEPH, *Psychology and the Measure of Man.* New York: The Free Press, 1963.
SARTRE, JEAN-PAUL, *Being and Nothingness,* translated by Hazel E. Barnes. New York: Philosophical Library, 1956.
SKINNER, B. F., "Behaviorism at Fifty," in T. W. Wann (ed.), *Behaviorism and Phenomenology: Contending Bases for Modern Psychology,* pp. 79–97. Chicago: University of Chicago Press, 1964.
VERNON, P. E., "The Attitude of the Subject in Personality Testing," *Journal of Applied Psychology,* Vol. 18, 1935, pp. 165–177.
VICO, GIAMBATTISTA, *The New Science,* translated by Thomas Goddard Bergin and Max Harold Fisch. New York: Doubleday and Company, Inc., Anchor, 1961.

PART TWO

The Formation of Personality

9

Personality and the Biological Nature of Man

John O. Ellefson

Most of the data used in this paper come from recent field studies of nonhuman primates.[1] From these studies examples of intraspecific variations in personality, principally of temperament, will be given for several species of primates, and the possible adaptiveness of these variations will be discussed. Variations among groups of the same species in terms of modes of group temperament will then be similarly examined. The modal temperaments of the various species will be discussed in the context of the social organization of the species and the relationship of the social organization to modes of subsistence. Suggestions will then be made concerning the adaptive significance of the interspecific differences noted. Finally, trends in temperament within the biological order of primates will be discussed in the light of their potential importance to an understanding of the evolutionary emergence of man.

This paper is based upon four broad assumptions concerning biological aspects of human personality that the author regards as sound and defensible but which, for lack of time and space, will not here be defended:

(1) The concept of personality has some validity as a biological entity.
(2) Intraspecific differences in personality are influenced by individual genetic differences as well as by epigenetic influences.
(3) The modal or normative personalities of species have adaptive significance; that is, norms of personality are the result of an adaptive process, an interplay between natural selection and the genetic variation intrinsic to sexual reproduction and mutation through time in populations.
(4) Interspecific homologies and functional similarities in personality exist to a degree that allows meaningful statements concerning their significance which apply in some degree across taxa.

Most fieldworkers in primatology have been impressed with individual variations in characteristic patterns of interaction among the members of social groups of nonhuman primates, and have reported their observations under the various captions of personality, temperament, character, and comportment. The parameter in question has been loosely defined, but there is general agreement that variations occur among nonhuman primates in habitual modes of social interaction, that these represent an important dimension of the social life of nonhuman primates and that, in at least some aspects, the modes of behavior resemble the parameters of personality used to describe habitual modes of interpersonal interaction of human beings.

Jolly (1967:1) summarizes the prevailing attitude among students of the social behavior of nonhuman primates concerning the functional communality of a personality parameter within the Order of Primates: "Men, apes, Old and New World monkeys, and some prosimians live in permanent groups in which each individual must recognize and adjust its behavior to the character of other individuals." According to Jolly (1967), temperament or character traits have been important in primate evolution because they integrally relate to the interindividual interactions that are the basis of social organization. Differences in temperament among species will accordingly affect social interactions and thus also affect social organization. The differences in temperament and social organization observed among species of primates ultimately reflect different adaptations to different modes of subsistence.

INTRASPECIES VARIATION

General agreement that the concept of personality may be applied to all primates has not led fieldworkers to a detailed quantification of personality and its related variables among nonhuman primates. Statements about personality differences are in large part impressionistic, based upon one or two quantified variables. One reason for this relative neglect of personality assessment in field studies has been an overriding concern with collecting data on general social behavior and general ecology, which have been regarded as more fundamental and thus more important information. Investigators studying species that have been the subjects of little observation under natural conditions expectably tend first to collect the data regarded as basic.

Jay (1963:1965) describes the personalities of adult males and females in a group of langurs, *Presbytis entellus*, on the basis of observations of differences among them in maternal behavior, tolerance for the proximity of other members of the group, and intensity of reactions, gestures, and vocalizations. She provides evidence that every adult male in the group may be distinguished from every other adult male because of variations in social interactions. These differences can be thought of as constituting unique personalities. Jay also reports that a female's temperament affects her interest in infants and her ability to handle them appropriately.

Writing on "paternal care" among Japanese macaques, *Macaca fuscata,* Itani (1959) entitles one section of his paper "The Personality of the Protecting Individuals." This passage describes the personalities of various adult males, using the variables of sociability (general ability to make peaceful or friendly contacts with other group members), aggressiveness, and interest in spending time in the center of the group (centripetality being correlated positively with status). Males were ranked high or low in each variable. A high rating in these variables correlates positively with a high status of dominance. The personalities were then ordered by rank according to the amount of "paternal" care given by individuals in each category. There is some evidence that those individuals showing a high degree of paternal care are changing status and are using paternal care as a means of moving upward socially. Paternal behavior of carrying immature offspring allows a central position in the group even to males of low positions of dominance.

Schaller (1963:80) describes individual differences among mountain gorillas, *Gorilla gorilla berengei,* in the following way: "Free living gorillas exhibit great individual variation in their affective behavior, and the spectrums of emotions exhibited by the members of the same group to my presence varied from excitement to seeming disinterest; in other words, there were nervous individuals and calm ones, aggressive individuals and shy ones." He states that adult females were generally more placid in their reactions to him than adult males and that young adult males were more varied in their reactions than older males.

Schaller's judgments concerning differences in affective behavior appear to have been largely based on reactions of animals to his presence rather than on their styles of interacting among themselves, but presumably the temperamental differences thus determined also apply in relations of gorillas to other gorillas.

The existence of variations of personality within social groups of nonhuman primates leads to the question of the adaptive significance of the variations. Aside from the presumed advantage of genetic variation within a population in providing potential flexibility to meet the vagaries of changing pressures of selection, it is not clear whether polymorphism in personality has selective value. If polymorphism has such value, is it specific or general; that is, does selection favor any one of the polymorphisms or does it favor a particular set of forms? Polymorphism in personality may be seen as advantageous in filling efficiently the various roles in a primate society. We should note, however, that sexual dimorphism, age (young or old), and close association during immaturity with mothers of various personalities (influencing status, high or low) ensure that eight types of "personalities" will always exist. These eight types would be sufficient to fill the roles of most nonhuman primate societies. What is probably occurring in these primate societies is selection toward a modal personality, perhaps bimodal, male and female. In sexually reproducing species, the resultant genetic variation is actually under constant selective pressure toward reduction. Much of socialization in these societies (as is also perhaps the case in most human societies) involves shaping the extremely large number of constitutional types into the relatively few roles required for social life. The phenotypic variation we see is only a small fraction of the possible range of genetic variation in a society or population.

The above situation might be described as the occurrence of variations in personality *in spite of* strict socialization and strong selective pressures operating against the full genetic range of expression. Evidence among rhesus monkeys, *Macaca mulatta* (Kaufmann 1965), and baboons, *Papio cynocephalus* (Hall and DeVore 1965), suggests that males who rank high in the dominance hierarchy are responsible for a disproportionately high number of pregnancies as compared with low-ranking males. Because ranking is partly or wholly dependent on fighting ability among rhesus monkeys (Sade 1967) and probably also among baboons, one would expect much more uniformity of male temperament than is the case. One mechanism working against a sharp modality is that female rhesus monkeys within a group do not become pregnant or give birth at a disproportionate rate matching their disparate dominance rankings (Kaufman 1967). Furthermore, personality comprises many traits, the genetic bases of which are probably located on several (if not all) chromosomes, and these chromosomes segregate independently during meiosis. These factors tend to buffer the effects of strong selection in one direction for temperament, resulting in continued variation.

Summarizing these field observations, it may be said that differences in personality exist among nonhuman primates. Various of the traits are used to enhance individual recognition, role differentiation, and dominance ranking; that is, in ordering the relationships among group members that form social organization. Sexual reproduction ensures that the genetic components of personality variation will be present even in the face of strong selective pressure diminishing variation. It seems probable that the particular variation occurring at any given time is of minor adaptive significance. This does not deny that genetic variation contributing to variation in personality has been important in the evolution of primate social organization or that the modal personality of any population is the result of natural selection and is therefore of great adaptive significance.

INTERGROUP VARIATION AND PERSONALITY

Individual personalities in one group may affect interactions of that group with other groups and the adaptive response of the group in patterns of subsistence. Group differences in intergroup reactions may largely reflect the personalities of single or a few group members, or they may be reflections of the modal personalities of groups. The influence of individual personalities upon intergroup contact is usually the most striking in cases of territorial aggression; that is, when one group attempts to displace another group spatially. Such displacement is often done to gain food and has obvious adaptive significance, both short and long term. A classic example of active vying for limited resources is provided by the colony of rhesus monkeys established on Cayo Santiago, Puerto Rico by C. R. Carpenter in 1938. When the monkeys were first released, the 34-acre island did not provide adequate space or natural foods for the colony. The monkeys formed into five groups. A group that included an unusually robust male, Diablo (Carpenter 1942), who fought and even killed males of other groups (Rioch 1967, quoting conversations with Carpenter), was able to displace other groups and gained access to the entire island. Although this kind of fighting would be maladaptive if population density were low in proportion to the supply of food, it is highly adaptive when the population is so great that equal sharing of food results in starvation of the entire population. It is significant that when Diablo was experimentally removed from the group (caged), the group could no longer range freely over the island. It is not known whether Diablo's habitual modes of interaction changed to fit the situation on Cayo Santiago or whether he was behaving as he always had. Nevertheless, his prowess demonstrates how extreme personality types are sometimes advantageous to the individual, to his group, and ultimately to the population.

Less dramatic than the above example, but still instructive, are data on intergroup behavior of gibbons (Carpenter 1940; Ellefson 1967a, 1967b). Gibbon groups comprise one adult male, one adult female, and their young. These groups live in adjoining territories which they defend against one another. Adult males are the primary protagonists in intergroup conflicts. Males vary in their ability to displace other males and the groups from disputed sources of food in the no-man's land between territories. Dominant males thus gain a disproportionate amount of food from disputed sources for themselves and their mates and offspring. Generally, antagonism between males spaces the groups of the population economically, but when food is scarce, individual differences would allow the survival of some groups at the expense of others, insuring survival of the population.

Researchers have also been impressed by the effects of individual personalities on the particulars of social organization, giving each group distinctive traits, its own structural idiosyncracies. The most comprehensive studies of these kinds of group differences and their possible relationship to personality have been conducted by personnel of the Japan Monkey Center observing Japanese macaques. Paternal caretaking behavior and its correlation with personality discussed earlier in this chapter occurs in only two of the many groups of Japanese macaques so far studied (Itani 1959). This kind of group difference may be greatly influenced by differences of personality among the dominant males in each group because, among groups of Japanese macaques, dominant males have a generally pervasive effect on over-all social organization (Itani *et al.* 1963).

Researchers of the Japan Monkey Center have collected a wealth of information on various innovations in food habits and the spread of such innovations among macaque groups. Their data show how the inventiveness of individuals with respect to new foods and how the receptivity of individuals to new foods influence group adaptibility to varying opportunities for subsistence. Individuals react differently to the opportunities for inventiveness in this respect, and the groups to which they belong benefit or fail to benefit accordingly (Kawamura 1959; Miyadi 1964; Tsumori 1967).

Students of primate social behavior have suggested that differences in dominant modal personalities could be the result of different selective pressures arising from different subsistence requirements in different ecological settings within the range of distribution of the species. Perhaps pressures of selection differentiate modal personalities in different areas and these modal types are in turn influenced by forms of socialization peculiar to different habitats. It seems probable that these adaptive processes continually interact, allowing particular adjustments to subsistence requirements by each group in its particular home range. This flexibility within a species allows a relative maximizing of numbers by enabling groups and other subpopulation units to adjust more efficiently to the differential challenges of particular micro-habitats.

SPECIES AND MODAL PERSONALITIES

In addition to distinctive individual variations in personality among nonhuman primates, field primatologists report impressions of the existence of modal personalities, often designated as temperament, that characterize species. It is thought that these differences relate in some fundamental way to the different modes of subsistence of each species. Statements concerning correlations between personality, social organization, and modes of subsistence have necessarily been general and, for the most part, have been offered as tentative hypotheses of heuristic value. These hypothetical correlations have most often concerned arboreal and terrestrial living and the presence or absence of pressure from predators. Washburn and DeVore (1961) state that a causal correlation exists between the aggressive temperament of adult male baboons and the pressure from predators in their largely terrestrial life on the African savannah. Jay (1965:249) suggests that a major factor accounting for differences in the temperaments and the forms of social organization of rhesus monkeys and langurs is a difference in pressure from predators:

> Among African baboons as among Indian rhesus macaques there is strong selective advantage for powerful aggressive adult males with large canines, and

for forms of social behavior that produce constant alertness and increase the ability of the group to react quickly to danger. These are essential factors in the effective defense of plains-living baboons. For a baboon, life in a group is necessary to survival. This is not so for a langur, as is evident from the small proportion of adult males that can and do live apart from a bisexual social group.

At the time they were offered, these suggestions were warranted by the data available, but it is now realized that the circumstances are more complex. Among primates are several subordinal lines of specialization each of which shows considerable internal variation among species in social organization, and patterns of subsistence (Washburn 1966). In her study of lemurs, Jolly (1966; 1967) describes a variety of social organizations and temperaments occurring among these prosimians that parallels the grades of complexity that are seen in the evolutionarily more advanced suborders of primates (apes and man, New World monkeys and Old World monkeys).

Crook and Gartlan (1966) sort various primate species into different grades according to complexity of social organization and ecological adaptation. Although I do not agree completely with their delineation of grades or their choices of species within each grade, it is clear that such grades are distinguishable and that they cut across phylogenetic lines. This parallelism and cross-cutting of taxa is to be expected within the subordinal lines because, although each line has its own general diagnostic features of gross anatomy, there have been many specializations in each species or genus. It is not surprising that these specializations have often been changes in social behavior, and consequently social organization, because adaptation through social organization is a hallmark of the primates, and splitting within the order has involved variations on this theme.

Available data on the anthropoid apes contain some information suggesting the significance of these differences in temperament, social organization, and subsistence patterns. Reynolds (1965:704) argues that the differences in temperament between chimpanzees ("volatile, lively, excitable") and gorillas ("morose, sullen placid") is "most clearly related to difference in social organization and foraging pattern." Reynolds' summary (1965:704–705) concerning differences in organization and patterns of subsistence follows:

> The gorilla is less arboreal and less frugivorous than the chimpanzee; it lives in permanent groups while the chimpanzee does not, does not exhibit the vocal chorusing typical of chimpanzees, has a more stereotyped display than the chimpanzee. Chimpanzees are better able to exploit dry-season zones than gorillas. Their food supply is located in different places at different times of the year while the gorilla's is not, so that food-finding is a greater problem for the chimpanzee than it is for the gorilla. The looser social organization and development of group chorusing in chimpanzees may be a response to the difference in the pattern of food distribution.

The common white-handed gibbon, *Hylobates lar,* provides a third distinctive pattern of temperament, social organization, and subsistence patterns among the Pongidae (Carpenter 1940; Ellefson 1967a). Adult gibbons are highly antagonistic toward other adult gibbons except their mates. This pervasive antagonism results in a dispersal of small groups. Territorial boundaries of each group are actively defended by a mated pair (primarily the male) against encroachment by neighboring groups. Antagonism is somehow overcome between the mated pair, probably through grooming and sexual behavior, and they are able to tolerate one another, occupy the same territory, and procreate while retaining an air of aloof individuality. The gibbon groups, the homologues of human nuclear families in terms of numbers, age, and sex categories of their members, are closed social units. The maximum size is six individuals. Territorial size is small, 50 to 300 acres. Gibbons feed from an estimated 200 or more species of plants, and individual plants of many species tend to be dispersed rather than clumped.

The traits of the gibbon contrast markedly with those of the chimpanzee, yet both forms are apes that are primarily arboreal (gibbons are almost exclusively so), mainly fruit eating, and live in tropical rain forests. The key to the differences between them may lie in the details of their different patterns of subsistence.[2] Crook (1964; 1965) has found interesting correlations between subsistence patterns and social organization among birds that suggest instructive analogies in the behavior of chimpanzees and gibbons. Crook's findings show, among other things, that birds living the year-round in pairs in a common territory which they defend show sexual and seasonal monomorphism (as do gibbons, but not chimpanzees) and eat foods that are either cryptic or dispersed rather evenly over the habitat, whereas birds that flock during at least some seasons of the year show sexual and seasonal dimorphism and eat foods that appear in scattered clumps. The differences in social organization and temperament of the chimpanzees and gibbons are probably not due simply to the fact that chimpanzees' food is in abundant clumps during some seasons of the year (Goodall 1965; Reynolds and Reynolds 1965) and that the gibbons' diet is dispersed. The functional analogies with circumstances reported to exist among birds are striking enough, however, to suggest the value of long field studies (ten years or more) on each species of primate with considerable emphasis on the details of ecology including the patterns of dispersal of major foods.

IMPLICATIONS WITH RELATION TO EARLY MAN

The differences among species of nonhuman primates in modal personality (temperament), social organization, and patterns of subsistence have profound implications with respect to attempts to infer the nature of the social behavior of early forms of man. It is useful to enumerate all traits that have been important throughout the evolution of primates, but reliance upon such common denominators is misleading in reconstructions of particular phyletic lines. Similarly, the inclusion of traits from distantly related species of primates to formulate a concept of a conglomerate ancestral population is also suspect. Man arose from one ancestral anthropoid species among which specializations in temperament and social organization distinguishing them from contemporaneous, related species of primates undoubtedly already existed. The differences among the species of anthropoid apes in these adaptive specializations presents a serious problem of choice in formulating a model for reconstructing early hominid social behavior.

Because available evidence is scanty, only a tentative choice of species for a model may be made, but I think it is necessary to choose a single species. In the matters of complex subsistence patterns, complex social organization, and proximity to man of phylogenetic relationship, the chimpanzee *(Pan satyrus)* offers the best choice. My use of the chimpanzee as the model implies the usual disclaimer concerning its direct ancestral relation to man, and depends for validity on the assumption that the modern chimpanzee resembles the common ancestor of chimpanzees and man in the traits being discussed. To the degree that specializations have evolved among chimpanzees in the relevant parameters after the splitting of the common ancestral stock, the arguments presented here are, of course weakened.

The following aspects of chimpanzee life should be included in the model:

(1) *Pan satyrus* has the widest distribution of any single species of anthropoid apes. The habitat ranges from climax tropical rain forest in West Africa to riverine semideciduous forest bordering the savannah in East Africa. The basic social organization of chimpanzees is flexible enough to allow efficient exploitation of these different habitats. Although Goodall (1965) and Reynolds and Reynolds (1965) report highly similar organizations among chimpanzees in both transitional, deciduous woodland-gallery rain forests and in rain forests, there are verbal reports that personnel of the Japan Monkey Center studying chimpanzees along the savannah forest edge in Uganda have found groups that are well defined and spatially cohesive in contrast with the loosely organized populations described by Goodall and the Reynolds. If these reports are accurate, they indicate that chimpanzees have the capacity to alter their social organization to meet subsistence requirements of different habitats and perhaps to meet increased pressure from predators.

(2) Chimpanzees make and use tools to help get foods (Goodall 1965). Tool use and tool making involve learning; the continuity from generation to generation of tools and techniques depends upon learning.

146   The Formation of Personality

Epigenetic flexibility of this kind has allowed a wide distribution of *Pan satyrus* without further specialization and subsequent speciation.
(3) Among chimpanzees, a division of labor between males and females exists beyond the givens of sexual reproduction and infant rearing. Adult males range more widely during foraging than females, and are thus more likely to locate the scattered clumps of fruit trees bearing seasonal fruits. Finding foods of this kind often precipitates vocalizing by males, and chimpanzees from the surrounding areas then congregate, feed, and join in the chorus of vocalizations (Goodall 1965; Reynolds and Reynolds 1965).
(4) Chimpanzees share food. An infant begs for food from its mother, and the mother either hands it food or allows it to take food from her mouth (Van Lawick-Goodall and Van Lawick 1965). Chimpanzees also beg from one another when one is eating a monkey or hare it has killed.
(5) Chimpanzees are gregarious. Although their temperament is volatile, they show a high proportion of friendly conspecific contacts as compared with agonistic contacts. There is much elaborate, friendly social contact, which forms strong bonds allowing relationships to persist over long periods of separation. Subgroups within the population mix freely, separate, reconstitute, and so on as subsistence demands change daily, weekly, and seasonally.

Edge-of-forest living, a tool tradition, flexibility of social organization as an adaptation to diversified habitats, a division of labor regarding subsistence activities, food sharing, and a volatile but basically friendly temperament are thus all aspects of the mode of life of this single species of nonhuman primate.

Chimpanzees offer a model for reconstructing the life ways of early man that is much more complex and subtle than most anthropologists had thought ten years ago. Several large gaps still remain, however, between information supplied by this model and the specializations involved in hominization. Among these are the circumstances leading to the development of bipedalism and the elaboration of techniques of making tools that characterize *Australopithecus* as well as modern and other extinct forms of man. Bipedalism may have arisen in connection with life at the edge of the forest (Washburn and Shirek 1967) which, in conjunction with the elaboration of tool traditions, allowed a later colonization of the savannah by species of *Australopithecus*. This change to a terrestrial way of life involving an increase in pressure from predators and a gradual shift in subsistence patterns *may* have been accompanied by profound changes in temperament toward heightened aggressiveness, but I think this possibility has been overstated.[3] Whatever increase may have occurred in propensity for aggression must have been counterbalanced by pressures for communal cooperation. The hominid phyletic line has been characterized by a remarkable lack of speciation. Among factors that may have inhibited speciation are the development of increased adaptibility in social organization allowing the colonization of habitats without speciating and the greater and greater advantages for survival coming from the diffusion among groups of learned patterns of subsistence, including tool technology. Whether such diffusion implies tolerance of strangers or conquest is currently moot.

SUMMARY

On the basis of observations made in the field, I have here argued that the concept of personality may validly be applied to nonhuman primates, and I have presented data on the subjects of intraspecific variations in personality and specific modal personalities among these primates. Certain data and theoretical considerations suggest to me that many differences in personality occur in spite of the pressures of natural selection toward a modal type. Among field observers of nonhuman primates, a general impression exists that there are differences in the modal temperaments of species and that these differences are somehow related to differences in ecology, but available data are insufficient for making definitive statements about the details of such correlations. Until such correlations can be made in detail, we cannot fully understand the adaptive significance of particular temperaments in particular social organizations meeting particular requirements of subsistence. To answer this question, additional and lengthy field observation is necessary. In the meantime, inferences about the human condition drawn from data on nonhuman primates should be received only as the tentative approximations they are meant to be.

NOTES

(1) This chapter is selective rather than comprehensive in its coverage of available information on personality among the nonhuman primates. Data were selected partly to show the range of existing information and partly to illustrate theoretical issues that I think are important in reconstructing the evolution of human social organization. Because many of the ideas presented here arose in discussions over the past few years with other fieldworkers, acknowledgement of the originators of the ideas is sometimes not made. I hope such omissions will not be viewed as slights or plagiarism by those originators, whom I cannot always identify with certainty. I wish to acknowledge a special debt to Sherwood L. Washburn along with a general indebtedness to my fellow graduate students in the Department of Anthropology, University of California, Berkeley, and to my colleagues in primatology.
(2) I am grateful to Lewis Klein, Department of Anthropology, University of California, Berkeley, for introducing me to Crook's work and for delineating the specifics of the gibbon-chimpanzee comparisons.

(3) The epitome of overstatement and premature extrapolation is contained in two popular books by Robert Ardrey, *African Genesis* and *The Territorial Imperative.* See a review of the latter by J. Ellefson, (1967[c]).

BIBLIOGRAPHY

ARDREY, H., *African Genesis.* New York: Delta Books, 1961.
———, *The Territorial Imperative.* New York: Atheneum Publishers, 1966.
CARPENTER, C. R., "A Field Study in Siam of the Behavior and Social Relations of the Gibbon (*Hylobates lar*)," *Comparative Psychology Monographs,* Vol. 16, No. 5, 1940.
———, "Characteristics of Social Behavior in Non-Human Primates," *Transactions of the New York Academy of Sciences,* Vol. 4, No. 8, 1942, pp. 248–258.
CROOK, J. H., "The Evolution of Social Organization and Visual Communication in the Weaver Birds (Ploceinae)," *Behaviour,* Suppl. No. 10, 1964.
———, "The Adaptive Significance of Avian Social Organizations," *Symposia Zoological Society of London,* No. 14, 1965, pp. 181–218.
———, and J. S. GARTLAN, "Evolution of Primate Societies," *Nature,* Vol. 210, No. 5042, 1966, pp. 1200–1203.
ELLEFSON, J. O., "A Natural History of Gibbons in the Malay Peninsula," unpublished doctoral dissertation, University of California, Berkeley, California, 1967[a].
———, "Territorial Behavior in the Common, White-Handed Gibbon, *Hylobates lar,*" in P. Jay (ed.), *Patterns of Primate Behavior: Adaptation and Variability.* New York: Holt, Rinehart and Winston, Inc., 1967[b].
———, Review, *The Territorial Imperative,* by Robert Ardrey, New York: Atheneum Publishers," *Psychological Record,* Vol. 17, No. 3, 1967[c], pp. 437–440.
GOODALL, J., "Chimpanzees of the Gombe Stream Reserve," in I. DeVore (ed.), *Primate Behavior: Field Studies of Monkeys and Apes,* pp. 425–473. New York: Holt, Rinehart and Winston, Inc., 1965.
HALL, K. R. L., and I. DEVORE, "Baboon Social Behavior," in I. DeVore (ed.), *Primate Behavior: Field Studies of Monkeys and Apes,* pp. 53–110. New York: Holt, Rinehart and Winston, Inc., 1965.
ITANI, J., "Paternal Care in the Wild Japanese Monkey, *Macaca fuscata fuscata,*" *Primates,* Vol. 2, No. 1, 1959, pp. 61–93.
———, K. TOKUDA, Y. FURUYA, K. KANO, and Y. SHIN, "The Social Construction of Natural Troops of Japanese Monkeys in Takasakiyama," *Primates,* Vol. 4, No. 1, 1963, pp. 1–42.
JAY, P., "The Ecology and Social Behavior of the Indian Langur Monkey," unpublished doctoral dissertation, University of Chicago, Chicago, Ill., 1963.
———, "The Common Langur of North India," in I. DeVore (ed.), *Primate Behavior: Field Studies of Monkeys and Apes,* pp. 197–249. New York: Holt, Rinehart and Winston, Inc., 1965.
JOLLY, A., "Lemur Social Behavior and Primate Intelligence," *Science,* Vol. 153, No. 3735, 1966, pp. 501–506.
———, *Lemur Behavior.* Chicago: University of Chicago Press, 1967.
KAUFMANN, J. H., "A Three Year Study of Mating Behavior in a Free Ranging Band of Rhesus Monkeys," *Ecology,* Vol. 46, 1965, pp. 500–512.
———, "Social Relations of Adult Males in a Free-Ranging Band of Rhesus Monkeys," in S. A. Altmann (ed.), *Social Communication Among Primates,* pp. 73–98. Chicago: University of Chicago Press, 1967.

KAWAMURA, S., "The Process of Sub-Culture Propagation Among Japanese Macaques," *Primates,* Vol. 2, No. 1, 1959, pp. 43–60.

MIYADI, D., "Social Life of Japanese Monkeys," *Science,* Vol. 143, 1964, pp. 783–786.

REYNOLDS, V., "Some Behavioral Comparisons Between the Chimpanzee and the Mountain Gorilla in the Wild," *American Anthropologist,* Vol. 67, No. 3, 1965, pp. 691–706.

———, and F. REYNOLDS, "Chimpanzees of the Budongo Forest," in I. DeVore (ed.), *Primate Behavior: Field Studies of Monkeys and Apes,* pp. 368–424. New York: Holt, Rinehart and Winston, Inc., 1965.

RIOCH, D. McK., "Discussion of Agonistic Behavior," in S. A. Altmann (ed.), *Social Communication Among Primates,* pp. 115–122. Chicago: University of Chicago Press, 1967.

SADE, D. S., "Determinants of Dominance in a Group of Free-Ranging Rhesus Monkeys," in S. A. Altmann (ed.), *Social Communication Among Primates,* pp. 99–114. Chicago: University of Chicago Press, 1967.

SCHALLER, G., *The Mountain Gorilla: Ecology and Behavior.* Chicago: University of Chicago Press, 1963.

TSUMORI, A., "Newly Acquired Behavior and Social Interactions of Japanese Monkeys," in S. A. Altmann (ed.), *Social Communication Among Primates,* pp. 207–220. Chicago: University of Chicago Press, 1967.

VAN LAWICK-GOODALL, J., and H. VAN LAWICK, "New Discoveries Among Africa's Chimpanzees," *National Geographic,* Vol. 128, 1965, pp. 802–831.

WASHBURN, S. L., "What is a Primate?" *Primate News,* Vol. 4, No. 2, 1966, pp. 6–7.

———, and I. DEVORE, "The Social Life of Baboons," *Sci. Amer.,* Vol. 204, No. 6, 1961, pp. 62–71.

———, and J. SHIREK, "Human Evolution," in J. Hirsch (ed.), *Behavior-Genetic Analysis,* pp. 10–21. New York: McGraw-Hill, Inc., 1967.

10

Toward a Neuropsychological Theory of Person

Karl H. Pribram

Not so long ago popular discourse employed such phrases as "she has a lovely personality," "he has a rigid personality." Today the mode of expression would more likely be "she is a lovely *person*" and so on. What was once an attributed function is now conceived as intrinsic structure.

My first reaction to this shift in the emphasis of discourse was that it portrayed the common and suspect process of reification of a function. There may be truth to this view. But I feel that in this instance the shift may reflect some deeper awareness.

Personality theory and the very concept of personality stem from the observation and study of inter- and intra-individual differences in attributes which occur among members of a social group. Most naturally the focus of description falls on the group. However, once these differences are established, inquiry turns readily to the identified individual—characteristic personalities become the characters of persons. Only a *person* can have character, an intrinsic structure, and the problem remains to develop methods for the objective analysis of this structure.

In keeping with the shift in emphasis in popular usage, scientific study has also grown through a phase of descriptive functionalism based on a single mode or level of observation. The present concern is beginning to deal multidimensionally with structure—structure conceived not as an invariant "res, a thing" but as the "organization of process" (For example, different characters or, perhaps better, different aspects of character, may be displayed according to circumstance). My interest fits this trend. For one time-honored means of studying organization is to analyze the mechanism which produces that organization. (Indeed, mechanism and structure are often treated as synonymous; but this synonymity falls heir to the problems of the reductionist fallacy). My aim here is to describe the results of recently performed neurophysiological and neuropsychological experiments and to delineate from these two dimensions relevant to the problem of "person."

SOME EXPERIMENTS

The experiments concern the control which an organism's central nervous system exerts over its input. Early observations showed that the configurations of the electrical responses in the input channels evoked by light or sound stimulation were different when an animal attended to the stimulation and when it was distracted (Hernandez-Peon et al. 1956a, 1956b). Also, electrical stimulation of efferent tracts (thought to serve motor functions), and even of some brain stem systems, resulted in changes in the amount of neural activity recorded from afferent fibers originating in receptors (Hagbarth and Kerr 1954:295–307).

In my laboratory a series of studies has extended these observations. Auditory and visual receptor mechanisms, for example, are each sensitive to activities occurring in the other (Spinelli et al. 1965:303–319; Weingarten and Spinelli 1966:363–376). Control over input can be originated in cortex—especially that cortex usually called "association" (Spinelli et al. 1965: 303–319; Spinelli and Pribram 1966:44–49). These results are important because they effect a drastically changed view of the functions of not only these cortical areas but of the entire brain itself. Until recently, sensory events were thought to initiate an input to the brain where a variety of such inputs were integrated or associated into more complex configurations. These, in turn, were thought to determine the movements, to regulate the motor apparatus, of the organism. This view was based on several premises: an empiricist, associationistic philosophy; a reflex arc conceptualization of the organization of reflex behavior; the presence of corticocortical connections via large tracts of nerve fibers.

I have elsewhere (Pribram 1960:1–40; Miller et al. 1960) detailed the evidence which leads to a revision of the reflex arc concept in favor of a servomechanism type of reflex organization. The experiments presented above add substantially to the body of results already established, which show that feedback is ubiquitous in the organization of the nervous system. In view of this fact, any simple stimulus-response, reflex-arc, model of brain-behavior organization—even when embellished by mediational stages—becomes untenable.

The cortico-cortical connections pose a more puzzling problem; their presence is an established fact. However, major connections are *not* from the receiving areas of the brain to the so-called association cortex. Rather, the pattern is that *every* cortical point is connected with its immediate neighbors by short, relatively fine, fibers and with more remote locations by longer and stouter ones. The functions in behavior of these connections are the puzzle: cutting through them by surgical removal of tissue (Chow 1954:762–1771) or by cross-hatching (Sperry et al. 1955:50–58; Pribram et al. 1966:358–364) has so far resulted in *no* detectable change in behavior.

By contrast, surgical removal (Pribram 1966:324–367) or cutting the input-output connections (Pribram *et. al.* 1966:365–1373; Wade 1952:179–207) of the so-called association areas produces profound disturbances in the problem-solving ability of primates.

Further, one of the major divisions of the "association cortex" is divisible into areas, each of which serves one or another sensory mode. Modality specificity of so-called association cortex has been amply documented: in somesthesis (Pribram and Barry 1956:99–106; M. Wilson 1957:630–635); taste (Bagshaw and Pribram 1953:399–408); audition (Weiskranz and Mishkin 1958:406–414; Dewson, Nobel, and Pribram 1966:151–159); and vision (Blum *et al.* 1950:53–100; Mishkin and Pribram 1954:14–20; Chow 1952:109–118). How can the notion that these areas serve an "associative" function be maintained in the face of this evidence?

Even that division of the association cortex—the frontal—which has been found to be nonspecific with regard to sensory modality (Pribram 1961:311–320) is specific for a particular type of problem-solving ability. Frontal cortex is involved in short-term memory processes (Pribram *et al.* 1964:28–55).

The inescapable suggestion derived from this series of experimental results parallels that derived from those delineating the "servo" nature of neural organization: a simple stimulus-response-association model of brain-behavior organization has become untenable.

However, the demonstration of efferent control of input provides the beginning of a plausible alternative. Instead of ever more complex integrations being effected in brain regions remote from input channels, the data suggest that these remote regions exert their influence downstream at various stations—controlling, programming, and organizing the events directly in the input channels per se. The effect obtained is similar to that produced in a computer program by the addition of recursive servolike, hierarchically-arranged loops established as subroutines.

Some facets of the nature of the efferent control have already been clarified. Ordinarily each input channel has a good deal of reserve redundancy in processing the information derived from the input; that is, a particular signal is carried over many parallel fibers. But the experiments mentioned have shown that the activity of the "association" areas of the brain can alter the amount of channel redundancy, the number of fibers used to carry a signal. Electrical stimulation of the cortex reduces redundancy (Spinelli and Pribram 1966:44–49); removal of this cortex has the opposite effect (Dewson *et al.* 1966:123–124). In addition, electrical stimulation of the frontal cortex (the part of the brain involved in short-term memory processes) has been shown to increase redundancy (Spinelli and Pribram 1967:143–149). As yet we have no evidence whether this increase is simply quantitative or whether some structuring of the redundancy is involved. These experiments show that the organism's input is influenced by the most recently developed portions of the central nervous system, and further, that two reciprocally-acting mechanisms of control exist.

The psychological effect of altering the amount and the structure of redundancy in an information processing system has not been fully explored but a few facts have been ascertained. For example, the greater the redundancy the greater the temporal resolution among input events; on the other hand, reduced redundancy leads to greater sensitivity to the complexities of input (Garner 1962:153, 161, 172, 183, 276). Thus, not only the clarity, but the very range of our perceptions seems to be under the control of this brain mechanism.

Though these findings are important to an understanding of the perceptual process they may be even more critical in molding our view of what is involved in motivation and emotion. This dividend comes in the experimental realization of the fact that organisms can respond to stimulation in ways which are not externalized as behavior. For the past half century behaviorism has pervaded psychology to the point where many tend to forget that an organism has in his repertoire reactions other than those immediately observable in behavior. Properly conceived neurophysiological research is especially potent in uncovering these "internal" reactions. Expectations, intentions, thoughts, and feelings are thus becoming legitimate topics for *objective* inquiry. As an important addition to the tools of behavioral research this neurologically oriented neomentalistic approach promises to enrich scientific psychology considerably. Here, let me focus on the relevance of the experiments described to the puzzling relationship between motivation and emotion.

THE EFFECTIVE-AFFECTIVE DIMENSION

According to the experimental results discussed above, one of the possible reactions an organism may have to a situation is to control the input initiated by that situation. Elsewhere, I have suggested (Pribram, 1967) that "e-motion" is manifest when an organism meets a situation by input control rather than through instrumental action. In this view, emotion, or what is now so aptly referred to by today's young as "a hangup," is not conceived to be an haphazard affair. Rather, just as action is motivated, that is, controlled, by the operation of a hierarchy of neural servomechanisms, programs or plans (Miller *et al.* 1960), so passion is e-moted, that is decontrolled by relinquishing or "pruning" smaller or larger segments or subroutines of these same programs, and restoring and strengthening earlier or simpler versions. As an example, take the interesting descriptions of the turning of the motive "love" into the emotion "in love" through separation as given by Reik (1941).

According to this analysis, then, one dimension along which a person's character may vary is the extent to which interaction with his environment displays action or passion—is effective or affective. Persons as *actors* effective, normal, and useful in their society have been chiefly considered by social scientists; exploration of the *passions* has been left to clinical psychologists and psychiatrists. Consequently, emotion, affect, has been suspect: we have come to think of it as somehow unhealthy, abnormal, futile. And yet, the error of this view is obvious. Attributes such as strength of character, creativity, and so on are known even by the layman to depend on the nonbehavioral reactions of a person to his situation. The techniques are at hand; there is no longer any good reason to withhold physiological observations from experiments made to investigate these processes, even by social scientists. The objective study of behavior can now be fruitfully complimented by the objective study of such nonbehavioral, internal, "mental" reactions of experimental subjects.

THE ESTHETIC-ETHICAL DIMENSION

For the purposes of this symposium I wish to elaborate more fully a second dimension which can be discerned from this set of neurophysiological and neurobehavioral experiments. This dimension deals with the fact that the brain contains a mechanism by which the amount of redundancy in a system, the amount of synchronous activity, can be governed. In the experiments cited, this regulation was shown to be effective over input, and there is evidence (Brooks and Asanuma 1965:674–681; 1965:247–278) that a similar effect operates on motor systems.

As already noted, the importance to the psychological process of redundancy regulation has as yet been only partially explored. On the input side, redundancy *reduction* is involved when interest and sensory *participation* are called forth: redundancy *enhancement* helps *focus and restrict* the organism's sensory interaction with the situation. The two processes are ordinarily balanced, for they converge on the same input mechanism, even on some of the same cells in the mechanism (Spinelli and Pribram 1967: 143–149). It is likely that the adjustment of this balance differs in different individuals in different situations.

Here, therefore, is an example of another dimension along which individual differences and differences among individuals may be produced from occasion to occasion. Some individuals are more inclined to sensory participation with their environment, and some situations tend to evoke participation more than others. Such evocation is the essence of esthetic endeavor, and for this reason redundancy reduction can be thought of as a mechanism underlying an esthetic mode of reaction. Its opposite, an increase in redundancy, tends to focus and remove the organism from participation and to turn him inward. He is therefore responsive more to his own neural organization than to the organization of his environment. This mode of reaction is characteristically displayed, for instance, when ethical considerations are involved (as when a person asks whether he is being true to himself).

A convergent line of evidence concerning this dimension comes from observations of behavior. Here, also, two processes are identified and the processes bear a resemblance to those already identified. In a recent study, Schachter (in press) examined the determinants of eating in obese and nonobese persons and showed that the obese person's eating is more under the control of external than of internal determinants, while the opposite is true of the nonobese person. In other words, most people eat when their physiological state demands; the gourmand responds to opportunity.

Another convergence comes from psychophysiological experiment. Lacey (1965:161–208) has used heart rate and other measures of autonomic nervous system reactivity to gauge the receptivity of an organism to stimulation. The evidence is that two modes exist—one "open" and one relatively "closed": "Cardiac deceleration accompanied and perhaps even facilitated ease of 'environmental intake' whereas cardiac acceleration accompanied or facilitated 'rejection of the environment.'" Data are presented to show that cognitive problem solving demanding "internal" work produces cardiac acceleration while situations demanding anticipatory vigilance, an "external orientation," are accompanied by cardiac deceleration. Clearly, an "open-closed" dimension is discernible in these results. It remains to be shown that the convergence with the recovery cycle data is real and not spurious: simultaneous recording of heart rate and evoked recovery functions in the two types of situation is an indicated next step.

The delineation of the esthetic-ethical dimension finds parallels in conceptions derived from still other types of observations. Developmental studies led Piaget to formulate the suggestion that two complementary processes guide cognitive growth. One process he labels *accommodation;* the other, *assimilation.* "In their initial directions, assimilation and accommodation are obviously opposed to one another, since assimilation is conservative and tends to subordinate the environment to the organism as it is, whereas accommodation is the source of changes and bends the organism to the successive constraints of the environment." (Piaget 1954:352) Thus, "the nursling's psychic activity is at first only simple assimilation of the external environment to the functioning of the organs. Through the medium of assimilatory schemata, at first fixed, then mobile, the child proceeds from this elementary assimilation to putting means and ends into relationships such that the assimilation of things to personal activity and the accommodation of schemata to the external environment find an increasingly stable balance. The undifferentiated and chaotic assimilation and accommodation which characterize the first months of life are superseded by assimilation and accommodation simultaneously dissociated and complementary."

(Piaget 1954:219) Accommodation thus resembles the effect which a neurologically-based redundancy reduction mechanism would be expected to exert; assimilation could well be effected by redundancy enhancement.

This convergence of conceptions does not in itself mean that accommodation is necessarily accomplished through redundancy reduction and that assimilation occurs through an increase in the synchronous operation of the organism's input mechanism. However, as hypotheses these possibilities can be fruitfully explored since the parts of the brain responsible for shifts in redundancy are known, as are the effects of removal of these parts on problem solving in adult primates. Thus, removal of the appropriate structure in young animals should have effects predictable from Piaget's formulation.

Other convergences come to mind. Factor analytic methods of studying subjects with brain lesions have been undertaken by Halstead (1947), Reitan (1966), and Teuber's group (Semmes et al. 1960). Of particular relevance here is the fact that most factor-analytic studies have yielded some sort of introversion-extroversion dimension. Petrie some years ago (1952) presented in detail carefully controlled evidence that frontal leucotomy leads to changes "on test measurements associated with the dimension of extraversion-introversion." The finding that these changes occur in the direction of greater extraversion is convergent with the model based on recovery-cycle here presented: removal of the influence of frontal lobe tissue leads to redundancy reduction in the input channels and hence "greater sensitivity to the complexities of the input." More recently (1967), Petrie has extended her work by devising a set of behavioral tests with which she has delineated additional ways of characterizing persons: a stimulus augmentor-stimulus reducer dimension and an autonomy-externally controlled dimension. She is at present engaged in a series of studies, using neurosurgical patients, aimed at relating her behavioral observations to their neural substates. Should this current work be combined with some simple neurophysiological observations, for example, elucidating recovery functions as in the experiments described here, another convergence among models could readily be accomplished. On the whole, electrophysiological data taken in conjunction with factor-analytic analysis should prove extremely fruitful. Pioneering studies of this sort have been undertaken. Pawlik and Cattell (1965:129–151) have analysed the organism's readiness to be aroused, and Barratt (1959a:63–66; 1959b:191–198) has investigated Lacey and Lacey's (1958:144–209) stabile-labile dimension of readiness to react.

Considerably more remote would be studies which relate the neurologically derived models with those based on social-cultural observation. Nonetheless, I believe such studies are possible. For example, Riesman (1955) has, from social-historical observation, delineated what he calls "inner-directed" and "other-directed" individuals. It could be that developmental exigencies mold some individuals along primarily redundancy-reducing, accommodative modes of communicative intercourse. And it could be that other circumstances yield primarily redundancy-enhancing, assimilative modes of communicative discourse. In this way a person (or even a whole population) would become primarily esthetic or primarily ethical in interpersonal interactions, depending on the formative culture.

Many questions can be raised within the framework of these observations: for instance, is inner- and other-direction synonymous with introversion and extroversion? Are there indeed more gourmands in other-directed societies, as the Schachter experiments might suggest, or is the relationship between inner- and other-direction specific to a reaction mode? Can the balance between esthetic and ethical sensitivity be altered by later experience or is there a limited "critical" period during development which "sets" the organism on one or another course? Do society and its culture determine not only the balance between the esthetic and ethical mode but also the emotional consequences of each reaction? In another paper, Melges and I (in press) tentatively proposed a classification of affects based in part on the difference between an ethical mode of reaction, which we called preparatory (or better, prerepairatory) and an esthetic mode which we called participatory. The suggestion was made that the affect associated with the ethical, preparatory type of reaction is, as a rule, pessimistic, whereas esthetic participation begets optimism. This suggestion was based on current clinical experience and attributed to the fact that the social outcome of participation was, on the basis of experience, appraised by an organism as potentially successful in establishing or reestablishing control, whereas preparatory maneuvers could, on the basis of experience, be expected to pose difficulties. However, this view is surely culture bound: participatory reactions are rewarded in a society populated by persons holding the Freudian point of view, but the preparatory mode is the more effective in a society subscribing to the Protestant ethic (Rieff 1959). In fact, those of an older generation often find the cocktail party the epitome of a demand for an almost exclusively participatory mode of intercourse—and hence a most trying experience accompanied by anxiety produced by the enhanced internal uncertainty and reduced redundancy necessary to be simultaneously open to a large number of information sources. For this earlier generation, the ethical mode of living true to one's principles proved a gratifying experience and thus led, in them, to optimistic affects.

In summary, then, two dimensions of "person" have been delineated from one set of neurobehavioral and neurophysiological results. I have here explored, for one of these dimensions, some possible convergences with other conceptions derived from other data and have suggested experiments and applications that come to mind as a result of the exploration. I have dwelled on convergences. An alternative would have been to spell out a more inclusive set of dimensions; I have eschewed this alternative—partly because I feel it would be premature to espouse it. But there is another reason for my choice. So much of scientific endeavor today is concerned with checking the reliability of conceptions by logical and experimental analytic procedure. Too often the validity of the conceptions remains either unquestioned or is dismissed by ridicule—as when a model is maligned as "reductive" or its converse, "soft." I urge that the validity of many conceptual systems can be tested by attention to convergences among them and by testing these convergences by performing experiments and observations in situations or contexts that combine elements from those which led to the original formulations. Without such synthesis through cross-disciplinary effort, science is likely to culminate in a tower of Babel where the many, by referring to the same event structured in different realms of discourse, fail totally to communicate.

Specific to our present concern is the fact that societies are made up of persons whose *brains* shape the interactive matrix. There should therefore be no barrier in using data from social observation, personality analysis and neurological experiment to come to a common understanding. In the spirit of this kind of cross-disciplinary endeavor, starting with a set of experimental results accomplished in my laboratories, I have described several areas where the investigation of "person" has led to an apparent convergence of concepts, a convergence which persuades follow-through: one such area would explore an effective-affective dimension, the other an esthetic-ethical dimension, along which persons may vary.

BIBLIOGRAPHY

BAGSHAW, MURIEL H., and K. H. PRIBRAM, "Cortical Organization in Gustation (Macaca mulatta)," *Journal of Neurophysiology*, Vol. 16, 1953, pp. 399–508.

BARRATT, E. S., "Relationship of Psychomotor Tests and EEG Variables at Three Developmental Levels," *Perceptual and Motor Skills*, Vol. 9, 1959a, pp. 63–66.

———, "Anxiety and Impulsiveness Related to Psychomotor Efficiency," *Perceptual and Motor Skills*, Vol. 9, 1959b, pp. 191–198.

BLUM, J. S., K. L. CHOW, and K. H. PRIBRAM, "A Behavioral Analysis of the Organization of the Parieto-Temporo-Preoccipital Cortex," *Journal of Comparative Neurology*, Vol. 93, 1950, pp. 53–100.

BROOKS, V. B., and H. ASANUMA, "Pharmacological Studies of Recurrent Cortical Inhibition and Facilitation," *American Journal of Physiology*, Vol. 208, 1965, pp. 674–681.

———, and ———, "Recurrent Cortical Effects Following Stimulation of Medullary Pyramid," *Archives of Italian Biology*, Vol. 103, 1965, pp. 247–278.

CHOW, K. L., "Further Studies on Selective Albation of Associative Cortex in Relation to Visually Mediated Behavior," *Journal of Comparative Physiology and Psychology*, Vol. 45, 1952, pp. 109–118.

CHOW, K. L., "Lack of Behavioral Effects Following Destruction of Some Thalamic Association Nuclei in Monkeys," *Journal of the Archives of Neurological Psychiatry*, Vol. 71, 1954, pp. 762–771.

DEWSON, J. H. III, K. W. NOBEL, and K. H. PRIBRAM, "Corticofugal Influence at Cochlear Nucleus of the Cat: Some Effects of Ablation of Insular-Temporal Cortex," *Brain Research*, Vol. 62, 1966, pp. 123–124.

GARNER, W. R., *Uncertainty and Structure as Psychological Concepts*. New York: John Wiley & Sons, Inc., 1962.

HAGBARTH, K. E., and D. I. B. KERR, "Central Influences on Spinal Afferent Conduction," *Journal of Neurophysiology*, Vol. 17, 1954, pp. 295–307.

HALSTEAD, W. C., *Brain and Intelligence: A Quantitative Study of the Frontal Lobes*. Chicago: The University of Chicago Press, 1947.

HERNANDEZ-PEON, R., H. SCHERRER, and M. JOUVET, "Modification of Electric Activity in Cochlear Nucleus During 'Attention' in Unanesthetized Cats," *Science*, Vol. 123, 1956[a], pp. 331–332.

———, and M. VELASCO, "Central Influences on Afferent Conduction in the Somatic and Visual Pathways," *Acta Neurologica Latino-Americana*, Vol. 2, 1956[b], pp. 8–22.

———, J. KAGAN, B. C. LACEY, and H. A. MOSS, "The Visceral Level: Situational Determinants and Behavioral Correlates of Autonomic Response Patterns," in P. H. Knapp (ed.), *Expression of the Emotions in Man*, pp. 161–208. New York: International Universities Press, 1963.

LACEY, J. I., and B. C. LACEY, "The Relationship of Resting Autonomic Cyclic Activity to Motor Impulsivity," in Solomon, Cobb, and Penfield (eds.), *The Brain and Human Behavior*, pp. 144–209. Baltimore: The Williams and Wilkins Company, 1958.

MILLER, G. A., E. H. GALANTER, and K. H. PRIBRAM, *Plans and the Structure of Behavior*. New York: Holt, Rinehart and Winston, Inc., 1960.

MISHKIN, M., and K. H. PRIBRAM, "Visual Discrimination Performance Following Partial Ablation of the Temporal Lobe: I. Ventral vs. Lateral," *Journal of Comparative and Physiological Psychology*, Vol. 47, 1954, pp. 14–20.

PAWLIK, K., and R. B. CATTELL, "The Relationship Between Certain Personality Factors and Measures of Cortical Arousal," *Neuropsychologia*, Vol. 3, No. 2, 1965, pp. 129–151.

PETRIE, A., *Personality and the Frontal Lobes*. London: Routledge & Kegan Paul Ltd., 1952.

———, *Individuality in Pain and Suffering*. Chicago: The University of Chicago Press, 1967.

PIAGET, J., *The Construction of Reality in the Child*. New York: Basic Books, Inc., 1954.

PRIBRAM, HELEN, and J. BARRY, "Further Behavioral Analysis of the Parieto-temporo-preoccipital Cortex," *Journal of Neurophysiology*, Vol. 19, 1956, pp. 99–106.

PRIBRAM, K. H., "Toward a Science of Neuropsychology: Method and Data," in R. A. Patton (ed.), *Current Trends in Psychology and the Behavioral Sciences*, pp. 115–142. Pittsburgh: University of Pittsburgh Press, 1954.

———, "A Review of Theory in Physiological Psychology," *Annual Review of Psychology*, pp. 1–40, Palo Alto, Calif.: Annual Reviews, Inc., 1960.

———, "Limbic System," in D. E. Sheer (ed.), *Electrical Stimulation of the Brain*, pp. 311–320. Austin, Texas: University of Houston Press, 1961.

———, "The New Neurology and the Biology of Emotion: A Structural Approach," *American Psychologist*, Vol. 22, 1967, pp. 830–838.

———, A. AHUMADA, J. HARTOG, and L. ROSS, "A Progress Report on the

160 The Formation of Personality

Neurological Process Disturbed by Frontal Lesions in Primates," in J. M. Warren and K. Akert (eds.), *The Frontal Granular Cortex and Behavior*, pp. 28–55. New York: McGraw-Hill Book Company, Inc., 1964.

———, S. R. BLEHERT, and D. N. SPINELLI, "The Effects on Visual Discrimination of Crosshatching and Undercutting and the Inferotemporal Cortex of Monkeys," *Journal of Comparative and Physiological Psychology*, Vol. 62, 1966, pp. 358–364.

———, and F. T. MELGES, "Emotion: The Search for Control," in P. J. Vinken and G. S. Bruyn (eds.), *Handbook of Clinical Neurology*, Amsterdam: North Holland Publishing Co., in press.

REIK, THEODOR, *Of Love and Lust*. New York: Grove Press, Inc., 1941.

REITEN, R. M., *Canadian Psychologist*, Vol. 7, No. 4, 1966.

RIEFF, PHILIP, *Freud: The Mind of the Moralist*. New York: The Viking Press, 1959.

RIESMAN, D., N. GLAZER, and R. DENNEY, *The Lonely Crowd*. New York: Doubleday & Co., Inc., 1955.

SCHACHTER, S., in David C. Glass (ed.), *Proceedings of the Russell Sage Foundation-Rockefeller University Conference on Biology and Behavior: Neurophysiology and Emotion*, in press.

SEMMES, J., S. WEINSTEIN, L. GHENT, and H. TEUBER, *Somatosensory Changes after Penetrating Brain Wounds in Man*. Cambridge, Mass.: Harvard University Press, 1960.

SPERRY, R. W., N. MINER, and R. E. MEYERS, "Visual Pattern Perception Following Subpial Slicing and Tantalum Wire Implantation in the Visual Cortex," *Journal of Comparative and Physiological Psychology*, Vol. 48, 1955, pp. 50–58.

SPINELLI, D. N., and K. H. PRIBRAM, "Changes in Visual Recovery Function and Unit Activity Produced by Frontal Cortex Stimulation," *Electroencephalography and Clinical Neurophysiology*, Vol. 22, 1967, pp. 143–149.

———, K. H. PRIBRAM, and M. WEINGARTEN, "Centrifugal Optic Nerve Responses Evoked by Auditory and Somatic Stimulation," *Experimental Neurology*, Vol. 12, 1965, pp. 303–319.

WADE, MARJORIE, "Behavioral Effects of Prefrontal Lobectomy, Lobotomy and Circumsection in the Monkey (Macaca mulatta)," *Journal of Comparative Neurology*, Vol. 96, 1952, pp. 179–207.

WEINGARTEN, M., and D. N. SPINELLI, "Changes in Retinal Perceptive Field Organization with the Presentation of Auditory and Somatic Stimulation," *Experimental Neurology*, Vol. 15, 1966, pp. 363–376.

WEISKRANZ, L., and M. MISHKIN, "Effects of Temporal and Frontal Cortical Lesions on Auditory Discrimination in Monkeys," *Brain*, Vol. 81, 1958, pp. 406–414.

WILSON, MARTHA, "'Effects of Circumscribed Cortical Lesions Upon Somesthetic and Visual Discrimination in the Monkey," *Journal of Comparative and Physiological Psychology*, Vol. 50, 1957, pp. 630–635.

11

Genetics and Personality

William R. Thompson

It seems to me that when a layman asks of a psychologist or a geneticist the question "Is personality inherited?" he is placing on the term "inherited" a meaning different from that placed on it by the professional scientist. What he usually wants to know is whether a given trait or set of traits are so embedded in his biological makeup as to show an expression that can readily be identified in his genetic relatives, for example, in his great-aunt Sally. The professional, however, will usually avoid framing his answer in these terms, since he knows already that genetic determination does not mean perfect stability of the phenotype and that heritability is, in any case, a property more of populations than of individuals. As Falconer (1960:160–167) has stated:

> It is important to realize that the heritability is a property not only of a character but also of the population and of the environmental circumstances to which the individuals are subjected. . . . . . So, whenever a value is stated for the heritability of a given character, it must be understood to refer to a particular population under particular conditions.

Thus, our hypothetical layman may find, to his surprise, that intelligence is highly heritable in Boston, Massachusetts, but hardly at all in Houston, Texas. Such a relativistic answer must inevitably dampen his enthusiasm and leave him with the feeling that if you ask a stupid question you get a stupid answer.

There is no question that estimates of heritability do vary a great deal from one tested sample to another; this applies especially to behavioral traits of personality and intelligence. Yet this is no reason to throw up our hands in despair. Perhaps the question implicitly framed by the layman is not such a silly one after all. In point of fact, as I shall try to show, the problem of how "fixed" a given trait is—as indicated by the variance of heritabilities it shows both for different populations of individuals or for single individuals in different environments—is precisely the problem on which those interested in the genetic basis of personality and intelligence should focus. The various measures that reflect these phenotypes are often sensitive to environment and may fluctuate considerably. It is this fact that makes it difficult to obtain any general estimates of the heritability of a character. Responsiveness to environment may go with high or low genetic determination. For genes can set not only the average level of expression of a given phenotype, but also its variability of expression, that is, its reaction norm and reaction range. How environment operates within the frameworks provided by genotype to mold certain personality characteristics represents to my mind one of the most interesting problems in modern psychology. In order to explicate this point more fully, let me now outline briefly the historical development of work on the genetics of personality so as to highlight some promising lines of research that now seem to be emerging.

EARLY WORK IN BEHAVIOR GENETICS

In a recent and excellent review of the history of behavior genetics, G. E. McClearn (1962) opens with a quotation from Darwin concerning the genetic transmission of a rather peculiar piece of behavior. The case was brought to Darwin's attention by his half-cousin Francis Galton, and I should like to report it here.

> A gentleman of considerable position was found by his wife to have a curious trick, when he lay fast asleep on his back in bed, of raising his right arm slowly in front of his face, up to his forehead, and then dropping it with a jerk so that the wrist fell heavily on the bridge of his nose.

A curious trick indeed. Even more curious is the fact that:

> Many years after his death, his son married a lady who never heard of the family incident. She, however, observed precisely the same peculiarity in her husband; but his nose, from not being particularly prominent, has never yet suffered from the blows. .... One of his children, a girl, has inherited the same trick (Darwin 1872).

Galton and the many others who followed him were able to offer many similar cases in support of the idea of natural inheritance of personality and intelligence. Such characteristics as "eminence," "practical business habits," "energy," "independence of character," "truthfulness," and "taste for science" were all classed as showing a higher incidence in the relatives of probands than in unrelated groups. Gun (1930a, 1930b), for example, claimed that genetically "efficiency" was the key trait in the personalities of members of the Tudor royal family, whereas "tactless obstinacy" dominated the Stuart character (cf. Fuller and Thompson 1960).

Though such observations as these have turned out to have some degree of validity, it can hardly be doubted that they did not involve suitable control of environmental influences which might also be expected to promote similarity within family groups.

163 Genetics and Personality

The earlier workers in the field were, of course, quite well aware of this problem, but were so impressed with the supposed influence of genotype that they tended to discount the importance of environment. One of Galton's arguments to this point was based on the alleged superiority of England over America in respect to the incidence of really eminent intellects. If environmental influences were really critical, then America, with its open, democratic form of society, should provide a situation in which high ability should flourish. The opposite should be the case in England, with its more repressive social life. Since this clearly was not the case—a rather bland assumption on the part of Galton—genes rather than environment must be mainly responsible for intelligence. Galton's argument is a rather interesting one but cannot be taken very seriously.

The historical phase that followed these early attempts with the pedigree method did not, however, do much to correct this situation. Its main contribution lay in the use of more precise methods of phenotype measurement and in more precise ways of representing degree of similarity. These improvements paralleled, of course, the rise of the testing movement in Britain and the United States of which the main method involved the assessment of intrafamily similarity in respect to some measurable psychological trait as reflected in the correlation coefficient. The possibility of obtaining an estimate or degree of likeness between relatives was a major step forward. At the same time, with the exception of a few studies (*cf.* Fuller and Thompson 1960), most of the work employing this general method did not represent any great improvement over the pedigree approach so far as separating out hereditary from environmental influences.

Perhaps the greatest step forward was taken by the introduction of the twin method, that is, the comparison of similarity or concordance in monozygotic and dizygotic pairs. Such a comparison assumes that environment will act in the same manner on each pair. This notion, as we will indicate shortly, may not in fact be correct, though it seemed a reasonable one to entertain at least provisionally.

Using the twin method, Carter (1935) found that several scales of the Bernreuter Personality Inventory showed reasonably high heritability. As indicated in Table 11-1, these included especially neuroticism, self-sufficiency, dominance, and self-confidence. A later study by Portenier (1939), however, obtained results that were in agreement only in respect to self-sufficiency. In all five of the other scales, siblings were more similar than twins. It is true that of the latter only two pairs out of twelve were monozygotic and consequently the study has little relevance to the heritability of personality. It does, however, represent a most interesting commentary on the manner in which family environment operates on fraternal twins as opposed to siblings. Apparently, parents tend to act in such a way, when faced with twins, as to make them more different in their personalities than they should be genetically. Presumably, they do this in an effort —conscious or unconscious—to preserve the individuality of each member

TABLE 11-1

Twin Similarities in Personality Traits as Measured by the Bernreuter Personality Inventory (Carter 1935).

	Mz	Dz Like sex	Dz Unlike sex
Neuroticism	.63	.32	.18
Self-sufficiency	.44	−.14	.12
Introversion	.50	.40	.18
Dominance	.71	.34	.18
Self-confidence	.58	.20	.07
Sociability	.57	.41	.39

of the pair. This finding has been recently confirmed by Wilde (1964), who reports the same effect for dizygotic twins raised apart. These turned out to be more similar in four out of five trait dimensions tested than members of pairs reared together. Curiously enough, the opposite held true for monozygotic pairs; those reared apart being less similar than those reared together in four out of the five traits tested. It is difficult to explain this result if it is one that has some degree of generality. Wilde's results are shown in Table 11-2.

TABLE 11-2

Intrapair Similarity of Personality in Mz and Dz Twins Reared Together or Apart (Wilde 1964).

Trait	Mz Together	Mz Apart	Dz Together	Dz Apart
Psychoneurotic complaints	0.55	0.52	−0.14	0.28
Functional body complaints	0.46	0.75	−0.05	0.64
Introversion-extraversion	0.58	0.19	0.19	0.36
Test-taking attitude	0.48	0.46	0.33	0.49
Masculinity-femininity	0.45	0.44	−0.34	0.30

More recently R. T. Smith (1965) has attempted to assay similarities between members of monozygotic as against dizygotic twin pairs in respect to a large number of behavioral patterns that were deliberately chosen to represent environmental rather than genetic influences. These included such items as: "eating between meals," "time of going to bed," "number of sports played," "active in clubs," and so forth. Smith's results showed that monozygotics do show greater intrapair similarity for such characteristics as compared with dizygotics. The data shown in Table 11-3 illustrate this point.

TABLE 11-3

Proportions of Twin Pairs Concordant for Selected Habits (Smith 1965)

Habit	Mz	Dz
Eating between meals	75.0	61.6
Snack before bedtime	55.7	64.4
Time usually go to bed	66.7	64.4
Time usually get up	67.0	59.7
Dressing alike	64.4	40.3
Study together	40.2	15.3

We may note in passing a point not shown in the table, namely, that female identicals tend to show more concordance than do male identicals. This difference does not hold up as well in the case of fraternal pairs. Thus, hereditary and environmental influences that determine twin similarity in behavioral traits are confounded rather seriously; and before we can really draw firm conclusions about the heritability of behavioral traits as educed from twin concordances, it will be necessary to devote a great deal more study to the kinds of lives members of twin pairs lead, particularly their social interaction with each other and with their siblings and parents. Such work is now being initiated at several centers, including the author's home institution, Queen's University.

The second historical phase which we are discussing was also characterized by a great deal of work on the inheritance of temperament in lower animals. Two main procedures were used: the comparison of pure strains and the artificial selection of particular behavior traits. Both have essentially demonstrated that almost all traits of personality studied in mice or rats shows strong genetic determination. An example is the trait of so-called emotionality. One measure of it that has been used a good deal is incidence of defecation in an open field, the rationale being that animals tend to lose control over elimination in situations that evoke strong fear. This also appears to be true of human beings when subject to severely stressful situations, as in battle. Both Hall (1938) and, later, Broadhurst (1960) were able to select strains of rats showing a high or low incidence of defecation in an open field, that is, emotional and nonemotional strains, respectively. And, according to Broadhurst (*Cf.* Broadhurst and Eysenck 1965), who has preferred to refer to his lines as "reactive" and "nonreactive," the selected trait generalizes quite widely to other tests. Thus a broad and important dimension of personality is directly dependent on genotype. Many studies on inbred mouse strains have given support to this conclusion.

Recent work by Bignami (1964) usefully supplements the studies on emotionality. This investigation has shown that susceptibility to avoidance conditioning can also be selected in rats. Such a measure undoubtedly reflects some components of temperament or emotionality. Furthermore, since environment, although clearly a contributing factor, can be fairly well controlled with animal subjects, these kinds of studies offer more convincing proof than those using human beings of the heritability of personality characteristics.

BEHAVIOR GENETICS TODAY

In its third historical phase behavior genetics, having pointed to the heritability of many psychological traits in the domains of personality and intelligence, both normal and abnormal, is now edging towards the consideration of several important problems. These in turn arise out of a confrontation with a number of conclusions that seem inescapable.

In the first place, the genetic picture that usually has emerged from work on the transmission of behavior traits tends to be highly complex. This is due, at least partly, to the fact that the phenotype being studied can seldom be described in terms of simple categories as could the morphological characters on which the Mendelian models were based. Most psychological dimensions, at least as commonly assessed, are seemingly caused by polygenes rather than by major genes. This probably applies even to the severe forms of mental illness, for example, schizophrenia and manic-depression. Though their expression does seem to depend on genotype, the patterns of incidence they show in the relatives of probands does not conform to any simple genetic models.

It is also true, as a summary by Gottesman and Shields (1966) has recently shown, that concordance estimates vary widely between different investigations, some being as high as 80 percent or better (Kallman 1953), others being as low as zero (Tienari 1963). The strong impression given by an inspection of the literature on the inheritance of schizophrenia is that a highly complex syndrome is involved, one that has a number of underlying components, each of which may vary independently of the other in its intensity or severity. Much the same is true of most other traits commonly studied, both normal and abnormal.

A second conclusion, coordinate with the first, is that perhaps this lack of orderliness in terms of *genetic transmission* is, in any case, not important. To show that a trait is carried by a single autosomal dominant may be satisfying to a geneticist and also of some practical usefulness to a medical person giving genetic counseling. But it is of little real interest to psychologists, since it is not a finding that points in any directions that are germane to their interests.

Our main focus must be on the understanding of behavior and only secondarily on genes. Certainly, even in biology, it is a fact that the work of Mendel has turned out to have its greatest importance through the light it has shed on events going on at the cellular level in the chromosome. Thus modern genetics is more concerned with the biochemical operations of genes than with whether the incidence of characters in breeding populations fits a Mendelian model. In behavior genetics the same holds true. Certain properties of genes may well hold great interest for a psychologist, but it is doubtful that these are considered important by the geneticist or the biochemist.

A third conclusion is obvious enough: both heredity and environment are important in fixing the expression of traits of personality and intelligence. It is foolish to take sides on the question of which is more important in *general,* though people still do this; but is important to develop empirical statements as to how the two sets of causes contribute separately and in interaction to the variance of any particular piece of behavior, both between and within individuals. More than just a statistical exercise is involved here. If we can assess the degree of fixity or lability of various traits, we will then have a better idea of the main directions in which we should further explore. Were it to be firmly established, for example, that aggressiveness was a relatively fixed genetic character, there would be little point in devoting much effort to an analysis of how it is affected by such environmental variables as parental discipline, frustration, sociological factors, and the like. It is undoubtedly true that for some traits, genetic influence is trivial, and for others, environmental influence is trivial. Which is true in any particular case is a matter for empirical decision.

As I have already stated, confrontation with these conclusions has led behavior geneticists to focus their attention on two critical problem areas. These relate first to the definition of the phenotype studied and secondly to the fluidity, plasticity, or changeability of the phenotype. Let me discuss each of these in more detail.

CURRENT PROBLEMS IN BEHAVIOR GENETICS

The Complexity of Behavior

Personality is usually defined most broadly in terms of dispositions to act towards various sectors of the world in certain ways. Thus we may say of a person that he is moody, or lively, or ambitious, or kindly, and so on. The trouble is that once a compilation of such adjectives is undertaken, there is almost no end to it. Consequently, most psychologists attempt to derive, by one method or another, master dispositions or traits that may be used to describe personality in a more economical fashion. In the present context the question must be raised as to whether such master traits as these are in any sense more meaningful from a genetic point of view than the more particulate behaviors which they are known to underlie.

The problem of dividing up the phenotype into rational or "natural" components is a thorny one. In the area of psychometrics, the technique most widely used to reduce the complexity of some psychological domain has been factor analysis. However, the so-called factors that emerge from applications of this method are only units in a mathematical sense and we have no reason to suppose that they will make more genetic sense than do the raw tests from whose intercorrelations they are educed. Thus it is empirically true that the heritability estimates for tests are of about the same order of magnitude as those of factors (Thompson 1966). Nor do we have any reason to suppose that whatever genetic mechanisms underlie the transmission of factors are in any way simpler.

In the realm of intellectual abilities, it does seem that there is such a thing as general intelligence, this being inferred from the fact that most tests of intelligence, including those dealing with so-called primary factors, tend to correlate with each other. But from the work that has been done there is little indication that this is in any way unique in its dependence on or independence of hereditary factors. For it must be recognized that any factor is simply a kind of average of coefficients of correlation and that any correlation or covariance can be partitioned, as can a variance, into genetic and environmental components. Which of these is the larger in any particular case will depend on the heritability of each of the tests being correlated. Consequently, the heritability of a factor must depend completely on the heritabilities of the tests on which it is based. The general formula for computing the genetic and environmental components of a phenotypic correlation is given as follows: (Falconer 1960: 315):

$$r_P = h_x h_y r_G + e_x e_y r_E$$

where r_P = phenotypic correlation between two tests
h_x, h_y = heritabilities of tests x and y

r_G = additive genetic contribution to phenotypic correlation
e_x, e_y = environmental components of variances of tests x and y
r_E = environmental contribution to phenotypic correlations

Application of this formula sometimes yields surprising results. For example, we find the phenotypic correlation of 0:30 between fleece length and fleece weight in sheep is due largely to environmental (and nonadditive genetic) factors. The additive genetic correlation is only —.02. There is every reason to suppose that such results may also apply in the case of many psychometric correlations or factors. One way of finding this out would be to construct separate correlation matrices for the genetic and environmental components of a set of phenotypic correlations. Factor analyses of these matrices should then yield factors that are truly genetic and other factors that are truly environmental.

Although this method has not been directly tried, Vandenberg (1965) and Loehlin (1965) have used rather similar procedures in their twin studies. Both have obtained some indication that many traits of personality and intelligence that are strongly determined by heredity apparently have duplicates—one might say "isomers"—arising from environmental causes. For example, Loehlin (1965) finds two factors of emotionality: a hereditary one centered on impulses and impulse control, and an environmental one centered on response (presumably learned) to environmental restriction and threat. Likewise, Loehlin and Vandenberg (1966) and Cattell (1943, 1963) claim to have obtained evidence supporting the notion of hereditary intelligence factor and an environmental intelligence factor, these being best measured by nonverbal and verbal tests, respectively.

If confirmed, these findings are extremely interesting since they allow us to start to make some sense out of the confusing kind of information we have at present. Such procedures may begin to make clear why some seemingly simple traits such as "self-control" or "intellectual efficiency" show no significant heritability (Gottesman 1967). Others of apparently great complexity, however, show very high heritability; these include vocational preferences measured by the Strong Interest Inventory, for example, "osteopath," "physicist," "mathematician" (in women only), and "personnel director" (in men only). Likewise, achievement need, shyness, religious attitudes, self-acceptance, originality and psychological mindedness, all show significant F ratios between monozygotic and dizygotic twin pairs (Gottesman 1967; Vandenberg and Kelly 1964).

In the face of such curious results, there is obviously some onus on the behavior geneticist to gear his tests more closely to genetic criteria, using methods of the kind suggested above. If this can be done, it may well turn out that the surprisingly high heritability of such a personality trait as "desire to be an osteopath," for example, is a reflection of some really fundamental disposition at work, even though this seems unlikely on the face of it.

One such disposition, strongly rooted genetically, does not seem to be emerging from many studies (Eysenck 1956; Gottesman 1963; Wilde 1964; Vandenberg 1966). This is the bipolar trait commonly known as introversion-extraversion, though its real identity may have more to do with the basic social posture an individual takes toward his fellows. A number of studies now seem to agree in the conclusion that this may be as strongly heritable as general intelligence and to be perhaps a trait that underlies many of the different forms of behavior we commonly associate with the domain of personality and temperament. No doubt there will also be found eventually other such master traits that form the basic natural units from which personality is compounded.

The Fluidity of Traits

If it is granted that some of the surprising results described above—such as the relatively high heritability of "desire to be an osteopath"—may be explained by reference to the taxonomy of behavior, another possibility presents itself. This represents, in fact, the second major focus of contemporary behavior genetics. I refer to the problem of behavior plasticity and its control by genotype-environment interaction. Most estimates of heritability have been calculated on identical and fraternal twins reared together. Such a procedure, as I have already pointed out, makes assumptions about the uniformity of parental treatment that may well be unjustified. I have cited the work of Portenier (1939), Wilde (1964) and Smith (1965) in this connection. The question remains, however, open to investigation. Further work by Wilde has recently shown that in a situation of conformity of the Asch-Crutchfield type members of twin pairs do not differ from nontwins in respect to their mutual conformity. That is to say, when given the opportunity to conform in a problem-solving situation, twins are no more dependent on each other than are unrelated persons. It may still be, however, that members of twin pairs, because of their long exposure to an age-peer, are more socially sensitive than nontwins. This hypothesis still remains to be tested, and its validity may help us to make more sense out of the data on twin similarity and the general process by which persons are moulded by environments.

The extent to which such moulding is possible is itself, of course, controlled by genotype. Some individuals will deviate more readily than others from the personality that their genotypes best predict. There is some evidence, admittedly rather ambiguous but arising from several different investigations, to indicate that females may be less plastic in this respect than males. Thus Osborn and DeGeorge (1959) showed that females showed higher heritabilities than males in 11 out of 18 morphological measures. In respect to somatotypes, females were higher than males in "total somatotype," "ecotomorphy," and the masculinity-femininity index. They were lower on mesomorphy and equal to males on endomorphy. Similarly, on a number of personality scales administered by Vandenberg (1966) and by Gottesman (1967), including the Stern High School Activities Index, the California Psychological Inventory, and the Comrey Personality and Attitude Factors, females showed significant monozygotic-dizygotic F ratios for about twice as many measures as did males. Some of the more startling results are summarized in Table 11–4 from Gottesman (1967). Another study by Gottesman (1963) using the MMPI and the Cattell HSPQ test, however, has yielded the opposite results. Thus the situation is ambiguous enough yet to require further exploratory work before a definite conclusion can be stated.

TABLE 11–4

Sex Differences in Heritabilities for Different Scales of the California Psychological Inventory (Gottesman 1967)

Scale	Female	Male
Responsibility	.50	00
Self-control	.47	00
Achievement via Independence	.46	00
Intellectual efficiency	.46	00
Sociability	.56	.39
Dominance	.42	.51

A good deal of work done with lower animals also indicates that plasticity is genetically controlled. Thus some of the various inbred strains of mice are known to differ significantly in their responsiveness to environmental stimulation (Lindzey, Lykken, and Winston 1960). C57 Blacks, for example, are notably more sensitive than other strains. Responsiveness is particularly evident when there is residual effect of trauma administered early in life. This brings us to the next point.

If the expression of a genotype may be altered by environment, so also can it be changed by developmental factors. Again we find that it is difficult to make any general statement about the constancy of expression with age. Some basic traits such as those demarcated in infants by Rutter, Korn, and Birch (1963) appeared to be very unstable over the three-year period during which they were studied in twins. Recent work of Freedman (1965) hits directly at the problem. In an attempt to find what he calls "building-blocks" for an adequate theory of personality, he has looked for the existence in very young infants of behavior sequences analogous to these so-called patterns of fixed-action studied by ethologists in lower animals. Two types of behavior on which he has particularly focused his attention are the smiling response and the fear response to strangers. These might be considered to reflect basic tendencies in human beings to social approach and avoidance. Freedman has found from his studies that concordance in respect to both these types of behavior is greater in monozygotic than in fraternal twins, thus suggesting the operation of hereditary influence on dispositions that are probably prototypic for much of the later social behavior of human beings. Follow-up studies on such twins would be most informative and useful, helping us to find out just how environment can act on these early dispositions and just how stable they are during development. At an older age level, Gottschaldt (1960) has reported results for a large number of personality characteristics (mood, vital energy, thinking capacity, level of abstraction) measured on twin pairs at adolescence and later on in adulthood. Not only were these traits remarkably stable over this time, but also the ratio of monozygotic within-pair variances increased with age. In other words, development acted in such a way as to increase the heritability of these traits.

The lines of research outlined above, dealing with sex and development as factors influencing genetic expression, must serve to illustrate the kind of work that is being done and can be done on the nature of genotype-environment interaction. I hope I have made it clear that it is a problem area that, to my mind, is basic to our understanding of the relation between genotype and personality.

CONCLUSION

Two problem areas which have been briefly discussed—the complexity of behavior traits and the fluidity of behavior traits—now seem to be of central importance to contemporary behavior genetics in general and to the genetic study of personality in particular. Careful empirical analysis of both should do much to give to the concept of "heritability" a meaning more pertinent to the interests of the psychologist and also of the layman than any it now possesses. As a "populations" concept, it is certainly useful in many different ways; but the psychologist is perhaps interested less in whole groups than in the individuals who make them up. Likewise, the layman's inclination is to wonder, idiosyncratically, "What is my makeup? How fixed is it? Can I transcend it?" These questions, after all, represent basic issues with which the behavioral sciences are concerned.

BIBLIOGRAPHY

BIGNAMI, G., "Selection for Fast and Slow Avoidance Conditioning in the Rat," *British Journal of Psychology,* Vol. 17, 1964 (abstract).

BROADHURST, P. L., "Experiments in Psychogenetics," in H. J. Eysenck (ed.), *Experiments in Personality.* London: Routledge & Kegan Paul Ltd., 1960.

———, and H. J. EYSENCK, "Emotionality in the Rat: a Problem of Response Specificity," in C. Banks and P. L. Broadhurst (eds.), *Studies in Psychology.* Aylesbury, Bucks, England: Hazell Watson & Viney Ltd., 1965.

CARTER, H. D., "Twin Similarities in Emotional Traits," *Character and Personality,* Vol. 4, 1935, pp. 61–78.

CATTELL, R. B., "The Measurement of Adult Intelligence," *Psychological Bulletin,* Vol. 40, 1943, pp. 153–193.

———, "Theory of Fluid and Crystallized Intelligence: a Critical Experiment," *Journal Educational Psychology,* Vol. 54, 1963, pp. 1–22.

DARWIN, C., *The Expression of the Emotions in Man and Animals.* London: John Murray, 1872.

EYSENCK, H. J., "The Inheritance of Extraversion-Introversion," *Acta Psychologica,* Vol. 12, 1956, pp. 95–110.

FALCONER, D. S., *Introduction to Quantitative Genetics.* New York: The Ronald Press Company, 1960.

FREEDMAN, D., "An ethological approach to the genetical study of human behavior," in S. G. Vandenberg (ed.), *Methods and Goals in Human Behavior Genetics.* New York: Academic Press, Inc., 1965.

FULLER, J. L., and W. R. THOMPSON, *Behavior Genetics.* New York: John Wiley and Sons, Inc., 1960.

GOTTESMAN, I. I., "Genetic aspects of intelligent behavior," in N. R. Ellis (ed.), *Handbook of Mental Deficiency.* New York: McGraw-Hill, Inc., 1963.

———, "Genetic variance in adaptive personality traits," *Journal of Child Psychology and Psychiatry,* 1967.

———, and J. SHIELDS, "Contributions of twin studies to perspectives on schizophrenia," in B. A. Maher (ed.), *Progress in experimental personality research,* Vol. 3. New York: Academic Press, Inc., 1966.

GOTTSCHALDT, K., "Das Problem der Phanogenetick der Personlichkeit," in P. Lersch and H. Thomas (eds.), *Personlichkeits forschung und Personlichkeits theorie, Handbuch der Psychologie,* Vol. 4. Gottingen: Hofgrefie, 1960, pp. 222–280.

GUN, W. T. J., "The Heredity of the Tudors," *Eugenics Review,* Vol. 22, 1930a, pp. 111–116.

———, "The Heredity of the Stewarts," *Eugenics Review,* Vol. 22, 1930b, pp. 195–201.

HALL, C. S., "The Inheritance of Emotionality." *Sigma Xi Quarterly,* Vol. 26, 1938, pp. 17–27.

KALLMAN, F. J., *Heredity in Health and Mental Disorder.* New York: W. W. Norton & Company, Inc., 1953.

LINDZEY, G., N. D. T. LYKKEN, and H. D. WINSTON, "Infantile Trauma, Genetic Factors and Adult Temperament," *Journal of Abnormal Social Psychology,* Vol. 61, 1960, pp. 7–14.

LOEHLIN, J. C., "A heredity—environment analysis of personality inventory data," in S. G. Vandenberg (ed.), *Methods and Goals in Human Behavior Genetics.* New York: Academic Press, Inc., 1965.

LOEHLIN, J. C., and S. G. VANDENBERG, "Genetic and Environmental Components in the Covariation of Cognitive Abilities: an Additive Model," *Research Report, Louisville Twin Study,* No. 14, 1966.

McCLEARN, G. E., "The Inheritance of Behavior," in L. Postman (ed.), *Psychology in the Making.* New York: Alfred A. Knopf, Inc., 1962.

OSBORN, R. H., and F. V. DeGEORGE, *Genetic Basis of Morphological Variation.* Cambridge, Mass.: Harvard University Press, 1959.

PORTENIER, L., "Twinning as a factor influencing personality," *Journal of Educational Psychology,* Vol. 30, 1939, pp. 542–547.

RUTTER, H., S. KORN, and H. F. BIRCH, "Genetic and Environmental Factors in the Development of Primary Reaction Patterns," *British Journal of Social and Clinical Psychology,* Vol. 2, 1963, pp. 161–173.

SMITH, R. T., "A Comparison of Socio-environmental Factors in Monozygotic and Dizygotic Twins, Testing an Assumption," in S. G. Vandenberg (ed.), *Methods and Goals in Human Behavior Genetics.* New York: Academic Press, Inc., 1965.

THOMPSON, W. R., "Multivariate Analysis in Behavior Genetics," in R. B. Cattell, *Handbook of Multivariate Experimental Psychology.* New York: Rand McNally & Company, 1966.

TIENARI, P., "A Psychiatric Twin Study," *Acta Psychiatrica Scandinavica,* Vol. 39, 1963, pp. 169, 393–397.

VANDENBERG, S. G., "Innate abilities, one or many? A new method and some results," *Acta Geneticae Medicae et Gemellologicae,* Vol. 14, 1965, pp. 41–47.

———, "Hereditary factors in normal personality traits (as measured by inventories)," *Research Report, Louisville Twin Study,* No. 19, 1966.

———, and L. KELLY, "Hereditary components in Vocational preferences," *Acta Geneticae Medicae et Gemellologicae,* Vol. 13, 1964, pp. 266–267.

WILDE, G. J. S., "Inheritance of Personality Traits," *Acta Psychologica,* Vol. 22, 1964, pp. 37–51.

12

Influences of Childhood and Adolescence

Mary Ellen Goodman

Over the last four decades a considerable number of anthropologists have contributed to development of a subdiscipline called "psychological anthropology" or, more usually, "culture and personality." The emergence of psychological anthropology was in a sense inevitable. As specialists in the study of culture, most anthropologists find it impossible to ignore the fact that culture is created, learned, shared, and transmitted by living, breathing human beings. Describing a culture at a given time amounts to generalizing about human behavior, past and present, and about its enduring results as embodied in a tradition and in artifacts. The living members of a society have learned some or many parts of this tradition, and older members can be observed in the process of transmitting it to younger ones. To say this is to say also that some or many parts of the tradition have become integral to each of the members of the society; these parts figure in that constellation of the inner man known as personality.

We see culture—some part of it, at least—in each living personality. But that is not all. Some cultural anthropologists seem to say that it is all, or very nearly all, there is to see. Their enthusiasm for the cultural order of natural phenomena and their absorption in this order have betrayed them into a skewed perspective. If we take a balanced view of the living personality, we must see that it reflects other influences and antecedents in addition to those of the cultural order. It reflects man's biologically given heritage, capacities, and inclinations. It is affected by the conditions and potentialities of its physical environment. It is affected also by social environment, for example, by the number, ages, proximities, and attributes of other persons.

Moreover, what we see in the living personality is an infinitely dense and elaborate interweaving—an incalculably intricate tangle—of all these antecedents and influences. In each of the major antecedent-influence categories (biological, physical environmental, social, and cultural) great numbers of specifics will underlie and be represented in a personality system. And because of the endless possibilities with respect to combinations of these specifics, and the variables of chronology, the combinations will be precisely the same in no two individuals. Not even identical twins can be precisely the same because from birth they move separately and their experiences will inevitably differ to slight or great extent.

Having taken note of all these complexity-producing factors we have not yet come to the most elusive and unpredictable of them. It resides in the fact that our subject—the living personality—is more than a sum of antecedents and influences. There is in him a "demand for autonomy" (Allport 1955), a restlessness, and creativity. He is more than an enormously complex result and product of enormously complex forces. He is also, in himself, a cause and a force. So, at any rate, many of us are convinced, and on grounds of an entirely empirical and naturalistic sort. Else Frenkel-Brunswik (Adorno, Frenkel-Brunswik *et al.* 1950) stated the conviction in these words:

> Although personality is a product of the social environment of the past, it is not, once it has developed, a mere object of the contemporary environment. What has developed is a *structure* within the individual, something which is capable of self-initiated action upon the social environment and of selection with respect to varied impinging stimuli; something which though always modifiable is frequently very resistant to fundamental change (p. 6).

We have noted that no two personalities will be identical. This of course does not rule out interpersonal and intergroup similarities. Family, class, caste, regional, tribal, national, and even wider similarities are real, in spite of the fact that they may be overstated. Prejudice, including the racial variety and the xenophobias, is in part a matter of overstatement with respect to both similarities ("they" are stupid, lazy, immoral, and so on) and differences ("we" are in these matters quite unlike "them"). Interpersonal similarities extend even to all humans now alive, to all earlier representatives of our species, and still further, though over the long time likenesses become attenuated.

The intricacies of the culture-personality relationship present to scholars a variety of perplexing problems. None is more crucial or more argued than those bearing on the genesis of personality. No "laws" governing the influences of culture on personality have been established, yet psychologists and anthropologists alike recognize that such influences are at work in every society, and that some of their results are apparent. In part the difficulty is the same one that so often frustrates students of human behavior: it is their inability to prove what they know or have good reason to believe is true. The solution has not yet been found in quantification—in "the thickets of statistical correlations" and more elaborate devices (Allport 1960:10). That route has led not infrequently to elaborate trivialization. Worse, it has deflected time and talents, and sometimes approximated a pseudoscientism which discredits the whole enterprise. But the solution has not been found in free speculation either, nor is it likely to be. In psychological anthropology an uncritical acceptance of truth-by-assertion generalizations has sometimes dignified and perpetuated a second variety of pseudoscience.

In this discussion we take what I believe to be a middle course, accepting as "probable"—as tentatively established—those generalizations which represent inductions from a sizable body of data. Space is limited, and it will be used mainly for reviewing these probables, as they appear in the light of present knowledge, rather than for describing long-discussed generalizations of increasingly dubious validity. To these we shall refer only in passing and for clarification by contrast.

We shall consider generalizations relating to (1) enculturation mechanics and processes, and the associated form and content features of sociocultural influences; (2) the range and variety of sociocultural influences, the variable cultures to be found among the young, and the varieties of culturally patterned expectations with respect to the nature and behavior of children and youth.

The reader should understand that this review presents what seem (to the writer) the generalizations currently best established. Space permits neither the presentation of supporting data (in significant amount), nor of the qualifications and counter views which would appear in a refined and extended treatment of our topic.

ENCULTURATION MECHANICS AND PROCESSES

The society and culture in which he finds himself become evident to a child in manifold, repetitive ways, some strident and some subtle. (See, for example, Mead's ample report [1953] on the "early influences that mold the Arapesh personality.")

Each child absorbs the culture accessible to him, but he also selects among the elements and alternatives of that culture, and he improvises on or beyond them (by invention, innovation, and re-combination).

What I have called "absorption" has been described more elegantly as "empathic participation" (Church 1966:290). Church writes:

> Through empathic participation they [babies] take on cultural styles and values, they form cultural identifications so that they come to be like the people around them. . . . [They pick up] the styles of their families, but in idiosyncratic ways that suit and express their own individual temperaments (1966: 290).

These modes of enculturation (absorption, selection, and improvisation) are possible for the child because he is a social creature and a sentient one as well. From birth he hears, sees, touches, and hears about other people.

Through these media of communication the culture of a society and of subsocieties is spread out before him. "All the socialization techniques employed by the adults are probably less effective in the modification of the child's behavior than the observation and imitation through which the children gradually absorb the skills, customs, and values of their group" (Minturn and Hitchcock 1963:331).

The child must absorb the culture of his group if he is to survive and to become socially adult. He does so because it is in the nature of man to learn from others of his kind. He cannot do otherwise than learn the culture in which he is embedded (some part of it, at any rate), because it is ordinarily the only culture accessible.

But he learns selectively because to do so is in his nature as an individual; he finds certain aspects of his culture difficult, impossible, uncongenial, and others easy, attractive, congenial. Inherent temperament and talents underlie selectivity, and inclination toward improvisation as well.

Though in this discussion our focus is on society and culture as they influence the child and the youth, it must not be forgotten that "influence" is a two-way street. Chombart de Lauwe (1966:247) reminds us:

> The child is "socialized" not only by his family and by school [in societies boasting such formalities], the adolescent not only by the spontaneous groups in which he participates, and the adult not only by the associations, the unions and the parties that he joins. Each one also brings an original contribution to the social milieu in which he lives. Some children very early have an extremely strong personality that stamps the whole family climate and often, through it, networks of relatives, friends and neighbors.

The persons who make up the child's social world are (a) those of his personal community, (b) those of his immediate community, and (c) those of his vicarious community. These three circumferences of an individual's social universe are, from his point of view, (a) the people he cares about, (b) the people he meets, and (c) the people he knows or hears about. These communities widen and change in composition as the child grows, learns, and moves about.

As a child's contacts widen toward the vicarious community, frequency and intensity of personal community interactions will be reduced. Immediate community interactions will be correspondingly increased, and there may be interactions in what was earlier the vicarious community.

By age six, or thereabout, the child's personality will have assumed enduring contours. Later experiences will develop detail within these contours, perhaps alter them to some or a considerable degree. However, these later developments must occur either within or against the early configuration. There is in much of human development a "sequential nature. Each characteristic is built on a base of that same characteristic at an earlier time or on the base of other characteristics which precede it in development . . ." (Bloom 1964:215).

By age ten personality is generally so well established that:

> . . . whatever pattern of moral behavior and character structure a child shows at ten years of age, he is far more likely than not to display into late adolescence; and, our belief is, for the rest of his life. . . . [While] there is *room* for change in later life. . . . prolonged, deep-going influences would be necessary to effect such a change, and . . . such influences are not likely to occur in the average person's life (Peck and Havighurst 1960:157).

The early formation of personality is possible, indeed inevitable, because of human intelligence as well as human sensitivity. Both are strikingly manifest in the young child's perceptivity with respect to the world around him. By age six, often earlier, children are likely to be well aware of prevalent social categories, quite able and ready to classify individuals in terms of these categories, and well on the way toward full development of the relevant value-attitude systems prevalent among the adults of their society. Fraser (1966:76) says, in his report on the Malay villagers of South Thailand: "Before six years of age most of the basic values are instilled in the child by precept and example." This observation is by no means unusual. Moreover, these values will persist. It has been shown, for example, that the level of achievement motivation developed in early childhood usually persists into adulthood (Moss and Kagan 1961).

The weight of such evidence is overwhelming, yet there are developmental psychologists still wedded to antithetical notions. (See Piaget 1948 and 1954; Piaget and Inhelder 1956) Concerning egocentricity; Piaget has held that before age eleven children—all children, presumably—are so egocentric that they are unable to understand or to accommodate to the needs and feelings of other persons. And concerning morality; until he is seven or eight the child is capable only of the "morality of constraint" or "the principle of moral realism"; that is, if his behavior coincides with the standards of his society, it is because he is doing what he must or what the consequences would dictate. It is difficult to understand how a lifetime study of children can have led to conclusions so out of accord with commonplace experience and observation or with the cross-cultural record. The explanation may lie partly in Piaget's dependence upon data drawn from the behavior of children in contrived or hypothetical rather than in "real life" situations, and of children in but one society. Whatever the reasons: "Undoubtedly, as many authorities have concluded, Piaget unjustifiably minimized the influence of the child's social environment" (Berkowitz 1964:50), and underestimated the young child's social sensitivities and acuities.

Recent studies go far to establish that children learn early many basic facts of their sociocultural worlds. Awareness of race and race differences, along with associated culturally patterned values and attitudes, are developed in most children (U.S.) by age five. (Goodman 1952 and 1964; Trager and Radke-Yarrow 1952; Landreth and Johnson 1953; K. Clark 1955; and others). Concepts of property—its ownership (including yours/mine distinctions), of standards for behavior, of interpersonal rights and obligations; of good and bad are well developed in middle-class urban American children by age five (Goodman and Cockrell 1958). The ability to classify people in terms of such social categories as kinship, occupational status, and foreign/nonforeign identity is well established in urban middle-class Japanese children of five to six years (Goodman, Huzioka, and Matsuura 1956).

Kreitler and Kreitler have shown that in four to five-and-one-half year olds "the level of information about sexual differences and the readiness to talk about sexuality are much higher than usually assumed" (Kreitler and Kreitler 1966:363). Their subjects were children in Israel most of whom have parents who were born and reared elsewhere (in Yeman, Iraq, Syria, Persia, Libya, Morocco, Russia, Poland, Lithuania, Hungary, Rumania, Germany, Holland, Denmark, England, and the U.S.). This study shows, the authors report, that:

> . . . the sexual concepts of the children deviate in essential points from the concepts ascribed to them by Freud and Piaget. Freud's theory about the infantile belief in the universality of the penis was refuted directly by our results. . . . In regard to Piaget, it is noteworthy that his theory about the artificialistic concept, to which he ascribes great importance, was in no way confirmed. . . . It can no longer be claimed that insufficient causal thinking (Piaget) or infantile libidinal development (Freud) hinder the adequate sexual enlightenment of children (Kreitler and Kreitler 1966:376–377).

Obviously the average adult in any society will "know" more than the average adolescent, and the latter more than the average child. It is hardly surprising that recent research should show that "the thought of the adolescent is not only more logically complex than that of the child but that it is also more flexible and mobile" (Elkind 1966:493). But the child too is knowledgeable, logical, and flexible, if ordinarily to a lesser degree.

FORM AND CONTENT FRAMES OF REFERENCE

The sociocultural influences basic to personality development are commonly discussed in terms resolvable into either *form* features, or *content* features.

Form features are matters especially of the who, when, and how of child rearing: who holds the infant, how frequently, in what manner; who sleeps with the child, for how many years, under what circumstances is he ousted from this customary bed? It is such specifics of *form* with which many students of child rearing and its effects long have been preoccupied. Beatrice Whiting expresses this preoccupation when she writes, in her introduction to the massive cross-cultural studies directed by John Whiting at the Harvard Laboratory of Human Development: "It is assumed that different patterns of child rearing will lead to differences in the personality of children . . ." (B. Whiting 1963:5). Like many other students of socialization, such as Kardiner (1939 and 1945), J. Whiting has been especially interested in body relationships and functions. He has contributed significantly to the extensive literature concerning weaning, toilet training, and the sexuality of childhood and adolescence (Whiting and Child 1953). It has been assumed that because of their biological primacy these body functions must be necessarily of emotional primacy also, and that they must therefore represent the wellsprings of human personality.

> . . . writers of this conviction have taken as proved the genetically and biologically oriented psychoanalytic assumption that the specific channeling of infantile physiological urges by parents produces specific psychological constellations in the individual (Sewell 1952:150).

In the last two decades this "psychoanalytic assumption" has been subjected belatedly to systematic testing. William Sewell concludes, in assessing his own major effort in this direction:

> Certainly, the results of this study cast serious doubts on the validity of the psychoanalytic claims regarding the importance of the infant disciplines [feeding, weaning, toilet training, sleeping arrangements] and on the efficacy of prescriptions based on them (1950:159).

This does not lead Sewell to argue that experiences during infancy are unimportant with respect to personality development. He concludes, rather:

> It is entirely possible that the significant and crucial matter is not the [infant training] practices themselves but the whole personal social situation in which they find their expression (1950:159).

This conclusion is congruent with the cross-cultural view of childhood and adolescence, and with a large body of data and interpretations in psychology as well as anthropology.

In the *form* emphasis frame of reference, with its focus on body and emotions, there has been little room for consideration of mind and reasoning. A different frame of reference is apparent in the growing trend toward "rediscovering the mind of the child . . ." (Martin 1960). With it goes a rediscovery of the child as active agent in the process of enculturation, rather than as passive vehicle and as victim of his body's imperatives (as he is usually viewed in the body-and-emotion frame of reference). Martin writes:

> . . . there is in the making a cognitive theory of behavior and development. It would view the child not merely as a passive victim of either his environmental history or of his biological nature, but as one who strives to be the master of both his nature and his history. It will thus emphasize the unique characteristic which makes that mastery a possibility, namely, intelligence (1960:75).

Recent work by Joseph Church (*Three Babies: Biographies of Cognitive Development*) opens the way toward promising studies:

> . . . of the early cognitive correlates of cultural differences, whether it be in such respects as style of movement, as pointed out by Mead and Macgregor (1951:181–186), or in the timing of postural development (Geber 1958), of posture and walking (Dennis and Najarian 1957), and of visually directed grasping (White 1963). We have additional evidence of the effects of early rearing experience from the literature of infra-human development (see, for instance, Denenberg 1962). There is every reason to suppose that cultural differences in cognition, which are very conspicuous in adults, will also begin to appear quite early in ways that can be investigated formally and quantitatively (1966:293).

The *content* features of sociocultural influences are a matter not so much of the who, when, and how as of the *what* of child rearing: what types of behavior does the child see and sense around him; what types of persons and personalities is he taught to admire and emulate; what is expected of him as a child and as a youth?

Scholars concerned with these content features are likely to be concerned also with the cognitive and active aspects of the developing personality. Among the modes of enculturation, selection and improvisation are seen to be potentially as important as absorption. The former (selection and improvisation) more than the latter (absorption) imply and require conscious, rational activity on the part of the child. This is not to say, however, that selection or improvisation can be wholly free of either affective or nonrational elements.

Form features (weaning, toilet training, training affecting sex and aggression, puberty rites) do of course differ cross-culturally. But these differences can be overstated by scholars preoccupied with them and relatively indifferent to content features. Anthropology offers much evidence that personality development is affected early and permanently by such content features as patterned concepts with respect to goals, ideals, and values. Specifics of child care and training will reflect, convey, and reinforce these content features. But primacy lies on the side of the content freatures. Hsu (1948) illustrates my point when he describes basic content elements in the culture of a traditional Chinese community, elements which importantly affect the formation and development of personality in that community. Hsu writes:

Influences of Childhood and Adolescence

> ... the most basic element of the culture is the father-son tie, which is characterized by authority on the part of the parent and filial piety on the part of the son. All other relationships in the family have this tie as their basic point of reference. . . . [Another] basic pattern is competition. . . . This competition is strictly circumscribed by the authority of parents, ancestors, and tradition. . . . The same forces of authority and competition also operate outside family and kinship groups as represented by: (a) holders of various ranks in the bureaucratic hierarchy, (b) rich and poor, and (c) literati and the illiterate (1948:276–277).

THE RANGE AND VARIETY OF SOCIOCULTURAL INFLUENCES ON PERSONALITY DEVELOPMENT

Sociocultural influences reach the child through his every perception and experience, but in early childhood these are likely to involve the members of his personal community. The sheer quantitative bulk of influences mediated by his personal community is in itself an explanation for the primacy of the personal community in the life of the child. But there is another and equally significant explanation: relationships in the personal community are largely primary (face-to-face, sustained, intimate, informal, personalized, sentiment laden). Relationships having this qualitative character appear to be, universally, peculiarly influential in the life of the child and of older persons, too.

The child's personal community is that group of people he cares about and on whom he can rely "for support and/or approval" (Henry 1958: 827). The effective personal community—effective, that is, in transmitting patterned values and standards—is enduring and cohesive. In it the child receives affection, supervision, discipline (Glueck and Glueck 1950). This we can state with assurance because of the proven relationship (in several urban-industrial societies) between these variables and ineffective transmission of patterned values and standards resulting in delinquency (Craig and Glick 1963).

Composition of the child's personal community is cross-culturally variable. For young children in a majority of societies it will include, ideally at least, their natural parents, who will be spouses. It is hardly necessary to argue that, from the child's point of view, relationships between a young child and his parents are normally of preeminent importance. Moreover:

> The conjugal family pattern is . . . in close adjustment with what we know of the optimum conditions for personality development in the young individual. Apparently the infant requires a large measure of affection and adult response over and above the satisfaction of its physiological needs . . .
> As the child grows older the presence of siblings plays an important role in its socialization . . . (Linton 1949:23–24 *passim*).

Children and adolescents, as well as infants, require evidence of affectionate and concerned response from others. But this need can be met by grandparents or aunts and uncles, as well as by natural or foster parents and siblings. There must be a personal community if sociocultural influences are to be effectively transmitted, but its size and composition vary with culture as well as with the vicissitudes of life (desertion by father, premature death of mother, and so on). In such matrilineal societies as the Trobriands, maternal uncles figure importantly in the child's personal community, and their role is culturally prescribed.

Ordinarily the young child's closest ties are with his mother, but even this relationship is subject to cultural definition. Mead (1960:126) reports that "an army of relatives" shared in the socialization of Samoan children, with the result that neither parent was notably influential. Read says:

> ... the social horizons of a small Ngoni child [Nyasaland] were never of a narrow type, restricted to his individual family. The care of a child, especially between the time of weaning and the coming of second teeth, was the concern of a number of women in addition to his own mother, from whom he was snatched away at weaning, and, for a time at least, kept away from her household for eating and sleeping (M. Read 1960:69).

Grandparents may play the roles of great importance, as they do among the Washo (Lake Tahoe region).

> These oldsters were particularly helpful in caring for and instructing the children as they were weaned and forced to depend less and less on their mother.... Even today an unusual warmth exists between relatives three generations apart, which seems to reflect this old relationship ... (Downs 1966:40).

In traditional societies especially, though by no means exclusively, sociocultural influences are likely to be mediated most strongly along the same-sex axis. Father, uncles, and sometimes older brothers and friends will teach a boy the skills and lore which men must know. Girls are instructed mainly by the older females with whom their ties are strong. In urban-industrial societies, with their heavy emphasis on formal education, these same-sex axes are weakened but still clearly discernible.

The "autonomous nuclear family" (Blitsten 1963) characteristic of urban-industrial societies presents the child with a relatively shrunken personal community. But this, like other structural variations, is tolerable; effective enculturation can still be achieved so long as the child possesses a truly personal community, however small. Lacking it he is unlikely to develop an integrated personality and a sturdy superego.

THE CULTURES OF CHILDHOOD AND YOUTH

Cultural differences notwithstanding, children and youth everywhere are, and must be, exposed to at least these aspects of culture:

(1) knowledge, attitudes, and practices designed to protect the child from injury and illness, natural and supernatural;
(2) knowledge, skills, habits and attitudes necessary if the child is to become an adult capable of coping with the environment and meeting the conditions for survival and necessary assistance to dependents;
(3) knowledge, attitudes, values, and practices intended to transform the ignorant and willful child into a "good citizen"—a person of admired character type—who has the admired qualities, who understands and respects others' rights, and who maintains the proprieties (e.g., in toilet habits and sex behavior) (Goodman 1967).

We have observed earlier that what children can and do learn of their culture, in the first few years of life, is impressive. Within even the first three years;

> ... they learn about objects and their attributes, about their locations and extensions and excursions in space, how they operate and what their functions are. They learn causal sequences, and they come to comprehend a host of relationships binding things together in both concrete and formal systems. They learn language, both passively, by listening to people talk in a concrete context of space and things and actions and emotions, and actively, so that the verbal materials to which they have been exposed—including the unspoken "rules" of grammar and logic, and all the exceptions to the rules—become the raw materials out of which they can shape crude symbolic versions of their experience (Church 1966:289).

In most traditional and folkish societies children of six or seven are expected to know the rules of proper behavior and to observe them with no more than occasional lapses. They are expected to participate to some extent in the necessary work of the adults around them, and to be repetitively practicing and refining the skills commanded by adults. Where formal education is a part of the traditional way of life, the child meets also the regimen of the school.

The child's early acceptance of cultural prescriptions and proscriptions is facilitated where these are clear, consistently spelled out, and systematically supported by adults. Wylie's report on the children of Peyrane, in the south of France, illustrates:

> ... all but the smallest children have their chores. ... The four-year-old child who has just started to school ... has no homework. He has no chores. The routine is hard, however, and he must accept it without complaining. He knows that complaining would not relieve him of the pressure, for no one

would listen to him. . . . He is told that he is old enough to face the school routine [8:30 A.M. to 4:00 P.M.], and he does so stoically. He is partially rewarded by his feeling of pride in being considered old enough, reasonable enough to accept the inevitable with resignation. For ten years, until the child is fourteen, the school routine is the most important part of his life. His parents, his teachers, his friends constantly remind him of its importance. Confronted by this unbroken social pressure, he accepts the school routine as a serious responsibility to which he must measure up. . . . To an American . . . the children of Peyrane seem incredibly well behaved. They are courteous, docile, gentle, cooperative, respectful. They seem deficient in daring, but on the other hand there is no malicious destruction of property by gangs of children. They are cruel-tongued to their equals, but they are gentle and patient with children younger than they. Above all they have a sense of dignity and social poise (1964:69, 83).

Wylie speedily learned that America children too can accept this traditional mode of enculturation and its expectations. He writes:

When we moved to Peyrane our older son was almost five years old, and naturally he was expected to go to school. Madame Girard [teacher] said we might do as we liked about sending him but she would be glad to have him. To us it seemed cruel to ask a five-year-old child to sit at a desk for six long hours a day listening to a language he did not understand, so we sent him at first only in the morning. After a few weeks, however, he asked if he might attend both morning and afternoon sessions. He said he liked the Peyrane school much more than the kindergarten he had attended at home. "At home we always had to keep playing all the time. Here we can learn real letters and numbers and things." (1964:57)

In the contemporary United States, and in other contemporary urban-industrial countries to varying degrees, segregation and role specialization by age are strongly patterned. The result is, as Maslow and Diaz-Guerrero have commented in their study of delinquency, that "the American child . . . [lives] by child values rather than adult values." Wylie's experience with his small son illustrates the fact that children themselves will, when they have a choice, elect to be challenged to practice the skills of adulthood. Some implications of the withholding of adult roles and expectations are pointed out by Maslow and Diaz-Guerrero:

American adults, especially fathers . . . have abdicated their ideal roles of structuring the world for the child, of providing him with a clear set of values—of "rights" and "wrongs" . . . thus leaving the child with the task of deciding right and wrong long before he is either willing or able to do so. . . . We postulate that juvenile violence, vandalism, cruelty, defiance of authority, and war against adults are not only a matter of growth dynamics of the standard Freudian variety, . . . but that they also imply a hostile and contemptuous lashing out in understandable retaliation against the adults who have failed them (1960:237–238).

The extent to which American children differ from even their cultural cousins in Britain has been noted by Farber (1953), who reports:

> The British child's behavior is strongly oriented toward not discommoding the tacitly superior adult world. The pressures are thus toward stepping into the preferable adult role in which he will become the central family figure, as soon as this is acceptable. The American child, in contrast, is more oriented toward his peer group of other children and in his contact with adults is rewarded for the "cute," spontaneous attention-getting childishness of his behavior. The adult state is not implicitly held up as the ultimately desirable goal. He [the child] is already the central family figure. Learning theory would indicate that with such reinforcement the tendency would be to retain the childhood role and behavior (249).

Since Farber wrote (1953), the culture of childhood and youth in Britain appears to have shifted rapidly in the direction of the American model. This has certainly been the case in Japan and probably in most other nations reached by the long arm of "Americanization." The model itself has become, meanwhile, only the more strongly and pervasively as Farber described it. "The adult state" is held up as attractive so long as it remains essentially the state of youth (free, independent but not economically responsible for self or others, amply provided with leisure and with "fun").

CULTURAL CONCEPTS AND GOALS FOR CHILDREN AND YOUTH

At the heart of child rearing, and at the crux of sociocultural influences on personality development, lie the culturally patterned ideas about children and youth. What *is* a child, in terms of inherent nature and capacities? What properly can be expected of him at various ages and stages? What kind of adult should he become if his parents and friends are to be pleased and happy with him in adulthood? In every culture there are answers to these questions, sometimes explicit and often quite implicit. It is a curious and rather amusing fact that the answers given by sophisticated "experts" differ about as widely as do the answers patterned in different cultures.

Differences among the experts must be attributed in part to an excess of zeal—a zeal which has betrayed the unwary into gross oversimplification. Dobzhansky (1957) says:

> Students of man have again and again succumbed to the temptation to simplify things by ignoring some of the variables. The scientific monstrosities of biological racism and of diaper anthropology are among the consequences (p. 18).

"Diaper anthropology" of course owes much to "the rigid ontogenetic stencils that derive from Freudianism," and to the fact that Freud produced a "doctrine of motivation anchored to neuro-anatomy" (Allport 1960:59). Allport adds:

> To him [Freud] motivation resided in the id [believed to be composed of organic tensions or drives, especially those of sex and aggression]. The conscious, accessible region of personality that carries on direct transactions with the world—that is, the ego—he regarded as devoid of dynamic power (p. 103).

That the roots of personality are neither so simple nor so organic is recognized today even by most psychoanalysts.

In the United States the "expert" concepts of the child, his nature and what should be expected of him, have shifted radically over time (Sunley 1955; Berkowitz 1964). Wolfenstein's tracing (1955) of these shifts from restrictive to permissive, from "goodness morality" to "fun morality," is more than amusing. It should alert us to the curiously erratic courses to which this kind of expertise has shown itself susceptible.

In the post-Revolutionary Soviet Union equally extreme shifts have occurred, but for very different and more readily understandable reasons. Mead and Calas (1955) note that the child training now approved by Soviet experts shows a "point-for-point congruence with Soviet political and social theory. . . . The child is expected to internalize the values of society and also to be continuously supervised by outside figures, to whom he is bound by feelings of love, trust, and respect" (pp. 195–196).

Culturally patterned (traditional and nonexpert) concepts of child nature and capacities exhibit greater stability. Even under the impact of strong acculturative forces, traditional views often die hard. Norman Chance's report on contemporary North Alaskan Eskimo culture (1966) illustrates such tenacity. He describes the traditional quality of parent-child relations among these Eskimo—the mutual warmth and affection, helpfulness and usefulness, the family cohesion and the participation of all its members in nearly all activities; ". . . parents rarely deny children their company or exclude them from the adult world." Chance continues:

> This pattern reflects the parents' view of child rearing. Adults feel that they have more experience in living and it is their responsibility to share this experience with the children, "to tell them how to live." Children have to be told repeatedly because they tend to forget. Misbehavior is due to a child's forgetfulness, or to improper teaching in the first place. There is rarely any thought that the child is basically nasty, willful, or sinful. Where Anglo-Americans applaud a child for his good behavior, the Eskimo praise him for remembering . . .
> Fathers participate almost as much as do mothers in modern family life, and in disciplinary matters they appear to fulfill much the same function that they do in Western society . . .
> In the less acculturated families, the father retains the dominant, rather than equal-participant, role. In these homes a child is expected to be restrained, quiet, and respectful in his father's presence.

Regardless of the degree of Westernization, more emphasis is placed on equality than on superordination-subordination in parent-child relations. A five year old obeys, not just because he fears punishment or loss of love, but because he identifies with his parents and respects their judgment . . .
Though a child is given considerable autonomy and his whims and wishes are treated with respect, he is nonetheless taught to obey all adults (1966:22–24 *passim*).

In these Eskimo concepts and practices there appears much that is widespread in folk and traditional belief and behavior affecting children. Implicit in the Eskimo child rearing are certain basic postulates very like those Hoebel (1960) reports from study of the Cheyenne way of life:

Children [excluding infants] have the same qualities as adults; they lack only in experience. . .
Children should, on their level, engage in adult activities. . . .
Children become adults as soon as they are physically able to perform adult roles (p. 99).

These postulates suggest a gradualist concept of movement toward full adult status and function, with implicit recognition of individual differences in rates of maturing. The gradualist concept is by no means unusual; Norbeck, Walker, and Cohen (1962) cite several cultures in which it appears: Araucanians, Lepcha, Tallensi, Trobrianders, Objibwa, Tiv, Samoans. All of these lack abrupt transitions and conceive of growing up as a gradual process extending from infancy even (Lepcha) into the midthirties. Other examples could be adduced.

"Ceremonial markers of passage from one social stage to another" (Norbeck, Walker, and Cohen 1962:478) are of course patterned in many cultures. But the nature and significance of such markers is extremely variable and extremely resistant to generalized interpretation, as Norbeck and others have shown. J. Whiting, R. Kluckhohn, and A. Anthony (1958) present an unconvincing case (Norbeck *et al.*) in attempting to support a psychoanalytically derived interpretation. They hold that male initiation ceremonies are functionally linked (as hostility-control devices) with practices presumably conducive to mother-infant son intimacy and therefore to tensions between father and son. But "as their research is presented, it concerns hypothetical conflict that is hypothetically resolved" (Norbeck *et al.*: 482).

Cohen (1964*a*; 1966) too finds Whiting's interpretations unacceptable, partly because of "Whiting's exclusive emphasis on infantile and childhood experiences as determinants of later behavior . . ." (Cohen 1966:355). But Cohen's own focus seems equally overdrawn. He appears to find "initiation ceremonies" a universal response to a universal need to "cope with the transition from childhood to adolescence" (1964*b*:11). Cohen's arguments rest on his conviction that body changes (hormonal) in the prepubertal and pubertal periods create developmental crises with which society must deal formally. That the changes occur no one doubts. But we know that they are treated very differently in different societies. They may be scarcely recognized; they may be celebrated before or after the fact, briefly or at length. They may be celebrated with more or less formality, "hazing" (Mead 1960; Whiting *et al.* 1953), or formal instruction. Little or much may be made of physiological maturing; this biological "given" of human life is culturally defined in an extraordinary variety of ways. Cohen unduly minimizes this range of variation.

We must reject also Cohen's view that "a sense of responsibility, consonant with the goals of the society, is implanted in the growing child" (1964b:11) *during* this "passage" (from childhood to adolescence). Without doubt this "sense of responsibility" is a crucial element in personality, and it may be importantly reinforced by rites of passage. But it is now well established, as we have noted earlier in this paper, that such elements develop from infancy and are already well shaped by age six or seven.

It is conceivable that rigorous and severe rituals may have a strong, even a reorienting impact on personality. So may other traumatic events. A striking change in personality may seem to be the result, but such a change is likely to be more apparent than real. Allport (1955) explains:

> It sometimes happens that the very center of organization of a personality shifts suddenly and apparently without warning. Some impetus, coming perhaps from a bereavement, an illness, or a religious conversion, even from a teacher or book, may lead to a reorientation. In such cases of traumatic recentering it is undoubtedly true that the person had latent within him all of the capacities and sentiments that suddenly rise from a subordinate to a superordinate position in his being. What he had once learned mechanically or incidentally may suddenly acquire heat and liveliness and motor power. What once seemed to him cold, "out there," "not mine" may change places and become hot and vital, "in here," "mine" (p. 87).

CONCLUSION

Sociocultural influences reach the infant and young child especially through his personal community, as its members provide for him life-sustaining care, as they give him attention and affection, and as they convey by precept and example the knowledge, skills, standards, and values of their society and subsociety, culture and subculture. Their dealings with him are shaped by culturally patterned concepts of his nature and capacities, and by culturally patterned expectations, goals and ideals for character in men and in women. The acuity of young children and the speed with which they absorb a culture, develop individual selectivity and tendencies toward improvisation are very great and often underestimated. By age six or seven the personality is likely to have assumed its major and largely enduring contours.

In later childhood and adolescence what was the child's immediate community will shift, in some part, into the orbit of his personal community. Some part of what was his vicarious community may shift into his immediate community. In small and traditional societies, as contrasted with large and urban-industrial societies, these shifts will involve only small numbers of people.

Transitions from childhood to adolescence and to maturity are in some societies ceremonially marked, though in widely differing ways and degrees. But a gradualist concept of movement through childhood toward full adult status and function is usual, even though a threshold may be celebrated.

Sociocultural influences differ greatly as between cultures, within a culture over time, and between individuals at a given time in a given society. There are cases in which a child happens to be exposed to influences of a preponderantly damaging sort. In our own society today such cases are disproportionately numerous in the lowest stratum of the socioeconomic system. Much of the "damage" resides in the fact that the developing personality is skewed away from cultural ideals for personality and from those personality attributes which facilitate attainment of the goods and statuses that Americans value.

Cultural influences, even cultural plus societal influences, are not the "all" of forces which combine to shape personalities. Nor do these forces ordinarily work wholly or even largely as repressive stencils within which personality is rigidly molded. The process of enculturation does of course induce conformity to custom, and that aspect of its working has been emphasized heavily in many studies. But the process has another and underemphasized aspect: it conveys knowledge, skills, and motivations for "creative becoming." There are then "two modes of becoming, the tribal and the personal: the one makes . . . [man] into a mirror [of his society and culture]; the other lights the lamp of individuality within [him]" (Allport 1955:35).

BIBLIOGRAPHY

ADORNO, T. W., ELSE FRENKEL-BRUNSWIK, D. J. LEVINSON, and R. N. SANFORD, *The Authoritarian Personality*. New York: Harper & Row Publishers, 1950.

ALLPORT, G. W., *Becoming, Basic Considerations for a Psychology of Personality*. New Haven, Conn.: Yale University Press, 1955.

———, *Personality and Social Encounter*. Boston: The Beacon Press, 1960.

BERKOWITZ, LEONARD, *The Development of Motives and Values in the Child*. New York: Basic Books, Inc., 1964.

BLITSTEN, DOROTHY R., *The World of the Family*. New York: Random House, Inc., 1963.

BLOOM, BENJAMIN S., *Stability and Change in Human Characteristics*. New York: John Wiley & Sons, Inc., 1964.

CHOMBART de LAUWE, PAUL-HENRI, "The Interaction of Person and Society," *American Sociological Review,* Vol. 31, No. 2, 1966, pp. 237–248.
CHURCH, JOSEPH, ed., *Three Babies: Biographies of Cognitive Development.* New York: Random House, Inc., 1966.
CLARK, K. B., *Prejudice and Your Child.* Boston: The Beacon Press, 1955.
COHEN, YEHUDI A., "The Establishment of Identity in a Social Nexus: The Special Case of Initiation Ceremonies and Their Relation to Value and Legal Systems," *American Anthropologist,* Vol. 66, No. 3, Part 1, 1964[a], pp. 529–552.
———, *The Transition from Childhood to Adolescence.* Chicago: Aldine Publishing Co., 1964[b].
———, "On Alternative Views of the Individual in Culture-and-Personality Studies," *American Anthropologist,* Vol. 68, 1966, pp. 355–361.
CRAIG, MAUDE M., and SELMA J. GLICK, "Ten Years' Experience with the Glueck Social Prediction Table," in *Crime and Delinquency,* pp. 249–261. New York: National Council on Crime and Delinquency, July 1963.
DOBZHANSKY, THEODOSIUS, "The Biological Concept of Heredity as Applied to Man," in *The Nature and Transmission of the Genetic and Cultural Characteristics of Human Populations.* New York: Milbank Memorial Fund, 1957.
DOWNS, JAMES F., *The Two Worlds of the Washo.* New York: Holt, Rinehart and Winston, Inc., 1966.
ELKIND, DAVID, "Conceptual Orientation Shifts in Children and Adolescents," *Child Development,* Vol. 37, No. 3, 1966, pp. 493–498.
FARBER, MAURICE L., "English and Americans: Values in the Socialization Process," *The Journal of Psychology,* Vol. 36, 1953, pp. 243–250.
FRASER, THOMAS M. JR., *Fishermen of South Thailand.* New York: Holt, Rinehart and Winston, Inc., 1966.
GLUECK, SHELDON, and ELEANOR GLUECK, *Unraveling Juvenile Delinquency.* Cambridge, Mass.: Harvard University Press, 1950.
GOODMAN, M. E., *Race Awareness in Young Children.* New York: P. F. Collier, Inc., 1964.
———, *The Individual and Culture.* Homewood, Ill., The Dorsey Press, 1967.
———, and DURA-LOUISE COCKRELL, *Emergent Citizenship—A Study of Four-Year-Olds.* 1958, (Mimeographed.)
———, Y. HUZIOKA, and H. MATSUURA, *Social Awareness in Young Children.* 1956, (Mimeographed).
HALLOWELL, A. I., "Culture, Personality, and Society," in A. L. Kroeber (ed.) *Anthropology Today,* pp. 597–620. Chicago: The University of Chicago Press, 1953.
HENRY, JULES, "The Personal Community and Its Invariant Properties," *American Anthropologist,* Vol. 60, No. 5, 1958, pp. 827–831.
HOEBEL, E. ADAMSON, *The Cheyennes.* New York: Holt, Rinehart and Winston, Inc., 1960.
HSU, FRANCIS L. K., *Under the Ancestors' Shadow: Chinese Culture and Personality.* New York: Columbia University Press, 1948.
KARDINER, A., *The Individual and His Society.* New York: Columbia University Press, 1939.
———, *The Psychological Frontiers of Society.* New York: Columbia University Press, 1945.
KLUCKHOHN, CLYDE, and O. H. MOWRER, "Culture and Personality: A Conceptual Scheme," *American Anthropologist,* Vol. 46, 1944, pp. 1–27.
KREITLER, HANS, and SHULAMITH KREITLER, "Children's Concepts of Sexuality and Birth," *Child Development,* Vol. 37, No. 2, June 1966, pp. 363–378.

LANDRETH, C., and B. C., JOHNSON, "Young Children's Responses to a Picture and Inset Test," *Child Development*, Vol. 24, No. 1, pp. 63–79, 1953.
LINTON, RALPH, "The Natural History of the Family" in Ruth Nanda Anshen (ed.), *The Family: Its Function and Destiny*, pp. 18–38. New York: Harper & Row, Publishers, 1949.
MARTIN, WILLIAM E., "Rediscovering the Mind of the Child: A Significant Trend in Research in Child Development," *Merrill-Palmer Quarterly of Behavior and Development*, Vol. 6, 1959–1960, pp. 67–76.
MEAD, MARGARET, "Early Influences that Mould the Arapesh Personality," in M. Mead and Nicolas Calas (eds.), *Primitive Heritage*, pp. 127–144. New York: Random House, Inc., 1953.
――――, *Coming of Age in Samoa*. New York: Mentor Books, New American Library, 1960 (First published 1928).
――――, and ELENA CALAS, "Child-Training Ideals in a Postrevolutionary Context: Soviet Russia," in Margaret Mead and Martha Wolfenstein (eds.), *Childhood in Contemporary Cultures*, pp. 179–203. Chicago: The University of Chicago Press, 1955.
MINTURN, LEIGH, and JOHN T. HITCHCOCK, "The Rajputs of Khalapur, India," in Beatrice B. Whiting (ed.), *Six Cultures*, pp. 207–361. New York: John Wiley & Sons, Inc., 1963.
MOSS, H. A., and JEROME KAGAN, "Stability of Achievement and Recognition Seeking Behaviors from Early Childhood through Adulthood," *Journal of Abnormal and Social Psychology*, Vol. 62, 1961, pp. 504–513.
NORBECK, EDWARD, DONALD E. WALKER, and MIMI COHEN, "The Interpretation of Data: Puberty Rites," *American Anthropologist*, Vol. 64, June 1962, pp. 463–485.
PIAGET, JEAN, *The Moral Judgment of the Child*. New York: The Free Press, a division of The Macmillan Company 1948. (Originally published by Harcourt, Brace in 1932)
――――, *The Construction of Reality in the Child*. New York: Basic Books, Inc., 1954.
――――, and B. INHELDER, *The Child's Conception of Space*. London: Routledge & Kegan Paul, Ltd., 1956.
READ, MARGARET, *Children of Their Fathers: Growing Up Among the Ngoni of Nyasaland*. New Haven, Conn.: Yale University Press, 1960.
SEWELL, WILLIAM H., "Infant Training and the Personality of the Child," *The American Journal of Sociology*, Vol. 58, September 1952, pp. 150–159.
SUNLEY, ROBERT, "Early Nineteenth-Century American Literature on Child Rearing," in Margaret Mead and Martha Wolfenstein (eds.), *Childhood in Contemporary Cultures*, pp. 150–167. Chicago: The University of Chicago Press, 1955.
TRAGER, H., and M. RADKE-YARROW, *They Learn What They Live*. New York: Harper & Row, Publishers, 1952.
WHITING, BEATRICE B. (ed.), *Six Cultures—Studies of Child Rearing*. New York: John Wiley & Sons, Inc., 1963.
WHITING, JOHN W. M., and IRVIN L. CHILD, *Child Training and Personality: A Cross-Cultural Study*. New Haven, Conn.: Yale University Press, 1953.
WOLFENSTEIN, MARTHA, "Fun Morality: An Analysis of Recent American Child-training Literature," in Margaret Mead and Martha Wolfenstein (eds.), *Childhood in Contemporary Cultures*, pp. 168–178. Chicago: The University of Chicago Press, 1955.
WYLIE, LAURENCE, *Village in the Vaucluse*. New York: Harper & Row, Publishers, 1964.

13

The Self and Adult Socialization

Howard S. Becker

Everyone knows what the self is. It seems to avoid nicely that brace of faults, one or the other of which afflict most concepts of social science. It is not merely a lay term, togged up with a new polysyllabic definition that conceals all the ambiguities of the original, though not very well. Nor is it totally esoteric, a barbarous neologism whose relation to anything known to ordinary men is questionable. (The concept of criminal, as social scientists habitually use it, nicely illustrates the first difficulty. Examples of the second can be found in any sociology textbook.)

The notion of the self avoids these troubles. It is not a term that plays a role in ordinary discourse so that it acquires emotional overtones or gets involved in questions that give rise to argument. On the other hand, it is not totally foreign. We immediately have an intuitive apprehension of the direction in which the concept points, a general idea of the kind of thing it must be. When a social scientist speaks of the self we feel, with some relief, that for a change we know what he is talking about.

He is talking, of course, about the essential core of the individual, the part that calls itself "I," the part that feels, thinks and originates action. Or is he? For despite the seeming clarity of the concept, people do not seem to agree on what they mean by it. This should not be surprising because, in fact, no concept can be defined in isolation. Any concept is, explicitly or implicitly, part of a theoretical system and derives its true meaning from its place in that system, from its relation to the other concepts of which the system is constructed. So the self means one thing in a sociologist's theory and another in a psychologist's, one thing (even among sociological theories) in a structural-functional theory and another in a theory based on symbolic interaction. When we accept the term intuitively we gloss over the differences it hides, differences due to the differing theoretical systems in which it has been embedded. Intuition conceals the disagreement we find when we explore the implications of the word.

In what follows I will approach the concept of self by suggesting the meaning it takes on in the framework of a theory of symbolic interaction, a theory that has long been of major importance in sociology. Of necessity, I will have to say a good deal about the symbolic character of human interaction, the nature of individual action, and the meaning of society before I can begin to speak of the self. But, having done so, I will then be able to proceed directly to the question of changes in the self during the years after childhood, a topic that has in the past few years become popular under the title "adult socialization."

SYMBOLIC INTERACTION

The theory of symbolic interaction achieved for a time a commanding position in American sociology. Its dominance arose from the presence of George Herbert Mead at the University of Chicago at the very time that sociology was establishing its first American beachhead there. Mead was a philosopher who developed a theory of society and the self as interdependent parts of the same process, a theory that became integral to the tradition of sociological research that grew up a little later around the figure of Robert E. Park. Mead's theory of symbolic interaction (as it has lately come to be called) provided, with assists from Dewey and Cooley, the basic imagery sociologists used in their work (Mead 1934; Dewey 1930; Cooley 1902).

Other sources of theoretical support for sociology eventually grew up to dispute the Chicago School. But Mead's theory still seems to me to provide a representation of the character of social life and individual action that is unsurpassed for its fidelity to the nature of society as we experience it. (Blumer 1966)

The theory of symbolic interaction takes as its central problem this question: How is it possible for collective human action to occur? How can people come together in lines of action that mesh with one another in something we can call a collective act? By collective act we should understand not simply cooperative activities, in which people consciously strive to achieve some common goal, but any activity involving two or more people in which individual lines of activity come to have some kind of unity and coherence with one another. In a collective act, to smuggle part of the answer into the definition, individual lines of action are *adjusted* to one another. What I do represents an attempt on my part to come to terms with what you and others have done, to so organize my action that you in turn will be able to respond to it in some meaningful way. Playing a string quartet embodies this notion of mutual adjustment of several individual lines of action. But so do less cooperative activities, such as arguing or fighting, for even in them we mutually take account of what each other does.

By asking how such collective actions are possible, the theory of symbolic interaction marks out a distinctive subject matter and gives a distinctive cast to the study of society. For we may, without exaggeration, regard all of society and its component organizations and institutions as collective acts, as organizations of mutually adjusted lines of individual activity, admittedly of great complexity. A city, a neighborhood, a factory, a church, a family—in each of these many people combine what they do to create a more-or-less recurring pattern of interaction. By focusing on the phenomenon of mutual adjustment, the theory raises two kinds of questions: first, what patterns of mutual adjustment exist, how do they arise and change, and how do they affect the experience of individuals? Second, how is it possible for people to adjust their actions to those of others in such a way as to make collective acts possible? Having raised the question of how collective action is possible, it answers briefly by referring to the phenomenon of mutual adjustment and then asks how that is possible.

The second question concerns us here. Mead, and those who have followed him, explained the mutual adjustment of individual lines of activity by invoking a connected set of conceptions: meaning, symbols, taking the role of the other, society and the self. Actions come to have meaning in a human sense when the person attributes to them the quality of foreshadowing certain other actions that will follow them. The meaning is the as yet uncompleted portion of the total line of activity. Actions become significant symbols when both the actor and those who are interacting with him attribute to them the same meaning. The existence of significant symbols allows the actor to adjust his activities to those of others by anticipating their response to what he does and reorganizing his act so as to take account of what they are likely to do if he does that. What we do when we play chess—think to ourselves, "If I move here, he'll move there, so I'd better not do that"—is a useful model, although it suggests a more self-conscious process than is ordinarily at work.

The actor, in short, inspects the meaning his action will have for others, assesses its utility in the light of the actions that meaning will provoke in others, and may change the direction of his activity in such a way as to make the anticipated response more nearly what he would like. Each of the actors in a situation does the same. By so doing they arrive at mutually understood symbols and lines of collective action that mesh with one another and thus make society, in the large and in the small, possible. The process of anticipating the response of others in the situation is usually referred to as taking the role of the other.

Our conception of the self arises in this context. Clearly the actions of a person will vary greatly depending on the others whose role he takes. He learns over time from the people he ordinarily associates with certain kinds of meanings to attribute to actions, both his own and theirs. He incorporates into his own activity certain regularized expectations of what his acts will mean, and regularized ways of checking and reorganizing what he does. He takes, in addition to the role of particular others, what Mead referred to as the role of the generalized other, that is, the role of the organization of people in which he is implicated. In Mead's favorite example, the pitcher on a baseball team not only takes into account what the batter is going to do in response to his next pitch, but also what the catcher, the infielders, and outfielders are going to do as well. Similarly, Strauss (1952), has argued that when we use money we are taking into account, as a generalized other, the actions of all those who we know to be involved in handling money and giving monetary value to things: storekeepers, bosses, workers, bankers, and the government.

The self consists, from one point of view, of all the roles we are prepared to take in formulating our own line of action, both the roles of individuals and of generalized others. From another and complementary view, the self is best conceived as a process in which the roles of others are taken and made use of in organizing our own activities. The processual view has the virtue of reminding us that the self is not static, but rather changes as those we interact with change, either by being replaced by others or by themselves acting differently, presumably in response to still other changes in those they interact with.

I have presented a complicated theory in a very summary fashion. The reader who is interested in pursuing it further may be interested in Mead's own writings, admittedly difficult, or may be satisfied with any of a number of good critical accounts already available. (See, for example, McCall and Simmons 1966.)

ADULT SOCIALIZATION

The current interest in adult socialization arose out of an attempt to generalize research in a great variety of fields on the changes that take place in people as they move through various institutional settings. Thus, some social psychologists had undertaken studies of the effects of participation in college life on college students; did the participation change them in any way? Others, out of an interest in the professions, had begun to explore the professional training of doctors, lawyers, nurses, and others. Still others, interested in medical sociology and social influences on mental health, had investigated the impact of mental hospitals and other kinds of hospitals on patients. Criminologists concerned themselves with the effects of a stay in prison on convicts, largely from a practical interest in how we might deal with problems of recidivism.

As workers in these different areas strove to find the general rubric under which all these studies might be subsumed and out of which might come propositions that were more abstract and more powerful, they were influenced by a desire common to most sociologists. They wanted to counter the common assumption that the important influences on a person's behavior occur in childhood, that nothing of much importance happens after that, observable changes being merely rearrangements of already existing elements in the personality. Since the term "socialization" had conventionally been applied to the formation of the personality in childhood, it seemed natural to indicate the belief that all change did not end with adolescence by speaking of "adult socialization," thus indicating that the same processes operated throughout the life cycle (Brim and Wheeler 1966; Becker and Strauss 1956; Strauss 1959; Merton, Kendall and Reader 1957).

The process of change indicated by the term can easily, and fruitfully, be conceptualized as a matter of change in the self. Our ways of thinking about our world and acting in it, arising as they do out of the responses of others we have internalized and now use to organize our own behavior prospectively, will change as the others with whom we interact change themselves or are replaced. These changes are precisely the ones students of adult socialization have concerned themselves with, though they have not always used the language of symbolic interaction or the self.

Two central questions have occupied students of adult socialization, each of them generating interesting lines of research and theorizing. The first directs itself outward, into the social context of personal change: What kinds of changes take place under the impact of different kinds of social structures? To put it in somewhat more interactionist terms, and spell out the process involved a little more fully, what kinds of situations do the socializing institutions place their new recruits in, what kinds of responses and expectations do recruits find in those situations, and to what extent and in what ways are these incorporated into the self? The second question, somewhat less studied, turns our attention inward: What kinds of mechanisms operate to produce the changes we observe in adults? I will take these up in order.

SOCIAL STRUCTURE The study of adult socialization began, naturally enough, with studies of people who were participants in institutions deliberately designed to produce changes in adults. The research was often evaluative in character, designed to find out whether these institutions actually produced the changes they were supposed to produce. Had students of professional schools, at the end of their training, developed the appropriate skills and attitudes? Did prisoners lose their antisocial character and become potentially law-abiding citizens? The studies done usually disappointed the administrators of the institutions studied, for they generally revealed that the desired results were not being achieved. This disappointment led to an inquiry into exactly what was going on, in the hope of discovering how these malfunctions could be avoided. Later inquiries were more complex, went beyond asking simply whether or not the institution achieved its purpose, began to raise more interesting questions, and produced some important discoveries.

One discovery was that the processes of change involved were more complicated than changing in a way that was not officially approved. Wheeler (1961) discovered, for instance, in a study of criminal attitudes among convicts, that their attitudes became more "antisocial" the longer they were in prison—until the date of their release approached. Then, confronted with the prospect of returning to civilian society, they rapidly shed the criminal orientation that the impact of prison had fostered in them. The curve of "criminalization," rather than being a straight line slanting up, was U-shaped. This indicated that one had to take seriously the obvious possibility that the curve of institutional influence might take any of a number of forms, each to be discovered by research rather than being taken for granted.

A second, and equally obvious, discovery was that to speak of "the institution" as producing change was a vast oversimplification. Institutions do not operate so monolithically. In order to understand the changes that took place one had to look at the structure of the institution in detail—at the particular relationships, both formal and informal, among all the participants, and at the kinds of recurring situations that arose among them. Thus, Stanton and Schwartz (1954) were able to show that mental patients responded dramatically to quarrels that took place between staff members of a mental hospital. A staff member might decide, against the opinion of others, that a particular patient would respond to intensive treatment. The staff member's intramural quarrel would lead him to invest vast amounts of time and effort on the patient and thereby produce radical improvement in the patient. But this investment also drove him out on a limb vis-à-vis his colleagues, and when he discovered his precarious situation, he clambered back to safety. The patient then returned to his original condition or, perhaps, to a worse one.

A third discovery, one that could easily have been predicted from early studies in industrial sociology, was that the people the institution was trying to socialize did not respond to its efforts as individuals, but might, given the opportunity, respond as an organized group. Thus, my colleagues and I, when we studied the socializing effects of a medical school, found it necessary to speak of *student culture*. (Becker, Geer, Hughes, and Strauss 1961) By this term we referred to the meanings and understandings generated in interaction among students, the perspectives they developed and acted on in confronting the problems set for them by the school, its authorities, and curriculum. The importance of this observation is that the school's impact does not strike the individual student, with his own unique feelings and emotions, directly. Rather, it is mediated by the interpretations given him by the culture he participates in, a culture which allows him to discount and circumvent some of the efforts of his teachers.

A fourth discovery was that the world beyond the socializing institution played an important part in the socializing process, affecting the amount of impact it had either positively or negatively. This is apparent in the earlier prison example, where the experience of prison actually produced a change in attitudes in a direction opposite to what was desired, this trend being overcome when the prospect of leaving the prison for the larger world loomed ahead. It was, in fact, only during the period when the influence of the outside world was minimized that prison had an influence. Similarly, Davis and Olesen (1963) and their colleagues have shown that the professional training of nurses is deeply marked by the nursing school's inability to shut out external influences, in the form of generalized cultural expectations that the girls will soon marry and never become practicing professionals.

As a consequence of these discoveries and rediscoveries, we can now look at the effects of socializing institutions with something of a model in mind. We know that the changes they produce in the self are likely to be complicated and many-faceted, the course in every case needing to be traced out empirically rather than assumed; we know that we must have detailed knowledge of the pattern of social relations within the socializing organization, as these impinge on the person being changed; we understand that we must see the process of socialization as at least potentially a collective experience, undergone by a group acting in and interpreting their world together, rather than as individuals; and we realize that we cannot ignore the influence of extraorganizational social groups. This gives us a framework for organizing research and a set of central concerns, each of which can be elaborated in specialized investigations.

As an example of the kind of elaboration possible, consider the question of the culture that grows up among those being socialized. (I gave as an example student culture, but it is important to realize that we may similarly have convict culture, patient culture, or a culture of any group confronted with the problem of having attempts made to influence their selves.) Such a culture may or may not develop, depending on the conditions of interaction among those being socialized. In the extreme case, if people cannot communicate they cannot develop a culture (though studies of prisons have shown that people are remarkably ingenious in devising methods of communication in unpromising circumstances). Less extremely, the kind of communication possible and the paths along which it can move will determine the degree and kind of culture that arise (Becker and Geer 1960).

This leads to analysis of how socializing institutions handle their recruits, as these affect communication possibilities. Wheeler has suggested two dimensions of prime analytic importance (Brim and Wheeler 1966). An institution may take recruits in cohorts, as most schools do when they admit a freshman class each fall, or it may take them in individually, as prisons and hospitals usually do. In the first instance, the recruits will face similar problems simultaneously, which maximizes the need for communication. In the second, each person will face his own problems alone; his fellows will either already have dealt with it and thus no longer be interested or will not be there yet and thus have no awareness of the problem, both tending to make communication more difficult.

The second dimension suggested by Wheeler distinguishes disjunctive from serial forms of socialization. In the first, one cohort or individual is released from the institution before another enters, so that communication is possible only outside the institution's walls; thus, delinquents might tell one another about the juvenile home before they enter it. In the second, several cohorts or individuals are present simultaneously, allowing the culture to be passed on rather than being developed anew, as happens when various perspectives on college life are passed on from one class to the next. Wheeler's analysis explores the consequences for the self of the various combinations of these dimensions that can arise.

Let me conclude our exploration of the effects of social structure by making the essential jump from the socializing institution, which may be taken as an extreme case, to social organizations generally, any of which can be analyzed as though it, in effect, were attempting to socialize its participants. That is, any social organization, of whatever size or complexity, has effects on the selves of those who are involved in its workings. By taking these effects as the object of our attention and viewing every organization, whatever its stated intentions as a socializing organization, we can see how society is perpetually engaged in changing the selves of its members. For every part of society constantly confronts people with new situations and unexpected contingencies, with new others whose role they must take, with new demands and responses to be incorporated into the generalized other. The self, as I remarked earlier, is constantly changing and, in this sense, the label "adult socialization" is a misnomer, suggesting as it does that the process occurs only occasionally and then only in special places.

Take the processes involved in the use of addictive and intoxicating drugs as an example. Throughout the history of any individual's experience with such drugs, society will confront him with situations that produce appreciable changes in the self. His initial willingness to experiment with drugs that are legally and morally forbidden comes about, typically, after he has begun to participate in circles where drugs are regarded as morally appropriate, as much less dangerous than popularly believed, and as productive of desirable kinds of experience.

When the person first takes any drug, the subjective experience he has will itself be a consequence of the anticipated responses he has learned to expect as a result of his interaction with more experienced users, responses he has incorporated into his self. For example, the novice marihuana user usually experiences nothing at all when he first uses the drug (Becker 1963:41–58). It is only when other users have pointed out to him subtle variations in how he feels, in how things look and sound to him, that he is willing to credit the drug with having had any effect at all. Similarly, Lindesmith (1947) has shown that people can be habituated to opiate drugs without becoming addicted, so long as no one points out to them the connection between the withdrawal distress they feel and the actual cessation of drug use. It is only when the withdrawal symptoms are interpreted as indicating a need for another shot, an interpretation often furnished by other users, and the shot taken with the predicted relief following, that the process of addiction is set in motion. When a drug-using culture exists, this process operates smoothly. When it does not, as appears to be presently true with respect to LSD-25, people are likely to have a great variety of symptoms, especially anxiety reactions, triggered by their surprise at unexpected effects (because they have not been forecast by participants in such a culture), which may lead to diagnoses of drug-induced psychosis (Becker 1967). Finally, drastic changes in the self may occur as changes in the user's social relations, incident to his drug use, take place. On the one hand, his use may involve him more and more deeply (though it will not necessarily do so) in participation with other users and deviants, whose responses, growing out of a shared culture, will lead him to see himself as one of them and to act more like them and less like any of the other social beings he might be. (This process seems most marked among opiate users, as it is among some homosexuals, and much less marked with users of marihuana.) On the other hand, the use of drugs may bring the person to the attention of authorities (mainly the police) who will brand him as deviant and treat him accordingly, thus inducing a conception of himself as the victim of uninformed outsiders. In either case, he is likely to come out of the process a more confirmed deviant than he entered. (Such processes, of course, do not always run the full course; we particularly need studies of the contingencies of social structure and interaction that lead away from the formation of deviant selves [Becker 1963:25–39].)

To repeat, this extended example serves simply as an instance of the utility of regarding all of society as a socializing mechanism which operates throughout a person's life, creating changes in his self and his behavior. We can just as well view families, occupations, work places, and neighborhoods in this fashion as we can deviant groups and legal authorities. All studies of social organizations of any kind are thus simultaneously studies of adult socialization.

MECHANISMS OF CHANGE   The second major area of research and theorizing in the study of adult socialization, less thoroughly explored than that of social structure, consists of the mechanisms by which participation in social organizations produces change. To introduce the topic, let me first mention that, in the view I have been presenting, stability in the self is taken to be just as problematic as change, so that we shall be looking at mechanisms that operate in both directions.

The general explanations of both stability and change in the self have been hinted at already in the discussion of interactionist theory and require only a slight elaboration. The person, as he participates in social interaction, constantly takes the roles of others, viewing what he does and is about to do from their viewpoint, imputing to his own actions the meanings he anticipates others will impute to them, and appraising the worth of the course on which he has embarked on accordingly. One important implication of this view is that people are not free to act as their inner dispositions (however we may conceptualize them) dictate. Instead, they act as they are constrained to by the actions of their coparticipants. To cite an obvious example, we use grammatical forms and words in accord with how others will understand them, knowing that if we become inventive and make up our own we will not be understood. The example indicates the limits of the proposition: It applies only when the actor wishes to continue interaction and have what he does be intelligible to others, or when he wishes to deceive them in some predictable way. But most social behavior meets this criterion and we need not concern ourselves with those rare instances in which communication is not desired.

The overall mechanism of change in the self, therefore, consists of the continual changes that occur in the person's notions of how others are likely to respond to his actions and the meanings he imputes to his own actions by virtue of the imputations others have made earlier. In his effort to continue interaction, to communicate, the person is continually confronted with his own wrong guesses on this score and thus with the need to revise the roles of others he has incorporated into his self.

This points the way to one specific mechanism of change, which has been called situational adjustment (Becker 1964). As the person moves into a new situation, he discovers that, just because it is new, it contains some unexpected contingencies. Everything does not work out as he expects. People respond to him in unanticipated ways, leading him to appraise what he is doing afresh. He gradually discovers "how things are done here," incorporates these new anticipations of the responses of others into his self and thus adjusts to the situation. He can then continue to act without further change in the self until he is precipitated into a new situation or until the situation changes beneath his feet.

The convicts studied by Wheeler (1961) provide an interesting example of this process. When they first enter prison they are ready to believe that crime does not pay. If it did, would they be there? But they enter an organization which is actually run by other prisoners. While prison administrators make rules and set policy, while guards attempt to enforce those rules and policies, the details of daily life come largely under the surveillance and control of the convicts' shadow government, to which prison officials largely abandon these tasks in return for peace and quiet in the institution. Convict culture is dominated by criminal values, by beliefs such as that crime does pay and that one should never snitch on a fellow inmate. To get along with the other prisoners, to play any meaningful part in what goes on and thus influence the conditions of one's own life, it is necessary to act in ways that are congruent with these beliefs and perspectives. Therefore, the longer one is in prison, the more "criminal" one's perspective.

By the same token, when one is about to leave the prison, it suddenly becomes clear that the world outside is, after all, not the prison and that it does not operate with the criminal perspectives that make collective action possible inside prison walls. The convict realizes that what works inside will probably not work outside, that his adjustment to prison ways will not enable him to interact easily with the people he will meet once he is out. In anticipation of the change in situation, he begins once again to adjust his self, changing it to incorporate the new responses of others he anticipates. (Wheeler did not study what happened to inmates once released. It may well be that the responses of other people include some the prisoners did not anticipate, so that they begin to move once more toward a criminal perspective.)

Situational adjustment is not very complicated, as explanatory mechanisms go. But it seems to explain a great deal of what can be observed of change and stability in the self. The self changes when situations change and remains relatively stable when they do not. Some aspects of the self, however, display great stability over a variety of situational pressures and this easily observable fact points to the need for other explanatory mechanisms. One which is congruent with the position taken here is the mechanism of commitment (Becker 1960).

A person is committed whenever he realizes that it will cost him more to change his line of behavior than it will to continue to act in a way that is consistent with his past actions, and that this state of affairs has come about through some prior action of his own. So committed, he will resist pressures to adjust to new situations that push him in a contrary direction, perhaps moving out of those situations where that is possible or else attempting to change the situation so that he can continue in the direction of his commitment.

A simple example of commitment is a man who is offered a new job but, on calculating its advantages and disadvantages, decides that the cost of taking the new job—in loss of seniority and pension rights, in having to learn a new set of ropes, and so on—makes it prohibitive. The trick in understanding commitment is to grasp the full range of things that have sufficient value to be included in the calculation. In analyzing occupational commitments, Geer (1966) has suggested the following as the minimal list of valuables by which people can be committed: specialized training, which can only be used in the particular occupation; generalized social prestige, which would be lost if one left the occupation; loss of face following an exhibition of being unable to continue at one's chosen work; perquisites of the job to which one has become accustomed; rewarding personal involvements with clients or coworkers; promotional opportunities and other career possibilities; successful situational adjustment to one's present way of doing things; and prestige among colleagues. We can discover how people are committed only by finding out from them which things have sufficient value for their loss to constitute a constraint.

The above list of committing valuables indicates clearly the importance of social structure for the commitment process. Commitment can only occur when there are things present in the environment which are valuable enough that their loss constitutes a real loss. But objects acquire that kind of value only through the operation of a social organization, which both embodies the consensus that ascribes major value to them and creates the structural conditions under which they achieve the necessary attribute of scarcity. If you can get a certain valuable anywhere and with great ease, it is no longer very valuable; but if the social structure makes it scarce, allowing it to be gained in only a few ways that are structurally guarded, it takes on greater value.

Commitment and situational adjustment are clearly of great importance, and each is congruent with a symbolic interactionist approach to the self and adult socialization. Other mechanisms have yet to be discovered and explored. We might speculate, for instance, that involvement will be another such mechanism. People sometimes create a new and at least temporarily stable self by becoming deeply engrossed in a particular activity or group of people, becoming involved in the sense that they no longer take into account the responses of a large number of people with whom they actually interact.

Just as in the case of commitment, one of the crucial questions in the analysis of involvements is how organizations are constructed so as to allow the mechanism to come into play. What kinds of special arrangements allow a person to become so involved in an object, activity, or group that he becomes insensitive to the expectations of others to whom we might equally, on the basis of propinquity and frequency of interaction, expect him to be responsive? Selznick's analysis of the "fanaticism" of grass roots recruits to the TVA suggests the direction such analyses might take (Selznick 1953:210–213). Their fanaticism consisted in always acting with the interests of their local community, and especially its businessmen, in mind, and systematically ignoring the considerations of national interest and bureaucratic constraint put forward by national TVA officials, both in Washington and in the field. They were able to maintain such a consistently one-sided perspective, which caused other agency officials to label them "fanatics," because all of their personal interests were bound up in the local community to which they knew they would return. They had no career or other interests in the national agency, so that the arguments and pleas of other officials (which took for granted that everyone had motives like theirs, actually unique to those who did have long term interests in the agency) meant nothing to them.

Generalizing from this case, we can look for the mechanism of involvement to operate whenever people are insulated from the opinions of others who, on the basis of common sense, we would expect to exert influence on them. Those others may be family members, as when an adolescent becomes so involved with his peers that he loses interest in what his parents think about his activities. They may be work associates, as in the TVA case. They may be such community representatives as the police, as when we speak of drug addicts being obsessed or totally involved in the activities surrounding drug use. Or we may have in mind some generalized conception of "public opinion," as when we wonder how people can do things that "everyone knows" are bizarre or unusual, such as being a nudist.

The structural conditions that produce such involvements consist of social arrangements which effectively isolate people from other opinion, which allow them to ignore the expectations of some of those with whom they interact. Physical isolation is the most obvious example: religious sects often attempt to move away from the rest of society, as the Mormons once did, thus protecting their members from the necessity of shaping their behavior in the light of the scandalized responses of others. People may also be isolated, as the grass roots fanatics in TVA were, in an organizational sense; though they interact with others, their organizational positions and interests are so different as to preclude the development of any sense of community or common fate. More subtly, a person may be taught by the members of a group he has joined how to discount the opinions of those he once took seriously. Drug users learn to do this, and so do young people who enter an occupation their parents disapprove. Or, to conclude this preliminary and incomplete catalogue, they may have an experience commonly defined in one way or another, as setting them apart from others: a serious illness, a religious conversion, an emotional trauma. In every case, the crucial fact is that the person's social relationships—whom he comes into contact with and what they expect of him—become patterned in a way that allows him to dismiss certain categories of people from the self process.

I have briefly indicated the nature of a few mechanisms of change in the self: situational adjustment, through which much of the day-to-day variation in behavior can be explained; commitment, through which the development of long-term interests arises; and involvement, a process of shutting out of potential influences. Much work, empirical and theoretical, remains to be done.

CONCLUSION

Work in the field of adult socialization has made several contributions to the study of personality. It is one of the developments that is helping to turn the theory of symbolic interaction, by filling it out with research and the differentiated network of propositions research brings with its findings, from a programmatic scheme into a usable scientific tool. By doing this, it also begins to make available to students of personality, by providing the necessary concepts, much of the rich body of data sociologists have accumulated. It has, finally, introduced all of us to some areas of society that had not heretofore been studied and in so doing enriched our understanding both of society and of the great variety of influences which play on the continual development of the self.

BIBLIOGRAPHY

BECKER, HOWARD S., "Notes on the Concept of Commitment," *American Journal of Sociology*, Vol. 66, July 1960, pp. 32–40.
———, *Outsiders: Studies in the Sociology of Deviance*. New York: The Free Press, a division of The Macmillan Company, 1963.
———, "Personal Change in Adult Life," *Sociometry*, Vol. 27, March 1964, pp. 40–53.
———, "History, Culture and Subjective Experience: An Exploration of the Social Bases of Drug-induced Experiences," *Journal of Health and Social Behavior*, Vol. 14, Winter, 1967, pp. 239–247.
———, and BLANCHE GEER, "Latent Culture: A Note on the Theory of Latent Social Roles," *Administrative Science Quarterly*, Vol. 5, Sept. 1960, pp. 304–313.
———, and ANSELM L. STRAUSS, "Careers, Personality, and Adult Socialization," *American Journal of Sociology*, Vol. 62, Nov. 1956, pp. 253–263.
———, BLANCHE GEER, ANSELM L. STRAUSS, and EVERETT C. HUGHES, *Boys in White: Student Culture in Medical School*. Chicago: The University of Chicago Press, 1961.
BLUMER, HERBERT, "Sociological Implications of the Thought of George Herbert Mead," *American Journal of Sociology*, Vol. 71, March 1966, pp. 535–544.
BRIM, ORVILLE G., and STANTON WHEELER, *Socialization After Childhood*. New York: John Wiley & Sons, Inc., 1966.
COOLEY, CHARLES HORTON, *Human Nature and the Social Order*. New York: Charles Scribner's Sons, 1902.
DAVIS, FRED, and VIRGINIA L. OLESEN, "Initiation Into a Women's Profession," *Sociometry*, Vol. 26, March 1963, pp. 89–101.
DEWEY, JOHN, *Human Nature and Conduct*. New York: Holt, Rinehart and Winston, Inc., 1930.
GEER, BLANCHE, "Occupational Commitment and the Teaching Profession," *The School Review*, Vol. 74, No. 1, Spring 1966, pp. 31–47.
LINDESMITH, ALFRED R., *Opiate Addiction*. Bloomington, Ind.: Principia Press, 1947.
McCALL, GEORGE J., and J. L. SIMMONS, *Identities and Interactions*. New York: The Free Press, a division of The Macmillan Company, 1966.
MEAD, GEORGE HERBERT, *Mind, Self, and Society*. Chicago: The University of Chicago Press, 1934.
MERTON, ROBERT K., PATRICIA KENDALL, and GEORGE READER (eds.), *The Student Physician*. Cambridge, Mass.: Harvard University Press, 1957.
SELZNICK, PHILLIP, *TVA and The Grass Roots*. Berkeley, Calif.: University of California Press, 1953.

STANTON, ALFRED, and MORRIS SCHWARTZ, *The Mental Hospital.* New York: Basic Books, Inc., 1954
STRAUSS, ANSELM L., "The Development and Transformation of Monetary Meanings in the Child," *American Sociological Review,* Vol. 17, June 1952, pp. 275–286.
——, *Mirrors and Masks.* New York: The Free Press, 1959.
WHEELER, STANTON, "Socialization in Correctional Communities," *American Sociological Review,* Vol. 26, Oct. 1961, pp. 697–712.

14

Personality Change in Middle and Old Age

William E. Henry

Problems of change and problems of continuities in personality are complexly interwoven. Whether one focuses upon the individual or upon larger units such as the family or other social group, disentangling the obviousness of continuing stabilities from the commonly less apparent changes is a difficult task. Part of the complexity lies in the fact that the processes involved are in themselves complex, and interactional in nature, whether one examines these in the interplay of events and people in a social system, or within the intricacies of inner psychodynamics in the private person.

A methodological preference for longitudinal observations, as opposed to cross-sectional observation, does not resolve the problems of choice between variables likely to show sameness over time and variables likely to show change. Nor will any choice of method resolve the question of whether repeated change in the life style of a single individual does not perhaps create its own continuity, a continuity of adaptive style, for example, observable as change or sameness depending upon one's conceptual stance. The very fact of an effort at education for adaptability creates a posture in which passing events and transitory anxieties are but minor fluctuations in the search for self-actualization. In that context, the most relevant observation is probably upon the fluctuations in the earlier years and the increasing continuity of an adaptive style in the later years. Such a perspective permits the perception of continuities in data which may appear fluctuating or chaotic at shorter range. But at the same time the realization of long-range goals, or an increasing sureness of problem solution, may obscure important alterations in the nature of problems as perceived by the individual in the resources which he uses for their contemplation and resolution. At the present time I believe we urgently need and do not now have a conceptual framework permitting us to examine changes and continuities over long spans of the lifeline. Within shorter ranges we can now choose to focus upon one set of issues or another, constantly running the hazard of allowing some stability to obscure change and some changes to overweigh a developing continuity. The most serious gap in our conceptual structure resides in the absence of data from the adult sphere and from our attendant tendency to examine adult issues, when we do, from the vantage point of ideas and concepts from the study of children and adolescents. The issue is not that some concepts from these fields may not indeed be relevant for the examination of adult or general life-span issues; the issue is rather that we do not know that they are, and that such studies of adulthood as exist and deal with personality changes tend to do so in terms which are specific to adulthood, thus confounding the problem of examining their relevance for other life periods.*

In most recent studies of adulthood, and especially of personality change, a focal issue is always the interplay of dynamic and situation, the interaction of person and role, of aim and social possibility. In one study of early adults in training in the mental health professions, preoccupations with nurturance needs presents a marked continuity over about a three-year span. At the same time, closer examination of these nurturance preoccupations shows considerable change in the contexts in which nurturance has saliency. There is a concern with the receiving of nurturance from parental figures in the early stages, through a marked ambivalence toward nurturance and training figures, to an end-point of the exercise of nurturance toward clients in a professional role. Here not only do inner dynamics change over a short time span, but they gain their greatest meaning when described in relation to the social events occurring at the same time. Whether these data are viewed as showing continuing concern with nurturance or developing change with the form and exercise of nurturance in differing social circumstances is a matter of choice.

It is, of course, undoubtedly true that at any age the interplay of inner dynamic and environmental press is important, and at any age the alternations in their relative saliency confound problems of description and prediction. Yet the middle adult periods, say from 30 to 60, seems most probably a period in which the focus upon the external, upon the social, is at a maximum, and further, a period in which inner changes become increasingly directed by the possibilities inherent in the life situation. By this I mean that the individual during this period is maximally involved in and engaged with the purposes and forms of social life, and tends to define his aims, his successes, and his purposes in these social terms. Not only do social forms and values come to direct his own affairs, he also comes to sponsor actively these values. As he actively attempts to direct his own life, similarly does he attempt the direction of the life of his colleagues and his children. Both stances, toward self and toward others, are not only active and instrumental ones, they are probably also stances which tend to max-

---

* For an excellent discussion of this issue see Neugarten, Bernice L. (14).

imize dominant values and minimize variations and alternative views. In this sense, they are stances which stabilize common modes of life, and in personal terms they are stances which are narrowing and consolidating. They tend thus to focus the individual more upon the utilization of outer events than upon the contemplating of inner events or the exploration of new values or new life styles. The common references to plateaus appearing in various measurements during adulthood, to consistency of expression of value and attitude, are probably real enough reflections of these consolidating phases. It is in this context that the common horror with which many adults view the vagaries of adolescence is probably more a measure of our investment in adult stable social values than it is an estimate of adolescent disdain for them. The work of the world is done by the middle-aged, acknowledging minor, highly publicized exceptions, and that work is one of outer-oriented instrumentality, of company policy, of believing in the maintenance of our values, and of conviction sufficiently intense to allow us to judge the deviations of our peers and of our children—and, as a matter of fact, the neighbor's children as well.

It is in this sense that one may speak of "engagement" with societal norms and forms during middle-age—a statement implying both active interaction and personal investment. It is in this same sense that I will later speak of "disengagement" in old age, implying a mixture of reduced interaction and personal investment (5, 11).

But this portrayal of the long haul of middle age, assuming the 30 to 60 I have suggested, suffers in part from an excessive emphasis upon the outer social actualities and in part from a failure to suggest any variations within it—either of kinds of middle-aged persons or of age-related changes within this period. It is at once too dull and too conscious, and appears to deny that preconscious contemplation of alternatives and vagaries so common to most people.

As an antidote, through possibly an overdose, I think it relevant to suggest that this period is one in which the greatest conscious and preconscious sense of self-awareness can develop. It remains to be shown that such a sense of identity is characteristic, or even common, among that broad range of kinds of people composing the mid-age cluster of any society. But it is a clear potentiality of the period, more so, I believe than the adolescent period with which the term identity is most commonly associated. I point out, as a bibliographic justification for its use in middle age, that Erikson proposed that identity, in the individual and communal context in which he uses it, cannot develop before the psychosexual issues of adolescence arise, and that after adolescence it is indispensable to that meaningful coherence of individual and communal consciousness that characterizes the optimal utilization of the adult years. As Erikson observes, in his discussion of the concept of identity in race relations

> Unless provoked prematurely and disastrously . . . . psychosocial identity is not feasible before the beginning, even as it is not dispensable after the end of adolescence, when the body, now fully grown, grows together into an individual appearance; when sexuality, matured, seeks partners in sensual play and, sooner or later, in parenthood; when the mind, fully developed, can begin to envisage a career for the individual within a(n) historical perspective—all idiosyncratic developments which must fuse with each other in a new sense of sameness and continuity (6, p. 160).

The central question for the study of adulthood, and its resolution in old age, may well be that of the degree to which identity is indeed established —identity perceived as "a subjective sense of an invigorating sameness and continuity" (6, p. 147).

Two special attributes of such a possible adult state are suggested by Sigmund Freud's address to the B'nai B'rith in 1926 (7), in his attempt to explain what bound him to Jewry in spite of his possessing "neither faith nor national pride."

> . . . it was my Jewish nature alone that I owed two characteristics that had become indispensable to me in the difficult course of my life. Because I was a Jew I found myself free from many prejudices which restricted others in the use of their intellect; and as a Jew I was prepared to join the Opposition and to do without agreement with the "compact majority."

In this statement there are perhaps three, rather than two, attributes, suggestive of the adult exercise of identity and applicable to men and women of less heroic stature. The first is the statement of a sense of personal history in a tradition not bound to the individual—"because I was a Jew." The second is the direct indication of free, unprejudiced, unbound use of talent and skill. And the third is the sense of autonomy implied in the awareness of a majority without need to be subservient to it.

The optional use of adulthood, and a use which cannot, I believe, be comparably made of any other major life period, is perhaps achieved in these ways—through an autonomy neither bound to nor hostile to a majority: an ability for the self-conscious, intentional, planned use of talent and skill; and a sense of history and purpose that locates the individual in a continuity. For Freud, Jewry provided that continuity, as after a time, his own intellectual development must have also. But I would take it that no such massive tradition is necessary, though undoubtedly that same tradition provides the historical perspective for lesser folk. Others may well find it in some comparable ethnic or religous tradition, in their relatedness of occupation, to family, or individual career line. Some may well gain a previously missing sense of continuity from their own immediate family. In fact, many of the stabilizations on adulthood, of adolescent identity diffusion, may well come from that interaction of individuality and communal purpose provided by the presence and development of children.

Conceivably, I am overimpressed with this portrayal of identity as an ideal, though certainly it seems more than a portrayal of the common, the normal—or perhaps it may indeed be seen as modal for certain as yet undefined subgroups. These might include some, but certainly not all, American upper middle-class professionals; or possibly some groups in other societies where cultural traditions have long continuity; or possibly groups in which intermixtures of hostility and achievement are of minimal intensity or where the transition from dependence to autonomy is more happily managed.

The question of whether identity, as phrased by Erikson, is an ideal state achieved only occasionally by certain individuals, or whether it can also be a common achievement of some socially defined entity, is probably researchable. It must be admitted, however, that Erikson is quite right in his comment that "attempts at transverting clinical concepts into quantifiable items subject to experimental verification are always undertaken at the risk of the experimenter" (6, p. 171).

The fuller, perhaps almost clinical, concepts of identity do nonetheless provide a broader and more fitting context for the instrumental engagement with societal norms that I earlier suggested as characteristic of this age span. They call attention to the crucial distinction between environmentally bound adherence to societal norms and an invigorating individuality in accord with social continuities.

An overlapping approach to this duality in adult personality may be seen in David Bakan's portrayal of agency and communion. In the broadest terms Bakan uses the term agency for the existence of the organism as an individual and the term communion for the participation of the individual in some larger organism of which he is a part. He admittedly conceives of communion and agency at a rather high level of abstraction, but sees manifestations of them in more specific terms.

> Agency manifests itself in self-protection, self-assertion, and self-expansion; communion manifests itself in the sense of being at one with other organisms. Agency manifests itself in the formation of separations; communion in the lack of separations. Agency manifests itself in isolation, alienation, and aloneness; communion in contact, openness, and union. Agency manifests itself in the urge to master; communion in noncontractual cooperation. Agency manifests itself in the repression of thought, feeling, and impulse; communion in the lack and removal of repression (1, p. 15).

One of the central elements of change in adults during the middle span may well be variations in the saliency of agency and communion, a variation independent of a level of identity—if identity may be seen at all as existing in degrees beyond a certain minimum rather than merely in a presence or absence.

Such concepts as agency and communion, particularly given their scope and level of abstraction, have the advantage of providing a conceptual generalness within which specific studies of more limited variables and particular samples may be given meaning. I have in mind here such findings as the prevalence of high instrumentality and achievement focus in 30-year-olds and an internal introspective orientation in 40- and 50-year-old business executives (18); the changes in age and sex role attributes assigned to men and women differentially by men and women during the 40-to-50-year span as opposed to those from 55 to 70 (16); the trend toward disengagement, seen as a contraction in outer world cathexes and an increase in interiority in ages over about 65 (5, 11, 17); personality changes suggested by the life review, a process posited as occurring in the very elderly (3); and the personality restructuring reported by Lieberman as related to distance from death in the elderly (12). Of course, these brief reports are by no means the only accounts of personality changes during adulthood and old age, but they are indicative of the kind of findings which are appearing. See in addition, Worchel and Byrne (19); Neugarten (13), Neugarten and associates (15).

The relevance of agency and communion to such findings resides in part in their more comprehensive coverage of areas of human motivation. Agency, as proposed by Bakan, covers far more than the delimited, though indeed more manageable variables such as instrumentality, and achievement. Communion similarly includes issues of social interaction but also calls attention to the feeling and affect elements of social union as well as other manifestations of the impulse to join and combine with other forces.

Their relevance to the adult sphere hinges upon what I would take to be a central concern of much adult life—the risk to a sense of social union inherent in lives of high instrumentality on the one hand, and the potential risk to a sense of social purpose and involvement in the world's work inherent in lives based exclusively upon the immediacy and socioemotionality of union without separateness and without instrumentality.

I suggested earlier a second deficiency to my portrayal of adult lives as dominated by investment in the social norms and that was the lack of variation among adults implied in such a portrayal. Beyond the obvious note that such a statement is a kind of average and that variation resides in the extremes, it would seem logical that the wide number of essentially normal adult lives would also differ in some more qualitative, stylistic ways. David Chiriboga (4) has recently attempted an investigation of Maslow's concept of self-actualization among a group of male adults selected as obviously successful in occupational terms. The sample is thus one maximizing some form of social contribution or occupational success. In this sense it is a sample skewed toward competence and success. This study is one directed by Bernice Neugarten and James Birren in which they are in part interested in examining the techniques and coping devices used by adults of demonstrated competence. As anticipated by my proposition regarding identity in adults, and by the anticipation of the relevance of self-actualizing properties in successful people, there is indeed a group of these adults who are adequately portrayed by autonomy, self-directed skill, responsible social interaction. This is a group making maximal use of the adult opportunity in directing their own efforts with a clear sense of their own sameness and continuity, and doing so clearly within the forms and conventions of their social groups. But this is only one group among this sample. There would appear to be at least two others, two other styles of being successful adults. The one represents a form of constricted adherence to goals of instrumentality and work success, without the sense of personal choice, without the joy of a sense of identity. They are a group not free to create an "opposition to the compact majority"; they are, in effect, the compact majority, bound to the conviction of agency and bound to their social norms more through a sense of need than of convenience and choice.

A third group is more directed toward impulse gratification, coasting nicely within the social conventions without undue attention to them and without concern for added achievement or self-actualization. This seems to be a fairly satisfied group, of good morale, where lives are by no means seen as finished, but who do not appear to be seeking either new experience or the opportunity to exercise talents and skills.

I would like to draw three conclusions for this admittedly preliminary study. The first is that the adult groups maximizing their autonomy within the framework of a firm sense of identity and a firm grasp upon the social realities do indeed exist. And they are a group which gives a particular sense of possibly overdetermined pleasure to the middle-class academician. They are in control of their own lives, using the social forms to personal ends but without rancor or resentment.

And, secondly, the very fact that they constitute only about a third of this special sample, suggests that they may perhaps be seen as representing a kind of ideal solution to the adult circumstance. They are hardly modal, even within this privileged sample—granted that the same life style may conceivably be found also among samples of a more routine nature.

And, thirdly, it becomes at once apparent that considerable variation in adult life styles will be found once other samples are studied in more detail.

I have treated the topic of personality change in middle life as it relates to what is usually called normal development, as opposed to equally justifiable treatments emphasizing change due to special environmental hazards, or arranged efforts at change. Within that very broad context, I have suggested the relevance of the concept of identity, the interaction of the concepts of agency and communion. I have attempted to lend some body and substance to my own observation regarding the social norm involvement of adulthood by suggesting that we have much to learn about how adults manage their lives during the 30 or so years of midlife.

The continuities of adulthood are fairly apparent, and the many observations of limited change in adulthood probably reflects these continuities. The question to be resolved is that of the degree to which these continuities obscure, for ourselves as adults or as investigators, the possibly many discontinuities. Change, when it is found, tends to appear more readily in that realm of behavior called personality than in social interaction or in adherence to social values (15).

Many of the discontinuities, in both social event and inner dynamic, of childhood and adolescence, have become apparent only when they are given meaning by the fresh conceptualization of an investigator. One very strong assumption, both socially and in theory, that the hurdles are over by late adolescence, may weaken as we probe into the placid plateaus of adulthood, and as we give thought to what in earlier phases are so apparently developmental tasks. Is there no reason to suppose that some events of adulthood do not have the power of change upon inner processes, do not require realignments of social action and motivation, do not present challenge or create anxiety? Indeed, major physical growth is over, some skill and knowledge have been attained, and a form of social living has been established. But is marriage only a social and sexual convenience; are children only things to be loved and instructed, without reactive effect upon the adult; are changes in occupation, in levels of responsibility in work and social commitment, only more or less time consuming; are not decreasing rates of gain in competence or social reward not anxiety producing; is the masculinity challenged by sexuality in adolescence not similarly challenged by its related decline in later adulthood; or the proof of femininity resident in having children not majorly reordered when the children achieve independence?

A major task for personality theory in the future is to consider these questions, to examine the fate of adolescent resolutions during adulthood, to examine afresh the discontinuities of adult life, and to provide us the kind of guidelines we have for childhood and adolescence, guidelines that will make of adulthood a period worthy of investigation.

I do believe that old age is a different phase, whether seen as a major form of change in social responsibilities—which it is—or as a form of change in inner dynamics—which I believe it is also. The main dynamic of that later phase resides in the gradual weakening of cathexes to social and other outer world events, and in the increased attention which the individual gives to interior processes, in nostalgic recollection and in present contemplation. Though here again it must be noted that there are styles of aging, which are major variations on this theme of disengagement (8, 9).

I would in fact prefer to think of old age as the later phases of adulthood, just because I suggest that the style of aging relates most clearly—as adolescence perhaps does to childhood—to resolutions adopted in the middle phases of adulthood.

BIBLIOGRAPHY

BAKAN, DAVID, *The Duality of Human Existence*. Skokie, Ill.: Rand McNally & Company, 1966.

BECK, R. J., "Personality, Values and the Career Line: A Study in the Development of Professional Identity," unpublished doctoral dissertation, Committee on Human Development, University of Chicago, 1965.

BUTLER, R. N., "The Life Review: an Interpretation of Reminiscence in the Aged," *Psychiatry*, Vol. 26, 1963, pp. 65–76.

CHIRIBOGA, D., "Self Actualization in Middle Age Males," unpublished manuscript, Committee on Human Development, University of Chicago, 1966.

CUMMING, M. ELAINE, and W. E. HENRY, *Growing Old*. New York: Basic Books, Inc., 1961.

ERIKSON, ERIK H., "The Concept of Identity in Race Relations: Notes and Queries," *Daedalus*, Winter, 1966.

FREUD, SIGMUND, "Address to the Society of B'nai B'rith," in *The Standard Edition of the Complete Psychological Works of Sigmund Freud*. London: Hogarth Press, 1953–1966; Vol. XX (1959) pp. 271–274.

HAVIGHURST, R. J., BERNICE L. NEUGARTEN, and S. TOBIN, "Disengagement, Personality and Life Satisfaction in the Later Years, in P. From Hansen (ed.), *Age with a Future*, pp. 419–424. Copenhagen: Munksgaard, 1964.

HENRY, W. E., "The theory of intrinsic disengagement," in P. From Hansen (ed.), *Age with a Future*, pp. 415–418. Copenhagen: Munksgaard, 1964.

———, "Some Observations on the Lives of Healers," *Human Development*, Vol. 9, 1966, pp. 47–56.

———, and M. ELAINE CUMMING, "Personality Development in Adulthood and Old Age," *J. Proj. Techniques*, Vol. 23, No. 4, 1959.

LIEBERMAN, M. A., "Psychological Correlates of Impending Death; Some Preliminary Observations," *J. Geront.*, Vol. 20, 1965, pp. 181–190.

NEUGARTEN, BERNICE L., "A Developmental View of Adult Personality" Chapter 12 in J. E. Birren (ed.), *Relations of Development and Aging*. Springfield, Ill.: Charles C Thomas, 1964.

NEUGARTEN, BERNICE L., "Adult Development: Toward a Psychology of the Life Cycle," address at American Psychological Association, 1966: submitted for publication, *Journal of Genetic Psychology*.

NEUGARTEN, BERNICE L., and associates. *Personality in Middle and Late Life*. New York: Atherton Press, 1964.

NEUGARTEN, BERNICE L., and D. GUTMANN, "Age-Sex Roles and Personality in Middle Age: A Thematic Apperception Study," *Psychol. Monogr.*, Vol. 72, No. 17 (whole No. 470), 1958,

ROSEN, JACQUELINE L., and BERNICE L. NEUGARTEN, "Ego Functions in the Middle and Later Years: A Thematic Apperception Study," *J. Geront.*, Vol. 15, No. 1, 1960, pp. 62–67.

SCHAW, L. C., and W. E. HENRY, "A Method for the Comparison of Groups: A Study in Thematic Apperception." *Genet. Psychol. Monogr.*, Vol. 54, 1956, pp. 207–253.

WORCHEL, P., and D. BYRNE, *Personality Change*. New York: John Wiley & Sons, Inc., 1964.

15

The Consequences of Early Bilingualism in Cognitive Development and Personality Formation[1]

A. Richard Diebold, Jr.

INTRODUCTION

I have not chosen to survey in this paper the full range of research devoted to language and verbal behavior and its possible contributions to the study of personality. The reason for the choice is not far to seek. The research interests and findings of the relatively new fields called "psycholinguistics" and "sociolinguistics" and the older field called "ethnolinguistics," are vast and varied; and as a whole, the contributions to the study of personality are more promising in future potential than in present fact.

Rather the focus will be on one topic, bilingualism and the psychology of the bilingual, and more specifically, on the matter of the consequences of early bilingualism in cognitive development and personality formation. I shall treat the topic as an exemplar of the significant advances which interdisciplinary research has made in the study of language behavior, and, in this case, with a problem which I believe has considerable import for the theory of personality formation.

The problem is neither novel nor trivial, and has the advantage of a ready translation into popular terms. Partly as a consequence of its obvious

---

[1] Much of the research upon which this paper is based was conducted at Harvard University under the auspices of the Department of Social Relations where the author was Assistant Professor of Social Anthropology and Linguistics (1961–1966). It was supported in part by research grants from the following sources: (1) a Faculty Grant from Harvard University's Ford International and Comparative Studies Fund (1966); (2) U.S. Office of Education (NDEA) grant No. OE 3-14-014 (1963-1966) administered jointly by Harvard University's Office for Reasearch Contracts and the Laboratory of Social Relations; (3) a Social Science Research Council Faculty Research Grant (1965).

Consequences of Early Bilingualism in Cognitive Development

relation to communicative difficulties and educational problems in large modern societies, the effects of bilingualism have come to be the subject for much debate. The collective sentiment about bilingualism in the United States has been at best ambivalent, a manifestation of the Anglo-American "melting pot" ethos. Educators, as a group which must cope with the practical problems of ministering to a population including a sizeable number of bilingual children, have been less ambivalent; indeed, their majority view is that bilingualism (as distinct from second-language learning in the school) is a damaging experience for the child, one which poses hurdles to the child's intellectual development and later emotional adjustment. Their arguments usually lead one to the conclusion that the trouble arises from "having too much in one's head," that some sort of deleterious conflict results from the bilingual child's being inputted with two different language codes, and that this linguistic conflict produces the very real evidence for intellectual deficit and personality problems which they are able to adduce in support of their contentions. (Let this be clear from the start: competent recent surveys of the literature [for example, Darcy 1953, 1963; Jensen 1962; Peal and Lambert 1962] do reveal that there is an association between bilingualism and lower intelligence ratings as well as certain types of personality dysfunction, when "somehow comparable" groups of monolinguals and bilinguals are compared.) Before 1950 there was little empirical data which could be drawn upon to refute this view, let alone any sophisticated experimental or interpretive research aimed at testing the notion that bilingualism itself was the cause of some of the evils cited.

My purpose here is to apprise the reader of two major fallacies in the popular argument: (1) that of interpreting an observed association in cause-and-effect terms, that is, that because P is observed to be associated with Q, it is necessarily true that P causes Q; and (2) that the majority of "somehow comparable" groups of monolinguals and bilinguals which have been compared as if bilingualism were the critical variable are in fact not "otherwise equally matched." Recent interdisciplinary research on bilingualism has produced conclusive results which oblige us to reject a linguistic etiology as an explanation for some of the cognitive and personality disorders associated with bilingualism.

THE CONCEPTS "INTERFERENCE" AND "DOMINANCE"

It is a psycholinguistic truism that all children, unless thwarted by various organic defects (such as deaf-mutism) or severe functional disorders (such as infantile autism) go through a developmental process characterized by certain fixed maturational sequences, and in the course of socialization and enculturation, begin to speak the language of the community wherein they live. There are unfortunately no statistics on the incidence in different societies concerning what at least some Americans intuitively feel to be an anomaly in this process of primary language acquisition, that in which the child learns not one, but two (or more) languages and thereby becomes a bilingual. The adult who emerges from this experience, if he continues to speak his two childhood languages, will most likely display a native-speaker's proficiency in both languages; that is, there will be in his linguistic performance no immediately observable *interference* in speech production in either language such as could be attributed to code *dominance* by the other. Such a proficient bilingual is believed to be the exception rather than the rule in the world's population of bilinguals, and it is instructive to contrast him with his more numerous bilingual fellows, so-called "subordinate bilinguals" whose backgrounds and actual linguistic performance betray a differential competence in their two languages. (In many cases, the differential competence stems from having learned a secondary language at some time subsequent to primary language acquisition.)

Although we will not be concerned with the subordinate bilingual in this study, it will be useful here to cite the "foreign accent" and "grammatical mistakes" in his secondary language as examples of what the concepts *interference* and *dominance* may refer to. If we examine the English spoken by native speakers of German, and the German of native speakers of English, we may discover in their speech deviations from native phonetic norms and syntactic rules which suggest "imperfect mastery" of the secondary language. Examples (i) and (ii) below show deviations from English models which a native speaker of German might produce:

(i) *phonological:* ("foreign accent")
for the utterance {*This is a fine state of affairs.*}, compare the subordinate bilingual's

[dɪsɪsəfaɪnšteːtəfəʔfeːʌs] with native English
[ðɪsɨzəfaɪnsteɪtəvəfeɚz].

(ii) *grammatical:* ("grammatical mistakes")
compare the utterance *{*When I walk the street along.*} with the acceptable English model {*When I walk along the street.*}.

Examples (iii) and (iv) show deviations from German models which a native-speaker of English might produce:

(iii) *phonological:* ("foreign accent")
for the utterance {*Sprechen Sie französisch?*}, compare the subordinate bilingual's

[sprɛkənzɪifrænzozɪš] with native German
[špreːxənziːfrantsöːziš].

(iv) *grammatical:* ("grammatical mistakes")
compare the utterance *{*Er kommt entlang die Straße.*} with the acceptable German model {*Er kommt die Straße entlang.*}.

The observable deviations of the nonnative speaker's replicas from the acceptable models as produced by a native-speaker (for example, *{*When I walk the street along.*} : {*When I walk along the street.*}) are instances of interlingual *interference*. These examples represent "conflict" between the phonological and grammatical rules ("habits") specific to the two languages, and the deviations themselves reveal a carry-over of linguistic habits from the (native) primary language into the secondary language. This interference in the secondary language is said to be symptomatic of *dominance* by the linguistic habits of the primary language.

It is heuristic to examine the different meanings which the terms dominance and interference carry. Given a community where two languages are in contact, the linguist will be interested in determining what subsequent changes in those languages can be attributed to this contact; many of the changes thus implicated would traditionally be called "linguistic borrowing." If the linguist speaks of dominance, it will refer to one of the *languages* being the principal donor and will imply that the other is the principal recipient of such interchange. The anthropologist or sociologist will be more concerned with the fact of language contact itself and with the *groups of speakers* so involved. They might focus on the demography of language usage and its consequences for social identities; on the social structure of the bilingual community; and on the relationship of bilingualism to intergroup communication and sociocultural change. If they speak of dominance, it will refer to the relative status of the two languages in contact, and their differing social functions. The psychologist typically will be more interested in the effects of bilingualization on the *individuals* thus enmeshed in language contact. When he speaks of dominance, it may refer to the realm of language behavior as measured by the speaker's relative competence and performance in his two languages. One central concern is how the bilingual acquires codes for two languages and then the extent to which he can utilize them as independent systems without interference and conflict between the two. This leads quite naturally to the special topics treated below: investigating the effects of bilingualism on cognitive development and personality formation.

Measuring linguistic and sociolinguistic dominance are relatively uncomplicated matters. The former seeks merely to determine for the bilingual whether, in speaking either language, there are any observable linguistic interference phenomena of the sorts exemplified in cases (i to iv) above, such as might be attributable to code dominance in the other language. (Various linguistic techniques and applications are contained in Diebold 1963; Haugen 1950, 1956; Lambert 1955; Mackey 1962, 1965,

1966; Weinreich 1953, 1957.) The output of such a comparative analysis of the bilingual's performance in his two languages, however, allows only of a decision as to whether he is "subordinate" or "proficient" in the senses mentioned above. Linguistic techniques alone cannot determine whether the proficient bilingual has differential competence in his two languages that might affect other behaviors depending upon which of the two languages were involved in less readily observable cognitive processes. Thus, if an apparently proficient German-English bilingual were basing his expectations about role behavior on the German model in example (xi) below, while speaking English in an American community, a linguistic analysis probably could not tap the cognitive conflict he would be experiencing (deriving from interference between models [xi] and [xii]).

A sociolinguistic analysis, investigating language usage in a bilingual community, could speedily resolve the question concerning sociological dominance (Barker 1947, 1951; Diebold 1961; Mackey 1966). The results of such an analysis would presumably include statements about the different social contexts in which the two languages were used (their "social functions"); the attitudes concerning that usage, as evidenced in "language loyalty" and maintenance of a less dominant language; and other relevant data about the communication network within and enmeshing the bilingual community (see Fishman *et al.* 1966; Gumperz 1962; Haugen 1966; Mackey 1966).

Determining psycholinguistic dominance is more problematic. To begin with, a typology of bilinguals which merely recognizes a continuum of linguistic interference in speech performance from zero (in the proficient bilingual) to "heavy" (in the case of a subordinate bilingual with very imperfect control of a secondary language) is too simplistic for our purposes. More revealing is to examine the potentially different types of linkage between interlingual word pairs in the bilingual's speech and the objects and concepts to which they refer. This requires two procedures: (1) a contrastive semantic analysis of the bilingual's two languages, employing traditional linguistic techniques as well as certain psycholinguistic techniques to be discussed below; and (2) a sociolinguistic analysis of the differential social functions of the two languages and, in particular, a specification of the possibly separate social contexts in which the two languages were first learned and then later used. Once this is done, we find that it is necessary to recognize two distinct "types" of proficient bilinguals: *compound bilinguals* and *coordinate bilinguals*. (The theoretical distinction itself is an old one; the specific terms "compound" and "coordinate" are taken here in the sense proposed by Ervin and Osgood 1954 and Weinreich 1953, which corresponds closely to the technical meaning they now carry in psycholinguistic research.)

Linguistically, the distinction between these two types can be repre-

223 Consequences of Early Bilingualism in Cognitive Development

sented by using the Saussurean model for a linguistic sign, a complex behavioral unit which is variously called a "word-and-its-object," a "label-and-its-referent," and so on; there are many synonymous terms. De Saussure's model (v) simply shows the learned linkage between the substance of a given speech formative (typically a "word," "morpheme," or "lexeme" in linguistic terminology) and its denotative and connotative meanings (= "meaning," "concept," "referent," "designatum,").

(v) a linguistic sign:

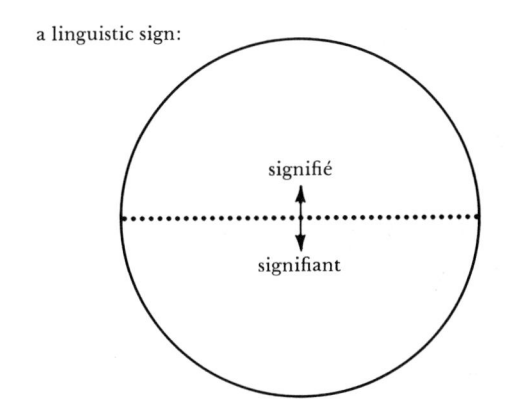

a linguistic sign:

signifié
signifiant

In de Saussure's terminology (1915), the *signifiant* is the physical property of the sign; the *signifié*, "that which is signified," is the associated meaning. For English, we find a speech formative with the acoustic (physical) image [dɔg], which is written *dog;* this signifiant is linked to an array of meanings, its signifié, which includes reference to tokens of the animal species *Canis familiaris,* as well as to various learned and idiosyncratic metaphorical extensions of this central denotative meaning to other objects. The signifié of [dɔg] will also include the connotative meanings associated with dogs, and these will include highly conventionalized components (deriving from culturally determined expectancies and values about these animals) as well as idiosyncratic components (that you may have an aversive reaction to dogs as a result of past unpleasant experiences with them, whereas your friend may not).

For the compound bilingual it is assumed that there is a more or less unitary semantic structure, such that many formatives from his two languages can be said to be true interlingual synonyms. This merging is shown in (vi) where a proficient German-English bilingual's signifiants *Hund* [hʊnt] and *dog* [dɔg] have a common signifié:

(vi)

Canis, etc.

[hʊnt]   [dɔg]

German   English

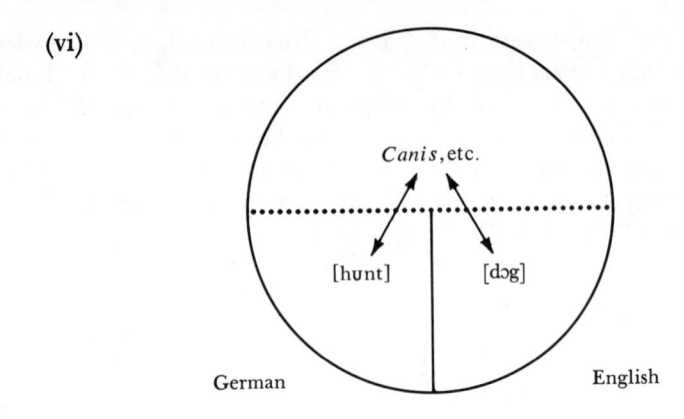

Figure (vii) depicts the separate linkage assumed for the coordinate bilingual:

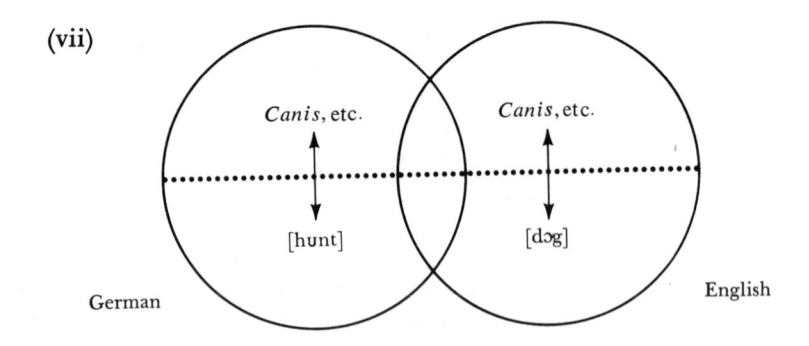

(vii)

Canis, etc.   *Canis*, etc.

[hʊnt]   [dɔg]

German   English

In the case of the coordinate bilingual there is not necessarily an identity between the signifiés of the semantically similar words *Hund* and *dog*. Moreover, it is not necessarily so that the coordinate bilingual will develop facility in rapid code switching, or that he will be adept in the recoding skill we call "simultaneous translation" (*cf.* Lambert, Havelka, and Gardner 1959; Paneth 1957). Thus in (vii) above, although there may well be an identity in central denotative meaning to *Canis familiaris*, the metaphorical extensions, associations, and connotative meanings might differ significantly in the two languages.

In this paper the focus will remain on the proficient bilingual who has acquired these word-meaning linkages in childhood, and "naturally" as opposed to later instruction in a classroom context. (There is general agreement that the process of later secondary language acquisition is qualitatively distinct from primary language acquisition, regardless of whether the latter involves one or two languages [*cf.* Lane 1962; Lambert 1963]). But it is interesting to contrast one type of subordinate bilingual with the compound and coordinate. This is the "type," which is often associated with formal second-language instruction, in which typically the incipient bilingual first develops a set of "translation equivalences" between his native and the target second language. Figure (viii) shows how these equivalences are first established between linguistic signs in the native language (here German) and signifiants in the foreign language (here English):

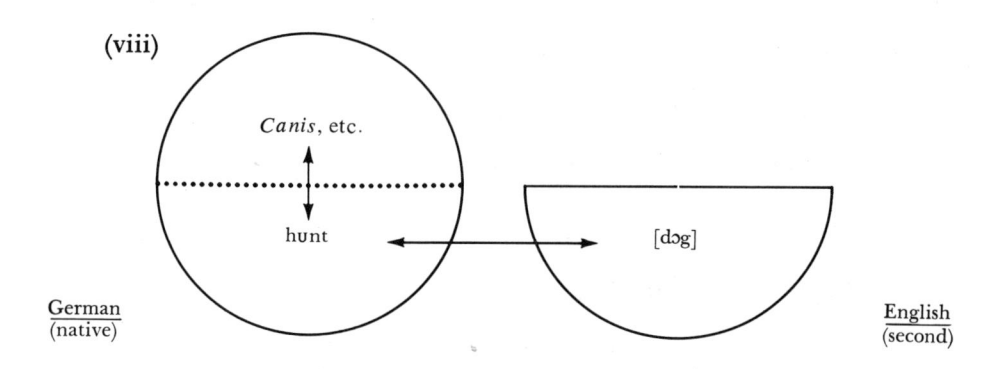

(viii)

Canis, etc.

hunt [dɔg]

German (native)   English (second)

We could figuratively describe this type or stage of subordinate bilingualism as being "compound" (compare [vi]) since there is, strictly speaking, a unitary semantic structure. But this apparent unity does not derive from two merged semantic structures which are potentially separable; the unitary content system is German, not German-English. Were we to analyze the connotative meanings and associations of the individual English words which the native German speaker had acquired, we would find that they deviate from a native English speaker's in the direction we would expect to find as modal for the German translation equivalents. This expectation is confirmed by several studies employing the "semantic differential" instrument (for example, Ervin 1961a; Lambert, Havelka, and Crosby 1958; Maclay and Ware 1961; Tanaka, Oyama, and Osgood 1963; Triandis and Osgood 1958). The theoretical consequences and observable effects of this sort of semantic interference in perception and cognition have been discussed in many studies (see Campbell 1964; Doob 1957; Triandis 1964).

In point of fact, however, we must also reject (or at least modify) the notion of a completely unitary semantic structure for compound bilinguals as well. If nothing else has been learned from two decades' discussion of the "Whorfian hypothesis," it is the realization that languages do differ greatly one from another (1) in their selection of criterial semantic features which must be grammatically and/or lexically marked, and (2) in their hierarchical lexical groupings, specifically in the ways in which superordinate categories are composed (see Bouman 1952–1953; Carroll 1963; Diebold 1965: Sec. 8; Fishman 1960). (It will remain for a more sophisticated "ethnoscience" to establish just what are the limitations on variability in these dimensions between languages; see the papers in Romney and D'Andrade, 1964.) Thus a careful contrastive analysis of even such closely reated languages as German and English suggests the possibility for semantic interference and attendant cognitive conflict for compound bilinguals. For a simple case of differential linguistic encoding of meanings, consider examples (ix) and (x) below:

(ix) recoding from German to English:

German *gemütlich* = English { ? }

German *Gemütlichkeit* = English { ? }

(x) recoding from English to German:

English *you* (singular) = German $\begin{cases} du \\ Sie \text{ (singular)} \end{cases}$

In the case of (ix), English has some sort of lexical inadequacy: the terms *gemütlich* ~ *Gemütlichkeit* have fairly precise meanings in a German speech community and carry very important affective connotations of "affability" and "empathy" useful for linguistic specification of interpersonal relations; but there are no translation equivalents in everyday English vocabulary (although equivalents may be found in some other languages, such as, Spanish *simpático* [adj.] ~ *simpatía* [noun]. Example (x) shows an interesting discrepancy in the available labels for the second-person singular category in pronouns (the alter in a face-to-face dyad) in which German has two possible translation equivalents, *du* ("intimate") and *Sie* ("formal"), corresponding to the single English term *you*. Pages could be devoted to describing the linguistic consequences (in terms of different obligatory grammatical inflections) as well as the sociolinguistic implications (in terms of specifying the social distance between two speakers; see, for example, Brown 1965: Chap. 2; Brown and Gilman 1960) which devolve upon selecting *du* as opposed to *Sie* in German.

A far more subtle type of interlingual misidentification is illustrated by examples (xi) and (xii) below; the case the examples concern is of special interest in this paper since it is intimately related to the stereotypes about personality and national character which German and at least American (if not British) nationals harbor about each other. As any German-English dictionary will confirm, German *Freund* and English *friend* are given as translations one for the other as if the terms were bilingual synonyms. (Historically speaking, the two words are of course "cognates.") And similarly German *Bekannte(r)* is offered as an equivalent of English *acquaintance*. In both German and American society a comparable number of the interpersonal contacts established outside one's kindred are labelled with

Consequences of Early Bilingualism in Cognitive Development

one or the other of the two terms available in each language (*Freund* : *Bekannte(r)* : : *friend* : *acquaintance*). But are these interlingual pairs in fact equivalent? The German national listening to an American speaking (even fluent) German will quickly know intuitively that they are not. And if he is xenophobic, the German may well conclude from the American's ubiquitous usage of *Freund* that Americans are brash and presumptuous in their interpersonal relations, and either shallow or insincere in their expressions of "friendly" sentiment. Conversely the American, upon perceiving it, may attribute this communicative static to his German host's being "too standoffish" or "formal." Thus the American in Germany who returns to his German university after a weekend skiing in Garmisch and announces *Ich habe ja viele neuen Freundschaften geschlossen,* will elicit from his German colleagues a response of firm and even antagonistic disbelief; for them, in the duration of a single weekend, regardless of one's affability (or *Gemütlichkeit*), it would typically be possible only to report *Ich habe ja viele nuen Bekanntschaften gemacht.* The discrepancy emerges in the role-network diagrams which follow. In both the German (xi) and American (xii) models, a propositus (=ego), the speaker, is shown surrounded by an identical number of alters with whom he has traffic. The closeness of each dyad is also constant between the models; the degree of closeness is indicated by the relative length of the lines connecting the various ego-alter dyads: greater length specifying greater social distance, such as might be quantified by testing for affect, measuring amount of interaction, and so on.

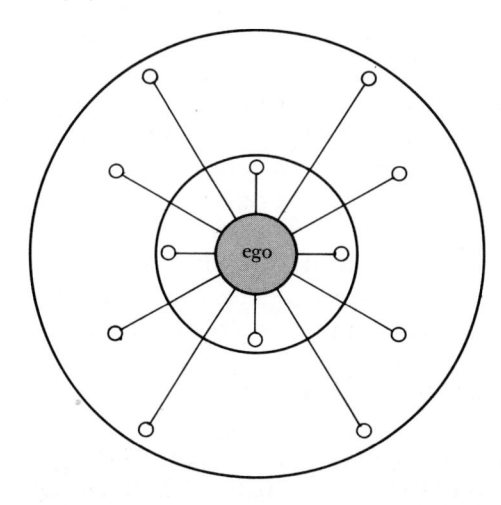

(xi) *German*

inner circle = *Freund*

outer belt = *Bekannte(r)*

(xii) *English (American)*

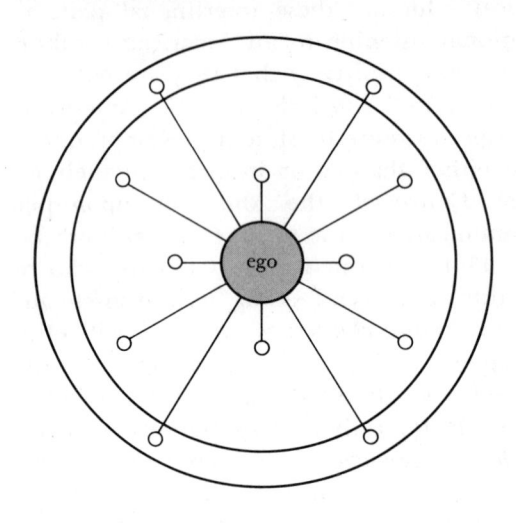

inner circle = *Friend*

outer belt = *Acquaintance*

Cursory inspection will identify the problem. The range of reference for German *Freund* (and *Freundschaft* "friendship") is much more restricted than it is for the accepted English translation equivalent *friend*. Every German's *Freund* in comparable situations in American society would be called a *friend*. The converse does not hold; many American *friends* would in comparable situations in German society be *Bekannten*. What cannot be so easily shown graphically are the differences in emotional meaning which are implied by this discrepancy; but here the prevarications of advertising help us. The travel advertisement in a German magazine which enjoins the reader to *Schließen Sie Freundschaft!* ("Make friends!") in some foreign country, elicits a different response from one which "correctly" reads *Machen Sie Bekanntschaft!* ("Become acquainted!"). (A somewhat analogous affective distinction is manipulated by American realtors who beguilingly extend the term *home* into linguistic contexts where most of us would say *house*). Among other connotations, *Schließen Sie Freundschaft* entails cultural expectations of *Gemütlichkeit* (see [ix]), which is at best optionally extended to the German tourist abroad. The obligatory semantic restrictions which operate in these German phrases are themselves interesting: *schließen* (used with *Freundschaft*) has strong connotations of entering into some binding contract which *machen* (used with *Bekanntschaft*) has not.

The sociolinguistic concomitants of bilingualism appear to be crucial. For the distinction between compound and coordinate, it is immediately apparent that the former type tends to result when two languages are acquired in a "fused" social context, that is, where the speech community offers the child equal and simultaneous exposure to two languages, and the later social functions of the two languages are minimally differentiated. It is also apparent that this type of bilingual community is relatively rare cross-societally, and when it exists, tends to be unstable through time. For the more typical sociolinguistic structure of the bilingual community is one in which one of the languages is sociologically dominant and in which the social functions of the two languages (for example, in the home as opposed to in the school) are maximally differentiated. In the latter more prevalent type of bilingual community, the social contexts and functions of the two languages are said to be "separated." (The sociolinguistic opposition "fused" : "separated" is developed in Lambert, Havelka, and Crosby 1958.) And it appears that this separated sociolinguistic background tends to produce coordinate bilinguals. The welter of further variables suggested by sociolinguistic analysis of the bilingual community is extensive. But it is not clear to date what implications some of these variables have for research with bilingual speakers. For example, does a separated context imply that the bilingual speech community is also bicultural, and, conversely, that a fused context implies relative cultural homogeneity within the bilingual community? What are the effects of language loyalty sentiments in a bicultural bilingual community wherein the sociologically dominant language is not the preferred one? In the last instance, what if there are (or are not) strong acculturative pressures which portend adaptive language shift and eventual monolingualism in successive generations? These and many other salient sociolinguistic variables have been treated in a wide range of studies: Bossard 1945; De Boer 1952; Diebold 1961; Fishman et al. 1966; Gumperz 1964; Herman 1961; Hoffman 1934; Pieris 1951; Soffietti 1955; Sapon 1953. What remains to be demonstrated is the significance of these sociolinguistic variables for the psycholinguistic investigation of the bilingual speaker.

The psycholinguistic evidence for distinctive types of proficient bilinguals is strong. Osgood and Ervin's (1954) original proposition was that language acquisition contexts, depending upon whether fused or separated, should result, in the process of language acquisition, in unitary representational mediators for interlingual synonyms in the former (= compound bilingualism), but distinct representational mediators for the latter (=coordinate bilingualism. Examples (xiii) and (xiv) illustrate Osgood and Ervin's conceptualization and are modified versions adapted from their 1954 statement. (The partial congruences with the Saussurean models [v–viii] are obvious.) G-sub = German; E-sub = English; $[S]_G$ and $[S]_E$ are potential interlingual synonyms. (For explanation of the learning theory processes represented in the models and further explication of the notation, see Diebold 1965:218, 219; Osgood 1963a:249–260, 1966.)

230   The Formation of Personality

(xiii) *compound representational mediators*

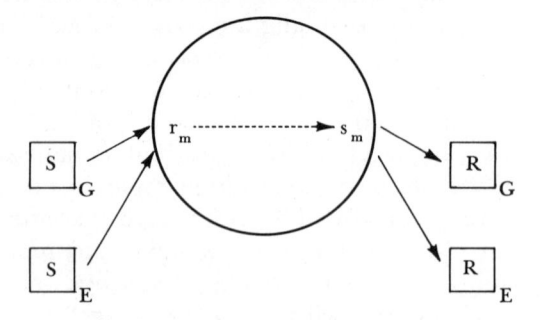

Comments: the association of $\boxed{S}_G$ and $\boxed{S}_E$ with the mediational response sequence $(r_m \to \to \to \to s_m)$ is equivalent; the $(r_m \to \to \to \to s_m)$ sets are unitary, having been acquired in a fused context.

(xiv) *coordinate representational mediators*

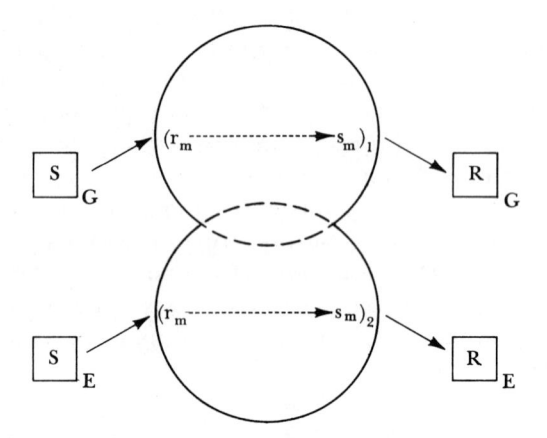

Comments: the $(r_m \to \to \to \to s_m)$ sets are not necessarily identical, having been acquired in separated contexts.

Much of the research seems to suggest that coordinate bilinguals (see [xiv] above), having learned and then using their two languages in separated contexts, have a correspondingly greater functional separation of their two linguistic systems as well as greater functional separation of the cognitive processes and other language-mediated behavior which relate to differential encoding of experience specific to one or the other language. Conversely, the compound bilingual seems to exhibit a greater merging of these systems and processes. Especially significant as evidence are the studies of semantic shifting and differential word associations which compare bilinguals with monolingual speakers of each of the two languages represented in him. The psycholinguistic evidence from these studies suggests that compounds have an intermediate semantic structure, whereas coordinates have associated with each of their languages semantic structures which are only slightly skewed from those of monolingual speakers of those languages. (See Ervin 1961a; Hofstaetter 1955; Jakobovits and Lambert 1961; Kolers 1963; Lambert, Havelka, and Gardner 1959; Lambert and Moore 1966; Lenneberg and Roberts 1956; Weinreich 1958.) To be sure, most of this research concerns different aspects of the signifiant-signifié linkage, such as codability and word associations. But there is also some evidence that recall and higher cognitive activities are differentially affected by which language the bilingual subject is obliged to use in the experimental task presented him; see Ervin 1961b; Peal and Lambert 1962. How much of these differences in coordinate bilinguals is to be explained by differential cognitive experience in his two languages (that mathematical calculations are performed exclusively in one language), and how much to an actual underlying (but undetectable) dominance in one language, pose knotty problems for future psycholinguistic research.

The most compelling evidence for differential dominance and the distinction between types of bilinguals comes from research into adventitiously acquired language disorders, especially the categories of organically based disturbances collectively called aphasia. (For a typology of these disorders, see Schuell and Jenkins 1959; recent general references to aphasia which contain sections dealing with bilingual aphasics include: Brain 1965; Goldstein 1948; Marx 1966; Weisenberg and McBride 1935; and several papers in de Reuck and O'Connor 1964.) It has long been recognized that some bilingual patients, after brain damage or during deteriorative senility, exhibit differential impairment to their two languages. If the literature on bilingual aphasia is reviewed (see Leischner 1948), there is considerable agreement in the reporting of individual case histories, that bilinguals who are demonstrably subordinate show greater deficit in their secondary language (see Bychowski 1919; Goldstein 1933; Herschmann and Pötzl 1920; Kauders 1929; Minkowski 1927; Pitres 1895; Pötzl 1930; Stengel and Zelmanowicz 1934). The interpretations of these observations vary; but most agree that the motor-productive and sensory-receptive habits associated with primary language acquisition (given continued usage of that language) confer greater resistance to language pathology after an aphasia-inducing trauma than is the case with the later learned habits associated with a secondary language. There is also evidence from these same sources that demonstrably proficient bilinguals (especially those who had simultaneously acquired two languages in childhood) tend to suffer equal damage to both languages. Presumably then, the explanation for the notion of greater stability of earlier learned linguistic habits has some relevance, and must be addressed within the framework of a maturational theory of language acquisition; see Lenneberg 1964, 1966. The most significant discovery was made, however, when Lambert and Fillenbaum (1959) reexamined case histories of proficient bilinguals who were aphasic, and found that compound and coordinate bilinguals were differentially impaired by aphasia; see also Fillenbaum, Jones, and Wepman 1961; Wepman and Jones 1966. In the cases thus analyzed, in which reliable information was available concerning the extent of the deficit and/or the extent of recovery, Lambert and Fillenbaum found that compound bilinguals suffered equal deficit while coordinates suffered differential deficit in their two languages. The question thus posed about which of the coordinate's two languages was most affected implicates a number of variables (some of which suggest undetected psycholinguistic dominance in one language) that include frequency of usage and the affective values attached to one or the other language. The last variable, discussed again below, is interesting since it corroborates the conclusions of an earlier study (Minkowski 1928) in which "language sentiments" were posited as independent variables equivalent in power with variables relating to early learning and frequency of subsequent usage.

Given this demonstrable evidence for various sorts of interference phenomena in the linguistic and in some language-mediated cognitive behavior of bilinguals, we can now ask what is its cumulative effect in cognitive development and personality formation?

EARLY BILINGUALISM AND COGNITIVE DEVELOPMENT

The language-acquiring child leaves something to be desired as a tractable subject; the experimental methods available for studying adult language behavior have a correspondingly limited utility with them. Most of our evidence for linguistic ontogeny is thus derived from detailed longitudinal studies, few in number however rich in the observational data recorded. It is therefore not surprising to find few references in the literature which deal with the simultaneous primary acquisition of two languages or very early "natural" learning of a second language. Much of the relevant literature as was then available (such as Ronjat 1913) was reviewed by Leopold (1948); earlier programmatic statements of research problems associated with child bilingualism are contained in Epstein 1915 and Stern 1923. To his own paragon longitudinal study of 1949 should be added several studies subsequent to Leopold's 1948 survey; principal among these is a paper by Burling (1959) and an interesting study by Imedadze (1960), which arrive at opposite conclusions about the child's developmental progress in functionally separating his two linguistic systems: Burling arguing for chronic interference and Imedadze for early achieved separation. Despite the want of extensive observational data on early bilingualism, there are nevertheless many statements which suggest that it is detrimental even to language acquisition itself: Travis, Johnson, and Shover (1937) purport to demonstrate a susceptibility to stuttering in early bilinguals; Beckey (1942) claims that speech development is retarded by early bilingualism; Duncan (1950) discusses an acquired articulatory abnormality which she relates to functional conflict deriving from code switching. Other studies, unfortunately few in number, have examined the sociolinguistic context of early bilingualism and adumbrate in their observations some of the major conclusions of this study; these include Braunhausen 1928; Covello 1937; Lambert 1956; McCarthy 1954; Sapon 1953; Tireman 1941, 1944.

We can summarize the output from much of the case-study research dealing with bilingualism in the child: it is focused on the readily observable phenomena of linguistic interference between and the separation of the two languages in the child's overt speech behavior. There has been almost no research into the development of correlated (but far less readily observable) language-based cognitive behavior such as concept formation. This is a glaring omission. For when we turn to the research dealing with the consequences of early bilingualism for later higher cognitive behavior, especially vis-à-vis "intelligence," we find an unmanageably vast body of literature. The remainder of this section will deal with the matters of measuring bilinguals' intelligence and of interpreting those measurements.

The terms "cognitive development" and "intelligence" are used here in a restricted sense. The former refers to what many authors call "intellectual growth," which I take to mean as the "processing [of] environmental events [dependent] upon the translation of experience into symbolic form" (Bruner 1964:13); that is, it refers to those cognitive activities (such as thinking and insight learning) which depend upon language and the extraordinary and distinctively human capacity for symbolically mediated learning and cultural transmission associated with it. The latter, "intelligence," in this paper although not in all of the literature cited, will refer to one dimension of cognitive development: the realized intelligence level of verbal children (or young adults) as measured by various standardized intelligence tests which relate actual performance to expected "mental age" performance and chronological age. Intelligence will thus refer to capacities achieved at a certain age; it will not refer to innate intellectual potential.

The topic itself has been incidentally treated in a number of linguistically oriented surveys of bilingualism, most notably in Christophersen 1948; Haugen 1956; Kainz 1956–1962; Titone 1964; Vildomec 1963; and Weinreich 1953. The specific topic of 'bilingualism and intelligence' has been reviewed in several recent and bibliographically rich surveys: Darcy 1963; Jensen 1962; Jones 1959; Lambert 1963; Peal and Lambert 1962. This second category in turn includes extensive discussion of many of the "classic" studies (Johnson 1953; Jones 1960; Pintner and Arsenian 1937;

Saer 1922, 1923; Smith 1932) as well as both older surveys and more recent replications (Arsenian 1937; Darcy 1953; Hoffman 1934; Jones and Stewart 1961; Mitchell 1937; Morrison 1958; Pintner 1932; Sánchez 1934).

The results of four major surveys of the literature dealing with bilingualism and intelligence (namely, Darcy 1953, 1963; Jensen 1962; Peal and Lambert 1962) reveal that the majority of earlier studies stand in agreement on one point: that when somehow "comparable" groups of monolingual and bilingual children were contrasted on verbal (as well sometimes as on nonverbal) intelligence tests, that the bilinguals scored significantly lower. Not all, but a majority of the earlier studies, many of which appeared to be based on sound experimental research, reached this conclusion. However, a number of the more sophisticated earlier studies (Johnson 1953; Jones and Stewart 1951) also reported that retarded development was evident only in verbal intelligence tests, and that monolingual-bilingual differences for nonverbal tests were insignificant. Few studies proposed a null hypothesis about the relationship of IQ scores to bilingualism, although there are notable exceptions (Arsenian 1945; Hill 1936; O'Doherty 1958). Virtually none of the experimentally sophisticated studies, with one important exception to be discussed below, proposed the converse, that early bilingualism produced any evidence of superior IQ ratings. Few studies of whatever category proposed definite hypotheses to account for the underlying cause of the bilingual children's lower scores, save to appeal to ill-defined notions about "mental confusion" and consequent retardation, derivative from the "unnatural" developmental task of acquiring two languages at the same time.

Haugen (1956, 1958) and Weinreich (1953), among others, anticipated the finding of a critical flaw in virtually all of the studies which concluded that early bilingualism directly caused subsequent lower intelligence: As Darcy (1963) and Peal and Lambert (1962) have now demonstrated, the allegedly matched monolingual and bilingual groups were in fact not comparable along several extralinguistic dimensions. Almost without exception, the monolingual groups in these studies (the children who gave significantly higher performances on standardized intelligence tests) were speakers of a sociolinguistically dominant language, dominant in the sense that it enjoyed greater prestige and greater communicative utility in the larger society from which the groups were selected. In the majority of these studies, it was further apparent that the bilinguals, regardless of their proficiency in the dominant language, were also disadvantaged by socioeconomic environmental factors specific to the lower status bicultural communities in which they were socialized. (In the United States, for example, this is typically the case of bilinguals who come from lower status immigrant enclaves in urban settings; compare Bossard 1945; Covello 1937; Fishman et al. 1966; Haugen 1956. Frequently in this country the acculturative pressures on such bicultural communities include deleterious racist

Consequences of Early Bilingualism in Cognitive Development

attitudes which become linked to any salient physical, cultural, or linguistic differences which distinguish the bicultural community from the larger Anglo-American society in which it is encysted; compare Hempl 1898; Johnson 1951; Levy 1933.) That these sociolinguistic factors can and do profoundly affect cognitive development generally and verbal skills specifically cannot be doubted; see the research of Bernstein (1961, 1964), John (1963; and John and Goldstein 1964), and Lawton (1963), to single out only a few of the relevant statements supportive of this generalization. Limitations of space prohibit further exposition and defense of the above summary assertion. But the author feels safe in insisting that the category of research referred to earlier (in which the monolingual groups are found to speak a sociolinguistically dominant language) has not taken into account all the variables which one must justifiably assume to be operative; and that those studies which followed through to conclude that as a variable bilingualism of itself produced intellectual deficit are beyond the pale of responsible inquiry.

When we consider individual bilinguals or groups of bilinguals in sociolinguistic contexts where their bilingual behavior (and/or bicultural background) does not automatically ascribe them lower status or cultural marginality within a larger monolingual community, the picture changes dramatically. The conclusions we can draw from one of the best controlled studies in the literature (Peal and Lambert 1962) is quite surprising. For Peal and Lambert found in their contrastive comparison of carefully matched monolingual and bilingual groups that bilingualism is associated with and may in fact facilitate significantly superior performances on both verbal and nonverbal intelligence tests. A portion of the experimenters' interpretive conclusions is interesting:

> The picture that emerges of the French-English bilingual in Montreal is that of a youngster whose wider experiences in two cultures have given him advantages which a monolingual does not enjoy. Intellectually his experience with two language systems seems to have left him with a mental flexibility, a superiority in concept formation, and a more diversified set of mental abilities, in the sense that the patterns of abilities developed by bilinguals were more heterogeneous . . . In contrast, the monolingual appears to have a more unitary structure of intelligence which he must use for all types of intellectual tasks (Peal and Lambert 1962:20).

Peal and Lambert's attempts to explain their surprising research results center on hypotheses (suggested by Leopold 1949 and independently corroborated by Imedadze 1960) relating to the early bilingual's being reinforced "to conceptualize environmental events in terms of their general properties without reliance on their [being encoded into] linguistic symbols" (Peal and Lambert 1962:14). This "detaching" of signifiés from signifiants apparently confers manifold advantages. While the relevance of this hypothesis to the bilingual's observed adroitness at the reorganization tasks involved in nonverbal intelligence tests is obvious, the relevance to his performance on verbal tests is no less oblique:

> At the very first stage of speech development in the bilingual child, when he first encounters the fact that an object can have two names, a separation of object and name begins. A word, when freed from its referent, can easily become the object of special attention (Imedadze 1960:67).

EARLY BILINGUALISM AND PERSONALITY FORMATION

We may now ask whether the bilingual's ventures in biculturalism predispose him to psychopathology, or whether his bilingualism facilitates emotional adjustment in the different social niches into which his language skills allow him entry. We have two disparate bodies of evidence: (1) one from studies of the relative differences in emotional adjustment in populations, comparing its monolingual and bilingual members; and (2) the other from individual psychiatric case studies in which the patient shows an adjustive failure associated with his bilingual background. Here, unfortunately, there are no surveys to aid in formulating the generalizations which follow.

The popular consensus about the effects of early bilingualism on personality integration and emotional adjustment is, again, that this bilingual experience is detrimental. The literature abounds in evidence which purports to show that the early bilingual does not function well as an older child or adult, and that he is especially subject to failures in conflict resolution characterized by a symptomatology for what we loosely call "alienation" or "anomie." If we take the better of the bad pronouncements on these matters, we find assertions such as Christophersen's (1948) that, where culture conflict prevails in a bilingual bicultural community, the bilingual is predisposed toward schizophrenia. But Christophersen's claim is an interesting one since it reveals as its rationale that notion which many of these pronouncements share, namely, the assumption of an implication chain: two languages imply two personality structures, which in turn imply psychodynamic conflict.

This implication chain can be examined critically at either end. For the first alleged entailment, there is only one relevant experimental study that the author is aware of: In a sample of proficient French-English bilingual speakers, Ervin (1964) discovered that strikingly different protocols were elicited by the TAT instrument from the same bilingual subject, and that the differences were correlated with which language was used in the elicitation procedures. In discussing the results of her study, Ervin mentions several obvious factors which might be operative in producing the contrasts in TAT content correlated with language choice. One is simply that her bilingual subjects had systematically different recall in their two languages, relating to the differential personal experiences, verbal preoccupations, and cultural values associated with the different social contexts in which each language was acquired and later used. This correctly implies that Ervin's subjects were coordinate bilinguals. And at least for coordinate bilinguals, with their separated linguistic systems and sociolinguistic backgrounds, we must provisionally concede that they may in fact have "two personalities", a concession which would at any rate be forced by the psychiatric evidence cited below.

Despite the absence of any concrete evidence concerning them, it is interesting to speculate whether compound bilinguals can similarly be said to have "two personalities." In the sense here implied, the author intuits that they have not, and predicts that a comparable projective-test experiment with compound subjects would result in more unitary responses.

If Ervin's study does permit us to infer two personality structures for some proficient bilinguals, we must then examine the second entailment: Granted differential encoding of past experiences in the two languages, do the bilingual's two experientially diverged personality structures perforce predispose him toward or actually induce conflict crises or psychopathology of any type? If we turn from individual to group psychodynamics, we can also ask whether this experience produces culture marginality?

Clinical evidence (much of it admittedly anecdotal) should incline one to the view that at least coordinate bilinguals have available a formidable defense mechanism denied monolinguals, namely, code-switching. Consider some bilingual responses: It is apparent that repression can be reinforced if the bilingual code-switches into the language with which less tramatic past experience and unresolved conflict is associated. Superego control can be weakened by the bilingual's acting out in the ontologically less charged language (without his necessarily becoming a psychopath). It is not facetious to add that this defense mechanism may pose an obstacle to psychotherapy or psychoanalysis, but that this problem is not so much the bilingual patient's as it is the psychiatrist's; the possible responses mentioned above, by themselves in many naturalistic social settings, could be highly adaptive functionally. It is the bilingual's exploitation of this defense mechanism which offers part of the explanation for the commonplace ambivalent stereotype about bilingual behavior—that it is "chameleon-like." Moreover, if code-switching is the potentially adaptive device this author believes it to be, it might account for the further impression that there is a low incidence of reactive schizophrenia in bilingual populations, despite epidemiological studies (for example, Hollingshead and Redlich 1958) which reveal a relatively higher incidence of schizophrenic patients from lower socioeconomic status groups (which in the United States include significant numbers of early bilinguals).

The analysts' problem mentioned in the paragraph above is not a trivial one. There does exist a scattered literature on the topic of choice of language for the analysis of the bilingual patient; studies perused by the author include Buxbaum 1949; Greenson 1950; Krapf 1955; Lagache 1956; Stengel 1939; Velikovsky 1934. These papers agree that the prognosis for successful treatment may devolve upon the analyst's decision which language to use and when to use it in his attempts to induce the patient to symbolize early, and even upon preverbal experience. Among the individual cases histories reported on, it appears that only two or three of the analysands described in the above papers were compound bilinguals, whereas the majority were clearly coordinate. Interestingly enough, the dysfunctional symptomatology of the former seemed to be more severe and the actual choice of language less important for therapeutic treatment. This last observation is my own and is impressionistic; there is insufficient evidence to offer it as a generalization. But it deserves of further inquiry, since the code-switching defense mechanism would logically seem adaptive only for the coordinate bilingual with his differentiated content system and separated sociolinguistic background.

Many other presently unanswerable questions require further research. The most striking relate to the underlying causes of the "alienation" and "anomie" anxiety syndromes to which many bilinguals with bicultural backgrounds do seem susceptible. It is not at all clear at the time of this writing whether the critical factors are exclusively sociolinguistic. Especially among my colleagues in anthropology whom I have consulted, there is a conviction that a linguistic cognitive etiology is basic.[2] Their interpretation is not the simplistic appeal to the bilingual's "having too much in his head" but a much more sophisticated argument based on concepts of cognitive perceptual incongruence; these concepts would include what psychologists discuss in terms of "contamination of categories," expectancy disconfirmations involving "double-bind" and "cognitive dissonance," and "perceptual disparity." If any of these concepts are relevant here, a number of interesting questions might be posed. Is there, for instance, a limit on the degree of cultural difference between two societies affecting the formation of a "fused" bilingual-bicultural community from which we could expect compound bilinguals? (To pose the question of another way: Is the reason that the compound bilingual is in fact a *rara avis* related simply to a limitation on the number of bilingual-bicultural combinations possible before cultural disparity enjoins "separated" contexts for language acquisition and usage?)

We return here to the question posed at the beginning of this section. Implicit arguments from clinical psychology to the contrary notwithstanding, the majority sentiment is still that early bilingualism can and frequently does produce emotional disorders in the child who is subjected to

---

[2] Grateful acnowledgment is especially due George D. Spindler for his insightful discussion of the theoretical role of cognitive incongruence in psychocultural marginality.

this socialization experience. If we examine those studies in which, again, somehow "comparable" groups of monolingual and bilingual speakers are contrasted, we do find a significantly higher incidence of maladjustment among the bilinguals (see Spoerl 1944, 1946). But in investigating emotional adjustment, unlike testing for intelligence, life-history information about the subject has long been recognized as an analytic prerequisite. And this information is immediately revealing of an essentially sociolinguistic basis for many of the observed emotional problems of the bilinguals studied. Many corroboratory statements support this conclusion; see Arsenian 1945; Bossard 1945; Devereux and Loeb 1943; Levy 1933; Raubicheck 1934. Thus if we critically examine bona fide cases of bilingual psychopathology, where the individual or group has been competently diagnosed, some variation on one common etiological theme emerges: This is basically a crisis in social and personal identity engendered by antagonistic acculturative pressures directed on a bicultural community by a sociologically dominant monolingual society within which the bicultural community is stigmatized as socially inferior and to which its bilingualism (historically viewed) is itself an assimilative response. The particular form which the conflict assumes varies; in some cases, cross-generation (parent-child) conflict is as destructive as that exerted by the conventionalized conflict between the monolingual and bilingual communities (see Fishman et al., 1966).

BIBLIOGRAPHY

ARSENIAN, S., *Bilingualism and Mental Development*. New York: Teachers College (Columbia University), 1937.
———, "Bilingualism in the Post-War World," *Psychological Bulletin* Vol. 42, 1945, pp. 65–86.
BARKER, G. C., "Social Functions of Language in a Mexican-American Community," *Acta Americana*, Vol. 5, 1947, pp. 185–202.
———, "Growing up in a Bilingual Community," *The Kiva*, Vol. 17, 1951, pp. 17–32.
BECKEY, R. E., "A Study of Certain Factors Related to Retardation of Speech," *Journal of Speech and Hearing Disorders*, Vol. 7, 1942, pp. 223–249.
BERNSTEIN, B., "Aspects of Language and Language Learning in the Genesis of Social Process," *Journal of Child Psychology and Psychiatry*, Vol. 1, 1961, pp. 313–324.
———, "Elaborated and Restricted Codes: Their Social Origins and Some Consequences," J. J. Gumperz and D. Hymes (eds.), *The Ethnography of Communication* (*American Anthropologist*, Special Publication), Vol. 66, No. 6, Pt. 2, 1964, pp. 55–69.
BOSSARD, J. H. S., "The Bilingual Individual as a Person—Linguistic Identification with Status," *American Sociological Review*, Vol. 10, 1945, pp. 699–709.
BOUMAN, A. C., "Das Problem der inneren Sprachform und die Psychoanalyse," *Lingua*, Vol. 3, 1952/1953, pp. 147–161.

BRAIN, (LORD), *Speech Disorders*. 2d ed. London: Butterworth & Co. (Publishers), Ltd., 1965.
BRAUNHAUSEN, N., "Le Bilinguisme et La Famille," in: *Le Bilinguisme et l'Éducation*, pp. 87–94. Genève, Luxemburg: Bureau International d'Éducation, 1928.
BROWN, R., *Social Psychology*. New York: The Free Press, a division of the Macmillan Company, 1965.
―――, and A. GILMAN, "The Pronouns of Power and Solidarity," in T. A. Sebeok (ed.), *Style in Language*, pp. 253–276. Cambridge, Mass.: Technology Press, M.I.T. and John Wiley and Sons, Inc., 1960.
BRUNER, J. S., "The Course of Cognitive Growth," *American Psychologist*, Vol. 19, 1964, pp. 1–15.
BURLING, R., "Language Development of a Garo and English Speaking Child," *Word*, Vol. 15, 1959, pp. 45–68.
BUXBAUM, E., "The Role of a Second Language in the Formation of Ego and Superego," *Psychoanalytic Quarterly*, Vol. 18, 1949, pp. 279–289.
BYCHOWSKI, Z., "Uber die Restitution der nach einem Schädelschuss verlorenen Umgangssprache bei einem Polyglotten," *Monatschrift für Psychiatrie und Neurologie*, Vol. 45, 1919, pp. 183–201.
CAMPBELL, D. T., "Distinguishing Differences of Perception from Failures of Communication in Cross-cultural Studies," in F. S. C. Northrup and H. H. Livingston (eds.), *Cross-Cultural Understanding: Epistemology in Anthropology*, pp. 308–336. New York: Harper & Row, Publishers, 1964.
CARROLL, J. B., "Linguistic Relativity, Contrastive Linguistics, and Language Learning," *International Review of Applied Linguistics in Language Teaching*, Vol. 1, 1963, pp. 1–20.
CHRISTOPHERSEN, P., *Bilingualism*. London: Methuen & Co., Ltd., 1948.
COVELLO, L., "Language as a Factor in Social Adjustment," in F. J. Brown and J. S. Roucek (eds.), *Our Racial and National Minorities*, pp. 681–696. Englewood Cliffs, N.J.: Prentice-Hall, Inc., 1937.
DARCY, N. T., "A Review of the Literature on the Effects of Bilingualism upon the Measurement of Intelligence," *Journal of Genetic Psychology*, Vol. 82, 1953, pp. 21–57.
―――, "Bilingualism and the Measurement of Intelligence: Review of a Decade of Research," *Journal of Genetic Psychology*, Vol. 103, 1963, pp. 259–282.
DE BOER, J. J., "Some Sociological Factors in Language Development," *Elementary English*, Vol. 29, 1952, pp. 482–492.
DE REUCK, A. V. S., and M. O'CONNOR, eds. *Disorders of Language*. London: J. & A. Churchill, Ltd., 1964.
DE SAUSSURE, F., *Cours de linguistique générale*. Paris: Payot, 1915.
DIEBOLD, A. R., Jr., "Incipient Bilingualism," *Language*, Vol. 36, 1961, pp. 97–112.
―――, "Code-Switching in Greek-English Bilingual Speech," in E. D. Woodworth and R. J. dePrieto (eds.), *Report of the Thirteenth Annual Roundtable Meeting on Linguistics and Language Studies (Georgetown University Monograph Series on Languages and Linguistics, No. 15)*, pp. 53–62. Washington, D.C.: Georgetown University Press, 1963.
―――, "A Survey of Psycholinguistic Research, 1954–1964," C. E. Osgood and T. A. Sebeok (eds.), *Psycholinguistics: A Survey of Theory and Research Problems* (2d ed.), pp. 205–291. Bloomington, Ind.: Indiana University Press, 1965.
DOOB, L. W., "The Effect of Language on Verbal Expression and Recall," *American Anthropologist*, Vol. 59, 1957, pp. 88–100.

DUNCAN, M. H., "Children of Foreign Tongues," W. Johnson (ed.), *Speech Problems of Children*, New York: Grune & Stratton, Inc., 1950, pp. 223–238.

EPSTEIN, I., *La pensée et la polyglossie*. Lausanne: Payot et Cie., 1915.

ERVIN, S. M., "Semantic Shift in Bilinguals," *American Journal of Psychology*, Vol. 74, 1961a, pp. 233–241.

———, "Learning and Recall in Bilinguals," *American Journal of Psychology*, Vol. 74, 1961b, pp. 446–451.

———, "Language and TAT Content in Bilinguals," *Journal of Abnormal and Social Psychology*, Vol. 68, 1964, pp. 500–507.

———, and C. E. OSGOOD, "Second Language Learning and Bilingualism," in C. E. Osgood and T. A. Sebeok (eds.), *Psycholinguistics: A Survey of Theory and Research Problems (Indiana University Publications in Anthropology and Linguistics, Memoir 10)*, 1954, pp. 139–146.

FILLENBAUM, S., L. V. JONES, and J. M. WEPMAN, "Some Linguistic Features of Speech from Aphasic Patients," *Language and Speech*, Vol. 4, 1961, pp. 91–108.

FISHMAN, J. A., "A Systematization of the Whorfian Hypothesis," *Behavioral Science*, Vol. 4, 1960, pp. 323–339.

FISHMAN, J. A., et al., *Language Loyalty in the United States*. The Hague: Mouton & Co., 1966.

GOLDSTEIN, K., "L'analyse de l'aphasie et l'étude de l'essence du language," *Journal de Psychologie Normale et Pathologique*, Vol. 30, 1933, pp. 430–496.

———, *Language and Language Disturbances*. New York: Grune & Stratton, Inc., 1948.

GREENSON, R. R., "The Mother Tongue and the Mother," *International Journal of Psychoanalysis*, Vol. 31, 1950, pp. 18–23.

GUMPERZ, J. J., "Types of Linguistic Communities," *Anthropological Linguistics*, Vol. 4, No. 1, 1962, pp. 28–40.

———, "Linguistic and Social Interaction in Two Communities," J. J. Gumperz and D. Hymes (eds.), *The Ethnography of Communication (American Anthropologist*, Special Publication), Vol. 66, No. 6, Pt. 2, 1964, pp. 137–153.

HAUGEN, E., "The Analysis of Linguistic Borrowing," *Language*, Vol. 26, 1950, pp. 210–231.

———, *Bilingualism in the Americas (Publications of the American Dialect Society, No. 26)*, University, Alabama, University of Alabama Press, 1956.

———, "Language Contact," E. Sivertsen (ed.), *Proceedings of the Eighth International Congress of Linguists*, pp. 772–785. Oslo: Oslo University Press, 1958.

———, "Dialect, Language, Nation," *American Anthropologist*, Vol. 68, 1966, pp. 922–935.

HEMPL, G., "Language Rivalry and Speech Differentiation in the Case of Race Mixture," *Transactions of the American Philological Society*, Vol. 29, 1898, pp. 31–47.

HERMAN, S. N., "Explorations in the Social Psychology of Language Choice," *Human Relations*, Vol. 14, 1961, pp. 149–164.

HERSCHMANN, H., and O. PÖTZL, "Bemerkungen über die Aphasie der Polyglotten," *Neurologisches Centralblatt*, Vol. 39, 1920, pp. 114–120.

HILL, H. S., "The Effects of Bilingualism on the Measured Intelligence of Elementary School Children of Italian Parentage," *Journal of Experimental Education*, Vol. 5, 1936, pp. 75–79.

HOFSTAETTER, P. R., "Über Ähnlichkeit," *Psyche*, Vol. 9, 1955, pp. 54–80.

HOLLINGSHEAD, A. B., and F. C. REDLICH, *Social Class and Mental Illness: A Community Study*. New York: John Wiley & Sons, Inc., 1958.

IMEDADZE, N. V., "K psikhologicheskoy prirode rannego dvuyazychiya" [On the Psychological Nature of Early Bilingualism], *Voprosy Psikhologii*, Vol. 6, 1960, pp. 60–68.
JAKOBOVITS, L., and W. E. LAMBERT, "Semantic Satiation among Bilinguals," *Journal of Experimental Psychology*, Vol. 62, 1961, pp. 576–582.
JENSEN, J. V., "Effects of Childhood Bilingualism," *Elementary English*, Vol. 39, 1962, pp. 132–143, 358–366.
JOHN, V. P., "The Intellectual Development of Slum Children: Some Preliminary Findings," *American Journal of Orthopsychiatry*, Vol. 33, 1963, pp. 813–822.
———, and L. S. GOLDSTEIN, "The Social Context of Language Acquisition," *Merrill-Palmer Quarterly*, Vol. 10, 1964, pp. 265–276.
JOHNSON, G. B., Jr., "The Relationship Existing between Bilingualism and Racial Attitudes," *Journal of Educational Psychology*, Vol. 42, 1951, pp. 357–365.
———, "Bilingualism as Measured by a Reaction-Time Technique and the Relationship between a Language and a Non-Language Intelligence Quotient," *Journal of Genetic Psychology*, Vol. 82, 1953, pp. 3–9.
JONES, W. R., "A Critical Study of Bilingualism and Nonverbal Intelligence," *British Journal of Educational Psychology*, Vol. 30, 1960, pp. 71–76.
———, and W. A. STEWART, "Bilingualism and Verbal Intelligence," *British Journal of Psychology (Statistical Section)*, Vol. 4, 1951, pp. 3–8.
KAINZ, F., *Psychologie der Sprache*, 5 vols. Stuttgart: Ferdinand Enke Verlag, 1956–1965.
KAUDERS, O., "Über Polyglotte Reaktionen bei einer sensorischen Aphasie," *Zeitschrift für die gesamte Neurologie und Psychiatrie*, Vol. 122, 1929, pp. 651–656.
KOLERS, P. A., "Interlingual Word Associations," *Journal of Verbal Learning and Verbal Behavior*, Vol. 2, 1963, pp. 291–300.
KRAPF, E. E., "The Choice of Language in Polyglot Psychoanalysis," *Psychoanalytic Quarterly*, Vol. 24, 1955, pp. 343–357.
LAGACHE, D., "Sur le polyglottisme dans l'Analyse," *La psychanalyse*, Vol. 1, 1956, pp. 167–178.
LAMBERT, W. E., "Measurement of the Linguistic Dominance of Bilinguals," *Journal of Abnormal and Social Psychology*, Vol. 50, 1955, pp. 197–200.
———, "Developmental Aspects of Second-Language Learning," *Journal of Social Psychology*, Vol. 43, 1956, pp. 83–104.
———, "Psychological Approaches to the Study of Language," *Modern Language Journal*, Vol. 67, 1963, pp. 51–62, 114–121.
———, J. HAVELKA, and C. CROSBY, "The Influence of Language-Acquisition Contexts on Bilingualism," *Journal of Abnormal and Social Psychology*, Vol. 56, 1958, pp. 239–244.
———, J. HAVELKA, and R. C. GARDNER, "Linguistic Manifestations of Bilingualism," *American Journal of Psychology*, Vol. 72, 1959, pp. 77–82.
———, and S. FILLENBAUM, "A Pilot Study of Aphasia among Bilinguals," *Canadian Journal of Psychology*, Vol. 13, 1959, pp. 28–34.
———, and N. MOORE, "Word-Association Responses: Comparisons of American and French Monolinguals with Canadian Monolinguals and Bilinguals," *Journal of Personality and Social Psychology*, Vol. 3, 1966, pp. 313–320.
LANE, H. L., "Some Differences between First and Second Language Learning," *Language Learning*, Vol. 12, 1962, pp. 1–14.
LAWTON, D., "Social Class Differences in Language Development," *Language and Speech*, Vol. 6, 1963, pp. 109–119.
LEISCHNER, A., "Über die Aphasie der Mehrsprachigen," *Archiv für Psychiatrie und Nervenkrankheiten*, Vol. 180, 1948, pp. 731–775.

LENNEBERG, E. H., "Language Disorders in Childhood," *Harvard Educational Review*, Vol. 34, 1964, pp. 152–177.

———, "Speech Development: Its Anatomical and Physiological Concomitants," E. C. Carterette (ed.), *Speech, Language, and Communication (Brain Function)*, Vol. 3, Berkeley, Calif.: University of California Press, 1966, pp. 37–66.

———, and J. M. ROBERTS, *The Language of Experience (Indiana University Publications in Anthropology and Linguistics, Memoir 13)*, 1956.

LEOPOLD, W. F., "The Study of Child Language and Infant Bilingualism," *Word*, Vol. 4, 1948, pp. 1–17.

———, *Speech Development of a Bilingual Child: A Linguist's Record*. 4 Volumes. Evanston, Ill.: Northwestern University Press, 1949. (1939–1949.)

LEVY, J., "Conflicts of Cultures and Children's Maladjustment," *Mental Hygiene*, Vol. 17, 1933, pp. 41–50.

MACKEY, W. F., "The Description of Bilingualism," *Canadian Journal of Linguistics*, Vol. 7, 1962, pp. 51–85.

———, "Bilingual Interference: Its Analysis and Measurement," *Journal of Communication*, Vol. 15, 1965, pp. 239–249.

———, "The Measurement of Bilingual Behavior," *Canadian Psychologist*, Vol. 7, 1966, pp. 75–92.

MACLAY, H., and E. E. WARE, "Cross-Cultural Use of the Semantic Differential," *Behavioral Science*, Vol. 6, 1961, pp. 185–190.

MARX, O. M., "Aphasia Studies and Language Theory in the 19th Century," *Bulletin of the History of Medicine*, Vol. 40, 1966, pp. 328–349.

McCARTHY, D. A., "Language Disorders and Parent-Child Relationships," *Journal of Speech and Hearing Disorders*, Vol. 19, 1954, pp. 514–523.

MINKOWSKI, M., "Klinischer Beitrag zur Aphasie bei Polyglotten," *Archives Suisses de Neurologie et de Psychiatrie*, Vol. 21, 1927, pp. 43–72.

———, "Sur un cas d'aphasie chez un polyglotte," *Revue Neurologique*, Vol. 35, 1928, pp. 361–366.

MITCHELL, A. J., "The Effect of Bilingualism in the Measurement of Intelligence," *Elementary School Journal*, Vol. 38, 1937, pp. 29–37.

MORRISON, J. R., "Bilingualism: Some Psychological Aspects," *Advancement of Science*, Vol. 56, 1958, pp. 287–290.

O'DOHERTY, E. F., "Bilingualism: Educational Aspects," *Advancement of Science*, Vol. 56, 1958, pp. 282–286.

OSGOOD, C. E., "Psycholinguistics," in S. Koch (ed.), *Psychology: A Study of a Science*, Vol. 6, pp. 244–316. New York: McGraw-Hill Publishing Company, Inc., 1963a.

———, "On Understanding and Creating Sentences," *American Psychologist*, Vol. 18, 1963b, pp. 735–751.

———, "Contextual Control in Sentence Understanding and Creating," E. C. Carterette (ed.), *Speech, Language, and Communication (Brain Function)*, Vol. 3. Berkeley, Calif.: University of California Press, 1966, pp. 201–229.

PANETH, E., "An Investigation into Conference Interpreting." Unpublished M.A. dissertation, London College, 1957.

PEAL, E., and W. E. LAMBERT, *The Relation of Bilingualism to Intelligence (Psychological Monographs, No. 546)*, 1962.

PIERIS, R., "Bilingualism and Cultural Marginality," *British Journal of Sociology*, Vol. 2, 1951, pp. 328–339.

PINTNER, R., "The Influence of Language Background on Intelligence Tests," *Journal of Social Psychology*, Vol. 3, 1932, pp. 235–240.

PINTNER, R., and S. ARSENIAN, "The Relation of Bilingualism to Verbal In-

telligence and School Adjustment," *Journal of Educational Research,* Vol. 31, 1937, pp. 255–263.
PITRES, A., "Étude sur l'aphasie chez les polyglottes," *Revue de Médecine,* Vol. 15, 1895, pp. 889–898.
PÖTZL, O., "Aphasie und Mehrsprachigkeit," *Zeitschrift für die gesamte Neurologie und Psychiatrie,* Vol. 124, 1930, pp. 145–162.
RAUBICHECK, L., "The Psychology of Multilingualism," *Volta Review,* Vol. 36, 1934, pp. 17–20.
ROMNEY, A. K., and R. G. D'ANDRADE (eds.), *Transcultural Studies in Cognition (American Anthropologist,* Special Publication), Vol. 66, No. 3, Pt. 2, 1964.
RONJAT, J., *Le développement du langage observé chez un enfant bilingue.* Paris: Champion, 1913.
SAER, D. J., "An Inquiry into the Effect of Bilingualism upon the Intelligence of Young Children," *Journal of Experimental Pedagogy,* Vol. 6, 1922, pp. 232–240, 266–274.
———, "The Effect of Bilingualism on Intelligence," *British Journal of Psychology,* Vol. 14, 1923, pp. 25–38.
SAPON, S. M., "A Methodology for the Study of Socio-Economic Differentials in Linguistic Phenomena," *Studies in Linguistics,* Vol. 11, 1953, pp. 57–68.
SÁNCHEZ, G. I., "Bilingualism and Mental Measures," *Journal of Applied Psychology,* Vol. 18, 1934, pp. 765–772.
SCHUELL, H., and J. J. JENKINS, "The Nature of Language Deficit in Aphasia," *Psychological Review,* Vol. 66, 1959, pp. 45–67.
SMITH, F., "Bilingualism and Mental Development," *British Journal of Psychology,* Vol. 13, 1923, pp. 270–282.
SOFFIETTI, J. P., "Bilingualism and Biculturalism," *Journal of Educational Psychology,* Vol. 46, 1955, pp. 222–227.
SPOERL, D. T., "The Academic and Verbal Adjustment of College Age Bilingual Students," *Journal of Genetic Psychology,* Vol. 64, 1944, pp. 139–157.
———, "Bilinguality and Emotional Adjustment," *Journal of Abnormal and Social Psychology,* Vol. 38, 1946, pp. 37–57.
STENGEL, E., "On Learning a New Language," *International Journal of Psychoanalysis,* Vol. 20, 1939, pp. 471–479.
———, and J. ZELMANOWICZ, "Über polyglotte motorische aphasie," *Zeitschrift für die gesamte Neurologie und Psychiatrie,* Vol. 149, 1933, pp. 292–311.
STERN, W., "Über Zweisprachigkeit in der frühen Kindheit," *Zeitschrift für angewandte Psychologie,* Vol. 30, 1923, pp. 168–172.
TANAKA, Y., T. OYAMA, and C. E. OSGOOD, "A Cross-Cultural and Cross Concept Study of the Generality of Semantic Spaces," *Journal of Verbal Learning and Verbal Behavior,* Vol. 2, 1963, pp. 392–405.
TIREMAN, L. S., "Bilingual Children," *Journal of Educational Research,* Vol. 11, 1941, pp. 340–352.
———, "Bilingual Children (II)," *Journal of Educational Research,* Vol. 14, 1944, pp. 273–278.
TITONE, R., *La psicolinguistica oggi.* Zürich: Pas-Verlag, 1964.
TRAVIS, L., W. JOHNSON, and J. SHOVER, "The Relation of Bilingualism to Stuttering," *Journal of Speech Disorders,* Vol. 2, 1937, pp. 185–189.
TRIANDIS, H. C., "Cultural Influences upon Cognitive Processes," L. Berkowitz (ed.), *Advances in Experimental Social Psychology,* pp. 1–48. New York: Academic Press, Inc., 1964.
———, and C. E. OSGOOD, "A Comparative Factorial Analysis of Semantic Struc-

tures in Monolingual Greek and American College Students," *Journal of Abnormal and Social Psychology*, Vol. 57, 1958, pp. 187–196.

VELIKOVSKY, I., "Can a Newly Acquired Language become the Speech of the Unconscious? Word-plays in the Dreams of Hebrew Thinking Persons," *Psychoanalytic Quarterly*, Vol. 21, 1934, pp. 329–335.

VILDOMEC, V., *Multilingualism*. Leyden: A. W. Sythoff, 1963.

WEINREICH, U., *Languages in Contact: Findings and Problems (Publications of the Linguistic Circle of New York, No. 1)*, 1953.

——, "On the Description of Phonic Interference," *Word*, Vol. 13, 1957, pp. 1–11.

——, "Research Frontiers in Bilingualism Studies," E. Sivertsen (ed.), *Proceedings of the Eighth International Congress of Linguists*, pp. 786–797. Oslo: Oslo University Press, 1958.

WEISENBURG, T., and K. E. McBRIDE, *Aphasia: A Clinical and Psychological Study*. New York: The Commonwealth Fund, 1935.

WEPMAN, J. M., and L. V. JONES, "Studies in Aphasia: A Psycholinguistic Method and Case Study," E. C. Carterette (ed.), *Speech, Language, and Communication (Brain Function)*, Vol. 3. Berkeley, Calif.: University of California Press, 1966, pp. 141–172.

16

The Study of Personality in Primitive Societies

John J. Honigmann

I

European missionaries and other travelers in far-off lands had noted remarkable features in the psychological make-up of primitive people long before anthropologists added psychology to their discipline's multifaceted viewpoint. Once anthropology emerged as a distinctive scientific field, early in the 19th century, travelers continued to provide theory builders with most of the information about the world's more exotic people. Professional anthropologists themselves became fieldworkers only during the final quarter of the last century. In 1901 appeared one of the earliest publications of psychological findings presented in an ethnological context, a report issued by the Cambridge Anthropological Expedition to Torres Straits (1901). Written by a number of eminent British psychologists and ethnologists, the volume stands as a benchmark in the development of what has come to be known as psychological anthropology. The expedition itself is notable for beginning a still continuing trend whereby psychologists and psychiatrists occasionally follow anthropologists into exotic parts of the world to study psychological processes in natural settings. The investigators set out in 1898, after Alfred Haddon, an ethnologist, had persuaded several of his academic colleagues to lay aside their books and lectures and to sail with him for the islands lying in the strait between New Guinea and Australia. Haddon himself had been to Torres Strait before and knew the area as a favorable spot for conducting psychological experiments. The Papuan inhabitants had emerged only 30 years before from what Haddon called a "completely savage state . . . absolutely untouched by civilization." Here, he promised his colleagues, was a fine natural setting in which to test the keen eyesight and other powers of primitive people such as had often attracted the admiration of travelers. The scientists indeed found plenty of willing subjects during their 12 months' stay. Most of that time they lived in a single small community and took scientific advantage of their growing intimacy with the native subjects. Like modern anthropologists carrying on participant observation, the Cambridge scientists utilized their growing familiarity with the islanders to enrich their information. In that way they improved their ability to interpret their test findings, that is, to see them in a natural, cultural frame of reference. They tested the islanders for visual acuity, color vision, color naming, visual illusions, smell and taste, reaction time, and similar "mental characteristics" and compared the results to findings available from Europeans and other control groups. That comparative information was on hand to use for this purpose indicates how quick experimental psychology had been to adopt a comparative approach. For instance, back in 1865 the American army was comparing the visual acuity of Negro and white soldiers recruited for the Civil War. In their report the Cambridge scientists could show that travelers who had credited primitive people with extraordinary sensory acuteness generally made no attempt to disentangle physiological mechanisms from experience or cultural conditioning. Indeed, with respect to vision, the Torres Strait expedition, using apparatus somewhat like the optometrist's eye chart, found the islanders' visual acuity to be superior to that of normal Europeans, but not to any marked degree. The Papuans' powers of observation (as distinguished from visual acuity in the strict sense) turned out to be even more remarkable and in every way worthy of the travelers' admiration. The natives spying a boat on the horizon could recognize its rigging and other features when the expedition's members could barely make out a vessel. William Halsey Rivers ascribed such visual ability to practice that makes "the savage . . . an extremely close observer of nature." On the other hand, Charles Myers blames the islanders' poor ability to distinguish musical tones on *lack* of practice. The musical resources of their culture left them unfamiliar with European musical notes, instruments, and other elements of Western musical culture that would have enabled them to exercise skills of the kind for which they were tested. The explanation has a familiar ring. Social scientists have since employed it many times to criticize the use of culture-bound tests in circumstances where experience has not endowed the subjects with the skills being tested. That the islanders quickly learned to improve their ability to distinguish tones, testifies to their adaptability and denies any deep-seated mental sluggishness. Rivers, however, took another view of the people's intelligence. The islanders' nearly exclusive preoccupation with sensory objects, he wrote, hindered their mental development; a conclusion to which a German ethnologist, Johann Ranke, had also come as a result of extended fieldwork in South America. Rivers theorized that the human body operates with a limited amount of energy. If too much is spent on the sensory functions, "it is natural that the intellectual superstructure should suffer." This theory sounds close to the "genital economics" which Joseph Unwin some years later borrowed from Freud to explain why many primitives have low cultures: they waste too much energy in premarital and postmarital sexuality, not conserving or sublimating enough to build civilizations.

II

The application of psychology to ethnological materials changed greatly in the 30 or 40 years between the return of the Cambridge Expedition from Torres Strait and the emergence of culture and personality study as an anthropological speciality. What happened in those three or four decades owes much to the impressive ability of psychoanalytic theory to reveal unexpected significance in the facts of culture. One way to continue tracing the growth of psychological anthropology and to show the insight provided by a psychodynamic viewpoint is to contrast two anthropologists' conceptions, separated by 25 years, of the culturally patterned nature of dreams.

In 1936 Paul Radin published an account of the highly stereotyped dreams that some American Indians induce by fasting, isolation, and concentration. Typically, such dreams feature a supernatural being who often assumes the guise of an animal that promises henceforth to help the dreamer. Radin offers a very simple theory to account for dreams that recur so similarly in tribal societies like the Ojibwa, Ottawa, and Cree. Stereotyped dreams, he says, conform with a focal interest of the cultures in which they occur. They are strongly expected, highly valued, and the person is taught to await them. Even though the dreamer is asleep and out of ordinary contact with other people, his dreamwork responds to social expectations he has internalized. In 1961 a young anthropologist Roy G. D'Andrade, who was also interested in the relationship between culture and personality, again considered the effect of culture on dreaming. He did not limit himself to American Indians but treated a worldwide panel of societies. Also, the theory with which he worked was much more complex and explicit than Radin's.

D'Andrade sees culture reaching into a person's unconscious by arousing anxiety. Consequently, dreams are culturally patterned defensive maneuvers which enable a person to adapt to his anxiety-provoking cultural situation. To illustrate, when life in a society promotes anxiety about being alone and on one's own, then, D'Andrade hypothesizes, dreams that seek and control supernatural power—Paul Radin's dreams of the supernatural helper—will be culturally patterned in that society. To test this prediction, D'Andrade collected information about dreams in cultures likely to promote considerable anxiety about isolation and being on one's own and compared this data with dreams from cultures less likely to induce that kind of stress. Obviously D'Andrade did not do fieldwork in the more than 50 societies that constituted his sample, but consulted ethnographies that had been written about them by other anthropologists. In fact, he did not even have to read the books and articles themselves but could locate cultures for which the necessary information was available by consulting files of data located in several parts of the United States. Those files make it possible to retrieve data about more than 250 world cultures, drawn from several thousand ethnographic sources, conveniently translated into English if necessary, neatly broken down by topic, and classified in numbered categories.

How could D'Andrade recognize societies whose ways of life arouse anxiety about isolation and self-reliance? As likely evidence of such feelings, he first chose the custom of a boy at marriage moving from his parents' home to live elsewhere. Surely men in such a society would experience that kind of anxiety. Second, he reasoned that hunting, collecting, and fishing rather than agriculture and cattle husbandry would very likely promote anxiety about isolation and being on one's own. Taking the first indicator—a boy leaving his parental home at marriage—D'Andrade found that 80 percent of the 21 societies in which a boy at marriage shifts from one local group to another put value on dreams about supernatural helpers compared with 40 percent of the 25 societies in which a boy leaves his parental home after marriage but continues to reside in the same village or local group as his parents, and only 27 percent of 11 societies in which he and his wife stay in the same household as his parents. These figures support the hypothesis. Comparison of tribes without agriculture and those with agriculture and animal husbandry also yielded results that conformed with the prediction. Stereotyped dreams about supernatural helpers not only conform with social expectations, as Radin explained; they are encouraged by cultures in which isolation and self-reliance instigate tension in personality. The evidence in favor of the hypothesis in turn supports the proposition, derived from psychoanalytic theory, that dreams represent culturally patterned defense mechanisms which enable a person to adapt to anxiety-provoking situations.

I cite these two approaches to dreams about supernatural helpers, emphasizing the dates when they were published, to illustrate how interest in the relationship between culture and personality has changed. The changes have been partly a result of new theories imported into anthropology and psychology and partly a consequence of the fairly elaborate ways that have been devised to test psychological theories cross-culturally. Radin barely began to study the working of culture on the level of personality. D'Andrade used a series of culturally different primitive societies to test psychological assumptions. True, the anthropologist cannot test by drastically manipulating ways of life in order to see what changes follow in personality. But he can use the primitive world, together with other cultures, to compare a large number of situations. He then observes if the crucial variable he is examining occurs in significantly different degree in conjunction with varying cultural conditions. The method of cross-cultural testing still faces serious problems, some of which I shall mention later. Undeniably, however, it has greatly expanded our knowledge about personality dynamics and shown new value in the detailed facts brought back from fieldwork in primitive societies.

The psychological questions anthropologists, psychologists, and other social scientists came to ask in the isolated, primitive communities during the years following the Torres Strait expedition rarely again pertained so exclusively to sensory acuity and the other matters that had engrossed the Cambridge scientists. In addition to adding human capacities such as learning, dreaming, and adaptation under stress to their orbit of attention, later students of human behavior in primitive social settings also attended primarily to factors of motivation and to emotional aspects of personality. Of course, members of the expedition had caught glimpses of an unfamiliar motivational life in their Papuan subjects. For example, they noted that when the islanders performed poorly, they quickly lost interest in the tests. Haddon complained that the natives sought to take all they could get from the visitors but in return showed little gratitude. William McDougall observed that the islanders could withstand minute amounts of experimentally induced pain better than members of the expedition. But the scientists lacked a psychological theory to explain such interesting behavior. Conscious and unconscious motives and unconscious equivalences, together with their sources in early childhood became major interests in comparative psychological research and spawned the subdiscipline that has come to be known as culture and personality (Kluckhohn 1944).

Some observers who went into the field to investigate primitive personality sought to grasp the "whole" personality of a people, looking for systemic relationships among psychological characteristics. Others concentrated on more limited, though still pervasive, features; for example, Allan Holmberg (1950), working among the Sirionó of eastern Bolivia, gave his attention to the hunger drive, comparing it with the patterning of the sex drive.

The observers varied in the concepts of personality they employed. Often they limited their orbit of interest to the covert processes that could be inferred from observable data or from the responses given to projective tests. By this definition, the acts and verbalizations of people are not themselves regarded as part of personality; only the underlying motives and similar processes as such. Others went into the field with an inclusive definition of personality, one that called attention to both covert phenomena, especially those with motivating power, and overt indicators of such covert states, including details of dress, posture, and, of course, what people do and say (Honigmann 1967:Ch. 3). Researchers have generally found it worthwhile to look at tangible, material products of behavior in primitive societies, like the designs, houses, or images that people make. Although artifacts are not part of personality, they provide clues to underlying psychodynamics. The validity of such clues must, of course, be verified by noting the degree to which they are consistent with inferences that can, with theoretical justification be drawn from other overt indicators. Folktales, although not usually created by the same generation that recounts them, likewise afford insight into the personality of their bearers (Fischer 1963).

III

The scientists of the Torres Strait expedition literally moved their laboratories from Cambridge and reestablished them in the southwest Pacific Ocean. Anthropologists still call the primitive communities they study their laboratories. And the image is a good one, for the diverse cultural conditions that primitive societies embody are ideally suited to test scientific generalizations about mankind. Bronislaw Malinowski (1927) used the Trobriand Islanders that way when he looked to see if their social arrangements conspired to arouse that conflict of incestuous love and jealous hate called by Freud the oedipus complex. Undertaking one of the earliest psychoanalytical analyses of personality of non-Western peoples, he recognized none of the tensions that in his opinion drove European youngsters to the verge of recapitulating the tragic destiny of King Oedipus. In Malinowski's opinion, cultural conditions in the Trobriand islands that contrast with those found in Europe rule out the oedipus complex, at least in the form described by Freud. In the islands, the mother's brother and not the child's father wields disciplinary authority. The father is a mild protective figure and not an awesome, dominant patriarch feared by his wife and children. Also, the Trobrianders are free of the sexual puritanism that complicates growth in Europe. Hence, children develop to self-confident, sexual maturity without passing through the same agonizing oedipal struggle that Freud's patients recalled and in some cases were still living through.

The fact that Malinowski had actually lived with the islanders whose psychic life he analyzed did not impress contemporary psychoanalysts, who found his conclusion scientifically naive. Without setting foot in the Trobriands, they explained away his argument and presciently undecked the camouflage which the oedipus complex adopts there. In the long run, however, Malinowski and other anthropologists, who experienced difficulties using the oedipus complex and other psychoanalytic concepts in their research, helped to transform orthodox psychoanalysis. The new schools of psychoanalytic thought that grew up ascribed a much greater role to culture in shaping personality than Freud had.

Knowledge is confirmed through testing but originally it grows through opportunities for surprise and discovery, and through imagining possibilities which our everyday lives supply only poorly. Primitive societies, cut off from contact with the great civilizations of Asia and Europe and having worked out their own plans for existence, have showered social science with hypotheses about personality, its formation, and its integration with culture. They inform us more fully than our own limited experience about what it means to be a human being. Each primitive culture demonstrates a new facet of what man has made of himself and, what is even more important, each promises what man can become. I don't mean that we can create our future by grafting this or that institution of primitive culture on our way of life or directly copy exotic values that excite our admiration. Cultures do not allow such simple grafting from one to another. Anthropologists are apt to find that the trinket, bit of cuisine, or habit brought back from the field transforms itself nearly unrecognizably in the setting of their own culture or else is soon buried out of sight. Primitive cultures help us chart prospective change in ways that are subtler than simple transplanting. The diversity that anthropology discovers in the primitive world informs us about the breadth of human plasticity. We learn not to mistake the unwitting nature of cultural evolution or the fixity of human development for rigidly controlled biological determinism. As Margaret Mead (1928) came to know Samoan girls and watched their easy transition into adolescence, she confirmed her suspicion that features in Western culture are responsible for often making that period of life a point of stress and strain. In a society like ours that clamors for hard and fast choices, adolescence, being a time when mental and emotional maturity begins, is bound to be filled with difficult conflicts. Margaret Mead's experience in Samoa recommended that we educate our young people for choice, bring them to adolescence with an open mind and flexible habits of thought, by teaching them that many possibilities are open, no one of which is sanctioned above its alternatives. Once man fulfills certain basic conditions—like eating, sleeping, and protection from the cold—he is bound to follow no predestined path in selecting his goals and values. In such ways, study of primitive societies and of the personalities within them enhances our conception of human freedom. For Stanley Diamond (1963), primitives possess what our civilization has lost, namely, "the immediate and ramifying sense of the person" and the presence of authentic individuation which is one of the conditions for personal growth. The point is, primitive cultures inform us about the variability of human nature and in doing so they demonstrate that it is possible to live more satisfactory lives.

Only as long as we regard primitive people in all respects as human as ourselves can we use them to learn about human nature and cite them as object lessons in human mutability. By holding primitives to be one with ourselves, we in effect hold human nature constant. It is culture that varies from one human group to another, and experience makes the difference in how people learn to behave. Behavioral variation in turn, gives assurance that human nature can be changed, and that neither our lives nor the lives of any of our contemporaries need follow their current patterns.

IV

While the assumption of mankind's psychic unity is old, not all observers of the primitive world have shared it to the same degree. For a time Claude Lévy-Bruhl (1925) did not. He castigated the "English school" of E. B. Tylor for postulating the universal identity of the human mind and then, on the basis of that "false" axiom, proceeding to explain how the mind could produce the fantasies with which primitive magic and religion are replete. Contrary to what Tylor believed, men did not invent the soul to account for their dreams and then logically proceed to generalize the soul concept into ideas of imposing deities. Primitives, Lévy-Bruhl insisted, ignore logic as we know it. They believe that a witch can be asleep next to her husband and at the same time off doing mischief. They can accept such preposterous ideas because their mentality is utterly different from ours. They think prelogically. Confronted by an unusual event, we look for antecedents and in doing so distinguish between natural and supernatural causes. They, on the other hand, immediately look for occult and invisible powers at work, for they live in a world where everything is undifferentiated and related to everything else. We objectify nature; they, feeling themselves fully participants in nature, do not; consequently, a wife's conduct at home influences her husband's fate in battle and even controls the growth of the garden. According to Lévy-Bruhl, the logical, modern mind evolved gradually as the collective prelogical mentality ceased to dominate individual thought. When the personal ego became clearly differentiated from the group in which the individual had formerly been absorbed, the rest of nature and the gods also came to be set apart from man and relatively independent of him. In his later years Lévy-Bruhl (1949), bowing to inescapable criticism, modified his theory to the extent of denying that a fundamentally different, evolutionarily earlier system of logic characterized primitive people. He admitted that "participation thinking" crops up so often in civilized man that it cannot be considered a peculiarity limited to any stage of culture. In other words, he accepted the conclusion that primitive modes of thought are derived from experience and are not products of some essentially different kind of human nature. But he still lumped primitive people together, ascribing a higher degree of participation thinking to them all, as if social experience were precisely alike from one primitive society to another.

There have been, and still are, other anthropologists who have few misgivings about lumping all primitive cultures together and who maintain that primitive people follow relatively distinct thought-ways or cultivate a special kind of world view. Franz Boas (1938:Ch. 12) said that the mind of primitive man, being socially dominated and emotionally loaded, allows the most heterogeneous phenomena—animals, religious concepts, social groups, and emotional states—to be associated together with impunity. Normal civilized men, however, through the sheer force of reason overcome such emotional, socially determined associations. Stanley Diamond (1963) takes a dim view of the idea that primitive communities differ too much between themselves to allow them to be generally labeled by a few common characteristics. In small-scale primitive societies, he believes, we discern primary human nature. With their communalistic economics; traditional bases of leadership; informal, customary law-ways; thoroughgoing conservatism; tight interlocking of religion, economics, social structure, and other aspects of culture, and kinship basis of social relations they encourage special modes of thought. Primitives think concretely, in terms of existence rather than essence, nominalistically, and personalistically. In their good nurturance of infants; their many-sided, enjoyable personal relationships; intellectual alertness; ability to incorporate deviants in privileged ways into the social fabric, and direct engagement of nature, primitives enjoy richly satisfying lives that by contrast illumine "the dark side of world civilization which is in chronic crisis."

More than one anthropologist just back from the field has recoiled in shocked dismay from the civilization he left a year or two before, and in which he is now reluctant to become fully reincorporated. Its values and emphases appear gross and false in the light of others to which his personality became deeply attuned. Reverse culture shock numbs him; his rhythms and standards are still adjusted to another set of cultural routines. Such a familiar experience, which occurs to anyone who intensely has come to know another—not necessarily primitive—way of life nevertheless offers nothing in support of the noble-savage hypothesis. Too many monographs have been written to allow anyone to entertain the idea that primitive people enjoy uniformly happy lives any longer. True, such reports may be slanted by the way their authors, like journalists or psychiatrists, prefer to dwell on stress, conflict, disequilibrium, and pathology, but what they report is nevertheless empirically grounded and therefore can not be ignored.

Few primitive societies are saddled with the pervasive inadequacies of the Alorese, a people crippled by defensive inhibitions, confusions, mistrust, anxiety, shame, fear, apathy, lack of enterprise, repressed hatred, and inability to understand one another (Du Bois 1944; Kardiner 1945). Much of their condition, the psychoanalyst Abram Kardiner believes, arises from the poor nurturance extended to them during the critical period of infancy and childhood. Despite the fact that Alorese society has no need to cope with actual food shortages, Alorese children remain chronically hungry, especially during the wet season when gardening occupies every woman to the exclusion of everything else. Children grow up, Kardiner says, with personal strengths sufficient only to maintain their culture on a very thin thread, and with just enough resources to conceal from themselves their own wretchedness. As I have said, few primitive communities support such thoroughly unsatisfying lives. On the other hand, not many primitive groups have been described as being replete with happy qualities. We have the Mountain Arapesh whom Margaret Mead (1935 and 1961) characterizes as gentle, cooperative, warm, trusting, enthusiastic about the achievements of others, and more accustomed to expressing rage against their surroundings than against other persons. But this does not make the Arapesh an ideal of psychological adjustment. Their security is one constructed on a narrow base, precariously dependent on receiving love and help. Psychologically minded observers have also drawn a positive picture of the Plains Indians west of the Mississippi River as they lived prior to the frontiersman's arrival. The Comanche personality, for example, Kardiner (1945) reconstructs as having been endowed with a strong ego and lacking the concept that misfortune hinges on disobedience or sin. The competition of Comanche men with one another did not interfere with their security and their hostility, directed against enemies, was also so structured that it could not disrupt their culture.

The regularity with which anthropologists and culturally minded psychoanalysts have encountered bleak, unhappy, and even psychiatrically disturbed personalities in the world's primitive societies should not deceive us. Not only has the population been inadequately sampled; there is a good likelihood that serious bias attended the research. Margaret Mead (1952:435) describes us as listening intensively for distortion without also listening for the compensatory "fulfillment and blessings which come to each individual in the course of learning to be a human being in his particular culture." Stresses may well inhere in primitive societies, but so do gratifications.

For a time anthropologists were puzzled over how a supposedly objective science could characterize the same societies by practically opposite traits. One set of observers reports the Zuni and Hopi Indians to be tranquil, nonaggressive, cooperative, and modest while another viewpoint sees them as anxious, suspicious, hostile, and ambitious (Bennett 1946). An amiable side of Kwakiutl life competes with the view that those North Pacific Coast Indians are obsessed with rivalry and competition (Codere 1956). When careful and accomplished fieldworkers who study the same society diverge on questions like these, no one can be branded wrong. They have all tested their interpretations against manifold empirical data in the standard manner that anthropologists follow to test their conclusions. To a considerable extent their divergence is due to what each selects for attention and to how he interprets what he sees. Incompatible, inexplicit value orientations guide the perception of different observers. To put it crudely, one observer enters the community prepared to find only evidence of social integration matched by personal adjustment; another expects to find individual and society in conflict and the social personality rent by tension. In a similar way, the primary focus on pathology that has characterized much anthropological work in culture and personality confines an observer's attention to facts of dysfunction, or at least leads him to reach such interpretations more readily than others. One thing is certain: we can never know a culture or a system of personality except through human bengs whose very modes of knowing are built into the knowledge they present. To try to get rid of the observer's role, especially in social science, is (as Jacques Barzun once said) like insisting that the actors go on, but play to an empty theatre.

v

Primitive people are no more fortunate than the rest of mankind in wholly escaping risk of psychiatric disorder. The important question, whether frequencies of such disorder actually run lower in isolated primitive than in civilized societies is not easily answered. One recent epidemiological survey executed among the Nigerian Yoruba—who can hardly be called isolated—at least provides some quantitatively ordered facts with which to advance the question from sheer speculation (A. H. Leighton *et al.* 1963). The researchers in Nigeria employed the same basic concepts and methods that they had used with Canadians in rural Nova Scotia. Some of the same investigators worked in both areas, thereby to a degree assuring comparable procedures. But by no means were study conditions matched perfectly. In Canada, out of a sample totalling 1010 persons the psychiatrists judged 57 percent to be, or sometime during their adult lives to have been, almost certainly or probably psychiatrically disturbed. Fifteen Yoruba villages provided a sample of 262 persons of whom 40 percent were similarly evaluated. In Canada, 33 percent of the sample were judged to have been sufficiently impaired for their symptoms to have significantly interfered in performing their work and other responsibilities. In Yorubaland, the comparable figure is only 15 percent. These comparisons suggest that in their adult lives Yoruba became mentally ill less often than rural Nova Scotians. It is, of course, also possible that the Western-trained psychiatrists found mental illness harder to detect and evaluate in Nigeria than in the more familiar cultural surroundings of Canada. At any rate, a larger proportion of the Yoruba sample falls into the "well" category; that is, it proved impossible to detect symptoms in the lives of 25 percent of the Yoruba sample compared with 17 percent of the Nova Scotians. In both Nova Scotia and Yorubaland, the prevalence of psychiatric disorder was smaller in socially well-integrated communities than in communities marked by poverty, poor leadership, cultural confusion, secularization, and similar signs of social disintegration. The researchers among the Yoruba took special pains to learn whether the extent of culture change in the 15 villages related to the prevalence of mental illness. Contrary to beliefs that had long prevailed in anthropology, they discovered that by itself the shift to new living patterns constituted no noxious factor as far as mental health is concerned. This important finding reinforces recent anthropological opinion which holds that change in primitive communities need not destroy personal well-being or social integration. Even rapid, wholesale change will not devastate members of a community if such change is guided by people's own inclination, a discovery that Margaret Mead (1956) made in Manus when she revisited that South Sea island in 1953 after a 25-year absence.

Note that epidemiologists are as confident about crossing cultural boundaries in diagnosing mental illness as they are in judging the prevalence of physical ailments, like malaria or cholera. Proponents of extreme cultural relativism used to claim that the mentally healthy person in one society might well turn out to be psychotic in another. In a sense, this is true. As Ruth Benedict (1934:275) says, the normal Kwakiutl contests of rivalry would be regarded as madness by the Zuni, with their deep-seated repugnance for dominance and the humiliation of others. However, experience proves Benedict wrong in predicting that "aberrant behaviour in either culture could never be determined in relation to any least common denominator of behaviour." The psychiatrist's yardstick, consisting of definitions and theory, allows him to determine exactly that. It is quite possible to diagnose mental illness across cultural boundaries. Clinical abnormality, then, is behavior which a psychiatrist has authority to define as disordered or abnormal. If we recognize his authority, then abnormal the behavior becomes, regardless of what people in the community themselves think and regardless of the fact that the mentally disturbed person may occupy a useful niche in the social structure. College students have complained to me about the unfairness of a definition that makes mental illness dependent on the professional judgment of an expert belonging to another culture. I can only reply that we need not be content with the way cross-cultural psychiatry is currently practiced, but at least we should understand the logic with which it operates (cf. Murphy 1965)

Much has been made of specialized forms of psychopathology nurtured in primitive cultures: wiitiko psychosis, with fantasies of being driven to cannibalism, among the Cree and Ojibwa Indians of eastern Canada; pibloktoq and incapacitating kayak-phobia among Eskimo; imitative Arctic hysteria in Paleosiberians, and frenzied running amok in Southeast Asia. Underneath the differing masks of these exotically titled disorders, social psychiatrists now recognize the familiar faces of all-too-common mental illnesses: obsessive-compulsive neurosis, hysteria, schizophrenia, and others. Only the content of the forms of disorder shifts, taking hints from cultural realities, like kayaking or cannibalism. But by and large, there are only so many modes of adapting under severe stress, and those modes recur from one part of the world to another. When the primitive's personality fractures, it is likely to give way along some of the same lines as in civilized commununities. Anthropology pursues comparative personality study with the aim of understanding behavior, normal and abnormal, in the fullest relevant cultural context: in terms of the primitive society's vision of its own life. Historical context—how the behavior came to be the way it is—is important but even more important is the cultural context obtained by asking questions such as the following: What ends do given personality characteristics consciously or unconsciously serve for the community or its members? Anthropologists are likely to find the shaman's possible psychopathology, so often debated, as less significant than the safety his encounters with the supernatural guarantee to his community. What meaning or value do people attach to normal or psychiatrically significant features of personality? I refer, of course, not to the deductive, theoretical meaning that personality traits possess for a foreign observer, but their existential meaning in the society itself. Cross-cultural psychiatric diagnosis has largely neglected such meaning. Such diagnosis too heavily distorts primitive reality to an unacceptable degree because it overlooks contextual understanding and ignores the successful adaptations even psychiatrically disturbed people sometimes make.

VI

Much personality research in primitive society has inquired into the social and cultural dynamics of personality formation. How, through the interaction of heredity and experience, does each community with a distinctive culture produce a different kind of people? The explanation with which anthropology made its debut in this area of personality study points to cultural patterning as the process whereby social personality is formed. Just as alien traits, like a folktale, religious ceremony, or pottery, drawn into a culture tend to become assimilated to the culture's "more or less consistent pattern of thought and action" (Benedict 1934), thereby acquiring distinctive meanings and sometimes even new, culturally compatible forms, so a culture affects the existence and conditions the thoughts and emotions of individuals born to it. Pueblo Indian culture, for example, bends its carriers to its dominant Apollonian emphasis of moderation, while the Dionysian values of Cheyenne, Blackfoot, and other Plains Indian cultures formerly brought people to strive to achieve the extreme limits of being. In like manner, the formalism of Samoan life, the tendency for situational behavior to be rigidly prescribed, impinges on individuals in such a way so that they learn to be unconcerned with originality, have little fear of failure, experience few deep or vivid emotions, and develop no intense personal loyalties (Mead 1928). Margaret Mead invoked the process called patterning in her book *Sex and Temperament* (1935), which she wrote to refute the idea that certain temperamental traits are "naturally" masculine and others "naturally" feminine. Whether men and women show different temperamental qualities is a matter of culture. A society may ignore the possibility of patterning different personalities for men and women or, like ours, it may constantly reiterate sexual differences. Mead best illustrates patterning by using the Mountain Arapesh, whose culture is oriented to the dominant idea of faithfully growing things—pigs, sago palms, taro, coconuts, wives, and children. The world is a garden that must be tilled, but tilled for others rather than for one's own gain. The ideal personality of men and women is congruent with the cultural emphasis put on growth. People are oriented away from self and directed toward a concern for others.

Patterning remains mainly a descriptive concept. Viewed as a process, it leaves personality formation largely unexplained. Social scientists interested in personality formation have preferred to devote their attention to socialization, enculturation, and learning, viewing those as the effective processes whereby personality is formed. In *Sex and Temperament,* for example, Mead examines the interpersonal influences that "mould" the Arapesh child. She draws attention to the primarily positive quality of Arapesh child care, in which relatively little attempt is made deliberately to curb him or interfere with his impulses; she stresses the rich satisfaction that adults lavish on his nurturance; reports the degree to which they encourage his dependence, and explains how lending children around and readily appeasing their discomfort enable them to develop a strong sense of trust in the world. Child-rearing practices allow an Arapesh youngster little opportunity to develop the feeling of being in active control of his environment; he need not demand feeding or initiate nursing; if he falls, he is picked up; he is not pushed to become independent; he must not master terror alone, and he receives no training in harshness or in ability to take it. Consequently, a passive, dependent, noninitiating, succoring, secure person ideally results from Arapesh upbringing. Perhaps because primitive societies have been slowly changing and homogeneous societies, in which childhood situations closely prefigure adult roles and duties, anthropologists and other social scientists studying socialization within them could afford to ignore the lifetime nature of that process, restricting themselves mainly to how the individual learns his culture in childhood. Personality formation, however, does not end at age 5, 7, or 12. Even in a primitive society, personality must continue to develop beyond the early years as a result of the individual's ceaseless transactions with the world and in consequence of his maturing capacities, cumulative experience, and continually altering social status.

Two major theoretical viewpoints have been employed in research on primitive societies to trace the sequence whereby in each generation culture comes to be embodied anew in the growing individual, shaping his behavior so that it conforms in some degree with the values and expectations of parents, peers, and other contemporaries. From psychoanalysis, as outlined by Freud and amplified or modified by his followers, comes the first theory. This holds that learning begins from the time an infant's body first encounters the society into which it is born. There are several versions of this theory associated, for example, with the names of Karl Abraham, Erik Erikson, Abram Kardiner, and John W. M. Whiting. In Whiting's very explicit version, cultural experiences occurring between a child and his socializers—experiences that either encourage or suppress aspects of the child's oral, anal, genital, dependence, or aggressive behavior—register in the child as feelings of gratification or as anxiety-laden deprivation. Such feelings, stemming from each of the five "systems of behavior," set up in the personality lasting characterological tendencies that subsequently reveal themselves in a variety of adult customs; for example, in ways of treating illness or in customary ideas pertaining to the cause of illness. Because young children's experiences differ from one culture to another, individuals in different societies become endowed with different personality characteristics. Whiting and his colleagues, among them Irvin L. Child (Whiting and Child 1953), have ingeniously tested this theory, using data from reports on a number of worldwide societies chosen partly because necessary information concerning some child-training practices was available on them. To make one such test, Whiting and Child reason that early gratification of any particular system of behavior sets up a lasting capacity in that system for satisfying experience. For instance, in a society that indulges nursing in babyhood and postpones weaning, the oral zone becomes habituated to meeting satisfaction. (Freudians would predict that the orally gratified person will grow up to be an optimist.) Now, to the degree that therapy allays the sense of danger arising from illness, therapy is a satisfying experience, regardless of the system of medicine according to which it is practiced. Therefore, Whiting and Child hypothesize, therapeutic practices in a society will tend to make use of behavior systems that have been, so to speak, fortified with a strong potentiality for experiencing satisfaction. In societies where the oral zone has been richly satisfied in early life, therapeutic practices will consist of swallowing something, it may be food, infusions of herbs, medicines, or other things. On the other hand, therapeutic practices will not make use of behavior systems that have been exposed to serious deprivation or frustration in childhood. The evidence from a worldwide sample of about 50 societies, while poor from the standpoint of statistical tests of significance, conforms with theoretical expectations. That is, in the societies tested, therapeutic practices do tend to employ behavior systems that have been conditioned in early life to yield high levels of satisfaction. Early deprivation or frustration is theoretically held to be filled with anxiety. Early deprivation endows particular systems of behavior with a readiness for unpleasant experience, loading them with a potential to experience threat or danger. From childhood on, the frustrated system becomes enveloped with a pessimistic aura of danger. Holding that satisfaction resulting from early gratification sets up a lasting capacity to experience predominantly satisfaction in a given behavioral system, Whiting and Child expected that because therapy gratifyingly allays the sense of danger arising from illness, therapy will tend to utilize behavior systems that were strongly indulged in earlier life. Conversely they expect that because theories of illness give rise to a sense of danger, such theories will tend to make use of behavior systems that early life has endowed with a high potential to experience threat or danger. Results bear out the hypothesis. For example, in societies where early socialization with respect to aggression is severe, people tend to blame aggression or aggressive acts, like disobedience to spirits, for illness.

In order to test the hypothesis, the satisfying or frustrating quality of socialization practices in different cultures receive numerical ratings. Thus, the Polynesian Marquesans, Melanesian Dobuans, and South African Thonga are rated high in the degree of anxiety likely to be engendered by the severity of early practices connected with the oral zone. They receive the highest scores—17, 16, and 15 respectively—of any of the 39 societies rated on this variable. All three conform with the prediction that follows from the theory; that is, they use oral explanations for the onset of illness. A Dobuan so dreads poisoning by malicious sorcery that he will never accept food except from a few people whom he knows and trusts (Fortune 1932:137). The South Pacific Kurtatchi and Ontong-Javanese both receive the lowest score for the presumed degree of oral socialization anxiety. Each receives a score of 6 on this variable. However, oral explanations of illness are present among the Kurtatchi (contrary to prediction), while being expectably absent among the Ontong-Javanese. In other words, the relationships that Whiting and Child trace between child rearing and adult personality are not necessary and inevitable but represent statistical probabilities.

In my opinion, the biggest shortcoming in Whiting and Child's brilliant demonstration of the role that early child rearing plays in personality formation lies in the way their method neglects clinical evidence of actual personality states. The published reports from which the testers derive their information were often written by observers unequipped with psychological training and not imbued with much clinical insight. The authors draw their conclusions about personality sets in childhood simply from the degree to which child-training practices appear to gratify or frustrate such systems in children. A towering mass of inference is erected on what may in the first instance be poor observation by an investigator ill-equipped even to study child rearing. The numerical ratings assigned to socialization practices *sound* precise and are the combined product of three independent judges, but too frequently they depend on very unprecise data informed by poor clinical ability.

When Whiting and his associates trace adult forms of behavior back to early life, they do not always stop with the child-rearing practices. Assuming that child rearing depends on a society's living arrangements, which determine such things as the time a mother has available to devote to child care, her inclination to indulge the child, or the values she attaches to his early independence, anthropologists have begun to look for specific cultural conditions which influence the child-rearing process. They have learned, for example, that in a primitive community where people accumulate their food through farming or animal husbandry, children experience the strongest pressure to be responsible and obedient. There, however, they are somewhat spared from the necessity to develop a strong achievement drive or to become strongly self-reliant. People who obtain food through hunting and collecting insist strongly on achievement and self-reliance, more so than on responsibility and obedience. These examples illustrate how the technological or maintenance system of a culture exerts an influence on child-rearing practices and thereby encourages what are likely to be useful personality traits in its members (Barry, Child, and Barry 1959). Other research supports the theory that child-training practices affect personality by shaping the image children form of parents and parental roles. Such images are in turn projected in the conception of deities (J. Whiting 1959).

Numerous criticisms of the method of cross-cultural testing continue to be heard, including finding fault with the statistical procedure and sampling methods used and disputing the reliability with which the testers scan ethnographic sources. (See, Norbeck, Walker, and Cohen 1962; Fischer 1965:211.) Currently, some anthropologists favor controlled methods of comparison in which quite a small number of thoroughly studied primitive societies are carefully selected because they possess theoretically significant features. Or else field research is directed to a few well-chosen communities. The analysis of data is used to discover how some dependent factors vary in association with one of more crucial independent variables. A simple illustration may suffice. In West Africa, Siegfried Nadel (1952) studied two neighboring communities inhabiting the same geographical landscape and possessing witchcraft beliefs. However, in one witches are predominantly female and in the other not. Using the common theory that witchcraft constitutes an outlet for frustration, Nadel was able to show that in the community where witches are predominantly female, men are commonly frustrated by their wives' trading activities, which seriously complicate marriage relationships. Such tensions, however, are not aroused in the neigboring community. Whiting himself has made great effort to obtain full and careful information about child training and associated conditions in order to pinpoint dynamics of personality formation in a number of carefully chosen communities. He sent out specially trained fieldworkers equipped with an explicit observation guide prepared to insure comparable attention to a number of significant variables (J. Whiting *et al.* 1966). The results brought back by the field teams have been published (B. Whiting 1963) and analysis of the data has begun (Minturn and Lambert 1964).

A second major theoretical viewpoint that has been used to account for personality formation derives, like Whiting's, from psychoanalysis but has received much less confirmation through testing. I will sketch it briefly. This viewpoint, which has been largely cultivated by Margaret Mead (1953, 1954, 1955) and persons associated with her, assumes that events of a cultural nature occurring to an infant as early as his first days of life mediate information passing between a child and his caretakers. Such informal and often inexplicit communication constitutes the process that implants culture anew in each growing organism, thereby patterning the specific kind of human nature that is desired by a particular society. The way an Arapesh child is held and passively fed, for example, constitutes the earliest lesson he receives in passivity, a lesson that will be reiterated many times in other contexts of his later life. An observer who uses this theory must pay close heed to the smallest details of child care. It is of little use to note simply that babies are nursed or swaddled. Precise context and form of nursing or swaddling, including cultural attitudes behind such practices, must be specifically known in order to decode the messages being transmitted through those channels. In place of doing as Whiting and Child do, proceeding from one culture to another and abstracting from behavior a few common elements (like the gratification or frustration of the child's oral zone), Margaret Mead urges attention to all the subtle characteristics of child rearing that are pregnant with meaning for children in particular social systems. The theory does not hold single modes of child training to constitute self-sufficient causes of characterological traits. It conceives of socialization as a circular or self-regenerative process that works through many learning situations, repeating the same message. The child, even a newborn one, through his behavior stimulates his socializers to act. As they respond to him in traditional fashion, he learns to modify his behavior in terms of messages he "reads" in their response. If they treat him as though he were helpless and ought to be passive, he (allowing for temperamental differences from one child to another) acts in a compatible manner, passively. By doing so, he reinforces their traditional perception of him and perpetuates certain culture patterns. Those culture patterns are already present when he is born; they have been there perhaps for centuries, and now they are communicated to him while at the same time he reinforces the pattern in his socializers.

Many difficult problems confront this theory. To what extent is a small child capable of perceiving attitudes that lie embedded in his caretakers' actions? How far does an infant's cognitive immaturity insulate it from parental attitudes? The viewpoint must also guard against the fallacy on which it verges; namely, conceiving adult-child communication as repeating itself from one generation to another, like the mechanisms of genetic inheritance. Parents do not merely repeat their own socialization or perpetuate the culture they once learned to embody. Even in an isolated primitive society life alters, and the changes brought about by culture change affect children, presenting them with new situations to which they normally adapt by mastering new forms of behavior.

VII

Studies made of socialization and personality in primitive societies trouble some people because the authors are often content to find and report only a single clear-cut pattern of personality in each society they visit. At a quick glance, it looks as if anthropologists were perpetuating the fallacy that the members of a society are all alike. This impression is misleading. Anyone who has spent months or years living closely with a group of people, no matter how strange their culture, sees that individuals differ. The apparent homogeneity implied by the ethnographic report is an unintentional consequence of the anthropologist's holistic method. He approaches primitive cultures as wholes and regards the people who give that culture its life, in whom it has its only being, as each embodying the whole to the extent that they individually participate in it. Such a point of view emphasizes that each person embodies his culture in a unique manner, but also maintains that by virtue of having been reared in a common culture each bears common aspects of the culture's stamp on his character. Anthropologists then devote themselves to abstracting those aspects, but tend to ignore individual differences or to relegate them to a minor place in the report. Yet, a problem remains. The ethnographer describes a type of person, a type he constructs out of his lengthy sojourn in a community. Exactly what kind of type is it? Is it a modal type? That is, does the configuration of personality he describes replicate itself in a majority, or even a plurality, of the community? Or is it an ideal type, to which absolutely no one conforms? With an ideal type, everybody may share certain of the typical characteristics, albeit in different degree. An ideal type sums up all those characteristics that came to the observer's attention and that he thinks it useful to include.

Anthony F. C. Wallace (1952) took pains to work up a truly modal type of personality for the Tuscarora Indians living in New York State. Using the Rorschach test to make his analysis, he found that exactly 37 percent of his sample of 70 adult men and women (20 percent of the adult population) fell within the modal range, and another 23 percent were so close around the modal range that they could be considered as represented by the modal type. That is, only 42 out of 70 of his subjects share the Tuscarora modal personality. They see life and its problems in terms of broad, loose generalities. They represent the typical Tuscarora Indian who thinks with stereotypes and reacts to stereotypes rather than to the concrete details of new situations. The typical Tuscarora is rigid, subsuming all stimuli into general categories. The external world threatens him, so he prefers to withdraw, responding by preference introversively to stimuli that arise from within. His difficulty in adapting his behavior smoothly to external circumstances arises from his relatively truncated emotional development. Sixty percent of Wallace's Tuscarora sample conform with this type. The remaining 40 percent fall within the modal range for some of the features on which this description of modal personality is based, but in others they depart further from the mode and so must be regarded as statistically deviant.

Few observers have duplicated Wallace's effort to find the modal personality of a primitive society (see, however, L. Spindler and G. Spindler 1961). Partly the failure to do so stems from the fact that few people have relied heavily on the Rorschach or other psychological tests which lend themselves to precise measurement and interindividual comparison. Also, many fieldworkers do not observe systematically from one person to another the way a psychological test demands. Some anthropologists, in fact, claim that if they were to isolate specific personality traits and rate individuals on specific attributes of behavior, they would cut out valuable potentialities in their own distinctive method of research. Furthermore, they point out, sampling and extensive interviewing will not work in some primitive communities. These fieldworkers prefer to describe a personality that is more like an ideal type than a modal type. It embraces those aspects of personality frequently encountered in a community which together are rarely or never found in any single representative of the culture. Even so-called deviants (who, anyhow, are deviant only with respect to certain items of behavior, not in everything) embody some of these personality features, having been affected by the culture in which they were reared.

Despite my interest in knowing more about the amount of interpersonal variability that occurs within a single society, I believe much still remains to be learned from perceptive, responsible fieldworkers of any discipline who, as Margaret Mead, A. I. Hallowell, or Erik Erikson have done, study primitive societies holistically and in their reports draw unimodal patterns of personality. Yet, I hope that anthropologists who prefer this approach will be dissatisfied enough with it to strive, by way of new standards of excellence, fresh devices of fieldwork, and better reporting, to improve their ability to recognize and describe the way a whole culture reflects itself in a people's typical value system, typical cognitive modes of thought, and typical feelings. Meanwhile, more social scientists of any persuasion might well pay attention to the diversity of personality in a society and the alternative formative institutions responsible for such diversity. They might note how such internal diversity is organized to make for an orderly social life (Wallace 1961). One approach does not rule out the other; in fact, each contributes a welcome brand of understanding.

VIII

In the 70 years that have elapsed since the Cambridge Expedition sailed for Torres Strait, we have acquired substantial psychological insight into only a trifle of the societies that anthropologists call primitive. I have made a list of people for whom I could find one or more comprehensive studies of

TABLE 16–1

Primitive Societies for Which Major Studies of Personality Are Available [1]

Ethnographic Region and Society	Sources [2]
AFRICA [3]	
Dogon	Parin, Morgenthaler, and Parin-Matthèy 1963.
Ghanese	Field 1960; Lystad, 1960a 1960b.
Gusii (Nyansongo)	LeVine and LeVine 1962, 1963; Minturn and Lambert 1964:Ch. 16.
Katanga	Leblanc 1958, 1960.
Ovimbundu	Childs, 1949.
Swazi	Sherwood, 1961.
Yoruba	A. Leighton, Lambo, et al. 1963.
Zulu	Lee 1958; Loudon 1959; Scotch 1961.
EAST EURASIA	
Lepcha	Gorer 1938.
Tanala	Kardiner 1939:Ch. 7–8.
NORTH AMERICA [4]	
Apache (Mescalero)	Boyer 1962, 1964.
Cherokee (Eastern)	Holzinger 1961.
Comanche	Kardiner 1945:Ch. 3–4.
Eskimo (Frobisher Bay)	Honigmann and Honigmann 1965.
Eskimo (Great Whale River)	Honigmann and Honigmann 1959; Ferguson 1962.
Eskimo (North Alaska)	Chance 1960, 1965, 1966; Chance and Foster 1962.
Eskimo (Nunivak)	Lantis 1953, 1959.
Hopi	Goldfrank 1945; Havighurst and Neugarten 1955; Simmons, 1942; Thompson 1950.
Iroquois (Tuscarora)	Wallace 1952.
Kaska	Honigmann 1949.
Klamath	Clifton and Levine 1961.
Kwakiutl	Benedict 1934:Ch. 6: Codere 1956.
Menomini	G. Spindler 1955; L. Spindler 1962.
Mixtecans (Juxtlahuaca)	Romney and Romney 1963; Minturn and Lambert 1964:Ch. 12.
Mohave	Devereux 1961 (see other references in this source).
Náhua (Tepotztlan)	Lewis 1951.
Navaho	Havighurst and Neugarten 1955; Kaplan 1954; Kluckhohn and Leighton 1949; D. Leighton and Kluckhohn 1947; A. Leighton and Leighton 1949; Vogt 1951.

Ethnographic Region and Society	Sources
Ojibwa (Chippewa)	Barnouw 1950; Hallowell 1955; Landes, 1937a, 1937b, 1938, 1961.
Papago	Havighurst and Neugarten 1955; Joseph, Spicer, and Chesky 1949.
Pokomám (San Luis Jilotepeque)	Billig, Gillin, and Davidson 1947–1948; Gillin 1951; Tumin 1952:Ch. 17.
Sioux	Erikson 1939, 1963:Ch. 3; Havighurst and Neugarten 1955; Macgregor 1946.
Slave (Lynx Point)	Helm, DeVos, and Carterette 1960.
Yurok	Erikson 1943, 1963:Ch. 4.
Zuni	Benedict 1934:Ch. 4; Goldfrank 1945; Havighurst and Neugarten 1955; Kaplan 1954; D. Leighton and Adair 1966.
INSULAR PACIFIC [5]	
Alorese	DuBois 1944; Kardiner, 1945:Ch. 4–9.
Arapesh	Mead 1935.
Australia (Central)	Róheim 1934.
Balinese	Bateson 1949; Bateson and Mead 1949.
Cook Islanders	Beaglehole 1957.
Dobuans	Benedict 1934:Ch. 3; Fortune 1932.
Iatmul	Bateson 1958.
Kwoma	Whiting 1941.
Manus	Mead 1930, 1932, 1956.
Maori	Beaglehole and Beaglehole 1946; Beaglehole and Ritchie 1958; Earle 1958; Mulligan 1957; James Ritchie 1957; Jane Ritchie 1957; Williams 1960.
Marquesans	Kardiner 1939:Ch. 5–6.
Pukapukans	Beaglehole and Beaglehole 1941.
Saipanese	Joseph and Murray 1951.
Samoans	Mead 1928.
Trukese	Gladwin and Sarason 1953.
Ulithians	Lessa and Spiegelman 1954.
SOUTH AMERICA	
Aymara	Tschopik 1951; Plummer 1966.
Caingang	Henry 1941.
Pilagá	Henry 1940; Henry and Henry 1940, 1944.
Sirionó	Holmberg 1950.

[1] Classification by regions follows Murdock 1957.
[2] Secondary sources are sometimes cited when they contribute in an important way to the analysis of data.
[3] For summaries see LeVine 1961; Doob, 1965.
[4] For summaries see Driver 1961:Ch. 24; Honigmann 1961.
[5] For summaries see Gladwin 1961; Burrows 1947.

personality in its cultural context (Table 16–1). Some of the references refer to very slim works indeed, but at least they constitute documentation of a distinctive mode of psychological being. The criteria by which I recognize "major" works on primitive personality vary from one region of the world to another, for where little information is to be had, even partial accounts assume magnified importance. A few of the writings dwell heavily on childhood and have relatively little to say about personality. However, I have eliminated some works of this type, like Margaret Read's (1959) work on Ngoni child rearing or Monica Wilson's (1951) account of how socialization is accomplished in Nyakyusa age-villages. Another kind of book, of which Ruth Benedict's classic *Patterns of Culture* (1934) constitutes an example, contributes little new data but probes extant cultural descriptions for insights of a psychological kind. I have included one or two such secondary sources when they are all we have for a people or when they constitute significant landmarks in research (as Benedict's book does for the Zuni and other Pueblo Indians). I have chosen to ignore many papers by psychoanalysts who, using primary sources on primitive cultures, scan them for expressions of personality processes in customs such as use of money, agriculture, or circumcision, and in folktales. Such work more often demonstrates versatility in exercising theory than it constitutes a serious essay into the dynamics and functioning of an exotic system of personality.

My survey reveals that the available literature (which is mostly in English) concentrates most heavily on two ethnographic regions: Oceania (insular Pacific) and North America. Even within each of those, gaps show up. A dearth of references, I would maintain, is not due wholly to the notoriously uncertain criteria for judging what is a primitive society or to the limits of my sampling, but indicates a culture area in which social scientists have plainly failed to carry out personality research. For example, only one major source reports on the Australian aborigines; we know little about personality in African societies, and extreme poverty faces us with regard to South and Central American Indians. In Asia, the whole of Siberia as well as the long mountainous rim of South and Southeast Asia are blank. Nobody can be sure about reasons for such sparse and uneven coverage but I will offer my ideas, looking mainly within the discipline of anthropology where we would expect to find the greatest effort concentrated. Undoubtedly, traditional frameworks for doing research grow up and are perpetuated from one generation to another in a region. For reasons not entirely clear, a psychological interest failed to wax strong among British-trained social anthropologists, who have dominated in the study of African societies and who strongly influenced the style of cultural anthropology in Australia. For Siberia, the situation can be ascribed in part to the violent repugnance that Soviet anthropologists feel for psychocultural research which, they maintain, commits the mistake of viewing behavior as exclusively determined by nonmaterial factors (Dunn 1965). A more general reason can be suggested to explain why anthropologists failed zealously to pursue personality research in all of the world's ethnographic regions. I refer to the quick decline of anthropological interest in culture-and-personality research after that subdiscipline attained its brief heyday, which prevented the field from recruiting new and additional fieldworkers. Although 70 years have passed since the Torres Strait expedition, intensive comparative research on personality in primitive societies is crowded into only a fraction of that time, having flourished between 1925 and 1950.

This leads to the question why, after only 25 years or so of effort, should the clock have run down. Partly, I suspect, because the comparative psychological approach encountered serious theoretical weaknesses that still prove difficult to surmount. For example, results of research in different communities quickly became repetitious and familiar due to the fact that researchers were mostly drawing heavily from the same theory, psychoanalysis, whose powerful concepts screen out too many distinctive features of exotic psychological life. Hortense Powdermaker (1966:54–55) tells in her recently published autobiography of meeting Géza Róheim, a psychoanalyst who made anthropology his avocation, while she was traveling to her first fieldwork station, and of noting with surprise that he seemed to know exactly what he would find among the Australian aborigines to whom he was going. As a result of the generality introduced by psychoanalytic theory, its use reveals rather few major differences in personality that match the strikingly large variations in culture plainly encountered from one society to another. Anthropologists, with a few exceptions, have always been unhappy with concepts that obscure another society's peculiar features. The science of man may aim toward universal generalizations, but such generalizations are supposed to come after giving full cognizance to psychological and other features that distinguish one system from another. Anthropologists value very highly obtaining what Malinowski called the native's own point of view—*his* vision of *his* life. Whether this ambitious goal is fully attainable or not, the psychological anthropologist's favorite theory has distinctly limited him in approaching his subjects in terms of their own, phenomenological structure of meanings and emotions. Psychoanalysis is far more apt to filter perception through an outwardly imposed matrix of deductively assigned meanings (*cf.* Preston 1963). Culture and personality simply could not marshal sufficient creativity to climb off the plateau where it found itself via a new, more suitable theory. The challenging barrage of criticism in the late 1940s and early 1950s, that charged culture and personality with undue subjectivity, impressionism, distortion, and other sins, further helped to break interest, with the result that research and the recruitment of new talent slowed down. The practitioners of culture and personality, with the exception of one or two (Mead 1954), showed little energy and ability to meet the challenge. They neither vigorously justified their approach nor refurbished some of their methods, both steps that might have reassured prospective followers (Honigmann 1961:126–128). Finally, within the discipline of anthropology the study of isolated primitive communities began to face competition from a growing engrossment with more complex societies, like those of India, peasant Europe, the Caribbean, and modern America. The major undertaking launched by John Whiting some years ago to explore relationships between child rearing and consequent differences in personality, chose only two or, at the most, three societies that can still be called primitive (B. Whiting 1963). With the trend toward studying culturally advanced people, fewer investigators have been available to visit societies whose primitive cultures are rapidly disappearing as they absorb more and more traits from the civilized world.

The primitive laboratories from which we have drawn lessons of what man is and can become are disappearing. Already in 1898, the Torres Strait expedition found people whom 30 years of missionary endeavor had left, to use its term, at least partly "civilized." How much deeper into the primitive world has Western influence driven since then, and especially during and after World War II! We can not claim that scholarship has mined primitive cultures so thoroughly that their disappearance is a matter of indifference. To record distinctive culture patterns that are still extant but rapidly vanishing, anthropologists are now preparing to launch an international crash program of salvage research, akin to the "salvage archeology" conducted in U.S. river basins about to be dammed and flooded. We have the means including 70 years of experience, to extend such a program of urgent research to personality. What we need in addition is a renewal of interest in comparative personality research sufficient to overcome competition furnished by other worthwhile problems and by research possibilities lying in more complex cultures located outside the primitive world.

BIBLIOGRAPHY

BARNOUW, VICTOR, *Acculturation and Personality Among the Wisconsin Chippewa.* The American Anthropological Association, Memoir 72, 1950.
BARRY, HERBERT, III, IRVIN L. CHILD, and MARGARET K. BACON, "Relation of Child Training to Subsistence Economy," *American Anthropologist,* Vol. 61, 1959, pp. 51–63.
BATESON, GREGORY, "Bali: the Value System of a Steady State," in Meyer Fortes (ed.), *Social Structure: Studies Presented to A. R. Radcliffe-Brown,* pp. 35–53. New York: Oxford University Press, 1949.
———, *Naven,* 2d ed. Stanford, Calif.: Stanford University Press, 1958.
———, and MARGARET MEAD, *Balinese Character: A Photographic Analysis.* Special Publications of the New York Academy of Sciences, Vol. II, 1942.
BEAGLEHOLE, ERNEST, *Social Change in the South Pacific: Rarotonga and Aitutaki.* New York: The Macmillan Company, 1957.
———, and PEARL BEAGLEHOLE, "Personality Development in Pukapukan

Children," in Leslie Spier, A. Irving Hallowell, and Stanley S. Newman (eds.). *Language, Culture, and Personality*, pp. 282–298. Menasha, Wis.: Sapir Memorial Publication Fund, 1941.
BEAGLEHOLE, ERNEST, and PEARL BEAGLEHOLE, *Some Modern Maoris*. Wellington: New Zealand Council for Educational Research, 1946.
———, and JAMES E. RITCHIE, "The Rakau Maori Studies," *Journal of the Polynesian Society*, Vol. 67, 1958, pp. 132–154.
BENEDICT, RUTH, *Patterns of Culture*. Boston: Houghton Mifflin Company, 1934.
BENNETT, JOHN W., "The Interpretation of Pueblo Culture: A Question of Values," *Southwestern Journal of Anthropology*, Vol. 2, 1946, pp. 361–374.
BILLIG, OTTO, JOHN GILLIN, and WILLIAM DAVIDSON, "Aspects of Personality and Culture in a Guatemalan Community," *Journal of Personality*, Vol. 16, 1947–48, pp. 153–187, 326–368.
BOAS, FRANZ, *The Mind of Primitive Man*, rev. ed. New York: The Macmillan Company, 1938.
BOYER, L. BRYCE, "Folk Psychiatry of the Apaches of the Mas Mescalero Indian Reservation," in Ari Kiev (ed.), *Magic, Faith, and Healing*, pp. 384–419. New York: The Free Press, 1964.
———, "Remarks on the Personality of Shamans. With Special Reference to the Apache of the Mescalero Indian Reservation," *Psychoanalytic Study of Society*, Vol. 2, 1962, pp. 233–254.
BURROWS, EDWIN G., "Functional and Psychological Studies in Polynesia," in Katharine Luomala, et al., *Specialized Studies in Polynesian Anthropology*, pp. 75–85. Bernice P. Bishop Museum, Bulletin 193, 1947.
Cambridge Anthropological Expedition to Torres Straits Reports. Vol. 2, *Physiology and Psychology*. New York: Cambridge University Press, 1901.
CHANCE, NORMAN A., "Acculturation, Self-Identification, and Personality Adjustment," *American Anthropologist*, Vol. 67, 1965, pp. 372–393.
———, "Culture Change and Integration: An Eskimo Example," *American Anthropologist*, Vol. 62, 1960, pp. 1028–1044.
———, *The Eskimo of North Alaska*. New York: Holt, Rinehart and Winston, Inc., 1966.
———, and DOROTHY A. FOSTER, "Symptom Formation and Patterns of Psychopathology in a Rapidly Changing Alaskan Eskimo Society," *Anthropological Papers of the University of Alaska*, Vol. 11, 1962, pp. 32–42.
CHILDS, GLADWYN, *Umbundu Kinship and Character*. New York: Oxford University Press, 1949.
CLIFTON, JAMES A., and DAVID LEVINE, *Klamath Personalities: Ten Rorschach Case Studies*. Eugene, Ore.: Department of Anthropology, University of Oregon, 1961.
CODERE, HELEN, "The Amiable Side of Kwakiutl Life: The Potlatch and the Play Potlatch," *American Anthropologist*, Vol. 58, 1956, pp. 334–351.
D'ANDRADE, ROY G., "Anthropological Studies of Dreams," in Francis L. K. Hsu (ed.), *Psychological Anthropology*. Homewood, Ill.: The Dorsey Press, 1961.
DEVEREUX, GEORGE, "Mohave Culture and Personality," *Character and Personality*, Vol. 8, 1939, pp. 91–109.
———, *Mohave Ethnopsychiatry and Suicide: The Psychiatric Knowledge and the Psychic Disturbances of an Indian Tribe*. Bureau of American Ethnology, Bulletin 175, 1961.
DIAMOND, STANLEY, "The Search for the Primitive," in I. Galdston (ed.), *Man's Image in Medicine and Anthropology*, pp. 62–115. New York: International Universities Press, Inc., 1963.

DOOB, LEONARD W., "Psychology," in Robert A. Lystad (ed.), *The African World*, pp. 373–415. London: Pall Mall Press, 1965.
DRIVER, HAROLD EDSON, *Indians of North America*. Chicago: University of Chicago Press, 1961.
DuBOIS, CORA, *The People of Alor*. Minneapolis: The University of Minnesota Press, 1944.
DUNN, STEPHEN P., "Some Preliminary Questions in International Anthropology," *Sovetskaia Etnografiia*, No. 6, 1965, pp. 76–91.
EARLE, MARGARET J., *Rakau Children: from Six to Thirteen Years*. Victoria University of Wellington Publications in Psychology, No. 11, 1958.
ERIKSON, ERIK H., *Childhood and Society*, 2d ed. New York: W. W. Norton & Co., Inc., 1963.
———, "Observations on the Sioux Education," *Journal of Psychology*, Vol. 7, 1939, pp. 101–156.
———, *Observations on the Yurok: Childhood and World Image*. University of California Publications in American Archaeology and Ethnology, Vol. 35, 1943.
FERGUSON, FRANCES N., "Great Whale River Eskimo Personality as Revealed by Rorschach Protocols," in John J. Honigmann (ed.), *Social Networks in Great Whale River*, pp. 80–99. National Museum of Canada Bulletin, No. 178, 1962.
FIELD, M. J., *Search for Security: an Ethno-psychiatric Study of Rural Ghana*. Evanston, Ill.: Northwestern University Press, 1960.
FISCHER, JOHN L., "The Sociopsychological Analysis of Folktales," *Current Anthropology*, Vol. 4, 1963, pp. 235–295.
———, "Psychology and Anthropology," in Bernard J. Siegel (ed.), *Biennial Review of Anthropology*, pp. 211–261. Stanford, Calif.: Stanford University Press, 1965.
FORTUNE, REO F., *Sorcerers of Dobu*. New York: E. P. Dutton & Co., Inc. 1932.
GILLIN, JOHN, *The Culture of Security in San Carlos*. Middle American Research Institute, The Tulane University of Louisiana, Publication No. 16, 1951.
GLADWIN, THOMAS, "Oceania," in Francis L. K. HSU (ed.), *Psychological Anthropology*, pp. 135–171. Homewood, Ill.: The Dorsey Press, 1961.
———, and SEYMOUR B. SARASON, *Truk: Man in Paradise*. Viking Fund Publications in Anthropology, No. 20, 1953.
GOLDFRANK, ESTHER S., "Socialization, Personality, and the Structure of the Pueblo Society," *American Anthropologist*, Vol. 47, 1945, pp. 516–539.
GORER, GEOFFREY, *Himalayan Village*. London: Michael Joseph Ltd., 1938.
HALLOWELL, A. IRVING, *Culture and Experience*. Philadelphia: University of Pennsylvania Press, 1955.
HAVIGHURST, ROBERT J., and BERNICE L. NEUGARTEN, *American Indian and White Children*. Chicago: University of Chicago Press, 1955.
HELM, JUNE, G. A. DE VOS, and TERESA CARTERETTE, *Variations in Personality and Ego Identification Within a Slave Indian Kin-Community*. Contributions to Anthropology, pt. 2, National Museum of Canada Bulletin, No. 190, 1960.
HENRY, JULES, *Jungle People, a Kaingáng Tribe of the Highlands of Brazil*. Locust Valley, N.Y.: J. J. Augustin, Inc., 1941.
———, "Some Cultural Determinants of Hostility in Pilagá Children," *American Journal of Orthopsychiatry*, Vol. 10, 1940, pp. 111–119.
———, and Z. HENRY, *Doll Play of Pilagá Indian Children*. American Orthopsychiatric Association, Research Monographs, No. 4, 1944.
———, and Z. HENRY, "Speech Disturbances in Pilagá Indian Children," *American Journal of Orthopsychiatry*, Vol. 10, 1940, pp. 362–369.
HOLMBERG, ALLAN R., *Nomads of the Long Bow*. Smithsonian Institution, Institute of Social Anthropology, Publication No. 10, 1950.

HOLZINGER, CHARLES H., "Some Observations on the Persistence of Aboriginal Cherokee Personality Traits," in William N. Fenton and John Gulick (eds.), *Symposium on Cherokee and Iroquois Culture*. Bureau of American Ethnology, Bulletin 180, 1961.
HONIGMANN, JOHN J., *Culture and Ethos of Kaska Society*. Yale University Publications in Anthropology, No. 40, 1949.
———, "North America," in Francis L. K. Hsu (ed.), *Psychological Anthropology*, pp. 93–134. Homewood, Ill.: The Dorsey Press, 1961.
———, *Personality in Culture*. New York: Harper & Row, Publishers, 1967.
———, and IRMA HONIGMANN, *Eskimo Townsmen*. Ottawa: Canadian Research Centre for Anthropology, University of Ottawa, 1965.
———, and IRMA HONIGMANN, "Notes on Great Whale River Ethos," *Anthropologica*, n.s. Vol. 1, 1959, pp. 106–121.
JOSEPH, ALICE, and VERONICA F. MURRAY, *Chamorros and Carolinians of Saipan, Personality Studies*. Cambridge, Mass.: Harvard University Press, 1951.
———, ROSAMOND B. SPICER, and JANE CHESKY, *The Desert People*. Chicago: University of Chicago Press, 1949.
KAPLAN, BERT, *A Study of Rorschach Responses in Four Cultures*. Papers of the Peabody Museum of American Archaeology and Ethnology, Harvard University, Vol. 42, 1954.
KARDINER, ABRAM, *The Individual and His Society*. New York: Columbia University Press, 1939.
———, *The Psychological Frontiers of Society*. New York: Columbia University Press, 1945.
KLUCKHOHN, CLYDE, "The Influence of Psychiatry on Anthropology in America During the Past One Hundred Years," in J. K. Hall, G. Zilboorg, and H. A. Bunker (eds.), *One Hundred Years of American Psychiatry, 1844–1944*, pp. 589–617. New York: Columbia University Press, 1944.
———, and DOROTHEA LEIGHTON, *The Navaho*. Cambridge, Mass.: Harvard University Press, 1946.
LANDES, RUTH, "The Abnormal Among the Ojibwa Indians," *Journal of Abnormal and Social Psychology*, Vol. 33, 1938, pp. 14–33.
———, "The Ojibwa of Canada," in Margaret Mead (ed.), *Cooperation and Competition Among Primitive Peoples*, rev. paperback ed., pp. 87–126. Boston: The Beacon Press, 1961.
———, *The Ojibwa Woman*. Columbia University Publications in Anthropology, No. 31, 1938.
———, "The Personality of the Ojibwa," *Character and Personality*, Vol. 6, 1937, pp. 51–60.
LANTIS, MARGARET, "Alaskan Eskimo Cultural Values," *Polar Notes*, Vol. 1, 1959, pp. 35–48.
———, "Nunivak Eskimo Personality as Revealed in the Mythology," Anthropological Papers of the University of Alaska, Vol. 2, 1953, pp. 109–174.
LEBLANC, MARIA, "Acculturation of Attitude and Personality Among Katangese Women," *Journal of Social Psychology*, Vol. 47, 1958, pp. 257–264.
———, *Personnalité de la femme Katangaise*. Louvain: Publications Universitaires, 1960.
LEE, S. G., "Social Influences in Zulu Dreaming," *Journal of Social Psychology*, Vol. 47, 1958, pp. 265–283.
LEIGHTON, ALEXANDER, H. T. ADEOYE LAMBO, CHARLES C. HUGHES, DOROTHEA C. LEIGHTON, JANE M. MURPHY, and DAVID B. MACKLIN, *Psychiatric Disorder Among the Yoruba*. Ithaca, N.Y.: Cornell University Press, 1963.
———, and DOROTHEA C. LEIGHTON, *Gregorio, the Hand-Trembler*. Papers

of the Peabody Museum of American Archaeology and Ethnology, Harvard University, Vol. 40, 1949.
LEIGHTON, DOROTHEA C., and JOHN ADAIR, *People of the Middle Place.* New Haven, Conn.: Human Relations Area Files, 1966.
———, and CLYDE KLUCKHOHN, *Children of the People.* Cambridge, Mass.: Harvard University Press, 1947.
LESSA, WILLIAM A., and MARVIN SPIEGELMAN, *Ulithian Personality as Seen Through Ethnological Materials and Thematic Test Analysis.* University of California Publications in Culture and Society, Vol. 2, 1954.
LE VINE, ROBERT A., "Africa," in Francis L. K. Hsu (ed.), *Psychological Anthropology,* pp. 48–92. Homewood, Ill.: The Dorsey Press, 1961.
———, and BARBARA B. LE VINE, "Nyansongo: A Gusii Community in Kenya," in Beatrice B. Whiting (ed.), *Six Cultures,* pp. 15–202. New York: John Wiley & Sons, Inc., 1963.
———, "Studying Child Rearing and Personality Development in an East African Community," in *Anthropology and Africa Today,* Annals of the New York Academy of Sciences, Vol. 96, Art. 2, 1962, pp. 620–628.
LÉVY-BRUHL, LUCIEN, *Les Carnets du Lucien Lévy-Bruhl.* Paris: Presses Universitaire de France, 1949.
———, *How Natives Think.* Translated by Lilian A. Clare. London: George Allen & Unwin Ltd., 1926.
LEWIS, OSCAR, *Life in a Mexican Village.* Urbana: University of Illinois, 1951.
LOUDON, J. B., "Psychogenic Disorder and Social Conflict Among the Zulu," in M. K. Opler (ed.), *Culture and Mental Health,* pp. 351–369. New York: The Macmillan Company, 1959.
LYSTAD, MARY HANEMANN, "Paintings of Ghanaian Children." *Africa,* Vol. 30, 1960 (a), pp. 221–237.
———, "Traditional Values of Ghanaian Children," *American Anthropologist,* Vol. 62, 1960 (b), pp. 454–464.
MACGREGOR, GORDON, *Warriors Without Weapons.* Chicago: University of Chicago Press, 1946.
MALINOWSKI, BRONISLAW, *Sex and Repression in Savage Society.* New York: Harcourt, Brace & World, Inc., 1927.
MEAD, MARGARET, "The Arapesh of New Guinea," in Margaret Mead (ed.), *Cooperation and Competition Among Primitive Peoples,* Revised paperback edition, pp. 20–50. Boston: The Beacon Press, 1961.
———, *Coming of Age in Samoa.* New York: William Morrow & Company, Inc., 1928.
———, *Growing Up in New Guinea.* New York: William Morrow & Company, Inc., 1930.
———, "An Investigation of the Thought of Primitive Children with Special Reference to Animism," *Journal of the Royal Anthropological Institute,* Vol. 62, 1932, pp. 173–190.
———, "National Character," in A. L. Kroeber (ed.), *Anthropology Today,* pp. 642–667. Chicago: University of Chicago Press, 1953.
———, *New Lives for Old.* New York: William Morrow & Co., Inc., 1956.
———, *Sex and Temperament in Three Primitive Societies.* New York: William Morrow & Co., Inc., 1935.
———, "Some Relationships Between Social Anthropology and Psychiatry," in Franz Alexander and Helen Ross (eds.), *Dynamic Psychiatry.* Chicago: University of Chicago Press, 1952.
———, "The Swaddling Hypothesis: Its Reception," *American Anthropologist,* Vol. 56, 1954, 395–409.

MEAD, MARGARET, "Theoretical Setting—1954," in Margaret Mead and Martha Wolfenstein (eds.), *Childhood in Contemporary Cultures,* pp. 3–20. Chicago: University of Chicago Press, 1955.
MINTURN, LEIGH, and WILLIAM W. LAMBERT, *Mothers of Six Cultures.* New York: John Wiley & Sons, Inc., 1964.
MULLIGAN, D. G., *Maori Adolescence in Rakau.* Victoria University College Publications in Psychology, No. 9, 1957.
MURDOCK, GEORGE P., "World Ethnographic Sample," *American Anthropologist.* Vol. 59, 1957, pp. 664–687.
MURPHY, JANE M., "Social Science Concepts and Cross-cultural Methods for Psychiatric Research," in Jane M. Murphy and Alexander H. Leighton (eds.), *Approaches to Cross-Cultural Psychiatry,* pp. 251–284. Ithaca, N.Y.: Cornell University Press, 1965.
NADEL, S. F., "Witchcraft in Four African Societies: An Essay in Comparison," *American Anthropologist,* Vol. 54, 1952, pp. 18–19.
NORBECK, EDWARD, DONALD E. WALKER, and MIMI COHEN, "The Interpretation of Data: Puberty Rites," *American Anthropologist,* Vol. 64, 1962, pp. 463–485.
PARIN, PAUL, FRITZ MORGENTHALER, and GOLDY PARIN-MATTHÈY, *Die weissen denken zuveil.* Zurich: Atlantis Verlag, 1963.
PLUMMER, JOHN S., "Another Look at Aymara Personality," *Behavior Science Notes,* Vol. 1, 1966, pp. 55–78.
POWDERMAKER, HORTENSE, *Stranger and Friend.* New York: W. W. Norton & Company, Inc., 1966.
PRESTON, RICHARD J., III, *Inherent and Imposed Structures and Writings of Edward Sapir.* M.A. thesis, Wilson Library, University of North Carolina at Chapel Hill, 1963.
RADIN, PAUL, "Ojibwa and Ottawa Puberty Dreams," in *Essays in Anthropology Presented to A. L. Kroeber.* Berkeley, Calif.: University of California Press, 1936.
READ, MARGARET, *Children of Their Fathers.* London: Methuen & Co., Ltd., 1959.
RITCHIE, JAMES E., *Basic Personality in Rakau.* Victoria University College Publications in Psychology, No. 8, 1957.
RITCHIE, JANE, *Childhood in Rakau: the First Five Years of Life.* Victoria University College Publications in Psychology, No. 10, 1957.
———, *Maori Families.* Victoria University of Wellington Publications in Psychology, No. 18, 1964.
RÓHEIM, GÉZA, *The Riddle of the Sphinx.* London: Hogarth Press, Ltd., 1934.
ROMNEY, KIMBALL, and ROMAINE ROMNEY, "The Mixtecans of Juxtlahuaca, Mexico," in Beatrice B. Whiting (ed.), *Six Cultures,* pp. 541–691. New York: John Wiley & Sons, Inc., 1963.
SCOTCH, NORMAN A., "A Preliminary Report on the Relation of Sociocultural Factors to Hypertension Among the Zulu." *Annals of the New York Academy of Sciences,* Vol. 80, 1960, pp. 1000–1009.
SHERWOOD, EDWARD T., "Swazi Personality and the Assimilation of Western Culture." Ph.D. dissertation, University of Chicago, 1961.
SIMMONS, LEO (ed.), *Sun Chief.* New Haven, Conn.: Yale University Press.
SPINDLER, GEORGE D., *Sociocultural and Psychological Processes in Menomini Acculturation.* University of California Publications in Culture and Society, Vol. 5, 1955.
SPINDLER, LOUISE S., *Menomini Women and Culture Change.* The American Anthropological Association, Memoir 91, 1962.
———, and GEORGE SPINDLER, "A Modal Personality Technique in the Study

of Menomini Acculturation," in Bert Kaplan (ed.), *Studying Personality Cross-Culturally*, pp. 479–491. New York: Harper & Row, Publishers, 1961.

THOMPSON, LAURA, *Culture in Crisis*. New York: Harper & Row, Publishers.

———, *Personality and Government*. Mexico, D.F.: Ediciones del Instituto Indigenista Interamericano, 1951.

TSCHOPIK, HARRY, JR., *The Aymara of Chucuito, Peru*. Anthropological Papers of the American Museum of Natural History, Vol. 44, Pt. 2, 1951.

TUMIN, MELVIN M., *Caste in a Peasant Society*. Princeton, N.J.: Princeton University Press, 1952.

UNWIN, JOSEPH D., *Sex and Culture*. New York: Oxford University Press, 1934.

VOGT, E. Z., *Navaho Veterans: A Study of Changing Values*. Papers of the Peabody Museum of American Archaeology and Ethnology, Vol. 41, No. 1, 1951.

WALLACE, ANTHONY F. C., *Culture and Personality*. New York: Random House, Inc., 1961.

———, *The Modal Personality Structure of the Tuscarora Indians*. Bureau of American Ethnology, Bulletin 150, 1952.

WHITING, BEATRICE (ed.). *Six Cultures*. New York: John Wiley & Sons, Inc., 1963.

WHITING, JOHN W. M., *Becoming a Kwoma*. New Haven, Conn.: Yale University Press, 1941.

———, "The Cross-Cultural Method," in Gardner Lindzey (ed.), *Handbook of Social Psychology*, 2 vols., pp. 523–531. Reading, Mass.: Addison-Wesley Publishing Co., Inc., 1954.

———, "Sorcery, Sin and the Superego: A Cross-Cultural Study of Some Mechanisms of Social Control," in *Symposium on Motivation*, pp. 174–195. Lincoln, Neb.: University of Nebraska Press, 1959.

———, and IRVIN L. CHILD, *Child Training and Personality*. New Haven, Conn.: Yale University Press, 1953.

———, et al., *Field Guide for a Study of Socialization*. New York: John Wiley & Sons, Inc., 1966.

WILLIAMS, JOHN SMITH, *Maori Achievement Motivation*. Victoria University of Wellington Publications in Psychology, No. 13, 1960.

WILSON, MONICA, *Good Company*. New York: Oxford University Press, 1951.

PART THREE

Personality under Stress and Change

17

Cultural Factors in Mental Illness

E. D. Wittkower and
G. Dubreuil

This symposium is devoted to the study of personality. Its subtitle is: an interdisciplinary appraisal. Most of the speakers have concerned themselves, and will concern themselves, exclusively or predominantly, with *normal* personality in relation to sociocultural environment. All speakers are, by discipline, psychologists or social scientists. Why then, it might be asked, should a psychiatrist be added to the list of speakers, and how does *abnormal* behavior fit in with the remainder of the program? In answering these questions it may be argued that much that applies to normal psychology, although in an exaggerated and distorted form, applies equally to abnormal psychology and that, indeed, as Freud has shown, much can be learned about man in interaction with his environment from persons who are mentally ill.

The task assigned to us is to deal with cultural factors in mental illness. These factors are relevant to the etiology of mental disease, to the clinical manifestations displayed, to the care and after-care of the mentally ill, and to community attitudes adopted toward them. Any of these phenomena may be studied in one given cultural unit or the vista of the observer may extend to other cultures. The latter approach, as it goes beyond one culture, has been named transcultural. (The term "cross-cultural," as we use it, has a methodological connotation. It refers to a comparison of psychiatric observations between at least two cultures.)

It is obviously impossible to cover all these areas within the time at my disposal. Consequently, we shall confine ourselves to dealing with causative (etiological) and symptom moulding (pathoplastic) considerations. Some preliminary remarks stating our conceptual orientation seem to be in order.

What is *culture?* For the purpose of this presentation, culture may be defined as the whole fabric of ways of living that distinguishes one human society from another. Culture is a blueprint of living that presents individuals of a society with modes of behavior, thought, and sentiment. Culture is essentially the product of history; it is transmitted relatively unchanged from generation to generation, and is, in this sense, a superorganic phenomenon. This means that culture can be analyzed without reference to individual biological and psychological idiosyncrasies. This also means that individuals who are born into a culture and who learn to share and afterwards to transmit its models of behavior are considerably determined in their personality by this culture, though these individuals also play a part in some social and cultural changes that occur during their lifetime.

How can the relationship between *culture* and *personality* be conceptualized? The relationship basically derives from the transmission from parents to children of attitudes toward life and of modes of perception. Parental values, attitudes, and controls that reflect cultural tradition are by precept, example, and practices of child training implanted in, and incorporated and absorbed by, the ego of the child, and form the driving force behind his conceptions of right and wrong—his superego. Both ego strength and superego severity are subject to variations. The question has been raised and debated whether there are societies whose members are predominantly guided by external authority (shame cultures) and others whose members have incorporated external authority in terms of morality, sense of duty, and control of aggressiveness (guilt cultures) (Piers and Singer 1953); just as there seem to be differences in cultures regarding living for the day—the mañana principle—versus emphasis on long-term perspectives.

Closely related to cultural differences in prevailing ego and superego structure are differences in ego defense mechanisms. It has been found that members of primitive societies are more apt to deny their objectionable impulses or to project them on to witches and sorcerers and to slip back—to regress—under stress to infantile modes of behavior than members of technologically advanced societies who unconsciously prefer such ego defense mechanisms as suppression, repression, reaction formation, and sublimation. However, collective projection of objectionable impulses also occurs in complex societies, such as the scapegoat hatred of the Jews in Nazi Germany and of the Negroes in some segments of the United States population.

What is *mental illness?* Perhaps the most acceptable definition is a subjective and/or objective disturbance in perception, thought, feeling, and behavior, sufficient to interfere with enjoyment of life, social interaction, and successful performance in various essential spheres. This definition denotes the *subjective* element in mental illness, that is, that an individual is as sick as he feels, for example, in hypochondriasis and anxiety states; the *objective* element, as in grandiose ideas of somebody believing that he is Jesus Christ; and the *degree of impairment*—for instance, fear of heights or the screaming of Beatle fans. All these are unusual, undesirable, and abnormal but are not severe enough to constitute mental illness.

Though mental illness exists everywhere, mental abnormality is not a supracultural phenomenon. Its recognition is a matter of cultural relativism. For instance, to believe that misfortune, illness, and death are caused by witches or sorcerers and even to kill the supposed evil-doers were normal centuries ago in Europe and are still regarded as normal in many primitive societies, just as going about nude, homosexuality, and transvestism, which we would regard as sexual perversions, are accepted modes of behavior in numerous non-Western societies.

Yet the cleavage between psychiatrists and native healers in the assessment of insanity is not as large as may be believed. According to native healers and the native population at large, a person is considered insane if his perceptions and beliefs go beyond those which are culturally shared, if they give rise to psychological suffering and inability to function effectively, and if the behavior displayed has a disturbing effect on others. Hence the native healers and the native population are usually quite capable of making a distinction between acceptable beliefs in magic and witchcraft and what we would call paranoid ideas.

What then is the relationship between *culture* and *mental illness?* As stated before, answers to this question will be given in the main body of our presentation.

A. ETIOLOGICAL CONSIDERATIONS

I. *Total Frequency*

It has been alleged, in rejection of the blessings of modern civilization, that primitive societies retain the last treasures of pristine bliss and that consequently these paradisiac cultures are free from mental illness. These assumptions are erroneous. No culture studied by psychologically minded anthropologists with or without the cooperation of psychiatrists has failed to reveal some sources of stress. But there is evidence, supported by Lin's study in Taiwan (Lin 1953) and Leighton's and Lambo's comparisons (Leighton *et al.* 1963) of Nova Scotia and Nigeria, that cross-cultural and cross-subcultural differences in the frequency of mental disorders exist. These differences can be accounted for only in cultural terms.

All cultures impose taboos, such as sexual taboos, which are intrinsically frustrating, and goals which compel individuals to delay some gratification. These constraints may be universal or confined to selective groups of the population. The negative effect of tensions arising from these constraints is somewhat lessened by psychological compensations for culturally standardized behavior, by training to tolerate them, by cultural mechanisms which serve as outlets, and by culturally institutionalized social niches for deviants and marginal individuals. A few examples may be given. Most people in the United States have learned to endure emotional tension arising from competition and from a much greater degree of social isolation than exists in most other cultures. Conversely, among the Pueblo Indians most individuals have acquired the capacity to tolerate tensions arising from constant immersion into enlarged family groups and from rigid conformity with values of social cohesiveness. In other societies, institutionalized trances, bull fights, and drinking provide socially sanctioned outlets for cultural tensions while priesthood or shamanism may serve as a refuge for individuals who find in their status many gratifications and even power over their fellow countrymen.

Such cultural mechanisms mitigate but do not eliminate factors of stress, which vary in intensity from culture to culture. Only some of these stress factors can be dealt with. They fall into three broad categories: cultural content, social organization, and sociocultural change. Cultural content refers to all beliefs, values, norms, attitudes, and customs in a people's culture. Social organization is the network of regular and relatively longstanding interactions between individuals and groups of individuals within a society. Sociocultural change means any modification undergone in the cultural content and in the social organization.

CULTURAL CONTENT Basically, the relationship between cultural content and mental disease lies in the degree of psychological tension and anxiety created between individuals and within individuals by certain cultural elements, which we shall discuss under six headings.

1. *Taboos.* Prominent among these elements is what may be called "cultural deprivation of basic gratifications." Such cultural deprivation exists when the number, type, and intensity of rules and taboos imposed by culture upon a population or upon certain social groups become so excessive that they frustrate the satisfaction of essential human needs. Such taboos may relate to food, aggression, sex, personal initiative, and political or religious authority. For instance, when a culture prescribes an excessive load of taboos upon women without proper compensations of prestige, as among some North African societies, it has been shown (Lewin 1958) that mental disorders in women are common. However, the pathogenic effect of taboos should not be overrated. They lead to mental disease not by themselves but rather in interrelation with other cultural elements, such as values.

2. *Value saturation.* No two individuals adopt the values of their society in an identical manner. While most individuals are reasonably guided in their thoughts, attitudes, and behavior by cultural values, some individuals are unable to accept the values and others become so imbued by them as to be almost intoxicated. This phenomenon may be called "value saturation." A typical example is the American who, though lacking in intellectual, emotional, and material capacity to become a good competitor in business, relentlessly devotes his whole life to the pursuit of values of high competence in business and to strenuous competition. In this case, psychological tension may assume such proportions that mental disease may ensue. It is probable that some cultures and subcultures tend to produce more satura-

tion than others. For example, Germany seems to have reached a very high degree of value saturation before and during the last war. It resulted in the collective murder of millions of Jews.

3. *Value polymorphism.* A third factor of cultural content that relates to frequency of mental disorder will be called *value polymorphism*. This refers to the coexistence, within the same cultural system or within the same individual, of antagonistic values.

There are three major aspects of value polymorphism: (a) It may encompass a culture as a whole. This occurs generally in complex societies where an individual may be confronted with different ideologies, moral norms, and religious dogmas. (b) It may relate to cultural discontinuity (Benedict 1949) and to role replacement (Wallace 1963). The passage from the status of son to the status of father entails a discontinuity in terms of values and roles, for example, from dependence upon others to the obligation to provide for others. This is a universal phenomenon. However, when a culture does not provide proper and clear strategies such as *rites de passage* for these changes in the individual's life cycle, or when the transitions and the roles themselves are ambiguously defined, the individuals may find themselves confronted with contradictory values, unable to choose those which could introduce them to their future statuses. The passage from adolescence to adulthood in Occidental cultures is a good example. (c) The third aspect of value polymorphism is the excessive exposure of individuals to simultaneous statuses. All human beings have simultaneous statuses: most adult females must be good daughters, good mothers, good wives, good daughters-in-law, and so on. Generally such status pluralism does not create excessive tensions. However, it can happen, especially in societies where value saturation exists, that some of these statuses become incompatible. For instance, the status of business executive burdens some individuals with so much responsibility that performance of their duties interferes with gratifications derived from other statuses such as fathers, husbands, and friends. Some cultures have taken care of value polymorphism by proper strategies which reduce anxiety. For instance, the Masai of Africa forbid marriage of young male adults engaged in military training and activities, but they allow them to have sexual relations with young unmarried females.

4. *Role deprivation.* The opposite of value polymorphism is role deprivation, a term which refers to withdrawal of culturally and psychologically significant statuses and roles from some categories of individuals in different cultures and in different situations. The most extreme case of role deprivation is the ritual killing or expulsion of individuals guilty of violating some taboo, as may happen in many primitive societies to those who commit incest. Other examples of role deprivation are the enforced retirement of the aged in Occidental societies, relegation of the aged to positions of uselessness in some primitive societies, such as the Eskimos and some

Australian tribes, and the discrimination suffered by some minority groups.

5. *Sentiments.* A fifth factor linked with mental disease is the system of sentiments which prevails in a particular society. Some cultures have been described, often with oversimplification, as impregnated by sentiments of jealousy, megalomania, fear of spirits and of people. For instance, in some African countries, such as Ghana, fear of black magic and of evil spirits is so universal and so pronounced that everybody is suspicious of everybody (Field 1960). There is good reason to believe that the more intense such sentiments are in a society, the more widespread will be mental disease.

6. *Basic personality structure.* The personality structure shared by most individuals of a society or subsociety may predispose them to mental illness in general and to some disorders in particular. For instance, in many Senegalese cultures children are trained in such a manner that their ego remains weak when they reach adulthood. This explains why Senegalese and members of other primitive African societies easily "go to pieces" if subjected to relatively minor stress. It has been shown in classical studies (DuBois 1944; Mead and MacGregor 1951) that the fragile personality of the Alorese can be attributed to the inconsistent child training by their mothers, and the schizoid characteristics of the Balinese to the withdrawal of affection from them in their childhood.

SOCIAL ORGANIZATION Two aspects of social organization relating to mental illness deserve special attention: anomie and rigidity.

1. *Anomie* refers to the lack of integration of social organization and is sometimes used synonymously with social disorganization. A relationship between anomie and increased frequency of mental disorders has been established. For instance, it has been demonstrated that unemployment and poverty in the slums of big North American cities and migration from rural to urban areas in Africa and South America are associated with high rates of mental illness. However, the correlation between anomie and mental disease is not simple. A variety of factors combine in bringing about anomie and associated mental disorders (Faris 1944). Movement of mentally ill persons into slum areas is one of these factors. Nonetheless, there is plenty of evidence that low standards of education, poverty, ethnic diversity, and especially migration tend to create tensions because they uproot the individual from his accustomed environment, deprive him of significant statuses and gratifying roles ("role deprivation"), and produce value polymorphism.

2. The extreme opposite of social disorganization is *social rigidity*. This term means that the overall social structure of parts of a society has become so inflexible that individuals must conform to prescribed social norms with little or no personal choice. Typically, in some small communities dominated by traditional values and by a social structure which imposes on individuals highly specific statuses and roles, individuals unable to knuckle

down to passive conformism feel so constrained that intense emotional tension ensues. They become marginal, delinquent, or psychologically disturbed. Some of them migrate to urban centers in the hope of finding proper niches. More often than not they experience various types of tension.

Social groups also become vulnerable to mental disease when they are reduced to positions of inferiority. Such seems to be the case for minority groups which have been "colonialized" by a more powerful majority group. It has been suggested that colonialized groups suffer from a complex of depersonalization; that is, many persons perceive themselves in accordance with the stereotypes which the dominant group entertains about them. This complex of depersonalization undermines and confuses their ego identity.

SOCIOCULTURAL CHANGE Much research has been carried out concerning the effect of sociocultural change on mental health.

Sociocultural change occurs everywhere, of course, but it varies in rate and nature according to a complex set of technological, economic, social, and cultural factors. It has been shown that sociocultural change does not necessarily produce adverse emotional reactions and that the speed of change is an essential factor. For instance, it has been suggested that in the United States the recent increase in mental illness in general and in juvenile delinquency in particular is due to rapid cultural change. This assumption seems to be justified because such change often results in anomie, especially in urban areas, in value polymorphism, and in role deprivation. The type of sociocultural change is also important. The case of colonialized people has been mentioned. It has been demonstrated that many primitive peoples living on the fringes of a complex society are subjected to stress which increases the frequency of mental illness. In brief, it can be concluded that sociocultural change is noxious to mental health if it produces one or more of the previously named sociocultural factors of anomie, role deprivation, and value polymorphism.

II. Relative Frequency

Differences in relative as well as absolute frequencies of mental disorders have been reported in cross-cultural and cross-subcultural comparisons (Carothers 1953; Field 1960; Collomb 1965). Obtaining reliable information on the frequencies of mental illness is difficult because of methodological problems. Bearing in mind that available data may not always be reliable, we may summarize information on relative frequencies as follows:

(1) Infectious psychoses, including general paralysis of the insane, are common in some parts of the world and rare in others.

(2) Schizophrenia is everywhere the most common functional psychosis requiring hospitalization.

(3) Manic-depressive psychosis is less common—or at least comes to the attention of psychiatrists less often—in underdeveloped countries than in developed countries.

(4) Suicide rates are unusually high in Japan, Sweden, Denmark, and Switzerland and are alleged to be low among African Negroes who, however, if emotionally disturbed, are apt to wander off into the bush and never come back.

(5) Postpartum psychoses are reported as frequent in some Asiatic and African countries, such as Mongolia, Tunisia, and Senegal.

(6) Gross forms of hysteria, such as hysterical blindness, deafness, convulsions, and paralysis, which have almost vanished in Euro-American countries, are common in such developing countries as India, Lebanon, Egypt, and Tunisia.

(7) Obsessive-compulsive neuroses have been reported as rare in rural areas of the African and Asiatic continents, though they are by no means uncommon in the big cities, for instance, of India.

(8) Various psychosomatic disorders, such as gastric ulcer, high blood pressure and bronchial asthma which are usually attributed to the hurly-burly of Western civilization, have been noted in substantial numbers among the bush population of Africa, just as impotence and painful menstrual periods (dysmenorrhea) are a common occurrence there.

(9) Presenile and senile psychoses are seen less often in developing than in developed countries.

(10) Sexual perversions are said to be less common—or at least more tolerated—in many developing and primitive societies than in advanced societies.

The explanation of some of these phenomena is obvious. For instance, it is obvious that in countries in which the risk of infection is abundant and in which medical services are inadequate, infectious psychoses are prevalent and that in countries in which the span of life is short, presenile and senile psychoses are rarely seen. Other phenomena require exploration. Schizophrenia, it is true, is ubiquitous, but it is conceivable and even likely that, as hinted at before, for reasons inherent in their cultures, in non-Western cultures different population groups are prone to be affected. Quiet, retarded depressives in many parts of the world are retained in, and looked after, by the family. The alleged rarity of depressive states among some peoples, such as Indonesians and Africans, may be accounted for by the protective effect of the extended family against mourning over loss of a loved person; by the effectiveness of funeral rites in working through object loss; by the effectiveness of projective mechanisms as a defense against depression, and by a predominance of a collective superego in primitive societies versus a predominance of an individual superego in Western and Western-type societies. The high frequency of postpartum psychoses in some of the countries named may be due to the great importance attached to fecundity, to the numerous taboos related to pregnancy and parturition, to the reality of the dangers of delivery, and to the high rate of infantile mortality. The frequency of gross forms of conversion hysteria among the uneducated in non-Western countries has been attributed to deficient control (repression) of objectionable impulses, and their recession in the West to the emancipation of women and to an increasing sophistication of the population. Panic states are by no means uncommon among primitive Africans but, owing to superego projection, they are states of fear rather than of anxiety. The infrequency of obsessive-compulsive neuroses in developing countries may be due to the disinclination of obsessive compulsives to seek psychiatric help, to leniency in toilet training, to externalization of a threatening superego in the form of popular beliefs and superstitions, and to absorption of obsessional defenses in culturally dictated rituals. Psychosomatic disorders in non-Western societies are still little explored; according to recent research in Senegal, their psychodynamics does not differ from that of Euro-Americans. As stated before, the diagnosis of sexual perversion depends on social conventions. If in a society, as among the Urubi Indians of Eastern Brazil, it is customary to go about naked with a ribbon tied around the penis, a gentleman thus attired can hardly be accused of indecent exposure.

B. PATHOPLASTIC CONSIDERATIONS

Information about cultural and subcultural differences in the symptomatology of mental disorders has been derived mainly from clinical interviews with patients in mental hospitals, and to a lesser extent with patients attending outpatient departments, and private patients. Hospital records have also been used for this purpose.

According to some observers, the clinical manifestations of mental disorders among primitive peoples, such as Australian aborigines, are so atypical that Western diagnostic categories are hardly applicable. Other observers stress similarities rather than dissimilarities in the clinical picture.

For the sake of this presentation, cultural and subcultural symptomatological differences may be discussed under the two divisions of "variants" and "unusual patterns."

I. Variants

Differences in the clinical manifestations of the major functional psychoses have been reported. It has been stated that *schizophrenia* in primitive African societies is quieter than in the Western world, "a poor imitation of European forms" as one author (Gordon 1934) puts it. Among Indian schizophrenics, catatonic body rigidity and negativism are reported to be unusually common, and less "method in madness" is said to be noticeable (Hoch 1959). Asiatic schizophrenics are said to be more withdrawn and less aggressive (Stoller 1959), and southern Italian patients less withdrawn and more aggressive (Parsons 1961) than their classical European counterparts. It is obvious that the content of delusions and hallucinations of psychotic patients is influenced by their cultures. For instance, an Eskimo who has not learned about the existence of Jesus Christ or General de Gaulle can obviously not imagine that he is either of them in his grandiose psychotic ideas. In Senegal a paranoid patient will accuse a sorcerer of bewitching him and will feel persecuted by spirits rather than by x-rays, radio, or television. It has been shown that persecutors vary with history, geography, religion, and sociopolitical developments. A study of changes in schizophrenic symptomatology during the last 100 years by an Austrian psychiatrist (Lenz 1964) reports that during the second 50 years ideas of persecution by God or the devil became infrequent and ideas of persecution by nonsupernatural agents more common. According to Japanese investigators, since the end of World War II paranoid schizophrenia has increased in Japan and paranoid delusions which formerly often concerned the emperor have changed to an increasing incidence of ideas about the United States, the Communist Party, radio, and television.

Possibly because it is socially disturbing, the manic phase of *manic-depressive* psychosis comes more often to the attention of psychiatrists in developing countries than the depressive phase (Carothers 1953; Gordon 1934). Symptoms of endogenous depression in their classical form—depression, mood change during the day, insomnia with early morning awakening, and diminution of interest in social environment—are most commonly found among Europeans irrespective of where they live. Atypical features have been noted in various non-European societies. Outstanding among these, according to our global survey (Murphy 1964), have been the rarity or absence of feelings of guilt, of self-accusation, and of expectation of punishment in depressed patients in non-Judeo-Christian cultures. Depressive ideas, as demonstrated by Indian patients, are characterized by a cultural coloring.

As for *psychoneuroses*, the frequency of gross forms of conversion hysteria and the rarity of obsessional neurosis in developing countries have been mentioned. Other common hysterical features in these societies are vague aches and pains, functional visceral disorders, and sensations of heat (reported from countries as far apart as India and Nigeria) which are based on prevailing folk beliefs. Acute anxiety reactions of short duration are more common in primitive societies than in advanced societies. These anxiety states are often precipitated by failure to perform customary rites and are attributed to the wrath of the gods or bewitchment. They are often accompanied by incoherence of thought amounting to confusion, and by hallucinatory and delusional activity. Generally, emotional involvement and tendencies to put morbid impulses, culminating in homicidal attempts, into action are greater in primitive societies than in highly developed societies.

What do all these findings mean? In trying to explain the differences described, one should bear in mind that (a) mental disorders in many developing countries—to some extent and in a manner not fully explained—are precipitated, aggravated, and influenced by such biological conditions as bacterial infection and vitamin deficiency; (b) most of the patients from whom conclusions are drawn have been examined in mental hospitals and, because of the willingness or the necessity in many countries to keep all but the grossly disturbing patients at home, they constitute a highly selected sample; and (c) cultural differences in thought, feeling, and behavior—and even in value orientation—between educated Westerners and educated, highly Westernized persons in non-Western societies become somewhat blurred, whereas uneducated people all over the world have certain characteristics in common, including weakness of ego control, unconscious preference for denial versus repression, and ample use of introjection, projection, and regression as ego defenses. Hence, in areas of the world where a large proportion of the population consists of illiterates, one finds certain traits of mental illness to be common: short, violent episodes of psychosis, a high frequency of gross forms of conversion hysteria, a rarity of obsessional neurosis, and a paucity of delusional content.

Various differences remain that lend themselves to cultural interpretation other than literacy versus illiteracy. For instance, the high frequency of social and emotional withdrawal in Indian schizophrenics, also observed in other Asiatic schizophrenics, may be related to the teachings of both Hinduism and Buddhism of withdrawal as an acceptable mode of reacting to difficulties. The frequency of catatonic rigidity and of negativism in Indian schizophrenics may similarly be seen as related to traditional passive-aggressive response to a threatening world. The maintenance of social contact in southern Italian schizophrenics, even when in advanced stages of schizophrenia, has been attributed to their traditional sociability and to their great family solidarity. No easy explanation can be offered for the rarity of feelings of guilt and of having sinned in depressed patients of non-Judeo-Christian cultures. The concept of sin is undoubtedly deeply rooted in the Jewish and Christian religions. Beyond this, the rarity of these feelings in other cultures is indicative of fundamental differences in ego and superego structure. If superego censure is projected on to the social environment, as has been demonstrated for primitive Africans, feelings of shame but no feelings of guilt are experienced.

II. *Unusual Patterns*

A special group of unusual symptom patterns constitute the so-called culture-bound disorders. To list them all would obviously serve little purpose. They have been variously classified in phenomenological terms and in terms of content. Following the lead of Yap (1966), we have divided them into fear reactions, rage reactions, and dissociation states. Only a few examples of each group will be presented.

1. *Fear reactions:*

Latah is a syndrome first described as occurring in Malaya, but recognized in many other parts of the world under different names. For instance, Yap holds that the "jumping Frenchman of Maine" belongs to the same clinical entity. Classical descriptions by Japanese and Western writers of the disorder called *imu* of the Ainus of Hokkaido, in northern Japan, resemble accounts of *latah*. *Imu* is a fright reaction usually set off in the Ainus by the sight of a snake. Middle-aged women of low intelligence, self-effacing, and submissive are most commonly affected by fright reactions of this kind. Domestic servants predominated among the sufferers in Java during the Dutch colonial regime.

At first the afflicted repeat their own words and sentences and then those of others, especially of persons in authority (echolalia). Later they repeat gestures and acts of others (echopraxia). At other times they do exactly the opposite of what other persons do (negativism). Eventually they compulsively use obscene language (coprolalia). Attacks of this disease may be precipitated by the word snake and by tickling. Some patients worsen, passing into severe obsessive-compulsive neurosis and even into psychosis. In others the disease remains static.

The disease has been interpreted as: (a) an expression of a conflict between submission and rebellion arising from "an unconscious connection between submission and a dreaded and desired passive sexual experience" (Aberle 1952); (b) as mocking behavior with an identification with the aggressor (Carluccio, Sours, and Kolb 1964); (c) as a primitive anxiety-relieving mechanism available to primitive peoples and to children in Western societies, but not to adult Western men (Arieti *et al.* 1959).

Susto or "magic fright" has been reported among Central and South American Indian tribes and non-Indian inhabitants of the Andean highlands of Peru, Bolivia, and Colombia. It most often afflicts infants and young children, although adolescents and, exceptionally, adults may also suffer an attack. The illness is attributed to contact with supernatural beings, or to breathing of "bad air" in dangerous places such as cemeteries, or to encountering strangers or animals that frighten the victim and cause him to fall to the ground. According to native belief, when one is frightened the soul leaves the body and is kidnapped by spirits or, in Peruvian belief, is absorbed by the earth. The illness is sometimes interpreted as a supernatural punishment for transgression.

The symptoms of *susto* are varied and can be divided into somatic symptoms (emaciation, loss of weight and strength, rapid heart beat, gastrointestinal disorders) and psychological symptoms (intense anxiety, hyperexcitability, generalized phobias, depression). Treatment consists of invocation of the absent soul, propitiatory offerings to the earth, and cleansing of the body by rubbing it with various plants or animals, especially with a guinea pig.

All observers agree that the onset and development of symptoms of *susto* result from a reaction to massive stress. According to sociocultural interpretation, the syndrome occurs when the victim finds himself in a situation where he is unable to fulfill adequately the social role standardized for him by his group (Rubel 1964). According to psychodynamic interpretation, the syndrome occurs in adjustive phases of infancy and childhood or in psychoneurotic conditions. Because the child is helpless and completely dependent on his parents for satisfaction, any experience of repudiation or abandonment produces intolerable tension in him and results in panic (Leon 1965).

Koro, also known as *suo-yang,* is a mental derangement which seems to occur only in Southeast Asia, particularly among the inhabitants of the Malay Archipelago and among southern Chinese who immigrated to this region. It is an anxiety state in which the patient is afraid that his penis will withdraw into his abdomen, resulting in his death. This anxiety usually has a very sudden onset; it is very intense. The condition may last for several days and even weeks. It is attributed by the afflicted to sexual overindulgence and especially to excessive masturbation. To prevent the withdrawal of the penis, the afflicted holds his penis in a viselike grip and is assisted in doing so by his wife, friends, and relatives. To release the penis even for an instant, in their belief, would be fatal. Some clamp the penis in a wooden box, or tie a red string around it. Linton (1956) reports a female equivalent of *koro* in Southeast Asia. Some female patients in Borneo feel that their breasts are shrinking and their labia are sucked inward, thus causing them to lose secondary sex characteristics.

Koro resembles in many respects the castration anxiety so common in the West. It differs in the way in which the threat to the genitals is experienced by the Chinese and in the manner in which the irrational fear is dealt with by the afflicted and members of his family. Causally it has been connected with the warnings frequently given by Chinese parents to children not to masturbate because masturbation will inflict grievous injury to their genitals. Psychodynamically the presenting symptom, as with the castration complex of the West, is based on an unresolved oedipal conflict; but as Rin (1963) has pointed out, the symptom is also deeply rooted in fundamental Chinese concepts of sexuality. The Chinese believe that it is due to an excess of what they call *yin,* the "female factor." Therefore, a medicine, such as powdered rhinoceros horn, containing the "male factor," *yang,* must be administered. At a still deeper level it has been suggested that the susceptibility of the Chinese to symbolic castration threats is related to their oral orientation and to fear of oral deprivation or starvation.

2. *Rage reactions:*

The classical example of a rage reaction is *amok*. This is another syndrome first described as occurring in Malaya and since observed in many other parts of the world, for example, Java, the Philippines, Africa, and Tierra del Fuego. It is confined to males characterized by withdrawn, quiet, inoffensive, and gentle behavior previous to the onset of the disease. It is precipitated by environmental difficulties usually of a frustrating nature. Physical and mental stress, such as acute infections, deprivation of sleep, heat, alcohol, and sexual excitement, may act as predisposing and reinforcing factors. Several phases of the disease have been described. After an initial phase during which afflicted persons become even more withdrawn than usual, comes a phase of meditation during which they lose contact with the world around them, have ideas of persecution, and are in a mood of anxiety and rage. This is followed by the phase of automatism—the *amok* proper. Suddenly they jump up, sometimes with a terrifying yell, grab daggers, and slash into anyone and anything they encounter. They often commit homicide, may mutilate themselves, and are not infrequently killed by their frightened neighbors. Those who survive gradually calm down, but, spontaneously, or in response to external stimuli, renewed outbursts of violence occur. Eventually, the afflicted reach a state of exhaustion. With recovery of consciousness they pass into a phase of depression. There is complete amnesia for the phase of automatism.

Somatic predisposing factors noted in some of the patients examined have been diagnosed psychiatrically as belonging to various disease categories (Zaguirre 1957). It has been suggested that *amok* occurs where people have a low tolerance for interpersonal stress (Yap 1966). Individually the *amok* attack seems to represent a breakthrough of repressed rage occurring in a cultural setting where such outbursts are to some extent tolerated. Reports (Yap 1966) that in Malaya and Java the incidence of *amok* fell after the authorities captured and jailed people stricken with the illness indicate that social measures can curb the frequency and the specific forms of such rage reactions.

3. *Dissociation states:*

Dissociation states are exemplified by *trance* and *possession*. These two conditions are closely related to each other though trance may occur without possession and possession without trance. The term dissociation in its psychological application denotes a process in which a group of mental activities breaks away from the main stream of consciousness and functions as a separate unit. States of dissociated consciousness may occur in a great variety of settings, under hypnosis, in spiritual séances, in hysteria, and in schizophrenia. In accordance with beliefs held in many primitive societies, possession means intrusion into the human body by outside agencies, such as animals, ancestors, spirits, and deities, which displace the proper human soul. The possessed person assumes the behavioral characteristics of the intrusive agent.

Temporary states of possession are an integral part of religious services in many parts of the world, for example, India, Indonesia, Africa, and Haiti. The possession that occurs during voodoo ceremonies in Haiti is typical. Suddenly, activated by the wild rhythm of the drum and encouraged by the priest, the *houngan,* a member of the congregation, passes into a trance. His face appears empty; he stares into space; and he acts and speaks like the god that possesses him. Remarkable feats which otherwise seem impossible, such as climbing a palm tree upside down, have been performed in this condition. Convulsive seizures frequently occur. Such states of possession usually last a few minutes; on recovery there is complete amnesia for behavior, thoughts, and feelings during the state of possession. Only a few members of the congregation become possessed. It is thought that the possession state, as observed in Haiti, is a phenomenon of suggestion in persons living in a culture which fosters submissiveness and hence suggestibility, and that the more suggestible a person is, the more likely he is to pass into a state of possession (Wittkower 1964).

Transient ceremonial states of possession of this nature are culturally sanctioned, institutionalized phenomena. They release emotion, relieve tension, mitigate feelings of guilt, and alleviate feelings of anxiety. They therefore have an adaptive function. Yet there are also states of prolonged, nonceremonial possession in Haiti and elsewhere which are pathological and are recognized as such by the indigenous population. An example of this kind of disorder is *kitsunetsuki* (Yonebashi 1964), which is based on certain traditional features of Shinto. Kitsunetsuki occurs in certain areas of Japan where the social order preserves traits of former feudal times, and attitudes of superstition and ignorance prevail. People affected by this disorder are believed to be possessed by foxes and are said to change their facial expressions accordingly. A whole family may be thus afflicted, and those stricken are feared and shunned by the whole community.

In the foregoing pages, an outline of cultural factors in mental illness has been given, and their relevance to the absolute and relative frequencies of mental disorders as well as their symptom-moulding effects have been discussed. The survey highlights the value of research in this area for both psychiatrists and social scientists. Benefits derived by both disciplines are of a theoretical nature, though for psychiatrists there are also practical implications in the handling of patients and in planning mental health services. Research in these areas requires cooperation between psychiatrists and social scientists—in the field and in the later analysis and evaluation of findings. Such cooperation is not easy. It entails problems of research leadership and dovetailing of data obtained by disciplines that are different in primary foci of interest, in theoretical orientation, and in methodologies.

The very facts that I have been invited to address this conference and that this presentation has been prepared jointly by an anthropologist and a psychiatrist are indicative of the growing endeavors to bridge the gap between the two disciplines.

BIBLIOGRAPHY

ABERLE, DAVID F., "Arctic Hysteria and Latah in Mongolia," *Transactions of the New York Academy of Sciences*, Vol. 14, Ser. 11, 1952, pp. 291–297.
ARIETI, SILVANO, and M. JOHANNES METH, "Rare, Unclassifiable, Collective and Exotic Psychotic Syndromes," *American Handbook of Psychiatry*, Vol. 1, 1959, pp. 546–563.
BENEDICT, RUTH, "Continuities and Discontinuities in Cultural Conditioning," in C. Kluckhohn and H. A. Murray (eds.), *Personality in Nature, Society, and Culture*, pp. 414–423. New York: Alfred A. Knopf, 1949.
CARLUCCIO, C., JOHN A. SOURS, and LAWRENCE C. KOLB, "Psychodynamics of Echoreactions," *Arch. Gen. Psychiat.*, Vol. 10, 1964, pp. 623–629.
CAROTHERS, J. C., "The African Mind in Health and Disease: A Study in Ethnopsychiatry," *World Health Organization Monograph Series*, Vol. 17, 1953.
COLLOMB, H., "Assistance psychiatrique en Afrique: Experience Senegalese," *Psychopathologie Africaine*, Vol. 1, No. 1, 1965, pp. 11–84.
DuBOIS, CORA, *The People of Alor*. Minneapolis: University of Minnesota Press, 1944.
FARIS, R. E. L., "Ecological Factors in Human Behavior," in J. McV. Hunt (ed.), *Personality and the Behavior Disorders*, Vol. 11, pp. 736–757. New York: The Ronald Press Company, 1944.
FIELD, M. J., *Search for Security*. Evanston, Ill.: Northwestern University Press, 1960.
GORDON, H. L., "Psychiatry in Kenya Colony," *Journal of Mental Science*, 1934, Vol. 80, pp. 167–170.
HOCH, E., "Psychiatrische Beobachtungen und Erfahrungen an indischen Patienten," *Praxis*, Vol. 48, Nov. 1959, pp. 1051–1057.
LEIGHTON, A. H., T. A. LAMBO, CH. C. HUGHES, O. C. LEIGHTON, J. M. MURPHY, and O. B. MACKLIN, *Psychiatric Disorder among the Yoruba*. Ithaca, N.Y.: Cornell University Press, 1963.
LENZ, H., *Vergleichende Psychiatrie, Eine Studie über die Beziehung von Kultur, Soziologie und Psychopathologie*. Vienna: Wilhelm Maudrich Verlag, 1964.
LEON, CARLOS, "El 'Espanto': sus Implicaciones Psichiatricas," *Transcultural Psychiatric Research Review*, Vol. II, April 1965, pp. 45–48.
LEWIN, BRUNO, "Die Konfliktneurose der Mohammedanerin in Agypten," *Zeitschrift fur Psychotherapie und Medizin*, Vol. 8, No. 3, 1958, pp. 98–112.
LIN, TSUNG-YI, "A Study of the Incidence of Mental Disorder in Chinese and Other Cultures," *Psychiatry*, Vol. 16, No. 4, 1963, pp. 313–336.
LINTON, RALPH, *Culture and Mental Disorders*. Springfield, Ill.: Charles C Thomas, Publisher, 1956.
MEAD, MARGARET, and F. C. MAC GREGOR, *Growth and Culture*. New York: G. P. Putnam's Sons, 1951.
MURPHY, H. B. M., E. D. WITTKOWER, and N. A. CHANCE, "Crosscultural Inquiry into the Symptomatology of Depression," *Transcultural Psychiatric Research Review*, Vol. I, April 1964, pp. 5–18.

PARSONS, A., "Some Comparative Observations on Ward Social Structure: Southern Italy, England and the United States," *Transcultural Psychiatric Research Review*, No. 10, April 1961, pp. 65–67.

PIERS, G., and M. B. SINGER, *Shame and Guilt*. Springfield, Ill.: Charles C Thomas, Publisher, 1953.

RIN, HSIEN, "Koro: a Consideration on Chinese Concepts of Illness and Case Illustrations," *Transcultural Psychiatric Research Review*, No. 15, Oct. 1963, pp. 23–30.

RUBEL, ARTHUR J., "The Epidemiology of a Folk Illness: Susto in Hispanic America," *Ethnology*, Vol. 3, 1964, pp. 268–283.

STOLLER, A., "Assignment Report on the Mental Health Situation in Thailand," *W.H.O. Regional Office Document*, SEA/Ment., May 1959.

WALLACE, A. F. C., *Culture and Personality*, p. 186. New York: Random House, Inc., 1962.

WITTKOWER, E. D., "Spirit Possession in Haitian Voodun Ceremonies," *Acta Psychotherapeutica*, Vol. 12, No. 72, 1964.

YAP, P. M., "Culture-Bound Reactive Syndromes," presented at the conference on Mental Health in Asia and the Pacific, March 28–April 1, 1966, East West Center, Honolulu, Hawaii.

YONEBAYASHI, T., "Kitsunetsuki," *Transcultural Psychiatric Research Review*, Vol. I, Oct. 1964, pp. 95–97.

ZANGUIRRE, J. C., "Amuck," *Journal of the Philippine Federation of Private Med. Practitioners*, Vol. 6, 1957, pp. 1138–1149.

18

The Family and Personality in Crisis

A. B. Hollingshead

This paper is concerned with the structure of family relations and the mental status of one of its principal members during a period of crisis. Viewed theoretically, individuals are members of family groups throughout their lives. In fact, the identification of every person with one or more family groups transcends the life arc of the individual. We all have ancestors and most older persons have descendants. Ancestors project the past into the present; descendants carry the present into the future. In this sense, each person's identity is a part of his family's heritage as long as he is regarded as a member of the kin group. In the course of a normal life cycle the individual in our society is a member of two family groups—the family of orientation into which he is born and the family of procreation which he creates when he marries. Speaking generally, the family is the socially approved unit for the creation and training of the oncoming generation. In this sense, the nuclear family of father-mother-and-child is a key unit in the structure of our society. It is the matrix within which socialization takes place and personality develops. This position has been established in the literature,[1] and I shall not discuss it further here.

Before I turn to the research on which this paper is based, it is pertinent to mention that during recent years psychologists, psychiatrists, and sociologists have become interested in the systematic study of interdependencies between the social structure of families and the mental status of their members.[2] A major objective of these studies is to build an empirical base for broad theories which accurately reflect the conditions and processes of personality development insofar as they are related to experiences in the family.[3] These studies should eventually demonstrate those dimensions of personality that are attributable to heredity or experience, or their interaction, in the production of a healthy or a disturbed personality. A proximate objective is to learn how society can control deviant behavior. The immediate goal is to determine how we can give meaningful therapy to disturbed personalities. In this connection, a major thrust of the current massive national movement to construct community mental health centers is an offshoot of the efforts of lay leaders, psychologists, psychiatrists, social workers, and sociologists to retain disturbed persons in the family rather than to hand them over to custodial or correctional institutions for indefinite periods of time.[4]

The research I shall discuss in this paper concerns families containing within them a physically ill adult. The crisis which the families faced was the hospitalization of a principal member. The research was designed so that each randomly selected sick person would be a principal member of a family of procreation. *A principal member* is defined as either the husband or the wife of a pair of spouses who live in the same household. To be included in the study, the principal member who was ill had to be admitted to either the medical or surgical service of a large, metropolitan, general hospital in New England. Of the 161 families in the study, 81 are represented by the hospitalization of the wife and 80 by the hospitalization of the husband. Each husband or wife was selected randomly from among the aggregate of patients who met our specifications. (The essential specifications were: married, Caucasian, between 40 and 64 years of age, conscious upon admission, and a resident of the state.) The research was carried out by a team headed by a physician [5] and a sociologist (the present writer), assisted by nurses, sociologists, and younger physicians.[6] Participation in the study was voluntary on the part of the patients, their physicians, the spouses, and other family members.

As soon as we had selected a patient, we asked his physician if we could include him in our study. We then asked the patient and his spouse for their approval. As soon as we had gained the consent of the three key persons—physician, patient, and spouse—we were ready to gather data about the family and its constituent members.

The many kinds of data we assembled on each patient and his family were prepared for analysis by two different procedures. Specific items of information whether quantitative, for example the amount charged for board and room in the hospital, or qualitative, such as the accommodation in which the patient was housed, were coded and punched on cards for data-processing machines. To take advantage of the vast quantity of vivid experiences related by respondents and the behavior we observed, we designed a 48-question assessment schedule. Each assessment question gave us an answer derived from a synthesis of all the data we had accumulated on the patient, the spouse, and the family. The information needed to answer each question was gathered by the physician and the sociologist while reading the entire record of a particular family. In this process we often read and reread the record, discussed specific points, and, where we disagreed, reexamined the record. Thus, the answer to each question on the assessment schedule reflects consensus between the two principal researchers.

The collection of data from the patient, the spouse, other family members, physicians, nurses, and ancillary staff was a time-consuming enterprise. Using schedules, we interviewed each person, observing behavior and recording who the participants were in each interaction as well as the subject matter and the mood, intensity, and feeling of each conversation. We were in direct, face-to-face contact with the patient, the spouse, and the family members on an average of 70 hours. In addition, some 5 to 6 hours were given over to interviews with physicians, nurses, and hospital staff who were caring for the patient. After discharge from the hospital each patient was visited in his home.

Now that I have stated our interests and outlined some essential research procedures, I shall present a few findings on the sociobiographical composition of the study group. The husbands have a mean age of 54 years and the wives 51 years. Both the husbands and the wives are predominantly native-born Americans; only 20 percent were born in a foreign country. Within the native-born segment, two out of three were born and reared in New England. The spouse pairs exhibit a high percentage of first marriages for both partners; only 18 percent of either the husband or the wives have been married before. There are children in 91 percent of the families. Parents in their forties and early fifties may have growing children still living in the parental home; children of parents in their later fifties and early sixties seldom live at home. The families reside in single households for the most part, either in individual residences or apartments. Only 13 percent share their homes with persons other than members of the nuclear family group, these extra persons being, in most instances, aged relatives or young children of a relative; few homes have boarders or nonrelatives who live with the family. Socioeconomically, these families range from the wealthy with an annual income of $100,000 and more to the very poor who eke out an existence on public welfare.

From the beginning of the study of each family until the conclusion of the fieldwork, we were concerned with behavior—of the spouses to one another, of the parents to the children, and of the children to the parents—and the actions of family members in their relationships with nurses, physicians, and other hospital personnel. The stories family members told us about themselves and other persons in the family and in the community also were of interest in helping us understand the family. The adjustment of family members to one another, to the neighborhood, and to the larger community is a discernible dimension of the social environment in which these families are enmeshed and the way it affects the structure of family relationships.

On the basis of all the data we accumulated, we made an assessment of the adjustment of family members to the social situations in which they function. We grouped our judgments of family adjustment into three categories: *adjusted, moderately maladjusted,* and *severely maladjusted.*

The Family and Personality in Crisis

The first estimate of a family's adjustment on this three-point scale was made by the physician and the sociologist independently. When their assessments differed on a family, each restudied the detailed materials gathered on all members of the family. Then the two judges met and arrived at a collaborative evaluation of the family's adjustment. Within each of the three categories, specific behaviors vary from family to family but there are no essential differences in our judgment of how to categorize a family.

To give the reader an understanding of what we mean by *adjusted*, *moderately maladjusted*, and *severely maladjusted* families, I shall now present statements of particular family situations. Critical identifying characteristics have been altered to protect the privacy of each family, and we have given fictitious names to the families.

Mr. and Mrs. Ash represent an *adjusted* family. We saw them for the first time in the hospital room to which Mr. Ash had been taken on a stretcher a few hours before. Mr. Ash greeted us with a weak smile on his pallid face. Mrs. Ash, who was carefully groomed and neatly dressed, was cordial but guarded in her behavior. We told them their physician had given his consent for us to approach them to take part in a study we were making, and they readily agreed to cooperate.

Mr. Ash is the foreman of a crew of some 30 men working on outdoor projects. He has been employed continuously by the state for almost 25 years and is within a few months of retirement on a pension. Almost every evening and on weekends Mr. Ash works around the 5-room house they bought several years ago in a newly developed section of their town. He has a workshop in the basement where he repairs household appliances for his wife and other family members and toys for the children in the area. He is known in the neighborhood as the man to go to when you want something fixed. He looks forward, with only a certain measure of anxiety, to his retirement when he plans to spend all his time refinishing furniture and following his other hobbies.

Mr. and Mrs. Ash are practicing Roman Catholics. Both were widowed when they married some 15 years ago. Mrs. Ash lost her first husband about 20 years ago; she had no children. Mr. Ash and his first wife had two sons and two daughters and they adopted two sons. After his first wife died, Mr. Ash lived alone with his children. Upon remarriage, he and the six children moved into the 14-room home his present wife had inherited from her parents. The present Mrs. Ash completed the rearing of the children. She saw that they all finished high school, obtained jobs, and, as time passed, were married and began to raise families of their own. In due course her ancestral home was sold, and the couple built their present smaller home.

Mr. Ash has been an active participant in community affairs since he was a young man. As a youth he played on the town's baseball team. Later he helped promote amateur athletics among the young men of the town. He has been a member of the town's volunteer fire department for some 25 years. Mrs. Ash has been a member of women's groups in the church and the community. She is particularly interested in aid to crippled children, as she suffered from a severe malady of unknown origin when she was a child.

Mrs. Ash is the social and business manager of the family, a point of pride with her husband. He has handed her his paycheck on payday ever since they were married. He says, "She never wastes a nickel and she gets five-and-a-half cents' worth out of every nickel." He never worried about the hospital bill, as the family had insurance; he told us, "Mother has the money. When I walk out of this hospital every cent of the bill will be paid in cash."

The six families of procreation stemming from this family all live in the community and all have children of their own. The different families visit one another almost every week; in addition, there is lively telephone communication between them. Both Mr. and Mrs. Ash look forward to the time when one or another of the older grandchildren marries and has children. They anticipate with pleasure becoming great-grandparents.

Mr. Ash reports that this is his first hospitalization and that he has never been sick "a day in my whole life." The onset of his illness was sudden, unexpected, and dramatic. After returning together from Mass they sat down to have breakfast. Mrs. Ash noted that Mr. Ash was pale and his hands and arms were shaking. Although he insisted that he was all right, she went into another room and called their oldest son on the telephone; she also telephoned their physician to ask him to "come over right away." When she returned to the living room she found Mr. Ash stretched out on the floor. She hurriedly telephoned the fire department for the emergency ambulance and the church for their priest. Within a few minutes the physician, the oldest son and his wife, the priest, and the ambulance all converged on their home.

While Mr. Ash was in the hospital, Mrs. Ash visited him daily. Every evening she telephoned the oldest son's wife to tell her of "Papa's" progress. There was close communication between the several family members. When Mr. Ash was able to have visitors the family members came in rotation. Before he left the hospital all of his children, their spouses, and his 14 grandchildren had come to see him. After his return home, Mrs. Ash each day made a report about his condition to one of the children in a system of communication decided upon by the family so that Mr. Ash would not be annoyed by telephone calls from all of them.

Mr. and Mrs. Ash are very close emotionally. They live for one another, for the children, and for the grandchildren. Their adjustment within the family, to the neighborhood, and to the community is wholesome. Mr. Ash's physician characterized him as "John Q. Citizen, U.S.A." Throughout the hospitalization and during the home visits afterward, we heard or observed nothing that led us to believe there is any disruptive tension in this family.

The Beech family represents those judged to be *moderately maladjusted*. Mr. Beech is a minor official in a small construction company. He and his wife and their teenage son and daughter live in a six-room house in one of the suburban towns. The family moved to this community from a nearby state at the end of World War II when Mr. Beech took a job with his present company. The two parental families had lived in the same town and the same neighborhood. Mr. and Mrs. Beech had played together when they were small children, gone to school together, courted, and eventually married. Their move to this area occurred when their elder child, the daughter, was a baby. It was their first effort to become independent from their parental families. However, sometime after they came to this city, Mrs. Beech's widowed mother moved here to be near her daughter, although she does not get along well with her son-in-law. Before long Mr. Beech's parents moved here also so that the elder Mrs. Beech could be close to her son.

When the young couple first moved to this community, they rented an upstairs flat in which they had some unpleasant experiences. The man who owned the property lived downstairs. For amusement, he several times locked Mrs. Beech out of her apartment while her small daughter was inside. On other occasions he locked Mrs. Beech in the basement where she had gone to do the laundry. Before they could find adequate housing, Mrs. Beech became a "nervous wreck" and Mr. Beech developed a stomach ulcer. Since that time Mr. Beech has suffered periodically from intestinal difficulties which his physician attributes to his nerves. Mrs. Beech realizes her husband is susceptible to emotional upsets when things do not go well for him, when his mother fills him with "her goodies," or when the children make demands on the family.

For several months before Mr. Beech's admission to the hospital, their life situation had been growing worse. Mr. Beech made a series of mistakes in estimating the cost of jobs on which his firm made bids; in one two-week period the firm lost five jobs upon which he had made estimates. The year before, the firm had not given him a bonus, and to make matters worse the teen-age son and daughter were demanding many luxuries their parents could not afford. As Mr. Beech became more tense and worried, he made more mistakes on his job. Mrs. Beech claimed she had to act like a "policewoman" to keep him away from his mother and the food she insisted he eat when he visited her.

The day before the hospital admission, Mrs. Beech had gone on a shopping trip with her mother. According to Mr. Beech, the two women had gone all over town spending money. A family argument about expenses developed at the dinner table. Although Mr. Beech had an uneasy stomach afterward, he went to visit his parents. His mother, in her accustomed manner, gave him lemonade, popcorn, and peanuts. About 10 P.M. he returned home and retired, but awoke in the middle of the night with a "terrible gut ache." This was followed by uncontrollable bowel movements. As the hours wore on, the diarrhea and the "gut ache" continued, and anal bleeding was observed, at which point the family physician was called.

When we first contacted this family, Mr. Beech was lying in his hospital bed in apparent discomfort. His wife was sitting on one side of him holding one hand and mopping his brow with a handkerchief; his mother was sitting on the other side of the bed holding the other hand; she, too, was mopping his brow with a handkerchief. Throughout Mr. Beech's hospitalization his mother-in-law did not come to visit, but his mother came at the beginning of visiting hours each day and stayed until the hospital personnel forced her to leave. In referring to her son, she always called him "my baby." On one occasion, Mr. Beech turned to our observer and said sarcastically, "Yeah, some baby!" He told us privately he wished his mother would stay at home but he could not tell her so.

The Beeches are nominal Protestants although they do not go to church. Mrs. Beech is a member of several women's organizations. Mr. Beech belongs to a lodge and occasionally attends meetings. The children appear to get along well with their parents and grandmothers. The daughter has a "steady boyfriend" who came with her to the hospital to visit Mr. Beech. The maladjustment in this family revolves around intergenerational relationships. The two older women compete with one another for the attention of their children and grandchildren, and there are strained relations between the younger and the older Mrs. Beech as well as between Mr. Beech and his mother-in-law. The emotional involvement of Mr. and Mrs. Beech with one another, with their mothers, and their mothers-in-law, as well as the demands of the children for status symbols and Mr. Beech's difficulties on the job are evidences of moderate maladjustment.

The Catalpa family is judged to be *severely maladjusted*. We first encountered Mrs. Catalpa sitting up in bed in the hospital, under an oxygen tent from which she had pulled the edges loose. We soon learned that she was deaf; when she desired to talk or hear, she put on her hearing aid; when she did not want to communicate with us, her family, or hospital personnel, she removed it. Before we could understand what she was saying, we had to wait until she took from under her pillow a complete set of false teeth and inserted them in her mouth.

Admission to the hospital culminated a long sequence of unhappy events in Mrs. Catalpa's life. The immediate antecedent incidents started about three weeks earlier when Mrs. Catalpa had pain in her chest, difficulty in breathing, feelings of faintness, and no energy. As she was alone when this attack occurred, she slumped down in a chair and "fell asleep." When her husband came home tired and irascible, a quarrel ensued because she did not have the housework done or his supper ready. Mr. Catalpa claims he tried to get her to go to the public health officer in their town—the only physician they had had any contact with after some 30 years of residence in the community. However, she said she did not want a doctor and her husband did not insist. Mrs. Catalpa told us, "I have always been in good health." She continued to have trouble breathing, coughed violently, and felt weak, so she purchased some cough medicine. Her condition worsened as the days passed. On the Saturday night before she was brought to the hospital, Mr. Catalpa came home drunk; they quarreled, he continued to drink, and sometime during the evening Mrs. Catalpa "fell asleep again" in her chair. The oldest son and wife happened to stop in at the rural slum home and found Mr. Catalpa stretched out on the floor in a drunken stupor and Mrs. Catalpa very ill. The son drove to the house of the town's public health physician and asked him to come to see his mother immediately. The physician was given directions to the house. However, although he promised to come that night, he did not arrive until about 11 A.M. on Sunday. According to the family, the physician looked at Mrs. Catalpa, collected ten dollars, and left to call an ambulance. When the ambulance arrived, Mr. Catalpa was still drunk. Mrs. Catalpa came to the hospital alone in the ambulance, delivered to the emergency service by the ambulance attendants. No member of her family came with her. The oldest son and his wife arrived several hours later.

Mr. and Mrs. Catalpa's ancestral families have lived in New England for several generations. They were born in the same community in another state and attended the same elementary school. During World War I, as a teen-ager, Mr. Catalpa joined the army. When he was discharged, he returned to the rural community of his childhood and married his 15-year-old neighbor. Some seven months later the first child was born and, in rapid succession, 14 more children followed. Early in their marriage they decided to come to this community because "there was plenty of work here." Mr. Catalpa found a job as a laborer in a coal-yard. Every year a new baby arrived. The family moved often, as they did not pay the rent; during one three-year period they moved eight times. When things became too hard, Mr. Catalpa left home for several months at a time. During one of these interludes Mrs. Catalpa and eight of their children lived in one room. (There is some evidence that a male friend shared the room with her and the children.) In time, Mr. Catalpa returned and moved his family to an adjacent town where they lived in a shack while he did catch-as-catch-can labor on farms. A few years later, the family went on "town charity." They remained on it for ten years during which time two children died. One, a patient for several weeks in the hospital where we did our research, was returned to the family, supposedly well, but died during the night of his first day at home. Mr. Catalpa wrapped him in a blanket and came to the hospital. He attacked the intern in the Emergency Room, accusing the hospital of killing the child. However, as he told us, "Two bulls got to me first and knocked me unconscious."

A year or two later, a visiting nurse came to their home to talk to them about their oldest daughter. According to the Catalpas, the nurse had "a paper" that said the girl was to be sent to a school in Boston. Several weeks later, they learned the girl had been committed to a state mental institution. She has remained there throughout the intervening years. The Catalpas are very bitter at what they consider their poor treatment by medical and welfare agencies.

The twelve living children of the Catalpas have given them "no end of trouble." The oldest son, who has never gotten along well with his father, "ran away from home" to join the army during World War II. On several occasions he beat his father when he found him drinking. A younger brother became a juvenile offender with a long record of arrests and sentences; he has been in every male correctional institution in the state. While his mother was in the hospital he was in "safekeeping" in the state prison. Another brother and a sister became intimate, and the girl gave birth to an illegitimate child; this child was taken from the family by the Welfare Department. The girl had a second child whose paternity we could not ascertain. This child she took with her when she married and left the family home. Mrs. Catalpa complained bitterly that all her children married "foreigners." The oldest son, she told us, married a "Pole"; others married "Germans," "Italians," "Irish," and so on. According to her, one daughter even married a "half-Irish half-Indian boy." One son married a girl who bore him two children; this girl divorced the Catalpas' son, married him again, divorced him a second time, and married another Catalpa son; she divorced this son and married a third son. "Now," said Mrs. Catalpa, "she's trying to have a go at Dad." (This latter opinion may be a fantasy, but the earlier multiple marriages and divorces did occur.) Another son accused his wife of having affairs with other men. One night he followed her and caught her having intercourse in a car with a strange man. One daughter separated from her husband, was "taken back," and then "got kicked out again" when he learned she had become pregnant while they were separated.

Although the Catalpas exhibit the severest forms of maladjustment, we could have substituted a number of other families who are as miserably disorganized. All of the families in this extreme group have one or more members who are severe alcoholics; they identify with no community institutions; there is poor communication among family members; and, finally, the members refuse to share joint responsibilities.

I shall turn now from the family situation to a consideration of the mental status of the spouse who is the patient. To recapitulate, each patient was admitted to a general hospital for the treatment of a physical illness which a physician sponsoring the admission believed to be treatable by the art and science of either internal medicine or surgery. In passing, I mention that physicians recognize two dimensions in each individual: the *soma* and the *psyche*. The *soma* or physical aspects of an individual—sex, age, height, color, and bodily contours—are easily observable. Attributes expressive of the *psyche*—personal feelings, manner of speech and thought, attitudes toward self and others, emotional sets, moods, reactions to the environment and other persons, in short the *selfness*—are less discernible. Nevertheless, they are a vital part of the personality. An individual afflicted with an illness defined by a physician as treatable by medication, surgery, or a combination of the two is likely to be sent to a general hospital. Such a patient may also be disturbed mentally and be in as great a need of professional help for his emotional difficulties as he is for his physical difficulties. However, the mental aspects of his illness may be overlooked.

We desired from the beginning of the study to make a systematic evaluation of each patient's mental status during two points in time: first, the probable mental status before he became afflicted with his present illness; and, second, the mental status as it was observed to be during the period of hospitalization. Ideally, this dimension of the study should have been carried out by a psychiatrist. In reality, a pilot study of patients and families, combined with discussions with internists and surgeons, led us to the conclusion that the incorporation of a psychiatric examination in the protocol would jeopardize the study. Fear of psychiatrists was a constant threat to many patients and to a considerable number of internists and surgeons as well. We eventually decided to base our assessment of mental status on a number of interrelated factors: the life history of the patient before this illness as told to us by the patient and the spouse separately; the patient's behavior during hospitalization; and, finally, the behavior of the patient and the spouse during home visits. The data upon which we made our assessment of the patient's mental status were collected over a period of weeks, usually months. After all the data were assembled, the physician and the sociologist made independent judgments of a particular patient's behavior and his expressed moods, feelings, and attitudes toward himself, the spouse, other family members, physicians, nurses, the hospital and other pertinent institutions, and persons. When we differed in our assessments, the whole record was restudied by each of us; we then discussed our individual evaluations of the person's mental status until we reached agreement.

We summarized mental status into four categories: *mentally healthy, moderately disturbed, severely disturbed,* and *psychotic.* Unfortunately, restrictions of time and space do not permit me to illustrate each mental status category with case materials comparable to the materials on family adjustments. However, the important fact, mentioned earlier, is that assessments of mental status were made for each patient at two points on the life arc: the first is concerned with his pre-illness personality, the second with his mental status during the time he was in the hospital. We concluded that prior to their present illness 9 percent of the patients were mentally healthy, 29 percent were moderately neurotic, 49 percent were severely neurotic, and 13 percent were psychotic.

We now raise a question crucial to social psychiatry: Is family adjustment related to mental status in the pre-illness phase of the patient's life? To answer this question, family adjustment is cross-tabulated with the mental status of each patient before the onset of his present illness. The data on interpersonal adjustments in the family and mental status are presented in Table 18–1.

TABLE 18–1

Relationships between the Prehospital Mental Status of the Patient and Adjustment in the Family of Procreation

Mental Status of the Patient	Maladjustment in the Family (in percentages)		
	None or Slight	Moderate	Severe
Mentally healthy	59	7	1
Moderately disturbed	41	60	8
Severely disturbed	—	33	67
Psychotic	—	—	24
N =	17	55	89

$p < .01$; $C = .83$.

These data demonstrate that persons who are assessed as mentally healthy in the pre-illness phase of their life arcs belong, in very large part, to families whose members are adjusted to one another and to their life situations. At the other end of the scale, all the psychotic patients belong to severely maladjusted families. The moderately neurotic patients are members of families who are, for the most part, either adjusted to one another or only moderately maladjusted. The corrected coefficient of contingency of .83 indicates the high order of correlation between family adjustment and the mental status of one of its principal members, either the husband or the wife. I am making no assumptions regarding independence and dependence of the two factors under examination—family adjustment and mental status. At the moment all I can say is that I do not know the answer. My tentative guess would be that they are concomitants of one another; that is, maladjustments in interpersonal relations exacerbate personality problems. These, in turn, react upon the internal structure of the family, and maladjustment is accentuated. Further research may be able to give a definite answer. I point out, in passing, that sex is not a significant factor in either family adjustment or mental status.

Mental status is considerably different during hospitalization in comparison with the preillness phase of the patient's life arc. No person was judged to be mentally healthy while in the hospital: 25 percent were assessed as moderately neurotic, 53 percent were severely neurotic, and 22 percent were psychotic. Nevertheless, there was continuity from the pre-illness phase to the in-hospital phase. One third of the persons who were judged to be mentally healthy in the pre-illness phase of their lives were assessed as moderately disturbed in the hospital, whereas 60 percent exhibited severely disturbed behavior and 7 percent were overtly psychotic. At the other end of the mental status gradient, one person who was assessed as psychotic before the present illness revealed only mildly disturbed behavior in the hospital and two persons who were clearly psychotic prior to this illness appeared to be severely neurotic while they were in the hospital. However, 86 percent of the persons who were given a mental status rating of psychotic before the present illness continued to behave in psychotic ways while they were in the hospital. The percentage figures for each mental status category at each specified time are presented in Table 18–2.

TABLE 18–2

Preillness Mental Status of Each Patient Compared with In-Hospital Mental Status

Pre-illness Mental Status	In-Hospital Mental Status (in percentages)			
	Mentally Healthy	Moderately Disturbed	Severely Disturbed	Overtly Psychotic
Healthy	—	12	11	3
Moderately disturbed	—	41	33	6
Severely disturbed	—	44	54	40
Psychotic	—	3	2	51
N =	0	41	85	35

$p < .01; C = .64$.

The corrected coefficient of contingency of .64 shows that the relationship between the mental status of the patients from the pre-illness period to the time of hospitalization is strong but not completely congruent with their observed behavior.

Two different but interrelated questions pertinent to in-hospital mental status are: (1) Are the patients aware of their mental disturbance? (2) Are the spouses aware of the patients' emotional disturbance? To answer briefly, the patients realize they are worried, tense, anxious, and threatened by their illness, and some realize they face imminent death; 52 percent have a correct perception of the threatening factors that encompass them. These patients give a coherent account of their fears. An additional 45 percent know they are upset, scared, resigned, or fighting their emotions, but they have only a partial perception of the real meaning of their anxieties. The remaining 3 percent have little or no insight into their situations. The spouses differ from the patients regarding their comprehension of the emotional problems besetting the patients. However, 43 percent perceive correctly the emotional disturbance of the patient; this is in contrast to the 52 percent of patients who have a correct self-awareness. The complementary figures for partial perception of emotional disturbance are 45 percent for the patients and 53 percent for the spouses; 2 percent of the spouses show no understanding of the patient's difficulties.

Full or partial awareness of the patient's mental disturbance in the hospital is linked closely to the presence or absence of empathy between the patient and the spouse as well as between the patient and other members of the family. Empathy, the ability to identify with another person, is an important element in family relations. To put oneself in the position of the sick member and help him solve his problems is integral to the social support associated with family life. Ideally, husbands and wives should be empathic in their relationships with one another. In our sample, some three husbands and wives out of five do exhibit empathy in their relationships with one another. Most of the remainder do to a certain extent, but there are a number of families in which empathy between the spouses is nonexistent. Empathy between the patient and members of the family other than the spouse follows a pattern very similar to that evidenced by one spouse with the other. To be specific, 57 percent of the patients are empathic with members of their families exclusive of the spouse. There is evidence of some empathy between 31 percent of the patients and other members of their families, but in 12 percent there is no evidence of empathy between the patient and any other member of his nuclear family. In this 12 percent, the relations between the members are so chaotic the aggregate hardly merits the designation *family*. The several individuals recognize one another as members of a kin network, but they definitely do not have empathic feelings for one another. For example, Mrs. Catalpa was alienated from all members of her family except the oldest son's wife who was mildly sorry for her. When Mrs. Catalpa was discharged from the hospital, this daughter-in-law attempted to rally Mrs. Catalpa's daughters to help their mother during her convalescence. Each daughter promised to go to the parental home and help care for her mother. However, not one of them actually came during the three weeks Mrs. Catalpa needed their help. The need for help ended the day Mr. Catalpa came home from work and found his wife dead on the floor. She was given a very economical funeral and buried in the cheapest lot in the town cemetery. Four months after her death Mr. Catalpa moved from the little shack where they had lived to a rooming house in a slum. During the next eight months not a single member of the family visited him. The abandonment of the father by the sons and daughters and in-law members of the family after Mrs. Catalpa's death marked the last step in a series of events that severed the parental generation from the oncoming generation.

By way of summary, I restate that this paper has focused attention on a very selected part of a large study of interrelations among family members and the treatment of illness in a hospitalized husband or wife. I have been concerned here with the structure of family relations and the mental status of one of its members during a crisis. The discussion is based on two issues: (1) the correlation between the ways family members adjust or fail to adjust to one another and the presence or absence of mental disturbance before the development of the illness which resulted in the hospitalization; (2) the change in the probable mental status before illness of each person during the crisis of hospitalization.

Families that were judged to be adjusted met the crisis of hospitalization with little or no alteration in the structure of family relationships. The support of the family often aided the patient in the handling of his emotional disturbance. In families judged to be moderately maladjusted, tensions were usually exacerbated by the crisis, and the mental status of the patient usually showed greater disturbance. In families that were judged to be severely maladjusted, family relationships often deteriorated into complete chaos. During the crisis of hospitalization the principal member of such a family usually became severely disturbed and sometimes psychotic. On the whole, during hospitalization the patient is more disturbed mentally than he was in the premorbid period. Patients are more aware of their disturbance than the spouses, but there is also excellent insight on the part of many spouses into the personality disturbance of the patients.[7]

NOTES

(1) Talcott Parsons and Robert F. Bales, *Family, Socialization, and Interaction Process*, New York: The Free Press, 1955; Robert D. Hess and Gerald Handel, *A Psychosocial Approach to Family Life*, Chicago: The University of Chicago Press, 1959; Robert F. Winch, Robert McGinnis, and Herbert R. Barringer

(eds.), *Selected Studies in Marriage and the Family,* New York: Holt, Rinehart, and Winston, 1962; Irving A. Hallowell, "Culture, Personality, and Society," in A. L. Kroeber (ed.), *Anthropology Today: An Encyclopedic Inventory,* pp. 597–620, Chicago: The University of Chicago Press, 1953 (The Hallowell paper includes an extensive bibliography on this subject and the footnotes are particularly pertinent.); John W. M. Whiting and Irvin L. Child, *Child Training and Personality: A Cross-Cultural Study,* New Haven, Conn.: Yale University Press, 1953.

(2) Lloyd H. Rogler and August B. Hollingshead, *Trapped: Families and Schizophrenia,* New York: John Wiley and Sons, 1965; John P. Spiegel and Norman W. Bell, "The Family of the Psychiatric Patient," in S. Arieti (ed.), *American Handbook of Psychiatry,* Vol. I, especially the bibliography pp. 114–149, New York: Basic Books, Inc., 1951; Yi-Chiang Lu, "Contradictory Parental Expectations in Schizophrenia," *Archives of General Psychiatry,* Vol. 6, 1962, pp. 219–234.

(3) Theodore Lidz, George Hotchkiss, and Milton Greenblatt, "Patient-Family Hospital Interrelationships: Some General Considerations," in Milton Greenblatt, Daniel J. Levinson, and Richard A. Williams (eds.), *The Patient and the Mental Hospital,* pp. 535–543. Glencoe: The Free Press, 1957.

(4) The first session of the 89th Congress (1965) enacted 59 laws touching on some aspects of the mental health field. These 59 laws involve 23 departments or agencies of the federal government. The National Institute of Mental Health has compiled a list of these 59 laws. The list or catalog is unpublished.

(5) Raymond S. Duff, M.D.

(6) The research reported here is being supported by Grant NU 00012, Division of Nursing, Bureau of State Services, United States Public Health Service. The complete report of the study is available in: Raymond S. Duff and August B. Hollingshead, *Sickness and Society.* New York, Harper & Row, 1968.

(7) A comprehensive theoretical statement of interdependences between the nuclear family, physical and mental illness, and their treatment is found in Talcott Parsons and Renee Fox, "Illness, Therapy, and the Modern American Family," in E. Gartley Jaco (ed.), *Patients, Physicians, and Illness,* pp. 234–245. New York: The Free Press, 1958.

19

The Personality of Social Deviants

William M. McCord

In this paper, I deal with a subject as elusive as "the character structure of poltergeists," for social scientists have neither reached a consensus about the personality of deviants nor can scholars even agree on the apparently simple matter of defining "deviance."

Schuessler and Cressey, for example, reviewed 113 studies of criminals and concluded that a criminal personality type did not exist (Schuessler & Cressey 1950). Similarly, in dealing with alcoholism, Syme examined all of the existing literature up to 1957 and felt forced to assert, "There is no warrant for concluding that persons of one type are more likely to become alcoholics than another type" (Syme 1957). Equal skepticism exists among psychiatrists concerning the supposedly distinct personality group labeled as schizophrenics; many analysts believe that the concept is merely a wastebasket into which highly diverse people are dumped (Arieti 1959). With good (but, in my opinion, insufficient) reason, one influential school of thought maintains, therefore, that *no* generalizations about the personality patterns of deviants can be propounded.

The very concept of deviance itself has rightfully been questioned. The lay public normally considers deviants—criminals or drug addicts or homosexuals—as either evil or diseased. This moralistic definition has little meaning since virtually all of us have, at one time or another, committed actions of which our society officially disapproves. Porterfield (1946), for example, anonymously questioned University of Texas students and found that 100 percent privately admitted committing at least one crime. The Kinsey report has amply demonstrated the extent of sexual deviations in our society. And Becker's study of marijuana users showed that, despite being so-called dope fiends, they could hold good jobs, maintain families, and lead outwardly "normal" lives (Becker 1963). The extent of private undetected deviance, then, is enormous and we cannot use either a simple concept of moral condemnation or one based on a statistical variation from the norm to label a person as criminal, queer, or crazy.

However, all societies do in fact define certain people as outside the pale of acceptable behavior and in turn punish, ostracize, or hospitalize them. The process by which one becomes a public deviant has been considerably clarified by Tannenbaum (1951), Lemert (1951), Kitsuse (1962), and, particularly, by Becker (1963) in his excellent book *Outsiders*. "Social groups create deviance," Becker has observed, "by making the rules whose infraction constitutes deviance and by applying those rules to particular people and labeling them as outsiders" (Becker 1963:9).

I would like to use this definition in examining three major groups in our society—criminals, alcoholics and psychotics—whose behavior is either legally punished, morally condemned, or treated as a disease. I have chosen to deal with only these three types of deviants since it is their behavior which, at this point in history, most clearly disturbs the public and which results in most extensive attempts to change their behavior.

If a somewhat modified version of Becker's concept is applied, criminals, alcoholics, and psychotics become "deviants" in this fashion:

(1) A group within American society, usually a majority, has defined the rules of acceptable behavior. (The fact that these rules vary from time to time hardly requires reiteration: homosexuality in America is a crime, in Greece it was not; abortion in America is a crime, in Japan it is not; believing that one is a Messiah in America is a psychosis, in ancient Jerusalem it was not.)

(2) The group who defines the rules has the power to enforce them and exercises this power. (*Who* has power obviously changes: strikes were illegal until the working class organized itself; polygamy was legal in Mormon communities until Utah became a state of the union; prohibitionists temporarily succeeded in labeling drinking a crime until they lost their influence as an effective pressure group.)

(3) The dominant group must catch the person breaking a rule and publicly label him as a deviant. ("Deviant" behavior—*if* undetected and unsanctioned—goes on all about us. The rich little old lady living off a private income can, for example, drink a quart of bourbon a day without being incarcerated as an alcoholic.)

Through this process by which a particular group in power enforces its conceptions of right and normal behavior upon others, millions of Americans have become officially branded as criminals, drunkards, or crazy people. In turn, an elaborate system of laws, police, prisons, drunk tanks, Alcoholics Anonymous groups, and mental hospitals have come into existence. Since the turn of the century, various schools of thought have arisen to explain the nature of the deviant and, therefore, to propose ways of curing or changing him. An elementary understanding of these differing approaches constitutes the first step in comprehending contemporary views concerning the personality of social deviants.

SOME CONTEMPORARY VIEWS ABOUT DEVIANTS

At the risk of oversimplification—since the opinions of various theorists about deviance often overlap and complement each other—one may contend that there are five schools of thought concerning deviance:

(1) *Deviance viewed as a reaction to anomie:* Beginning with Durkheim's classic work on suicide, many social scientists have regarded deviant behavior as a person's reaction to a social situation of strain, conflict, or disequilibrium (Durkheim 1951). Merton, for example, has suggested that American society demands that all people achieve "success" but that not all people have the same means for fulfilling this high, ill-defined goal. In reaction to this frustrating situation a disadvantaged American—say, a lower-class Negro—may react in a number of possible ways. He may retreat into the hallucinatory world of drugs or he may use disapproved means, such as running a numbers racket, to achieve the supposedly legitimate goal of "success" (Merton 1957). Cloward and others have applied this theory to the explanation of why particular groups (slum dwellers) are more susceptible to delinquency than are others (the upper class) (Cloward 1959). Such a distinctly sociological theory has many advantages: it can go far in explaining different rates of crime between various nations and in explicating differences in the incidence of mental disorders in various subsections of American society.

(2) *Deviance viewed as a reaction to subcultures:* A second, closely allied tradition has attempted to clarify another basic question: Why does a person who is subjected to some form of societal frustration choose one outlet as opposed to another? Sutherland and Cohen, among other scholars, have attempted to answer this issue (Sutherland and Cressy 1960; Cohen 1955). Sutherland stated: Criminals learn how to be criminal from other criminals. To the degree a person "differentially associates" with criminals, the more likely he is to learn the techniques and rewards of such behavior. This may seem a truism today, but in Sutherland's time his work effectively dispelled prevalent notions that all criminals were morons or biologically maladjusted. From Sutherland's point of view, criminals were simply normal people, undistinguished from others except by the fact that they had the opportunity to learn criminality. Cohen considerably refined this position by pointing to the existence of delinquent subcultures: gang societies with their own values. Further, he explained why such subcultures arise amongst lower-class boys who, in the Merton terminology, cannot possibly "succeed" in the usual middle-class milieu.

Scholars of this persuasion have served a useful function in describing such subcultures, whether they be those of the delinquent, the professional thief, the homosexual, or the drug addict. Their work has swept away several myths: particularly that such deviant groups are necessarily pathological or disorganized.

(3) *Deviance viewed as a process of "commitments":* Among the most sophisticated commentaries about deviance are the works of Becker (1963), Goffman (1961), Erikson (1966), and Schur (1965). They adhere to the basic point, as stated by Becker, that "deviance is . . . a consequence of the application by others of rules and sanctions to an 'offender'. The deviant is one to whom that label has successfully been applied" (1963:9). Several important consequences follow from acceptance of this premise. Schur points out, for example, that the very process of being stigmatized as a deviant may increase a young person's chance of committing himself to the form of behavior which powerful groups in society disapprove (Schur 1965). One relevant illustration: once a boy is labeled as a delinquent and is sentenced to a typical reform school, his chances of continuing in a criminal career considerably increase (McCord, McCord, and Zola 1959). Also, once an adult person is stigmatized as deviant, the possibility goes up that he will behave in the way society expects. As Goode has observed in comparing psychotics incarcerated in modern mental hospitals, as opposed to ordinary asylums: "When treated like 'crazy people', psychotics behave that way much more frequently" (1966:207).

Scholars of this school, then, concentrate upon the interaction between the deviant and his society. They recognize that the process of becoming a burglar, a homosexual, or a drug user represents various commitments: a progressive series of steps where the person gradually becomes initiated and then increasingly involved in his deviant world. Beyond this, writers like Becker (1963) and Goffman (1961) point out that the process of commitment is actually begun and often furthered by exactly those institutions designed to change deviants.

(4) *Deviance viewed as a psychological predisposition:* Commencing with Freud, many scholars have attempted to explain the unique backgrounds and psychological characteristics which predispose individuals to participate in deviant behavior. Often sociologists have regarded this approach as the polar opposite of the three schools of thought which have previously been discussed. Yet this need not be so. Indeed, in my opinion, it is only through a melding of psychology and sociology that we can create a truly comprehensive theory of deviance. A strictly sociological approach, for example, finds great difficulty in explaining the behavior of a child who—despite the fact that he lives in a slum neighborhood, associates with a gang and is exposed to criminal models—never becomes a delinquent. Equally, the pure sociological approach has difficulty in explaining the behavior of a person such as Charles Whitman, who recently killed 18 people from the tower of the University of Texas. Whitman had been a model of propriety, a Boy Scout, and a good student until he suddenly exploded into violence. To explain this man, we cannot turn to such social factors as

experience in a delinquent subculture. We are forced to go much more deeply into the particular personality of the individual before we can even hope to reach any explanation of his murderous tendencies.

Fortunately, a body of work is growing which, in the best of eclectic fashions, unites sociology and psychology in the study of deviance. Jackson's proposition of a "double-bind" theory of schizophrenia, Pittman and Snyder's investigations of alcoholism, the Gluecks' research on delinquency, and Cohen's recent attempts to unify theories of deviance and social control epitomize an interdisciplinary attack on the problems of deviance: a position which recognizes the importance of social interaction and yet probes deeply into the psychological predispositions of the deviant (Glueck and Glueck 1950; Jackson 1960; Cohen, 1966).

(5) *Deviance viewed as a biological predisposition:* A final question needs to be posed: since men obviously differ in their biological needs, capacities and structure, do these differences predispose an individual to a particular form of deviance? Some writers have attempted to reduce all deviant behavior into a neat biological explanation. Ordinarily, these doctrines have been swept away by subsequent research. A classic example would be Lombroso (1912) who described criminals as possessing particular, atavistic biological traits. Goring's more careful investigations demolished this theory (1913). Similar attempts to explain alcoholism as a biochemical defect or homosexuality in terms of a hormonal imbalance have met with little success.

Yet this certainly does not mean that the biological approach to the study of deviance should be totally abandoned. Psychotic behavior, in particular, seems most susceptible to some form of genetic and/or biochemical explanation. Kallman (1938), for example, has presented convincing evidence that a genetic factor operates in the production of schizophrenia. Osmond has postulated plausible theories relating psychoses to faulty metabolism of epinephrine (Osmond & Smythies 1954). Most recently, biochemists have suggested that a serotonin deficiency may help to explain psychoses (Wooley and Shaw 1954). (Interestingly, this hypothesis was derived from the finding that LSD interfered with serotonin functioning.)

I am not, by any means, suggesting that all personality deviations—even those as extreme as psychotic behavior—can be explained biologically. Distinguished scholars contend that the biological basis of even schizophrenia is unestablished (Jackson 1960). Nonetheless, this avenue of investigation certainly needs to be pursued in the future.

No single theory, it seems to me, has yet succeeded in explaining all forms of deviant behavior. Biochemical hypotheses seem useful in investigating psychoses, but irrelevant in explaining a Harlem gang. The subcultural approach may explain much of the behavior of delinquents, but adds little to understanding the lonely schizophrenic. The tradition which stresses the concept of anomie can help to explicate America's high rate of alcoholism, but does not inform us about what motivates a particular alcoholic to abandon his family in favor of skid-row life. Only a true "behavioral science"—one which unites biological, social, and psychological perspectives—can lead to a full comprehension of the personality of social deviants. I would like to outline the conclusions of one interdisciplinary attempt to accomplish this goal: the research based upon the Cambridge-Somerville experiment.

This experiment has been fully described in various publications; consequently, I shall only briefly summarize the nature of the project (Powers and Witmer 1951). In 1935 Dr. Richard Clarke Cabot of Harvard selected 650 boys from Cambridge and Somerville, Massachusetts. These boys came largely from lower-class environments. In an attempt to prevent delinquency, half of the children were given social counseling, medical and educational aid, and various other services. As a control group, the rest were left to the usual devices of the community.

In the progress of the project a vast fund of information was gathered about the boys. For a period of seven years social workers regularly visited their homes, psychiatrists and psychologists interviewed the children and their parents, physicians carried out physical examinations, and various social agencies contributed information about the boys and their families.

At the commencement of the project the boys averaged nine years of age. None of them had yet been officially labeled as criminal, alcoholic, or psychotic. Beginning in 1956 a systematic follow-up study of the adult behavior of the boys was begun (and continues today). The men were traced through a variety of community agencies—courts, public health clinics, Alcoholics Anonymous, social agencies, mental hospitals, and so on. Thus, on the one hand, measures of the adult deviant behavior of the men were secured and, on the other hand, the project had produced a mass of information about the background and personality of the men, which had been independently recorded when they were children. Approximately 40 percent of the men had a public criminal record, 10 percent had been labeled as alcoholic, and 5 percent had been incarcerated in mental hospitals. The remainder were outwardly nondeviant.

The experiment had several advantages for studying the development of deviant patterns: (1) Information had been gathered not only on the physical, but also the social and psychological natures and background of the men. (2) The information had been secured before the subjects had been officially defined as either "deviant" or as "normal." (3) Consequently, the usual retrospective bias which hinders many studies was eliminated (for example, since the alcoholics were studied long before they started drinking one could estimate the physical nature of the children before the excessive drinking took its physiological toll).

From the results of the Cambridge-Somerville study, it became quite apparent that the backgrounds and personality of the various deviants—before they became deviant—differed substantially. They differed not only from the conformist boys, but also, as children, the potentially violent criminal was a quite different person from the potential alcoholic or the withdrawn schizophrenic. Naturally, these conclusions must be hedged with many qualifications: this was a special sample selected in part because someone predicted potential deviance. Half the sample was originally chosen as "normal" boys and half as "potentially maladjusted" boys. These judgments were made by the boys' teachers, ministers, and others in close contact with them. The predictions were wrong: equal proportions of supposedly normal and supposedly abnormal boys did, in fact, become deviant. In itself, this is an interesting commentary on the "self-fulfilling" theory of deviance, that is, once labeled by his community as deviant, the child behaves in that fashion. In this case, the community judgment of the child was irrelevant to whether he became a violent criminal, alcoholic, or schizophrenic. The boys came from a particular social segment of one geographical area; and they lived through a special period of history when America experienced both a depression and a war. The results therefore should be taken with a grain of salt but they are suggestive of future interdisciplinary, longitudinal research. Keeping this caution in mind, let us briefly summarize the social psychology of three groups of deviants: violent criminals, alcoholics, and schizophrenics.

THE VIOLENT CRIMINAL

Any sophisticated discussion of crime must distinguish amongst the many types of people lumped under the label of criminal: they range from professional thiefs to kleptomaniacs, from psychopaths to those with a neurotic compulsion to pass bad checks, from one-time offenders to those who truly make a career of crime. It would be naive to assume that all such people have similar personalities (although, in a previous publication, I have pointed out that there are in fact some similarities in their backgrounds) (McCord, McCord, and Zola 1959). Because of this variability I would like to discuss only one type of criminal: the individual who commits acts of personal violence. Here again one would expect variations from those who commit a "crime of passion" to those who run a "Murder, Inc." Yet, surprisingly, similar themes appear to run through the background and character of violent criminals.

From the Cambridge-Somerville group, 14 men committed murder or assault with intent to murder. (Obviously, we are dealing here only with those who are caught and labeled for such crimes. No generalizations can, of course, be made about undetected murderers.) They contrasted in background and in nature with the noncriminals *and* with other criminals who eschewed violence. (In this and succeeding sections dealing with the Cambridge-Somerville study the contrasts reported are statistically significant beyond the .05 level.)

Specifically, the potential murderers came from homes devoid of love. Their mothers either neglected them utterly or tried to dominate every aspect of their life. Their fathers were generally highly aggressive men (who quite often had a criminal record themselves); they taught the child, at least implicitly, that one could express violent tendencies without inhibition. Typically, the parents disciplined the potentially violent criminals in an erratic manner: sometimes they overlooked a childhood transgression entirely while at other times they punished the same action with physically brutal methods. We found that the violent criminals did not necessarily emerge from a delinquent subculture, their intelligence was average, and they did not differ from others in any physical or neurological characteristics. As children, the potential murderers were often—outwardly—quite "normal" boys who did well in school. A few, however, exhibited sadistic tendencies, such as torturing animals.

From this evidence, several tentative conclusions concerning the personality of violent criminals can be offered. Typically, such people feel rage against their parents (and, by extension, towards other human beings). They often suppress these violent feelings, as children, underneath a facade of mildness. When, eventually, they do commit an act of extreme violence, their behavior can best be conceptualized as an act of symbolic revenge against their parents: a way of repaying the world for the beatings, cruelty, and domination which they experienced as children.

Sophisticated observers can easily diagnose these violent tendencies early in the life of the child. Counselors of the Cambridge-Somerville project, for example, had access to various psychological tests of the children. The counselors predicted that 16 boys would commit acts of aggression later in life. Of the 14 persons in the sample who had been judged as violent criminals 20 years later, only 1 was not included in this group of 16. Thus, our society may well have the knowledge to predict murder long before it happens.

THE ALCOHOLIC

As a group, alcoholics contrasted sharply with the violent criminals, in both original environment and personality (McCord, McCord, and Gudeman 1960). From the Cambridge-Somerville sample 51 men were identified as alcoholics. Operationally, we defined alcoholics as men who had either been arrested twice for public drunkenness, joined Alcoholics Anonymous, contacted a social agency for the treatment of alcoholism, or had been committed to a mental hospital on a diagnosis of alcoholism. (Clearly, such a definition omits the "secret" alcoholic. Also, since the measures were applied when the men were generally in their early 30s, the results do not necessarily pertain to men who become labeled as alcoholics later in life.)

In childhood, the typical alcoholic was reared in a middle-class family full of stress and quarreling. Usually, he had been raised by a mother who alternated between loving indulgence and overt rejection, who was likely to see herself as a "martyr" whose own interests she had begrudgingly sacrificed to the interests of her family and who tended to react to crisis in an escapist manner. The typical father of the potential alcoholic was a cool, distant man. In reacting to the pressure of a critical situation—such as the loss of a job—the father withdrew from reality (sometimes by drinking but equally often by such a simple mechanism as falling into a long sleep). The potential alcoholics did not differ biologically from other children, except that they more often exhibited signs of neurological disorder.

In childhood, therefore, the typical alcoholic lived in a highly ambivalent environment where, on the one hand, his mother sometimes indulged him but, on the other hand, would at times berate him and fail to come to his aid in critical situations. The boy's father talked disparagingly of the mother's failings. In addition, the father failed to fulfill the usual American image of male behavior. Rather than being "responsible" and "courageous," these fathers collapsed in the face of even the most minor threats.

During adolescence, the typical alcoholic reacted to his situation by creating a facade of self-reliant manhood. He tended to be aggressive, outwardly self-confident, and highly independent. In other words, the potential alcoholic accepted the American stereotype of masculinity and then played the role to the hilt. Underneath, however, psychological tests revealed that the prealcoholic felt inferior and desired to be cared for in a dependent fashion.

In adulthood, the prealcoholic searched for various channels to express his twin desires to be independent and to be loved. In our society it is most difficult for men to satisfy these contradictory desires. The imbibing of alcohol, however, is a major outlet available to such a person. When intoxicated he achieves feelings of warmth, comfort, and omnipotence: his desire to be loved is satisfied. At the same time he maintains his image of independence and self-reliance. The hard drinker in American society is pictured as tough, extroverted, and manly—exactly the masculine virtues the alcoholic strives to incorporate in his own self-image.

The potential alcoholic may manage to remain at a moderate stage of drinking for years, unless he goes through two other experiences:

(1) His desire to be dependent is severely frustrated. This may happen, for example, when a previously satisfying marriage in which the wife served essentially as a substitute mother collapses. If this occurs, such an incident has a profound meaning for the potential alcoholic: it indicates to him that adulthood, like childhood, is fraught with situations where his desire to be loved cannot be satisfied.

(2) His self-image as a highly independent man is severely attacked. Many events, such as the loss of a job, can undermine the potential alcoholic's desire to appear masculine and self-sufficient. Such an experience undermines the potential alcoholic's already precarious self-image.

If someone who is characterized by a potentially alcoholic personality syndrome passes through these stages, his destiny as an addict seems assured. In the Cambridge-Somerville experiment, for example, it was possible to isolate four types of backgrounds which correlated with adult alcoholism. Although no quantified prediction was made at the time, it is useful to note that 93 percent of those whose backgrounds were regarded as favoring alcoholism before middle age did in fact become alcoholics by this time (McCord, McCord, and Gudeman 1960:95).

THE PSYCHOTIC

Twelve subjects in the Cambridge-Somerville experiment were diagnosed as "functional psychotics" in their early manhood and incarcerated in a mental hospital. (The psychotics were given different labels: paranoid, schizophrenic, manic-depressive, and so on. We discuss them as a unit for two reasons: (1) The various labels are notoriously changeable; and (2) in fact, important differences between the different categories did not appear in our data.) The very small number of psychotics may well render the sample as atypical—at best, therefore, our conclusions concerning this group can only indicate some hypotheses to be tested in a longitudinal fashion on a larger, more representative group of psychotics. Nonetheless, even in dealing with this small sample, a distinctive pattern emerged which distinguished the psychotics from a control group of "normal" people, as well as from the alcoholics and the violent criminals (McCord, Porta, McCord 1962).

Typically, the psychotics were raised by a "smothering" mother: a mother who loved her son, guided his every activity, tried to protect him from the outside world, and, in general, dominated the child. In contrast, the fathers of the prepsychotics were passive, ineffectual men. None of them actively demonstrated love for the child. The fathers, in turn, were dominated by their wives who, reversing the usual pattern, made all the basic decisions for the family. Six of the pre-psychotic boys came from families with a history of mental disorder.

As children, the prepsychotics exhibited feelings of inferiority and loneliness. They had little to do with other children. When faced with a minor crisis (such as a bad grade in school), the prepsychotics tried to "run away" from the problem rather than by handling it in an effective, realistic fashion. None of the children, however, showed signs of the delusions and hallucinations which were to plague them later in life.

Thus, the prepsychotics were encouraged—indeed, forced—to become exceptionally dependent upon their mothers. Presumably, this led them to view dependent relationships as the normal form of human interaction and to develop a set of expectations that other human beings should and would treat them in the same fashion. Further, the prepsychotics were deprived of a stable masculine model: if they identified with their fathers at all, they were presented with a model of ineffectual escapism and passivity. Because of their sheltered existence, the prepsychotics lacked training in human interaction. They were not allowed to participate in a variety of roles, to gain knowledge of others' reactions, or to practice different techniques for mastering their environments.

When the prepsychotics reached manhood they were confronted with a number of situations—dating, marriage, military service, a career—which demanded that they assume independent responsibility for their lives. Because of their lack of training for responding to such situations, the prepsychotics responded with confusion, fear, and eventually by psychotic withdrawal. Thus, by this interpretation, a psychosis is fundamentally an attempt to reestablish an early dependent environment, the only kind of milieu for which the person has been conditioned and in which he feels relatively comfortable and secure. Uneducated to meet crises and, perhaps, unable to do so by a genetic predisposition, the psychotic crumbles in the face of his problems and seeks to return to a symbolic state of maternal love and domination.

Naturally, the results of this study could be interpreted in a number of alternative ways. One could argue that the parental characteristics are themselves genetically determined. By this interpretation parental behavior would not be regarded as independently causal, but merely as symptomatic of an underlying disorder affecting both parents and child. It might also be suggested that the child's behavior may determine, rather than result from, the parents' behavior. From this point of view the innate "peculiarities" of the prepsychotic child (such as his feelings of inferiority) elicit certain typical reactions from the parents. One could easily make a case, for example, that the withdrawn behavior of the child leads the mother to define her son as different and to respond to his inadequacies by becoming overprotective and smothering. (This "vicious circle" theory of deviance has great utility but it can hardly be stretched to explain how the prepsychotic child could provoke his father into playing a generally passive, submissive role in the family.) While not denying the validity of other possible theories, the evidence from this research tends to indicate that early familial relationships which heighten the person's dependent needs and destroy his ability to master his environment, particularly when linked with a presumed genetic predisposition, play a central role in promoting psychoses.

CONCLUSIONS

The various portraits I have drawn of violent criminals, alcoholics, and psychotics are in no sense intended as definitive statements concerning the personality structure of these various types of deviants. At best, the Cambridge-Somerville studies can serve simply to suggest new approaches both to the study of deviance and to public policy. Nonetheless, a review of these and other recent studies of deviants leads, it seems to me, to these conclusions:

On the Level of Scientific Research

(1) No single, overarching explanation for deviant behavior can be defended. Obviously, criminals, alcoholics, and psychotics are quite different people, although they happen to have in common the fact that society has publicly stigmatized them. Theories which help to explain one form of behavior, such as membership in a delinquent gang, have little, if any, relevance to explicating the biochemical basis of psychotic hallucinations. To advance our knowledge, more "middle-range" studies need to be conducted of particular forms of deviance: these, in turn, may lead to "middle-range" theories which clarify the nature of special types of behavior.

(2) To understand the entire process by which one becomes a particular sort of deviant, more longitudinal studies are required: ideally, studies which would commence in babyhood and end only with the death of the subjects. Only such studies can really go far in explaining why a person is predisposed to some form of deviant behavior; how he is initiated into it; and how, eventually, he may abandon it. The literature is replete, for example, with studies of delinquent gangs; yet we know relatively little about children before they join the gang, or of how the gang changes them, or why—as 65 percent do—children leave the gang (McCord, McCord, and Zola 1959).

(3) Contrary to the prevailing sociological view, the Cambridge-Somerville research suggests that certain personality characteristics predispose a person to choose a course of deviant behavior. Judging on the basis of the research concerning alcoholics and violent criminals, these personality characteristics are established rather early in life, as a reaction to experiences within the familial environment.

(4) Equally clearly, however, such a predisposition does not, in itself, determine the person's life. For example, the functional psychotics described in this paper emerged from a particular type of home and had an unusually high incidence of mental disorder in their ancestry. Yet, an additional 23 boys had, apparently, exactly similar backgrounds but did *not* become labeled as psychotics. In other words, while a predisposition to psy-

chosis may exist, any number of intervening factors—the person's adolescent experiences, marriage, career, and so on—apparently affect whether or not the predisposition blossoms into a true psychosis. This is a murky but very important area for future research: to determine the exact interaction between the person's basic character, presumably created in childhood, and the later social experiences which he undergoes.

(5) It is clear that closer collaboration between the different sciences is needed to advance our knowledge concerning deviants. The border lines between the different social sciences are, fortunately, evaporating but as yet there is very little collaboration between the physical and the social sciences. It seems evident, for example, that we cannot comprehend the various mental disorders unless social scientists, biochemists, geneticists, and psychiatrists ally themselves in a joint attack upon the problem.

On the Level of Public Policy

(6) Existing knowledge concerning social deviance must somehow be translated into public policy by lawyers, politicians, journalists, and the general public. On the basis of the Gluecks' research, we have good reason to believe that criminal behavior can be predicted very early in life (Glueck and Glueck 1959). If we assume that future research confirms this discovery, issues of both social and philosophical concern will inevitably arise. Perhaps the most difficult problem will be how American society should utilize this knowledge. What limits, under our tradition of freedom, should be imposed? We may soon be faced with the momentous choice between either intervening in a child's family, perhaps forcibly—and thus altering our conception of the parents' right to raise their own children—or of abstaining from intervention even though we *know* that certain types of environments basically injure children and eventually threaten society. All those concerned with directing public policy in American life must soon begin to face issues such as these; as yet, the debate has not even begun.

(7) Lawyers, in particular, must somehow find means of reconciling the American legal system with new knowledge derived from the social sciences. To pose just a few of the dilemmas: Does it make sense to apply the M'Naghten rule as a test of criminal responsibility when the Gluecks' research has demonstrated that criminality can be predicted many years before its onset solely from knowledge of forces which are totally independent of the rational (or irrational) condition of the criminal's mind at the moment of his offense (McCord 1960)? Is it reasonable to retain "drunk tanks" as means of controlling alcoholism, when we have every reason to believe that jailing a drunk increases his chances of addiction (Wallace 1965)? What social good is served by continuing to define homosexuality between consenting adults as a crime (Schur 1965)? Reform of the law must proceed hand-in-hand with advances in the behavioral science; other-

wise, our courts will continue to operate ineffectually on outmoded 18th century conceptions of human nature and "proper" behavior.

(8) Finally, it seems clear that existing social agencies should, ideally, devote much more of their energies to the prevention of truly serious forms of deviant behavior, such as murder, than they currently do. If we can identify the potential murderer early in life, it seems the height of irrationality to ignore him until only *after* he has taken his victims. Similarly, why should society condemn alcoholics to skid row or potential psychotics to mental hospitals, without attempting first to change those circumstances which lead to these forms of self-destruction. I am aware of all of the difficulties which accompany a policy of prevention: the very labeling of the individual as a possible deviant may increase his proclivities in that direction; the various behavioral sciences have not perfected exact methods of prevention; existing institutions already have too few resources to deal with their current problems; and the public has, as yet, little inclination to spend money for, say, child guidance clinics when it derives so much more vicarious satisfaction from watching the majestic process of the law in punishing a confirmed criminal.

These are no mean obstacles. Yet the resources and demonstrated flexibility of American society are sufficient for the task of implementing effective preventive policies. And I have sufficient faith in the rationality of mankind to believe that once the people are informed as to the true nature and origins of social deviance, they will eventually respond with humane and enlightened measures.

BIBLIOGRAPHY

ARIETI, SILVANO, "Schizophrenia," in *American Handbook of Psychiatry*, Vol. 1, Chap. 23. New York: Basic Books, Inc., 1959.
BECKER, HOWARD S., *Outsiders*, Chap. 4. New York: The Free Press, 1963.
CLOWARD, RICHARD A., "Illegitimate Means, Anomie, and Deviant Behavior," *American Sociological Review*, Vol. 24, 1959.
COHEN, ALBERT K., *Delinquent Boys*. New York: The Free Press, 1955.
―――, *Deviance and Control*. Englewood, Cliffs, N.J.: Prentice-Hall, Inc., 1966.
DURKHEIM, EMILE, *Suicide*. New York: The Free Press, 1951.
ERIKSON, KAI T., *Wayward Puritans*. New York: John Wiley and Sons, Inc., 1966.
GLUECK, SHELDON and ELEANOR GLUECK, *Predicting Delinquency and Crime*. Cambridge, Mass.: Harvard University Press, 1959.
―――, *Unraveling Juvenile Delinquency*. Cambridge, Mass.: Harvard University Press, 1950.
GOFFMAN, ERVING, *Asylums*. Chicago: Aldine Press, 1961.
GOODE, WILLIAM J., *The Dynamics of Modern Society*, p. 207. New York: Atherton Press, 1966.
GORING, CHARLES, *The English Convict*. London: His Majesty's Stationery Office, 1913.

JACKSON, DON, *The Etiology of Schizophrenia.* New York: Basic Books, Inc., 1960.
KALLMAN, FRANZ J., *The Genetics of Schizophrenia.* Locust Valley, N.Y.: J. J. Augustin, Inc., 1938.
KITSUSE, JOHN, "Societal Reaction to Deviance: Problems of Theory and Method," *Social Problems,* Vol. 9, 1962.
LEMERT, E. M., *Social Pathology.* New York: McGraw-Hill, Inc., 1951.
LOMBROSO, CESARE, *Crime, Its Causes and Remedies.* Boston: Little, Brown and Company, 1912.
McCORD, WILLIAM, "Review of Predicting Delinquency and Crime," *Stanford Law Review,* Vol. 13, 1960.
———, JOAN McCORD and IRVING ZOLA, *Origins of Crime.* New York: Columbia University Press, 1959.
———, JOAN McCORD and JON GUDEMAN, *The Origins of Alcoholism.* Stanford, Calif.: Stanford University Press, 1960.
———, JUDITH PORTA and JOAN McCORD, "The Familial Genesis of Psychoses," *Psychiatry,* Vol. 25, 1962.
MERTON, ROBERT K., *Social Theory and Social Structures.* New York: The Free Press, 1957.
OSMOND, H. and J. SMYTHIES, "Schizophrenia: A New Approach," *Journal of Mental Science,* Vol. 29, 1954.
PORTERFIELD, AUSTIN L., *Youth in Trouble.* Austin, Tex.: Leo Potisham Foundation, 1946.
POWERS, EDWIN and HELEN WITMER, *An Experiment in the Prevention of Delinquency.* New York: Columbia University Press, 1951.
SCHUESSLER, KARL F. and DONALD R. CRESSEY, "Personality Characteristics of Criminals," *American Journal of Sociology,* Vol. 55, 1950.
SCHUR, EDWIN M., *Crimes Without Victims.* Englewood Cliffs, N.J.: Prentice-Hall, Inc., 1965.
SUTHERLAND, EDWIN H. and DONALD R. CRESSEY, *Principles of Criminology,* 6th ed. Philadelphia: J. B. Lippincott Company, 1960.
SYME, LEONARD, "Personality Characteristics of the Alcoholic," *Quarterly Journal of Studies on Alcohol,* Vol. 18, 1957.
TANNENBAUM, FRANK, *Crime and the Community.* New York: McGraw-Hill, Inc., 1951.
WALLACE, SAMUEL, *Skid Row as a Way of Life.* Totowa, N.J.: Bedminster Press, 1965.
WOOLEY, D. W. and E. SHAW, "A Biochemical and Pharmacological Suggestion about Certain Mental Disorders," *Science,* Vol. 119, 1954.

20

Psychocultural Adaptation

George D. Spindler

INTRODUCTON

Like most of my colleagues in this symposium, I want to build some models and test their application. My concern is with those psychological processes most intimately linked with culture change, and I will be primarily concerned with change set in motion by the confrontation of divergent cultural systems. I regard this process as adaptive, and see the psychological and cultural dimensions as interdependent and inseparable.

The amount of work accomplished in this area is small; the unsolved problems unlimited. No more significant arena for interdisciplinary collaboration exists, given the world revolution we are all caught up in. Everything that we know or can learn from the behavioral sciences is potentially relevant. There is no special psychology of cultural change, since change is the normal state for any organism or system. What we must study are the acute phases of adaptation that are concomitant with the worldwide explosion of ideas, technology, and population in our time.

I will present three processes, and two of them may be seen as more limited dimensions of the first. They are: the interdependence of the psychological system and the cultural system, and the implications of convergence and divergence in these systems for adaptive change; the search for identity under conditions of radical change where there is confrontation between divergent systems; and the attempt to reestablish cognitive control under conditions of radical change where there is confrontation between divergent systems. I am less concerned with reviewing what we have done than with what we need to understand better. I illustrate the first process with a summary of a long-term, controlled comparative study of the Menomini Indians of Wisconsin and the Blood Indians of Alberta, conducted by Dr. Louise Spindler and myself (G. Spindler 1955; L. Spindler 1962; G. and L. Spindler 1965). The inferences I draw from this research are still in a raw state since the study is not yet complete. The second and third processes I shall relate to a response to radical change that has been termed reactive movements. I shall end with a methodological note.

First, some brief definitions. By *cultural system* I mean the ordering of persons into groups, roles, and statuses, the ecological adaptation, and the traditional patterns for behavior in all spheres of activity. I intend that this term shall cover what is usually referred to as social organization and culture. By *psychological system* I refer to those aspects of the organization of biopsychic resources within persons that are most intimately linked with the cultural system. These most intimate linkages I shall at times refer to together with the term *psychocultural system*. I am mindful of Anthony Wallace's criticism of an assumption of psychological uniformity and accept his stricture that complementarity in roles and their psychological concomitants are essential to the maintenance of social systems (Wallace 1961). But I also regard psychological and cultural systems as linked in the sense that certain psychological characteristics must be widely distributed within the membership of a cultural system if that system is to endure. These shared features include cognitive orientations, even specific patterns of thought, and control of affect.

Many anthropologists and some psychologists have researched aspects of the functional interdependence of psychological and cultural systems (though social system is usually substituted for the latter and with somewhat different meaning). Several reviews have covered this ground, particularly those of Alex Inkeles (1954, 1961), and De Vos and Hippler (1967). Especially relevant to the first process to be discussed and to the Menomini-Blood comparison to follow is the work of De Vos (1965) and Caudill and De Vos (1956). Since De Vos brings this work into focus in his paper in this symposium, I need only to make its relevance explicit.

De Vos demonstrates that among the Japanese the need for achievement appears to converge with that which operates in our own society, but that its concomitants are quite different. In the case of the Japanese, little value is placed on individualistic self-realization and much value placed on affiliation with familistic groupings to which one's success brings pride, a valence that fits the Japanese social structure. There is convergence in motivations, so Japanese succeed in America, and the Japanese nation has industrialized more rapidly than any other Eastern power (for this and other reasons), but the sources for the energy of this convergent motivation are quite different in the respective cultural systems.

MENOMINI–BLOOD COMPARISION

In the case of the Japanese, motivations converge with the success requirements, and this is also true of the Blood Indians. In the case of the Menomini the relevant psychological processes are radically divergent. It seems to me that the location and description of these kinds of relationships are of extreme importance both to the development of theories of psychocultural adaptation and to the practical exigencies of community development and transcultural communication. I have chosen the Menomini–Blood comparison because it is, to my knowledge, one of the very few controlled comparative studies available. The fact that both of these populations are American Indian may raise some eyebrows, for these are usually enclaved groups in a special dependent relationship to the external society. There are advantages as well as disadvantages involved in their choice as illustrative cases. I believe that examination of them produces hypotheses applicable elsewhere.

We did long-term field studies of these two tribal communities with a variety of techniques, including the Rorschach projective test, life history interviews, extensive participant observation, and a new form of eliciting technique that we have called the Instrumental Activities Inventory (G. and L. Spindler 1965). We also utilized ethnohistorical data to establish probable cultural and psychological continuities with the past. Our purpose is to compare the relationship between manifest cultural change (that is, changes in material culture, group membership, religious practice, subsistence, house and furnishings, and so on) and psychological adaptation, in both its perceptual-cognitive and affective dimensions.

For analytic purposes we divided the Menomini population into five acculturative categories, approximating real groups in the Menomini community. They are: the native-oriented, whose way of life exhibits identifiable continuities with the aboriginal past; the Peyote Cult, a stabilized form of reactive movement (a phenomenon I will discuss later) organized as a chapter of the Native American Church and representing a working synthesis of Christian and native patterns of belief and ritual; the ungrouped transitionals, who carry on some vestiges of the traditional culture but who are mainly poor White * in their life way; and the acculturated personnel, subdivided into lower status and elite. The former are adapted to a laboring-class standard of behavior and achievement. The latter are adapted to an achievement-oriented middle or even upper-middle class standard. They represent a radical departure, both culturally and psychologically, from the other segments of the Menomini population.

The psychological configuration of the native-oriented Menomini fits the cultural system of that group, and to the extent that system is a valid projection of the past, fits also the traditional Menomini culture (G. Spindler 1963). The key role expectations of this cultural system center upon restraint and control in interpersonal behavior, and dependence upon supernatural power rather than upon individual achievement. Competitive be-

---

* I will use "White" and "Whiteman" frequently to denote the dominant, usually broadly middle-class oriented, non-Indian population. I do not infer by this that non-Whites are necessarily excluded from membership in the dominant cultural system (though this is a moot point). I use these terms because the Indians use them.

havior, aggressive, self-gratifying achievement, boasting are all highly deviant behaviors. These behaviors are punished, and therefore controlled or eliminated by witchcraft. The key social control of this group is witchcraft, exercised, as Louise Spindler has demonstrated, not by deviant persons, but by respected and powerful elders (L. Spindler 1967), thus reinforcing the central values of the cultural system directly.

Our psychological data show clearly that the Menomini in the native-oriented group operate with deep internal controls over aggression. The people are inward-oriented, not achievement-oriented; they lack overt emotional responsiveness but are sensitive to the nuances of interpersonal relations; they are fatalistic in orientation, and exhibit quiet endurance under stress or deprivation, a pattern Louise Spindler has termed "latescent" (L. Spindler 1962). There is no marked evidence of anxiety or internal conflict, nor of free-flowing spontaneity.

The Peyotists are a special case. They are highly committed to the ideology and ritual of Peyotism stressing rumination about one's self, sins, and salvation, attainment of power individually and through partaking of Peyote in an acceptant mood. There is significant relaxing of controls over emotions and overt expression of feelings, with public crying during testimonials and rituals and bids for collective expressions of sympathy, which are offered freely.

The ungrouped transitionals are characterized by very uneven adjustments to the vicissitudes of transformational culture change. Some are striving for an orderly way of life, towards goals recognizable in the surrounding non-Indian community; others are withdrawn and mostly just vegetate; others go on destructive rampages, during or between drunks. Beating, murders, illegitimacy, dirt and disorder are a way of life for many in the latter group. The Menomini transitionals are like human populations everywhere who have lost their way; for them neither the goals of the traditional or the new culture are meaningful.

The acculturated, and particularly the elite, are radically different from any of the other groups. The roles they occupy demand punctuality, regular hours of concentrated work, orderly behavior and planning, pride in material possessions and economic status. The psychological data on them shows that they are emotionally open, but not disorganized. They utilize their emotional energy in the attainment of goals—personal success, material acquisition—approved of by middle-class persons in the surrounding communities. They are concerned about production and competition. They react to environmental pressures in a controlled but aggressive manner. They are also more anxious and tense than the native-oriented, but this anxiety is focused, rather than diffuse (as it is among the transitionals).

The acculturated Menomini deny their identity as Indians and specifically disclaim any relationship to "those Indians"—the members of the native-oriented group. Most of them do not speak their own language. The few who do rarely use it. Their homes and possessions are indistinguishable from those of Whites in nearby towns.

It is evident that the radical departure represented by the elite acculturated in the acculturative continuum of the Menomini occurs in both the manifest and psychological phases of adaptation. In order to "make the grade" on the terms of American middle-class culture the elite had to learn to stop being Menomini and learn how to be middle-class, achievement-oriented Americans. This reorganization occurred in depth and was not merely an overt adjustment. This statement applies whether a selective process requiring several generations or an adaptive process requiring only one is involved.

We hypothesized that this same personality reformulation would occur in other situations where the conditions of acculturation and culture change were approximately the same. We chose the Blood Indian reserve in Alberta because, in its external features, the Blood community in its milieu resembled the Menomini community in its milieu. In both cases there were the isolated reservation community, the prejudicial attitudes of surrounding Whites, and the unique feature of a highly productive industry using rich natural resources found within the boundaries of the reservation: in the Menomini case, the lumber industry and the mature forest; in the Blood case, the cattle and wheat growing and the productive high plains on their immense reserve in southern Alberta. We believed that the reason the acculturated Menomini elite represented a psychological as well as socioeconomic transformation was because success, recognizable on the terms of the dominant culture, was available to them, and in their own community, so that they could identify with the goals of this culture. Their psychological resources were organized around this identification. Their roles required it. The Blood, too, have this kind of opportunity. The elite ranchers and entrepreneurs among the Blood are no less successful on Whiteman terms than the managers of the lumber industry among the Menomini.

We approached the Blood community with the expectation that we would find an acculturative continuum ranging from native-oriented to the elite acculturated similar to that found among the Menomini. We did find significant socioeconomic differences within the population, and we were able to subdivide our sample into four socioeconomic categories on the bases of indices such as house type and condition, subsistence pattern and income, and possessions, ranging from a low status to an elite category. We were also able to distinguish two extremes in acculturation—old timers who spoke little or no English and identified with the traditional culture in many obvious ways, and youngsters who spoke good English (but still speak their native language), who had been in school for years, and identified overtly with little or nothing regarded by them as traditional. But the bulk of the population was culturally in the middle ground between these two extremes. Most of the Blood still speak their own language, most belong to (or as women are affiliated with) age-grade societies, most attend Indian kinds of social gatherings, such as the seasonal dances in Indian style put on by the age-grade societies. Various other manifestations of cultural unity in the direction of a relatively traditionalistic orientation are apparent, such as the popularity of the hand game, the annual attendance at the Sun Dance, the membership maintained in the sacred horn society and the women's Mohtokay, the observance of in-law avoidances.

Our first surprise, then, was that acculturative adaptation and socioeconomic status were not concomitant among the Blood, as they were among the Menomini. In the Blood population there was an observable, underlying, cultural homogeneity, which among the Menomini was notable for its absence.

The analysis to date, still incomplete, indicates that the underlying cultural homogeneity is accompanied by psychological homogeneity. I do not mean to say that the Blood are lacking in individualism. They are highly individualistic, and there are sharp individual differences in the profiles of emotional and intellectual adaptation. But these differences are not concomitant with discriminations along socioeconomic lines and there are some features that appear consistently. Success, on Whiteman terms, does not require psychological reformulation among the Blood, as it does among the Menomini, despite the apparent external similarity of the situations of the two populations.

The explanation for this marked difference in the two populations cannot lie in a single factor. There are differences in their relations with the respective governments, differences in the pressure of the surrounding non-Indian populations, some differences in time scaling. But in our opinion these differences are less accountable for the observed phenomenon than the fact that the Blood and the Menomini exhibit very different psychological configurations, and that of the Blood is convergent with the requirements of our cultural system in a critical area.

The native-oriented Menomini operate with deep internal controls over aggression, are not overtly responsive emotionally, and are not achievement-oriented. The Blood are openly aggressive, their emotions come comparatively quickly to the surface, they are vigorous in their perception of the world about them, they have high endurance but are not passive in their acceptance of fate, and they are much concerned with personal success and display. These features appear among rich and poor, the overtly less and more acculturated, and most notably among the young Blood (16 to 24 years) studied intensively by Anthony Fisher (1966).

These features fit the traditional cultural system of the Blood as we are able to reconstruct it from contemporary observation, from earlier ethnographies, and from ethnohistorical documents, as well as the contemporary community. The Blood were roving plainsmen, buffalo hunters, warriors.

They counted coup on their enemies, and boasted about it afterwards in public recitals. They were shrewd traders, and managed to keep the European fur merchants under control for over a century. And they took pride in acquiring and keeping many horses, in feeding many guests, in having a large tepee and good equipment. There were rich men among the Blood. Given the patterns of generosity, their wealth was (and still is) continuously redistributed. Their way of life differed greatly from that of the Menomini, and so did their psychology.

In the broad terms in which I am speaking now, it is apparent that the Blood personality features described are more congruent with the demands of our cultural system than those described for the Menomini. Our system demands the controlled use of aggression for personal achievement, and places high value upon personal success displayed in part through the acquisition of material goods.

It is our thesis, then, that some of the Blood are able to make an overt adaptation to the demands of the surrounding Whiteman cultural system without a corresponding psychological reformulation because they already have certain of the required psychological features. To be sure, there are marked differences between Canadian-American and Blood Indian psychological systems. The Blood are literal minded, pragmatic, and autonomous in ways that would be very deviant in the Whiteman system. And they are not conditional thinkers. The imaginative projection into *if* and *should* or *could* is rare. This latter feature is a handicap in economic development planning, and in the success striving of individuals. Nor am I making the claim here that whenever convergent features of the kind described are present there will be a successful adaptation, with or without psychological reformulation. If I did, I would have to explain the miserable condition of the Sioux, the Kwakiutl, and other Indian tribes as well as that of many other peoples about the world where parallels may be demonstrated. Adaptation is the result of many factors, and political, social, or environmental factors may outweigh the psychological potential for nondisruptive adaptation. But weighing all the factors, the best explanation for the observed fact that those Blood who are successful on Whiteman terms are psychologically not distinguishable from the rest of the Blood population and that no psychological reformulation in depth occurred among them appears to be in the terms that I have proposed. What is important is that given the opportunity, some of the Blood could make the adaptation at relatively low psychological cost and without losing their identity. The Menomini could not.

REACTIVE MOVEMENTS

This leads to the discussion of reactive movements. By reactive movements I mean those reactions to rapid change that sweep through whole populations and particularly where radically divergent cultural systems confront each other. Reactive movements are to be viewed as exaggerated forms of ordinary response to change. What happened with the Xhosa (South Africa) is an example.

> The Xhosa first showed their opposition to Europeans and their culture by fighting. There were a series of "Kafir Wars." In 1856–57 came the cattle-killing. Nongqawuse, a girl of 15 or 16, reported to her uncle (a diviner) visions of men who told her that people must consume their corn, cease to plant, and kill their cattle, and then, on a certain day, the ancestors would rise armed with guns and spears, and with the help of a whirlwind, Europeans would be swept into the sea. At the same time kraals would be full of cattle, and store-huts piled high with grain. Several other women and girls in different parts of the country reported similar visions. The people were also urged to destroy any material of sorcery they possessed. Many Xhosa, and a few Thembu, killed their cattle and refrained from planting. . . . Eventually vast numbers died from starvation, and others, weak and emaciated, entered the Colony in search of food and work. (Hunter 1936:159)

Melanesia has been the scene of reactive movements of an especially extreme type. One of the most spectacular was the Vailala madness which broke out in the Gulf of Papua after World War I.

> This movement involved a kind of mass hysteria, in which numbers of natives were affected by giddiness and reeled about the villages. So infectious was it that almost the whole population of a village might be affected at one time. The leaders of the movement poured forth utterances in "djaman" ("german"), which were in fact a mixture of nonsense syllables and pidgin English. Sometimes these were incomprehensible, but sometimes the leaders gave intelligible utterance to prophecies and injunctions. The central theme of the former was that the ancestors would soon return to the gulf in a ship, bringing with them a cargo of good things. The leaders of the movement communed with them by means of flagpoles, down which messages were transmitted to the base where they were received by those who had ears to hear—an obvious adaptation of the idea of a wireless mast. Elaborate preparations were made to receive the ancestors, and offerings of food for them were placed in special houses under the control of the leaders (Piddington 1957:739).

The prophets of the movement claimed that they were told by ancestors to have the people abandon the old ceremonies and burn the bullroarers and masks associated with them. This behavior is frequently associated with reactive movements of the more extreme type.

In a less dramatic form this is what the Manus did, studied by Margaret Mead at 2 periods 25 years apart. They virtually threw away their old culture in the interim, moving their houses from stilts in the lagoon to high ground, where they were laid out to conform to the plan of a military camp, changing their clothes, eliminating ceremonies, in order to take on what they perceived to be the Western pattern of behavior transmitted to them mainly by military troops in World War II (Mead 1956). Perhaps transformational culture change is always a reactive movement. The essential difference between the Cargo Cult reaction, of which the Vailala madness was one, and what the Manus did, is that the latter were more realistic in their procedures. But I believe that the underlying processes were parallel.

But these movements take many forms. Only some emphasize the discarding of old patterns of behavior and belief and the wholesale appropriation of new ones from the dominant cultural system. Another kind of reactive movement affects a synthesis of patterns and elements from both the dominant and subordinate cultural systems. This type is represented by the Peyote Cult among the Menomini. I quote from my own observations, written just after attending a number of meetings in the early 1950s.

> In the center of the tepee ground is a carefully laid fire of clean split staves, the ashes of which are swept at dawn into the form of a dove or mythical "Waterbird." . . . There is a half-moon altar of sand between the leader's place and the hearth, with a small pedestal for the "master" Peyote, and an indented line drawn along the top of the half-moon's ridge to symbolize the difficult and narrow path the Peyote member must follow through life.
>
> Christian symbols are apparent in the material structure and paraphernalia, as well as in the prayers and speeches. The tepee's poles represent Jesus Christ and the disciples. The staff is carved with crosses. The prayers and many of the songs are directed to Christ by name. The leader sometimes crosses his breast with his hand before lifting the blessed water to his lips in the sacred silver cup. The basic conception, premises, and procedures, however, are native North American, if not specifically Menomini.
>
> The ultimate declared purpose of taking peyote is to acquire the power with which it has been invested by the Creator (kese·maneto·w). This power cannot be obtained by merely consuming peyote. It comes to one only when the person approaches it in a proper state of humility and after long preoccupation and concentration. If the person is "filled with sin," the medicine will only make him ill, but once the peyote power is acquired, it will enable him to do wondrous things and serves to protect him from evil, including sorcery.
>
> The atmosphere during the first half of the meetings is serious, intense, and quiet. Toward midnight the voices become more emotional, and the drumming more rapid. The songs become a cry for help. The prayers become pleas for salvation, for aid and relief from fears, doubts and guilt feelings. Men pray aloud, give testimonials at certain periods in the ceremony, and frequently break into tears.
>
> Each man seeks his revelations and salvation, and gains power individually. There can be, it is claimed, no instruction in the Peyote way; this must come to the individual through his own experience in meetings. It is the Indian's own religion and was here "before Columbus," and must be learned the "Indian way." Much of this instruction is gained in visions, and some in dreams. But all members are aided in their striving for revelation, knowledge, and "cleansing of sins" by the efforts of the group in concert—through collective and individual prayers, singing, and drumming, and the maintenance of a sacred atmosphere throughout the meeting. (G. Spindler 1958)

These manifest aspects of the ritual in its setting, and of the behavior of the members, are reinforced by a highly standardized ideology, which most members can reproduce when stimulated to do so. To illustrate, the Whiteman has taken the land and everything in it from the Indian by force. As a consequence he is rich. His clothes look good, he has a good car, a big house, and so on, while the Indian is always poor, his children are ragged, he drives a rattletrap car and lives in a shack. But God compensates through the gift of peyote to the Indians. God gave them a medicine, a religion, a way of worship that is exclusive with them. So let the Whiteman have his material things. The Indian has a greater spiritual gift. Peyote is like a mirror held up before one's face. You learn about yourself. You can learn only by taking peyote, not through books, or from teachers. Peyote shows man the path to right living, cures him of sickness, gives him power to combat evil forces.

I have used the term "reactive movements" to include both the Cargo Cult and Peyote types to emphasize that the forms of reaction to the confrontation of divergent cultures (usually the Euro-American system and a technologically less developed one) labeled reformulative, nativistic, revitalizing, or reaffirmative by anthropologists, have underlying features in common. These features, as I see them, are the *search for identity* and the *attempt to reestablish cognitive control*. These processes become acute when there is a threat to the existing way of life, but are present (I hypothesize) as constants in all human beings as members of cultural systems. I will refer back to reactive movements as I discuss these processes.

Among many other writings, I have been particularly influenced by Anthony Wallace's works on revitalization movements (1956a), on mazeway reorganization (1956b), and on the psychological validity of componential analysis (1965); by Thomas Gladwin's paper on culture and logical process (1964); and Ward Goodenough's discussions of identity change (1963). For recent relevant developments that are influential (though in places tangential) to the lines of reasoning developed here, interested readers will be well advised to examine three recent issues of the *American Anthropologist:* one edited by John Gumperz and Dell Hymes (1964), another by E. A. Hammel (1965), and the third by A. Kimball Romney and Roy G. D'Andrade (1964); and Hymes' *Reader in Linguistic Anthropology* (1964).

THE SEARCH FOR IDENTITY

The search for identity can be regarded as the continuing attempt of persons to seek for reassurance that they are who they want to be. In a stable situation people want to be what their culture tells them they should be. Identity is more complex than this, however, and is composed in part of one's own image of self, in part of one's perception of others' estimates, in part of the rationalization of discrepancies between the two. The form of, and emphasis upon, these estimates, images, and rationalizations are provided for the individual by his culture. The specific individual content is always idiosyncratic within the limits of the form. A community or group shares a collective identity insofar as its members share images and perceptions of others' estimates because of their membership and refer to this membership as part of their self-image, for example, "I am a_____." One of the major ways in which the Euro-American cultural system affects the members of underdeveloped societies is that the basis for identity can be destroyed or badly damaged. Given the overwhelming technological superiority of the Western system, the reaction of less well-equipped peoples is frequently that they must be inferior and that this applies to their minds as well as to their artifacts and rituals. The words of one of my Blood Indian informants illustrate what I mean.

> You White people have a different kind of brain. Your mind is open to everything. You learn new things all the time. You're always inventing something. We Indians just lived. We took what God put on this earth in its regular form and just used it. We didn't change nothing. You White people, you're smart. The Indians are the lowest class of people on earth. We're even lower than the Black man.

It was clear that this Blood Indian was not what he wanted to be, and that he regarded himself and his culture as inferior. He is ambivalent, however. He hates himself for feeling inferior, envies the Whiteman and what he can do with his technology, but his pride keeps flickering and so he must derogate the Whiteman.

> You people come over here, teach us everything. The clothes we wear, the tools we use, the cloth, the seeds, all what we have and do—you people made it. We can't make nothing. Even those trees there you planted. That tree there (he pointed to a half-dead elm) —your people would look at it and say it had some disease. Then you would find out what caused it and cure it, or cut the tree down so the disease won't spread. Indian people would never think of that. They just live. We don't know nothing.
>
> You people made writing, so you don't have to remember nothing. I guess that's why you White people have such bad memories. I notice I can tell you something one day, if you don't write it down you don't remember it the next. We Indians remember everything that happens, even when we were little kids, it's all clear.
>
> Your people have dentists to fix your teeth. You need them because you eat dead food. Before you come over here we Indians all had good teeth. You people have Doctors that can cut a person up and put him back together again. You have factories to make cars, everything you need. You have scientists and they take what's in the ground and make atom bombs. Some day there's going to be a terrible war and you'll blow yourselves all up. Then maybe we'll be the only ones left around.

The identity of this thoughtful, articulate man, whose upbringing put him clearly within the framework of the traditional culture, but whose maturing years of experience made him into a marginal man of the classic type, is uncertain. He shares his uncertainty with his colleagues, and with multitudes of others whose cultural foundations of identity have been destroyed or seriously shaken by the world revolution.

I believe that we can see the linkage between the search for identity and reactive movements. The Xhosa looked for help from their ancestors, in their past identity and strength. They killed their cattle to show their faith in this miraculous salvation. In the Vailala madness the language (djaman), and the technology (the "wireless" poles, ship, cargo) are an attempt to identify with the alien cultural system. The destruction of ceremonial masks and abandonment of traditional ceremonies seem to be a way of symbolically declaring the old identity dead.

The Peyote Cult is somewhat different. Here a new identity is sought, one that turns its back on the old (Peyotists do not participate in the traditional Medicine Lodge or keep medicine bundles or bags), but does not turn completely toward the new. The Peyotists understand the blocks against their complete identification with the Whiteman's way, so they synthesize a new identity that is different from what is available in either the subordinate or dominant cultural system. The Peyote Cult is a workable rationalization of a conflict situation where the old identity is virtually destroyed but where the route to a new one that is wholly commensurate with the dominant cultural system is blocked.

COGNITIVE CONTROL

The search for identity is paralleled by the attempt to establish new cognitive controls. Perhaps the former is a part of the latter process.

The work of A. Irving Hallowell has provided us with essential background in his publications on the world view and cognitive orientation of the Saulteaux Ojibwa, beginning most specifically in 1937, with his "Temporal Orientation in Western Civilization and in a Preliterate Society," and continuing to the present. I quote Hallowell:

> The fact that the geographical locale of these Indians is on the Berens River in a subarctic physical environment, that they hunt, trap, and fish for a living ... is of less moment from the standpoint of our present discussion than the content of their beliefs about the nature of the surrounding world ... Their native belief system ... defines the ... environment in which they live, and no purely objective account would be sufficient to account for their behavior in relation to this physical environment (Hallowell 1942:5).
>
> Thunder Birds and monster snakes ... are important items in the behavioral environment of these Indians. Since from our point of view thunder is part of their physical environment and monster snakes are not, we might be

inclined to make a distinction between them. But if we do this we are making *our* categories a point of departure. (1942:6)

Human beings in whatever culture are provided with cognitive orientation in a cosmos; there is "order" and "reason" rather than chaos . . . if we pursue the problem deeply enough we soon come face to face with a relatively unexplored territory—ethnometaphysics. Can we penetrate this realm in other cultures? (1960:50)

All cultures provide a cognitive orientation toward a world in which man is compelled to act. A culturally constituted world view . . . by means of beliefs, available knowledge and language, mediates personal adjustment to the world through such psychological processes as perceiving, recognizing, conceiving, judging, and reasoning. It is a blueprint for a meaningful interpretation of objects and events . . . (1963:106)

Mary Black of Stanford University has just finished a study of the Ponemah Chippewa of Red Lake, Minnesota (the Chippewa are stateside Ojibwa) that applies ethnoscientific methods to the problems raised with such perceptiveness by Hallowell on the basis of less replicable but more comprehensive research procedures. A condensed description of the ethnoscientific methods she used is likely to be misleading. Her theoretical position and methodology stem most directly from the work of Charles Frake (1962) and Duane Metzger and Gerald Williams (1963). She applied to her informants in 500 hours of interviewing a controlled eliciting procedure using native terms for the purpose of getting from them with high reliability a Chippewa taxonomy (classification system) of living beings, with particular attention to the "persons" category. Her results confirm a substantial portion of Hallowell's descriptions of the same categories and groupings in the Saulteaux Ojibwa belief and thought, and deviate from them in interesting ways. Most important for our purposes, the Ojibwa taxonomy for living things arranges objects, such as certain stones (at certain times), spirits, men, and animals, in a way that is very divergent from the Western taxonomy and that is arranged in one of its most consistent and meaningful forms according to the Chippewa belief in possession and exercise of "power" by living entities and the "respect" accorded to them on the basis of this power. This power we would regard as "supernatural" power, and in fact our ethnographies of people like the Chippewa and Ojibwa (such as the Menomini) use this term. But in the Chippewa-Ojibwa system there is no supernatural in the sense we use it. This is our imposition of meaning upon their belief system.

The important inference is that each psychocultural system is made up in part of a unique way of viewing, sorting, and synthesizing the things and events believed to exist in the world. This is the cognitive process. Cognitive control is the maintenance of the organization of this process. The concept as used here is related to Anthony Wallace's "Principle of Conservation of Cognitive Structure" (Wallace 1961:161), but differs in the wider scope of its application, since the conservation model is addressed to the failure to abandon particular views of reality even in the face of direct evidence of inutility rather than to the appropriation of new cognitive elements or the synthesis of new and old. The concept of cognitive control is also related to Leon Festinger's (1957) inference of drives to reduce "cognitive dissonance." The term "cognitive control" has been used by others, notably G. S. Klein (1962), whose work centers attention upon typical individual strategies of perceiving, remembering, and thinking, and particularly upon tolerance for unrealistic experience and upon flexible-constricted control. (I am indebted to Robert Koff [1966] for calling my attention to Klein's work in a discussion of this paper.) Klein's work places cognitive control in the general framework of psychoanalytic ego psychology, and does not relate the concept to cultural process.

It should be noted that I am not making the assumption that a taxonomic system or any totality of systems in a single culture is equivalent to cognitive structure. The relationship between cognitive structure and taxonomies elicited by ethnoscientific methods is a matter of considerable discussion. I am making the assumption that such taxonomies are a significant dimension of the cultural materials with which we perceive and think, and that they may well be one of the best indices to cognitive convergence and divergence in psychocultural systems.

I hesitate here, for we are far from being able to put thinking processes and cultural forms together with anything more than metaphors, and when we add affect and motivation the complications seem unbearable. Nevertheless, we cannot avoid the inference that one of the central processes in the adaptation to the impact of an alien cultural system must be cognition, in its broadest sense, including viewing, sorting, and synthesizing in order to produce a relevant response.

The linkage between cognition and culture is indeed intimate, if we accept Ward Goodenough's definition of culture which was given in a pioneering paper that contributed significantly to the development of ethnoscience and cognitive anthropology: ". . . it does not consist of things, people, behavior, or emotions. It is rather an organization of these . . . It is the forms of things that people have in mind, their models for perceiving, relating, and otherwise interpreting them." The perceiving, sorting, and synthesizing is done in the brain, as Dr. Pribram makes clear, but the "form of things" is cultural insofar as these forms are shared. Problems are solved in predictable ways in given communities, choices are made and there is a limitation upon their range, because man thinks in the categories and with the content provided by his culture.

Given the uniqueness of the cognitive process in each psychocultural system, and the central role of cognition in instrumental choices leading to action, then one of the central processes in culture change is released when a "native" thinker is confronted with an alien and dominant cognitive system. The problem is essentially simple to grasp (but not simple for the "native" who has to solve it); that is: how to learn to think in such a way as to act effectively in the framework of perceived reality imposed by the new cultural system when the old cognitive organization is very divergent from the new one. It may be impossible to move from one to another while keeping the old one intact or even partially intact.

A seemingly very acculturated and very successful Blood Indian once told me, "I have to think about some things in my own language and some things in English. Well, for instance, if I think about horses, or about the Sun Dance, or about my brother-in-law, I have to use my own language. If I think about buying a pickup truck, or selling some beef, or my son's grades in school, I have to think in English." His thought language was parallel to his role taking. He was bilingual, bicultural, and bisected. His life was segmentalized in both its external and internal dimensions. Blackfeet and English are separated by great lexical and semantic differences. His two languages were learned in very different social contexts. The linguistic divergence appears to represent, in this case, cognitive divergence. That he mastered both segments of these divergent systems so well is a tribute to his great intelligence and energy. His mastery also reflects the general convergence in affect controls and success-display orientation described previously, and his motivation to succeed in both worlds. The latter is of special significance in the context of our discussion of the Menomini-Blood differences. Blood were more frequently motivated to succeed in both dimensions, and despite the difficulties inherent in this form of segmental adaptation, did so. We cannot long divorce cognition from motivation in our attempts to understand psychocultural adaptation.

A segmentalized adaptation of this kind is possible for some persons from some cultural systems, particularly where motivational as well as cognitive convergences may be operating. Further, since the language usages and the semantic contexts of this usage are role defined in limited instrumental social contexts the whole system need not be learned; consequently, all potential divergencies will not be encountered. We need to know much more about the conditions of successes and failures in segmentalized adaptation. It is probably true, however, that the human brain is not capable of handling effectively all of the complexities produced by attempts to resolve sharply divergent cognitive systems as whole systems and that the same stricture applies to certain types of segmental resolution.

As Wallace (1962) points out, there is probably a fairly definite limit to the complexity of conceptual discriminations possible for human beings. (See also his paper in this symposium.) Native cognitive systems are probably usually more complex than we realize them to be for we have dealt so far mostly with the byproducts of the cognitive process (artifacts, rituals, kinship systems, and so on) and not with the structure and process of thinking itself. Confront a native who is already operating with a complex cognitive system with another that is equally complex and divergent in a conflicting way and the result may be failure—a breakdown in the ability to think at all. His cognitive control may be threatened and disaster face him, for without cognitive control man is doomed. He has no ability to predict, to plan, to choose, to put first things first, to keep his wits about him.

Some of the brighter persons learn, as a number of Blood have done, to handle both systems on a segmentalized basis, but probably less efficiently than if they were handling only one. This process is very difficult under circumstances where very wide divergencies exist between systems, or where motivation is lacking to master the problems created by the divergence.

In other cases, perhaps where the confronting systems are wildly divergent or discongruent, a form of collective madness temporarily ensues—as in the Cargo Cult. Attempts are made to eliminate crucial reference points of the old cognitive system at the same time an attempt is made to secure the accoutrements of a new one miraculously. Cognitive complexity and conflict are therefore temporarily reduced and control temporarily established, or at least the illusion of control is established. Some such formulation is tempting at least. The notion that reactive movements of the type described are attempts at reestablishing cognitive control is not unrelated to the notion that they are attempts at establishing a new identity. Perhaps these are different dimensions of the same process, or different terms for the same dimensions.

In the Menomini Peyote Cult, cognitive control is reestablished by producing a new psychocultural system from the materials of both the established and the new systems. This will work in limited areas of confrontation, but probably not in all. The Menomini Peyotists do well at synthesis in the area of ritual and beliefs about power and supernatural beings, salvation and sin. They do not do any better than any of the rest of the Menomini in the area of occupational or domestic management. The cognitive components of the roles that are instrumental in our cultural system are so discongruent with theirs that there is no way to synthesize them with the equivalent components in the native cultural system. Nevertheless, the control established by synthesis in the domain of the Peyote Cult serves to reduce anxiety and increase security. Without the Peyote Cult many of the Menomini Peyotists would be highly anxious, and in the case of one definitely psychotic member, participation in Peyote rituals temporarily seems to make him "sane." I believe that his insanity is in part a product of culture conflict, a process we now can translate into confrontation of discongruent cognitive systems, and that the temporary reestablishment of cognitive control relieves the condition.

The attempt to establish and maintain cognitive control is a universal and constant process in human life. Any cultural system, in fact, may be seen as the product of such an attempt over a period of time.

When divergent cognitive systems confront each other in the perceiving, thinking, and action of members of the confronting cultural systems, the need for cognitive control is accentuated because the effectiveness of this control is challenged as well as the very assumptions about reality upon which it is based.

Reactive movements are merely acute forms of a universal process. We might even characterize the native-oriented Menomini as a reactive movement in this sense. The members of this group have maintained barriers against the penetration of the alien system by reaffirming the traditional culture as they understand it in order to maintain cognitive control by exclusion. Heretofore we have been inclined to see the culture of this group as consisting of elements from the aboriginal culture that survived due to the sheer inertia of cultural forms. But this was a description of a state, not an exploration of process. The cognitive control model helps us to explain the staying power of cultures as well as their transformation.

Present-day Pueblo societies in our own Southwest, Hutterite societies in our West and in Canada, Amish communities in the East are all interpretable as intensive, long-term attempts to maintain cognitive control under conditions of discongruent confrontation. The Birch Society appears to be essentially a cognitive-complexity-reducing reactive movement. Its ideology eliminates many of the complications of twentieth-century life. We might hypothesize that modern youth who do not wash, who wear peculiar clothes, and disregard amenities are engaging in a kind of reactive movement the function of which is to establish cognitive control by reducing the number of role demands and avoiding complex expectations directed at young people by adults. Doubtless they are also searching for identity. Possibly when identity is found, cognitive complexity is reduced, and control becomes possible. Perhaps the pervasive belief in flying saucers and visitations of beings from other planets is a kind of reactive movement—an attempt to maintain a cognitive control we feel to be threatened by our perplexing world. Our own problems are too painful, too complex, too incapable of solution. The way out is to introduce a totally alien dimension into the equation, where our towering technology is seen as child's play by beings of infinite intelligence and skill. They will save us, or destroy us, but at least we will not have to solve our own problems. If a Cargo Cult, why not unidentified flying objects? (I want to make it clear, however, that this interpretation of the belief in extraterrestial visits may be valid even if there are "real" flying saucers.)

SUMMARY

The central thesis running through the three parts of this paper is that of the consequences of the confrontation of divergent psychocultural systems. In the discussion of the Menomini-Blood comparison, emphasis was placed on the most global dimensions of this process—the broad motivational and affective factors that influence adaptation to the conditions imposed by a divergent and dominant psychocultural system. In the discussion of the search for identity and the attempt to establish cognitive control, emphasis was placed on two processes that fall within the broad framework established in the prior discussion but which stress the intellectual processes. Identity was described as a central aspect of all psychocultural systems and one that is decisively challenged in confrontations of divergent systems. Reactive movements, a general class of intensified response to divergent confrontation, can be seen as attempts, in varying degrees of intensity, to establish a new identity commensurate with the new conditions of life, or to reassert the validity of the old identity. Cognitive control, it was asserted, is a central process in the establishment and maintenance of all psychocultural systems. Identity may be considered (tentatively) as a dimension of cognitive control. Reactive movements can then be seen as accentuated attempts to regain cognitive control that is threatened by the confrontation of divergent psychocultural systems. Whether reactive movements ensue or not, however, the attempt to retain cognitive control can be seen as a central adaptive process.

The adaptive processes involved in reestablishing cognitive control (or maintaining control under threat) appear to be: (1) through attempts at exclusion of divergent cultural materials, as in the Menomini native-oriented group; (2) through synthesis of materials from the confronting systems in selected domains, as in the Menomini Peyote Cult; (3) through segmentalization of materials from the confronting systems as appropriate to role behavior in limited social contexts, as in the case of the bilingual Blood; (4) through attempts at more or less total rejection of the established psychocultural system and a sweeping embrace of the new, as in the Cargo Cult (an extreme form of the process), or in the adaptation of the Manus (a more widespread form). Striving for order and reduction of complexity and conflict, as well as the rationalization of perceptions, beliefs, and symbols to the form of the new identity, appear to be underlying processes.

In conclusion, it is important that we regard what I have discussed as exploratory models. They appear to have some explanatory power in the chosen contexts in which I have applied them. Despite the assertive tone of my analysis (a style that has its semantic advantages), I must remind the reader that the unsolved logical and empirical problems are legion. We do not really know much about cognition in the context in which I have placed it, though the psychologists have much more to say about it in other, more limited (and more manageable) contexts, than I have had opportunity to indicate. We are not by any means certain about what the upper limits of conceptual discrimination and mastery of cognitive complexity in the human brain may be. Dr. Pribram's research may give us a needed answer here. Nor do we know nearly as much as we need to know about the relationship of language to cognition, or the interdependency of language and nonlinguistic symbols, taxonomic systems, and cognition. Though again, psycholinguists have more to say about these relationships than I have had opportunity to indicate. And I have left almost entirely aside any consideration of social interaction excepting to imply, as Frake makes explicit (1961) with respect to taxonomies, that cognitive structures and the forms of their use are learned in and are fulfilled in social contexts. Surely we need the help of social psychology and sociolinguists here. The analytic structure I have tried to develop is entirely open-ended and provides merely an orientation towards further study.

A METHODOLOGICAL NOTE

Assuming that these problems are significant as well as researchable, then we are faced with the selection of research procedures. I suggest that there is not and never will be a good substitute in anthropological research for long-term participant observation, for the conditions of everything we want to know about can only be observed *in situ,* and with as little alteration as possible. But given this somewhat pious utterance, we then must ask, "what next?" Our own approach has been to use projective instruments to elicit responses from which cognitive as well as affective and motivational processes may presumably be inferred. The Rorschach is such an instrument. Our use of it is tangential to the conventional applications of it as an instrument for personality assessment of individuals in our own society. We are using standardized but culturally ambiguous stimuli to elicit culturally variant responses. The results are cryptic and difficult to assess, but seem to furnish data that are sufficiently abstracted from the highly unique cultural-relevant response (as in life histories) to permit controlled comparisons of culture cases. We have recently developed another technique which we have termed the Instrumental Activities Inventory, which presents stimuli in the form of line drawings intended to elicit choices of possible social actions leading to socially recognizable goals, and elicit the rationale concerning the relationships between these instrumental means and the ends to be gained. The instrument must be redrawn for each culture area in which it is used, for, in contrast to the Rorschach, it is imperative that the eliciting stimuli be culturally relevant. We have used this procedure with the Blood, and last summer with the Mistassini Cree, and Robert Edgerton pioneered a related and prior technique with our Menomini sample (Goldschmidt and Edgerton 1962). We see the results as complementary to Rorschach-elicited data. The Rorschach elicits, it might be said, from deep inside the cognitive and affective process, where goods from the storage place called the unconscious are continually being brought up. The Instrumental Activities Inventory elicits from the area of cognition most directly linked with social decision making.

Some of our colleagues and students are beginning to use ethnoscientific procedures to elicit data relevant to problems of cognitive control and culture change. The precision of this approach has merit. The greatest limitation is in the difficulties in joining affective and motivational forces, as well as problem-solving processes, with the essentially static cognitive structures presumably represented by taxonomies elicited (for example) about ladino weddings, disease symptoms, plants, beer making, or kinship. We suggest that one useful approach may be to combine a projective methodology with that of ethnoscience, or more broadly speaking, with that of formal ethnography.

One of the great challenges for the scientific study of man today is to devise ways of describing and analyzing his mind—the structure and process that stands behind the material forms of culture and social action. The dramatically diverse psychocultural systems created by man out of his incredible capacity for making reality out of fantasy (and vice versa) are disappearing under the crushing avalanche of Western technology, science, industrialization, and education. There is no greater task in psychological anthropology (or anthropological psychology) than the scientific study of these esoteric systems and their variant modes of adaptation to this advance.

BIBLIOGRAPHY

BLACK, MARY, "An Ethnoscience Investigation of Ojibwa Ontology and Worldview." Unpublished Ph.D. dissertation, Stanford University, 1967.

CAUDILL, WILLIAM, and GEORGE DE VOS, "Achievement, Culture and Personality: The Case of the Japanese Americans," *American Anthropologist*, Vol. 58, No. 6, 1956, pp. 1102–1126.

DE VOS, GEORGE A., "Achievement Orientation, Social Self-Identity, and Japanese Economic Growth," *Asian Survey*, Vol. 5, No. 12, 1965, pp. 575–589.

———, and ARTHUR HIPPLER, *Cultural Psychology: Comparative Studies in Human Behavior.* In press.

FESTINGER, LEON, *The Theory of Cognitive Dissonance.* New York: Harper & Row, Publishers, 1957.

FISHER, ANTHONY, "The Young Blood Indians and Their Perceptions of Cultural Alternatives." Unpublished Ph.D. dissertation, Stanford University, 1966.

FRAKE, CHARLES, "The Ethnographic Study of Cognitive Systems," in Thomas Gladwin, William C. Sturtevant (eds.), *Anthropology and Human Behavior.* Washington, D.C.: The Anthropological Society of Washington, 1962.

———, "The Diagnosis of Disease Among the Subanum of Mindanao," *American Anthropologist*, Vol. 63, No. 1, 1961, pp. 113–132.

GLADWIN, THOMAS, "Culture and Logical Process," in Ward Goodenough (ed.), *Explorations in Cultural Anthropology*, pp. 167–178. New York: McGraw-Hill, Inc., 1964.

GOLDSCHMIDT, WALTER, and ROBERT EDGERTON, "A Picture Technique for the Study of Values," *American Anthropologist*, Vol. 3, No. 1, 1961, pp. 26–45.

GOODENOUGH, WARD H., *Cooperation in Change.* New York: Russell Sage Foundation, 1963.

GOODENOUGH, WARD H., "Cultural Anthropology and Linguistics," in Paul L. Garvin (ed.), *Report of the Seventh Annual Round Table Meeting on Linguistics and Language Study.* Georgetown University, Monograph Series on Language and Linguistics, No. 9, 1957, pp. 167–173.

GUMPERZ, JOHN J., and DELL HYMES (eds.), *The Ethnography of Communication,* special issue of *American Anthropologist,* Vol. 66, No. 6, Part 2, 1964.

HALLOWELL, A. IRVING, "Temporal Orientation in Western Civilization and in a Preliterate Society," *American Anthropologist,* Vol. 39, 1937, pp. 647–670. Reprinted in A. I. Hallowell, *Culture and Experience,* pp. 216–235. Philadelphia: University of Pennsylvania Press, 1955.

———, *The Role of Conjuring in Saulteaux Society.* Philadelphia: University of Pennsylvania, 1942.

———, "Ojibwa Ontology, Behavior, and World View," in S. Diamond (ed.), *Culture in History.* New York: Columbia University Press, 1960. Reprinted in Bobbs-Merrill Reprint Series in the Social Sciences, A101.

———, "The Ojibwa World View and Disease," in I. Galston (ed.), *The Image of Man in Medicine and Anthropology.* New York: International Universities Press, Inc., 1963.

HAMMEL, E. A., (ed.), *Formal Semantic Analysis,* in Special Publication of the *American Anthropologist,* Vol. 67, No. 5, Part 2, 1965.

HUNTER, MONICA, *Reaction to Conquest.* London: International Institute of African Languages and Cultures, 1936.

HYMES, DELL, *Language in Culture and Sociology: A Reader in Linguistics and Anthropology.* New York: Harper & Row, Publishers, 1964.

INKELES, ALEX, "National Character and Modern Political Systems," in F. L. K. Hsu (ed.), *Psychological Anthropology,* pp. 172–208. Homewood, Ill.: The Dorsey Press, 1961.

———, and D. J. LEVINSON, "National Character: The Study of Modal Personality and Sociocultural Systems," in G. Lindzey (ed.), *The Handbook of Social Psychology,* pp. 977–1020. Reading, Mass.: Addison-Wesley Publishing Company, Inc., 1954.

KLEIN, G. S., "Tolerance for Unrealistic Experience: a Study of the Generality of Cognitive Control." *British Journal of Psychology,* Vol. 53, 1962, pp. 41–55.

KOFF, ROBERT H., "The Relationship Between Two Cognitive Controls and Selected Voluntary and Involuntary Behavior." Unpublished Ph.D. dissertation, University of Minnesota, 1966.

MEAD, MARGARET, *New Lives for Old.* New York: William Morrow & Co., Inc., 1956.

METZGER, DUANE and GERALD E. WILLIAMS, "A Formal Analysis of Tenejapa Ladino Weddings," *American Anthropologist,* Vol. 65, No. 5, 1963, pp. 1076–1101.

PIDDINGTON, RALPH, *An Introduction to Social Anthropology,* Vol. II. London: Oliver and Boyd, Ltd., 1957.

ROMNEY, KIMBALL A., and ROY G. D'ANDRADE (eds.), *Transcultural Studies in Cognition,* a Special Publication of the *American Anthropologist,* Vol. 66, No. 3, Part 2, 1964.

SPINDLER, GEORGE D., *Sociocultural and Psychological Processes in Menomini Acculturation.* Berkeley, Calif.: University of California Publications in Culture and Society, Vol. 5, 1955.

———, "Personal Documents in Menomini Peyotism," in Bert Kaplan (ed.), *Primary Records in Culture and Personality,* Vol. II, No. 13. Madison, Wis.: University of Wisconsin Press, 1958.

———, "Personality, Sociocultural System, and Education Among the Menomini," in G. Spindler (ed.), *Education and Culture*, pp. 351–399. New York: Holt, Rinehart, and Winston, Inc., 1963.

SPINDLER, GEORGE D., and LOUISE SPINDLER, "Researching the Perception of Cultural Alternatives: The Instrumental Activities Inventory," in Melford E. Spiro (ed.), *Context and Meaning in Cultural Anthropology*, pp. 313–337. New York: The Free Press, 1965.

SPINDLER, LOUISE S., *Menomini Women and Culture Change*, American Anthropological Association, Vol. 64, No. 1, Part 2, Memoir 91, 1962.

———, "Menomini Witchcraft," in DeWard Walker, Jr., (ed.), *American Indian Witchcraft*. (To be published in 1968)

WALLACE, ANTHONY F. C., "Revitalization Movements: Some Theoretical Considerations for Their Comparative Study," *American Anthropologist*, Vol. 58, No. 2, 1956[a], pp. 264–281.

———, "Mazeway Resynthesis: A Biocultural Theory of Religious Inspiration," *Transactions of the New York Academy of Sciences*, Vol. 18, Series 11, 1956[b], pp. 626–638.

———, *Culture and Personality*. New York: Random House, Inc., 1961.

———, "Culture and Cognition," *Science*, Vol. 135, No. 3501, 1962, pp. 351–357.

———, "The Problem of the Psychological Validity of Componential Analysis," in E. A. Hammel (ed.), *Formal Semantic Analysis*, Special Issue of the *American Anthropologist*, Vol. 67, No. 8, 1965, pp. 229–248.

21

Achievement and Innovation in Culture and Personality

George A. De Vos

INTRODUCTION: INSTRUMENTAL AND EXPRESSIVE BEHAVIOR IN SOCIAL CHANGE [1]

Today rapid social change is taken for granted. Forces of change are manifestly at work from within as well as without in every culture. No matter how isolated previously, societies throughout the world are now gradually being absorbed in an interrelated world society with a pervasively secularized set of implicit values. Even the seemingly disparate and clashing ideologies of socialism and capitalism when examined closely are found to be based on similar premises and to have similar goals. They differ only in the economic and political means advocated for their realization.

Although the major forces at work in this gradual, worldwide homogenization of values are economic and political in nature, an examination of change in economic or political terms alone cannot sufficiently explain what occurs in particular cultural settings. Economic or political theory cannot by itself account for the peculiarly different responses of individual cultures to the economic and political forces pressing them toward accelerated social change. The nature of the perceived challenge and the adequacy of the response are highly different depending on the culture. To the objective observer, it becomes quickly apparent that both the previous cultural history and the psychological peculiarities of a people must be considered significant as forces impeding or facilitating change. What is sometimes less apparent is that these peculiarities have to do more with "expressive" than with "instrumental" aspects of culturally determined behavior.

---

[1] Instrumental behavior is directed toward a goal. Expressive behavior is an end in itself; its "meaning" is to be found in the activity itself (*cf.* Parsons, Talcott, and Bales, Robert, *Family Socialization and Interaction Process*, New York: The Free Press, 1955).

It has been relatively easy for anthropologists to classify, categorize, and conceptualize the instrumental aspects of culture. Man has used considerable ingenuity and rationality to cope with the essential difficulties of any of the highly diverse geographic or social environments within which he has found himself. Whatever the culture, much of man's behavior becomes understandable when one views it as directed toward realizing some understandable economic or social-political end. It has been much harder to comprehend man's behavior cross-culturally when various forms of expressive behavior are considered.

In addition to adapting himself rationally to the demands of his natural and social environment, man must also be considered a peculiarly irrational animal. He creates for himself curious problems and complexities uncalled for by any direct, simple need for either survival or social dominance. Expressively, man is a religious, artistic, and playful animal as much as he is a political or economic animal. Man developed not only into a Promethean rebel, a violator of nature, and a killer of his own kind, but into a dreamer and an idealist.

These aspects of man's nature are difficult to fathom and are not often included satisfactorily into social science theory. Each observer, as he examines the behavioral motives in cultures other than his own, finds it difficult to shed his own implicit values which subjectively color his perception of man's expressive nature. Although he may well comprehend the rational elements of another culture, his own unexamined, irrational values make a truly relativistic approach virtually impossible when it comes to studying expressive behavior. Man's behavior is never limited to establishing a means for survival. What starts out as utilitarian in a culture, such as particular techniques used in making artifacts, eventually becomes an end in itself and in this sense "expressive." The shape of artifacts, grammatical structures, or modes of artistic representation readily become cherished in themselves not merely as utilitarian forms but as social values and may end up becoming something quite nonutilitarian. Changes gradually occurring in previously functional aspects of culture may come to be governed more by a sense of style than by a continuing sense of utilitarian adaptation.

We can observe psychologically that all men are motivated. The social scientist, whatever his specialized discipline, works with some more or less well-differentiated, explicit theory of human motivation. Few would hold that man's behavior is totally guided by the immediate, external sanctions of his society. Most recognize the presence of internal motivations or "needs" that govern and direct human action. One such generally recognized need is a need to achieve or accomplish. This is usually considered as leading to an emphasis on instrumental rather than expressive elements in behavior since achievement implies the realization of a future goal rather than being simply an end in itself.

It is necessary for the survival of any culture that the younger generation become motivated to take on prescribed or expected roles. In this sense all individuals are achievement oriented when they conform with the cultural pattern in which they grow up. To grow up, one must want to act like an adult and direct behavior towards some form of future accomplishment.

Achievement motivation, as it is usually defined in modern societies, is not static; it implies some system of social stratification in which individuals do not repeat the past role of a parent but tend to behave so as to acquire higher status through a capacity to take risks, to excel, or to innovate. It is only in a fairly elaborate culture, however, that political or economic conditions are complex enough to present a choice in alternative roles. In complex social systems, higher status may usually be obtained by acquiring wealth or some developed capacity to dominate by the manipulation of personal or group power. Behavior carefully guided toward a goal of higher status is by definition highly instrumental.

In every culture, higher status can also be gained in ways more subtle than economic or political achievement by individuals who exemplify or express the sacred values or the basic, unquestioned values of the society, either for their own sake or as a means to an end. No society, however instrumentally oriented, is without its exemplars of the ideal, as personified variously in the social roles of the scientist, the artist, the teacher, and religious leader.

Innovation or invention in social behavior is not limited to the political and economic spheres; it may take the form of religious innovation or social reform. Llewellyn and Hoebel (1941) and Barnett (1959) give examples among American Indians and New Guinea natives, respectively, of how social change can occur essentially in the realm of values rather than in the political or economic spheres. Llewellyn and Hoebel discuss the emergence of certain patterns of law among the Cheyenne while Barnett discusses various changes in addition to the economic and political brought about by religious innovation in New Guinea. These two anthropological studies present case examples of changes that may come about as the result of the rise of particular charismatic leaders operating within the context of the expressive aspects of the culture, who, through these means, obtain eventual political dominance. The sociologist Weber (1925) was well aware of the expressive aspects of leadership in his discussion of the charismatic leader and his influence in social innovation.

Static societies discourage such innovation. They maintain themselves by fairly rigid prescriptions of fixed adult roles which define the limits of aspiration for each generation. When status is ascribed rather than achieved, individual motivation toward excellence is not directed toward any form of innovation; rather, the enhancement of status occurs only through the realization of a previously well-defined role. It is only when social change occurs or when some form of continual, dynamic disequilibrium occurs in a society that we begin to think of achievement motivation in its modern sense.

As has been pointed out in different contexts by Tönnies (1940), Redfield (1956), Riesman (1950), and others, many societies today are moving with increasing acceleration from folk societies with traditional cultures based on a network of ascribed statuses of kinship to societies of the "market place," where one can attain status only through some form of self-initiated, personal achievement requiring well-directed and integrated motivation toward meeting social standards supported by internalized values or by sanctions exercised by other members of society.

Achievement itself can be a form of personal validation. As such, it must be considered as motivated by some psychological patterning which guides behavior in accord with a value system. This fusion of internalized needs for achievement and the necessity for personal validation through economic success is what seemingly occurred in northern Europe, as discussed by Max Weber (1925) and R. H. Tawney (1926). This fusion also occurred in Japan during the Meiji period (1868–1912). During this period of self-conscious, government-directed modernization, there occurred among many of the former samurai a transmutation of quasi-religious, feudal social values into an entrepreneurial ideology directing behavior into lifelong patterns of economic activity that contributed to rapid economic development (Bellah 1957; Hagen 1962; De Vos 1965).

There has been an increased awareness among scholars of the role of cultural differences in modern economic development. These cultural differences, however, cannot be understood without further exploration of underlying psychological mechanisms. Robert LeVine, in his introduction to his recent monograph on achievement motivation in Nigeria, summarizes our point of view well:

> It has become increasingly clear that a high rate of economic development in a country cannot be guaranteed by the presence of abundant natural resources, capital, and even skilled manpower. Consequently serious attention has been paid to the suggestion that psychological, and particularly motivational, factors may be importantly involved.
> The 'psychological position' is that an individual drive to excel is required for the entrepreneurial activity which converts resources, capital, and manpower into production and—eventually—income. Where this drive is strong and widespread in a population, the economy will develop rapidly through the cumulative push of entrepreneurial actions; where the drive is weak or infrequent, economic advance will be slow. Proponents of this psychological position attribute differences in the rate of economic growth, between the 'have' and 'have-not' nations and between rapidly industrializing nations like Japan and those countries which have lagged behind, to corresponding differences in the incidence of this drive to excel among the national populations concerned. Particular ethnic groups specializing in trade have been singled out as having more of this motive than do their neighbors within some of the un-

derdeveloped countries. Thus a psychological factor—an acquired drive for excellence or need to achieve—is held to be unevenly distributed in the human species and to be at least partly responsible for the major national and other group differences in economic growth which are so conspicuous in the contemporary world (1966:1).

COMPARATIVE RESEARCH ON ACHIEVEMENT MOTIVATION

As noted by Crandall (1963), the concept of achievement motivation as a psychological variable in the educational and occupational activities of adults had some status in psychology for some time before Murray's use of the variable "need achievement" in the analysis of TAT stories and the subsequent application of this concept to cross-cultural research by David McClelland and others. Reviewing its prior use, Crandall notes that both Alfred Adler and Kurt Lewin made much of achievement-motivation as a central need. Lewin discussed achievement in terms of levels of aspiration. Even previously, Alfred Adler spoke of a need for achievement as a compensatory motivation derived from the childhood experience of inferiority in relation to adults. Nevertheless, from the standpoint of cross-cultural research, David McClelland must be recognized for having been, over the past 15 years, the individual most to be credited with developing a stimulating line of research on achievement-motivation in a variety of cultures.

With G. A. Friedman, McClelland (1952) published the results of a cross-cultural study of the relationship of child-rearing practices to achievement-motivation as it appeared in the folktales of a number of American Indian tribes. They analyzed the imagery of these tales as they symbolically reflected some form of achievement need. John Atkinson, R. A. Clark, and McClelland (1953) published an account of what they called the achievement-motive and its associated behavior as related to particular forms of childhood socialization. An example of their line of thought follows. A mother of a high achiever teaches her son self-reliance and personal competition with a standard of excellence. As an adult, the son will continue to seek out tasks that reflect these now internalized standards. He will prefer tasks with a moderate amount of risk and a high degree of personal responsibility. Such an individual likes to pursue energetic, instrumental activity toward goals. He avoids situations in which the task is either too easy or is so difficult as to preclude any chance of success except through luck. He has a need for accurate feedback on results so that he can know how well he is functioning. Such an individual may become depressed with failure, even when he has no great control over outcome. When failure may possibly result from personal inadequacies, he strives very hard to compensate for or overcome the effects of such inadequacies. McClelland (1955) noted later that an entrepreneurial role is the one which seems best to suit men that fit his operational definition of high need achievement.

Winterbottom (1958) is credited with developing a fairly tight research design to help test out the relationship of need achievement and socialization in American culture. Using a series of psychological tests, she divided a group of boys into high need and low need achievement types. She then systematically analyzed the child-rearing practices of their mothers, and found striking confirmation of the general hypotheses of McClelland and his associates. She discovered that mothers of the boys of high need achievement continually stressed the importance of the child's ability to take care of himself and make his own decisions at an earlier age than the mothers of the boys classified as low need achievers. In this study the class variable was held constant, and, since possible differences among the fathers were ignored, American fathers were not considered to be an important variable in socialization.

There is some controversy concerning the effect of the father on need achievement. Rosen and D'Andrade (1959) suggest that influences can occur when an authoritarian father interferes excessively with his son's attempt at mastery; by so doing he inhibits the eventual development of high need achievement. Bradburn (1963a) suggests that in certain societies, such as Turkey, socialization is more fully in the hands of the father than of the mother; hence, the father's role is much more important. Where the father concerns himself minutely with the son's behavior, as in Turkey (and as seems true in Algeria, Egypt, and other Moslem countries), variations of the father's behavior toward the children may have at least no less effect than variations of the mother's behavior toward them. Bradburn (1963b), in commenting on Winterbottom's research, also notes some need to qualify findings derived from the study of white, middle-class Americans.

Training involved in achievement orientation is threefold: "independence" training per se; "mastery" training; and "caretaker" training. According to McClelland (1961), only variations in types of mastery and independence training can be shown to correlate cross-culturally with need achievement. D'Andrade (1959), in examining the development of need achievement, stresses that it is the affective concern conveyed by the mother to the child in her attempts at independence training which produces high need achievement. In fact, what appears to be independence training can under certain conditions be construed by the child as a form of rejection on the part of the mother if it is not at the same time accompanied by a very positively affective concern over successful acts of independence. It is the nature of this concern itself which induces an internalization of standards of excellence.

Turning from considerations of theory to those of method we find that McClelland's influence has here been equally strong. In 1953 he made a detailed exposition of his scoring system. Child, Storm, and Veroff (1958) further applied McClelland's methods to a total of 52 cultures and found to their satisfaction a definite correlation between folktales and particular socialization practices. They made use of ethnographic records concerning child rearing as a means of seeking out correlations between particular practices and the manifest content of the folktales.

Parker (1962) used a similar method in analyzing and comparing Eskimo and Ojibwa mythology in terms of achievement motivation. He pointed to the greater amount of individual achievement orientation to be found in Ojibwa culture. Conversely, the Eskimos appear to be more concerned in many instances with affiliation than with achievement. Parker's results support Landes' (1938) previous conclusions concerning Eskimo personality.

Others have attempted historically to apply McClelland's methods to an analysis of need achievement by turning to written literature. Cortes (1960) made a study of shifts in achievement motivation in Spain from the thirteenth to the eighteenth centuries by analyzing popular Spanish literature. Bradburn and Berlew (1960) similarly related the era of English industrial growth to concurrent themes found in the popular literature of the time. DeCharms and Moeller (1962) suggested that observable variations in achievement themes of American children's readers are related to fluctuations in American economic expansion from 1800 to 1950.

Barry, Child, and Bacon (1959), using materials from relatively simple cultures, found interrelationships between types of subsistence patterns and childhood training that led them to infer that societies dependent on hunting and gathering for food are more interested in training children toward independence and self-reliance than are societies with technologies permitting them to accumulate and store food. LeVine (1963) takes exception to the somewhat simplistic attempt to use Hull's reinforcement theory as an explanation for this interrelationship. He points out that one cannot compare the very simple cultures examined by Barry, Child, and Bacon with other cultures employing a more complex technology. For example, differences between Poland and England with respect to achievement-motivation can hardly be reduced to questions of basic subsistence.

Rosen (1959) has made an extensive comparison of ethnic variations in achievement using samples of Canadians, Italians, Greeks, Jews, Negroes, and white New England Protestants. He concludes that class and ethnic factors are more important than religious affiliations in explaining observed differences. Rosen (1962) also used TAT scores for need achievement to compare Brazilians and Americans. He infers from his data that differences in childhood training are the principal factors that distinguish the achievement behavior of the two cultures. American culture, compared with that of Brazil, more pervasively stresses independence, autonomy, and self-reliance, and induces the child to compare himself competitively with idealized standards of excellence.

McClelland's recent volume *The Achieving Society* (1961) reviews a number of other related studies in more detail. Throughout, he finds a relationship between entrepreneurial behavior and modes of child rearing which stress early independence and a sense of personal mastery. As one of his conclusions, he cites evidence which seems to support Weber's postulated relationship between Protestantism and capitalist economic activity.

More recently, Hagen (1962) the economist, borrowing loosely from McClelland and other sources, has proposed a general theory explaining different responses to economic development in a number of cultures on the basis of some form of status deprivation. Status deprivation serves as a stimulus to a particular minority of the population, inducing it to undertake compensatory forms of innovation, some of which relate to the eventual economic development of the entire society.

A particular social segment separated by religious or ethnic distinctions may be affected by a withdrawal of proffered status. Some such groups may become demoralized and manifest various forms of deviance or social pathology. Such groups may also be prompted to find alternative means of reestablishing themselves. Minority groups can become either positively or negatively innovative in such a way as to produce some form of social change which eventually brings about change in the total society. Hagen considered the situations in which innovation occurs in the economic sector in a way that generates general economic development. Hagen considers types of authoritarian or nonauthoritarian personality fostered within innovating minorities to be of crucial importance in this process. He draws a great deal on previous studies of need achievement and, unfortunately, to some extent, somewhat oversimplifies his discussion of the psychological variables involved. Nevertheless, taken as a whole, Hagen's theory offers a direct challenge to other economists who are accustomed to ignoring the significant psychocultural variables in their observations of how economic development is supposed to occur. Elsewhere I have criticised some of the specifics of Hagen's theory as applied to Japanese modernization (De Vos 1965). As a whole, however, I find that Hagen does afford us a very valuable insight into the complex manner in which differences in social status and socialization experiences within the social segments of a society bring about tensions and disequilibria relieved only by some form of social change.

A COMPARISON OF ACHIEVEMENT AND INNOVATION
AS RELATED TO ETHNIC VARIATIONS IN NIGERIA

Perhaps nowhere in the world is social change as dramatic as in the new nations of Africa where a wide variety of political and economic experiments are being conducted by governments wishing to transform their new nations from a conglomeration of tribal entities into modern pluralistic societies. As noted by LeVine, in his volume *Dreams and Deeds* (1966), one can observe the relative rise of particular ethnic or tribal groups in Africa characterized by energy, achievement strivings, and enterprise. Often cited in this context are the Kikuyu of Kenya, the Chagga of Tanganyika, the Ewe in Ghana, the Bamileke in Cameroun, and the Ibo in Nigeria. LeVine sees these groups as noted for both their opportunism and their industry in responding to the new situations created by the Europeanization of Africa during the past century.

LeVine decries the widespread stereotypes of the African. In fact, LeVine suggests that in contrast with folk and peasant people in other parts of the world, Africans generally have been responsive to economic incentives and have been eager to acquire an education whenever it has been offered. In many supposedly remote villages, there is a quick comprehension of the need for material improvement. There was a great deal of migration and resettlement of new lands by African societies before the advent of white dominance. A number of African cultures were characterized by movement and instability. There is no dead hand of tradition holding back Africans from taking advantage of the more recent changes now taking place. LeVine notes, however, that there is a very conspicuous difference between the African concept of work and achievement and that characteristic of northern Europe. Freedom from work is a prerogative of high status in Africa. The necessity to do something oneself indicates that a person lacks the status to have someone else do it for him. Status is manifest through a demonstration of the power to command the labor of others. A person can demean himself by doing some minor menial task for himself. This concept of how one validates status, therefore, is of considerable consequence in determining the steps taken toward economic development.

The ethnic division of Nigeria provided LeVine an opportunity to study the interrelationship of personality, social values, and economic enterprise among its three largest ethnic segments, the Hausa, the Ibo, and the Yoruba. Each group has a distinctive culture and each has come to play a major role in the development of contemporary Nigeria. The Hausa, as orthodox Moslems, tend to be rather conservative although very politically oriented. They generally lack much formal education or any form of urban sophistication, but their numbers have allowed them to play a dominant political role in the new Nigerian state. The Yoruba are the most urbane of the three. They have had the longest history of Westernization and education. They have been exposed for a long period of time to Christian missionary work and have contributed disproportionately to the professions and the civil service in Nigeria. They comprised the majority of the Africans of high status during the British colonial period. LeVine characterizes their behavior as a combination suggesting Victorian respectability and a somewhat spendthrift pursuit of pleasure. The Ibo are energetic newcomers who within a few decades have come to challenge rather successfully the Yoruba's previous supremacy as a professional and civil service elite. The Ibo were leaders in the struggle for Nigerian nationalism and have produced the greatest number of political and social radicals.

LeVine describes how the political scientist Coleman (1958), in order to understand the Nigerian historical-political scene, found it necessary to compare the different factors of personality of these three major groups as these interrelated in a general push within Nigeria toward economic and social mobility. Coleman found that in the traditional Ibo society there is much internalized pressure toward upward mobility. Among the Ibo there is a fairly close correlation between the individual acquisition of wealth and the exercise of legitimate political power. This contrasts with Hausa society, which was more tightly knit and emphasized ascribed status that allowed much less mobility. The Yoruba, unlike the Ibo, were prevented by consideration of status from flexibly adapting themselves to change brought about by formal education and from taking clerical positions or other service roles which seemed to them demeaning.

Different social values are ascribed to particular types of behavior within the three groups. For example, today among the Ibo the ambitious person is admired whereas the passive one is accorded little respect. Among the Ibo upward mobility is directly related to economic role performance. Life among the Ibo traditionally was highly competitive. In contrast, the traditional Hausa status system emphasized much greater differences in the distribution of wealth, power, and prestige by inheritance. Among the Hausa today, upward mobility in social status is primarily achieved through competition for political office. Personal loyalties are politically rewarded. One can obtain higher social status by obedience, loyalty, and submissiveness to superiors. Generally, therefore, a rise in status was obtainable among the Hausa primarily through the continued success of a patron of high status, whereas among the Ibo it was through one's own success.

The question of which system offered greater incentives for status mobility is not easily resolved. Among the Hausa, political office led to wealth; among the Ibo acquisition of wealth led to political power. The Hausa status system was politically oriented while the Ibo one was occupationally oriented. In analyzing the very complex form of status mobility of the Yoruba, the third major Nigerian society, LeVine concluded that this society provided an environment that would possibly reward independent occupational achievement but at the same time would put a greater emphasis on ascribed status than Ibo society did. Although there were opportunities for status mobility for independent men with particular occupational skills, it was equally clear that there were hereditary restrictions against reaching any of the higher positions. Among the Yoruba there was more scope for success through some form of subservient sycophancy than existed in Ibo society. Therefore, LeVine hypothetically saw the Ibo at one extreme and the Hausa at another with the Yoruba intermediate with reference to the possible development of need achievement.

LeVine was interested in testing these observations by conducting some controlled research on adolescents to see if these postulated differences would be observable in samples of achievement. He tested high school students from the top grades of the leading non-Catholic men's schools in the provincial cities of each ethnic group. (These groups were roughly equivalent to junior college groups in the United States.) In all, LeVine tested a total of 65 Hausa, 139 Yoruba, and 138 Ibo, using dream material collected in the classroom. He was unconcerned whether or not the dreams were genuine descriptions of events; what he wanted was spontaneous fantasies, which he scored independently using the McClelland-Atkinson scoring system for need achievement. LeVine developed a research design paying heed to questions of reliability in scoring procedures. His findings concerning achievement as reflected in dreams were in full accord with his hypotheses. As a further check, he used essays obtained from the same students, which were compared with respect to the relative frequency that obedience and social compliance were emphasized by members of the three groups. Again the results supported LeVine's hypotheses. Recently, a disproportionately large number of Ibo have been receiving higher education and moving into professional occupations. Throughout, the postulated higher need achievement of the Ibo is substantiated in both thought and behavior.

THE CULTURAL CONTEXT OF ACHIEVEMENT: JAPANESE
SOCIALIZATION AND NEED ACHIEVEMENT

In 1947 I was one of a group of social scientists [2] interested in various aspects of the experience of relocated Japanese-Americans of the West Coast who settled in the Chicago area during World War II. American-born Nisei made an obvious, positive occupational and social adjustment in the face of a blatant act of ethnic and racial discrimination in the midst of war hysteria that resulted in their deportation from California. A large number of the younger generation of these Japanese-Americans in the Chicago area entered white-collar and professional occupations. Just as the Japanese nation had taken on the ways of the West in its rapid, self-conscious industrialization, Japanese immigrants and their children in the United States gave evidence—occupationally at least—of breaking through the barrier of color discrimination in the United States. Again, as illustrated in the above discussion of Nigeria, neither sociological theories about discrimination nor economic theories alone can explain the acculturation of the Japanese-American in the United States and in such Latin American countries as Brazil, or the economic development of Japan. A psychological theory related to the socialization of human motivation also is necessary.

However, the model presented by McClelland and others does not seem

---

[2] Included in various phases of cooperative, interdependent research were Charlotte Babcock, William Caudill, Adrian Corcoran, George De Vos, Estelle Gabrielle, Allan Jacobson, Setsuko Nishi, and Lee Rainwater.

to work for Japan. In the samples of TAT materials obtained by Caudill (1952 and 1956) in Chicago and in the subsequent collaborative research with the TAT done by myself and research colleagues at Nagoya University in Japan (De Vos 1960, 1961, 1965), we found a pervasive preoccupation with achievement and accomplishment, no matter where or what group of Japanese was tested. But their achievement imagery differs from that of American samples in the context within which it appears (Wagatsuma, unpublished ms.). Throughout, the Japanese materials show high need affiliation, and this conflicts with American reports, which usually suggest a negative correspondence between the appearance of need achievement and need affiliation.

It is obvious that these differences relate to differences in experiences of socialization in American and Japanese cultures. The generalizations made by McClelland, Winterbottom, and others concerning the socialization pattern that is characteristic for high need achievement differs greatly from observations made of the common experiences of Japanese children. The Japanese child is not trained toward independence or self-reliance in a manner characteristic of non-Japanese who manifest high need achievement in the United States (Caudill 1966a, 1966b; Doi 1955, 1960a, 1960b).

Ezra Vogel (1963) and William Caudill (1966a) made intensive, detailed observations of mother-child relationships in middle-class families in Japan. Vogel's observations of the mother's interaction with children of school age attests to the relative lack of any American type of independence training for Japanese children of this age. There is an intensity of concern for educational achievement on the part of the Japanese mother, and this is imparted to the child in a manner quite different from anything that occurs in the American household. The mother and child act almost as one in meeting the demands of the school.

In Japan, the family rather than the individual has tended to be the traditional unit. Success for oneself only was considered a sign of excessive, immoral egoism. One learned to aim at high standards of performance as a quasi-religious act of dedication. One lost one's selfish feelings in the pursuit of goals benefiting the family. The family, not only the self, suffered the consequence of any failure. I have discussed elsewhere (De Vos 1960) how a subjective sense of need to repay the parents for their self-sacrificing care is a very strong moral imperative impelling the individual toward achievement. The sense of dedication of individual Japanese, the nature of group cohesiveness, and group processes within the Japanese community all require one to pay attention to how the need for social belonging is structured in Japanese economic development as well as in the individual need to achieve (De Vos, unpublished ms.).

Motives related to affiliation and nurture play a continuous role throughout the life cycle. In my formulations concerning Japanese need achievement, I give much more attention to cultural patterns operative in the structuring of guilt than is done in McClelland's theory. I am as concerned with the social sense of belonging as it manifests itself in Japanese culture as is McClelland with a sense of self-reliance and individualism as it is manifest in Americans.

ROLE DEDICATION AND ECONOMIC DEVELOPMENT

In considering economic development, McClelland somewhat single-mindedly emphasizes the role of individualistically oriented entrepreneurial behavior. McClelland's suggestion (1961:302) that Hermes is the most suitable figure in Greek mythology to represent the achieving personality symbolically is rather a curious concept from the view point of Japanese concepts of how to achieve in the context of social dedication. In addition to being a messenger and an athlete, Hermes was given to "entrepreneurial" activities aided by his capacities to be an outrageous liar and thief as well as a trickster. This suggests to my way of thinking an individualistically oriented concept of need achievement which, if present only by itself in a culture even among a large number of individuals, would hardly contribute optimally to national economic development. To illustrate: Chinese who have immigrated to other sections of Asia have been eminently successful as merchants and entrepreneurs, but within China itself social and historical circumstances made China an easy prey to the incursions of colonial powers. The fact that the Chinese value system emphasized only the immediate family and de-emphasized any wider sense of social integrity or honesty in service of the national entity was a crucial factor in helping to explain both the political collapse and the lack of general economic development of China in the late nineteenth and early twentieth centuries. The rampant corruption in the Chinese government until the recent take-over by the Communists made both resistance to foreign incursions and internal modernization impossible. A second example is provided by India, where one today finds good evidence of individualistic need achievement in particular subgroups which has not brought about widespread economic development. Ethnic minorities of India such as the Parsees and the Jains manifest a high degree of individual entrepreneurial activity. Like the Chinese, Indians in minority enclaves overseas in Africa and Asia have a great deal of economic prowess. Nevertheless, counter forces within Indian culture prevent a high rate of economic development on the Indian subcontinent itself.

McClelland holds that national economic development is instigated internally in populations high in entrepreneurial virtues of self-reliance and initiative. Need achievement is ideally embodied in a socially mobile, expediential, instrumentally oriented personality type dedicated to the pursuit of selfish gain. McClelland's theory of economic development is the psychological counterpart of Adam Smith's "Wealth of Nations" theory of free enterprise. As such it is as one-sided a vision of social processes derived from an implicit nineteenth-century rationalist ideology as is the instrumentally oriented communist interpretation of history, which is built upon the idea of a progressive political and economic exploitation of subordinate groups by a power elite. Neither variety of rationalist-individualist theory can be applied with cogency to what occurred in Japan.

Economic development in Japan depended not only on individuals ready to take chances to further their individual aims but also on the cooperative, concerted efforts of many people, distributed throughout all ranks of a rigidly stratified society, who were imbued with a relatively high sense of mutual trust and a sense of social responsibility. The desire for individual social mobility of itself is not necessarily conducive to a social climate that results in economic development if there is no fair level of integrity in government bureaucracies and if the legislative and judicial processes are subject to widespread corruption. Japanese society developed very little sense of class alienation during its major phases of modernization. Japanese need achievement indirectly influenced overall economic development by stimulating individuals to actualize themselves in such roles as teacher and civil servant as well as in the roles of merchant or entrepreneur. One cannot overemphasize the need to take a look at the total cultural configuration and the various alternative roles through which achievement motivation is directed. Dedication to a wide variety of occupational roles on all levels within a national entity is necessary to promote economic development.

There is no doubt that McClelland's model well suits American culture, but it is less applicable elsewhere. Even from the limited perspective afforded by projective materials in a culture such as that of Japan, one gains the impression that human psychology as it influences history cannot be so engagingly reduced to a single paramount motivation.

Examining what can be determined by somewhat less focused quantitative approaches to projective test materials than those used by McClelland, I find a complex configuration of internalized values impelling individual Japanese to act the way they do. This configuration is common to Japanese artists, scientists, scholars, government officials, and soldiers as well as businessmen or entrepreneurs. The elements comprising the configuration include more than achievement motivation; however, one cannot gainsay its strong central influence.

In emphasizing a particular type of socialization related to need achievement, McClelland tends to ignore the question of how such a need can be intermeshed with other varying expressive cultural values. Elsewhere (De Vos 1965), I have noted the striking parallels between the internalized quasi-religious ethics of the Japanese that led many of the early business leaders in the Meiji period to feel a sense of social purpose which strongly resembles the Protestant sense of self-actualization through hard work and success.

Robert Bellah (1957) has noted such similarities in his volume on Tokugawa religion. One must note a singular difference between Europe and Japan. In the nineteenth century, individualism was a reigning ideology in western Europe, but in Japan there was no overriding concern with salvation in relation to a personal God. The Japanese found his overriding sense of purpose in a dedication to his occupational and vocational role somewhere within the hierarchical Japanese social structure.

The Western ideal of personal self-realization apart from family or social group has been foreign to the Japanese system of thought up until very recently, except among a small group of alienated intellectuals. The ultimate goals of Japanese life centered on noninstrumental, quasi-religious concepts of family continuity. Legally and morally, individuals in nineteenth-century Japan defined themselves in the context of familial roles and their attendant obligations and expectations. The point to be made here, going back to my introductory remarks about the lack of attention to the expressive elements in culture, is that in Japan actualizing oneself through some meeting of social challenges took place within the context of strong needs of nurture and affiliation. The dedication to social service in one form or another in the performance of a designated role even on the low rungs of the status ladder is a strong traditional social value which today remains based on the same psychological motivation as formerly even though it is redirected into new social purposes. For example, this expressive need to direct behavior instrumentally toward long-range goals, was once directed among people of the former samurai class toward service as a warrior-administrator. Later, similar psychological motivations were transferred into entrepreneurial activities by many samurai when their previous social role was abolished during the Meiji period. The government turned its attention to consciously directed programs of economic and political modernization and found recruits psychologically primed to undertake the new challenges of their changing culture.

One can understand a great deal of Japanese achievement motivation as couched in terms of a continuing need to belong and to participate cooperatively with others, as well as of mutual needs for nurture and affect, that united individuals in bonds of family and in a variety of pseudo-kinship ties called *oyabun-kobun* relationships (Bennett and Ishino 1963) (in literal translation, "parent role–child role" relationships). Internalized sanctions make it difficult to conceive of letting down one's family, one's social group, or one's occupational superiors. In turn, those in positions of authority must paternally take care of those for whom they have responsibility (Abegglen 1958). These motives are as strong for the Japanese as any sense of individual accomplishment. The achievement drive of the Japanese must be seen as motivated by irrational, unconscious forces as well as by the immediate benefits to be derived by economic success. The sense of validating the self through sustained work is transmuted into modern goals instead of ancient purposes.

In the West, the sense of satisfaction in rational, autonomous, and individualistic behavior is "expresive" of a value orientation, and instrumental behavior and expressive needs are congruent in many Westerners whose behavior is oriented toward economic accomplishments. It is only when there is some such congruence between the instrumental and expressive natures of goal-directed behavior in a sufficiently large number of people within a society that one can talk about an "achieving" society. McClelland and his associates have successfully described how particular socialization patterns common within the United States contribute to such a syndrome. We would argue on the basis of the Japanese evidence, however, that other culturally determined syndromes psychologically different in some respects may also lead to economic development without being as directly individualistic or rational in nature. In short, the system of classical economics developed in Britain and the United States to some degree must be seen as an ethnoeconomics with an implicit enthnopsychology as a motivational base. Its emphasis on the source of human motivation—as is also true for communist theory generally—is too much dependent on an individualistically motivated, instrumental view of human nature. McClelland's concept of need achievement has the virtue of seeing some internally motivated processes as antecedent to goal-directed behavior, but his emphasis on achievement as something generally counterposed inversely to a strong need affiliation is ethnocentric. His hypotheses concerning underlying patterns of socialization make good sense in a Western setting but do not necessarily hold for other societies.

LeVine's study of achievement motivation and social change in Nigeria gives examples of differences in achievement behavior in three different cultures in one nation. In the studies of the Japanese-American minority in the United States and of Japanese in Japan, we find expressed in the projective materials obvious effects of the cultural tradition and a pattern of socialization leading to considerable concern with achievement although it is cast in a quite different context from that of American society. Let us now turn to some psychocultural considerations in particular ethnic minorities related to a failure to achieve in spite of expressed desires to take on the values of the dominant segments of an achievement-oriented society.

ACHIEVEMENT MOTIVATION, NEGATIVE SOCIAL SELF-IDENTITY,
AND MINORITY STATUS

The sustaining social ideology in most of the complex, pluralistic societies, such as the United States, is that all social strata and all ethnic subdivisions should be imbued with sufficient achievement motivation to undergo a sustained period of vocational training after puberty to equip the oncoming generation with the specialized skills necessary to maintain a very complex, technological society. The ideal of maintaining a high degree of technological competence among the entire society is obviously not realized. There are psychologically as well as sociologically limiting forces that inhibit optimal educational and vocational advancement of members of particular groups within the society. Various forms of social dislocation and deviancy in every society inhibit the optimal exploitation of the natural environment and the optimal allocation of human resources.

Deviations from optimal expectations are especially apparent among certain ethnic minorities. These ethnic minorities may be barred from full participation by barriers of caste or racial discrimination. Achievement behavior with or without this complication is influenced also by other factors that cause different ethnic minorities to be distributed disproportionately into one or another social class level. It has sometimes been erroneously concluded that differences in social and occupational distribution are due simply to different values placed upon economic success by different ethnic groups. But one often finds in economically depressed groups considerable concern with their marginal economic position and a strong wish to better their position.

Complex, internalized concepts of self in relation to society operate where systems of social stratification exist. Differences in the possible intensity of values must be considered, as well as differences related to various forms of discrimination and lack of opportunity. But one must also consider how a sense of social self-identity comes to be internalized among members of a minority group. A number of psychological problems arise as a result of experiences of socialization among members of disparaged ethnic groups, and these may inhibit achievement.

One finds both advantaged and disadvantaged ethnic minorities within most pluralistic societies. Some minorities come to play specialized roles of one sort or another. Jews, Parsees, Chinese, Armenians, and Hindu Indians are examples of groups taking on entrepreneurial-commercial functions in minority enclaves in a number of different societies in Africa, Asia, and Europe. They are groups which are usually considered also to give other evidence of high need achievement. Jews, Chinese, and Parsees all put a fairly heavy emphasis on making use of opportunities for gaining advanced education.

There are also many examples of degraded and defeated ethnic or caste minorities. In Pacific settings such as New Zealand and Hawaii, and in African societies such as Rhodesia in South Africa, white colonists have established cultures in which defeated indigenous groups became ethnic minorities regardless of their relative numbers. Members of these minority groups have been forced to evaluate themselves as subordinate to the dominant Europeans. Negroes originally brought into Brazil as slaves are today economically possibly much worse off in a Brazilian society relatively free of the rigidities of color caste than are American Negroes living within a society which has not as yet freed itself from caste restrictions. Throughout the former Spanish colonies of Latin America, there is generally a well-maintained cultural separation between the native Indians and the descendants of the Spanish conquerers. Looking at the problem from a psychological as well as a sociological perspective, in all these instances one can find in the subordinate segments of these nations internalized psychocultural impediments to achievement that are as compelling as the obvious continuing force of discriminatory practices on the part of the elite.

The plight of the Maori in what is often considered to be a relatively harmonious pluralism in New Zealand is a case in point. Ausubel's research in New Zealand (1965a, 1965b) carefully documents the fact that there are no really significant differences in the stated achievement objectives of Maori youth and those of New Zealanders of European ancestry (the so-called Pakeha). Using a battery of questionnaires, Ausubel found that conscious, attitudinal differences by themselves would not account for the facts that Maori do less well in school, drop out of school earlier than do Pakeha and have a rate of adjudicated juvenile delinquency four times that of the Pakeha. These differences are not due solely to external forces related to discrimination but also to unconscious, internal psychological characteristics influencing the structuring of need achievement and the capacity to direct behavior toward long-range goals. Unfortunately, Ausubel made no use of projective tests such as the TAT to obtain indirect, unconscious evidence relating to need achievement.

Adolescent problems called "juvenile delinquency" that come to the attention of the police in New Zealand, as elsewhere, are usually evidence of social alienation and, as such, are a negative index of aptitudes for, or inclinations toward, actualizing school and vocational goals. There is evidence of considerable social alienation among Maori youth. The high delinquency rate among adolescent Maori compares with that recently found in some American ethnic minorities. A disproportionately high number of Hawaiian youths of Polynesian ancestry are in trouble with the police. On the mainland, Negroes and Mexican-Americans are generally low in achievement and high in juvenile delinquency. Statistics for the state of California show a rate of juvenile delinquency among Mexican-Americans five times as great as that among youths of European descent, and among Negroes a rate four and one-half times as great.

In all these instances, several generations of people have suffered from discrimination—enough to influence patterns of socialization. In sharp contrast is the social behavior of the children of Japanese immigrants. These immigrants brought with them no established stigma of inferiority. Instead, they brought a sustaining cultural tradition stressing education and behavior oriented toward long-range goals. Their children were socialized within the context of strongly integrated family units. The descendants now have a high level of education (averaging over two years of college) and a low delinquency rate (in California approximately one-fiftieth that of the majority group).

We must note, however, that in Japan itself one finds the differentiating effect of individual minority status on some Japanese adolescents. In the city of Kobe, the rate of juvenile delinquency among the Korean minority group was found to be at least seven times as great as that of the Japanese majority group; among descendants of the former pariah caste (called *Burakumin* or Eta) [3] of Japanese the rate was at least three and one-half times as great (De Vos and Wagatsuma 1966). In spite of full legal equality, Japanese Burakumin continue to experience various forms of social and economic discrimination that in effect continually remind them of a supposed biological inferiority as descendants of an infra-human social caste. Examination of various studies of the Burakumin reveals that wherever systematic comparisons using such measures as I.Q. tests or achievement tests have been made, the children do poorly compared with children of the majority population. This difference occurs even when the children tested are in integrated schools. Customs of socialization of Burakumin differ from those of Japanese of the majority group (De Vos and Wagatsuma 1966), but the most important difference between the two groups that relates to achievement is the strong evidence among the Burakumin of internalized feelings of self-identification as members of an inferior social group, an attitude which must be considered as having considerable influence on their school and vocational behavior.

Important social identification of the self may be with one's peer group. In a very revealing study of attitudes toward health in a Mexican-American community in California, Margaret Clark (1959) brings out forcefully what one may infer in related problems of social self-identity among Mexican-Americans. She cites a number of cases of tensions related to school achievement in a family in which the parents are unsuccessful in having a child take a positive attitude toward school. Special considerations of language and other factors of socialization are involved, but there is also the strong effect of loyalty to a reference group of peers that is part of a minority group. Such loyalty can override any values the parents may hold concerning the potential accomplishment of the child in school. Boys who wish to be accepted by their own group cannot take a positive attitude toward their schoolwork without chancing an alienation from the group. Any positive school behavior is interpreted by peers as a capitulation to the alien "Anglo" world.

A study of a family of Slavey Indians of Canada (Helm and De Vos, ms.) comparing parents and children on the basis of the results of projective tests and other ethnographic data provides an example of the effect of peer

---

[3] The former Japanese outcastes are usually known outside of Japan as Eta, but within Japan itself, this term is today even more pejorative than the term "nigger" in the United States and is no longer used in polite speech. The more neutral term *burakumin* is a contraction of the term *tokushū burakumin*, "people of special communities."

groups and of what seems to be the future unsuccessful acculturation of two Indian boys. The father was reared in an Anglican mission school and the mother showed obvious, sustained interest in having her two boys take on white values of accomplishment. These Indian parents, however, could not overcome the strong social influence of the boys' peer group. Although the parents have produced personality traits of an obsessive-compulsive nature in both their children, they had not succeeded in having their boys manifest any need achievement as expressed either symbolically in the TAT or behaviorally in school.

Alan Coult (personal communication), in the course of his ethnographic work on the Mescalaro Apache, witnessed an instance where a particular Indian youth was given a scholarship for advanced schooling. The reaction of his peer group was to interpret the boy's prompt acceptance as a threat to their own collective sense of self-identity as nonachievers. Thereupon, they killed his dog and beat him up severely.

CONCLUSION

These examples are sufficient to indicate that the study of achievement motivation must be seen as part of a total cultural context that may spur or inhibit achievement. When achievement motivation is examined in particular cultures, it must be related to available social roles. In a plural society it has to be seen in the context of various ethnic or cultural traditions and the history of particular groups that have resulted in their special forms of intergroup relationships. The study of achievement must ultimately be related to the effects of these cultural and historical influences on the prevailing processes of socialization within these special groups. It must also be related to socialization processes in the primary family and to the ways in which social self-identity of the adult is developed and maintained within the context of peer groups and other reference groups. Cross-cultural comparison of need achievement, whether of total societies or minority segments of particular societies, is meaningless without due attention to the complex differences of both cultural and personality configurations involved. There is obvious need for the development of techniques, as represented by the work of McClelland and his associates, for quantitative measurement of the relative degree of concern with achievement motivation. We must also, however, apply quantitative measures to other aspects of the cultural context to gauge adequately the interrelationships of need achievement and economic and social behavior.

BIBLIOGRAPHY

ABEGGLEN, J. G., *The Japanese Factory: Aspects of Its Social Organization.* New York: The Free Press, 1958.

BARNETT, H., "Peace and Progress in New Guinea," *American Anthropologist,* Vol. 61, 1959, pp. 1013–1019.

BARRY, H. H., I. L. CHILD, and MARGARET BACON, "Relations of Child Training to Subsistence Economy," *American Anthropologist,* Vol. 61, 1959, pp. 51–63.

BELLAH, ROBERT, *Tokugawa Religion.* New York: The Free Press, 1957.

BENNETT, JOHN and IWAO ISHINO, *Paternalism in the Japanese Economy; Anthropological Studies of Oyabun-Kobun Patterns.* Minneapolis: University of Minnesota Press, 1963.

BRADBURN, N. M., "The Cultural Context of Personality Theory," in J. M. Wepman and R. W. Heine (eds.), *Concepts of Personality,* pp. 333–360. Chicago: Aldine Publishing Co., 1963b.

———, "Need Achievement and Father Dominance," *Journal of Abnormal and Social Psychology,* Vol. 67, No. 5, 1963a, pp. 464–468.

———, and D. E. BERLEW, "Need for Achievement and English Industrial Growth," *Economic Development and Cultural Change,* Vol. 10, 1960, pp. 8–20.

CAUDILL, WILLIAM, "Japanese American Personality and Acculturation," *Genetic Psychology Monographs,* Vol. 45, 1952, pp. 3–102.

———, and GEORGE DE VOS, "Achievement, Culture and Personality: The Case of the Japanese Americans," *American Anthropologist,* Vol. 58, No. 6, 1956, pp. 1102–1126.

———, and DAVID PLATH, "Who Sleeps by Whom? Parent-Child Involvement in Urban Japanese Families," *Psychiatry,* in press.

———, and HELEN WEINSTEIN, "Maternal Care and Infant Behavior in Japanese and American Urban Middle Class Families," in Rene Konig and Reuben Hill (eds.), *Yearbook of the International Sociological Association.* Switzerland: Broz, 1966[a].

CHILD, I. L., T. STROM, and J. VEROFF, "Achievement Themes in Folk Tales Related to the Socialization Practice," in J. W. Atkinson (ed.), *Motives and Fantasy Action in Society.* Princeton, N.J.: D. Van Nostrand Company, Inc., 1958.

CLARK, MARGARET, *Health in a Mexican-American Community.* Berkeley, Calif.: University of California Press, 1959.

COLEMAN, JAMES, *Nigeria: Background to Nationalism.* Berkeley, Calif.: University of California Press, 1958.

CORTES, J. B., "The Achievement Motive in the Spanish Economy Between the Thirteenth and the Eighteenth Centuries," *Economic Development and Cultural Change,* Vol. 9, 1960, pp. 144–163.

CRANDALL, V. J., "Achievement," in H. Stevenson, J. Kagan, and C. Spiker (eds.), *Sixty-Second Yearbook of the National Society for the Study of Education.* Chicago: University of Chicago Press, 1963.

DECHARMS, R., and G. H. MOELLER, "Values Expressed in American Children's Readers 1800–1950," *Journal of Abnormal Social Psychology,* Vol. 64, 1962, pp. 136–142.

DE VOS, GEORGE, "Achievement Orientation, Social Self Identity and Japanese Economic Development," *Asian Survey,* Vol. 5, No. 12, 1965, pp. 575–589.

DE VOS, GEORGE, "The Relation of Guilt Towards Parents to Achievement and Arranged Marriage Among the Japanese," *Psychiatry,* Vol. 23, No. 3, 1960, pp. 287–301.
———, "Role Narcissism and the Etiology of Japanese Suicide," Unpublished manuscript.
———, "Social Values and Primary Relationships in Niiike," *Occasional Papers,* Center for Japanese Studies, University of Michigan, 1965, pp. 53–91.
———, and JUNE HELM, "The 'Protestant Ethic' in a Northern Athabascan Indian Community; A Family Unit Study of Acculturation Stress," Unpublished manuscript.
———, and HIROSHI WAGATSUMA, "Psycho-Cultural Significance of Concern over Death and Illness Among Rural Japanese," *International Journal of Social Psychiatry,* Vol. 5, No. 1, 1959, pp. 6–19.
——— and ———, *Japan's Invisible Race.* Berkeley, Calif.: University of California Press, 1966.
———, and ———, "Value Attitudes Toward Role Behavior of Women in Two Japanese Villages," *American Anthropologist,* Vol. 63, No. 6, 1961, pp. 1204–1230.
DOI, L. TAKEO, " 'Jibun' to 'Amae' no Seishinbyori, (Psychopathology of 'Jibun' and 'Amae')," *Journal of Psychiatry and Neurology,* Vol. 62, 1960[a], pp. 149–162.
———, "Naruchishizumu no riron to jiko no hyosho. (Theory of Narcissism and the Psychic Representation of Self)," *Japanese Journal of Psychoanalysis,* Vol. 7, 1960[b], pp. 7–9.
———, "Some Aspects of Japanese Psychiatry," *American Journal of Psychiatry,* Vol. 111, 1955, pp. 691–695.
HAGEN, E., *On the Theory of Social Change: How Economic Growth Begins.* Homewood, Ill.: The Dorsey Press, 1962.
LANDES, R., "The Abnormal Among the Ojibwa," *Journal of Abnormal Social Psychology,* Vol. 33, 1938, pp. 14–33.
LE VINE, R. A., "Behaviorism in Psychological Anthropology," in J. M. Wepman and R. W. Heine (eds.), *Concepts of Personality,* pp. 361–384. Chicago: Aldine Publishing Co., 1963.
———, et al., *Dreams and Deeds: Achievement Motivation in Nigeria.* Chicago: University of Chicago Press, 1966.
LEWIN, K., et al., "Level of Aspiration," in J. Hunt (ed.), *Personality and the Behavior Disorders,* pp. 333–378. New York: Ronald Press Company, 1944.
LLEWELYN, K. H., and E. A. HOEBEL, *The Cheyenne Way.* Norman, Okla.: University of Oklahoma Press, 1941.
McCLELLAND, D. C., *The Achieving Society.* Princeton, N.J.: D. Van Nostrand Company, Inc., 1961.
———, "Some Consequences of Achievement Motivation," in M. R. Jones (ed.), *Nebraska Symposium on Motivation.* Lincoln, Neb.: University of Nebraska Press, 1955.
———, and G. A. FRIEDMAN, "A Cross-Cultural Study of the Relationship Between Child-Rearing Practices and Achievement Motivation Appearing in Folk Tales," in G. E. Swanson, et al. (eds.), *Readings in Social Psychology,* pp. 243–249. New York: Holt, Rinehart and Winston, Inc., 1952.
———, et al., *The Achievement Motive.* New York: Appleton-Century-Crofts, 1953.
PARKER, S., "Motives in Eskimo and Ojibwa Mythology," *Ethnology,* Vol. 1, 1962, pp. 516–523.
REDFIELD, R., *Peasant Society and Culture.* Chicago: University of Chicago Press, 1956.

RIESMAN, DAVID, *The Lonely Crowd*. New Haven, Conn.: Yale University Press, 1950.

ROSEN, B. C., "Race, Ethnicity and the Achievement Syndrome," *American Sociological Review*, Vol. 24, 1959, pp. 47–60.

———, "Socialization and Achievement Motivation in Brazil," *American Sociological Review*, Vol. 27, No. 5, 1962, p. 623.

ROSEN, B. C., and R. G. D'ANDRADE, "The Psycho-Social Origins of Achievement Motivation," *Sociometry*, Vol. 22, 1959, pp. 185–218.

TAWNEY, R. H., *Religion and the Rise of Capitalism*. New York: Harcourt, Brace & World, Inc., 1926.

TÖNNIES, F., *Gemeinschaft und Gesellschaft*. New York: American Book Company, 1940.

VOGEL, EZRA, *Japan's New Middle Class*. Berkeley, Calif.: University of California Press, 1963.

WAGATSUMA, HIROSHI, "Japanese Values of Achievement: The Study of Japanese Inhabitants of Three Japanese Villages of Means of TAT," Unpublished Master's thesis, University of Michigan, 1956.

WEBER, MAX, *Wirtschaft und Gesellschaft*, 2d ed., 2 vols. Tubingen: J. C. B. Mohr, 1925.

WINTERBOTTOM, MARIAN, "The Relation of Need for Achievement to Learning Experiences in Independence and Mastery," in J. W. Atkinson (ed.), *Motives and Fantasy Action in Society*. Princeton, N.J.: D. Van Nostrand Company, Inc., 1958.

Closing Address

Problems and Progress in the Study of Personality

Margaret Mead

Being given a chance at the last word, and an unscripted last word, of course offers a frightful temptation to argue with all of my predecessors. I am going to be careful not to do that.

A symposium such as this, which has attempted to condense in a very short, rapid period all the different and best things that are being thought upon the subject of personality, can be treated as a kind of indicator of the state of the whole field. It can be treated archeologically; I can look back through the four decades of culture and personality that I have participated in. It was very conspicuous in this discussion that psychoanalysis lies at the bottom of the lowest stratum. Dr. LaBarre gave us a traditional interpretation, and, incidentally, he was the only person who really mentioned the body here—bodies have been "out" for a very long time. Conceivably the body is going to come back in by way of drugs. We had no mention of drugs except peyote, but of course peyote was here. There is almost nothing that I can say was not here but what was here appeared in many different shapes. I think learning theory probably got the shortest shrift—and we got extraordinarily little about new developments in learning theory and about the interplay between older forms of learning theory and new forms of motivational theory and such things as locality imprinting, and many of the cross referencings of ethology. Again you could not say these matters were not present, but they were present almost imperceptibly.

The 1940s were characterized, as far as I am concerned, by the growth of cybernetics and of communication and information theory; these too were taken for granted and only mentioned from time to time. I myself felt a little bit like a ghost except when Dr. Honigmann characterized my relationship to cybernetics so gracefully. It was a fair statement, I think, of the difference that cybernetics has made. Until the development of cybernetics, we thought of the child as an end product of a linear assembly line. The child was born and *adults did things to it* until finally it became an adult who *did things to other people*. It was really the whole set of circular conceptions that came in with cybernetics, that made us realize that the child, shaped by its culture, is also a vivid component in the perpetuation of society in societies that are changing slowly and of change itself in societies that are changing rapidly.

I've always thought of the 1950s as characterized by what we were going to learn from ethology. And here again, in this discussion, virtually the whole of ethology had to be carried by Irven DeVore, in a 20-minute speech covering the most recent things that we have learned from comparative primatology. We had to skimp considerably upon the other problems that have been raised by comparative animal psychology which includes other creatures besides the primates and these problems were implicit in DeVore's discussion but, of course, could not be discussed in detail. So a fair number of issues that are of importance to the world today, and that are getting a great deal of discussion (such as the relationship between aggression and pair formation and war) did not come into the discussion as much as they might have.

I had expected that the 1960s were going to be primarily a period of neurophysiological research, covering what we have found out about the human brain. Here again, Dr. Pribram had to carry the whole burden of brain research. There was not time to give anything like the explication that I am sure will be given in Dr. Pribram's publication of what our developing knowledge of the brain is going to contribute to our understanding of these problems.

In a sense this is all archeology. A research style disappears and there is a tendency to leave it in the lower strata of the kitchen midden and not dig it up any more, as we work with the present, most fashionable style. Of course, there was striking emphasis on identity. Identity and cognition, I think, are the two recurrent themes of this symposium. Certainly we needed to discover that there was such a thing as cognition—which we knew quite well in the 1920s, before it got completely swamped. When that happened, everything from child-training manuals to the most erudite discussions dealt with nothing but the various zones of the body. I agree with Dr. Honigmann that zonal discussion got infernally boring, but the expression of the pregenital character of man *is* boring. Possibly the reason it is boring is that it is universal, relatively invariable and so very old. It is one of the aspects of original or human nature, of which Dr. Wallace talked, that are so omnipresent that the expressions in each society, although they may seem temporarily exotic, eventually become monotonous. In this respect, I think the whole of the psychoanalytic discussion of pregenital development of character is very comparable to a study of sex. (Sex is *the* most boring subject to study of any that I know. Years ago when I came back from Samoa, Dr. Wissler told me that if I would just stick with sex, I would be scientifically secure. Of course, what he meant by that assurance was that I would get very good funding from the National Research Council. I said that I was not going to stick with it, because it was too dull. You do not get more than one new point on sex *per* culture. You take all the trouble to go and live among the mosquitoes, and maybe get malaria, and learn a language, and study a whole community, only to come back with one small detail. It is not worth it.)

However, I do think it important to say, as we look at this lowest stratum of our various theoretical approaches, that the kind of repudiation of *Totem and Taboo* (1918) which was popular in anthropological circles 20 years ago, did not take into account all that we now know about early man and primate behavior. Although Freud used bad anthropology, the fault should not be laid at Freud's door. The anthropologists he relied upon simply did not know very much. If we looked again at *Totem and Taboo,* which most of its critics do not do, we would find that there was a basic understanding on Freud's part of a very early hominid period, which continues to be expressed in the evolutionary sequences of *Homo sapiens* (Mead 1963). There are modern expressions of some of these problems, very modern ones, that are important to consider. If the biological invention of latency is seen as a lengthened period of learning that was sufficient to permit man to use his developing brain in a constructive way, it must be considered one of the biological essentials for the emergence of human civilization. In this light, the fact that the age of puberty is dropping four months a decade is something we cannot ignore. I do not believe we could do very well without latency, and the film "The Lord of the Flies" was a remarkably good statement of what we might be up against without it. Consequently, many of these earlier discussions have to be looked at again. I think that there has been a little bit too much of a sense of progression here, and of leaving a period completely behind us, instead of considering the latest work being done in each of the fields that have been successively important. Of course, I am only reacting to the spoken word, and everybody here had a long paper he was not able to deliver, filled with magnificent things that we will be able to read later. But reacting to the selections that were made here by the various speakers I felt there was a tendency to think, "We had psychoanalysis—in fact we have got it—but we do not have to think much about it any more, and a little bit of it is pretty passé. Then we had learning theory, and frustration and aggression, along with the depression, and we do not have a depression now—we hope—and so we do not have to pay much attention to that any more," instead of looking at the very complex cross-referencing now possible in other kinds of studies of learning. And then it seemed as if they meant to say: "We had communication theory, and information theory, and redundancy, and all those things." These also are being taken for granted. But they are not being followed through into their present state and their present implications as much as they might be. Here again one paper carried the whole burden.

Dr. Diebold's paper carried the whole burden of psycholinguistics, ethnemics and semiotics, just to mention a few things we were given a glimpse of in his very able presentation.

There is something else I missed, and yet it was here too, though only for a minute. I missed quite acutely the computer. The only time the computer came in was in two slides Dr. Pribram presented, and a couple of words like "programming". This does not necessarily mean that each contributor who read a paper may not spend his life with a computer. As far as I know, all of them may. But somehow, what we can do with a computer, such as the possibility of handling enormous numbers of variables and no longer being restricted to fourfold tables, and the rest of those little interim devices, did not come through in the papers as much as it might have.

Alex Inkeles gave a paper several years ago in which he claimed we would never be able to handle more than seven variables. This statement seems as remote today as the claim that man would never see the other side of the moon. The possibilities of simultaneous consideration of a very large number of variables making it possible to deal with some of the richness of which Gardner Murphy spoke so vividly, in my opinion was not given as much definition as it might have had. We are going to be moving into a period in which, if we can only handle a multitude of simultaneous observations and solve the problem of coding such observations, we will be able to solve a great many more complex problems.

Partly because getting the whole field of personality into this short period was such a strenuous undertaking, we have been confronted with the very rapid coding that is provided by words (anybody who has tried to learn anything from television knows *how* rapid words are). But we have not dealt here explicity with all the possibilities open to us for accurate machine recording of behavior or with the possibilities of computer graphics which will soon permit the transfer of direct visual observations, as they already do for direct auditory observations, into manageable, simultaneous forms. When Dr. Diebold talked about differences in the kinds of speech of people who are bilinguals, of course his material had been recorded on tape, and he had with him beautiful samples of the kinds of speech he described. And Dr. DeVore arrived with a film on baboon behavior which we did not see because there was not time. The use of film makes it possible to preserve and code enormous numbers of observations, totally beyond any work that has ever been done by observation with pencil and paper, or by checking little check-lists, or by getting three judges to judge anecdotes.

All this is present, in a sense; it is all known to the people who are working here, but since we do not have the time to listen to tapes or look at movie film in a symposium of this length, it may be forgotten. We may think that a great many of the problems that have come up here are problems on which separate disciplines have been working as hard as they could, using their particular methods on pieces of the problem, and that it will not be necessary in the future to have as much isolation as we have had in the past. I think we want to say, as did one of the speakers: "We need a science of behavior, not a bunch of behavorial sciences." I think the only way that we can hope to have this is to have shared materials that we can work on with our variety of conceptual schemes and methods of analysis. If you consider everything that has been said here, we have everything we need. We have students of culture; and we have students of the individual, in various forms of interpersonal interaction; we have students of child development; we have students of the structure of social situations, and those who are prepared to relate the structure of social situations to the larger economic and world scene. But we do not put them together. And we have not as yet a device which—whenever anybody is working on one little piece of this picture—defines those aspects of the situation that he is not dealing with. Instead of saying, as Dr. Strauss did, "Sociologists are not interested in personality," I would prefer to say that sociologists put this kind of personality in black boxes, and then say, "We're going to treat this as a series of black boxes. We know there is something inside the black boxes, but for our analysis this is not relevant." In the same way it would help if those who are working on the structure of small group situations and on the social structures inside our own society could include their awareness that the whole of American culture is relevant, and that they would not get the same kinds of social structures in another society. This does not actually mean they have to study every culture, but they should include them conceptually if we are going to have a single science. As each approach is experimented with and explicated, each should include those other parts of the picture that are known to exist, but are not going to be included in the particular research. What has happened with the division between disciplines is that each discipline has gone off with its own methods, and we have had a great deal of difficulty in getting students and members of any one of the disciplines to keep up with the others.

This brings me to another question not dealt with here. That is the problem of retrieval of information. I do not think that we quite realize, partly because of the erudition of many of our speakers, that we are trembling on the edge of a new era of information retrieval. This is of great importance, especially in a field which, as Dr. Price-Williams has said, is rather overendowed with categories and definitions. We are so helpless in our attempt to retrieve information at present, that we are dependent on each person's particular knowledge of particular parts of the whole. But this situation is not going to continue. There is not any reason why, within ten years, we cannot have a form of information retrieval that will give us a simultaneity which we do not have now. Instead of the sequential little bits of insights, and repeated insights, and forgotten insights, and rediscovered insights which are so characteristic of the human sciences, we ought to be able, in ten years, to dredge them all up at once and take a look at them, and not waste as much time as we do now in rediscovery.

I think all the way through this discussion I have sensed a tension that has been recurrent between those who want to do justice to the unique, whether it is the unique human person or the unique culture, and those who want to generalize and universalize in a variety of ways. Perhaps this attention to uniqueness, which is important, is one reason why thinking in the social sciences (or the human sciences, as I prefer to call them) goes round and round and round, and is, on the whole, so extraordinarily non-cumulative. Each worker, certainly each anthropologist with a new tribe, has to rediscover everything. If he is in the contemporary style and has done a very careful study of the native categories, he then finds he has to recategorize everything else so all we get is a repetition of insight, instead of any accumulation of exact knowledge and propositions on which we can build.

Perhaps one of the most exciting leads we can follow was in what Dr. Pribram said about looking for convergences. If we could now take all of the different kinds of relevant data which have been accumulated in this general field under a variety of rubrics and really begin to submit them to some kind of analysis so that we could work out congruences and convergences, we might very well take another step forward. Whether that step is exactly the same one that Dr. Price-Williams was talking about, I rather doubt. I am laying stress on shared materials, rather than on a shared conceptual scheme, and on the possibility that if we have enough shared materials, it will be possible for us to work out better, more shareable conceptual schemes. It has been our experience in multidisciplinary research that if you take a group of people who represent different disciplines, and who have no shared materials, they can argue from now until kingdom come and never get any work done at all. If you give them a few interviews or a film or a careful and exact description of a situation, they can go to work (Mead and Metraux 1953). Mechanical methods of observation employing carefully made sound film give us the means to eliminate the problem of the different kinds of observers and the biases of the different kinds of observers. Such observations can be replaced by objective recorded materials that everyone can agree are subject to analysis. I miss, although it came up a few times, any discussion of replication in complex situations and the fact that we are dependent, of course, on the growth of experimental designs to work on many of our complicated hypotheses. We have not begun to exploit the fact that with a fully recorded situation, recorded by mechanical means which eliminate observer bias and everything that the observer's culture, conceptualizations, and sensory modalities bring in to confuse the picture, it is the cameras and the sound track that are recording what is there. So the *analysis* of the situation can be replicated indefinitely, and as we gain more conceptual sophistication, we can continue to learn from the same very exact record of a situation which is not reproduceable in life, but which can be replicated by repeated study.

This symposium is to me a very dramatic occasion—dramatic because such a large number of people responded to Dr. Norbeck's invitation. (He lost only a very few of those he asked, and I am requesting that he publish their names so we will know they were invited. For later history, one likes to know things like that.) We can look at this symposium in terms of the challenges that are going to be presented in this field in the next 20 years and how we will respond to them. At the moment none of us is being asked to do very much. But we should consider, as a kind of precursor of future activity what happened in World War II, for the sciences that were concerned with this general field *did* come forward in World War II. We were able to deal with the questions that were put to us—questions that were soluble by the human sciences but were not soluble by, say, the United States Army. In World War II a large group of anthropologists, psychiatrists, psychologists, and sociologists went to work under the pressure of a particularly felicitously phased war which we could all feel was worth fighting. I hope we will never again fight a war of that size. We were able to take what was known at that period and put it at the disposal of agencies that could use the information. Whether it was a question of internal morale, of finding strengths in the people of occupied countries, of planning for various treatments of defeated countries, of predicting enemy behavior, of planning for the demobilization of our troops, we did these things and we did them adequately and well (Mead and Metraux 1965). And we worked together in a way that no one would have predicted. This was true both in England and in the United States. Now for 16 years no one in authority has asked us to do anything that has amounted to very much. Nevertheless, we may ask what we, as a group of behavioral scientists, with all the various sorts of eruditions and insights that we have assembled here, would be prepared to say if any institution with power really asked for precise help, or asked us to organize major projects to deal with present world problems. The tremendous rapidity of change, the impact of the population explosion—and the complete change in the definition, therefore, of appropriate human reproductivity—the spread of urbanization, the change in our whole viewpoint that has come about with space exploration, what automation is going to do in changing our whole society—all these pose large-scale questions and problems with which everyone here is familiar. But are we prepared to aid in their solutions if asked? If we made up a team of any five people here, or any ten, would we be prepared with the methods of research and analysis needed to present our findings in a way that would be useful? Of course, it is only one test of the state of a science to ask whether it can be applied or not. But the human sciences can never avoid human problems. They cannot avoid them, partly because unless the rest of the society supports their efforts, the human sciences cannot proceed very far (Mead 1964).

Dr. Kaplan pleaded for a humanization of psychology, and it seems to me that we must consider the relation of the state of our assembled sciences to a science of human behavior in terms of what we would be ready to do. What could we do? What size chunks could we deal with? How many of us could take a particular area of specialization and sophistication and generalize it so that it would be relevant to the whole world? What answer would we give, if we were asked today about policies which might affect the entire world, and peoples of the very simplest level as well as the peoples of the most complex level—those caught in our modern cities and those on the mountain tops in New Guinea? Would we be prepared to think about them all at once (because they are all within one communicating network today) in such a way that we could help draft policies, or help in directing new forms of research and exploration? Could we bring to bear what we know now, after 50 years of work, on problems that affect the whole human race at a time when the race is becoming one people and when action taken on any part of this planet (and this includes the exposition of a theory as well as attempts at applications) may be significant for all the rest of the world? It is only one measure of the state of our sciences, but I think it is a possible measure, and so I commend it to you as such. If we think of what happened during World War II when we had a really tremendous speedup of our ability to bring what we knew in particular fields to the problem of the day, we realize what a little world it was and what small problems they were compared with those which face us now. If we can think of what happened then as a kind of white heat that was generated by warfare and danger, if we can think of what is going to confront us in the next 25 years as hopefully generating another kind of white heat but nevertheless a heat of urgency, then we can put what we can do in perspective.

The most striking thing that will be happening to this particular focus of culture and personality that we have all been working with here, is that change is going to be so rapid that we will not have a generation in which to adjust to it. The change will have to occur within a generation, which is of course a point that Dr. Henry emphasized when he discussed the discovery of the middle-aged adult. It is no longer going to be a question of our fashioning children who then, as they are fashioned, become creatures who evoke from us behavior we would be incapable of unless they had learned part of it from us (Mead 1964). We are going to be fashioning children who are going to be different from any human beings who have ever been—from whom we are going to have to be able to learn things that we would not otherwise know. Although there have been premonitions of it in the past, this is going to be a totally new model of human experience.

For millennia it has been the experience of the elders, passed on to the children, that has bound culture together. Now we have got to tie in with this experience of the elders an ability (we do not know how to cultivate yet) to learn from the children who will have an experience that no one has ever had before. We must do so if we are to design the kinds of society for which there have been no precursors and for which we have no models.

BIBLIOGRAPHY

FREUD, SIGMUND, *Totem and Taboo*. New York: Moffat, Yard, 1918; reprinted 1960, New York: Vintage Books, Random House, Inc.

MEAD, MARGARET, "Psychologic Weaning: Childhood and Adolescence," in Paul Hoch (ed.), *Psychosexual Development in Health and Disease*, pp. 124–135. New York: Grune & Stratton, Inc., 1949.

———, "*Totem and Taboo* Reconsidered with Respect," *Bulletin of the Menninger Clinic*, Vol. 27, 1963, pp. 185–199.

———, *Continuities in Cultural Evolution*. New Haven, Conn.: Yale University Press, 1964; reprinted 1966, New Haven, Conn.: Yale University Press.

———, and RHODA METRAUX (eds.), *The Study of Culture at a Distance*. Chicago: University of Chicago Press, 1953.

———, and ———, "The Anthropology of Human Conflict." in Elton B. McNeil (ed.), *The Nature of Human Conflict*, pp. 116–138. Englewood Cliffs, N.J.: Prentice-Hall, Inc., 1965.

BIOGRAPHICAL SKETCHES OF AUTHORS

HOWARD S. BECKER. Professor of Sociology at Northwestern University, Howard S. Becker received his doctoral training at the University of Chicago. His interests in sociology include community studies, social problems, and the sociology of education. Among his various publications are the books *Boys in White: Student Culture in Medical School* (1961, co-author), *Outsiders: Studies in the Sociology of Deviance* (1963), and *Social Problems, A Modern Approach* (1966).

DANIEL BELL. Daniel Bell was awarded the Ph.D. in Sociology by Columbia University, where he is now Professor of Sociology, and Chairman of the Department of Sociology in Columbia College. Dr. Bell's distinguished and varied career includes ten years of service as an editor of *Fortune*. He is the author of the well-known books *Work and Its Discontents* (1956), *The End of Ideology* (1960), and *The Reforming of General Education* (1966), and editor of *The Radical Right* (1963).

G. DUBREUIL. Awarded the M.A. in Psychology by the Université de Montréal, Guy Dubreuil has also undertaken graduate study in the field of anthropology, at Columbia University and at the Musée de l'Homme in Paris. Presently Associate Professor of Anthropology at the Université de Montréal, Dubreuil's research and publications have emphasized community studies and the subject of personality and culture in French Canada and the West Indies.

GEORGE A. DE VOS. Professor of Anthropology and chairman of the Center for Japanese and Korean Studies, at the University of California, Berkeley, George A. De Vos was awarded the M.A. in Anthropology and the Ph.D. in Psychology by the University of Chicago. His subsequent professional work has combined the views and methods of anthropology and psychology. One of his principal scholarly interests has been the subject of the personality of the Japanese and its formation. His most recent major publication, in coauthorship with Hiroshi Wagatsuma, is entitled *Japan's Invisible Race: Caste in Culture and Personality* (1966).

A. RICHARD DIEBOLD, JR. One of the youngest participants in the symposium, Diebold is an anthropological linguist who received his doctoral training at Yale University and is now Associate Professor of Anthropology at Stanford University. His principal scholarly interests are psychological and social aspects of linguistics. His publications concern various subjects relating to language and personality and include the book *Linguistic Anthropology* (in press).

JOHN O. ELLEFSON. John O. Ellefson, a primatologist, is a Research Associate and Post-Doctoral Fellow in the Department of Psychiatry of the Stanford University School of Medicine. The youngest contributor to this volume, Ellefson received the Ph.D. in Anthropology from the University of California at Berkeley and has done field research in the Malay Peninsula. His doctoral dissertation is entitled *A Natural History of Gibbons in the Malay Peninsula* (1967).

MARY ELLEN GOODMAN. Professor of Anthropology and Sociology at Rice University, Dr. Goodman was awarded the Ph.D in Anthropology at Radcliffe College. Her numerous activities include authorship of a weekly column on social problems for the *Houston Post* and many civic activities. She was named Woman of the Year by Delta Zeta sorority in 1963. Dr. Goodman's interests in research include the study of values and their transmission, the socialization of children, and urban problems. She is the author of the books *Race Awareness in Young Children* (1964), *The Individual and Culture* (1967), and many shorter writings.

WILLIAM E. HENRY. Professor of Psychology and Chairman of the Committee on Human Development at the University of Chicago, William E. Henry was awarded the Ph.D. by the University of Chicago. Among his honors are appointments as Ford Distinguished Visiting Professor at the University of Wisconsin and at Michigan State University. His many publications on aspects of personality, the formation of personality, and techniques of research connected with personality include the books *The Analysis of Fantasy: The Thematic Apperception Technique in the Study of Personality* (1956), and *Growing Old* (1961, coauthor).

A. B. HOLLINGSHEAD. Dr. Hollingshead is William Graham Sumner Professor of Sociology at Yale University. Awarded the doctorate by the University of Nebraska, Dr. Hollingshead has since conducted extensive research and is the author of many well-known publications. These include *Human Ecology* (1938), *Elmtown's Youth* (1949), *Social Class and Mental Illness* (1958), and *Trapped: Families and Schizophrenia* (1965). Among his honors is the MacIver Award for distinguished research, awarded in 1959.

JOHN J. HONIGMANN. Research Professor and Professor of Anthropology at the University of North Carolina, John J. Honigmann was awarded the doctorate in anthropology by Yale University. He has long been interested in research on personality and has conducted field investigations among the Indians and Eskimo of Canada, in West Pakistan, and in Austria. He is the author of many scientific papers and several books, including *Culture and Personality* (1954), *The World of Man* (1959), and *Understanding Culture* (1963).

BERT KAPLAN. Awarded the Ph.D. in Psychology by Harvard University, Bert Kaplan subsequently taught at the University of Kansas and at Rice University, and is presently Professor of Psychology at the University of California, Santa Cruz. His interests in research have included preventive psychiatry and methods and techniques of using projective tests. He has conducted extensive field research among the Navajo Indians. His publications include the books *Studying Personality Cross-Culturally* (1961, editor), and *The Inner World of Mental Illness* (1964, editor).

WESTON LaBARRE. Professor of Anthropology at Duke University, Weston LaBarre was awarded the doctorate in anthropology by Yale University. He has also had extensive training in psychiatry and was the first recipient, in 1958, of the Geza Roheim Memorial Award for Distinguished Contributions to Psychoanalysis and the Social Sciences. His numerous publications include the monographs and books *The Peyote Cult* (1938), *The Human Animal* (1954), and *They Shall Take Up Serpents: Psychology of the Southern Snake-Handling Cult* (1962).

WILLIAM M. McCORD. William McCord was awarded the Ph.D. in Social Science by Harvard University and presently holds the Lena Gohlman Fox chair as Professor of Sociology at Rice University. His special fields of interest are social psychology, social philosophy, and social change in developing nations. Now engaged in research on developing nations and Negro social psychology, he has also conducted extensive research on social problems of criminality, alcoholism, and juvenile delinquency. His publications include the books *Psychopathy and Delinquency* (1956, coauthor), *Origins of Crime* (1959, coauthor), *Origins of Alcoholism* (1960, coauthor), *The Psychopath* (1964, coauthor), *The Springtime of Freedom* (1965), and *Mississippi: The Long Hot Summer* (1965).

MARGARET MEAD. Curator of Ethnology at the American Museum of Natural History, New York, and Adjunct Professor of Anthropology at Columbia University, Margaret Mead was awarded the Ph.D. in Anthropology by Columbia University. An outstanding pioneer in research in culture and personality, Dr. Mead has been extremely active in research, writing, and lecturing, and has been the recipient of many honorary degrees and other awards of merit. Her field research, beginning with a study of Samoan culture, has given her a rich acquaintance with many societies, especially those of Oceania. She is the author of numerous papers and over a dozen books and is also coauthor and editor of additional books. Among her best-known books are *Coming of Age in Samoa* (1928), *Sex and Tem-*

perament in *Three Primitive Societies* (1935), *Male and Female* (1955), and *New Lives for Old* (1961).

GARDNER MURPHY. Director of Research, Menninger Foundation, Topeka, and holder of the Dr. Henry March Pfeiffer Research-Training Chair in Psychiatry, Gardner Murphy received his doctoral degree in psychology from Columbia University. His multiple interests in research include the subjects of social aspects of urban renewal, human potentiality for creation, psychotherapy, and extrasensory perception. Some of his recent books are *Human Potentialities* (1958), *Development of the Perceptual World* (1960, coauthor), and *Freeing Intelligence Through Teaching: A Dialectic of the Rational and the Personal* (1961).

EDWARD NORBECK. Professor of Anthropology, Chairman of the Department of Anthropology and Sociology, and former Dean of Humanities at Rice University, Edward Norbeck received his doctoral training at the University of Michigan. Director of the symposium on personality from which this volume is derived, Norbeck is the author of many articles and several books, which include *Takashima, A Japanese Fishing Community* (1954), *Pineapple Town—Hawaii* (1959), *Religion in Primitive Society* (1961), *Prehistoric Man in the New World* (1964, coeditor), and *Changing Japan* (1965).

DOUGLASS PRICE-WILLIAMS. Douglass Price-Williams was awarded the Ph.D. in Psychology by the University of London and came to the United States in 1962. He is presently Professor of Psychology and Chairman of the Department of Psychology at Rice University. His interests in psychology include the subjects of perception of space-time relationships, cognitive development, and various other aspects of cognition as well as social psychology in general. He has conducted field research in Africa and Central America. His publications include the book *Introductory Psychology: An Approach for Social Workers* (1958).

KARL H. PRIBRAM. Karl H. Pribram was awarded the degree of Doctor of Medicine by the School of Medicine, University of Chicago and is also holder of the Diplomate, awarded by the American Board of Neurological Surgery. He is presently United States Public Health Service Research Professor in the Department of Psychiatry and Psychology at Stanford University. Dr. Pribram has conducted extensive research relating to neuropsychology, neurophysiology, and neurosurgery. A prolific writer, he is the author of many scientific papers and contributor to many books in the fields of his interests.

GEORGE D. SPINDLER. Professor of Education and Anthropology, and Executive Head of the Department of Anthropology at Stanford University, George D. Spindler received his doctorate in anthropology from the University of California at Los Angeles. In collaboration with his wife, Louise, he has conducted field research among the Menomini, Chippewa, Winnebago, Blackfeet, and Blood Indians and among German villagers. The author of many writings, Dr. Spindler is also the editor of many books and a past editor of the journal *American Anthropologist*. Among his publications are *Sociocultural and Psychological Processes in Menomini Acculturation* (1955), *Education and Culture: Anthropological Approaches* (1963, editor and contributor), and, the most recent, *Culture in Process* (1967, coauthor).

ANSELM STRAUSS. Professor of Sociology at the University of California Medical Center in San Francisco, Anselm Strauss received his doctoral training at the University of Chicago. He is the author or coauthor of a wide range of publications in sociology and social psychology including the books *Social Psychology* (1954), *Mirrors and Masks* (1958), *Awareness of Dying* (1956), and *Discovery of Theory* (1966).

W. R. THOMPSON. Dr. Thompson received his doctoral training in psychology at the University of Chicago and is now Professor of Psychology and Head of the Department of Psychology at Queen's University, Kingston, Ontario. He has conducted research in various subjects of experimental psychology and genetics, including genetics of behavior, development, and exploratory behavior. He is author of scientific papers on these subjects and coauthor of the book *Behavior Genetics* (1960).

ANTHONY F. C. WALLACE. Awarded the Ph.D. in Anthropology by the University of Pennsylvania, Anthony F. C. Wallace is now Professor of Anthropology and Chairman of the Department of Anthropology at the same institution, and is also Senior Research Scientist at the Eastern Pennsylvania Psychiatric Institute. His scholarly interests include various subjects relating to personality, human reactions to stress, the role of religion in human life, and Iroquois Indian culture. His abundant writings include the books and monographs *The Modal Personality Structure of the Tuscarora Indians, as Revealed by the Rorschach Test* (1952), *Culture and Personality* (1961), and *Religion: An Anthropological View* (1966).

E. D. WITTKOWER. Professor of Psychiatry and Director of the Section of Transcultural Psychiatric Studies at McGill University, Montreal, Dr. Wittkower received the degree of Doctor of Medicine from the University of Berlin. A past president of the American Psychosomatic Society, he now serves as vice-president of the Canadian Psychoanalytic Society, and is the author or editor of many writings on psychiatric subjects. He is presently coeditor of *Transcultural Psychiatric Research Review and Newsletter*.

NAME INDEX

Abegglen, J. G., 362
Aberle, David F., 290
Abraham, Karl, 84, 260
Adler, Alfred, 81, 86, 352
Adorno, T. W., 176
Allport, Gordon W., 15, 88, 95, 96, 97, 110, 176, 188, 190, 191
Anthony, A., 189
Ardrey, Robert, 148
Arieti, Silvano, 290, 310, 311
Arnheim, R., 28
Arnold, Matthew, 105
Arnold, Thomas, 114
Arsenian, S., 233, 234, 239
Asanuma, H., 154
Asch, Solomon, 99, 170
Atkinson, John, 352, 358
Auden, W. H., 84
Ausubel, David P., 365

Babcock, Charlotte, 358
Bacon, Margaret, 354
Bagehot, Walter, 119
Bagshaw, Muriel H., 152
Bakan, David, 213, 214
Baldwin, J. M., 31
Bales, Robert F., 309, 348
Barker, Ernest, 105, 106, 222
Barnett, H., 350
Barratt, E. S., 156
Barringer, Herbert R., 309
Barry, H. H., 262, 354
Barry, J., 152
Barzun, Jacques, 256
Becker, Howard S., 57, 198, 199, 200, 201, 202, 203, 204, 311, 312, 314
Beckey, R. E., 233
Bell, Daniel, 103
Bell, Norman W., 310
Bellah, Robert, 351, 362
Benedict, Ruth, 89, 107, 108, 251, 258, 268, 283
Bennett, John W., 255, 362
Bentley, A. F., 31, 32
Berger, Stanley, 125, 126
Bergson, Henri, 33
Berkowitz, Leonard, 179, 188
Berlew, D. E., 354
Bernstein, B., 235

Bignami, G., 166
Binet, Alfred, 22, 28
Birch, H. F., 171
Birren, James, 214
Black, Mary, 338
Blitsten, Dorothy R., 184
Bloom, Benjamin S., 179
Blum, J. S., 152
Blumer, Herbert, 195
Boas, Franz, 91, 253
Börne, Ludwig, 105
Bossard, J. H. S., 229, 234, 239
Bouman, A. C., 225
Bowie, Robert, 117
Bradburn, N. M., 353, 354
Brain, Lord, 231
Braunhausen, N., 233
Brenman, M., 25
Brentano, Franz, 129
Brickner, Richard, 107
Bridgman, P. W., 19
Brim, Orville G., 198, 200
Broadhurst, P. L., 166
Brooks, V. B., 154
Brown, R., 100, 226
Bruner, J. S., 93, 233
Bryce, Lord, 106
Bucher, Rue, 57
Burling, R., 232
Buxbaum, E., 238
Bychowski, Z., 231
Byrne, D., 214

Cabot, Richard Clarke, 316
Calas, Elena, 188
Campell, D. F., 225
Cannon, W. B., 86
Carluccio, C., 290
Carothers, J. C., 285, 288
Carpenter, C. R., 141, 144
Carr, E. H., 111
Carroll, J. B., 225
Carter, H. D., 163, 164
Cattell, R. B., 22, 156, 169, 171
Caudill, William, 327, 358, 359
Chamberlain, Houston Stewart, 105
Chance, Norman, 188
Chapman, John, 117

389

Name Index

Child, Irving L., 92, 181, 260, 262, 263, 310, 353, 354
Chiriboga, David, 214
Chombart de Lauwe, Paul-Henri, 178
Chomsky, Naom, 49
Chow, K. L., 151, 152
Christophersen, P., 233, 236
Church, Joseph, 177, 182, 185
Claparéde, E., 31
Claridge, G., 98
Clark, K. B., 180
Clark, Margaret, 366
Clark, R. A., 352
Cloward, Richard A., 313
Cockrell, Dura-Louise, 180
Codere, Helen, 255
Cohen, Albert K., 313
Cohen, Mimi, 189, 262
Cohen, Yehudi A., 190
Coleman, James, 357
Collomb, H., 285
Cooley, Charles Horton, 55, 99, 195
Corcoran, Adrian, 358
Cortes, J. B., 354
Coult, Alan, 367
Covello, L., 233, 234
Craig, Maude M., 183
Crandall, V. J., 352
Cressey, Donald R., 311, 313
Crook, J. H., 143, 144, 147
Crosby, C., 225, 229

Dalton, Melville, 58
D'Andrade, R. G., 225, 248, 335, 353
Darcy, N. T., 233, 234
Darwin, Charles, 20, 26, 70, 71, 162
Darwin, Erasmus, 20
Davis, Fred, 58, 59, 200
de Beauvoir, Simone, 120
DeBoer, J. J., 229
DeCharms, R., 354
DeGeorge, F. V., 170
de Reuck, A. V. S., 231
DeSaussure, F., 223
Descartes, René, 66, 117, 122, 123
Deutsch, Karl, 120
Devereux, George, 239
DeVore, Irven, 44, 140, 374, 376
De Vos, George A., 327, 351, 355, 358, 359, 361, 366
Dewey, John, 31, 32, 113, 195
Dewson, J. H., 152
Diamond, Stanley, 252, 254
Diaz-Guerrero, R. D., 98, 186
Dicks, Henry V., 107, 108
Diebold, A. R., Jr., 221, 222, 229, 376
Dilthey, Wilhelm, 122, 130
Dobzhansky, Theodosius, 187
Doi, L. Takeo, 359

Doob, L. W., 225
Downs, James F., 184
DuBois, Cora, 90, 254, 284
Duff, Raymond S., 310
Duncan, M. H., 233
Dunn, Stephen P., 268
Durkheim, Emile, 313

Ebbinghaus, Herman, 26
Edgerton, Robert, 345
Eggan, Fred, 91
Elkind, David, 180
Ellefson, John O., 137, 141, 144
Epstein, I., 232
Erikson, Erik H., 47, 211, 213, 260
Erikson, Kai T., 314
Ervin, S. M., 222, 225, 229, 231, 236, 237
Eysench, H. J., 166, 170

Falconer, D. S., 161, 168
Farber, Maurice L., 187
Faris, R. E. L., 284
Featherstone, H. L., 111
Fechtner, G. T., 26
Fenichel, Otto, 85
Ferenczi, Sandor, 84
Festinger, Leon, 339
Field, M. J., 284, 285
Fillenbaum, S., 232
Fischer, John L., 251, 262
Fisher, Anthony, 331
Fisher, Ronald A., 26, 35, 36
Fishman, J. A., 222, 229, 234, 239
Fox, Renee, 310
Frake, Charles, 338, 344
Fraser, Thomas R., Jr., 179
Freedman, D., 171, 172
Frenkel-Brunswik, Else, 176
Freud, Anna, 32
Freud, Sigmund, 17, 19, 21, 22, 24, 26, 32, 36, 41, 66, 71, 72, 74, 75, 83, 84, 106, 127, 180, 186, 212, 248, 260, 314, 375
Friedman, G. A., 352
Fromm, Erich, 47, 108
Fronde, J. A., 105
Fuller, J. L., 162, 163

Gabrielle, Estelle, 358
Galton, Francis, 22, 162, 163
Gardner, R. C., 224, 231
Gardner, Riley W., 98
Garner, W. R., 153
Gartlan, J. S., 143
Geer, Blanche, 199, 200, 204
Geertz, Clifford, 110
Giddings, Franklin H., 120
Gill, M. M., 25
Gilman, A., 226
Gladwin, Thomas, 335

Name Index

Glaser, Barney, 61
Glick, Selma J., 183
Glueck, Eleanor, 183, 315, 323
Glueck, Sheldon, 183, 315, 323
Goffman, Erving, 47, 60, 129, 314
Goldschmidt, Walter, 345
Goldstein, K., 231, 235
Gordon, H. L., 287, 288
Gorer, Geoffrey, 107, 108, 114
Goring, C., 315
Goodall, J., 144, 145, 146
Goode, William J., 314
Goodenough, Ward H., 47, 335, 339
Goodman, M. E., 180, 185
Gottesman, I. I., 166, 169, 170, 171
Gottschaldt, K., 172
Green, J. R., 105
Greenblatt, Milton, 310
Greene, Graham, 120
Greeson, R. R., 238
Gudeman, Jon, 318, 320
Guilford, J. P., 19
Gumperz, J. J., 222, 229, 335
Gun, W. T. J., 162

Haddon, Alfred C., 93, 246
Hagen, E., 351, 355
Hagbarth, K. E., 151
Hall, B., 166
Hall, Calvin S., 95, 166
Hall, K. R. L., 140
Hallowell, A. I., 46, 265, 310, 337, 338
Halstead, W. C., 156
Hammel, E. A., 50, 335
Handel, Gerald, 309
Hartley, E. L., 25
Hartshorn, H., 32
Haugen, E., 221, 222, 233, 234
Havelka, J., 224, 225, 229, 231
Hayek, F. A., 88
Hebb, D. O., 26, 29
Heiden, Konrad, 86
Heider, Fritz, 99
Helm, June, 366
Hempl, G., 235
Henry, Jules, 183
Henry, William E., 380
Herman, S. N., 229
Hernandez-Peon, R., 151
Herodotus, 103, 120
Hess, Moses, 105
Hess, Robert D., 309
Hilgard, E. R., 25
Hill, H. S., 234
Hippler, Arthur, 327
Hitchcock, John F., 178
Hoebel, E. Adamson, 189, 350
Hoch, E., 287
Hofstaetter, P. R., 231

Holmberg, Allen, 250
Hollingshead, A. B., 237, 310
Honigmann, John J., 250, 270, 373
Hotchkiss, George, 310
Hsu, Francis L. K., 49, 182
Hughes, E. C., 57, 199
Huizinga, Johann, 111
Hull, Clark, 18, 354
Husserl, Edmund, 123, 125, 129, 130, 132
Huzioka, Y., 180
Hymes, Dell, 335

Imedadze, N. V., 232, 235, 236
Inhelder, B., 179
Inkeles, Alex, 54, 56, 103, 107, 109, 110, 115, 116, 327, 376
Ishino, Iwao, 362
Itani, J., 139, 141, 142

Jackson, Don, 315
Jaco, Gartley E., 310
Jacobson, Allan, 358
Jakobovitz, L., 231
James, Henry, 119
James, William, 16, 20, 27, 31
Janet, Pierre, 24
Jay, P., 138, 142
Jenkins, J. J., 231
Jensen, J. V., 233, 234
John, W. R., 235
Johnson, B. C., 180
Johnson, G. B., Jr., 234, 235
Johnson, W., 233
Jolly, A., 138, 143
Jones, Ernest, 84, 85
Jones, L. V., 232
Jones, W. R., 233, 234
Jung, Carl G., 81, 86, 96, 100

Kagan, Jerome, 179
Kainz, F., 233
Kallman, Franz J., 166, 315
Kant, Immanuel, 16, 31, 122
Kaplan, Bert, 121, 125, 380
Kardiner, Abram, 47, 49, 90, 91, 107, 180, 181, 254, 260
Kauders, O., 231
Kaufmann, J. H., 140
Kawamura, S., 142
Keith, Sir Arthur, 106
Kelly, L., 169
Kemenyi, J. G., 51
Kendall, Patricia, 198
Kerr, D. I. B., 151
Kiev, Ari, 87
Killian, Lewis, 59

Name Index

Kitsuse, John, 312
Klein, G. S., 339
Klein, Lewis, 147
Kluckhohn, Clyde, 88, 114, 250
Kluckhohn, Richard, 189
Koff, Robert, 339
Koffka, K., 19, 28
Kohler, W., 31
Kolb, L. C., 290
Kolers, P. A., 231
Korn, S., 171
Krapf, E. E., 238
Kreitler, Hans, 180
Kreitler, Shulamith, 180
Kroeber, A. L., 85, 88, 100, 310
Kykker, N. D. T., 171

LaBarre, Weston, 85, 114, 373
Lacey, B. C., 155, 156
Lacey, J. I., 155, 156
Lambert, W. E., 221, 224, 225, 229, 231, 232, 233, 234, 235
Lambert, Wm. W., 262
Lambo, T. A., 281
Landes, R., 354
Landreth, C., 180
Lane, H. L., 224
Lawton, D., 235
Leighton, A. H., 256, 281
Leischner, A., 231
Leites, Nathan, 108, 119
Lemert, E. M., 312
Lenin, 119
Lenneberg, E. H., 100, 231, 232
Lenz, H., 288
Leon, Carlos, 291
Leopold, W. F., 232, 235
LeVine, R. A., 351, 354, 355, 356, 357, 358, 363
Levinson, Daniel J., 103, 107, 109, 110, 115, 116, 176, 310
Levy, J., 235, 239
Levy-Bruhl, Claude, 253
Lewin, Bruno, 282
Lewin, Kurt, 21, 29, 32, 352
Lidz, Theodore, 310
Lieberman, M. A., 214
Lin, Tsung-yi, 281
Lindesmith, Alfred R., 201
Lindsay, A. D., 103
Lindzey, Gardner, 95, 107, 171
Linton, Ralph, 107, 115, 183, 291
Lipset, S. M., 119
Llewelyn, K. H., 350
Loehlin, J. C., 169
Lombroso, Cesare, 315
Lowenthal, Leo, 119
Lu, Yi-Chiang, 310

Lykker, N. D. F., 171
Lyons, Joseph, 129, 130

McBride, K. E., 231
McCall, George J., 197
McCarthy, D. A., 233
McClearn, G. E., 162
McClelland, D. C., 352, 353, 354, 355, 358, 359, 360, 361, 363, 367
McCord, Joan, 314, 317, 318, 320, 322
McCord, William M., 314, 317, 318, 320, 322, 323
McDougall, William, 250
McGinnis, Robert, 309
McKeon, Richard, 104
MacGregor, F. C., 284
Mackey, W. F., 221, 222
Maclay, H., 225
Malinowski, Bronislaw, 42, 92, 251
Martin, Norman, 57
Martin, William E., 181, 182
Marx, O. M., 231
Maslow, A. H., 110, 186, 214
Matsuura, H., 180
May, M. A., 32
Mead, George Herbert, 31, 55, 60, 97, 99, 195, 196, 197
Mead, Margaret, 42, 49, 51, 92, 108, 177, 182, 184, 188, 190, 252, 255, 258, 259, 263, 265, 269, 284, 333, 375, 379, 380
Melges, F. T., 157
Melville, Herman, 119
Mendel, Gregor, 167
Menkowski, M., 231
Mercado, S. J., 98
Merton, R. K., 54, 198, 313
Metraux, Rhoda, 378, 379
Metzger, Duane, 338
Meyerson, Martin, 113
Miller, Daniel, 99
Miller, G. A., 151, 153
Miller, George, 51
Minkowski, M., 232
Minturn, Leigh, 178, 262
Mishkin, M., 152
Mitchell, A. J., 234
Miyadi, D., 142
Moeller, G. H., 354
Moore, N., 231
Moreno, J. L., 29
Morison, Elting E., 119
Morris, James, 112
Morrison, J. R., 234
Moss, H. A., 179
Mullahy, P., 99
Murphy, Gardner, 32, 257, 376
Murphy, H. B. M., 288
Murray, Harry A., 22, 23, 28, 32, 35, 114

Name Index

Murray, Henry, 352
Myrdal, Gunnar, 119

Nadel, S. F., 94
Neugarten, Bernice L., 210, 214
Newcomb, T. M., 99
Nishi, Setsuko, 358
Nobel, K. W., 152
Norbeck, Edward, 189, 262, 379

O'Connor, M., 231
O'Doherty, E. F., 234
Odbert, H. S., 95, 96
Olesen, Virginia L., 200
Opler, Marvin K., 87
Osborn, R. H., 170
Osgood, C. E., 222, 225, 229
Osmond, H., 315
Oyama, F., 225

Paneth, E., 224
Park, Robert E., 55, 195
Parker, S., 354
Parsons, A., 288
Parsons, Talcott, 54, 97, 119, 309, 310, 348
Pavlov, I. P., 17, 23, 26, 36
Pawlik, K., 156
Peal, E., 231, 233, 234, 235
Perelman, M. A., 25
Petrie, A., 156
Piaget, Jean, 21, 155, 156, 179, 180
Pintner, R., 233, 234
Pieris, R., 229
Piers, G., 280
Pitres, A., 231
Plato, 89
Poe, Edgar Allan, 119
Popper, Karl, 88, 94, 100
Porta, Judith, 320
Portenier, L., 163, 170
Porterfield, Austin L., 311
Pötzl, O., 231
Powdermaker, Hortense, 269
Powers, Edwin, 316
Preston, Richard J., 269
Pribram, Karl H., 150, 151, 152, 154, 157, 339, 343, 374, 376, 378
Price-Williams, Douglass, 88, 377, 378

Quint, Jeanne, 61

Radcliffe-Brown, A. R., 91, 99
Radin, Paul, 248
Radke-Yarrow, M., 180
Rainwater, Lee, 358
Rank, Otto, 81, 86
Raubicheck, L., 239
Read, M., 184, 268
Reader, George, 198

Redfield, R., 351
Redlich, F. C., 237
Reik, Theodor, 153
Reiten, R. M., 156
Reynolds, F., 143, 144, 145, 146
Reynolds, V., 143, 144, 145, 146
Rieff, Philip, 157
Riesman, David, 109, 119, 156, 351
Rin, Hsien, 291
Rioch, D. McK., 141
Rivers, W. H. R., 93, 94
Roberts, J. M., 231
Roehm, Ernst, 86
Rogler, Lloyd H., 310
Roheim, Geza, 43, 269
Romney, A. K., 225, 335
Ronjat, J., 232
Rorschach, Hermann, 22, 28, 72, 125, 126, 130, 264
Rosen, B. C., 353, 354
Rostow, W. W., 119
Rubel, A. J., 291
Rutter, H., 171

Sade, D. S., 140
Saer, D. J., 234
Sanchez, G. I., 234
Sanford, R. N., 176
Santayana, George, 117
Sapon, S. M., 229, 233
Sarason, Irwin G., 90
Sartre, Jean-Paul, 124, 128, 129
Schachter, S., 155
Schaller, G., 139
Schaffner, Bertram, 107
Schuell, H., 231
Schuessler, Karl F., 311
Schur, Edwin M., 314, 323
Schwartz, Morris, 199
Sears, R. R., 99
Segall, M. H., 93
Seligman, C. G., 96, 100
Selznick, Phillip, 205
Semmes, J. S., 156
Sewell, William H., 181
Shaw, E., 315
Sherif, M., 29
Shields, J., 166
Shirek, J., 146
Shover, J., 233
Simmons, J. L., 197
Simpson, George, 56
Singer, Milton, 89, 280
Skinner, B. F., 19, 23, 127
Smigel, Erwin, 57
Smith, Adam, 360
Smith, F., 234
Smith, R. T. 165, 170
Smythies, J., 315

Name Index

Snyder, Louis L., 106
Socrates, 103
Soffietti, J. P., 229
Sours, John A., 290
Sperry, R. W., 151
Spiegel, John P., 310
Spindler, George D., 238, 265, 326, 328, 334
Spindler, Louise, 265, 326, 328, 329
Spinelli, D. N., 151, 152, 154
Spiro, M. E., 43, 49, 89, 97
Spitz, Rene, 44
Spoerl, D. T., 239
Staton, Alfred, 199
Stengel, E., 231, 238
Stephin, Karin, 85
Stern, W., 232
Stewart, W. A., 234
Stoller, A., 287
Stone, Gregory, 60
Strauss, Anselm L., 197, 198, 199, 377
Strom, T., 353
Sullivan, Harry Stack, 99
Sunley, Robert, 188
Sutherland, Edwin H., 313
Syme, Leonard, 311

Tanaka, Y., 225
Tannenbaum, Frank, 312
Tawney, R. H., 351
Teuber, H., 156
Thayer, L., 30
Theophrastus, 103, 104
Thomas, W. I., 32, 55, 110
Thompson, W. R., 162, 163, 168
Tienari, P., 166
Tireman, L. S., 233
Titone, R., 233
Tocqueville, Alexis de, 120
Tolman, Edward C., 18, 24
Tönnies, F., 351
Trager, H., 180
Travis, L., 233
Triandis, H. C., 225
Trilling, Lionel, 105
Trollope, Frances, 120
Tsumori, A., 142
Turner, Ralph, 60
Tylor, E. B., 253

Unwin, Joseph, 247

Valéry, Paul, 117, 118
Vandenberg, S. G., 169, 170, 171
Van Lawick, H., 146
Veblen, Thorstein, 113

Velikovsky, I., 238
Vernon, P. E., 129
Veroff, J., 353
Vico, Giambattista, 122, 131
Vildomec, V., 233
Vogel, Ezra, 359
von Uexküll, J., 32

Wagatsuma, Hiroshi, 359, 366
Wagner, Richard, 105
Walker, Donald E., 189, 262
Wallace, Anthony F. C., 45, 47, 50, 51, 90, 264, 265, 283, 327, 335, 338, 340, 374
Wallace, Samuel, 323
Ware, E. E., 225
Washburn, S. L., 43, 143, 146, 147
Watkins, J. W. N., 89
Weber, Max, 350, 351, 355
Weingarten, M., 151
Weinreich, U., 222, 231, 233, 234
Weisenberg, T., 231
Weiskranz, L., 152
Weinstein, L. G., 156
Wepman, J. M., 232
Wertheimer, Max, 18, 28
Westermarck, Edward, 94
Wheeler, Staton, 198, 200, 201, 203, 204
Whiting, Beatrice, 181, 262, 270
Whiting, John W. M., 48, 49, 92, 181, 189, 190, 260, 262, 263, 270, 310
Whorf, B. L., 100
Wilde, G. J. S., 164, 170
Williams, Gerald, 338
Williams, Richard A., 310
Wilson, M., 152
Wilson, Monica, 268
Winch, Robert F., 309
Winston, H. D., 171
Winterbottom, Marian, 353, 359
Wissler, Clark, 374
Witkin, H. A., 98
Witmer, Helen, 316
Wittkower, E. D., 293
Wolfenstein, Martha, 119, 188
Wolff, W., 28
Woodworth, R. S., 25
Wooley, D. W., 315
Worchel, P., 214
Wylie, Laurence, 185

Yap, P. M., 289, 292
Yonebashi, T., 293

Zaguirre, J. C., 292
Zelmanowicz, J., 231
Zola, Irving, 314, 317, 322

SUBJECT INDEX

Accommodation, cognitive process of, 155–157
Achievement motivation, 10, 214, 262, 327, 340, 342–343, 348–367
   and cultural context, 367
   and ethnic minorities, 363–367
   in Japan, 358–363
   and juvenile delinquency, 365–366
   methods of study of, 353–358
   in Nigeria, 355–358, 363
   theories of, 350–353
   See also Economic development
Acculturation, and personality, 326–344
Adolescents, personalities of, 185–191
Adults, personalities of, 8, 194–207, 209–216
   See also Middle age, Old age
Agency, concept of, 213–214
Alcoholics, 73–74, 282, 318–320
   and family life, 319
   personalities of, 311, 312, 315, 316, 318–320
Amish, 342
Anecdotal veto, 42–43
Amok, 292
Anomie, and psychosis, 284
   and social deviance, 313
Anorexia nervosa, 74
Anthropology, contributions to the study of personality by, 41–52
Apes (see Primates, nonhuman)
Assimilation, cognitive process of, 155–156
Attitude, concept of, 95–96

Baboons, 140, 142–143
Basic personality structure, 91–92, 107
   as source of tension, 284
   See also Modal personality
Behavioral genetics, 161–172
   history of, 162–167
Behavioral traits, genetic elements in, 161–172
   of lower animals, 165–166
   environmental influences on, 167
Behaviorism, 27–28
Bernreuter Personality Inventory, 163
Biculturism and language, 236–239

Bilingualism, 218–239
   and cognitive development, 232–236
   and intelligence, 219, 233–239
   and personality formation, 236–239
   psycholinguistic factors in, 229–232
   sociolinguistic concomitants of, 228–229
Bilinguals, code-switching of, 237
   compound and coordinate, 222–239
   semantic structure of, 225–227
Biological factors in personality (see Genetics, Neuropsychology, Primate nature of man)
Blood Indians, 326, 327–332, 336–337, 340, 341, 342, 343, 344
   personality of, 330–332
Brain, and personality (see Neuropsychology)

California Psychological Inventory, 171
Cambridge Anthropological Expedition to Torres Straits, 8, 246, 247, 248, 250, 251, 265, 269
Cambridge-Somerville study, 316–322
Canalization, concept of, 24–25
Cargo Cult, 334, 335, 341, 343
Castration complex, 76, 77, 78–79
   and mental illness, 291
Central nervous system, and human nature, 46–48
   See also Neuropsychology
Character, concept of, 108–109
   types of, 108–110
   See also National character
Child training, 7–8, 175–191
   and achievement motivation, 352–355, 359
   and adult personality, 261
   in primitive societies, 259–263
   and psychosis, 284
Children, personalities of, 175–191
   See also Child training
Chimpanzees, 143–146
Code-switching, of bilinguals, 237
Cognition, 10, 110, 150–158, 218–239, 374
   and culture, 43, 50–51, 339–340
   and language, 100

395

Subject Index

Cognitive control, 337–343
Cognitive development and bilingualism, chapter 15
Cognitive dissonance, 238, 339
Cognitive processes, 132, 155–156, 338–341
Cognitive styles, 98
Commitment mechanism, 204–205
Communication-information theory, 30
Communion, concept of, 213–214
Componential analysis, 335
Compulsive obsessives (*see* Obsessive compulsion)
Comrey Personality and Attitude Factors, 171
Concordance estimates, variation in, 166
Conditioning, classical, 23–24
  operant, 23–24
Contamination of categories, concept of, 238
Couvade, 77
Conversion hysteria, 67–68, 79, 287, 288, 289
Coprolalia, 290
Cortico-cortical connections and brain behavior, 151–153
Criminals, personalities of, 9–10, 311–318
Cross-cultural research, 19–20, 22–23, 27, 110, 131, 279
  in psychiatry, 257–258, 285–287
  tests in psychological theories in, 249–250
Cultural determinism, 89–90, 94–95
Cultural discontinuity, 283
  See also Middle age, Old age
Cultural and psychological systems, interdependence of, 327–332, 344
Cultural relativism, 27–28, 280
Cultural system, definition of, 327
Culture
  and cognition, 339–340
  cognitive structure of, 43, 50–51
  definition of, 279–280
  and the individual, 99
  and mental illness, chapter 17
  and national character, 106–108
  patterns of, 106–107, 258–259, 263
  and psychological functions, 92–93
  superorganic concept of, 90, 280
Culture and personality research
  as anthropological specialty, 248, 250, 269
  definition of, 88–89, 100
  history of, 91–93, 106, closing address
  See also Personality and Culture
Culture change, and mental health, 285
  and personality, 326–344
  See also Innovation
Cultures, holistic concepts of, 107
Culturological view of personality, 88–93

Cybernetics, 373
Cyclopean family, 85

Defense mechanisms, 82, 109, 237, 280
  of bilinguals, 237
  of ego, 67–69
Deviance disavowal, 58–59
Deviants, social (*see* Social deviance, Social deviants)
Disengagement from social norms, concept of, 211
Dissociation states, 292–293
Documentation, research use of, 97–98
Dominance, linguistic concept of, 219–221
Double-bind, concept of, 238
Dreams, cultural patterning of, 248–249
  symbolism in, 75
Drug addicts, personalities of, 313, 314

Echolalia, 290
Echopraxia, 290
Ecology, 32–34
  of nonhuman primates, 137–144
Economic development, and achievement motivation, 355–363
  and role dedication, 360–363
  See also Achievement motivation
Ego (*see* Freudian psychology)
Electra complex, 79–80
Empathic participation, 177, 182
Enculturation, community interaction during, 178–179, 191
  improvisation in, 177, 182, 190
  mechanics and processes of, 177–180
  in primitive societies, 259
Engagement, concept of, 211
Erotomania, 69
Eta, 366
Ethnolinguistics, 218
Ethology, 373–374
Evolution of man (*see* Primate evolution)
Existentialism, 6
Experimental psychology (*see* Psychology)
Extroversion, concept of, 96
  genetic inheritance of, 170

Familiarity, in perception, 93
Family, and mental health, 296–309
  and personality, 296–309
  See also Child training, Psychotics, Social deviance, Twins
Fear reactions, as forms of psychosis, 290–291
Feedback theory, 32
Free association, 82
Freudian psychology, 65–84
  See also Freud, Sigmund, in Author Index

Subject Index

Genetics, and personality, 161-172
  See also Behavioral genetics
Genotype, 162, 163, 166, 170
  and environment, interaction of, 172
Gestalt psychology, 28
Gibbons, 141, 143-144
Gorillas, 139, 143-144
Guilt, and mental illness, 289
Guilt cultures, 280

Hausa, 356-358
Heredity, and personality, 7
  See also Behavioral genetics
Heritability, differences in definition of, 161
Homosexuality, 68, 71, 78, 86, 280, 311, 313, 314, 323
Human nature, anthropological contributions to the study of, 41-52
  and personality, 92-93
  See also Behavioral genetics, Neuropsychology, Primates
  and primitive peoples, 252-254
Hutterites, 342
Hypochondriasis, 280
Hydraulic theory of the libido, 85
Hypnosis, 74
Hysteria, 74
  frequency of, 286-287
  See also Conversion hysteria

Ibo, 356-358
Id (see Freudian psychology)
Identity, concept of, 43, 46-48, 253, 374
  and adjustment, 335-337, 343
  in middle and old age, 211-213
  See also Self, self-identity
Idiographic approach to personality, 15, 24, 37
Impression management, concept of, 60-61
Imprinting, 24-25
Improvisation, in enculturation, 177, 182, 190
Imu syndrome, 290
Incest taboos, 76
Individualist view of personality, 5, 88-92
Information retrieval, 377
Information theory, 30, 373, 375
"Inner-directed" personality, concept of, 109, 157
Innovation, in social behavior, 177, 350-351, 355-358
  See also Achievement motivation
Instrumental Activities Inventory, 328, 344
Intelligence, genetic influences on, 163, 168, 169
  of twins, 169
Interference, linguistic concept of, 219-221

Introspection, as a research method, 28-29
Introversion, 96, 157
  genetic inheritance of, 170
Invention, 177
Investment, concept of, 24-25

Japanese, achievement motivation of, 358-363
  personality of, 107, 108
Juvenile delinquency, 313-315
  and achievement motivation, 365-366
  and personality, 9-10
  and social change, 284

Kitsunetsuki, 293
Koro, 291

Language, and cognition, 343-344
  and culture, 100
  and personality (see Bilingualism, Bilinguals)
Langurs, 138, 142-143
Latah syndrome, 290
Learning theory, 373, 375
Life styles, 209, 215

Macaques, 139, 140, 141
Manic-depression, 74, 320
  frequency of, 286
  genetic inheritance of, 166
  variant forms of, 288
Manus, reactive movement among the, 333, 343
Maori, 365
Masturbation, 79-80
  and mental illness, 291
Mazeway reorganization, 335
Megalomania, 69
Mendelian models, 166-167
Menomini Indians, 326, 327-332, 334-335, 341, 342, 343, 344
  personality of, 328-330
Mental health, and the family, 296-309
  See also Psychosis
Mental illness (see Psychosis)
Methodology in the study of personality (see Personality)
Middle age, personality in, 209-216
  continuities and discontinuities of personality in, 215-216
Minority groups, and mental illness, 285
  and personality, 10
Modal personality, 4-5, 264-265
  of nonhuman primates, 142-144
  See also Basic personality structure, Culturological view of personality, National character
Monkeys (see Primates, nonhuman)
Morphology, 21, 26

Subject Index

Motivation, 131–132
  See also Achievement motivation

Narcissism, 80
Nation, concept of, 104, 108, 110–111
Nationalism, definition of, 111
National character, 5, 97, 98, 103–132
  of the Chinese, 114
  of the English, 112, 114
  Greek concepts of, 103–104
  history of concept of, chapter 7
  of the Yugoslavians, 111–112
National Conciousness, 118, 120
National Creed, 118
National Imagoes, 118–119
National Style, 118–120
Native American Church, 328
Need achievement, 358–367
  See also Achievement motivation
Need affiliation, 359–363
Neurophysiological aspects of personality, 7, 11, 150–158, 374
Neuropsychology, convergences with other fields of concepts in, 157–158
  effective-affective factors in, 153–154, 157
  esthetic-ethical factors in, 154–155, 157
  factor-analytic studies in, 156
  and personality, 150–158
Neurosis, Freudian views of, 66–84
  variant forms of, 288
  See also Mental health, Psychosis, Psychosomatic illness
Nomothetic approach to personality, 15, 37
Nurturance needs, 210

Obsessional neurosis, 288, 289
Obsessive compulsion, 74, 290
  frequency of, 286–287
Oedipus complex, 65, 72, 73, 76, 80, 83–84, 86, 251
Old age, personality in, 8, 209–216
  continuities and discontinuities of personality in, 215–216
"Other-directed" personality, concept of, 109, 157

Paranoia, 68–69, 71, 74, 320
  variant forms of, 288
Parapsychology, 26
Pathoplastic factors in mental illness, 279, 287–289
Perception, 93
Perception-cognition, theory of, 28
Perceptual disparity, concept of, 238
Personality, abnormal, 8–9, 278–324
  and acculturation, 10, 326–345

Personality, (*continued*)
  anthropological contributions to the theory of, 41–52, 91
  biological aspects of, 6–7, 65–66, chapters 9–11
  concepts and methods in the study of, 4–6, 17–33
  comparison of anthropological, psychological, sociological, and psychoanalytic views of, 88–100
  continuities and discontinuities in, 215–216
  and culture (*see* Culture and personality)
  and culture change, 9, 326–345
  culturological view of, 88–93
  definitions of, 15, 88–100
    See also Modal personality, Basic personality structure
  individual versus modal concepts of, 5, 88–93
  integration of, 5–6, 34
  and language (*see* Language)
  and the life cycle, 175–216
  neuropsychological approaches to the study of, 150–158
  phenomenological approach to study of, 127–131
  of primitive peoples, 8, 93, 246–270
  primatological contributions to the study of, 137–148
  psychiatric contributions to the theory of, 65–84
  psychological contributions to the theory of, 15–38
  sociological contributions to the theory of, 5, 6, 54–63
  concept of trait of, 95–96
  See also Culture and personality
Perversions, sexual (*see* Sexual perversion)
Peyote Cult, 328–329, 334–335, 337, 341, 343
Phenomenology, 28–29
  and personality, 127–131
Phenotypic correlation, genetic and environmental components of, 168–169
Physiology, and personality, 26, 43, 45–46
  See also Behavioral genetics, Neuropsychology
Polymorphism, and personality, 139–140
Possession, states of, 292–293
Postpartum psychosis, frequency of, 286–287
Primal horde, 65, 85
Primate evolution, and human personality, 144–148
Primate nature of man, 43–44, 144–148
Primates, nonhuman, 137–148
  intergroup variation among, 140–142

Subject Index

Primates, (continued)
   intragroup variation among, 138–140
   modal personalities of, 142–144
Primitive medicine, 281
Primitive society, child training in, 259–263
   mental illness in, 285–294
   personalities of members of, 93, 246–270
   See also Acculturation
Projection, 67
Projective techniques, 81–82, 92–93, 97–98
Prosimians (see Primates, nonhuman)
Psychiatry, contributions to the study of personality by, 65–84
   and study of mental illness, 279–294
   See also Freudian psychology
Psychic determinism, 81
Psychoanalysis, assumptions of, 81–82
   contributions to the study of personality by, 4, 65–84, 375
   problems of, 80–81
Psychocultural adaptation, 326–344
   See also Acculturation, Culture change
Psychocultural system, definition of, 327
Psycholinguistics, 218, 344
Psychological anthropology, 246
Psychological systems, definition of, 327
   and cultural systems, interdependence of, 327–344
Psychologisms, 89
Psychology, contributions to the study of personality by, 15–38
   methods of, 15–37
   clinical, 19, 22–23
   comparative, 20–21
   cross-cultural, 19–20, 22–23, 27
   developmental, 19, 21, 22
   experimental, 19, 23–26, 247
   quantitative, 19, 26–27
Psychometrics, 168
Psychoneurosis (see Neurosis)
Psychophysics, 26
Psychosis, and bilingualism, 236–239
   biological factors in, 289
   cross-cultural comparison of frequency of, 285–287
   cultural factors in, 279–294
   definition of, 280–281
   and family structure, chapter 18
   Freudian views of, chapter 5
   in primitive society, 255–257
   postpartum, 286–287
   and social deviance, 320–321
   and social organization, 284–285
   See also Anomie
   types of, 286–293
Psychotics, and family life, 320–321
   personalities of, 312, 314–315, 320–322

Psychosomatic illness, frequency of, 286–287

Race, and national character, 105–106
Rage reactions, as mental illness, 292
Reactive movements, 332–335, 342, 343
Redundancy, in neuropsychology, 152–153, 154, 156, 157
Reflex arc concept of brain behavior, 151
Religious movements (see Reactive movements)
Revitalization movements, 335
   See also Reactive movements
Rhesus monkeys, 140, 141, 142–143
Rites of passage, 189–190, 191, 283
Role conflict, 59
Role dedication, and economic development, 360–363
Role deprivation, 283–285
Role playing, 60–61, 196–197, 202–203
Role replacement, 283
Role theory, 97
Rorschach test, 72, 81–82, 83, 125–126, 328, 344
Russians, personality of, 107, 108

Salience, in perception, 93
Scapegoating, 280
   See also Witches
Schizophrenia, 66, 73, 286, 289, 310, 320
   and bilingualism, 237
   double-bind theory of, 315
   frequency of, 285
   genetic transmission of, 166–167
   variant forms of, 287–288
Self, self-identity, 194–207, 363–367
   See also Identity
Self-realization, concept of, 110
Senile and presenile psychosis, frequency of, 286–287
Sex differences in psychological traits, 171
Sexual perversion, 280, 311
   frequency of, 286–287
   See also Homosexuality
Sexuality, Freudian concepts of, 71–73
Shamanism, 282
Shame cultures, 280
Sin, and mental illness, 289
Situational adjustment, 203–205
Smiling response, 172
Social change, and mental illness, 284
   and personality (see Acculturation, Anomie)
Social deviance, 311–324
   as biological predisposition, 314–315
   concept of, 311–317
   etiological views of, 313–317, 322–323
   and anomie, 313
   as a process of commitment, 314

Social deviance, (continued)
  and public policy, 323–324
  as reaction to subcultures, 313–314
Social deviants, personalities of, 317–320
Social psychology, 29, 55
  See also Psychology
Social rigidity, and psychosis, 284
Socialization, 48–50
  of adults, 194–207
  of children, 175–190
  and communication, 200–201
  and need achievement, 358–367
Society, meaning of, 195–197
Sociolinguistics, 218
Sociology, contributions to the theory of personality by, 5, 6, 54–63
Sorcery (see Witchcraft)
Stern High School Activities Index, 171
Stimulus-response concept of brain behavior, 151
Stress, categories of, 282–285
  and personality, 279–344
  See also Acculturation, Psychosis, Social deviance
Strong Interest Inventory, 169
Sublimation, 71
Subtle stage theory, 109
Suicide, frequency of, 286
Superego (see Freudian psychology)
Susto, 290–291
Suo-yang, 291
Symbolic content of thought, 69–70
Symbolic interaction, theory of, 195–197
Symbolism, in human interaction, 195–197

Taboos, 280–283, 286–287
  and psychosis, 286–287
  as source of stress, 282

Thematic Apperception Test, 82, 354, 359, 365, 367
Toilet training, 76–77, 182
  and psychosis, 287
Torres Straits expedition (see Cambridge Anthropological Expedition to Torres Straits)
Totemism, 85
Trance, states of, 282, 292–293
Transference, in psychoanalysis, 74, 82–83
Transvestism, 280
Twins, studies of, 163–166
  personalities of, 163–164
  familial influences on traits of, 163–165

Unconscious, psychoanalytic concept of the, 81–82

Vagina dentata, 77
Vailala madness, 333, 337
Value polymorphism, 283, 284, 285
Value saturation, 282–283
Values, formation and transmission of, 179–180, 183, 190

Witchcraft, 280–281, 288
  as cause of illness and misfortune, 281, 288
Weaning, 92, 182
Womb envy, 77

Xhosa, reactive movement among the, 333, 337

Yoruba, 356–358

BF
698
.S77